Praise for *Career Development and Counseling: Putting Theory and Research to Work,* Second Edition

"Outdoing even their excellent first edition, Brown and Lent have strengthened the emphasis on scientifically-informed career practice and on issues of diversity, individual differences, and social justice. This volume is an essential resource for the library of anyone interested in the field of career development, assessment, and counseling and should also prove invaluable for graduate students interested in immersing themselves in some of the best work being done today in the field of career development and counseling."

Nancy E. Betz, PhD
Professor, Department of Psychology
The Ohio State University

"In this second edition, Drs. Lent and Brown continue to shape career development discourse and illustrate the ongoing significance of the fields of career development and counseling in the 21st century. Woven into the fabric of each chapter are multicultural and practice implications, addressing the complex sociocultural issues salient in career development. This edition will help both researchers and practitioners alike to better understand, investigate, and promote the role of work in people's lives."

Angela Byars-Winston, PhD
Associate Professor of Medicine, School of
Medicine and Public Health
University of Wisconsin–Madison

"This handbook is a great resource for the student, experienced practitioner, and the researcher in the areas of career counseling and vocational psychology. The coverage of career development theory is detailed and current, and the handbook provides a comprehensive review of approaches to the practice of career counseling. I highly recommend this valuable contribution to the literature."

Gail Hackett, PhD
Provost and Executive Vice Chancellor for Academic Affairs
University of Missouri, Kansas City

"*Career Development and Counseling* is a must-have for any researcher in vocational psychology or career counseling or anyone who wishes to understand the empirical underpinnings of the practice of career counseling. If you wish to know why good career counseling works, this is the book for you."

Mark Pope, EdD, MCC
Professor and Chair, Department of
Counseling and Family Therapy
University of Missouri–Saint Louis
Former President, National Career
Development Association &
American Counseling Association
Editor, *The Career Development Quarterly*

Career Development and Counseling

Putting Theory and Research to Work

Second Edition

Edited by
Steven D. Brown
Robert W. Lent

WILEY

John Wiley & Sons, Inc.

Library of Congress Cataloging-in-Publication Data:

Career development and counseling : putting theory and research to work /
edited by Steven D. Brown, Robert W. Lent.—2nd ed.
    p. cm.
  Includes bibliographical references and index.
ISBN 978-1-118-06335-4 (cloth)
ISBN 978-1-118-22222-5 (ebk.)
ISBN 978-1-118-23627-7 (ebk.)
ISBN 978-1-118-26097-5 (ebk.)
  1. Career development. 2. Vocational guidance. 3. Counseling. I. Brown, Steven D. (Steven Douglas), 1947– II. Lent, Robert W. (Robert William), 1953–
   HF5381.C265273 2013
   331.702—dc23
                                                                                    2012017192

For Elaine and Ellen

Contents

Preface

THIS EDITION OF *Career Development and Counseling: Putting Theory and Research to Work*, like the first edition, has as its primary goal the promotion of scientifically informed career practices. It is, therefore, intended to be helpful to a wide audience of students, practitioners, and researchers who are interested in basing their work on the best that science and theory have to offer—science and theory emanating directly from vocational psychology as well as other disciplines that can inform career practice.

This edition of the text maintains continuity with the first edition in several ways. First, Section One is devoted to major theories of career development, choice, and adjustment that (a) either have received direct empirical attention or are derived from other, well-studied theories and (b) have clear implications for practice. Although the theories we include have received varying amounts of research support, all have the potential to generate new empirical knowledge as well as practical applications. As in the first edition, our goal was not to provide encyclopedic coverage of all available theories, but rather to focus selectively on those that appear to be empirically viable and useful in practice.

Second, this edition also includes separate sections devoted to the assessment of important career constructs and occupational information systems (Section Three) and to interventions for working with career issues across the life span (Section Four), which are mainstay topics of vocational psychology and career development. Third, we asked authors to be selective, scientific, and interdisciplinary in their coverage—to highlight assessment devices, information tools, and interventions that have garnered some scientific support and that have clear implications for practice—and to incorporate literatures from other fields of inquiry (e.g., industrial/organizational psychology, personality psychology) that can inform career research and practice.

Despite these continuities with the first edition, this edition departs from the earlier one in several important ways. The most prominent change in this edition is that we have reconfigured Section Two to focus to a greater extent than in the first edition on the roles of diversity, individual differences, and social factors in the career development process. This edition, therefore, contains separate chapters devoted to gender, race/ethnicity, social class and poverty, sexual minority identity, disability status, personality, and relational factors.

An additional change is that we now include an introductory chapter to set the table for the book by defining the purview of career development, discussing the importance of career counseling in the 21st century, and offering a brief history of career science and practice. This chapter is intended to encourage students to see the unique role of work in people's lives, its interface with other life domains (e.g., family, education, leisure), and the value of assisting people to surmount hurdles to occupational functioning. It is also intended to dispel myths and biases that sometimes surface regarding career counseling and to encourage a view of career development and counseling as vital, relevant areas of scholarship and practice.

We also, frankly, wanted to improve this edition's ability to speak directly to practitioners. Although the first edition, like this one, was developed to promote scientifically based practices, the practice implications of some chapters in the first edition were not always sufficiently clear. Thus, we asked all authors, regardless of specific topic, to think carefully about the practice implications of their chapters and to end their chapters by summarizing in a clear and concise way some of the most important practical take-home messages of their chapters.

We have many people to thank for their help throughout this process. First, we thank all of the students who have taken our courses and who continue to shape our thinking about how to teach career development and counseling in ways that are scientifically informed and useful to practitioners. Second, we are grateful to have had a gifted group of contributing authors whose chapters taught us a great deal and who were exceptionally open to editorial dialogue. Third, we appreciated the valuable input we received at various stages of the book from Ellen Lent and Mark Savickas, who served as sounding boards for particular topics and provided feedback on some of the chapters that we ourselves had authored. Fourth, we were grateful for the superb help we received from Rachel Livsey, our editor at Wiley, and her editorial assistant, Amanda Orenstein. Finally, we (as always) thank our families, friends, and colleagues for their support and inspiration. We could not have completed this edition of *Career Development and Counseling: Putting Theory and Research to Work* without them.

Steven D. Brown
Robert W. Lent
March 30, 2012

Contributors

Saba Rasheed Ali, PhD
University of Iowa
Iowa City, IA

Becky L. Bobek, PhD
ACT
Iowa City, IA

Steven D. Brown, PhD
Loyola University Chicago
Chicago, IL

Ellen S. Fabian, PhD
University of Maryland
College Park, MD

Nadya A. Fouad, PhD
University of
Wisconsin–Milwaukee
Milwaukee, WI

Paul A. Gore Jr., PhD
University of Utah
Salt Lake City, UT

Jo-Ida C. Hansen, PhD
University of Minnesota–Twin
Cities
Minneapolis, MN

Mary Ann Hanson, PhD
ACT
Iowa City, IA

Paul J. Hartung, PhD
Northeast Ohio Medical University
Rootstown, OH

P. Maggie Hauser, MA
Southern Illinois University
Carbondale
Carbondale, IL

Mary J. Heppner, PhD
University of Missouri–Columbia
Columbia, MO

Andreas Hirschi, PhD
University of Lausanne
Lausanne, Switzerland

Barbara Noblin James, MEd
Indiana University
Bloomington, IN

Jing Jin, MA
University of Illinois at
Urbana-Champaign
Champaign, IL

LaRae M. Jome, PhD
University at Albany,
State University of New York
Albany, NY

Janice E. Jones, PhD
Cardinal Stritch University
Greendale, WI

Cindy L. Juntunen, PhD
University of North Dakota
Grand Forks, ND

Neeta Kantamneni, PhD
University of Nebraska
Lincoln, NE

Alexandra R. Kelly, MS.Ed
University of Utah
Salt Lake City, UT

Maureen E. Kenny, PhD
Boston College
Chestnut Hill, MA

Richard T. Lapan, PhD
University of
Massachusetts–Amherst
Amherst, MA

Robert W. Lent, PhD
University of Maryland
College Park, MD

Wade C. Leuwerke, PhD
Drake University
Des Moines, IA

Mary Beth Medvide, MA
Boston College
Chestnut Hill, MA

A. J. Metz, PhD
University of Utah
Salt Lake City, UT

Margaret M. Nauta, PhD
Illinois State University
Normal, IL

Roxanna Pebdani, PhD
University of Maryland
College Park, MD

Susan D. Phillips, PhD
University at Albany,
State University of New York
Albany, NY

Kipp R. Pietrantonio, MA
University of North Dakota
Grand Forks, ND

Jeffrey P. Prince, PhD
University of California,
Berkeley
Berkeley, CA

Steven B. Robbins, PhD
ETS
Princeton, NJ

Patrick J. Rottinghaus, PhD
Southern Illinois University
Carbondale
Carbondale, IL

James Rounds, PhD
University of Illinois at
Urbana-Champaign
Champaign, IL

Mark L. Savickas, PhD
Northeast Ohio Medical
University
Rootstown, OH

Madalyn Schneider, MA
Southern Illinois University
Carbondale
Carbondale, IL

Jane L. Swanson, PhD
Southern Illinois University
Carbondale
Carbondale, IL

Sherri L. Turner, PhD
University of Minnesota–Twin
Cities
Minneapolis, MN

Susan C. Whiston, PhD
Indiana University
Bloomington, IN

CHAPTER 1

Understanding and Facilitating Career Development in the 21st Century

ROBERT W. LENT AND STEVEN D. BROWN

W HY DO PEOPLE WORK? What role does it play in our lives? Why should counselors and psychologists focus on work behavior? What do they have to offer people who are in the process of preparing to enter the world of work, adjusting to the workplace, experiencing problems or major changes in their work lives, or preparing to leave the work role? How does work relate to other life roles? Should work be seen as an impediment or as a complement to involvement in family and other life domains? Is counseling for work issues any different than counseling for other issues?

These are all questions that captivate and challenge those who study work behavior from a psychological perspective or who seek to assist students, workers, and retirees in the process of preparing for, entering, surviving or thriving within, or exiting from the work world. Not surprisingly, such questions form the foundation of this book, which is aimed at introducing students (and reacquainting professionals) in the helping professions with the literature on career development and counseling. This literature includes foundational and evolving theories of work and career behavior, research on a host of work-related constructs, and efforts to translate theory and research into practical efforts to help people experience optimally satisfying and successful work lives.

This chapter is designed to set the stage for the rest of the book by briefly considering the role of work in people's lives, sketching the conceptual and professional boundaries of career development and counseling, discussing some of the myths and realities that surround the field, and describing its historical context and contemporary challenges. Our primary goal is to convince the reader that work and career is one of the most important domains of life that counselors and psychologists can study—and that it is also one of the most meaningful targets of intervention in our roles as counselors, therapists, educators, and advocates. Freud was said to have equated mental health with the capacity to love and to work. Although these capacities may not truly be sufficient to define mental health, it is clear that work has a central location in many people's lives—one that frequently intersects with other life roles and that can have an immense impact on one's overall quality of life.

WHY DO PEOPLE WORK?

It seems fitting to begin by considering the reasons that people work and the various roles that work can play in their lives. At first glance, the question of why people work may seem silly or moot—the sort that only academics perched up in their ivory towers might ask. People work because they have to, don't they? They need the money that work provides to put food on the table and a roof over their heads. This may be true for most adults, but work as a means of survival does not tell the whole story, at least not for everyone. As the old saying goes, people do not live by bread alone.

WORKING TO LIVE OR LIVING TO WORK? THE DIFFERING ROLES OF WORK IN PEOPLE'S LIVES

In this section, we briefly consider various sources of work motivation.

Work as need fulfillment. One way to view the question of why people work is through the lens of Abraham Maslow's (1943) famous hierarchy, where human needs range from those that focus on basic survival (e.g., the need for food) all the way to self-actualization (e.g., the need to realize one's inner potential). Maslow's hierarchy is often pictured as a pyramid, with more basic needs (e.g., food, safety, security) at the bottom. In this view, the satisfaction of basic needs provides a foundation for meeting higher-order social and psychological needs, such as friendship, intimacy, self-esteem, and personal growth.

One of the problems in applying such a needs hierarchy to work motivation is that it may be used to imply that some reasons to work are somehow nobler or loftier than others or that poor people work only because they *have to* (i.e., to survive) while those better-off work because they *want to* (i.e., to satisfy higher-order needs). To avoid such a bind, one can simply view Maslow's needs as reflecting a range or list of reasons why people work, without the added assumption that they are necessarily hierarchical in nature. Thus, in addition to meeting basic survival needs, work can provide the context for fulfilling (at least a portion of) one's needs for security (e.g., enhancing the material comfort of one's family), social belonging and intimacy, personal esteem (e.g., providing a sense of personal worth and accomplishment), purpose, and self-actualization. People may be motivated to work for any combination of these reasons; they are not mutually exclusive or necessarily hierarchical, except to the extent that basic survival is obviously a prerequisite for fulfilling other needs. Rounds and Jin (Chapter 15, this volume) provide a more complete consideration of work needs and values, including their role in the selection of particular forms of work.

Work as an individual's public identity. Beyond Maslow's hierarchy and the issue of need fulfillment per se, work may also serve other, perhaps less obvious roles in people's lives, particularly if we expand the question to "what do people get from working?" and if we highlight the role of culture in work. For example, tied to the esteem and self-actualization bases of work is the issue of identity, which can have both public and private significance. Perhaps particularly in individualistic or Western societies, work can be seen as an expression of one's public image. Note how often people in the United States ask each other, "What do you do?" (i.e., what form of work do you do?) when they meet someone new. One's occupation can be a shorthand way of announcing one's social address (e.g., education, social class, prestige). Fair or not, what one does for a living is often viewed as an essential part of who one is as a person.

Work as personal identity or self-construction. Work-as-identity can also be an expression of self-image, a means through which people "implement a self-concept," in the words of Donald Super (Super, Savickas, & Super, 1996, p. 139). This may be most obvious in artistic forms of work. For example, we typically think of artists as expressing themselves through the things they create. But self-expression or, more expansively, using work to become the sort of person one imagines—to construct a self—can be a potent source of motivation in any form of work. Taking Super's thoughts about work motivation a step further, Edward Bordin, another influential career writer, emphasized people's capacity to seek work that they find intrinsically interesting or from which they can derive pleasure. To illustrate his point, Bordin (1994, p. 54) asked, "Is a professional athlete working or playing?"

Such views of work motivation are sometimes criticized with the argument that many people are not free to choose work that expresses anything more than the need for a paycheck or that not everyone is lucky enough to be able to do work that is pleasurable. One may ask whether those who work for a minimum wage, in unskilled jobs, in fast-food restaurants, on assembly lines, or in coal mines have the luxury of "playing" at, or implementing their self-concepts through, work. There is little question that lack of economic resources can limit one's choice of work or that jobs may differ in their obvious outlets for self-expression.

However, it is not hard to think of less affluent persons who find meaning, dignity, and enjoyment in their work. The notions of work as a calling (e.g., as a way to help others or to serve a higher power) or as an opportunity to construct and tell one's life story (Savickas, Chapter 6, this volume) capture the sense that work can play extremely valuable, self-defining roles in people's lives, regardless of social class and even when performed under difficult or harsh conditions. One can easily, from an external perspective, see someone else's life story as mundane, boring, or marked only by exploitation. However, that same story may be far more intriguing and meaningful to the person who is living it.

Work as normative expectation, group identity, and social contribution. In more collectivist cultures, work may be seen as an expression of group as well as personal identity. For example, choice of work may be made less on a personal basis and more in collaboration with members of one's family, tribe, or community. Consideration may be given to the needs of the collective and to selecting work that serves (and reflects positively on) the group and preserves relational harmony. Such functions of work may be seen, perhaps, as extensions of Maslow's (1943) focus on security, social, esteem, and actualization needs—but with the focus on benefits for the group rather than for the self alone.

Of course, prevailing social norms in most societies maintain that one *must* work if one is able to do so. It is a strong expectation conveyed by social agents in the family, school, and other social institutions. This norm is well-captured by the early rock-and-roll hit "Get a Job," in which the singer comically bemoans the social pressure to find work. Indeed, those who fail to find work are often derided with labels such as bum, shirker, lazy, good-for-nothing, or couch potato—especially if their failure to find work is attributed to their character or to a lack of effort. The power of this social norm can be seen in the internalized anger, frustration, and other adverse reactions unemployed persons often experience. This normative aspect of work may be seen as a special instance of Maslow's social belongingness need.

Work as existential response and aid to mental health. From an existential point of view, work may be seen as a way to structure one's time and construct personal meaning in an otherwise meaningless universe. Kierkegaard, the famous philosopher, spoke of work as a means by which people may find distraction from their self-consciousness, especially from thoughts of their own mortality. Although perhaps not the most upbeat idea, such a view of work may nevertheless help to explain why some people become so heavily invested in their work, sometimes to the point of work addiction, and why many become depressed when the loss of the work role, either through involuntary layoff or retirement, erodes their sense of life structure or meaning. Several social problems, like delinquency, may also stem partly from, or be exacerbated by, lack of access to suitable work. The old adage "an idle mind is the devil's workshop" captures the value of work as a way to structure time, maintain mental health, and promote prosocial behavior. The concept of psychological "flow" (Csikszentmihalyi, 1990) demonstrates how pleasurable it can be to become so absorbed in one's work activities that one becomes oblivious to the passage of time or to one's own sense of self-awareness.

In sum, people work for a variety of reasons, especially to earn a living, honor and contribute to their families and communities, achieve self-growth, establish a public identity, and structure their lives. Many of the ideas we have presented on why people work or what they derive from working can really be reduced to two venerable philosophical positions. In the *hedonic* view, people are motivated to survive and to experience as much personal pleasure (and to avoid as much pain) as possible. This position subsumes Maslow's survival, security, and esteem (and, perhaps, love and belongingness) needs. In the *eudaimonic* view, people are motivated to "live the good life," not merely the "happy life." Doing good is elevated above feeling good. A premium is placed on approaching work as an opportunity to achieve growth, purpose, meaning, and social contribution. The eudaimonic position subsumes Maslow's focus on aesthetic and cognitive needs (e.g., knowledge, goodness, justice) and self-actualization (or developing one's inner potential).

WORK VIS-À-VIS OTHER LIFE DOMAINS AND ROLES

Paid work is but one of life's domains, though it is the focal point of many people's waking lives—if not in terms of psychological investment, then at least in terms of hours spent. Assuming an 8-hour workday, many full-time workers spend at least a third of most weekdays at work—as much or more time as they spend sleeping or engaged in just about any other activity. And this estimate does not include the many additional hours or days that some people put into their work, above and beyond the traditional workweek. If work accounts for a third of a typical workday and sleep accounts for another third, that means all other activities (e.g., leisure, parenting, volunteering) are compressed into the remaining third or are put off until the weekend—assuming that one is not doing paid work then, too. Many people also think about their work when they are not at work. It is no wonder, then, that work can be seen as having the potential to conflict with or overshadow other life roles, like family members. Yet psychological research increasingly acknowledges that work and other life roles also have the potential to enrich one another (see Heppner, Chapter 7, this volume.)

Super was perhaps the first vocational theorist to view career development in the context of other life domains or roles and note that, in addition to their roles as workers, people can be invested in student, family, romantic, leisure, volunteer, and other life roles. Because work can interface with these other roles, it makes sense to reframe career planning as life-career planning or "life design" (Savickas, Chapter 6, this volume). Such a broadened view suggests that people consider how central or peripheral a role paid work will play in their lives. It also opens the door to extending interventions, for example, to those who perform unpaid work or who wish to enrich their leisure or civic lives. (In a literal sense, *occupations* can be seen as any activities that occupy people's time and energy—or as roles that people occupy—regardless of whether such activities or roles involve paid compensation.)

Super also emphasized the notion of role salience, which implies that work, or any other life role, can vary in its centrality or importance for any given individual and at different stages of life. This insight reminds us that work is not *the* most valued role for everyone. (See Hartung, Chapter 4, for coverage of Super's ideas regarding life-career development.) Such a perspective is extremely liberating, allowing for a less work-centric view of people's lives, freeing career counselors to view their clients as whole people with interests and commitments outside of work, and providing a valuable link to the study of women's career development (Richardson, 1993). Historically, men have often been socialized to focus primarily on their work trajectories, giving less thought to other life domains, whereas women have been more likely to view their work lives in the context of other central life roles, such as romantic partner or parent. Life-career planning and the allowance for differential role salience simultaneously challenges the traditional, male career pattern as *the* way to define career development, normalizes alternative ways to pursue work, honors the feminist commitment to equality, and offers the possibility of more flexible choices for women and men alike.

The What, When, Where, and How of Work

To this point, we have mainly focused on the *why* of work—the reasons why people work—and how work relates to other life domains or roles. In so doing, we have been discussing the general forces that impel, or motivate, people to work. And we have so far sidestepped the crucial what, when, where, and how questions: *what* specific form of work people either choose or feel compelled to do, the *how* of choice making (the process through which the individual and/or important others make work choices), the *when* of work decisions (points at which key work choices are made), and the *where* of work (the impact of the environment on choice and subsequent work outcomes).

Much of this book is devoted to addressing these very questions. The major theories of career development, contained in the first section of the book, all grapple with these questions to varying degrees. For example, the theories of person–environment fit (see Swanson & Schneider, Chapter 2, and Nauta, Chapter 3) tend to emphasize the what and where questions (i.e., the content of work that people do and the role of the environment in attracting them to or repelling them from certain forms of work). The developmental theories (see Hartung, Chapter 4), meanwhile, highlight the how and when questions (e.g., the ages or stages at which work-related decisions are made and the processes by which these decisions are aided or stifled). The chapters in the second section of the book emphasize key person and social factors (e.g., gender, social class) that often play into work "choices" and affect how people lead their work lives. The chapters in the third section focus on psychological and social attributes that career counselors often assess when assisting people to select or adjust to work. And the chapters in the final section involve interventions that extend theory and research to practice—the how of facilitating life-career development.

- Parenthetically, we placed the word *choices* in quotation marks in the last paragraph to highlight the point that work decisions are not always—in fact, are *often* not—a matter of purely free choice. Some people in certain cultural and economic contexts may assert greater personal agency in selecting their work than do others. In some contexts, "choice" is severely limited by financial or other constraints. In other contexts, choices may be made primarily by important others (e.g., family members). And in all cases, the environment has something to say about what work people will be allowed to do and for how long. Vroom (1964) observed that "people not only *select* occupations, they *are selected for* occupations" (p. 56). Thus, employers, admissions committees, and others serve as gatekeepers that help to determine initial and continued access to particular work and educational paths.

WHAT IS A CAREER? WHAT IS CAREER DEVELOPMENT?

To this point, we have been using the term *work* as the most inclusive way to refer to the subject matter at the center of this book. *Work* may also be less laden with excess conceptual and cultural baggage than are other terms used to describe the same essential area of human functioning. Some writers have, in fact, suggested that the field of vocational psychology be recast as "work psychology" or the "psychology of working" (Blustein, 2006). We appreciate this argument, but we also find the older terms—*vocational psychology, career counseling*, and so forth—still serviceable, if occasionally problematic. We decided to retain "career development and counseling" in the title of this book to maintain continuity with a large body of literature that has accumulated on the study and promotion of work behavior. But it is appropriate at this stage to define our terms more carefully.

WORK, JOB, OCCUPATION, VOCATION, CAREER—WHAT'S THE DIFFERENCE?

Work refers to the domain of life in which people provide services or create goods, typically (though not always) on a paid basis. It can also refer to the specific activities that one performs for pay or on a volunteer basis (i.e., volunteer work). In most societies, work is associated with the period of life after formal schooling (although some students engage in work as well as academic roles) and before retirement, or disengagement from work. *Job* is a specific work position held over a defined period of time (e.g., being a quality inspector at one factory for 10 years). Although *job* and *career* are sometimes used synonymously in popular discourse, vocational psychologists often use the term *career* to refer to a sequence or collection of jobs one has held over the course of one's work life. In this sense, people may hold different types of jobs over the course of a single career. However, it is also common to use *career* in a more limited sense to refer to one's involvement in a particular job family (e.g., engineering), which may include multiple jobs (e.g., being an engineer at company A for 10 years and at company B for another 10 years). It is in this sense that one can speak of a *career change*, a shift from one job family to another (e.g., from engineer to teacher).

Other terms commonly used to refer to work behavior include *occupation* and *vocation*. Both of these terms are often used interchangeably with *career*. For example, many writers speak of occupational choice, vocational choice, or career choice as meaning the same thing. But each of these terms, particularly *vocation* and *career*, also come with some excess baggage, at least in the view of some writers. *Vocation* is sometimes viewed as an antiquated term. It originated from the Latin verb *vocare*, "to call," and historically has been used in some religious circles to refer to a divine calling to pursue a religious path. *Vocation* was later used to refer to secular forms of work as well, and leaders of the vocational guidance movement (e.g., Parsons, 1909) sought to assist people in locating jobs that would best match their personal qualities and be satisfying. In more recent times, the term *vocation* has been associated with vocational/technical (as opposed to "academic track") education and is sometimes used to refer to jobs that do not require higher education. As a result, clients may sometimes be a bit confused about how someone identified as a *vocational* counselor or psychologist can help them select or adjust to a *career* path. Still, *vocation* has had staying power as a generic term.

Career may have a more contemporary feel than *vocation* and is more commonly used in popular discourse. Potential clients may be more likely to understand why they might see someone called a career counselor as opposed to a vocational counselor, and many professionals in our field prefer to refer to themselves as career counselors or psychologists. However, some writers find the term *career* objectionable on political or socioeconomic grounds and argue that it implies choice and privilege and that not everyone who works has a subjective sense of career. According to this line of reasoning, careers imply higher-status work. Thus, engineering is a career, but housepainter is not because the former requires more education and tends to command greater prestige and more favorable work conditions and pay.

Although we are sensitive to this argument, we are not sure that the term *career* necessarily implies all these things (or that housepainters would agree that they do not have careers). Moreover, it is hard to dismiss the term without also dismissing the extensive literature with which it is associated. In short, *career* is a compromise that most professionals in the field have been willing to make in the absence of an alternative term that meets with universal acceptance. Yet it is well for readers to be aware of the controversy that sometimes surrounds it.

What Is Career Choice and Development?

Career development can be seen as a process that encompasses much of the life span—one that begins in childhood (and includes the formal and informal experiences that give rise to talents, interests, values, and knowledge of the world of work), continues into adulthood via the progression of one's career behavior (e.g., entry into and adjustment to work over time), and culminates with the transition into, and adjustment to, retirement. It is a concept designed to capture the dynamic, changing nature of career or work behavior and is sometimes used as incorporating *career choice* and at other times as distinct from it. Career choice may be seen as the process of selecting and entering a particular career path, whereas career development refers to one's experience before, during, and (especially) after career choice. The period before initial career choice may overlap with one's educational life.

Some writers conceive of this period of academic or educational preparation as a part of the larger career development process; others treat it as distinct from, but conceptually related to, career development. Of course, career choice is not necessarily a static or one-time process. Many people revise their career choices over time for various reasons (e.g., to pursue work that better fits their interests and talents, to shift paths after involuntary job loss, or to reenter the workforce after raising children). Career choice, in turn, often has at least two phases: setting a choice goal and then taking steps to implement this goal, for instance, through additional training or a job search process.

Career *development* is sometimes used synonymously with career *advancement* or *management*. We see these terms as somewhat distinctive, however. Career advancement implies a linear process or one in which the individual progressively improves his or her career standing over time, as in the metaphor of climbing a career ladder. Career management connotes a situation in which the individual is actively engaged in directing the course of his or her own career development; that is, it implies a view of the person as active agent, anticipating and adjusting to new opportunities and behaving proactively to cope with negative situations. Career development, by contrast, connotes a continuous stream of career-relevant events that are not necessarily linear or positive in impact and that may or may not be subject to personal agency (e.g., being born into poverty, losing a job due to the bankruptcy of one's company). Although development ordinarily implies forward movement, it also holds the potential for devolvement or regression as well as progress.

Super, the dean of the developmental career theorists, described a number of life stages through which careers were assumed to evolve (growth, exploration, establishment, maintenance, disengagement; see Hartung, Chapter 4), and other developmental theorists also point to distinct stages or life periods that are crucial to career choice and development (e.g., Gottfredson, 2005). The current book is organized with three larger developmental periods in mind, namely, the periods prior to work entry (e.g., see Turner & Lapan, Chapter 19, and Whiston & James, Chapter 20), during work entry (e.g., Jome & Phillips, Chapter 21), and after work entry (e.g., Lent & Brown, Chapter 22; Bobek, Hanson, & Robbins, Chapter 23), which may well involve a recycling through periods of retraining/preparation and entry into new career paths.

WHAT IS CAREER COUNSELING AND HOW IS IT DISTINCTIVE?

We use the term *career counseling* in this book, as will most of the chapter authors, to refer to services offered to ameliorate or prevent problems with work behavior, regardless of the prestige or level of education associated with a given work option. In this section, we describe the purview of career counseling, other services that may augment or overlap with it, and the relation of career and personal counseling.

FORMATS AND FOCI OF CAREER COUNSELING

Career counseling typically takes place between an individual client and counselor, though many career counselors also employ group counseling or workshops, particularly in educational settings in which a number of clients are dealing with common developmental challenges (e.g., academic or career-related choices). Career counseling can be directed at a fairly wide range of client presenting problems, but these may largely be captured within three larger categories:

Help in making and implementing career-related decisions. Helping clients make career choices is probably the most popular image of career counseling. It entails assisting clients in deciding among various career paths as well as educational or training options (e.g., academic majors) that may have career relevance. Some clients enter counseling needing assistance to identify viable career options, with few if any firm ideas about which direction they might like to pursue. In some cases, clients have prematurely eliminated options that may, in fact, suit them well. Other clients enter with a dizzying array of options in mind and hope for help in narrowing their list. Yet other clients may have already made at least a preliminary decision about their educational or career direction and would like the counselor's assistance either in confirming the wisdom of this choice or in putting their choice into action, for example, by helping them locate and obtain employment in their chosen field. Whiston and James, Chapter 20, and Jome and Phillips, Chapter 21, focus, respectively, on counseling for making and implementing career choices.

Although career choice counseling is often pursued by students anticipating the period of work entry, it is also often sought by adult workers wishing to change directions (or sometimes forced to do so by circumstances) and by persons planning to reenter the paid workforce after a period of primary engagement in other life roles (e.g., parenting). For these reasons, it may overlap with the career transition focus of career counseling, discussed later in this section. In addition, counselors in school settings often focus on orienting children and adolescents to the world of work, helping them gain self-understanding, and aiding their academic performance. Such activities, which are intended to prepare students to ultimately make and implement satisfying choices (Turner & Lapan, Chapter 19), may be part of the developmental aims of vocational guidance and career education services.

Help in adjusting to work and managing one's career. Another common focus of career counseling involves work adjustment concerns, such as coping with dissatisfaction with one's job or difficulties with work socialization or performance. These problems may be manifest at any point after work entry. Sometimes they occur during the early period of transitioning from school to work as people discover that their new job is not exactly what they expected to find or that they are having a difficult time meeting the expectations of their employer. At other times, work dissatisfaction or performance issues may occur at later periods, for example, when people gradually come to feel stifled by a lack of variety or advancement opportunities or when a promotion places them in a novel situation where their current skills are challenged by new job requirements. Counseling to promote work satisfaction and performance must contend with the many reasons an individual may be unhappy at work as well as the many reasons supervisors or coworkers may be unhappy with the individual (see Lent & Brown, Chapter 22).

Help in negotiating career transitions and work–life balance. Some people seek or are referred for career counseling specifically for help in making the transition from school to work, from one form of work or career path to another, or from work to retirement or other life roles. The issue of career transitions is complex and multifaceted because such transitions may be either voluntary (e.g., based on a desire to do something "more meaningful" or to engage in "career renewal") or involuntary (e.g., due to job layoff), experienced as either developmentally on time and expected or unplanned and premature, and be anticipated with great worry or, in other cases, great excitement. Of course, whereas some clients may seek counseling preemptively to improve their work lives before things go wrong, many seek counseling with a sense of urgency or crisis after a negative life event has occurred or seems imminent. Career transition issues are addressed by Bobek and colleagues in Chapter 23.

Some clients also seek assistance in coping with the challenges of managing multiple roles or maintaining work–life balance. Although their reasons for counseling may not be stated exactly in those terms, these concerns may be implicit in such presenting problems as stress at keeping up with work responsibilities while caring for an ailing parent or dissatisfaction with one's relationship partner because he or she is perceived as not fulfilling a fair share of child care or homemaking responsibilities. Some counselors may view this class of presenting problems as not essentially a part of career counseling and rather as being within the realm of relationship counseling or even psychotherapy. We believe it clearly falls within the province of career counseling, particularly if one takes a broadened view of career–life counseling, seeing the work role as intersecting with other life roles (e.g., romantic partner, parent, family member). Several chapters in this book include consideration of work–life balance issues (e.g., Heppner, Chapter 7; Kenny & Medvide, Chapter 12; Lent & Brown, Chapter 22).

Our clustering of career presenting problems into three broad categories is, admittedly, somewhat arbitrary. Some problems do not fit neatly into only one category. For example, as we noted, some clients anticipating a career transition or dissatisfied with their current jobs may need to revisit career choice issues to consider whether a career change may better fit their current interests or life circumstances. Still, it is helpful to think of career counseling as encompassing multiple presenting issues that occur over the life span, from the preentry period of education and work preparation through entry into, adjustment to, and exit from the world of work. To be helpful to clients, counselors must ordinarily arrive at a mutual agreement with them on the goals and tasks of counseling. Taking a one-size-fits-all approach—by assuming, for example, that all career counseling involves career choice issues—may severely limit the ways in which a counselor can be helpful to his or her clients.

CAREER COUNSELING VIS-À-VIS OTHER CAREER SERVICES AND INTERVENTIONS

As Savickas (1994) has noted, career counseling is related to a variety of other services intended to promote people's career development, in particular, guidance, advising, education, placement, coaching, and mentoring. The first three of these are mainly identified with educational settings; the remaining three tend to be associated with work settings or with the transition from education to work. *Guidance* refers to the career-orienting activities typically provided by school counselors and teachers as they help students to become aware of the work world, of the value of planning, and of self-attributes that may relate to various career options. Career counseling as a formal specialty grew partly out of this guidance function. In recent years, computerized career guidance and information systems have been developed to automate or aid the guidance function (see Gore, Leuwerke, & Kelly, Chapter 18, this volume). *Advising*, typically associated with teachers and professors, is usually limited to selection of coursework and fulfillment of academic requirements but may involve less formal aspects, including advice regarding career options.

Career education usually refers to formal school-based programs, often at the middle and high school levels, aimed at introducing students to the world of work, assessment of career-relevant personal attributes, and exploration of career options that may fit one's personal attributes. It may also include a work component (e.g., placement in a relevant part-time job as a part of a school's career academy). Career education may be seen as an extension of the guidance function in that it is aimed at many of the same career-orienting and planning objectives, though often in a more structured and lengthier format. It differs from advising in that the focus is on career exploration rather than simply provision of advice or instructions on meeting academic requirements. A typical format for career education involves coursework facilitated by school counselors or teachers. Career planning courses are often offered at the college level as well to assist students in making academic and career decisions.

Placement, as the term implies, is focused on "placing" students or workers in particular jobs. It is concerned with helping people locate relevant job openings, mount effective job searches, and present themselves effectively to prospective employers (e.g., via resumes, job applications, and interview preparation). (On the work organization side of things, human resources professionals are involved in recruitment, screening, and selection of prospective employees.) Career counselors often provide services that overlap with those of placement personnel because both may assist people in implementing their career choices. Placement offices on college campuses are sometimes part of a larger career services center that offers both career counseling and placement. The advantage of such an arrangement is that it provides students with one-stop career assistance. In other cases, however, placement services may be located in a unit separate from counseling services.

Finally, coaching and mentoring are increasingly popular career services. *Coaching* has come to take on a number of different meanings in the career world. Often it is focused on assisting workers, particularly managers or executives, to improve their work performance or to promote their career progress within a given work organization (e.g., prepare for a new role or job). It may be practiced by service providers from a variety of professional backgrounds (e.g., counselors, vocational psychologists, organizational psychologists) and overlap substantially with career counseling. Alternatively, it may be offered by persons with relevant work content experience but no formal counseling or psychological training. *Mentoring* typically refers to the practice of pairing a newer worker with one or more experienced workers for the purposes of helping the newcomer adjust to the work environment, learn the ropes of his or her job, receive support and advice when work problems surface, have a model for negotiating work–life balance, and generally facilitate his or her career progress. Mentors and mentees may come together informally or be formally paired by the work organization.

It is apparent that career counseling can overlap with other career services. It is, therefore, important for career counselors to be familiar with these services so that they can facilitate clients' use of them as needed, for example, by making appropriate referrals to an academic advisor, a career class, or a placement office, or by helping clients identify mentors.

CAREER COUNSELING VIS-À-VIS PERSONAL COUNSELING AND PSYCHOTHERAPY

There are differing views about how career counseling relates to personal counseling and psychotherapy. Career counseling is clearly distinctive in some respects. Its most obvious distinction is the focus on one or two life domains, that is, preparation for work and functioning in work and school contexts. Thus, it involves specialized training elements and courses of study, for example, in career counseling and vocational psychology. However, the prevailing view within the counseling professions appears to be that there is often a false dichotomy between career and personal counseling (Hackett, 1993). This view is based on the observations that clients often present with multiple concerns (e.g., depression *and* difficulty making a career choice), that career issues are often intertwined with other life domains and roles (e.g., the difficulty of a romantic couple in making dual career decisions), that career problems can have emotional sides or consequences (e.g., stress, dissatisfaction), and that counseling can frequently rotate back and forth between career and other (e.g., personal, relational) life concerns.

Given the frequent overlap of career and personal counseling, it may be argued that the ideal scenario is for counselors and psychologists to be prepared, via training and experience, to deal with both career and personal concerns. Training, for example, only in personal counseling and psychotherapy can lead counselors and therapists to overlook or downplay the importance of work-related issues or to feel incompetent at dealing with them. It is, of course, imperative that one be able to recognize the limits of one's competence and, where those limits have been reached, to make responsible referrals. However, there are also advantages to receiving training of sufficient breadth in counseling and therapy so that one is truly competent to identify and deal with the more common career *and* personal problems with which clients are likely to present.

It is probably most helpful to view the career versus personal counseling controversy in terms of a continuum rather than a dichotomy, with more purely career-type concerns (e.g., career choice) at one end and more purely personal concerns (e.g., depression) at the other. In the middle of this continuum is where the two overlap or are interwoven (e.g., where choice is made more difficult by depression). A good example of how career issues can be relatively distinct from and, at other times, overlap with personal issues can be found within the types of clients who seek help with making career choices. Researchers have found that there are several types of career indecision (Brown & Ryan Krane, 2000) and that these can best be approached with different counseling strategies. For instance, some clients enter counseling with relatively focused, developmental problems in making a career decision. They do not generally experience decision-making problems but are having trouble with this one area. Not surprisingly, perhaps, such clients often do well in just five or fewer counseling sessions that are aimed exclusively at self-exploration, career information, and decision-making activities. Another type of career client enters counseling with a characteristic tendency to experience negative affect and to be indecisive in most life areas. To be maximally helpful, counseling with such clients may well involve more extensive efforts to deal with both their career and personal (e.g., cognitive and emotional) concerns.

SOME MYTHS AND REALITIES ABOUT CAREER COUNSELING

We have found that career counseling is viewed in stereotypic fashion by some of our colleagues in the helping professions. Common stereotypes include perceptions that career counseling is relatively simple, easy, formulaic, and brief; that it involves a "test 'em and tell 'em" approach in which assessments are mechanically assigned and interpreted and clients are quickly sent on their merry way; that computer programs can be used to substitute for career counselors; and that the effects of career counseling are not as impressive or meaningful as are those of personal counseling. In this section, we briefly address such perceptions and examine ways in which we believe they can mistake or distort the reality of career counseling.

CAREER COUNSELING AS SIMPLE, BRIEF, AND HIGHLY STRUCTURED

Is it true that career counseling is simple, easy, formulaic, and brief? The kernel of truth in this stereotype is that some clients do, indeed, profit from relatively brief, structured forms of career counseling. But it really depends to a great extent on the nature of clients' goals and presenting problems, on other qualities they bring to counseling, and on the methods counselors employ. As we noted before, research has found that many clients profit from five or fewer sessions of counseling aimed at career choice. Such rapid gains are most likely to occur when (a) clients' presenting problems are limited to making a career-related decision, (b) clients do not exhibit high levels of general indecisiveness or negative affect (i.e., global tendencies to experience feelings like depression and anxiety), and (c) counseling includes at least three of five critical ingredients (see Whiston & James, Chapter 20).

Many clients also profit from receiving more than five sessions of career counseling (Brown & Ryan Krane, 2000). In such cases, it is likely that their presenting issues extend beyond making a career decision (e.g., coping with work dissatisfaction or stress), that they present with other issues that affect their career development (e.g., chronic indecisiveness), or that their career concerns are complexly intertwined with personal (e.g., emotional) or relationship (e.g., work–family balance) issues. Such situations, which are quite common, stimulate the creativity of career counselors and underscore the need for them to be facile with both career and other forms of counseling. For example, counseling for work dissatisfaction often draws on many of the same strategies as would be employed with clients who seek help because of dissatisfaction in other areas of their lives (Lent, 2004). Career counseling need not be any less artful or spontaneous than other types of counseling—and clients frequently present with problems that cannot be neatly categorized as needing only one form of assistance.

THE ROLE OF FORMAL TESTING

Is it true that career counseling is synonymous with testing? The kernel of truth here is that career counselors often do employ formal assessments, particularly with clients who seek assistance in making a career-related decision. In fact, many clients have been told by advisors or others to go see a career counselor to "take that test that will tell you what you should do." Of course, no test can read a client's mind or future, much less make a decision for her or him, and some clients are displeased, if not entirely surprised, when they discover this reality. However, there *are* a number of assessment devices that can provide very useful information about clients' self-attributes (e.g., interests, values, abilities) in relation to educational and career options they are considering or can help them expand or narrow their range of options (see the chapters in the third section of this book). Although not as dramatic, perhaps, as gazing into a crystal ball, it can be very helpful to discover, for example, that one's interests resemble those of people who are satisfied working in health care settings. In fact, individualized assessment is one of the components that accounts for the effectiveness of career choice counseling (Brown & Ryan Krane, 2000). Career counseling for work adjustment and transition issues may also profitably employ formal assessment methods (Lent & Brown, Chapter 22; Bobek et al., Chapter 23).

Despite its documented utility, career counseling need not involve formal psychometric measures exclusively or even at all. Many career counselors use less formal ways of gathering information about clients, often in addition to psychometric measures, to aid the counseling process. For example, depending on the presenting issue, some counselors use card-sorting activities, fantasy workday exercises, career genograms, role plays, and a variety of other methods (Pope & Minor, 2000). Such options can stimulate their clients' thinking about career issues and make the process of career counseling more interactive, engaging, and creative—anything but the sterile, rigid, "test 'em and tell 'em" stereotype.

COUNSELORS VERSUS COMPUTERS

Is it true that whatever career counselors have to offer could be done more efficiently and just as effectively by a computer program? It is important to acknowledge that most people do not seek the services of a career counselor. Most make choices and solve other career-related problems on their own or with the support and guidance of parents, teachers, friends, work colleagues, or others. Computerized guidance and information systems and high-quality Internet resources are useful tools for many persons who do not seek career counseling and who have relatively uncomplicated, developmental needs. Such options can aid people in gathering career-relevant information about themselves and the world of work and, perhaps, in reconciling these two sources of information (see Gore et al., Chapter 18). Computerized and Internet-based options can also be useful adjuncts for people who do seek career counseling. Research indicates, however, that for such persons, access to computerized services alone, on average, yields less substantial effects than when they also meet with a counselor (Brown & Ryan Krane, 2000; Whiston, Brecheisen, & Stephens, 2003). In essence, counselors can still do things that computers do not, such as helping clients set and work toward career goals, assisting them in processing complicated computer-generated information, and aiding them in marshaling supports and overcoming barriers to implementing their preferred choices (Brown et al., 2003).

THE EFFECTS OF CAREER COUNSELING

Finally, how useful is career counseling compared to personal counseling (i.e., where the two forms of intervention are treated as relatively distinct)? Is it true that career counseling is somehow less impactful or meaningful? For several reasons, we believe it would be a mistake to trivialize the importance of career counseling. First, one's work can have a great impact on the kind of life one leads, both hedonically (e.g., materially) and eudaimonically (e.g., in terms of life meaning and purpose). As we noted earlier, work plays a central role in many people's lives. Its significance often goes well beyond the sheer amount of time and effort they put into their jobs or the size of the paycheck they receive. For many, work (or its absence) can have great psychological significance, with the potential to spill over into the nonwork parts of people's lives. For example, work-related stresses or conflicts can affect people's sense of well-being when they are not at work. Likewise, work colleagues become an important source of friendships and general social support for many people. Although some compartmentalize their lives more than others, when people feel stifled or unhappy in their work lives, they are often likely to be unhappy with their lives as a whole (see Lent & Brown, Chapter 22). And this can have implications for one's friends and loved ones as well. Thus, it would be difficult to overstate the value of counseling that can either prevent or remediate career-related problems.

Second, meta-analyses, which statistically combine the findings of many studies together, have found that the effects of career choice counseling actually rival and, in some cases, exceed the effects of personal counseling. For instance, the average person receiving career counseling tends to show as much gain as the average person receiving psychotherapy, especially if career counseling involves at least three of five critical ingredients (Brown & Ryan Krane, 2000; see Whiston & James, Chapter 20). We should not press this comparison too far because the gains assessed in career counseling and psychotherapy outcome studies tend to involve different sorts of outcomes (e.g., changes in career decidedness versus depression). However, career choice clients do show statistically and practically significant benefits from counseling—benefits that may well promote other aspects of personal well-being.

WHO DOES CAREER COUNSELING AND STUDIES WORK BEHAVIOR?

Career counselors and vocational psychologists are not alone in their interest in career development issues. There are many facets to work behavior, and these are, accordingly, studied by a variety of professions. Thus, it is useful to appreciate the larger lay of the land. *Career counselors* often have master's degrees in counseling, with a focus on career issues. They may have studied in programs accredited by the Council for Accreditation of Counseling and Related Educational Programs. *Vocational psychologists* typically have doctoral degrees in counseling psychology. Their academic programs may have been accredited by the American Psychological Association. Vocational psychology has, historically, been a central part of the larger specialty of counseling psychology rather than an entirely separate specialty area. Practicing vocational psychologists often consider themselves as career counselors, as well as more general therapists. Some vocational psychologists prefer the title "career psychologist." Some of the key professional journals read by career counselors and vocational psychologists are the *Journal of Vocational Behavior, Journal of Counseling Psychology, Career Development Quarterly, Journal of Career Assessment*, and *Journal of Career Development*.

In addition to those trained specifically as career counselors and vocational psychologists, a variety of other master's-level counselors, especially *school counselors*, *mental health counselors*, and *college counselors*, may provide career counseling or related career services. For example, school counselors may lead comprehensive career guidance programs or teach career education classes, in addition to doing individual or group counseling aimed at facilitating educational behavior or career planning. Some *social workers* also focus on occupational issues, for example, as personnel in employee assistance programs. Historically, social work emphasized vocational services in an effort to combat poverty, particularly in urban settings.

Within the realm of psychology, *industrial/organizational (I/O) psychologists* also study and, in some cases, intervene in work-related issues. In some ways, vocational and I/O psychologists are interested in opposite sides of the same coin. They each focus on factors that promote effective work functioning, but vocational psychologists are primarily concerned with person-focused outcomes (e.g., how to facilitate an individual's decisions), whereas I/O psychologists mainly emphasize outcomes of concern to work organizations (e.g., how to promote organizational productivity). Although they tend to approach work behavior from these differing person versus organization perspectives, their interests frequently overlap. For example, both specialties are concerned with issues of work satisfaction, performance, stress, the work–family interface, and workplace equity. The I/O psychologists are less likely to receive training in career counseling but are somewhat more likely to engage in organizational development and consulting activities. *Occupational health psychology*, a relatively new specialty, is concerned with factors that affect the psychological and physical health of workers (workplace safety, psychological burnout). Various other psychological specialties, such as *educational psychology* and *developmental psychology*, also study topics that overlap with vocational psychology.

Finally, several fields outside of psychology and the helping professions also share an interest in work behavior. In particular, *occupational sociology* (also referred to as industrial sociology or the sociology of work) focuses on work-related trends, such as technological change and employee–employer relations, that affect workers and families at a large group or societal level. *Labor economics* focuses on issues affecting employment levels, participation rates, income levels, and economic productivity (e.g., gross domestic product). Like occupational sociologists, labor economists tend to examine work-related outcomes and processes at a more collective level, rather than at the level of individual workers or work organizations. These fields emphasize different aspects of work behavior than do counselors and psychologists, but they share a concern with shaping public policies that promote the well-being of workers, though they may define well-being in social or economic, rather than in psychological, terms.

CAREER DEVELOPMENT AND COUNSELING:
PAST, PRESENT, AND FUTURE

The field of career development and the practice of career counseling have evolved rapidly over the past century. However, an interest in work behavior is hardly new. People no doubt began thinking about their work, what they liked and disliked about it, how to do it better or with greater rewards, how to handle conflicts with others at work, and so forth well before recorded history. Zytowski (1972) discovered books about occupations dating back to the late 1400s, and, of course, philosophers have long been preoccupied with the role and meaning of work in people's lives. A full-scale history of career development and counseling is beyond the scope of this chapter. Several writers have already traced the evolution of career development as a formal discipline from its early roots in vocational guidance, circa 1850, up through its current-day contributions and challenges. Some of these histories focus primarily on vocational psychology (Crites, 1969; Savickas & Baker, 2005), and some on career counseling (Crites, 1981; Miller & McWhirter, 2006), though the two areas are greatly intertwined with one another. There have also been intriguing histories of the pioneers of the vocational guidance movement, which formed the foundation for present-day career counseling and vocational psychology (Savickas, 2009).

One of the things that historians of career development agree upon is that Frank Parsons (1909) deserves credit as one of the field's key early figures. Parsons, a social reformer who was committed to raising the living standards of the urban poor, ran an early vocational service in Boston. He developed a deceptively simple three-step approach to vocational guidance that has been widely incorporated into subsequent formal theories of career development and counseling. In essence, he recommended that, in choosing a form of work, people be encouraged to (1) achieve a "clear understanding" of their personal attributes (e.g., interests, abilities) and (2) develop a knowledge of the requirements and conditions of different occupations and then (3) use "true reasoning" to consider how to reconcile these two sources of information. Modern-day career counselors may identify with a variety of theoretical positions and employ somewhat different terms and methods, but Parsons's simple formula still serves as a fundamental blueprint for the practice of career choice counseling,

Historians of the field also tend to agree that the two world wars of the 20th century—and the Great Depression in between them—were major influences on the field's evolution within the United States. In particular, the military needed assistance in assigning its recruits to different jobs in both wars, and the Veterans Administration was concerned with assisting returning veterans to adjust personally, educationally, and vocationally to civilian life after World War II. The Great Depression created an unparalleled challenge of returning people to work in some organized way. In addition, increasing industrialization and associated changes in the economy (e.g., shifts from agriculture to manufacturing) in many countries during the 20th century also created a need for proven methods of matching people with work options, attending to their productivity, and nurturing their satisfaction and loyalty. These challenges were a huge boon both to the development of psychological instruments that could systematically assess self and occupational attributes and to the creation of guidance and counseling methods. Assessment devices, like the present-day Strong Interest Inventory and the General Aptitude Test Battery, emerged from this early cauldron of activity. So did the development of career counseling methods based on directive and, eventually, person-centered approaches.

Once veterans returned from the world wars and the economy recovered from the Great Depression, there was a continuing need for career counseling and placement personnel. Subsequent societal and economic changes in the latter half of the 20th century (e.g., the increasing popularity of higher education, shifts in employment demand from manufacturing to service sectors) formed the historical context for the further evolution of the career development field. In more recent decades, there have been considerable changes in technology (e.g., the introduction of personal computers and the Internet), in the nature of work (e.g., increasing need for knowledge workers), in global economic competition, and in the structure of work organizations.

Observing such changes, many career writers have concluded that a new era in career development has dawned (e.g., Hesketh, 2000). The old psychological contract between worker and employer has been cast aside. Where many could once expect to work for a single employer for many years and feel confident that their loyalty and productivity would be rewarded appropriately, the new contract promises far less security and stability. Terms like *boundaryless careers, protean careers,* and *Me Incorporated* abound in the recent career literature, particularly among I/O psychology writers. These terms are based on the assumption that employers will continue to be motivated, for reasons of global economic competition, to retain smaller permanent workforces. They will, instead, draw on temporary, part-time, or contract workers to a much greater degree to create a flexible, just-in-time workforce that requires neither benefits nor long-term commitments—a cadre of workers who can complete particular projects and then move on.

The implication is that current workers, and especially those in the future, will need to be increasingly adaptable and resilient in their approach to work. The "Me Incorporated" notion refers to the need to treat oneself essentially as a private vendor who is responsible for finding new work, investing in one's own career development, developing new interests, and updating one's skills to remain employable under uncertain and constantly changing conditions. Some believe that the new contract will render obsolete current theories of career development and current approaches to career counseling. Although the context of work may be changing, we are convinced that current career theories still have relevance. People may have less stability in terms of where and when they work, but they still profit from identifying and accessing work options that are compatible with their work personalities (e.g., interests, talents, personal and cultural values) and in which they can perform successfully. We think this is a point that career futurists sometimes miss. If a career is based on the assumption that one will work for a particular employer over one's entire work life, then *that* restrictive notion of career may be dead (and was never truly viable for many workers). However, if *career* is defined, consistent with Super, as the sequence or collection of jobs held over one's work life, then the concept of career remains as alive as ever, but it is a concept owned by the worker rather than by the employer and requires no assumptions about the long-term stability of a particular job.

We are not sure that career choice and development theories really need to predict the exact job that a single individual will enter and stay in for life. What such theories have always done best is to help people to identify and adjust to an array of compatible work options. Beyond these traditional contributions, however, we do see a need for new theories and preventive-developmental interventions to help people negotiate a changing macroenvironment. Although the range of jobs people perform is still generally captured well within existing occupational classification schemes (see Gore et al., Chapter 18), how and where many jobs are performed (e.g., using computers, at home) is changing—and so is the need to prepare for periods of work instability and change. The time-tested Parsonian formula, though still viable, needs to be supplemented with new methods aimed at assisting students and workers in anticipating and coping with periods of flux and transition (Lent, in press). We are not sure it is a reasonable goal to transform all workers into entrepreneurial chameleons. Not everyone has entrepreneurial interests or talents, and poets do not easily turn themselves into engineers just to find the next job. But it may make sense to approach adaptability, resilience, and planning as qualities that, potentially, can be learned or strengthened through counseling and other forms of career intervention (e.g., career courses, workshops).

A FINAL WORD: CAREER DEVELOPMENT AS PRACTICE, SCHOLARSHIP, *AND* SOCIAL JUSTICE FORUM

We believe this is an exciting time to enter the field of career development. In fact, there have probably been few more momentous times in the field's history. In addition to meeting the external challenges of a changing work world, the field seems poised to transform itself from within. In particular, career counselors and vocational psychologists are, increasingly, meeting and working together with their counterparts across cultural and national boundaries as the larger profession—like the work domain that serves as their common focus—becomes more and more internationalized. The U.S.-based professional associations, like the National Career Development Association and the Society of Vocational Psychology, are not alone. International associations, like the International Association for Educational and Vocational Guidance and the International Association of Applied Psychology, are prospering. The field has clearly been infused with a great deal of vitality and energy, as career counselors and vocational psychologists around the world find new ways to study and promote career behavior.

It is important to emphasize that career development and counseling is both a scholarly *and* a practice field. That is, it is devoted to understanding work behavior *and* to applying this understanding to practices that directly enrich clients' lives. Although the ideal for many years in psychology has been to develop scientist-practitioners—that is, persons who attend to both of these spheres—the reality is that many professionals are drawn to one of them more than to the other. Indeed, this very awareness is a reflection of what has been learned about career behavior, for instance, that interests tend to favor choice of some work activities over others. Thus, those with primarily social interests may gravitate toward the counseling role, and those with stronger science interests may favor the research and scholarship roles. The field needs talented people to perform both roles, and it needs them to communicate well with one another so that scholarship remains responsive to practice and that practice is based on science as well as art. More and more, the field is also becoming aware of the need to invest a greater portion of its collective energy in advocacy and public policy efforts, including involvement with decision makers and leaders who formulate wide-ranging education and work policies. Such upstream advocacy may aid people's career opportunities and functioning at a systemic level, regardless of whether they ever seek formal career services.

As part of its science, practice, and advocacy missions, the career development field is also marked by a commitment to social justice and multiculturalism and to serving the needs of an increasingly diverse society and world. Indeed, concerns about social justice pervade the history of the career development field. They were prominent in the earliest days of the field, as social reformers sought to improve the lives of recent immigrants and others lacking economic privilege (Parsons, 1909), and they were a primary stimulus for the field's efforts during the middle and latter parts of the 20th century to better meet the needs of women, persons with disabilities, veterans, work-bound students, and other traditionally underserved clients from diverse social and economic backgrounds. Social justice remains a hallmark of the field, as evidenced by a continuing sensitivity to the ways in which diversity shapes people's career experiences (e.g., see the chapters in the second section of this book). In short, assisting people to obtain and succeed at work has long been seen as an essential way to improve the human condition and to promote equity.

CONCLUSION

We covered a fair bit of ground in this chapter. In particular, we noted a variety of roles that work may play in people's lives, from meeting basic survival needs through helping them to address meaning-of-life questions. We also defined several key terms, such as *career* and *career development;* identified the counseling and psychological professionals who are specifically trained to provide career counseling and related services; and noted a variety of other professions that share an interest in career development or work behavior. We considered some common myths and stereotypes surrounding career counseling, pointing out ways in which they may sometimes be accurate but more often are not. Finally, we described the field's historical context and some of its contemporary challenges and argued that a concern with social justice and a respect for human diversity have been key forces directing the field's evolution from its inception up through its present state. We welcome you to the field of career development and counseling and hope you will find it a great place to develop your own career.

REFERENCES

Blustein, D. L. (2006). *The psychology of working: A new perspective for career development, counseling, and public policy.* Mahwah, NJ: Erlbaum.

Bordin, E. S. (1994). Intrinsic motivation and the active self: Convergence from a psychodynamic perspective. In M. L. Savickas & R. W. Lent (Eds.), *Convergence in career development theories: Implications for science and practice* (pp. 53–61). Palo Alto, CA: Consulting Psychologists Press.

Brown, S. D., & Ryan Krane, N. E. (2000). Four (or five) sessions and a cloud of dust: Old assumptions and new observations about career counseling. In S. D. Brown & R. W. Lent (Eds.), *Handbook of counseling psychology* (3rd ed., pp. 740–766). New York, NY: Wiley.

Brown, S. D., Ryan Krane, N. E., Brecheisen, J., Castelino, P., Budisin, I., Miller, M., & Edens, L. (2003). Critical ingredients of career choice interventions: More analyses and new hypotheses. *Journal of Vocational Behavior, 62,* 411–428.

Crites, J. O. (1969). *Vocational psychology: The study of vocational behavior and development.* New York, NY: McGraw-Hill.

Crites, J. O. (1981). *Career counseling: Models, methods, and materials.* New York, NY: McGraw-Hill.

Csikszentmihalyi, M. (1990). *Flow: The psychology of optimal experience*. New York, NY: Harper & Row.

Gottfredson, L. S. (2005). Applying Gottfredson's theory of circumscription and compromise in career guidance and counseling. In S. D. Brown & R. W. Lent (Eds.), *Career development and counseling: Putting theory and research to work* (pp. 71–100). Hoboken, NJ: Wiley.

Hackett, G. (1993). Career counseling and psychotherapy: False dichotomies and recommended remedies. *Journal of Career Assessment, 1*, 105–117.

Hesketh, B. (2000). Prevention and development in the workplace. In S. D. Brown & R. W. Lent (Eds.), *Handbook of counseling psychology* (3rd ed., pp. 471–498). New York, NY: Wiley.

Lent, R. W. (2004). Toward a unifying theoretical and practical perspective on well-being and psychosocial adjustment. *Journal of Counseling Psychology, 51*, 482–509.

Lent, R. W. (in press). Career-life preparedness: Revisiting career planning and adjustment in the new workplace. *Career Development Quarterly*.

Maslow, A. H. (1943). A theory of human motivation. *Psychological Review, 50*, 370–396.

Miller, D. S., & McWhirter, E. H. (2006). The history of career counseling: From Frank Parsons to twenty-first-century challenges. In D. C. Capuzzi & M. D. Stauffer (Eds.), *Career counseling: Foundations, perspectives, and applications* (pp. 3–39). Boston, MA: Pearson.

Parsons, F. (1909). *Choosing a vocation*. Boston, MA: Houghton-Mifflin.

Pope, M., & Minor, C. W. (Eds.). (2000). *Experiential activities for teaching career counseling classes and for facilitating career groups*. Columbus, OH: National Career Development Association.

Richardson, M. S. (1993). Work in people's lives: A location for counseling psychologists. *Journal of Counseling Psychology, 40*, 425–433.

Savickas, M. L. (1994). Convergence prompts theory renovation, research unification, and practice coherence. In M. L Savickas & R. W. Lent (Eds.), *Convergence in career development theories: Implications for science and practice* (pp. 235–257). Palo Alto, CA: Consulting Psychologists Press.

Savickas, M. L. (Ed.). (2009). The 100th anniversary of vocational guidance [Special section]. *Career Development Quarterly, 57*, 3.

Savickas, M. L., & Baker, D. B. (2005). The history of vocational psychology: Antecedents, origin, and early development. In W. B. Walsh & M. L. Savickas (Eds.), *Handbook of vocational psychology* (3rd ed., pp. 15–50). Mahwah, NJ: Erlbaum.

Super, D. E., Savickas, M. L., & Super, C. M. (1996). The life-span, life-space approach to careers. In D. Brown, L. Brooks, & Associates. *Career choice and development: Applying contemporary theories to practice* (3rd ed., pp. 121–178). San Francisco, CA: Jossey-Bass.

Vroom, V. H. (1964). *Work and motivation*. New York, NY: Wiley.

Whiston, S. C., Brecheisen, B. K., & Stephens, J. (2003). Does treatment modality affect career counseling effectiveness. *Journal of Vocational Behavior, 62*, 390–410.

Zytowski, D. G. (1972). Four hundred years before Parsons. *Personnel and Guidance Journal, 50*, 443–450.

MAJOR THEORIES OF CAREER DEVELOPMENT, CHOICE, AND ADJUSTMENT

CHAPTER 2

Minnesota Theory of Work Adjustment

JANE L. SWANSON AND MADALYN SCHNEIDER

THE MINNESOTA THEORY of Work Adjustment (TWA) is considered a model of person–environment vocational fit, as is Holland's vocational-personality typology (see Nauta, Chapter 3, this volume). Both theories evolved from earlier trait-and-factor counseling (Chartrand, 1991; Rounds & Tracey, 1990), which, in turn, was based on Parsons's (1909/1989) social reform efforts at the turn of the 20th century. Further, both TWA and Holland's theory (as based on Parsons) may be described as "matching models" (Betz, 2008), in which vocational choice is maximized by specifying important characteristics of the individual and the environment and then attempting to find the best match or fit between individual and environment. The characteristics of individuals and environments that are considered to be important vary by theory. An additional component of matching models is that the degree of fit is quantified in some manner, and fit may then be used to predict central outcomes, such as the person's satisfaction or tenure.

Both TWA and Holland's model evolved within the discipline of vocational psychology yet share a conceptual foundation with the broader study of *person–environment psychology* (Dawis, 2000). This perspective is built on the assumption that there is a reciprocal relationship between people and their environments: People influence their environments, and environments influence the people in them (Walsh, Price, & Craik, 1992). Work is but one of many environments in which people interact—others include school, family, intimate relationships, living environments—all of which influence and are influenced by the individuals in them. Vocational psychology—its science and its practice—has embraced the tenets of person–environment psychology (Swanson & Chu, 2000), as evidenced by the TWA and Holland models of person–environment fit. In addition to being a model of person–environment fit, TWA may be considered a model of person–environment interaction (Dawis, 2005): The concept of *fit* describes the degree of similarity between a person and an environment, whereas the concept of *interaction* reflects the reciprocal influence between a person and an environment.

CORE CONCEPTS OF THE THEORY OF WORK ADJUSTMENT

The theory of work adjustment, as reflected in its name, has as its primary focus the process of adjustment to work environments, but it also can be used to help people make vocational choices (to be discussed in a later section of this chapter). In the original presentation of the theory and throughout its continued development, TWA has been characterized by careful attention to the structural characteristics of theory building. For example, Dawis and Lofquist (1984) presented 17 formal propositions and associated corollaries, which have guided subsequent work related to the theory. These propositions are presented in slightly paraphrased form in Table 2.1.

As a theory of person–environment fit, TWA focuses on the process of persons' adjustment to their work environments, including the characteristics of persons that predict their satisfaction with the work environment, as well as their level of satisfactoriness within the work environment. TWA actually consists of two models: a predictive model and a process model (Dawis, 2005). The *predictive model* focuses on the variables that explain whether individuals are satisfied with their work environments and whether they are satisfactory to their work environments, which in turn predicts individuals' tenure in their work environments. The *process model* focuses on how the fit between individuals and their environments is attained and maintained.

PREDICTIVE MODEL: PREDICTING *WHETHER* WORK ADJUSTMENT OCCURS

The predictive model comprises the core of TWA and is reflected in Propositions I through IX in Table 2.1. TWA proposes two sets of parallel characteristics. First, an individual has a set of needs and values that may (or may not) be met by rewards available in the work environment. Second, the work environment has a set of job requirements that may (or may not) be met by the skills and abilities that the individual possesses. Each of these intersections of an individual and his or her environment is described by the term *correspondence* or its lack, *discorrespondence*. If a person's needs are met by his or her work environment, then the person and

Table 2.1
Summary of Formal Propositions of the Theory of Work Adjustment

Proposition I: Work adjustment at any time is indicated by the concurrent levels of the person's satisfaction and satisfactoriness.

Proposition II: A person's satisfaction is predicted from the correspondence between his or her values and the environment's reinforcers, provided that there is also correspondence between the person's abilities and the environment's ability requirements.

 Corollary IIA: A person's values may be inferred from knowledge of his or her satisfaction and the environment's reinforcers.

 Corollary IIB: An environment's reinforcers may be inferred from knowledge of a person's values and his or her satisfaction.

Proposition III. A person's satisfactoriness is predicted from the correspondence between his or her abilities and the environment's ability requirements, provided that there is also correspondence between the person's values and the environment's reinforcers.

 Corollary IIIA: An environment's ability requirements may be inferred from knowledge of a person's abilities and his or her satisfactoriness.

 Corollary IIIB: A person's abilities may be inferred from knowledge of an environment's ability requirements and the person's satisfactoriness.

Proposition IV: Prediction of a person's satisfaction is moderated by his or her satisfactoriness.

Proposition V: Prediction of a person's satisfactoriness is moderated by his or her satisfaction.

Proposition VI: The probability that a person will leave an environment is inversely related to his or her satisfaction.

Proposition VII: The probability that an environment will fire a person is inversely related to his or her satisfactoriness.

Proposition VIII: A person's tenure is predicted from his or satisfaction and satisfactoriness.

 Given Propositions II, III, and VIII:

 Corollary VIIIA: A person's tenure is predicted from the correspondence between his or her values and the environment's reinforcers, and the correspondence between his or her abilities and the environment's ability requirements.

 Corollary VIIIB: A person's tenure is predicted from the correspondence between person and environment.

Proposition IX: Person-environment correspondence increases as a function of a person's tenure.

Proposition X: The correspondence between a person's style and the environment's style moderates the prediction of the person's satisfaction from the correspondence between his or her values and the environment's reinforcers, and the prediction of the person's satisfactoriness from the correspondence between his or her abilities and the environment's ability requirements.

Proposition XI: A person's flexibility moderates the prediction of his or her satisfaction from the correspondence between his or her values and the environment's reinforcers.

(Continued)

Table 2.1 (*Continued*)

Proposition XII: An environment's flexibility moderates the prediction of a person's satisfactoriness from the correspondence between his or her abilities and the environment's ability requirements.

Proposition XIII: The probability that a person will engage in adjustment behavior is inversely related to his or her satisfaction.

    Corollary XIIIA: A person's flexibility threshold may be determined from knowledge of this probability associated with his or her satisfaction.

Proposition XIV: The probability that an environment will engage in adjustment behavior is inversely related to the person's satisfactoriness.

    Corollary XIVA: An environment's flexibility threshold may be determined from knowledge of this probability associated with the person's satisfactoriness.

Proposition XV: The probability that a person will quit an environment is inversely related to his or her perseverance.

    Corollary XVA: A person's perseverance threshold may be determined from knowledge of this probability associated with his or her quitting the environment.

Proposition XVI: The probability that an environment will terminate (fire) an individual is inversely related to its perseverance.

    Corollary XIVA: An environment's perseverance threshold may be determined from knowledge of this probability associated with the environment's terminating a person.

    Given Propositions VIII, XV, and XVI:

Proposition XVII: A person's tenure is predicted jointly with his or her satisfaction, satisfactoriness, and perseverance, and the environment's perseverance.

Source: The propositions are adapted from Dawis (2005) with slight alterations in wording; the original numbering is preserved.

---

environment are in correspondence; if not, then they are in discorrespondence. Likewise, if the work environment's requirements are met by the person, then the person and environment are in correspondence; if not, then they are in discorrespondence. The former situation determines the individual's level of *satisfaction* (or dissatisfaction) with the work environment; the latter refers to the individual's level of *satisfactoriness* (or unsatisfactoriness) to the work environment. Said another way, an individual has needs, and the work environment has rewards; if needs and rewards (or reinforcer patterns) correspond, then the individual is satisfied. Likewise, an individual has abilities, and the work environment has ability requirements; if abilities and ability requirements correspond, then the individual is considered satisfactory. These relationships are illustrated in the left side of Figure 2.1.

TWA emphasizes the measurement of abilities and values to facilitate the match of individuals' characteristics with the characteristics of the work environment (the assessment of these concepts is discussed is a later section). In the parlance of TWA, abilities are "reference dimensions of skills" (Dawis,

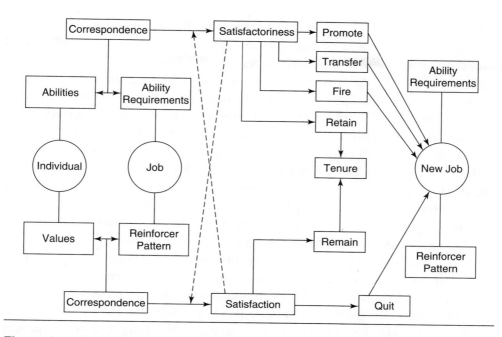

Figure 2.1   Prediction of Work Adjustment
("Prediction of Work Adjustment") in *A Psychological Theory of Work Adjustment*, by R. V. Dawis and L. H. Lofquist (Minneapolis: University of Minnesota Press, 1984) p. 62. Reprinted with permission.

2005); that is, abilities are the more general dimensions underlying specific skills. For example, verbal ability is the general dimension underlying demonstrated reading comprehension and vocabulary. In a similar fashion, values are the general dimensions underlying specific needs. TWA includes six core values: *achievement* (using one's abilities and having a feeling of accomplishment), *comfort* (feeling comfortable and not feeling stressed), *status* (achieving recognition and being in a dominant position), *altruism* (being of service to others and being in harmony with others), *safety* (having a stable, ordered, and predictable work environment), and *autonomy* (being independent and having a sense of control) (Dawis, 2002).

If an individual is both satisfied and satisfactory, then the individual and his or her environment are in a state of harmonious equilibrium, and work adjustment has been achieved. If, however, the individual is dissatisfied, unsatisfactory, or both, then a state of disequilibrium exists. This disequilibrium serves as a motivational force, propelling some type of change to occur. The specific type of change depends on a number of other factors, to be discussed later. Thus, dissatisfaction serves a central motivational role in TWA. Dissatisfaction of either party—the person or the environment—represents a disequilibrium in the person–environment system and serves as the impetus for some kind of adjustment to occur.

Disequilibrium is an uncomfortable state that motivates actions that lead to reestablishment of equilibrium. As Dawis (1996) noted, "Satisfaction motivates 'maintenance' behavior; dissatisfaction motivates adjustment behavior" (p. 87). Adjustment behavior may take one (or more) of four avenues (Dawis, 2002): Two of the options are present when individuals are dissatisfied with their environments, and two of the options are present when individuals are unsatisfactory (and therefore the environment is dissatisfied with them). The ideal state is when a person is satisfied *and* satisfactory, leading to maintenance behavior. However, a person could be satisfied yet unsatisfactory, dissatisfied yet satisfactory, or both dissatisfied *and* unsatisfactory. These latter three states lead to adjustment behavior.

If people are dissatisfied, they have two possible choices: attempting to change the environment or change themselves. They may be able to influence the environment to change the number or kinds of reinforcers that it provides, for example, by requesting a salary increase or a change in work tasks. Alternatively (or in conjunction with environmental change), workers could change the number or kind of needs that they require, such as changing their expectations about salary or rethinking how they interact with a difficult coworker. Ultimately, individuals must decide whether to stay in the current work environment or leave for another environment.

If individuals are unsatisfactory, they have two possible choices: increasing their level of skill or expanding their skill repertoire to meet the requirements of the environment or attempting to change the environment's expectations. Moreover, the environment has several possible actions, with the ultimate outcomes of retaining or terminating the individual.

Although TWA focuses on both the individual and the environment, the theory clearly emphasizes what the person experiences: The term *satisfaction* refers to an individual's satisfaction with his or her job, whereas the term *satisfactoriness* refers to an individual with whom the work environment is satisfied. Tenure occurs when an individual is both satisfied and satisfactory (Dawis, 2005) (see the center portion of Figure 2.1).

In addition to these basic predictions, TWA proposes a number of moderating relationships and variables. As depicted by the dotted X in the center of Figure 2.1, the processes of correspondence, satisfaction, and satisfactoriness influence one another. That is, workers' levels of satisfaction with their work environment is predicted to influence their level of satisfactoriness to the work environment; if workers are satisfied, then they are more likely to perform at a satisfactory level, whereas if they are not satisfied (i.e., if their needs are not being met), then they are less likely to perform at a satisfactory level. Conversely, if individuals are performing at a level that the environment judges to be satisfactory, then they are more likely to be satisfied than if they are performing at an unsatisfactory level.

Another type of moderator variable included in TWA is personality style, which describes how individuals characteristically interact with their environments. TWA proposes four styles: celerity, pace, rhythm, and endurance. *Celerity* describes how quickly one responds or the speed with which an individual initiates interaction with the environment. A person with high celerity responds quickly to the environment, perhaps even impulsively, whereas a person with low celerity moves slowly in interacting with the environment. *Pace* refers to how intensely one responds to the environment. Once an individual chooses to act on the environment, then pace describes the rate of interaction, such as high or low energy. *Rhythm* is the pattern of the pace of one's response, such as steady, cyclical, or erratic patterns, and *endurance* refers to sustaining the pattern of response to the environment, namely, how persistently one responds. These four personality style variables help explain why individuals with similar values and abilities exhibit different behaviors within the same work environment (Swanson & Fouad, 2010). These style variables also can be used to describe the environment, thus leading to a description of the correspondence between an individual and his or her environment. For example, an individual with a high degree of celerity would be in greater correspondence with an environment that requires a similar level of celerity than an environment with low celerity. Although the four style variables are not included in the model in Figure 2.1, these variables and the level of person–environment correspondence they produce are important to consider.

PROCESS MODEL: PREDICTING *How* WORK ADJUSTMENT OCCURS

The process model adds to TWA's ability to predict work adjustment by focusing on *how* adjustment occurs and *how* it is maintained. Recall that discorrespondence between people and their environments serves to motivate behavior; the process portion of TWA defines the parameters and outcomes of that motivational force. Recall, too, that discorrespondence refers to either the individual being dissatisfied with the work environment, the individual being unsatisfactory to the work environment, or both. TWA proposes that individuals' adjustment styles characterize how they react to the occurrence of discorrespondence, as illustrated in Figure 2.2.

Adjustment style consists of four variables: flexibility, active adjustment, reactive adjustment, and perseverance. *Flexibility* refers to how much discorrespondence people will tolerate before they reach a threshold of dissatisfaction that leads to some type of adjustment behavior. Individuals vary in the amount of flexibility that they will exhibit before their mismatch with the environment becomes too great, but eventually discorrespondence may exceed their tolerance and individuals move into an adjustment mode.

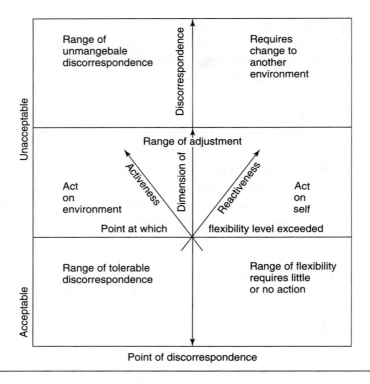

Figure 2.2   Relationships Between Adjustment-Style Dimensions
("Relationship Among Adjustment-Style Dimensions") in *Essentials of Person Environment Correspondence Counseling*, by L. H. Lofquist and R. V. Dawis (Minneapolis: University of Minnesota Press, 1991) p. 19. Reprinted with permission.

Once an individual's flexibility level has been exceeded, adjustment behavior can be characterized as either active or reactive.

In *active* adjustment, the individual acts on the environment in an effort to decrease discorrespondence (such as by trying to change the available rewards and/or trying to change what the environment requires). In *reactive* adjustment, the individual acts on himself or herself to reduce the amount of discorrespondence (such as by changing his or her own needs and/or skills). Activeness and reactiveness are not mutually exclusive; rather, an individual might use both modes of adjustment. Finally, *perseverance* refers to the length of time that an individual is willing to persist in a discorrespondent environment after engaging in adjustment behavior. An individual who quits the job after a brief attempt at change is characterized as low in perseverance, whereas an individual who persists despite repeated or lengthy attempts at change is considered high in perseverance.

Adjustment styles are relevant to the environment, too. Environments differ in how much discorrespondence they will tolerate between an individual's abilities and the environment's ability requirements before judging the person as unsatisfactory (flexibility). When an environment's flexibility threshold is exceeded, it engages in either active (e.g., provide additional training to improve the person's abilities) or reactive (e.g., move the person into a more ability-correspondent position). Some environments may fire a discorrespondent employee more quickly than others (perseverance).

All four of these adjustment style variables are hypothesized to vary among individuals and work environments and are important factors in predicting adjustment behavior. The concepts of active and reactive adjustment modes and of flexibility and perseverance are thus useful in predicting what an individual is likely to do when he or she is dissatisfied with a job. The active and reactive adjustment modes can also provide options for counselors and clients to consider to improve clients' levels of work satisfaction. Flexibility and perseverance are viewed as fluctuating characteristics: An individual may be flexible and able to tolerate discorrespondence on one day but then be unable to tolerate it the next, thus entering into adjustment mode. Despite fluctuations, an individual is likely to develop a characteristic adjustment style over time, which may be evident in multiple arenas of his or her life.

The illustration of adjustment behavior in Figure 2.2 demonstrates the influence of the four adjustment style variables. The vertical line in the center of the figure represents the range of discorrespondence that an individual (or an environment) might experience, with zero discorrespondence at the bottom of the line and extreme discorrespondence at the top of the line. Moving up the center line represents an increase in discorrespondence, as that amount begins at an acceptable or tolerable level. As the increase in discorrespondence exceeds an individual's level of flexibility—or becomes intolerable or unacceptable—then he or she embarks on adjustment behavior, either active or reactive. The individual continues with adjustment attempts until he or she has reached the limit of his or her perseverance, at which point the amount of discorrespondence has become unmanageable, and he or she will leave the environment.

For example, a woman who has a strong desire for autonomy is dissatisfied by the level of close monitoring provided by the supervisor in her new job, yet she is flexible in tolerating this discorrespondence because she believes her supervisor will reduce monitoring after a training period. However, her supervisor continues close monitoring even when she has demonstrated her skill, and the employee experiences dissatisfaction. When the employee's dissatisfaction reaches an intolerable level, she will then attempt to make an adjustment. She may choose to talk with her supervisor about her frustration (active adjustment) and/or decrease her feelings of dissatisfaction by changing how she interprets her supervisor's behavior (reactive adjustment). If she is successful, then she will feel satisfied (achieve correspondence and restore equilibrium). If, however, her supervisor continues to closely monitor her work, and she continues to feel dissatisfied, she will need to decide whether to persevere in her job or leave for another position (either in the same organization or at a different organization).

The concepts found in the predictive model interact with those in the process model. According to TWA, people's levels of satisfaction mostly depend on how their values correspond to the reinforcers provided by the environment. However, workers' levels of satisfaction also depend on their satisfactoriness as well as on their flexibility. In other words, if a person is unsatisfactory (the environment is dissatisfied with the individual), the individual's satisfaction can no longer be predicted as well by the correspondence between his or her values and the environment's reinforcers. Further, the greater an individual's flexibility, the easier it is for the environment to satisfy the individual (Dawis, 2002). In a similar fashion, an individual's satisfactoriness depends mostly on how his or her abilities correspond to the requirements of the environment. However, an individual's satisfactoriness also depends on his or her level of satisfaction, as well as the flexibility of the environment. In other words, if a person is dissatisfied, then the individual's satisfactoriness can no longer be predicted as well by the correspondence between his or her abilities and the environment's requirements. Further, the greater the environment's flexibility, the more tolerant it will be with a lower level of correspondence between an individual's abilities and the environment's requirements.

ASSESSMENT OF TWA CONSTRUCTS

A strength of the theory of work adjustment is the amount of attention that its authors have devoted to developing psychometrically sound measures of its central constructs. Unfortunately, however, many of these measures are not widely available and so have not been adopted by career practitioners. However, as Dawis (2005) noted, the theory is not wedded to use of these specific measures, and, in fact, using measures developed outside of a theoretical framework may provide more robust evidence on the theory's validity and practical utility. Indeed, because TWA focuses on the correspondence between person variables and environmental variables, any measures that provide a way to quantify that correspondence may be used within the context of TWA constructs. In this section, we briefly discuss the measures developed by Dawis and his colleagues, as well as other measures.

The role of vocational interests in TWA is less direct than in other theories of vocational choice. Dawis (1996) described interests as "more complex variables that are functions of the simpler TWA variables" (p. 92) of abilities and values. Specifically, if interests are defined as liking or disliking different activities (Hansen, 2005; Chapter 14, this volume), then abilities influence what activities an individual chooses to try and/or continue to pursue, and values influence an individual's liking or disliking. Assessment of an individual's interests is a common component of career counseling and may be used as a mechanism for discussing a client's abilities and values.

Needs and values. Assessing work-related needs and values is frequently an important part of career counseling (see Rounds & Jin, Chapter 15, this volume). Within the context of TWA, the Minnesota Importance Questionnaire (MIQ; Rounds, Henley, Dawis, Lofquist, & Weiss, 1981) was developed to measure an individual's needs and values. The MIQ measures 20 work-related needs and produces in scores on six values: (1) *Achievement*, consisting of Ability Utilization and Achievement; (2) *Altruism*, consisting of Co-workers, Social Service, and Moral Values; (3) *Autonomy*, consisting of Creativity and Responsibility; (4) *Comfort*, consisting of Activity, Independence, Variety, Compensation, Security, and Working Conditions; (5) *Safety*, consisting of Company Policies, Supervision–Human Relations, and Supervision-Technical; and (6) *Status*, consisting of Advancement, Recognition, Authority, and Social Status.

The MIQ profile provides two different types of information. First, intraindividual (ipsative) scores on the 20 needs and six values are plotted relative to one another. Second, comparisons are made between an individual's values profile and patterns of reinforcers empirically derived for a variety of occupations. The latter yields a list of occupations in which a person is likely to be satisfied. The MIQ materials and scoring are available through the Vocational Psychology Research website at the University of Minnesota (http://www.psych.umn.edu/psylabs/vpr/default.htm).

Another option for assessing an individual's needs and values is the Work Importance Profiler (WIP), available via O*NET, the online occupational information database of approximately 1,000 occupations developed by the U.S. Department of Labor (http://www.onetonline.org). The WIP is based on a ranked version of the MIQ and produces scores on six values—Achievement, Independence, Recognition, Relationships, Support, and Working Conditions—that correspond to the six MIQ values, as well as scores on 21 needs (the 20 MIQ needs plus Autonomy). The O*NET provides links to its database of occupations on the basis of the six values; for example, one can browse occupations that match a specified set of work values, such as Achievement and Independence, or search for a specific occupation and then determine the characteristic needs and values of individuals in that occupation (see also Rounds & Jin, Chapter 15, this volume).

Measures of work-related values other than the MIQ and the O*NET's WIP include Super's Work Values Inventory (Nevill & Super, 1986; Zytowski, 2006). Another method of addressing work-related values within career counseling is a values card sort. A card sort consists of a set of cards, each imprinted with a work-related value, which clients place into categories according to their importance. Because a card sort is completed during a career counseling session, it provides a mechanism for in-session discussion of the client's important values, the origin of these values, and how values are related to other career-related information such as interests and skills.

Work satisfaction. In TWA, "satisfaction" is conceptualized as the correspondence between an individual's values/needs and the reinforcers offered by the environment. In some ways, satisfaction in TWA is a derived variable that can be inferred from the match between an individual's values and an environment's reinforcers. For instance, good correspondence between values and reinforcers implies satisfaction. However, satisfaction can also be measured directly by asking individuals about the degree to which they like their work environments, either overall or specific aspects (see Lent & Brown, Chapter 22, this volume). Early in the evolution of TWA, the researchers developed a measure of work satisfaction, the Minnesota Satisfaction Questionnaire (MSQ; Weiss, Dawis, England, & Lofquist, 1967). The MSQ provides scores on 20 facets of job satisfaction, as well as three summary scores (Intrinsic, Extrinsic, and General Satisfaction). The 20 facets parallel the scales on the MIQ (with the exception of the MIQ Autonomy scale). This measure has been used primarily in research and is not generally used in practice settings. It, too, is available through the Vocational Psychology Research website (http://www.psych.umn.edu/psylabs/vpr/default.htm).

More generally, the study of job satisfaction has received substantial attention within the domain of industrial/organizational psychology (Fritzsche & Parrish, 2005; Swanson, 2012; Zedeck, 2010), where a main focus is the organizational antecedents and consequences of job satisfaction (Landy & Conte, 2010). In contrast, there is a relative lack of attention to job satisfaction within vocational psychology. Lent (2008) examined job satisfaction from the perspective of vocational psychology. He noted that job satisfaction "may be viewed as an integral part of work adjustment and overall mental health" (p. 462). Lent defined *job satisfaction* as "people's cognitive constructions of their work enjoyment" (p. 463), highlighting the cognitive and affective components that constitute satisfaction. Lent and Brown (Chapter 22, this volume) also describe how organizational psychology research on job satisfaction can be used to inform career counseling practice.

Many measures of job satisfaction have been developed for use in a variety of settings, focusing on both global (overall feelings about a job) and facet (specific aspects of a job) satisfaction (Fritzsche & Parrish, 2005). For example, the Job Descriptive Index (JDI; Smith, Kendall, & Hulin, 1985) consists of 72 items that measure satisfaction with five aspects of a job (work, pay, promotions, supervision, and coworkers). Lent and Brown (Chapter 22, this volume) describe this and other measures of job satisfaction more fully.

Satisfactoriness.   Another measure developed as part of TWA, the Minnesota Satisfactoriness Scales (MSS; Gibson, Weiss, Dawis, & Lofquist, 1970) was designed to measure 28 variables of job satisfactoriness and is completed by an individual's work supervisor. The MSS yields scores on five scales: Performance, Conformance, Dependability, Personal Adjustment, and General Satisfactoriness. The MSS is available from the Vocational Psychology Research website (http://www.psych.umn.edu/psylabs/vpr/default.htm). Although the MSS as originally designed would not often be used as part of a career intervention, it or another measure of job performance could be used as a self-assessment tool. For example, clients and counselors could use the MSS in session to assess how clients perceive their performance on these five dimensions of satisfactoriness and to facilitate discussion of the accuracy of clients' perceptions.

RESEARCH SUPPORT FOR THE THEORY OF WORK ADJUSTMENT

Dawis (1996) and Dawis and Lofquist (1984) provide thorough overviews of the early research support for TWA. Their reviews will be briefly visited here, followed by a review of more recent research on TWA constructs and propositions, as well as areas in which further research support is warranted.

GENERAL SUPPORT FOR TWA PREDICTIONS

General research on person–environment fit has served as a foundation for the study of work adjustment. In TWA specifically, the primary concepts include those defined earlier: person–environment correspondence, satisfaction, satisfactoriness, and tenure. Some of the variables receiving research attention include work personality variables (e.g., abilities, values, personality style), work environment variables (e.g., reinforcer systems, ability requirements, environment style), indicators of work adjustment (e.g., satisfaction and satisfactoriness), and correspondence between personality and environment. Although there have been instruments constructed specifically for use with this theory, such as the Minnesota Satisfactoriness Scales, other instruments have also been used to support the theory and its applicability to real people and places of employment (Dawis & Lofquist, 1984).

Much TWA research, using both TWA-specific measures and other more general measures of person–environment fit constructs, has focused on the prediction of satisfaction, satisfactoriness, work adjustment, and tenure. Results have indicated strong support for the interactions between these constructs, which maps well onto the first eight formal propositions of TWA (Dawis, 1996; see Table 2.1). For example, Dawis (1996) described the studies supporting the hypotheses that satisfaction and satisfactoriness are predicted by person–environment correspondence (Propositions II and III). Although this first set of TWA propositions has received empirical support, the second set (Propositions X through XVII), geared toward the roles of personality style, adjustment style, and flexibility of both the individual and the environment, remains in need of research attention (Dawis, 1996).

RESEARCH PERTAINING TO DIVERSE POPULATIONS

In addition to personality styles and flexibility, research on the use of TWA with diverse populations remains another area in which expansion is needed. Swanson (1996) emphasized the importance of demonstrating the ability of person–environment fit theories, such as TWA, to explain and predict work satisfaction, satisfactoriness, and tenure across diverse groups (e.g., gender, race, ethnicity, and culture). Following this recommendation, a few studies have shown support for the use of TWA with culturally stigmatized groups, such as lesbian, gay, and bisexual (LGB) populations (Lyons, Brenner, & Fassinger, 2005); African American employees (Lyons & O'Brien, 2006), and individuals with mental retardation (Chiocchio & Frigon, 2006). Using a measure of perceived person–job and person–organization fit developed by Saks and Ashforth (1997), Lyons and colleagues (2005) found that perceived correspondence predicted satisfaction and the probability of remaining in the current work environment for lesbian, gay, and bisexual individuals. This support held true even in the presence of informal heterosexism in the workplace, which is an example of a unique barrier that stigmatized populations experience in workplaces. Results of the study indicated that the persons' perception of correspondence between their values and the work environment reinforcers mediated the relationship between workplace heterosexism and job satisfaction (Lyons et al., 2005). That is, the experience of heterosexism resulted in lower levels of satisfaction because it tended to reduce employees' sense of fit with the work environment.

In a similar study with African American employees, Lyons and O'Brien (2006) reported that perceived person–environment fit explained 43% of the variance in job satisfaction and 17% of the variance in intentions to quit.

Perceived racial climate, however, did not moderate or mediate the relationship between fit and satisfaction or turnover intentions, supporting the primacy of perceived person–environment correspondence. Further, qualitative analyses coded for TWA values and racial climate indicated the TWA value of comfort was cited most often as contributing to job satisfaction, whereas racial climate was cited least often. Chiocchio and Frigon (2006) also demonstrated support for the use of TWA in a sample of adults with mental retardation, for whom both satisfactoriness and satisfaction together predicted tenure 16 weeks after starting a job. These studies suggest the usefulness of TWA in explaining the work experiences of different groups of people.

Research on the process model (e.g., on the roles of personality styles, adjustment styles, flexibility, and perseverance) has been much more limited than research on the predictive model. Several writers have suggested that attention to personality factors might enhance TWA by providing a more holistic picture of what the individual brings to the interaction between the person and environment. Hesketh and Griffin (2005), for example, suggested that such factors as mental health, general well-being, knowledge as well as skills, abilities, and higher-order needs or values need to be considered to more fully understand the adjustment strategies that people employ and various options to enhance career success across diverse populations (Renfro-Michel, Burlew, & Robert, 2009). Although additional research is needed (especially on the process model and the validity of TWA in culturally diverse populations), TWA's theoretical concepts offer potential benefit for practitioners. In the next section, we discuss some of the applications of TWA.

APPLICATIONS OF TWA

The theory of work adjustment can be applied to better understand current work trends, stages of career development, and career adaptability for culturally diverse populations. As Griffin and Hesketh (2005) discuss, it is common, or even expected, that contemporary organizations will experience environmental change. These changes will have an effect on everyone involved in the workplace. Environmental change may lead to organizational expansion, reduction, or shifts in power or resources. These changes are likely to alter the reinforcements and requirements that characterize the environment. Therefore, the environment may no longer correspond with what the individual employee originally brought to the interaction. On the other side of the coin, shifts occurring for the individual (e.g., life changes such as a medical diagnosis, having a child, or a variety of other events or shifts in values or priorities) may render reinforcers that were previously valued by an individual much less reinforcing. When such discorrespondence occurs, the workplace or the individual will be required to adjust to restore satisfaction and satisfactoriness. Adjustment may consist of active, reactive, or tolerant behavior by either the organization or the individual (Griffin & Hesketh, 2005). TWA may be a useful framework within the current career climate to enhance understanding of the continuous change process and how it impacts individuals, the environment, and the interaction between the two.

TWA also intersects with the positive psychology movement, which has natural connections to the broader field of vocational psychology. This movement includes a greater focus on mental health, well-being, and life satisfaction. It is widely recognized that job satisfaction is closely interconnected with overall life satisfaction (Lent, 2008; Lent & Brown, Chapter 22, this volume; Swanson, 2012). With satisfaction as one of TWA's key components, there is an inherent connection between TWA and positive psychology (e.g., Eggerth, 2008). TWA depicts how environmental reinforcers, satisfactoriness, and other factors feed into a person's job satisfaction, which in turn may have an impact on individuals' overall levels of life satisfaction and mental health. Thus, the application of TWA for persons experiencing dissatisfaction at work may at the same time alleviate psychological distress and promote greater life satisfaction and well-being, one of the goals of the positive psychology movement.

CAREER ISSUES THROUGHOUT THE LIFE SPAN

As one of the primary theories of person–environment fit, TWA can be useful in the early stages of career exploration and development to help individuals identify an array of occupational possibilities in which they may achieve satisfaction and success in the future. According to TWA, an effective strategy with adolescents and young adults is to identify their major work-related needs, values, skills, and abilities, as well as occupational possibilities that correspond with their values and abilities (Dawis, 2005), which should promote more satisfying and satisfactory choices. Attention to person–environment fit during initial entry into a career field may also lead to higher-quality employment experiences (Saks & Ashforth, 2002).

By focusing on work adjustment, TWA can also be useful in counseling persons who are currently dissatisfied with their work environments or who are judged as unsatisfactory in their current jobs. TWA provides some clear hypotheses about sources of dissatisfaction and unsatisfactoriness that can provide directions for counseling. For example, a practitioner familiar with TWA would explore with dissatisfied clients their major work-related values and how well these are being met in their work environments.

Should need–reinforcer discorrespondence be identified, the client could then explore and implement different active and reactive strategies to achieve greater correspondence. Should these strategies fail, then the counselor might work with the client to identify more value-correspondent jobs or occupations. Additionally, clients' levels of flexibility would also be considered. Clients who are characteristically inflexible are likely to report dissatisfaction with seemingly minor levels of discorrespondence and may require close attention to value–reinforcer correspondence in exploring future job or occupational possibilities.

Similarly, in working with clients who are judged to be performing poorly at work (unsatisfactory workers), TWA would suggest an exploration of the clients' abilities and the degree to which these abilities match the ability requirements of their current jobs. And again, should discorrespondence be evident, counselors would explore with clients different active and reactive strategies that may be employed to achieve greater satisfactoriness. Counselors would also help clients explore and identify alternative jobs or occupations in which the client is more likely to achieve satisfactory performance. Lent and Brown (Chapter 22, this volume) provide some additional suggestions about how TWA and other theories can be applied in working with clients experiencing problems of job satisfaction and satisfactoriness.

Recent work has explored the applicability of TWA to promoting adjustment to retirement (Harper & Shoffner, 2004). For individuals reaching the age of retirement, adjustment is not only probable but also probably unavoidable. No matter what life after retirement will look like, there are likely to be differences from the world of work that the individual currently experiences. The ultimate goal for most individuals is to achieve satisfaction in their postretirement lives. Thus, TWA could be used in working with individuals who are planning for retirement or experiencing difficulties in adjusting to retirement by exploring how their major needs and values are being satisfied in their postretirement lives and how they might implement their abilities in this new developmental stage.

Using TWA With Diverse Clients

As mentioned in the previous section regarding research support for TWA, there remain limited empirical data on the application of TWA to many specific populations. However, this does not necessarily mean that TWA lacks benefit for working with a diverse clientele. There are several examples of applying TWA concepts with specific populations, drawing on authors' experiences as career practitioners. TWA has been used to conceptualize career issues for people who have HIV/AIDS (Dahlbeck & Lease, 2010), symptoms of anorexia nervosa (Withrow & Shoffner, 2006), and the specific challenges experienced by lesbian women (Degges-White & Shoffner, 2002). Each of these authors discussed the dynamic nature of the person and the environment, as well as their interaction. For example, chronic health status issues for persons living with AIDS/HIV may affect previous levels of abilities and skills and lead to a reevaluation of needs and values; TWA would be useful in framing related work adjustment issues. Withrow and Shoffner (2006) described the personality and behavioral characteristics of women with disordered eating symptoms as leading to "precarious person–environment correspondence" (p. 366), in which the achievement of job satisfaction and satisfactoriness exacerbates eating disorders. In applying TWA to lesbians, Degges-White and Shoffner (2002) described the relationship between being "out" in the workplace and four critical aspects of TWA: job satisfaction, person–environment correspondence, the importance of workplace reinforcers, and abilities. These unique challenges may also be apparent for gay, bisexual, and transgendered workers. Research discussed earlier (Lyons et al., 2005) suggested that the experience of heterosexism in the work environment might have a significant impact on LGB workers' perceptions of fit and, therefore, their satisfaction with their jobs.

Analysis of the challenges to successful career choice and adjustment of unique groups of individuals such as those just discussed highlights the usefulness of TWA tenets. The central concepts of TWA—that person–environment correspondence leads to favorable outcomes and that discorrespondence leads to adjustment behavior—provide a core framework that can be used to understand and work with diverse clients encountering difficulties with work adjustment.

Career counseling from the TWA perspective addresses the two aspects of correspondence: the client's satisfaction with his or her job or occupation and the client's satisfactoriness within his or her work environment. Counselors using TWA as a theoretical framework would begin by identifying the needs and abilities of the client. These characteristic needs and abilities are unique starting points, and so counselors would explore the specific nature of the client's abilities and needs, as well as the degree of satisfaction and satisfactoriness resulting from the degree of fit between a client and his or her environment. Counseling from the perspective of TWA is primarily focused on discorrespondence and the resolution of clients' discorrespondence with their environments through career choice and adjustment.

Lofquist and Dawis (1991) suggested several questions to guide a counselor's work with clients from the framework of TWA. First, what is the match between clients' abilities and the ability requirements of their jobs? Clients' abilities may be too high or too low for the position. Second, what are clients' subjective evaluations of their abilities and the discorrespondence they are experiencing with requirements of the work environment? Is there a discrepancy between self-estimated and actual abilities or between the perceived and actual environmental requirements? Third, what is the match between clients' needs and the rewards offered by the environment? Fourth, are clients actually both satisfied with and satisfactory in their work environments but experiencing difficulties in nonwork domains? These questions translate TWA tenets into testable hypotheses to pursue in career counseling (Swanson & Fouad, 2010).

A unique aspect of TWA is that counselors may focus on characteristics of work (and nonwork) environments to a greater degree than in other theories (Juntunen & Even, 2012). Such a focus allows counselors and clients to determine the degree of correspondence between environmental requirements and rewards and an individual's abilities and needs.

INTERVENTIONS IN ORGANIZATIONAL SETTINGS

TWA also has potential applications for work organizations. For example, personnel assessment may be a primary area in which TWA could be used. TWA has had a history of application within personnel assessment and evaluation of job performance. Much job performance evaluation has focused solely on measures of individuals' capabilities (see Lent and Brown, Chapter 22, this volume). TWA, however, depicts job performance as a measure of the interaction between a person's ability and the demands or requirements of the workplace (Dawis, 1980). Therefore, finding ways to assess job performance within the actual environment, rather than solely the person's capability to perform job like tasks, would be an incorporation of TWA into performance evaluation. TWA could also be used in other interventions, such as organizational leadership and management aimed at creating a positive work climate and promoting workplace support (Griffin & Hesketh, 2005). The creation and employment of organizational-level interventions is equally important as interventions aimed at individuals because TWA emphasizes the needs and requirements of each within the adjustment process.

CASE EXAMPLE

To further examine how TWA may be used in working with clients, we discuss the case of Jasmine. Jasmine is a 19-year-old single, heterosexual Latina. She is an only child and has a close, supportive relationship with her mother, a social worker, who lives three hours away. Jasmine is a sophomore in college, currently majoring in interior design. She sought career counseling because she recently began to question her choice of major but is unsure of other majors or careers she might like to pursue.

Interior design has been her dream career since the age of 10, and Jasmine never considered alternative career paths. She reports finding enjoyment in organizing and decorating rooms and in seeing others' happiness as a result of her creativity.

Jasmine has always been a good student, earning As and Bs throughout high school, as well as in her first semester of college. However, during the past two semesters, she has begun earning Cs, which Jasmine attributes to the types of courses she has been taking for her major. These courses consist of architecturally based classes requiring knowledge of "angles and math" that she is "not able to understand," despite the hours she reports spending on assignments and projects. She has begun feeling unexcited about her work and misses the experience of being artistically creative with colors, themes, and objects within a room. She has begun to perceive designing the structure of a room as overly restrictive. Jasmine wishes to receive help in deciding whether to continue with her interior design major.

TWA can aid in the understanding of Jasmine's current experiences of discorrespondence with her major through exploring both her satisfaction and satisfactoriness as contributing forces. In terms of satisfaction, Jasmine reported that she enjoyed interior design based on the process of organizing rooms, creating color schemes and themes, and seeing others' enjoyment. In terms of TWA values, these reflect independence and achievement, including ability utilization (making use of her artistic abilities), achievement (being able to see what she has accomplished), creativity (being able to try her own ideas), and social service (doing things for others).

Her creativity needs of artistic expression are currently not being met in the courses she is taking, causing her to have low levels of satisfaction. In terms of satisfactoriness, the interior design major requires an architecturally based skill set that does not match Jasmine's repertoire of abilities, resulting in low satisfactoriness.

Goals of career counseling with Jasmine may be (a) clarifying her needs in a work environment, (b) increasing understanding of her abilities and how they relate to interior design or other academic majors, and (c) ultimately making a decision regarding whether to remain in her current major or change to a different major. These goals work together within the TWA framework to first understand what factors are important for Jasmine to experience correspondence with an academic major or career and then aid in identifying what Jasmine can do to obtain satisfaction and tenure in a given environment. These goals can be obtained through exploration of both the self and the environment. For example, exploring past experiences and environments in which Jasmine has felt her needs were met, as well as those in which she felt her needs were not sufficiently met, may provide important information regarding the flexibility and variation of Jasmine's needs. Such an exploration may provide greater insight into which needs are necessary for Jasmine to experience satisfaction within an environment.

Jasmine could also take the O*NET Work Importance Profiler (WIP) to help in the identification of her major work-related values (see Rounds & Jin, Chapter 15, this volume). One advantage of the formal value assessments that can be obtained by the MIQ or WIP is that they provide a rank-ordering of values that may aid individuals who have a hard time discriminating among important values and needs. For example, Jasmine may feel that relationships with coworkers and using her creative abilities are equally important to her, whereas the WIP might suggest that achievement is more important to her than relationships with coworkers. Using assessment tools such as the MIQ or WIP also may bring needs and values to the forefront of discussion with Jasmine, such as having high scores on working conditions that lead her to consider the importance of needs such as pay and job security.

Exploring and identifying Jasmine's abilities and the skill requirements of the occupation of interior design, as well as other potential options, can also be used to predict the occupational areas in which Jasmine is likely to be most satisfactory. Finally, identifying ways in which Jasmine may change her current environment (e.g., adding art classes to her course load to meet her need for artistic expression) may also be a beneficial intervention in finding ways to increase satisfaction and correspondence without changing to a completely new major and career path.

CONCLUSIONS AND PRACTICE IMPLICATIONS

As evidenced throughout this chapter, TWA has great potential for understanding the experiences of clients presenting with career choice issues and for assisting clients (whether individuals or organizations) in increasing work adjustment. In this section, we offer take-home tips for career professionals in using TWA.

1. TWA is a well-constructed theory with possible applications across the career life cycle. It can be used to help people (a) forecast the types of occupations in which they may achieve satisfaction and satisfactoriness, (b) select among different occupational possibilities, (c) achieve (or reachieve) satisfaction and satisfactoriness in the current work environment and identify work environments that might be associated with greater satisfaction and satisfactoriness, and (d) aid in the retirement adjustment process.

2. In all cases, TWA suggests that clients be helped to identify their major work-related (or retirement-related) needs, values, and abilities.

Theories vary in the concepts they deem most important; values and abilities constitute the primary focus of TWA.

3. TWA is a person–environment fit theory. Thus, it is also important to help clients identify work environments that appear to be correspondent with their major work-related needs, values, and abilities. There are a variety of occupational information systems that can be employed for this purpose, including the Minnesota Occupational Classification System and the O*NET data bases (see Gore, Leuwerke, & Kelly, Chapter 18, this volume).

4. Discorrespondence may occur for either the person or the environment. Clients may enter career counseling expressing dissatisfaction with their jobs or career choices, but counselors are advised to remember that individuals also may be unsatisfactory; that is, the environment may be dissatisfied with the person. The concepts of TWA provide a ready framework for attending to both aspects of dissatisfaction.

5. Some research suggests that the theory has cross-cultural validity, especially in the predictions of satisfaction among LGB individuals and African Americans. Thus, value-reinforcer correspondence seems an important target for counseling LGB and African American clients who are looking for satisfying career options or experiencing dissatisfaction in the workplace. TWA seems also relevant to other groups as well, but research is limited.

6. Finally, fully informed and comprehensive career counseling will incorporate other empirically supported theories and research along with TWA in helping people make satisfying and satisfactory career choices and achieve workplace and retirement adjustment. For example, Rounds (1990) found that value-reinforcer correspondence (from TWA) and RIASEC congruence (from Holland's theory) did a better job of predicting work satisfaction than did either correspondence or congruence alone. We also identified some ways in which concepts drawn from other theoretical approaches (such as positive psychology) and attention to contextual factors may help develop more complex approaches to understanding and assisting clients.

REFERENCES

Betz, N. E. (2008). Advances in vocational theories. In S. D. Brown & R. W. Lent (Eds.), *Handbook of counseling psychology* (4th ed., pp. 357–374). Hoboken, NJ: Wiley.

Chartrand, J. M. (1991). The evolution of trait-and-factor career counseling: A person X environment fit approach. *Journal of Counseling and Development, 69,* 518–524.

Chiocchio, F., & Frigon, J. Y. (2006). Tenure, satisfaction, and work environment flexibility of people with mental retardation. *Journal of Vocational Behavior, 68,* 175–187. doi:10.1016/j.jvb.2004.11.004

Dahlbeck, D. T., & Lease, S. H. (2010). Career issues and concerns for persons living with HIV/AIDS. *Career Development Quarterly, 58,* 359–368.

Dawis, R. V. (1980). Personnel assessment from the perspective of the theory of work adjustment. *Public Personnel Management, 9,* 268–273.

Dawis, R. V. (1996). The theory of work adjustment and person–environment-correspondence counseling. In D. Brown, L. Brooks, & Associates (Eds.), *Career choice and development* (3rd ed., pp. 75–120). San Francisco, CA: Jossey-Bass.

Dawis, R. V. (2000). The person–environment tradition in counseling psychology. In M. E. Martin Jr., & J. L. Swartz-Kulstad (Eds.), *Person–environment psychology and mental health: Assessment and intervention* (pp. 91–111). Mahwah, NJ: Erlbaum.

Dawis, R. V. (2002). Person–environment correspondence theory. In D. Brown & Associates (Eds.), *Career choice and development* (4th ed., pp. 427–464). San Francisco, CA: Jossey-Bass.

Dawis, R. V. (2005). The Minnesota theory of work adjustment. In S. D. Brown & R. W. Lent (Eds.), *Career development and counseling: Putting theory and research to work* (pp. 3–23). Hoboken, NJ: Wiley.

Dawis, R. V., & Lofquist, L. H. (1984). *A psychological theory of work adjustment.* Minneapolis: University of Minnesota Press.

Degges-White, S., & Shoffner, M. F. (2002). Career counseling with lesbian clients: Using the Theory of Work Adjustment as a framework. *Career Development Quarterly, 51,* 87–96.

Eggerth, D. E. (2008). From theory of work adjustment to person–environment correspondence counseling: Vocational psychology as positive psychology. *Journal of Career Assessment, 16,* 60–74. doi:10.1177/1069072707305771

Fritzsche, B. A., & Parrish, T. J. (2005). Theories and research on job satisfaction. In S. D. Brown & R. W. Lent (Eds.), *Career development and counseling: Putting theory and research to work* (pp. 180–202). Hoboken, NJ: Wiley.

Gibson, D. L., Weiss, D. J., Dawis, R. V., & Lofquist, L. H. (1970). Manual for the Minnesota Satisfactoriness Scales. *Minnesota studies in vocational rehabilitation, XXVII.* Minneapolis, MN: University of Minnesota.

Griffin, B., & Hesketh, B. (2005). Counseling for work adjustment. In S. D. Brown & R. W. Lent (Eds.), *Career development and counseling: Putting theory and research to work* (pp. 483–505). Hoboken, NJ: Wiley.

Hansen, J. C. (2005). Assessment of interests. In S. D. Brown & R. W. Lent (Eds.), *Career development and counseling: Putting theory and research to work* (pp. 281–304). Hoboken, NJ: Wiley.

Harper, M. C., & Shoffner, M. F. (2004). Counseling for continued career development after retirement: An application of the theory of work adjustment. *Career Development Quarterly, 52,* 272–284.

Hesketh, B., & Griffin, B. (2005). Work adjustment. In W. B. Walsh & M. Savickas (Eds.), *Handbook of vocational psychology: Theory, research, and practice* (3rd ed., pp. 245–266). Mahwah, NJ: Erlbaum.

Juntunen, C. L., & Even, C. E. (2012). Theories of vocational psychology. In N. A. Fouad, J. A. Carter, & L. M. Subich (Eds.), *APA handbook of counseling psychology.* Washington, DC: American Psychological Association.

Landy, F. J., & Conte, J. M. (2010). *Work in the 21st century: An introduction to industrial and organizational psychology* (3rd ed.). New York, NY: Wiley.

Lent, R. W. (2008). Understanding and promoting work satisfaction: An integrative view. In S. D. Brown & R. W. Lent (Eds.), *Handbook of counseling psychology* (4th ed., pp. 462–482). Hoboken, NJ: Wiley.

Lofquist, L. H., & Dawis, R. V. (1991). *Essentials of person–environment-correspondence counseling*. Minneapolis: University of Minnesota Press.

Lyons, H. Z., Brenner, B. R., & Fassinger, R. E. (2005). A multicultural test of the theory of work adjustment: Investigating the role of heterosexism and fit perceptions in the job satisfaction of lesbian, gay, and bisexual employees. *Journal of Counseling Psychology, 52*, 537–548. doi:10.1037/0022–0167.52.4.537

Lyons, H. Z., & O'Brien, K. M. (2006). The role of person–environment fit in the job satisfaction and tenure intentions of African American employees. *Journal of Counseling Psychology, 53*, 387–396.

Nevill, D. D., & Super, D. E. (1986). *The Values Scale: Theory, application, and research*. Palo Alto, CA: Consulting Psychologists Press.

Parsons, F. (1989). *Choosing a vocation*. Garrett Park, MD: Garrett Park Press. (Original work published 1909)

Renfro-Michel, E. L., Burlew, L. D., & Robert, T. (2009). The interaction of work adjustment and attachment theory: Employment counseling implications. *Journal of Employment Counseling, 46*, 18–26.

Rounds, J. B. (1990). The comparative and combined utility of work value and interest data in career counseling with adults. *Journal of Vocational Behavior, 37*, 32–45. doi:10.1016/0001–8791(90)90005-M

Rounds, J. B., Henley, G. A., Dawis, R. V., Lofquist, L. H., & Weiss, D. J. (1981). *Manual for the Minnesota Importance Questionnaire*. Minneapolis: University of Minnesota.

Rounds, J. B., & Tracey, T. J. (1990). From trait-and-factor to person–environment fit counseling: Theory and process. In W. B. Walsh & S. H. Osipow (Eds.), *Career counseling: Contemporary topics in vocational psychology* (pp. 1–44). Hillsdale, NJ: Erlbaum.

Saks, A. M., & Ashforth, B. E. (1997). A longitudinal investigation of the relationships between job information sources, applicant perceptions of fit, and work outcomes. *Personnel Psychology, 50*, 395–427.

Saks, A. M., & Ashforth, B. E. (2002). Is job search related to employment quality? It all depends on the fit. *Journal of Applied Psychology, 87*, 646–654. doi:10.1037/0021–9010.87.4.646

Smith, P. C., Kendall, L. M., & Hulin, C. L. (1985). *The job descriptive index*. Bowling Green, OH: Bowling Green State University.

Swanson, J. L. (1996). The theory *is* the practice: Trait-and-factor/person–environment fit counseling. In M. L. Savickas & W. B. Walsh (Eds.), *Handbook of career counseling theory and practice* (pp. 93–108). Palo Alto, CA: Davies-Black.

Swanson, J. L. (2012). Work and psychological health. In N. A. Fouad, J. A. Carter & L. M. Subich (Eds.), *APA handbook of counseling psychology*. Washington, DC: American Psychological Association.

Swanson, J. L., & Chu, S. P. (2000). Applications of person–environment psychology to the career development and vocational behavior of adolescents and adults. In M. E. Martin, Jr., & J. L. Swartz-Kulstad (Eds.), *Person–environment psychology and mental health: Assessment and intervention* (pp. 143–168). Mahwah, NJ: Erlbaum.

Swanson, J. L., & Fouad, N. A. (2010). *Career theory and practice: Learning through case studies* (2nd ed.). Thousand Oaks, CA: Sage.

Walsh, W. B., Price, R. H., & Craik, K. H. (1992). Person–environment psychology: An introduction. In W. B. Walsh, K. H. Craik, & R. H. Price (Eds.), *Person–environment psychology: Models and perspectives* (pp. vii–xi). Mahwah, NJ: Erlbaum.

Weiss, D. J., Dawis, R. V., England, G. W., & Lofquist, L. H. (1967). Manual for the Minnesota Satisfaction Questionnaire. *Minnesota Studies in Vocational Rehabilitation* (No. XXII), 1–119. Minneapolis: University of Minnesota, Industrial Relations Center.

Withrow, R. L., & Shoffner, M. F. (2006). Applying the theory of work adjustment to clients with symptoms of anorexia nervosa. *Journal of Career Development, 32,* 366–377. doi:10.1177/0894845305284706

Zedeck, S. (Ed.). (2010). *APA handbook of industrial and organizational psychology.* Washington, DC: American Psychological Association.

Zytowski, D. G. (2006). *Super Work Values Inventory-revised: Technical manual.* Retrieved from http://www.kuder.com

CHAPTER 3

Holland's Theory of Vocational Choice and Adjustment

MARGARET M. NAUTA

W HEN JOHN HOLLAND INTRODUCED a theory of vocational choice in 1959, his goal was to present a framework that would be practical for counselors and clients to use. His work as a career counselor in educational, military, and clinical settings helped provide Holland with a sense of what was needed and what would be useful. He concluded that simplicity was critical: If a theory was too complex for counselors to explain and for clients to remember and reflect on, it ran the risk of being underutilized. Therefore, Holland strove to articulate a theory that would be sufficiently robust to explain important outcomes and yet simple enough to be user-friendly. It is safe to say he accomplished this goal with resounding success. Holland revised and refined his theory numerous times based on results from empirical studies he and others conducted to test elements of the theory. Now Holland's theory is generally regarded as among the most influential theories guiding career counseling and practice.

This chapter serves as an introduction to Holland's (1997b) theory of vocational choice and is divided into three major sections:

1. An overview of the theory and its predictions
2. A summary of research on the theory, including its applicability to diverse populations
3. A discussion of how the theory can be applied to career issues that arise over the life span with diverse populations

The chapter concludes with a series of take-home messages that summarize for practitioners the key parts of the theory and their implications for career interventions.

OVERVIEW OF THE THEORY

The essence of Holland's theory is that both people and environments can be described in terms of their resemblance to six model, or theoretical, types. The interrelationships among the types provide the basis for several predictions about the kinds of careers people will choose, how satisfied they will be with their work, how well they will perform in their work, and the ease with which they will be able to make career decisions.

THE SIX TYPES OF PERSONS AND ENVIRONMENTS

According to Holland, by late adolescence most people can be characterized in terms of how closely they resemble each of six basic personality types: Realistic, Investigative, Artistic, Social, Enterprising, and Conventional (commonly abbreviated with the acronym RIASEC). Each type has a unique constellation of preferred activities, self-beliefs, abilities, and values, as summarized in Table 3.1. Readers are encouraged to consult Holland (1997b) for more detailed descriptions of the personality types.

Describing how the RIASEC personality types develop was not a central goal of Holland's, but he suggested they are likely the result of a complex interaction among "a variety of cultural and personal forces including peers, biological heredity, parents, social class, culture, and the physical environment" (Holland, 1997b, p. 2). Based on these influences, Holland believed people first begin to prefer some activities over others, and then these preferences become strong interests and areas of competence that lead them to seek some experiences and to avoid others. This further reinforces their interests and abilities such that over time, the interests, areas of competence, and resulting self-beliefs become dispositional and can be used to make predictions about people's future choices and behaviors.

In arguing for the presence of six basic types, Holland did not assert that people represent only a *single* type. Many individuals have a dominant type that they most closely resemble plus one or more additional types (called *subtypes*) that they also resemble to some degree. Accordingly, Holland recommended using the rank-ordering of all six types to describe people. Considering all possible combinations of the rank-ordered six types, there are 720 different personality profile patterns that can exist. Therefore, while providing simplicity by allowing us to think about individuals in terms of six dimensions, the theory actually allows for quite a bit of complexity and diversity among those individuals. In practice, many counselors use a three-point code—called a Holland code—that is made up of the first letters of the three types a client most resembles. Thus, if a client most resembles the Social type, but also shows a reasonable degree of resemblance to the

Artistic and Enterprising types in descending order, he or she would have a three-point Holland code of SAE.

To assess a client's resemblance to the RIASEC types, counselors can use instruments developed by Holland and his colleagues, including the Vocational Preference Inventory (VPI; Holland, 1985b) and the Self Directed Search (SDS; Holland, Fritzsche, & Powell, 1994). RIASEC scales have also been created for almost all major career interest inventories, including the Strong Interest Inventory (SII; Donnay, Morris, Schaubhut, & Thompson, 2004), the Unisex Edition of the ACT Interest Inventory (Swaney, 1995), and the Armed Services Vocational Aptitude Battery (U.S. Department of Defense, 1994) (see Hansen, Chapter 14, this volume). These instruments provide RIASEC *interest* scores, which are more narrowly defined than are the broader RIASEC *type* scores from the SDS (which include information about other personal attributes, in addition to interests), but, in practice, interest and type scores are usually used in the same way. In addition, the RIASEC dimensions serve as the organizing framework for instruments measuring other career-relevant constructs, such as people's beliefs about their abilities (e.g., the Skills Confidence Inventory; Betz, Borgen, & Harmon, 2004).

Holland proposed that, like people, work and educational environments can also be categorized in terms of their resemblance to the six RIASEC types. Each environment type presents unique opportunities and tends to require different skills of its incumbents (see Table 3.1). Readers can consult Gottfredson and Holland (1996) and Holland (1997a) for more complete lists and detailed descriptions of the environment types. As with people, some environments are quite complex and resemble multiple RIASEC types, so again the rank-ordering of multiple types is useful, and three-point Holland codes are often used to describe environments as well.

One way to determine an environment's type is on the basis of the personalities of the people working in it because, as Holland explained, "where people congregate, they create an environment that reflects the types they most resemble" (Holland, 1997b, p. 3). Thus, an environment comprising mostly workers with CRE personalities would be considered a CRE environment. Alternatively, an environment can be described based on the types of activities in which people in it usually engage. The Position Classification Inventory (PCI; Gottfredson & Holland, 1991) allows employees or supervisors to rate the frequency with which a job involves various activities, values, and perspectives that are grouped by RIASEC type. Three-point Holland codes are also available for hundreds of occupations in the *Dictionary of Holland Occupational Codes* (*DHOC*; Gottfredson & Holland, 1996); ancillary materials to the SDS, such as the *Occupations Finder* (Holland, 1996) and *Educational Opportunities Finder* (Holland, 1997a); and in many

Flatter

Table 3.1

Characteristics of Holland's RIASEC Personality and Environment Types

Realistic

Preference for working with: things

Personality characteristics: frank, practical, focused, mechanical, determined, rugged

Preferred/typical activities and skills: mechanical, manual, physical, and athletic tasks

Sample careers: Fitness trainer, firefighter, mechanic, builder, farmer, landscaper

Sample majors: criminal justice studies, athletic training, construction management

Values: tradition, freedom, independence

Investigative

Preference for working with: things and ideas

Personality characteristics: analytical, intellectual, reserved, independent, ambitious

Preferred/typical activities and skills: working with abstract ideas, solving intellectual problems, collecting data

Sample careers: biologist, researcher, physician, mathematician, computer systems analyst

Sample majors: botany, engineering, mathematics, premed, food technology

Values: independence, logic, scholarly achievement

Artistic

Preference for working with: ideas and people

Personality characteristics: complicated, original, impulsive, independent, expressive, creative

Preferred/typical activities and skills: using imagination, creative expression

Sample careers: artist, musician, actor, creative writer, photographer

Sample majors: art, theater, graphic design, music

Values: aesthetic experience, self-expression, imagination, nonconformity

Social

Preference for working with: people

Personality characteristics: cooperative, helpful, empathic, kind, tactful, warm, sociable, generous

Preferred/typical activities and skills: interacting with and helping people, teaching, guiding

Sample careers: teacher, clergy, counselor, nurse, school bus monitor

Sample majors: nursing, education, counseling, social work

Values: altruism, ethics, equality

Enterprising

Preference for working with: data and people

Personality characteristics: persuasive, energetic, sociable, adventurous, ambitious, assertive

Preferred/typical activities and skills: leading, managing, persuading, and organizing people

Conventional

Preference for working with: data and things

Personality characteristics: careful, conforming, conservative, responsible, controlled

Preferred/typical activities and skills: ordering, attending to details

Table 3.1 *(Continued)*

Sample careers: manager, lawyer, business administrator, politician	*Sample careers*: accountant, banker, actuary, editor, office manager, librarian
Sample majors: prelaw, business management, political science	*Sample majors*: business, accounting
Values: tradition, economic achievement, ambition	*Values*: tradition, ambition, obedience, economic achievement, comfort

Source: Adapted from Gottfredson and Holland (1996), Holland (1997a, 1997b), Prediger (1982).

other sources of occupational information, including the U.S. Department of Labor–sponsored O*NET database (see Gore, Leuwerke, & Kelly, Chapter 18, this volume).

PREDICTIONS BASED ON RELATIONSHIPS AMONG THE TYPES

In striving for a theory that was simple enough to be widely used, Holland willingly sacrificed some detail and predictive power. He maintained that a more complex theory involving more than six types or more constructs would be impractical. Nevertheless, Holland recognized that it was important to acknowledge the limits of the theory and to place it in context. Therefore, he introduced his theory with an "other things being equal" (1997b, p. 12) qualifier, explaining that the theory is useful for understanding individuals' career choices *after* controlling for age, gender, social class, and other influences that limit opportunities or the range of careers a person can or does consider.

After the influence of these other factors has been accounted for, Holland suggested that the interrelationships among the RIASEC personality and environment types allow us to make several predictions about people's career choices, satisfaction, and performance. Four important constructs related to these predictions are congruence, differentiation, consistency, and identity.

Congruence. The most important part of Holland's theory is the idea that an individual's personality is better suited to some environments than to others. He asserted that people search for and enter environments that permit them to "exercise their skills and abilities, express their attitudes and values, and take on agreeable problems and roles" (p. 4). In other words, people seek environments that fit well with their personalities. Environments also seek good-fitting employees via their recruitment and selection of people with desired characteristics. Thus, like the theory of work adjustment (see

Swanson & Schneider, Chapter 2, this volume), Holland's theory is an exemplar of the person–environment fit (Dawis, 2000) approach.

Holland used the term *congruence* to refer to the degree of fit between an individual and his or her current or projected environment with respect to the RIASEC types. The more similar the personality is to the environment, the more congruent are the two. A person with an RIA personality working in an RIA environment has a very high level of congruence. That same individual working in an RIE environment would have slightly lower congruence, and that person in an SEC environment would have a very low degree of congruence.

In research and practice, congruence has been operationalized in many ways. The simplest measure considers only the match between the first letters of the person's and the environment's Holland codes, whereas other congruence indices consider the rank ordering of two or more personality and environment types (see Brown & Gore, 1994; Camp & Chartrand, 1992; Young, Tokar, & Subich, 1998, for summaries and evaluations of congruence indices).

Holland theorized that congruence is a determinant of several important outcomes, including people's career aspirations and choices, work satisfaction, job stability, and performance. Specifically, he predicted that:

- People will tend to aspire to and choose educational and work environments that are congruent with their personalities.
- When people are in environments that are highly congruent with their personalities, they will be more satisfied and successful, and they will remain in those environments longer, resulting in greater stability (i.e., fewer job changes) over the life span.

Differentiation. A minority of people and environments resemble one RIASEC type almost exclusively (i.e., are "pure" types), whereas other people and environments are similar to many of the types. Holland used the term *differentiation* to describe the degree to which a person or environment is clearly defined with respect to the RIASEC types.

People with high levels of differentiation show a strong resemblance to one RIASEC type and little resemblance to other types, whereas people with low levels of differentiation have similar degrees of resemblance to many of the types. The lowest degree of differentiation is present in the profile of a person who receives identical scores on all six RIASEC scores when taking an inventory such as the SDS. Among people, Holland operationalized differentiation as the difference between the highest and lowest scores for the six types. Other differentiation indices, for example, the distance between the highest and lowest scores that comprise a person's three-point Holland code, have also been used (see Alvi, Khan, & Kirkwood, 1990, for descriptions of several differentiation indices).

Highly differentiated work environments have employees and activities that clearly align with one RIASEC type and few of the others. An example is an auto repair shop in which all of the employees are primarily engaged in hands-on, mechanical work that exemplifies the Realistic type, even though some may specialize in electronic systems, others in body work, and still others in engine repair. Environments made up of employees with varied RIASEC types or that require many different kinds of work activities have low levels of differentiation. An example is a medical office complex in which there are physicians (primary I type), nurses (primary S type), and medical records clerks (primary C type), whose work activities can be quite disparate. Work environment differentiation can be quantified by having employees or supervisors rate the environment with the PCI and then using indices that are analogous to those used to calculate personality differentiation.

Holland theorized that differentiation has implications for the process of career decision making and that it moderates the relationships between congruence and its outcomes. People with highly differentiated personalities should be drawn to a narrow range of occupational areas with which there is obvious congruence, but people with highly undifferentiated personalities can have difficulty making career decisions because they feel torn between multiple areas that are equally attractive (or equally unappealing, in the case of low, undifferentiated personality profiles). Likewise, because highly differentiated environments are more predictable (i.e., are easier to identify and involve more activities typically associated with a given type), they should more easily attract highly congruent employees. Accordingly, Holland predicted that:

- Personality differentiation is positively associated with ease of career decision making. Therefore, individuals with highly undifferentiated personalities may struggle to a greater degree with making career choices.
- The positive relationships between congruence and work satisfaction, success, and stability will be stronger when differentiation (either personality, environmental, or both) is greater.

Consistency. Each RIASEC type, whether personality or environment, has more in common with some types than with others. When examining the pattern of correlations among RIASEC scores, Holland and his colleagues (Holland, Whitney, Cole, & Richards, 1969) discovered a roughly circular ordering of types and subsequently presented what has become an icon in career development and assessment: the Holland hexagon (see Figure 3.1).

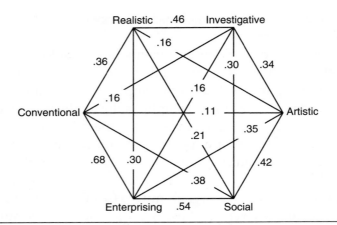

Figure 3.1 Holland's Hexagonal Model of the Relationships Among Personality and Environment Types

Source: From J. L. Holland, D. R. Whitney, N. S. Cole, & J. M Richards, Jr. (1969). *An empirical occupational classification derived from a theory of personality and intended for practice and research* (ACT Research Report No. 29). Iowa City, IA: American College Testing Program. Copyright 1969 by the American College Testing Program. All rights reserved. Reproduced with permission from ACT, Inc.

As shown by the correlations among the RIASEC type scores in Figure 3.1, when the RIASEC types are placed, in order, on the points around a hexagon, those on adjacent points (e.g., R and I) are more similar than those that are more distant (e.g., R and A). Those that are diametrically opposed (e.g., R and S) share the least in common. This underlying structure, or *calculus*—in which the RIASEC types are equidistantly located around the hexagon and there is an inverse relationship between distances on the hexagon and similarity—provides a means for determining the degree to which there is relative harmony versus discordance among the types a person or environment most closely resembles.

When the types that make up a person's or environment's Holland code are adjacent on the hexagon (i.e., are more similar), the person or environment has a high degree of what Holland called *consistency*. For instance, the Social and Enterprising types, while having distinct characteristics, share a common element of involving work with people (Prediger, 1982). A low level of consistency is present when the types making up a person's or environment's Holland code are diametrically opposed (e.g., I and E) and have little in common. For example, a highly inconsistent work environment requires a combination of interests and abilities that are rarely required in the same job and that few people have. Consistency is frequently calculated by examining the position of the first two letters of the three-letter person or environment Holland code on the hexagon, although more complex methods for determining consistency have also been used (see Strahan, 1987).

Among both people and environments, consistency is more the norm than the exception. For example, the *DHOC* lists only two occupations as having the highly inconsistent ACS Holland code, whereas over 80 are listed that have the highly consistent CER Holland code. As a result, people with more consistent personalities will be able to consider and choose from more occupations that allow them to express most of the key elements of their personalities. Similarly, highly consistent environments should be able to recruit from a larger pool of employees with highly congruent personalities. Accordingly, Holland predicted that:

- Consistency is positively associated with ease of career decision making. People with highly inconsistent personalities may be more challenged when attempting to find highly congruent environments.
- Consistency moderates the relationships between congruence and its outcomes. The relationships between congruence and work satisfaction, performance, and stability will be stronger when consistency (either personality, environmental, or both) is high.

Identity. Finally, Holland noted that some people and environments are more clearly defined and have more stability over time than do others. *Identity* refers to the degree to which a person has "a clear and stable picture of one's goals, interests, and talents" (Holland, 1997b, p. 5) and can be assessed using the Identity Scale of My Vocational Situation (MVS; Holland, Daiger, & Power, Holland et al., 1980). Strong environmental identity is present when an environment or organization has clear, integrated goals, tasks, and rewards that are stable over long time intervals. A work setting with a limited range of highly related positions that remain the same over time would have a strong, or crystallized, identity, whereas a work setting with varied positions that change frequently has a more diffuse identity. Holland indicated that one way to operationalize environmental identity is to take the inverse of the number of occupations within a work setting. For example, a small business with employees in four different occupations—such as salesperson, marketing executive, administrative assistant, and product designer—would have an identity of 0.25 (the inverse of 4).

Theoretically, identity is strongly related to differentiation and consistency because people or environments with high degrees of differentiation and consistency are expected to have clearer, stabler goals. In fact, Holland considered identity to be somewhat redundant with differentiation and consistency, but he thought identity provides a more direct measure of "how well a person defines himself or herself" (1997b, p. 33).

As with differentiation and consistency, Holland expected that:

- A stronger, well-defined identity promotes ease in career decision making.

- Identity moderates the relationships between congruence and its outcomes. Specifically, congruence will have stronger positive relationships with work satisfaction, stability, and performance when identity (either of the person, the environment, or both) is well defined.

SUMMARY

In summary, when all else is equal, Holland predicted that individuals who have highly consistent and differentiated personality profiles should have more crystallized identities, make career decisions with greater ease, and experience greater stability in their career trajectories. Those with less differentiated, less consistent profiles may have more diffuse identities, struggle more with career decision making, and have less stable career paths. He expected that people will seek environments that are congruent with their personalities, and when they do so, they will "probably do competent work, be satisfied and personally effective, and engage in appropriate social and educational behavior" (Holland, 1997b, p. 40). Likewise, environments characterized by a high degree of consistency and differentiation that possess a clear identity are expected to have employees with higher levels of satisfaction, stability, and productivity.

RESEARCH SUPPORT FOR HOLLAND'S THEORY

Holland's theory consists of easily quantifiable constructs and predictions that lend themselves well to scientific investigation. Consequently, hundreds of studies examining aspects of Holland's theory have been conducted. We now know a great deal about many parts of the theory, including its applicability to diverse populations. Several meta-analyses (Assouline & Meir, 1987; Spokane, Meir, & Catalano, 2000; Tracey & Rounds, 1993; Tsabari, Tziner, & Meir, 2005) and reviews of the empirical status of Holland's theory (e.g., Carson & Mowsesian, 1993; Holland, 1997b; Nauta, 2010; Spokane, 1985) provide a more in-depth analysis of this body of research, but some of the larger trends are summarized here.

RESEARCH ON THE TYPES AND THEIR INTERRELATIONSHIPS

Much research has been devoted to verifying that the RIASEC types exist among people and environments and that they possess the characteristics described by Holland (1997b). Researchers have also tested the degree to which the types and their interrelationships are invariant across segments of the population.

Existence of the types. Because Holland's theory relies on six types as the basis for matching people to environments, it has been critical to establish that the RIASEC types do, in fact, exist. Numerous studies have provided evidence that people's self-descriptions (e.g., on adjective checklists or interest inventories) cluster together in ways that resemble Holland's types. This has been shown to be true among a wide variety of individuals, including high school students (e.g., Holland, 1962), college students (e.g., Edwards & Whitney, 1972), and working adults (e.g., Rachman, Amernic, & Aranya, 1981). There is also support for the existence of the types among environments, because workers' and job analysts' descriptions of workplace requirements and rewards often group together in ways that resemble the RIASEC types when subjected to factor or cluster analyses (e.g., Donnay & Borgen, 1996; Rounds, Smith, Hubert, Lewis, & Rivkin, 1999). Of course, documenting the presence of the RIASEC types does not mean this is the *only* structure or valid mechanism for categorizing persons and environments, but Holland's six types do seem to provide a reasonable heuristic for doing so.

Relations to other constructs. Many studies have linked people's RIASEC scores with scores on measures of other constructs, and the findings have tended to be fairly consistent with Holland's descriptions of the types. For example, RIASEC scores are related in ways that are consistent with Holland's type descriptions to people's values (Williams, 1972) and life goals (Astin & Nichols, 1964), as well as to some of the Big Five personality factors (e.g., Larson, Rottinghaus, & Borgen, 2002) and measures of actual or perceived ability (e.g., Ackerman & Heggestad, 1997; Betz, Harmon, & Borgen, 1996). RIASEC environment types have also been shown to have many characteristics that are consistent with Holland's descriptions (Maurer & Tarulli, 1997), although there has been less research on the environment types than on the personality types. Overall, Holland's framing of the model RIASEC types as broad constructs (i.e., collections of interests and other attributes, like values and abilities) seems well founded.

Stability over time. Holland's conceptualization of the RIASEC personality types as being dispositional by late adolescence has also been critical to verify empirically. After all, it would be of little practical value to use the RIASEC types as the basis for seeking congruent future environments if people's resemblance to those types fluctuates tremendously. Studies have documented a good degree of stability for RIASEC type scores for late adolescents 'and adults over fairly short time periods. For example, the test–retest stability of RIASEC scores on the SDS for a sample that included high school students, college students, and adults ranged from .76 to .89 over periods of up to 12 weeks (Holland et al., 1994).

A larger body of literature has examined the stability of RIASEC *interests* (again, just one component of the Holland types) as assessed by instruments such as the SII. Because some of these studies have used lengthier follow-up intervals, they provide more useful information about the degree to which RIASEC scores can be considered traitlike. Consistent with Holland's dispositional view, findings from their meta-analysis of interest stability research led Low, Yoon, Roberts, and Rounds (2005) to conclude that RIASEC interests are reasonably stable between the ages of 12 and 40 and are comparable to personality traits and abilities in terms of their level of stability. Low and colleagues did find, however, that interests became noticeably *more* stable after the age of 18. Across studies that assessed RIASEC interests using retest periods of over 1 year, Low and colleagues found that Realistic and Artistic interests tended to be stabler over time than Enterprising and Conventional interests, but all the types exhibited sufficient stability to support the practice of RIASEC interest assessment in career counseling. Nevertheless, note that some individuals' interests change substantially over time (see Swanson, 1999). Holland (1997b) explained such fluctuations in terms of inconsistent, undifferentiated profiles or a more diffuse identity, but as will be discussed later, these explanations have received only mixed support.

Group differences. There appear to be some reliable differences in RIASEC score levels across segments of the population. The largest of these differences is with respect to gender. On most measures, women tend to outscore men on the Social type, and men tend to score higher than women on the Realistic type (e.g., Fouad, 2002; Tracey & Robbins, 2005). It is also not uncommon for women to score higher than men on the Artistic type (Fouad, 2002). Differences by age and racial/ethnic group tend to be fairly small in size. One study found that Asian Americans scored higher on measures of the Investigative type than did members of other racial/ethnic groups (Fouad, 2002), but most other studies (e.g., Fouad & Mohler, 2004) have not found such differences. The gender and racial/ethnic group differences in RIASEC scores probably reflect the different kinds of experiences and opportunities people have as they are growing up (Holland, 1997b).

The structure of types. A good deal of research—and much of the recent research on Holland's theory—has investigated the degree to which Holland's hexagon provides a good representation of the relationships among the RIASEC types. Not surprisingly, given that the hexagon figure was articulated on the basis of known correlations among RIASEC type scores, findings from many studies have generally supported the RIASEC ordering of types among people and environments. That is, types that are adjacent on the hexagon have consistently been found to be more strongly related than are nonadjacent types (e.g., Armstrong & Rounds, 2008; Darcy & Tracey, 2007). However, because there is less support for the fit of a strict model that specifies equal distances between the points of the hexagon (e.g., Armstrong, Hubert, & Rounds, 2003), many writers (e.g., Armstrong & Rounds, 2008; Darcy & Tracey, 2007) now refer more generally to a RIASEC circular ordering, or "circumplex," rather than to a hexagonal structure per se.

With a few exceptions (e.g., Rounds & Tracey, 1996), most studies have found that the fit of the RIASEC circumplex in mostly U.S. samples is either invariant or varies to a fairly small degree based on gender and race/ethnicity (Armstrong et al., 2003; Darcy & Tracey, 2007; Rounds & Tracey, 1993; Ryan, Tracey, & Rounds, 1996) and socioeconomic status (Ryan et al., 1996). Gender differences in the RIASEC structure may be more pronounced among individuals who are racial/ethnic minorities (Kantamneni & Fouad, 2011), however. In addition, the RIASEC model's fit appears to vary somewhat among people of different nationalities, especially in Asian countries (e.g., Armstrong & Rounds, 2008; Yang, Stokes, & Hui, 2005). The model also does not fit well in younger (elementary and junior high school) samples (Lent, Tracey, Brown, Soresi, & Nota, 2006; Tracey & Ward, 1998). Asian Americans and residents of Asian countries have also been found to exhibit lower levels of congruence with anticipated and chosen occupations than other racial/ethnic groups (Fouad & Mohler, 2004; Gupta & Tracey, 2005). Thus, counselors must be cautious when using the hexagon framework to interpret RIASEC scores with younger adolescents and with those residing in Asia. Otherwise, the framework seems to work well.

RESEARCH TESTING HOLLAND'S PREDICTIONS ABOUT WORK-RELATED OUTCOMES

Another critical area of research has examined the validity of Holland's predictions about work-related outcomes on the basis of his theory's constructs. Of these, Holland's predictions about outcomes associated with congruence have received the most attention.

Congruence in relation to choice, satisfaction, and performance. There is good evidence that RIASEC type and interest scores are predictive of many individuals' choices of college majors and careers (see Betz, 2008; Holland, 1997b). That is, people frequently choose majors and careers that are congruent with their dominant RIASEC type(s). Congruence with respect to the RIASEC types is also predictive of people's persistence or stability in college majors and occupations (e.g., Donohue, 2006; Tracey & Robbins, 2006). Moreover, people who change jobs often switch to ones that are more congruent with their personalities than the ones they left (Oleski & Subich, 1996). These findings all support Holland's basic assumption that people seek environments with which their personalities are congruent.

Meta-analyses have also supported Holland's prediction that person–environment congruence with respect to the RIASEC types is associated with favorable outcomes. These studies have confirmed that congruence is positively associated with job satisfaction (Assouline & Meir, 1987; Spokane et al., 2000; Tsabari et al., 2005) and, to a lesser extent, performance (Spokane et al., 2000; Tsabari et al., 2005). However, the sizes of these effects tend to be small. For example, Tsabari and colleagues' (2005) meta-analysis revealed a mean congruence–satisfaction correlation of .17, and Assouline and Meir (1987) found a mean congruence–academic achievement correlation of only .06. Although methodological limitations of studies and narrow samples may partially explain the modest relationships between congruence and work-related outcomes, it is clearly the case that congruence should be considered only one of many factors that predict important work-related outcomes.

Differentiation and consistency. Holland's differentiation and consistency hypotheses have received less attention than those regarding congruence, and from the studies that have examined differentiation and consistency as predictors of work-related outcomes (see Carson & Mowsesian, 1993), there is mixed empirical support for the theory. In fact, Holland (1985a) characterized this body of findings as "checkered" because there have been both positive and negative findings. Even among the studies that have found support for Holland's predictions that differentiation and consistency are predictive of career decision-making ease, career choice stability, and work satisfaction, the relationships tend to be fairly small in magnitude.

Identity. Holland's predictions about vocational identity's positive associations with differentiation and consistency, career decision-making ease, career stability, and performance have received fairly minimal empirical attention, perhaps because this construct was added only to later versions of the theory. As with the findings regarding differentiation and consistency, the pattern of findings regarding identity is best described as checkered. The hypothesized positive associations of identity to consistency and differentiation were not supported in one study (Leung, Conoley, Scheel, & Sonnenberg, 1992). Although having a stronger identity does seem to be associated with some benefits, such as readiness to make career decisions (Hirschi, 2007) and career decision-making self-efficacy (Gushue, Scanlan,

Pantzer, & Clarke, 2006), other studies (Blinne & Johnston, 1998; Leung, 1998) have yielded mixed or null results regarding the relation of vocational identity to predicted outcomes. Environmental identity was linked to job satisfaction in one study (Perdue, Reardon, & Peterson, 2007) but otherwise has received little empirical attention.

SUMMARY

In summary, there is empirical support for many aspects of Holland's theory. The presence of the RIASEC types has been well documented, and the types' interrelationships appear to be fairly consistent across major segments of the U.S. population, although the generalizability of the RIASEC model to those of Asian nationalities is less clear. RIASEC type or interest scores contribute substantially to the prediction of people's choices of college majors and careers, and congruence with respect to the RIASEC types is also associated with the stability of those choices. Congruence is positively related to work satisfaction and performance, although the magnitude of those relationships is not as substantial as Holland might have believed they would be. Support for Holland's predictions involving the secondary constructs of consistency, differentiation, and identity is less robust.

APPLICATIONS OF THE THEORY

When evaluating theories with respect to the degree to which they help career counselors and clients in practice, Holland's (1997b) theory is unsurpassed, as it serves as the guiding framework for more career interventions than any other theory.

CONTRIBUTIONS TO OCCUPATIONAL CLASSIFICATION AND CAREER ASSESSMENT

There is little doubt that Holland's theory has helped to transform the practice of career counseling. Prior to the theory's introduction, clients could take an interest inventory and receive scores that reflected their similarity to employees in various occupations. The challenge for counselors, however, was to help clients understand how those occupations fit together in some coherent way and to extrapolate beyond the limited number of occupations represented on the inventory itself. Holland's theory allows us to think about people and environments using a manageable number of dimensions, thereby facilitating clients' understanding of themselves and the world of work. In addition, Holland's instruments for assessing the RIASEC personality types, the introduction of RIASEC scales on major interest inventories (e.g., Campbell & Holland, 1972), and the development of parallel RIASEC environmental classification materials (e.g., the *DHOC*) have greatly improved clients' and counselors' ability to generate fairly comprehensive lists of possible careers that warrant consideration.

Because of this user-friendliness, Holland's theory has been widely adopted. It serves as the organizing framework for many self-help systems, such as the best-selling *What Color Is Your Parachute?* (Bolles, 1986). Holland's SDS and its supporting materials were designed for self-administration and interpretation, which has contributed to the theory's widespread use in educational and career workshops. Finally, Holland's theory frequently guides individual career counseling interventions (see Brown & Ryan Krane, 2000).

From the perspective of Holland's theory, career intervention involves using the RIASEC typology to characterize a client's personality in order to understand how she or he may best fit with the world of work. Typically, this is done using the SDS or an interest inventory that has RIASEC scales, although counselors can also gather information about a client's resemblance to the RIASEC types in a clinical interview. In such an interview, the counselor helps the client verbalize and explore her or his preferred activities, perceived competencies, self-beliefs, interests, values, and occupational daydreams. The counselor then explains Holland's model to the client, and together they work to determine the client's resemblance to each of the types. Regardless of the way in which the assessment occurs, an interpretation typically focuses on determining the client's three-letter Holland code. The client can then use environmental classification materials to explore environments with which his or her personality is fairly congruent. Counselors can also use the constructs of differentiation, consistency, and identity to help clients understand the sources of career decision-making difficulties they may be experiencing and to identify possible ways to reduce those difficulties. In general, counseling is intended to "create self understanding and stimulate more insightful and constructive planning" (Holland, 1997b, p. 199).

Using this general framework, counselors can address many kinds of client needs, including helping people who are seeking to make or remake educational or career choices, promoting greater career/work satisfaction and performance, preparing people to implement career choices, and promoting optimum career development among younger persons. The manner in which counselors who use Holland's theory might address each of these concerns is discussed next.

Working With Persons Who Are Seeking to Make or Remake Educational or Career Choices

Because it provides a parallel way for conceptualizing people and environments, Holland's theory is optimally suited for assisting people who are seeking to make initial or subsequent educational or career choices. Once a client's Holland code is known, a counselor can assist the client in consulting the *Occupations Finder*, the *Educational Opportunities Finder*, the *DHOC*, the O*NET database, and other environmental classification materials to explore occupations that are congruent with his or her three-letter Holland code. Because, at least after adolescence, RIASEC type scores tend to be fairly stable for most people, and because congruence is associated (albeit modestly) with work satisfaction and performance, the rationale for using this approach to match people to environments is solid.

When using Holland's theory as the basis for identifying potentially satisfying educational and work environments, clients and counselors must not use the theory in a more simplistic manner than it was intended. Several points are worth keeping in mind.

- First, a work environment need not be completely congruent with a client's personality to be rewarding. Although occupations with three-point Holland codes that are dramatically different from the client's personality might be tentatively eliminated to allow greater focus in career exploration, exploration for most clients would ideally be inclusive of occupations with several Holland codes. For example, a client with an ASI personality would be encouraged to consider and explore occupations with Holland types of all combinations of the ASI types (e.g., ASI, AIS, SAI, SIA), particularly if the person's profile does not show a high degree of differentiation (i.e., if the scores are not spread very far apart). Also, although in practice it is common to use three-point person and environment Holland codes, Holland recommended using the rank-ordering of all six types as part of an analysis of congruence. Depending on the degree to which the client also resembles types beyond the tertiary type, additional categories of occupations (e.g., ASE) may also be recommended for exploration.
- Second, although congruence is positively associated with favorable work-related outcomes, the strength of these associations is at best modest. Clearly, congruence can be an important determinant of work satisfaction for some people, but it is essential for counselors and clients to view congruence with respect to the RIASEC types as only one of many sources of information when matching clients to environments. RIASEC congruence might best help clients understand the kinds of educational or work environments whose employees will share the most in common with them or in which they will enjoy the typical work activities (i.e., intrinsic work satisfaction) (Prediger, 2000). Constructs from other theories, such as the theory of work adjustment (see Swanson & Schneider, Chapter 2, this volume), would be an appropriate supplement for

helping clients explore environments that would provide a match for their needs and values.

- Third, socialization and real or perceived barriers may have contributed to clients' having had limited experiences in areas that are nontraditional for persons of their race or gender. This would be reflected on inventories such as the SDS in terms of lower RIASEC raw scores for those nontraditional areas. A counselor would ideally work with a client to assess whether her or his inventoried RIASEC scores accurately reflect her or his authentic self. When it appears that external constraints may have impeded development in some areas that would be intrinsically rewarding, the counselor could then attempt to broaden career possibilities by helping the client consider how these barriers might be bypassed or how areas of potential interest might be reconsidered (for example, see the modified occupational card sort described by Lent, Chapter 5, this volume).

- Fourth, Holland's "other things being equal" qualifier is particularly important for work with clients who have constrained educational or career options due to economic reality, family wishes, and other barriers. In one sense, Holland's theory is limited because it assumes that people are relatively free to choose environments based on RIASEC congruence, an assumption that clearly does not hold for all clients. In another sense, the theory is quite flexible because it paints a picture of people and environments using broad strokes (the RIASEC types). Although a person may not have many degrees of freedom in options from which to choose, the theory suggests that maximizing congruence will be beneficial, so choosing from among the *most* congruent of available options would be advocated. Because occupations with varied prerequisites (e.g., levels of needed training or education) are present within each RIASEC type, maximizing RIASEC congruence may still be a consideration even when there are limited options from which to choose. Helping clients with limited options identify and remove barriers to congruent but currently unattainable options may be a way to help them expand their occupational possibilities.

For some clients who are seeking to make educational or career choices, engaging in self- and environmental exploration and identifying congruent environments may be a sufficient intervention. For others, Holland's secondary constructs of differentiation, consistency, and identity may be particularly useful to consider.

Increasing personality differentiation and helping to define more clearly the client's identity are common goals of counseling interventions if the client lacks direction as a result of feeling torn between multiple areas of comparable appeal. Helping clients achieve greater personality differentiation by gaining more varied experiences to learn what they like and dislike may be helpful in some cases. Using counseling sessions to explore in more depth the areas of comparable strength of interest may also yield additional information that helps clients prioritize some areas over others. Occupational card sorts, such as the Missouri Occupational Card Sort (Krieshok, Hansen, Johnston, & Wong, 2002), with Holland code classifications for various job titles may assist a client in exploring and articulating what it is about each RIASEC type that is appealing or unappealing. Finally, because negative affect (e.g., depression) can contribute to a low, undifferentiated RIASEC profile, counselors might screen for and treat mood disorders that suppress a client's interests or perceived competencies.

Promoting consistency is not typically a goal of career counseling, but Holland's consistency construct may nevertheless be useful in counseling. First, some clients may simply experience a sense of normalization when a counselor points to a highly inconsistent personality profile as a source of career decision-making difficulties. Likewise, clients with inconsistent personalities may feel conflicted about their current or future career plans, and their ambivalence can be validated by acknowledging both the pros and cons of having diverse interests. Second, although clients with highly inconsistent personality profiles may experience frustration to find that few environments are highly congruent with their personalities, counselors can help such clients think creatively about new career options or tweak existing options to maximize congruence. For example, environments with the highly inconsistent AC combination may be rare, but a client could brainstorm ways to maximize exposure to activities that involve the orderly and systematic manipulation of data (C activities) within a traditionally A environment, say, by cataloging and inventorying materials in an art library. For other clients, it may be helpful to recognize that although expressing highly inconsistent parts of one's personality may be difficult in a single job, taking on temporary work, combining part-time jobs, or making planned, periodic career changes can be legitimate options for some persons (Donnay et al., 2004). Finally, clients with inconsistent profiles can be encouraged to find other, perhaps avocational, outlets for parts of their personalities that are likely to be unexpressed through work. *The Leisure Activities Finder* (Holmberg, Rosen, & Holland, 1997)—an ancillary to the SDS that provides three-letter Holland codes for hobbies, sports, and other activities—may be useful toward this end.

PROMOTING WORK SATISFACTION AND PERFORMANCE

Another important application of Holland's theory involves working with people who want to experience greater job satisfaction and/or performance.

Although satisfaction and performance are clearly different outcomes, because Holland's predictions about sources of work satisfaction and success are the same, interventions targeting these outcomes are nearly identical.

The primary hypothesis from the perspective of Holland's theory is that a person who is dissatisfied and/or underperforming in work may have made a career choice that was incongruent with his or her personality in the first place, or there was a shifting of the primary RIASEC types within the person or the environment such that a once congruent career choice is no longer so. The latter would not be uncommon if, for example, the typical activities of a workplace changed after the introduction of some new technology.

As a first step, a counselor would gather information to assess the degree of RIASEC congruence between the client and his or her current work environment to test the low-congruence hypothesis. Because some work environments are quite complex or can be idiosyncratic, it is wise not to rely exclusively on existing environmental classifications (e.g., the *DHOC*) to determine the three-letter Holland code of the client's current environment. Rather, it is preferable to have the client estimate the time spent in various activities and to see if the person is in a special subunit that can be isolated and assessed (Holland, 1997b). It may also be useful to have clients complete the Position Classification Inventory as a way to develop a RIASEC code for their current jobs. Discussing the RIASEC types and the idea of congruence with a client may provide him or her with a framework with which to think about dissatisfaction or underperformance that may provide some new clarification and insight.

If the low-congruence hypothesis is supported, there are several options. The least intrusive option—and a reasonable first step to explore with a client—is to consider tweaking the work environment so that it is more congruent with the client's personality. In many work settings, there is some flexibility in how employees complete their jobs. A client could be encouraged to ask a supervisor about shifting responsibilities or taking on some new responsibilities that would increase congruence.

Subunits within an occupation can have different Holland codes because they comprise employees with different types or emphasize different activities. For example, although according to the *DHOC* the Holland code of the typical administrative assistant is ESC, within a large organization, some administrative assistants may have frequent direct contact with the public, whereas other administrative assistants' primary responsibilities involve little face-to-face contact with others and relatively greater emphasis on recording data. The former subunit would likely be more congruent with a client who has a strong resemblance to the Social type. Thus, it is possible for a client to move toward greater congruence without changing careers altogether. If such changes to the environment are unlikely or unappealing to the client, then a goal of counseling might be to explore other careers or jobs that might provide a better match, again using RIASEC environmental classification materials.

Theoretically, because Holland hypothesized stronger congruence–satisfaction and congruence–performance relations under conditions of high consistency, differentiation, and identity, working to promote a client's sense of identity may also be valuable, although the research support for these hypotheses is not strong. Nonetheless, for a client with a very low degree of personality differentiation or a poorly defined identity, there might be merit in promoting greater self-understanding and differentiation as a way of increasing the probability of shifting to a career that is more congruent. However, keep in mind the modest strength of congruence–satisfaction and congruence–performance relationships. RIASEC congruence is one consideration, but a counselor would wisely explore other sources of job satisfaction and performance as well (see Lent & Brown, Chapter 22, this volume).

Helping People Implement Career Choices

Holland's theory has the most direct applicability for working with clients to identify educational or career choices, but it also has some implications for helping people implement those choices. The primary goal of a counselor using Holland's theory to work with a client who is ready to implement a career choice is to identify and remove any barriers that would impede congruence seeking. Such barriers could be external, such as when family disapproval makes it difficult for a client with a highly differentiated Artistic personality to enter an Artistic work environment, or they could be internal, as when low confidence contributes to a client's reluctance to attend a job interview for a highly congruent position.

Holland's theory may also be applicable to the implementation of career choices by providing clients with a framework for describing to potential employers how their abilities and characteristics map onto the position employers are seeking to fill. For example, discussing transferable skills from a previous position may be easier when clients have a mechanism, such as the RIASEC types, for understanding the links between a previous work environment and a prospective work environment.

Promoting Optimum Career Development Among Children and Adolescents

The choice-making and choice-implementing applications previously described are primarily relevant for work with late adolescents or adults.

Indeed, this is the population that is the primary target for Holland's theory, and given that RIASEC type and interest scores are less stable in younger adolescents, using RIASEC scores to narrow career choice considerations with younger people is ill advised. Nevertheless, Holland's theory can be useful when working with younger adolescents to the degree that it provides them with a rationale for learning as much as possible about themselves and the world of work.

A counselor might help a younger client begin to think about himself or herself and the world of work in RIASEC terms and encourage her or him to seek opportunities related to each of the RIASEC areas, even if some areas do not hold much initial appeal. Conceptually, knowing which RIASEC types one does *not* closely resemble is important in the development of personality differentiation and a clear vocational identity. In addition, research has shown that thinking about career interests in terms of the RIASEC model is associated with career decision-making benefits, presumably because it helps people understand the career information that exists and enables them to use it better in their decision making (Tracey, 2008). Thus, interventions with younger persons might introduce them to the RIASEC framework so that they can use it as a schema within which to incorporate new information they acquire about themselves and the world of work.

CONCLUSIONS AND PRACTICE IMPLICATIONS

Holland's theory provides a straightforward means for classifying personalities and work environments. The following tips for practitioners summarize the ways in which the theory is commonly and most optimally applied.

- Practitioners seek to promote optimum career development by encouraging clients to learn as much as possible about themselves and work environments. By educating clients about Holland's theory and the RIASEC types, counselors give clients a parallel way for thinking about themselves and the world of work.
- Counselors assess clients' resemblance to the RIASEC types using a clinical interview, the SDS or VPI, and/or an interest inventory that has RIASEC scales.
- Using environmental classification resources, such as the *DHOC*, the *Educational Opportunities Finder*, or the O*NET database, counselors may assist clients in identifying potentially congruent educational and work environments. Obviously incongruent environments might be tentatively ruled out to help clients home in on a few potentially satisfying areas in which they are likely to perform well. Ideally, the generation of educational and career choice possibilities should, however, be

inclusive, involving not only environments with Holland codes that match the client's personality identically but also those with similar Holland codes.

- RIASEC congruence is associated with favorable work-related outcomes, including job satisfaction and performance, but not strongly so. Congruence can, therefore, be considered as one source of information, yet counselors must also work hard to help clients consider other sources of satisfaction and performance. Highly congruent occupations certainly warrant consideration but without the sense that they are specifically being prescribed by the counselor.

- Clients who are experiencing career decision-making difficulties may benefit from interventions designed to promote personality differentiation and the crystallization of vocational identity. Such interventions might involve gaining more experiences in diverse areas and prioritizing areas of interest via discussion and exploration.

- Clients with highly inconsistent personalities may need avocational outlets for expressing parts of their personalities because there may be few environments that will be highly congruent with all parts of their personalities. Alternatively, such clients might need to be creative in modifying existing positions to emphasize parts of themselves that are not well-represented in the environment or simply plan to change careers in the future to use parts of themselves that are not well expressed in an initial choice.

- Once clients have identified career choices, Holland's theory supports the practice of removing real or perceived barriers to promote the seeking of congruent work positions.

REFERENCES

Ackerman, P. L., & Heggestad, E. D. (1997). Intelligence, personality, and interests: Evidence for overlapping traits. *Psychological Bulletin, 121,* 219–245. doi:10.1037/0033-2909.121.2.219

Alvi, S. A., Khan, S. B., & Kirkwood, K. J. (1990). A comparison of various indices of differentiation for Holland's model. *Journal of Vocational Behavior, 36,* 147–152. doi:10.1016/0001-8791(90)90022-T

Armstrong, P. I., Hubert, L., & Rounds, J. (2003). Circular unidimensional scaling: A new look at group differences in interest structure. *Journal of Counseling Psychology, 50,* 297–308. doi:10.1037/0022-0167.50.3.297

Armstrong, P. I., & Rounds, J. B. (2008). Vocational psychology and individual differences. In S. D. Brown & R. W. Lent (Eds.), *Handbook of counseling psychology* (4th ed., pp. 375–391). Hoboken, NJ: Wiley.

Assouline, M., & Meir, E. I. (1987). Meta-analysis of the relationship between congruence and well-being measures. *Journal of Vocational Behavior, 31,* 319–332. doi:10.1016/0001-8791(82)90036-7

Astin, A. W., & Nichols, R. C. (1964). Life goals and vocational choice. *Journal of Applied Psychology, 48,* 50–58. doi:10.1037/h0048653

Betz, N. E. (2008). Advances in vocational theories. In S. D. Brown & R. W. Lent (Eds.), *Handbook of counseling psychology* (4th ed., pp. 357–374). Hoboken, NJ: Wiley.

Betz, N. E., Borgen, F. H., & Harmon, L. W. (2004). *Skills confidence inventory.* Mountain View, CA: CPP.

Betz, N. E., Harmon, L. W., & Borgen, F. H. (1996). The relationships of self-efficacy for the Holland themes to gender, occupational group membership, and vocational interests. *Journal of Counseling Psychology, 43,* 90–98. doi:10.1037/0022-0167.43.1.90

Blinne, W. R., & Johnston, J. A. (1998). Assessing the relationships between vocational identity, academic achievement, and persistence in college. *Journal of College Student Development, 39,* 569–576.

Bolles, R. N. (1986). *What color is your parachute? A practical manual for job hunters and career changers.* Berkeley, CA: Ten Speed.

Brown, S. D., & Gore, P. A. (1994). An evaluation of interest congruence indices: Distribution characteristics and measurement properties. *Journal of Vocational Behavior, 45,* 310–327. doi:10.1006/jvbe.1994.1038

Brown, S. D., & Ryan Krane, N. E. (2000). Four (or five) sessions and a cloud of dust: Old assumptions and new observations about career counseling. In S. D. Brown & R. W. Lent (Eds.), *Handbook of counseling psychology* (3rd ed., pp. 740–766). New York, NY: Wiley.

Camp, C. C., & Chartrand, J. M. (1992). A comparison and evaluation of interest congruence indices. *Journal of Vocational Behavior, 41,* 162–182. doi:10.1016/0001-8791(92)90018-U

Campbell, D. P., & Holland, J. L. (1972). A merger in vocational interest research: Applying Holland's theory to Strong's data. *Journal of Vocational Behavior, 2,* 353–376. doi:10.1016/0001-8791%2872%2990012-7

Carson, A. D., & Mowsesian, R. (1993). Moderators of the prediction of job satisfaction from congruence: A test of Holland's theory. *Journal of Career Assessment, 2,* 130–144. doi:10.1177/106907279300100203

Darcy, M. U. A., & Tracey, T. J. G. (2007). Circumplex structure of Holland's RIASEC interests across gender and time. *Journal of Counseling Psychology, 54,* 17–31. doi:10.1037/0022-0167.54.1.17

Dawis, R. V. (2000). The person–environment tradition in counseling psychology. In W. E. Martin Jr., & J. L. Swartz-Kulstad (Eds.), *Person–environment psychology and mental health* (pp. 91–111). Mahwah, NJ: Erlbaum.

Donnay, D. A. C., & Borgen, F. H. (1996). Validity, structure, and content of the 1994 Strong Interest Inventory. *Journal of Counseling Psychology, 43,* 275–291. doi:10.1037/0022-0167.43.3.275

Donnay, D. A. C., Morris, M. L., Schaubhut, N. A., & Thompson, R. C. (2004). *Strong Interest Inventory manual.* Mountain View, CA: CPP.

Donohue, R. (2006). Person–environment congruence in relation to career change and career persistence. *Journal of Vocational Behavior, 68,* 504–515. doi:10.1016/j.jvb.2005.11.002

Edwards, K. J., & Whitney, D. R. (1972). Structural analysis of Holland's personality types using factor and configural analysis. *Journal of Counseling Psychology, 19,* 136–145. doi:10.1037/h0032637

Fouad, N. A. (2002). Cross-cultural differences in vocational interests: Between-group differences on the Strong Interest Inventory. *Journal of Counseling Psychology, 49,* 283–289. doi:10.1037/0022-0167.49.3.282

Fouad, N. A., & Mohler, C. J. (2004). Cultural validity of Holland's theory and the Strong Interest Inventory for five racial/ethnic groups. *Journal of Career Assessment, 12,* 423–439.

Gottfredson, G. D., & Holland, J. L. (1991). *The Position Classification Inventory: Professional manual.* Odessa, FL: Psychological Assessment Resources.

Gottfredson, G. D., & Holland, J. L. (1996). *Dictionary of Holland occupational codes* (3rd ed.). Odessa, FL: Psychological Assessment Resources.

Gupta, S., & Tracey, T. J. G. (2005). Dharma and interest–occupation congruence in Asian Indian college students. *Journal of Career Assessment, 3,* 320–336.

Gushue, G. V., Scanlan, K. R. L., Pantzer, K. M., & Clarke, C. P. (2006). The relationship of career decision-making self-efficacy, vocational identity, and career exploration behavior in African American high school students. *Journal of Career Development, 33,* 19–28. doi:10.1177/0894845305283004

Hirschi, A. (2007). Holland's secondary constructs of vocational interests and career choice readiness of secondary students: Measures for related but different constructs. *Journal of Individual Differences, 28,* 205–218. doi:10.1027/1614-0001.28.4.205

Holland, J. L. (1959). A theory of vocational choice. *Journal of Counseling Psychology, 6,* 35–45.

Holland, J. L. (1962). Some explorations of a theory of vocational choice: I. One-and-two-year longitudinal studies. *Psychological Monographs, 76*(26, Whole No. 545), 49.

Holland, J. L. (1985a). *Making vocational choices: A theory of vocational personalities and work environments.* Englewood Cliffs, NJ: Prentice Hall.

Holland, J. L. (1985b). *Manual for the Vocational Preference Inventory.* Odessa, FL: Psychological Assessment Resources.

Holland, J. L. (1996). *The occupations finder.* Odessa, FL: Psychological Assessment Resources.

Holland, J. L. (1997a). *Educational opportunities finder.* Odessa, FL: Psychological Assessment Resources.

Holland, J. L. (1997b). *Making vocational choices: A theory of vocational personalities and work environments* (3rd ed.). Odessa, FL: Psychological Assessment Resources.

Holland, J. L., Daiger, D. C., & Power, P. G. (1980). *My vocational situation.* Palo Alto, CA: Consulting Psychologists Press.

Holland, J. L., Fritzsche, B. A., & Powell, A. B. (1994). *The Self-Directed Search technical manual.* Odessa, FL: Psychological Assessment Resources.

Holland, J. L., Whitney, D. R., Cole, N. S., & Richards, J. M. (1969). *An empirical occupational classification derived from a theory of personality and intended for practice and research* (ACT Research Report No. 29). Iowa City, IA: American College Testing Program.

Holmberg, K., Rosen, D., & Holland, J. L. (1997). *The leisure activities finder*. Lutz, FL: Psychological Assessment Resources.

Kantamneni, N., & Fouad, N. (2011). Structure of vocational interests for diverse groups on the 2005 Strong Interest Inventory. *Journal of Vocational Behavior, 78*, 193–201. doi:10.1016/j.jvb.2010.06.003

Krieshok, T. S., Hansen, R. N., Johnston, J. A., & Wong, S. C. (2002). *Missouri occupational card sort manual*. Columbia: University of Missouri.

Larson, L. M., Rottinghaus, P. J., & Borgen, F. H. (2002). Meta-analyses of Big Six interests and Big Five personality factors. *Journal of Vocational Behavior, 61*, 217–239. doi:10.1006/jvbe.2001.1854

Lent, R. W., Tracey, T. J. G., Brown, S. D., Soresi, S., & Nota, L. (2006). Development of interests and competency beliefs in Italian adolescents: An exploration of circumplex structure and bidirectional relationships. *Journal of Counseling Psychology, 53*, 181–191. doi:10.1037/0022-0167.53.2.181

Leung, S. A. (1998). Vocational identity and career choice congruence of gifted and talented high school students. *Counselling Psychology Quarterly, 11*, 325–335. doi:10.1080/09515079808254064

Leung, S. A., Conoley, C. W., Scheel, M. J., & Sonnenberg, R. T. (1992). An examination of the relation between vocational identity, consistency, and differentiation. *Journal of Vocational Behavior, 40*, 95–107. doi:10.1016/0001-8791(92)90049-6

Low, K. S. D., Yoon, M., Roberts, B. W., & Rounds, J. (2005). The stability of vocational interests from early adolescence to middle adulthood: A quantitative review of longitudinal studies. *Psychological Bulletin, 131*, 713–737. doi:10.1037/0033-2909.131.5.713

Maurer, T. J., & Tarulli, B. A. (1997). Managerial work, job analysis, and Holland's RIASEC vocational environment dimensions. *Journal of Vocational Behavior, 50*, 365–381. doi:10.1006/jvbe.1996.1549

Nauta, M. M. (2010). The development, evolution, and status of Holland's theory of vocational personalities: Reflections and future directions for counseling psychology. *Journal of Counseling Psychology, 57*, 11–22. doi:10.1111/j.1464-0597.2008.00375.x

Oleski, D., & Subich, L. M. (1996). Congruence and career change in employed adults. *Journal of Vocational Behavior, 49*, 221–229. doi:10.1006/jvbe.1996.0041

Perdue, S. V., Reardon, R. C., & Peterson, G. W. (2007). Person–environment congruence, self-efficacy, and environmental identity in relation to job satisfaction: A career decision theory perspective. *Journal of Employment Counseling, 44*, 29–39.

Prediger, D. J. (1982). Dimensions underlying Holland's hexagon: Missing link between interests and occupations? *Journal of Vocational Behavior, 48*, 59–67. doi:10.1016/0001-8791(82)90036-7

Prediger, D. J. (2000). Holland's hexagon is alive and well—though somewhat out of shape: Response to Tinsley. *Journal of Vocational Behavior, 56,* 197–204. doi:10.1006/jvbe.1999.1737

Rachman, D., Amernic, J., & Aranya, N. (1981). A factor-analytic study of the construct validity of Holland's Self-Directed Search test. *Educational and Psychological Measurement, 41,* 425–437. doi:10.1177/001316448104100221

Rounds, J., Smith, T., Hubert, L., Lewis, P., & Rivkin, D. (1999). *Development of occupational interest profiles for O*Net.* Raleigh, NC: National Center for O*NET Development.

Rounds, J., & Tracey, T. J. G. (1993). Prediger's dimensional representation of Holland's RIASEC circumplex. *Journal of Applied Psychology, 78,* 875–890. doi:10.1037/0021-9010.78.6.875

Rounds, J. B., & Tracey, T. J. G. (1996). Cross-cultural structural equivalence of RIASEC models and measures. *Journal of Counseling Psychology, 43,* 310–329. doi:10.1037/0022-0167.43.3.310

Ryan, J. M., Tracey, T. J. G., & Rounds, J. (1996). Generalizability of Holland's structure of vocational interests across ethnicity, gender, and socioeconomic status. *Journal of Counseling Psychology, 43,* 330–337. doi:10.1037/0022-0167.43.3.330

Spokane, A. R. (1985). A review of research on person–environment congruence in Holland's theory of careers [Monograph]. *Journal of Vocational Behavior, 26,* 306–343. doi:10.1016/0001-8791%2885%2990009-0

Spokane, A. R., Meir, E. I., & Catalano, M. (2000). Person–environment congruence and Holland's theory: A review and reconsideration. *Journal of Vocational Behavior, 57,* 137–187. doi:10.1006/jvbe.2000.1771

Strahan, R. F. (1987). Measures of consistency for Holland-type codes. *Journal of Vocational Behavior, 31,* 37–44. doi:10.1016/0001-8791(87)90033-9

Swaney, K. B. (1995). *Technical manual: Revised unisex edition of the ACT Interest Inventory (UNIACT).* Iowa City, IA: ACT.

Swanson, J. L. (1999). Stability and change in vocational interests. In M. L. Savickas & A. R. Spokane (Eds.), *Vocational interests: Meaning, measurement, and counseling use* (pp. 135–158). Palo Alto, CA: Davies-Black.

Tracey, T. J. G. (2008). Adherence to RIASEC structure as a key career decision construct. *Journal of Counseling Psychology, 55,* 146–157. doi:10.1037/0022-0167.55.2.146

Tracey, T. J. G., & Robbins, S. B. (2005). Stability of interests across ethnicity and gender: A longitudinal examination of grades 8 through 12. *Journal of Vocational Behavior, 67,* 335–364. doi:10.1016/j.jvb.2004.11.003

Tracey, T. J. G., & Robbins, S. B. (2006). The interest–major congruence and college success relation: A longitudinal study. *Journal of Vocational Behavior, 69,* 64–89. doi:10.1016/j.jvb.2005.11.003

Tracey, T. J. G., & Rounds, J. B. (1993). Evaluating Holland's and Gati's vocational interest models: A structural meta-analysis. *Psychological Bulletin, 113,* 229–246. doi:10.1037/0033-2909.113.2.229

Tracey, T. J. G., & Ward, C. C. (1998). The structure of children's interests and competence perceptions. *Journal of Counseling Psychology, 45*, 290–303. doi:10.1037/0022-0167.45.3.290

Tsabari, O., Tziner, A., & Meir, E. I. (2005). Updated meta-analysis on the relationship between congruence and satisfaction. *Journal of Career Assessment, 13*, 216–232. doi:10.1177/1069072704273165

U.S. Department of Defense. (1994). *Technical manual for the ASVAB 18–19 Career Exploration Program.* Chicago, IL: United States Military Enlistment Processing Command.

Williams, C. M. (1972). Occupational choice of male graduate students as related to values and personality: A test of Holland's theory. *Journal of Vocational Behavior, 2*, 39–46. doi:10.1016/0001-8791(72)90005-X

Yang, W., Stokes, G. S., & Hui, C. H. (2005). Cross-cultural validation of Holland's interest structure in Chinese population. *Journal of Vocational Behavior, 67*, 379–396. doi:10.1016/j.jvb.2004.08.003

Young, G., Tokar, D. M., & Subich, L. M. (1998). Congruence revisited: Do 11 indices differentially predict job satisfaction and is the relation moderated by person and situation variables? *Journal of Vocational Behavior, 52*, 208–233. doi:10.1006/jvbe.1997.1587

CHAPTER 4

The Life-Span, Life-Space Theory of Careers

PAUL J. HARTUNG

L IFE-SPAN, LIFE-SPACE THEORY FOCUSES on the content, process, and outcomes of career choice and development throughout the human life course (Super, 1953, 1957, 1990; Super, Savickas, & Super, 1996). The theory views career choice and development in three ways: (1) as movement over time through discrete developmental stages with accompanying developmental tasks that constitute the *life span*, (2) as arrangement of worker and other roles that constitute the psychosocial *life space* wherein people design their lives, and (3) as implementation of *self-concept* in work roles. Across the life span and within the life space, individuals, too, develop a sense of self in contexts of time and space. In this way, life-span, life-space theory comprises a creative synthesis of ideas and evidence culled from seemingly disparate theories and lines of research assembled along three primary segments: the longitudinal or chronological, developmental life span; the latitudinal or contextual, psychosocial life space; and the self and self-concepts. With development and psychosocial roles principal among its segments, the theory describes vocational behavior as fluid, dynamic, continuous, and contextual.

Offering a segmented differential-developmental–social phenomenological perspective on vocational behavior (Super, 1994), life-span, life-space theory also spawned a proven model and practical methods for career education and counseling (Healy, 1982; Super, 1983; Super et al., 1996). Counselors can use this model and its methods to assist children, adolescents, and adults with learning the attitudes, beliefs, and competencies necessary for successful career planning, exploration, decision making, and choice (Savickas, 2005,

2011a; Super, 1983). Today, without question, the theory ranks, along with the theory of vocational personalities and work environments (Holland, 1997; Nauta, Chapter 3, this volume), as one of the two most influential, empirically supported, and widely applied career theories in the history of vocational psychology and career development.

To fully understand the breadth and depth of vocational behavior and career development, career practitioners can benefit from knowing and possessing ability to apply the principles and practices of life-span, life-space theory in service of diverse client populations. Toward that end, this chapter describes the historical background, core principles, practical applications, and research findings in support of the theory. The chapter overviews and updates knowledge about and use of the theory to provide both retrospective and prospective understanding. Readers interested in further study would do well especially to consult the original (Super, 1953, 1957), penultimate (Super, 1990), and final (Super, 1994; Super et al., 1996) statements of the theory by its progenitor and prime architect: the late Professor Donald E. Super.

BACKGROUND OF THE THEORY

Life-span, life-space theory resulted from the work of Donald E. Super (for a biography, see Savickas, 1994). Super (1953) first articulated a theory of vocational development nearly 60 years ago. Name changes from the original "career development theory" to "developmental self-concept theory" and finally to "life-span, life-space theory" reflect the theory's evolution over this period (Savickas, 1997). Throughout this time, Super combined in one grand theory the fruits of existing research and his own empirical and conceptual work in three main areas: differential psychology, developmental psychology, and self-concept theory (for complete compendia of historical antecedents, see Savickas, 2007; Super, 1990, 1994). These three areas form the keystone segments of the theory.

DIFFERENTIAL PSYCHOLOGY

Prior to 1950, the paradigm for comprehending vocational behavior focused solely on the content of occupational choice from the objective perspective of individual differences. The individual differences, or person–environment (P-E) fit perspective advanced a *psychology of occupations* that assumed satisfaction and success resulted from a harmonious person–occupation match. Near mid-20th century, this perspective found its embodiment in a classic textbook that delineated psychological traits affecting vocational choice and classified occupational fields and levels structuring the world of work (Roe, 1956). By concentrating on *what* occupations individuals select, the three-part *matching* model of self-knowledge, occupational knowledge, and true reasoning between these two types of knowledge (Parsons, 1909) provided counselors with an understanding of vocational choices and an intervention scheme for fitting people to jobs in accordance with their unique interests, abilities, personalities, and other traits. This intervention scheme relied on using psychological tests and inventories, coupled with occupational information, to match people to jobs.

Applied to vocational behavior, differential psychology asserts that particular occupations suit particular types of people. In *The Republic*, Plato (360 BC) captured this view long ago by commenting: "No two persons are born exactly alike; but each differs from the other in natural endowments, one being suited for one occupation and the other for another." For many years, the individual differences perspective assumed that once matched to suitable jobs, people would experience success, satisfaction, and stability and never again need to make a vocational choice. Today, the matching model, best exemplified in Holland's (1997; Nauta, Chapter 3, this volume) preeminent theory of vocational personalities and work environments, continues to inform the practice of career intervention whereby counselors help individuals match themselves to jobs.

Advancing the matching model and reflecting his background as a differential psychologist, Super authored two books. In the first volume, Super (1942) synthesized existing knowledge about the practice of vocational guidance in the individual differences tradition and initially described his views on career choice as a developmental process. In the second book, Super (1949) compiled and interpreted research findings about the most prevalent psychological tests then used in vocational guidance to teach readers how to evaluate and use such tests themselves. Later, in life-span, life-space theory, Super (1980) adopted differential psychology to explain the content of occupational choice as a match between self and situation. He also used individual differences methods to develop psychometric inventories and scales to operationally define key constructs of the theory for use in research and practice.

Super's (1994) self-analysis of his more than 50-year publication record revealed his foundation in differential psychology that anchors life-span, life-space theory. This supported an earlier conclusion: "Super has never repudiated the differential approach; in fact, in many ways he led it" (Borgen, 1991, p. 284). Notable among his many contributions to differential career psychology, Super (1957; Zytowski, 1994), along with Lofquist and Dawis (1978), advanced work values as traits useful in vocational appraisal and guidance. Work values denote important satisfactions people seek both through the nature of the work they do (i.e., intrinsic values such as autonomy and intellectual challenge) and through the outcomes that can be obtained from work (i.e., extrinsic values such as money and prestige). Super developed the Work Values Inventory (Super, 1970; Zytowski, 2009) and Values Scale (Super & Nevill, 1985b) to measure work values in counseling and research settings (see Rounds & Jin, Chapter 15, this volume, for a discussion of these instruments).

DEVELOPMENTAL PSYCHOLOGY

By the mid-20th century, two phenomena stimulated emergence of a second paradigm to augment the matching model for vocational guidance. Unique to the growing profession of vocational guidance, one phenomenon involved increasing awareness of the lack of theory to guide practice (Ginzberg, Ginsburg, Axelrad, & Herma, 1951). A second, more widespread phenomenon concerned the shift within the United States, as well as in other countries, from an agrarian to a predominantly industrial and organizational society (Savickas & Baker, 2005). As individuals confronted mounting organizational work contexts, need arose to comprehend the process of occupational choice from the subjective perspective of the developing person. Beginning with his 1942 book, then in his 1952 presidential address to the Division of Counseling and Guidance (American Psychological Association), and then in his 1957 book, Super advanced a developmentally oriented *psychology of careers*.

By concentrating on *how* individuals move through a sequence of occupations, jobs, and positions in a career, Super (1953) offered a developmental theory of vocational behavior containing 10 propositions that increased to 14 in the theory's later statement (Super et al., 1996). In so doing, he followed the lead of Ginzberg and colleagues (1951), whose earlier groundbreaking developmental theory of vocational choice "prompted an explosion of career theories; almost one theory per year . . . for the next 20 years" (Savickas & Baker, 2005, p. 42). Super's (1942, 1949, 1957) syntheses of the existing literature, his 20-year longitudinal study of 100 ninth graders in the Career Pattern Study (Super, 1985), and his development of psychometric scales (e.g., Super, 1955, 1970; Super, Thompson, Lindeman, Jordaan, & Myers, 1979, 1988) supplied the foundational principles and constructs, mechanisms for empirical support, and applications of the theory. Primary among its core constructs, the theory advanced the concept of *career maturity* (Super, 1955) as an individual's readiness to cope with developmental career stage tasks. Subsequent theorizing would aptly replace the biological construct of career maturity with the psychosocial construct of career adaptability (Savickas, 1997; Super & Knasel, 1981).

Developmental career theory and the life-span, life-space approach as its chief exemplar augmented the individual differences perspective and matching model for vocational guidance. It did so by explaining the subjective processes of occupational exploration, choice, entry, and adjustment among individuals within contexts that offered mobility up organizational ladders. The developmental view, along with social role theory, explained how individuals manage worker and other roles over the life span and propagated the superordinate construct of *career* to denote "the sequence of occupations, jobs, and positions occupied during the course of a person's working life" (Super, 1963, p. 3). Whereas differential psychology focused interest on *what* traits differentially fit individuals for what occupations, developmental psychology placed concern on *how* the individual cultivates a career over time. Holland (1959, 1997) worked to articulate what would become the prototypical P-E fit theory in the differential psychology of occupations. Meanwhile, Super (1957, 1990) explicated what would become the quintessential life span theory in the developmental psychology of careers. As a segmental theorist taking components from different theories, Super always remained true to incorporating knowledge and concepts from multiple areas, including P-E fit, life span development, social learning, self-concept, and psychodynamic perspectives (Super, 1994).

Life-span, life-space theory eventually produced practical models and materials for assisting individuals across developmental age periods to learn the planning attitudes, beliefs, and decision-making competencies needed to make suitable and satisfying educational and occupational choices and to manage their careers over the life course (Healy, 1982; Super, 1983). What may be called the *managing* model of career education, then, offered counselors a scheme for assisting people to ready themselves to make career decisions and fit work into their lives (Savickas, 2011a). The managing model and its methods of career education and counseling supported the matching model and its methods of vocational guidance by focusing on preparing people to make effective occupational choices. A contemporary view on career management as interplay between individual and organization involving "multipoint decision making in time and space" (Hoekstra, 2011, p. 161) clearly reflects life-span, life-space theory.

Infusion of the developmental perspective via life-span, life-space theory spread roots deep and wide, moving the field of vocational psychology and the profession of counseling from a solely matchmaking, vocational guidance perspective to a managing, career development perspective. The continuing vigor of this perspective found embodiment some years ago in Jepsen's (1984) assertion: "Nearly all vocational behavior theorists and researchers seem to subscribe to some variation of the developmental viewpoint" (p. 178). As prime evidence, Holland (1959, 1973, 1997) attended substantially, if incompletely (Bordin, 1959), to the role of development in vocational behavior. Dawis (1996), too, in the theory of work adjustment described career development as "the *unfolding* of capabilities and requirements in the course of a person's interaction with environments of various kinds (home, school, play, work) across the life span" (p. 94). Following suit, many other career theories, including those described in this volume, attend to developmental processes. Predominance of the developmental perspective also prompted the National Vocational Guidance Association in 1985 to rename itself the National Career Development Association—a designation that remains today (Chung, 2008). Likewise, many career courses in graduate-level counseling and psychology programs across the United States and in other nations include the words *career development* in their titles.

SELF-CONCEPT THEORY

Along with differential and developmental psychology, Super used self-concept theory (Super, Starishevsky, Matlin, & Jordaan, 1963) as a third keystone to frame life-span, life-space theory. Drawing from the work of theorists such as Carl Rogers (1951), Super recognized that self-concept theory could help bind the seemingly disparate differential and developmental perspectives on human behavior into a cohesive, more robust explanation of vocational behavior and its development. Self-concept theory explains how individuals develop ideas about who they are in different roles and situations based on self-observations of their own unique personal characteristics and experiences, as well as on social interactions and feedback from others. As Super (1963) explained, "The concept of self is generally a picture of the self in some role, some situation, in a position, performing some set of functions, or in some web of relationships" (p. 18). For example, a person organizes her conception of herself as physically muscular, agile, and fast into the role self-concept of athlete. The content and outcomes of occupational choice, then, emerge as a function of individuals' attempts to implement their self-concepts in work roles (Super, 1957; Super et al., 1963).

Self-concepts refer to mental representations of self (Savickas, 2011c; Super et al., 1996). As such, self-concepts by their very nature form individuals' subjectively held perspectives on the self in a role. With regard to occupational choice and work adjustment, the self per se may be viewed from both objective and subjective perspectives. Psychometric test and inventory data allow counselors and researchers to view the self as an object by counting and categorizing vocational interests, abilities, and other traits that form a *personality*. These traits yield an occupational (Blustein,

Devenis, & Kidney, 1989) or vocational (Savickas, 1985) identity whereby individuals may be held up as objects to be matched to occupations that fit their particular characteristics. Objectively implementing a self-concept in a work role involves a process akin to P-E fit in the differential tradition. By experiencing the self as an object, individuals in effect declare, "This is *me*."

Alternatively, self-estimates of traits such as interests and abilities allow counselors and researchers to view the self as a subject by attending to the totality of an individual's unique experience or *personhood*. The whole of an individual's experience forms an occupational self-concept constituting life themes and the purpose work holds for oneself. Subjectively implementing a self-concept in a work role involves purposefully fitting work into a constellation of life roles in the developmental tradition. Experiencing self as subject, an individual in effect states, "*I* shape me." Combined, objective and subjective views on the self provide a lens for viewing how individuals publically declare and privately construe the content and outcomes of their vocational behaviors, developmental statuses, and life roles (Super et al., 1996).

Life-span, life-space theory underscores the point that individuals develop not just one but rather constellations of self-concepts, or ideas about themselves, based on experiences in a wide array of life spheres. The primary concern within life-span, life-space theory, of course, is the vocational sphere, wherein the individual rests at the center of career choice, development, and decision making. The individual as decider and constructor of perspectives on herself or himself attempts to implement a vocational self-concept in an occupational choice. Constructing a self-concept with regard to the work role involves a subjective process of making meaning of the objective content of one's lived experiences, personal characteristics, and social situation. Then, individuals use realism and reality testing to evaluate how well their chosen work roles incorporate their self-concepts in a continuing process of improving the match between self and situation.

The archway of career determinants (Super, 1990), seen in Figure 4.1, delineates a unique architecture of self and self-concept development and visually models the personal and situational factors that shape life-span, life-space development. The two columns comprise various psychological characteristics and social forces depicted as stones within each column. In theory, these personal and situational factors affect the life-career depicted by the arch that sits atop the two columns. Developmental stages of childhood and adolescence form the left end of the arch. Adulthood and senescence stages form the right end of the arch. In between rest self-concepts in roles such as child, student, and worker with the self as decision maker. The dynamic interplay between and among personal traits of the left-hand column and environmental factors of the right-hand column determines important vocational

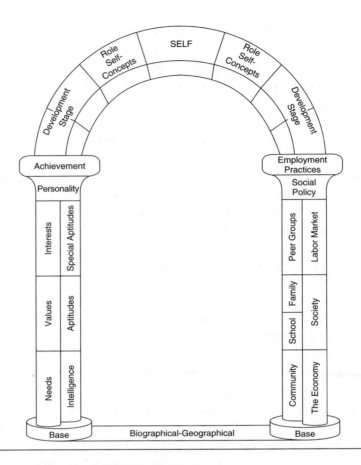

Figure 4.1 The Archway of Career Determinants

Source: From Super, D. E. (1990). A Segmental Model of Career Development: A life-span, life-space approach to career development. In D. Brown (Ed.), *Career choice and development* (2nd ed.; p. 200). San Francisco: Jossey-Bass.

outcomes in terms of movement through developmental stages, development of role self-concepts, and self-construction.

Super suggested that self-concept theory might be better replaced by personal construct theory (Kelly, 1955) to account for how individuals make occupational choices based on their own "personal assessments of the changing socioeconomic situation and of the social structure in which they live and function" (Super, 1990, p. 223). Using the language of personal constructs, Super believed, would move from self-concept theory as "essentially a matching theory" (p. 222) to a more social psychological conceptualization. Ultimately, self-concept theory within the life-span, life-space approach melds the individual differences and individual development perspectives to describe self-concepts as comprising objective and subjective self-views.

SUMMARY

By combining the three keystones of differential psychology, developmental psychology, and self-concept theory, the life-span, life-space approach focuses:

> on the differential psychology of occupations as contributory to a psychology of careers, on life stages and processes in vocational development, on patterns of career development, on the nature and causes of vocational maturity and its role in choice and adjustment, and on the individual as the synthesizer of personal data, the interpreter of experience, and the maker of decisions. (Super, 1969, p. 2)

These foundational emphases form the blueprints for configuring and comprehending the core principles of the theory.

CORE PRINCIPLES

Set against the backdrop of individual differences, individual development, and self-concepts, life-span, life-space theory organizes its core propositions and principles along two primary dimensions: chronological time and contextual space (for a list of the theory's 14 propositions, see Super et al., 1996). The life-career rainbow in Figure 4.2 depicts the theory's two dimensions, along which a vocational self-concept is developed, implemented, and adjusted. The theory's longitudinal time dimension, portrayed in the outer arcs of the rainbow, concerns the successful traversing of developmental career stages and associated tasks and transitions over the human life span from childhood through late adulthood. The theory's latitudinal space dimension, portrayed in the inner arcs of the rainbow, concerns the meaningful design of psychosocial roles within the life space, along with the situations that individuals confront within these roles. Together, the longitudinal and latitudinal dimensions of the theory mark the coordinates by which individuals chart their careers over the life span and within the life space.

LIFE SPAN: TRAVERSING CAREER STAGES, TASKS, AND TRANSITIONS

Human life follows a definite developmental sequence from conception to death, from womb to tomb. Every life begins at one point in time and ends at another in a prototypical way. Yet, the unique interactions of self and situation yield substantial individual variability within this sequence. Careers, too, begin and end in a chronological, developmental progression beginning

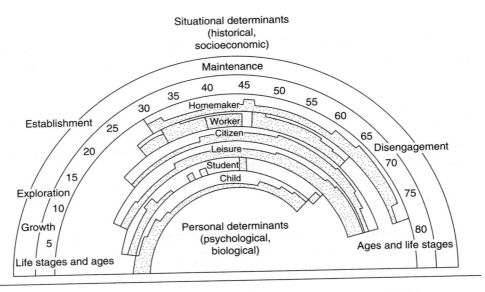

Figure 4.2   The Life-Career Rainbow: Six Life Roles in Schematic Life Space
Source: The Life-Career Rainbow: Six Life Roles in Schematic Life Space in D. E. Super (1990). A life-span, life-space approach to career development. In D. Brown (Ed.), *Career Choice and Development* (2nd ed., p. 212). San Francisco, CA: Jossey-Bass. Reprinted with permission of John Wiley & Sons, Inc.

in childhood vocational aspirations and ending in late adulthood superannu-ation. As with general human development, each individual career proceeds in its own unique way, following or diverting from the prototypical linear sequence of exploration, choice, entry, adjustment, and retirement. Careers may thus form stable, unstable, and multiple-trial patterns. The life span segment of life-span, life-space theory deals with the linear and nonlinear progression of careers over the life course in terms of developing, imple-menting, and stabilizing self-concepts in work and other roles (Super, 1990; Super et al., 1996).

Five developmental periods demarcate the stages of a career depicted in Figure 4.2. The childhood stage of career growth begins the cycle that proceeds through adolescent career exploration, young adult career estab-lishment, middle adult career maintenance (or management; see Hoekstra, 2011; Savickas, 2002), and late adult career disengagement. Each career stage presents discernible developmental tasks (or substages) that entail a primary adaptive goal. Developmental tasks convey socially and cul-turally expected responsibilities that individuals must meet with regard to developing a career. Completing all tasks associated with each stage builds a foundation for future success and reduces the likelihood of diffi-culties in later stages (Super et al., 1996). The ladder model of life-career stages and tasks in Figure 4.3 depicts the prototypical sequence of career

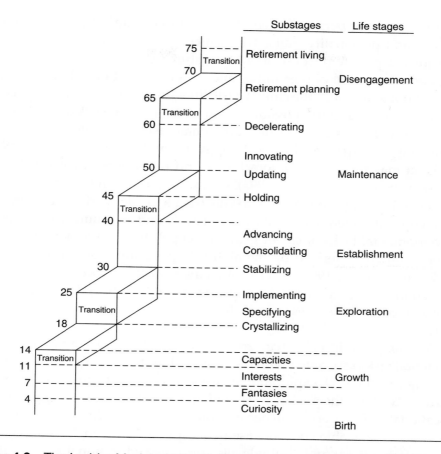

Figure 4.3 The Ladder Model of Life–Career Stages and Developmental Tasks
Source: Life Stages and Substages Based on the Typical Developmental Tasks, With Focus on the Maxicycle. From D. E. Super (1990). A life-space, life-span approach to career development. In D. Brown (Ed.), Career choice and development (2nd ed.; p. 214). San Francisco: Jossey-Bass.

development. The Adult Career Concerns Inventory (Super et al., 1988; http://www.vocopher.com) provides counselors with a measure of exploration, establishment, maintenance, and disengagement stages and tasks. In a prototypical linear pattern, each career stage constitutes approximate chronological ages and characteristic tasks that combine to form a "grand narrative" (Super et al., 1996, p. 135) about vocational development.

Growth. The career development grand narrative begins in childhood (Hartung, Porfeli, & Vondracek, 2005) with the life stage of growth. Spanning birth to age 13, this opening developmental period concentrates on the goal of forming an initial and realistic vocational self-concept, in part by identifying with significant others. The budding vocational self-concept reflects the child's formative answer to the question "Who am I?" in a mental representation of personal strengths, limitations, interests, values, abilities, talents, and personality traits. This self-concept contains the child's public picture and private purpose about the future role of work in his or her life. Society expects that opportunities and experiences afforded at home, play, and school will arouse the child's curiosities, fantasies, interests, and capacities to construct a future possible self to be realized in work and other social roles. Growth substages (or developmental tasks) for children (and adults revisiting growth) comprise developing *concern* about the future, *control* over decision making, *conviction* to achieve, and *competence* in work habits and attitudes (Savickas & Super, 1993). Children must learn to imagine, be self-responsible, and problem-solve to construct a viable work future consistent with cultural imperatives conveyed in family and community contexts. The developmental tasks of career growth compel the child to acquire a future orientation characterized by the ability to planfully look ahead (Savickas, 1997; Super et al., 1996). A critical element in this process is envisioning oneself in work and other roles and comprehending the relative salience, or importance, of these roles in one's life.

Exploration. Childhood career growth eventually gives way to new developmental tasks associated with the ensuing life stage of exploration. Encompassing ages 14 to 24, exploration focuses the adolescent and emerging adult (Arnett, 2004) on the goal of crystallizing, specifying, and implementing the vocational self-concept in an occupational role. *Crystallizing* means developing a clear and stable vocational self-concept reflecting one's preferences for occupational fields and ability levels. *Specifying* educational and vocational choices in line with the vocational self-concept results from broadly exploring preferred occupations and forming a vocational identity. Once specified, *implementing* an occupational choice entails preparing for and obtaining a position. During exploration, society expects that gathering information about self and occupations through part-time work, curricular and extracurricular experiences, and other activities will lead the adolescent and emerging adult to ultimately select an occupation to enter and thereby implement self in the work role. Traversing the exploration stage involves learning about the structure and opportunities of the world of work, initially implementing a vocational self-concept, and exploring occupations broadly through a capacity to look around (Savickas, 1997). Successful movement through exploration yields planfulness, curiosity to explore work roles, and knowledge about career decision-making principles and the occupational world.

Establishment. Career exploration yields occupational choice, work-role entry, and a new set of tasks in the succeeding life stage of establishment.

Traversing ages 25 to 44 in a prototypical pattern, establishment involves stabilizing, consolidating, and advancing the self-concept and a career pattern to develop a secure place in the world of work. Stabilizing involves settling into and securing a new position by performing competently and acclimating successfully to the work culture. This gives way to consolidating the position through sustained work productivity, interpersonal effectiveness, and adjustment. Eventually, individuals may pursue advancing to higher-level positions when possible. Stable self-concepts and career patterns result from successful establishment wherein the main goal concerns implementing the self-concept in the work role to yield both a means of earning a living and a meaningful way of living a life. Work devoid of meaning requires workers to realize their self-concepts in other roles such as parent, spouse, community member, and leisurite. Establishment in today's digital age of insecurity, uncertainty, and frequent job change often proves a more variable and protracted career stage (Savickas, 2011b).

Maintenance. Research supports renewal (Williams & Savickas, 1990) "as a transitional period between the establishment and maintenance stages" characterized by "questioning future direction and goals . . . [and] encountered primarily by younger maintainers" (p. 173). Successful career establishment at midlife therefore prompts a sustainability question. Individuals ask themselves whether they want to continue in their established positions until retirement. If not, they revisit prior tasks of exploration and establishment to make an occupational or organizational change. If so, they continue on with new tasks of career maintenance. Spanning ages 45 to 65, maintenance concentrates on the prime goal of building on the vocational self-concept developed, implemented, and stabilized in the foregoing career stages. Because people deal in various ways with the long-term prospects of continuing in their positions, maintenance stage tasks may be better termed "styles" or "strategies." For some people, maintenance involves a strategy of holding on to a secured position through continued job proficiency. For other people, maintenance constitutes updating knowledge and skills to enhance performance or innovating new and creative ways of performing to keep work vigorous and fresh. Innovating in particular may prevent career plateaus (Tan & Salomone, 1994) and mid-career changes due to job dissatisfaction. Like establishment, career maintenance may elude many workers in the contemporary global economy because of the effects of job loss, "dejobbing" that shifts work from jobs to assignments, corporate failure, and organizational restructuring.

Disengagement. The grand narrative of life span career development concludes in late adulthood with the disengagement stage. Encompassing ages 65 and older, disengagement presents the longtime worker with a major life transition to retirement (Shultz & Wang, 2011). This transition shifts the focus from self-concept development, implementation, stabilization, and enhancement in work roles to developing and implementing role self-concepts more fully in other domains, such as family, community, and leisure. Disengagement tasks present themselves in the form of *decelerating* workloads and productivity levels, *retirement planning* to organize finances and structure daily activities (Adams & Rau, 2011), and *retirement living* to answer questions of where to live, what to do, and how to revitalize and form new relationships outside the workplace. Individuals during disengagement may ask themselves, "What will retirement mean for me?" or "How will I adjust?"

Increased life expectancies, early retirement options, and cost-of-living concerns may prompt revisiting tasks of exploration and establishment to obtain bridge employment (Zhan, Wang, Liu, & Shultz, 2009) or develop encore careers (Freedman, 2007). Through bridge employment, workers engage in part-time, self-, or temporary employment after leaving full-time work to better sustain their mental and physical health, as well as their financial solvency. Encore careers replace retirement with engagement in alternative work that allows greater personal meaning, fulfillment, or social impact than prior work made possible. Recent theorizing has articulated eight metaphors that reflect various meanings of retirement ranging from "loss," characterized by purposelessness and threatened identity, to "transformation," characterized by adopting a new role, lifestyle, and identity (Sargent, Bataille, Vough, & Lee, 2011). Meanwhile, the changing nature of work and an unsettled economy couple to alter the very nature and long-term viability of retirement itself for many workers (Shultz & Wang, 2011).

Managing tasks, transitions, and traumas. Life stage success requires *career maturity*, a term Super (1955) coined to explain and measure progress in moving through the developmental stages and tasks particularly associated with exploration. Career maturity denotes attitudinal and cognitive readiness to make educational and vocational choices. Attitudinal readiness means active engagement in planning and exploring an occupational future. Cognitive readiness means possessing knowledge about occupations and how to make good career decisions. The Career Maturity Inventory (CMI; Crites, 1965; Crites & Savickas, 1995) measures global and specific dimensions of career maturity. Super and his colleagues (Super et al., 1979) subsequently constructed the Career Development Inventory (for a review, see Savickas &

Hartung, 1996) to also measure level of career choice readiness more broadly in terms of engagement in career planning and exploration, as well as knowledge about career decision making and the world of work. Counselors and researchers may find both measures available at http://www.vocopher.com.

Applied largely to research in and evolving from the Career Pattern Study (Super, 1985; Super & Overstreet, 1960), career maturity proved an apt term to denote increased choice readiness typically accompanying age and grade-level increases during the adolescent years. Despite attempts to apply the construct beyond the exploration stage, "the focus remained on a structural model of career maturity in adolescence" (Savickas, 1997, p. 250). Recognizing this constraint and the limitations inherent in using a biologically based term to describe a psychosocially based process, the theory eventually replaced career maturity with *career adaptability* (Savickas, 1997; Super & Knasel, 1981; Super et al., 1996). Career adaptability entails having the readiness and resources to cope with developmental tasks, career transitions, and work traumas across the entire life span (Savickas, 2005). Recent research has advanced and supported career adaptability along the three primary dimensions of planning, exploring, and deciding (e.g., Creed, Fallon, & Hood, 2009; Hirschi, 2009; Koen, Klehe, van Vianen, Zikic, & Nauta, 2010). The most recently revised version of the CMI produced an adaptability form that measures the dimensions of career adaptability for diagnostic work with school populations up to and including 12th grade (Savickas & Porfeli, 2011).

Career adaptability aids development as individuals cycle and recycle through the five career stages over the life span. These five career stages collectively provide an overarching structure of career development. Individually, each stage in fact serves a principal *function* in that it helps to achieve a particular purpose with regard to completing developmental tasks associated with growing, exploring, establishing, maintaining, and disengaging from work roles. Individuals visit and revisit the tasks associated with each function over the life course. Normative transitions such as voluntary job change and work-based traumas such as job loss prompt new growth, reexploration, and reestablishment. Activated by personal, social, or economic factors or a combination of these factors, transitions mark passage from one career stage or function to the next. Movement through the stages and tasks over chronological time constitutes the *maxicycle* of career development. Because people often *recycle* by revisiting developmental stages and tasks through which they have passed earlier in their lives, career development also may involve various *minicycles* of development. For example, an established career high school science teacher decides at midlife to transition to a different occupational field. Similarly, a 30-year-old veteran disengages from military service and transitions to work in civilian life, and a 42-year-old homemaker explores options for reentering the paid workforce. Such situations prompt new cycles of movement (i.e., recycling) through earlier career tasks. Each developmental age period, too, presents tasks of later career stages reflecting this cycling and recycling (Super & Thompson, 1981). For example, adolescence involves the disengagement task of giving less time to play and hobbies, and late adulthood presents the exploration task of finding a good place to live in retirement. The life span segment of the theory thus accounts for both linear and circuitous life-career patterns.

LIFE SPACE: ARRANGING SOCIAL ROLES

Every life needs a context, a structure to shape its development. Life structure comes in the form of a grand design of social roles arranged within various domains of human activity. Performing roles of worker, spouse or partner, volunteer, and leisurite in work, family, community, and play domains offers an identifiable and potentially meaningful life structure. Too little structure and inactivity across domains breeds ennui and various mental health problems. For example, work-role loss causes depression, anxiety, and lowered subjective well-being (Paul & Moser, 2009). Too much structure and overactivity breeds exhaustion and other problems. For example, work-role overengagement produces burnout (Maslach & Jackson, 1986) and conflict with roles in other domains such as family (Halbesleben, Harvey, & Bolino, 2009). Therefore, designing a life to achieve balance among roles becomes imperative for overall satisfaction and well-being (Niles, Herr, & Hartung, 2001). The life space segment of life-span, life-space theory deals with the context of career development within a web of social roles individuals occupy and enact over the life span (Super, 1990; Super et al., 1996). Depicted by the inner arcs of the life-career rainbow (Figure 4.2), the life space constitutes core roles individuals use to design their lives. Mindful of life's complex and context-rich nature, the theory thus situates career choice and development within this constellation of social roles.

Super (1980) proposed that nine major roles constitute the typical life structure in chronological order of child, student, leisurite, citizen, worker, spouse, homemaker, parent, and annuitant. In the example of Figure 4.2, the individual played six core roles over the life span. A typical life structure comprises two or three core roles, with other roles playing a negligible or no part (Super et al., 1996). Among these, the worker role typically represents a core role, given the cultural, social, and personal imperative to work. Yet, worker offers just one of several role possibilities. Rather than prizing the work role, life-span, life-space theory uses the construct of *role salience* to explain and consider the relative importance that individuals ascribe to various roles in the course of their lives. As measured by the Salience Inventory (Super & Nevill, 1985a; http://www.vocopher.com), role salience entails behavioral, emotional, and values components. These components denote how much one participates, feels invested, and expects to realize important outcomes in a given role. Role salience thus accounts for how a person may perform a great deal in a role (e.g., work long hours) and want much from it (e.g., receive good pay and benefits) yet not feel particularly devoted to it (e.g., would give up the work role for a life of leisure, family, and community activity if not for the money).

A host of factors shape levels of role salience and role viability within the many role contexts of human development. These factors include prevailing cultural value orientations, the changing nature of work, societal diversity, fluctuating economic conditions, gender and family expectations, social class, and occupational and other barriers (Blustein, 2006; Cook, 1994; Fitzgerald & Betz, 1994; Hartung, 2002; Richardson, 1993). Roles, too, interact to varying degrees in ways that may be complementary and supportive or conflictual and straining (Halbesleben et al., 2009). Family support may ease job stress, whereas work overengagement may strain family life. Individuals typically seek career counseling at times of role change and when they want to redesign their life structures into a different pattern of life roles (Super et al., 1996). Counselors, in response, must first recognize and address the relative importance that clients ascribe to various life roles, rather than assuming that the work role constitutes the main focus of the client's problems and concerns. Recent theorizing has elaborated on life roles as vehicles for developing a personal career identity and public career success (Hoekstra, 2011).

Self-Concepts: Developing, Implementing, and Adjusting Self

Across the life span and through the life space, individuals develop, implement, and adjust their self-concepts to optimally fit themselves to social roles (Super, 1951). The twin processes of traversing career stages and arranging social roles engage the individual in developing a vocational self-concept, applying it to the work role, and regulating it according to changes in self and circumstances. Self-concepts develop from a combination of heredity, social learning experiences, opportunities, and evaluations by self and others. The vocational self-concept reflects both personal (e.g., needs, values, and interests) and situational (e.g., economy, society, and labor market) factors. Occupational choice entails implementing a self-concept, work expresses the fullness of self, and career development encompasses a "continuing process of improving the match between self and situations" (Super et al., 1996, p. 139).

As we have seen, developing a vocational self-concept represents the primary adaptive goal or function of career growth for children and for adults recycling through this stage. Then, in exploration, the adolescent or adult recycler tries implementing the self in work roles. During establishment, the young or recycling adult who has implemented a vocational self-concept in a work role seeks to stabilize the self in a chosen occupation. As an established career progresses to maintenance, changes in self and circumstance prompt adjusting the work-role self-concept accordingly during middle adulthood. Reaching career disengagement, the adult in early retirement or late life relinquishes the work role and devotes energies to more fully developing, implementing, and adjusting self-concepts in other life roles.

Three of life-span, life-space theory's 14 propositions (see Super et al. 1996) deal directly with occupational choice as a function of self-concept. First, the theory proposes that self-concept development, implementation, and adjustment entail a lifelong process of decisions and redecisions. Self-concepts grow increasingly stable over the life span, lending coherence and continuity to one's life. Yet, they remain susceptible to change with time and experience. Second, the theory postulates that career development involves processes of developing and implementing occupational self-concepts. This occurs as the individual synthesizes and negotiates knowledge about self and experience to form more satisfying person–environment connections. Third, the theory suggests that individuals experience subjective success and satisfaction in work as a function of their ability to implement their vocational self-concepts in their occupational choices. Individuals more able to enact their self-concepts in work roles presumably experience greater fulfillment.

As the segment joining life span and life space, self-concept links person as decider to environment as decision. Recent work has delineated with remarkable acuity three perspectives on the self and self-concepts (Phillips, 2011; Savickas, 2011c). Individually, Phillips and Savickas each described the self in three unique terms. Phillips delineated self and self-concept as a collection of traits, as developing over time, and as decision maker. Meanwhile, Savickas portrayed the self as object in the form of personality, as subject in the form of personhood, and as project in the form of identity. Collectively, the conceptual works of Phillips and Savickas converge on the position advanced by and amenable to life-span, life-space theory that the self and self-concepts comprise differential, developmental, and constructionist dimensions (for more about constructionism and views on the self, see Savickas, 2011a, 2011c, Chapter 6 in this volume). The differential dimension reflects the view that objective knowledge about the content of self and vocational self-concept (i.e., personality traits or characteristics), combined with knowledge about occupations, promotes effective career decision making.

In the differential view, the self passively *matches* to occupations that it most resembles, comparable to an actor assigned to perform in a work role. The developmental dimension reflects the view that subjective reflection yields meaning (i.e., personhood) as the self and self-concepts surface, develop, and change over time. In the developmental view, the self actively *develops* through work roles, much like an agent who manages a career. The constructionist dimension, building on the differential and developmental perspectives, reflects the view that projective self-construction involves purposefully using work and career to design and shape experience. In the constructionist view, the self with even greater agency intentionally *decides* about and scripts the work role, akin to an author who writes a life-career story. The constructionist view on the self goes beyond matching and developing to also emphasize that the individual purposefully reflects on, shapes, and makes meaning of vocational choices and development.

In sum, life-span, life-space theory long sought to combine these three perspectives on self (i.e., differential, developmental, and constructionist) in one grand statement about career choice and development. Super harvested the fruits of P-E fit and life span career psychology, along with social role theory, to articulate the fundamental tenets of life-span, life-space theory. He also attended, albeit less deliberately and directly, to the roles of personal constructs (i.e., internal models of reality or beliefs people form about themselves and the world; Kelly, 1955) and narratives in career development and counseling. For example, he alluded to the merits of using personal constructs rather than self-concepts to connect the life span and life space segments. Super also articulated the thematic extrapolation method (Jepsen, 1994; Super, 1954) as a narrative career counseling intervention for ascertaining life themes to promote career choice and development. The Career Pattern Study collected life history data to capture the rich context and stories of a life-career. Ultimately, Super's passing in 1994 left to other theorists the goals of fully reconciling and synthesizing the differential, developmental, and narrative (or constructionist) dimensions of life-span, life-space theory. Savickas (2002, 2005, Chapter 6 in this volume) attempts this very synthesis in career construction theory.

EMPIRICAL SUPPORT

As the life-span, life-space approach has ranked among the dominant theories of career choice and development for over 60 years, so, too, has it prompted a wealth of empirical research about its propositions and principles. Leading the way, Super and his robust cadre of associates and students conducted sustained programmatic research during this period, most notably in the Career Pattern Study (Super, 1985; Super & Overstreet,

1960) and multinational work importance study (Super & Sverko, 1995). These efforts produced substantial evidence in support of many of the theory's concepts (for detailed reviews, see Betz, 2008; Borgen, 1991; Hackett, Lent, & Greenhaus, 1991; Hartung et al., 2005; Jepsen, 1984; Osipow & Fitzgerald, 1996). For example, results of the Career Pattern Study indicated general support for career maturity as a predictor of important outcomes such as career satisfaction, self-improvement, and occupational satisfaction. Findings also indicated that age-graded increases in career maturity occur as children and adolescents become more future-oriented, more actively engaged in exploring careers, and more knowledgeable about occupations and making career decisions. A comprehensive review of the child vocational development literature indicated significant progress in completing developmental tasks consistent with the career stages of growth and exploration (Hartung et al., 2005). Results of the work importance study (Super & Sverko, 1995) indicated support for the validity of constructs of work values and life-role salience across 12 nations. A review of the work importance study literature concluded that contextual factors such as developmental stage, gender, and culture affect role salience and work values (Niles & Goodnough, 1996). It also pointed out the counseling utility of these two concepts central to life-span, life-space theory.

A multitude of individual studies have also examined and provided at least reasonable support for aspects of the theory. Review and advancement of much of this work, as well as cross-cultural support, appears in a special issue of the *Career Development Quarterly* (Savickas, 1994). This special issue deals with the theory's key constructs, such as career development and maturity, exploration, adaptability, life roles, and work values. The research reviewed pertains to elements across the theory's three primary segments of life span, life space, and self-concepts. On balance, the special issue authors concluded that research generally supports these theoretical constructs and would benefit from use of more refined methodologies and inclusion of more diverse participant samples. Elsewhere, research has indicated that future orientation and planfulness promote career maturity and academic success (Lewis, Savickas, & Jones, 1996). A more recent study supported the proposed planning, exploration, and decision-making components of career adaptability (Creed et al., 2009).

Research has also supported the validity and reliability of the wide array of psychometric instruments that operationally define various concepts within life-span, life-space theory. For example, study findings strongly support the sensitivity and specificity of the Career Development Inventory as a measure of readiness to make educational and vocational choices and as an operational definition of Super's structural model of adolescent career maturity (Savickas & Hartung, 1996). Likewise, the Adult Career Concerns

Inventory provides a valid and reliable measure of attitudes about (Cairo, Kritis, & Myers, 1996) and progress toward completing (Niles, Lewis, & Hartung, 1997) developmental career stages and tasks during the adult years. Research also supports the Values Scale (Nevill & Kruse, 1996) and the Salience Inventory (Nevill & Calvert, 1996) as valid and reliable measures of work values and life-role salience, respectively (see Rounds & Jin, Chapter 15, this volume, for a discussion of these two inventories).

More broadly speaking, "the developmental segment is well documented, and data relative to the self-concept segment generally agree with the theory" (Super et al., 1996, p. 145). Literature reviews have both supported and advanced self-concept as important in career development and career intervention (Betz, 1994; Osipow, 1983). A review by Osipow and Fitzgerald (1996) concluded that the theory has substantial research and practice utility, as well as broad empirical support. A wealth of research specifically supports the roles of career maturity and exploratory behavior in promoting career choice and development (Hartung et al., 2005; Savickas & Hartung, 1996). A criticism of this and much research related to the theory has been an almost exclusive focus on the adolescent and young adult years, with little attention to childhood and middle and late adulthood. Hartung and colleagues (2005), however, reviewed a substantial body of literature supporting Super's views of the career development processes during the childhood and early adolescent years consistent with life-span, life-space theory. Beyond growth and early exploration stages, support of family, teachers, and friends fosters success in completing career exploration stage tasks, but later career stages of establishment, maintenance, and disengagement reflect more nonlinear processes in line with the life-span, life-space concept of recycling (see Betz, 2008). Critics have also pointed to inadequate consideration of factors such as gender and cultural context as a problem with the theory. In response, research has supported the cross-cultural validity of the career maturity construct (e.g., Leong & Serafica, 2001), and findings of the Work Importance Study indicated cross-national support for the constructs of life roles and work values (Super & Sverko, 1995). Conceptual work has also underscored the cultural dimensions and utility of the life roles and values constructs (Hartung, 2002).

Theory revision to include the life space and self-concept segments has also well attended to issues of gender, with particular focus on achieving balance among multiple life roles, especially for women. The theory's lack of testable hypotheses and its use as a post hoc way to interpret findings rather than an a priori frame for study design (Hackett et al., 1991) have limited true tests of its propositions. Despite a noted contemporary decline in its empirical study, the theory's tremendous breadth has for decades allowed researchers to apply it to considering, comprehending, and consolidating evidence about the vast complexity of vocational behavior and development in diverse contexts.

APPLICATION TO CAREER INTERVENTION

Reflecting the dictum "there is nothing so practical as a good theory" (Lewin, 1952, p. 169), the life-span, life-space approach offers a useful guide for career intervention. During 60 years of theory development, Super and his colleagues simultaneously devised methods and materials for assisting individuals to prepare for, enter, and adjust to work roles over the life span. This culminated in a model known as career-development assessment and counseling (C-DAC; Super, 1983). C-DAC systematically applies life-span, life-space theory's key components (i.e., the archway of career determinants, the life career rainbow, and the ladder model of career stages and tasks) to career intervention practice by blending elements of the differential, developmental, and self-concept segments of the theory into one comprehensive four-step scheme. The model's differential component reflects Parsons's (1909) matching model and Holland's (1997) person–environment fit theory. The model's developmental component directly reflects Super's (1990) life-span, life-space theory that recognizes the stages and roles that constitute a life career. The model's self-concept or personal construct component reflects the preferred use of a narrative approach in transitioning from career assessment to career counseling (Super et al., 1992).

ASSESSMENT BATTERY

Using a comprehensive career assessment battery, the C-DAC approach helps clients explore their life roles, developmental stages and tasks, career attitudes and knowledge, values, and interests within their unique life contexts. The C-DAC model offers counselors flexibility in using various measures in career assessment. A typical C-DAC battery includes the following four core measures to assess (1) role salience, (2) developmental concerns, (3) career maturity, and (4) work values and interests.

Role salience is typically assessed with Super and Nevill's (1985a; http://www.vocopher.com) Salience Inventory (SI). The SI measures the extent to which individuals participate in, commit to, and expect to realize values in five life roles: student, worker, citizen, homemaker (including spouse and parent), and leisurite.

The Adult Career Concerns Inventory (ACCI; Super et al., 1988; http://www.vocopher.com) assesses developmental concerns and attitudes. The ACCI's 4 scales and 12 subscales measure concerns related to the career stages and developmental tasks, respectively, of exploration (crystallizing, specifying, implementing), establishment (stabilizing, consolidating, advancing), maintenance (holding, updating, innovating), and disengagement (decelerating, retirement planning, retirement living). The ACCI can be used to measure developmental task mastery, as well as level of concern with developmental tasks (Niles et al., 1997).

Career maturity is usually assessed with the Career Development Inventory (CDI; Super et al., 1979; http://www.vocopher.com). The CDI measures readiness for making educational and vocational choices. The CDI has two parts: career orientation, with four scales that measure career planning (CP), career exploration (CE), career decision making (DM), and world-of-work information (WW); and knowledge of preferred occupation, with one scale measuring knowledge of preferred occupational group (PO). Three composite scores result from summing individual scale scores as follows: career development attitudes combines CP and CE; career development knowledge and skills combines DM and WW; and career orientation total combines CDA and CDK. Higher scores indicate greater career maturity.

The Values Scale (VS; Super & Nevill, 1985b; see Rounds & Jin, Chapter 15, this volume) is typically used to measure 21 basic intrinsic and extrinsic values people seek in work and life. A typical C-DAC assessment battery concludes with the Strong Interest Inventory (see Hansen, Chapter 14, this volume) to assess vocational interests.

INTERVENTION PROCESS

Counselors implement the C-DAC model in a four-step process of preview, depth view, data assessment, and counseling. This process begins with a *preview* that reviews any available data (e.g., school and prior counseling records), an initial interview to identify the client's presenting concerns, and the formation of a preliminary intervention plan. Central to this first step, the practitioner assesses work importance relative to the importance of life roles in other theaters, such as school, home and family, community, and leisure. This assessment may be done informally through dialogue and formally using the Salience Inventory. Ascertaining level of role salience indicates how individuals wish to arrange their life roles. Individuals high in work-role salience show readiness to maximally benefit from further career intervention. Those individuals low in work-role salience may need help with either orienting to the worker role and its importance as a central life task or with exploring and preparing for other life roles.

C-DAC's next step is a *depth view* that systematically measures career stage using the ACCI and career development level using the CDI. This process indicates how ready the individual is for career decision-making activities, such as identifying and exploring occupational interests and work values. Individuals low in career choice readiness need interventions to increase planfulness, exploratory behavior, and knowledge about decision making and the structure of work and occupations. Assessing readiness *before* assessing traits such as interests to match people to occupations is critical because, as Super (1983) stated, "Match-making is hardly likely to last unless those being matched are ready and willing" (p. 557). Once a client is ready for career decision making, attention turns to *data assessment*, measuring vocational interests, abilities, and values using appropriate inventories and scales. In a typical C-DAC battery, these instruments include the SII (Donnay et al., 2005) and the VS (Super & Nevill, 1985b).

C-DAC concludes in a fourth step of *counseling* that involves interpreting all of the assessment data to yield an integrated picture of the individual and a plan for action. An elaboration of the C-DAC model suggested also appraising cultural identity in the first step and considering cultural identity concerns throughout the process (Hartung et al., 1998). Interested readers may wish to study the original (Super, 1983) and subsequent descriptions and illustrations of the C-DAC approach (e.g., Hartung, 1998; Hartung et al., 1998; Niles & Usher, 1993; Osborne, Brown, Niles, & Miner, 1997; Taber & Hartung, 2002). Ultimately, C-DAC helps guide practitioners in teaching children, adolescents, and adults the planning attitudes, career beliefs, and decision-making competencies necessary for life-career success (Savickas, 2005, 2011a). The approach also assists individuals with completing developmental tasks and clarifying and implementing their self-concepts. As a comprehensive scheme for linking people to occupations that fit with their self-concepts and within the broader arrangement of their life roles, C-DAC offers a useful guide and method for career intervention.

CONCLUSIONS AND PRACTICE IMPLICATIONS

Despite having now passed the zenith of its own conceptual and empirical advancement, life-span, life-space theory remains "a sophisticated framework for comprehending the full complexity of vocational behavior and its development in diverse groups in manifold settings" (Super et al., 1996, p. 170). As evidence of its preeminent influence, concepts underlying life-span, life-space theory pervade much theoretical and applied work evidenced in many of the chapters of this volume and in other works (e.g., Blustein, 2006; Brown, 2002; Gottfredson, 2002; Guichard, 2005; Hoekstra, 2011; Vondracek, Lerner, & Schulenberg, 1986). Most notably, readers will find the central tenets, propositions, and practical materials of the life-span, life-space approach directly and substantially updated and advanced in the theory and practice of career construction (Savickas, 2002, 2005, Chapter 6, this volume), as well as in resources available free in an Internet-based career development and counseling resource, referred to as a career "collaboratory" (see Glavin & Savickas, 2010; http://www.vocopher.com). Such conceptual and practical advancement well befits the spirit of life-span, life-space theory as a fluid, contextual, and multidimensional approach to understanding and developing careers that remains open to continued renovation and refinement.

Life-span, life-space theory leaves practitioners with a useful guide and tools for practice. As a guide for practice, the theory reminds practitioners that career choice and development encompasses a lifelong, developmental process that begins in childhood and proceeds continuously over the life course. Each life stage presents particular problems to solve, and these problems may, and often do, surface and resurface in predictable and unpredictable ways at various age periods. By attending to the developmental nature of careers, counselors can assist clients to understand and deal with current and imminent developmental tasks to promote effective career planning, career exploration, career decision making, and work adjustment at all life stages. Practitioners can help clients ready themselves for designing their careers and navigating successfully through both anticipated transitions, such as from school to work, job to job, and work to retirement, and unanticipated work-based traumas, such as job loss, work disability, and job dissatisfaction.

Applying a developmental perspective on careers to career education and counseling practice, the theory also reminds practitioners to help clients arrange their work and other life roles into a livable and satisfying pattern. Recognizing that worker represents one of many psychosocial roles that people play helps counselors more effectively understand, assess, and intervene with clients relative to the multiple roles that form the basis of the life structure. Greater cultural relevance in practice can be achieved by exploring the unique meanings clients ascribe to life roles and helping them comprehend how society and their cultural backgrounds shape those meanings. By attending to the collection of traits that individuals possess, as well as the meaning and purpose those traits hold for the work role, counselors can help clients clarify and shape their self-concepts. With greater self-concept clarity, clients may experience an improved match between self and occupation, as well as a more purposeful implementation of self in work and other life roles. Life-span, life-space theory informed the development of many career assessment instruments. These measures, combined with the language for understanding career development that the theory offers, provide useful tools for fostering careers across the life span and through the life space.

REFERENCES

Adams, G. A., & Rau, B. L. (2011). Putting off tomorrow to do what you want today: Planning for retirement. *American Psychologist, 66,* 180–192.

Arnett, J. (2004). *Emerging adulthood: The winding road from the late teens through the twenties.* New York, NY: Oxford University Press.

Betz, N. E. (1994). Self-concept theory in career development and counseling. *Career Development Quarterly, 43,* 32–42.

Betz, N. E. (2008). Advances in vocational theories. In S. D. Brown & R. W. Lent (Eds.), *Handbook of counseling psychology* (4th ed., pp. 357–374). Hoboken, NJ: Wiley.

Blustein, D. L. (2006). *The psychology of working: A new perspective for career development, counseling, and public policy.* Mahwah, NJ: Erlbaum.

Blustein, D. L., Devenis, L., & Kidney, B. (1989). Relationship between the identity formation process and career development. *Journal of Counseling Psychology, 36,* 196–202.

Bordin, E. S. (1959). Comment. *Journal of Counseling Psychology, 6,* 44–45.

Borgen, F. H. (1991). Megatrends and milestones in vocational behavior: A 20-year counseling psychology retrospective. *Journal of Vocational Behavior, 39,* 263–290.

Brown, D. (2002). The role of work values and cultural values in occupational choice, satisfaction, and success. In D. Brown (Ed.), *Career choice and development* (4th ed., pp. 465–509). San Francisco, CA: Jossey-Bass.

Cairo, P. C., Kritis, K. J., & Myers, R. M. (1996). Career assessment and the Adult Career Concerns inventory. *Journal of Career Assessment, 4,* 189–204.

Chung, Y. B. (2008). National Career Development Association. In F. T. L. Leong (Ed.), *Encyclopedia of counseling, Vol. 4, Career counseling* (pp. 1582–1583). Thousand Oaks, CA: Sage.

Cook, E. P. (1994). Role salience and multiple roles: A gender perspective. *Career Development Quarterly, 43,* 85–95.

Creed, P. A., Fallon, T., & Hood, M. (2009). The relationship between career adaptability, person and situation variables, and career concerns in young adults. *Journal of Vocational Behavior, 74,* 219–229.

Crites, J. O. (1965). Measurement of vocational maturity in adolescence. *Psychological Monographs, 79* (Whole No. 595).

Crites, J. O., & Savickas, M. L. (1995). Revision of the Career Maturity Inventory. *Journal of Career Assessment, 4,* 131–138.

Dawis, R. V. (1996). The theory of work adjustment and person–environment correspondence counseling. In D. Brown & L. Brooks (Eds.), *Career choice and development: Applying contemporary theories to practice* (3rd ed., pp. 75–120). San Francisco, CA: Jossey-Bass.

Donnay, D. A. C., Morris, M. L., Schaubhut, N. A., & Thompson, R. C. (2005). *Strong Interest Inventory manual: Research, development, and strategies for interpretation.* Mountain View, CA: CPP Inc.

Fitzgerald, L. F., & Betz, N. E. (1994). Career development in cultural context: The role of gender, race, class, and sexual orientation. In M. L. Savickas & R. W. Lent (Eds.), *Convergence in career development theories: Implications for science and practice* (pp. 103–117). Palo Alto, CA: Consulting Psychologists Press.

Freedman, M. (2007). *Encore: Finding work that matters in the second half of life.* New York, NY: Public Affairs.

Ginzberg, E., Ginsburg, S., Axelrad, S., & Herma, J. (1951). *Occupational choice: An approach to a general theory.* New York, NY: Columbia University Press.

Glavin, K. W., & Savickas, M. L. (2010). Vocopher: The career collaboratory. *Journal of Career Assessment, 18,* 345–354.

Gottfredson, L. S. (2002). Gottfredson's theory of circumscription, compromise, and self-creation. In D. Brown (Ed.), *Career choice and development* (4th ed., pp. 85–148). San Francisco, CA: Jossey-Bass.

Guichard, J. (2005). Life-long self-construction. *International Journal for Educational and Vocational Guidance, 5,* 111–124.

Hackett, G., Lent, R. W., & Greenhaus, J. H. (1991). Advances in vocational theory and research: A 20-year retrospective. *Journal of Vocational Behavior, 38,* 3–38.

Halbesleben, J. R. B., Harvey, J., & Bolino, M. C. (2009). Too engaged? A conservation of resources view of the relationship between work engagement and work interference with family. *Journal of Applied Psychology, 94,* 1452–1465.

Hartung, P. J. (1998). Assessing Ellenore Flood's roles and values to focus her career shopping. *Career Development Quarterly, 46,* 360–366.

Hartung, P. J. (2002). Cultural context in career theory and practice: Role salience and values. *Career Development Quarterly, 51,* 12–25.

Hartung, P. J., Porfeli, E. J., & Vondracek, F. W. (2005). Child vocational development: A review and reconsideration. *Journal of Vocational Behavior,66,* 385–419.

Hartung, P. J., Vandiver, B. J., Leong, F. T. L., Pope, M., Niles, S. G., & Farrow, B. (1998). Appraising cultural identity in career-development assessment and counseling. *Career Development Quarterly, 46,* 276–293.

Healy, C. C. (1982). *Career development: Counseling through the life stages.* Boston, MA: Allyn & Bacon.

Hirschi, A. (2009). Career adaptability development in adolescence: Multiple predictors and effect on sense of power and life satisfaction. *Journal of Vocational Behavior, 74,* 145–155.

Hoekstra, H. (2011). A career roles model of career development. *Journal of Vocational Behavior, 78,* 159–173.

Holland, J. L. (1959). A theory of vocational choice. *Journal of Counseling Psychology, 6,* 35–45.

Holland, J. L. (1973). *Making vocational choices.* Englewood Cliffs, NJ: Prentice-Hall.

Holland, J. L. (1997). *Making vocational choices* (3rd ed.). Odessa, FL: Psychological Assessment Resources.

Jepsen, D. A. (1984). The developmental perspective on vocational behavior: A review of theory and research. In S. D. Brown & R. W. Lent (Eds.), *Handbook of counseling psychology* (pp. 178–215). New York, NY: Wiley.

Kelly, G. A. (1955). *The psychology of personal constructs*. New York, NY: Norton.

Koen, J., Klehe, U. C., Van Vianen, A. E. M., Zikic, J., & Nauta, A. (2010). Job-search strategies and reemployment quality: The impact of career adaptability. *Journal of Vocational Behavior, 77*, 126–139.

Leong, F. T. L., & Serafica, F. C. (1995). Career development of Asian Americans: A research area in need of a good theory. In F. T. L. Leong (Ed.), *Career development and vocational of racial and ethnic minorities* (pp. 67–102). Hillsdale, NJ: Erlbaum.

Lewin, K. (1952). *Field theory in social science: Selected theoretical papers by Kurt Lewin*. London, UK: Tavistock.

Lewis, D. M., Savickas, M. L., & Jones, B. J. (1996). Career development predicts medical school success. *Journal of Vocational Behavior, 49*, 86–98.

Lofquist, L. H., & Dawis, R. V. (1978). Values as second-order needs in the theory of work adjustment. *Journal of Vocational Behavior, 12*, 12–19.

Maslach, C., & Jackson, S. E. (1986). *Maslach Burnout Inventory manual* (2nd ed.). Palo Alto, CA: Consulting Psychologists Press.

Nevill, D. D., & Calvert, P. D. (1996). Career assessment and the Salience Inventory. *Journal of Career Assessment, 4*, 399–412.

Nevill, D. D., & Kruse, S. J. (1996). Career assessment and the Values Scale. *Journal of Career Assessment, 4*, 383–397.

Niles, S. G., & Goodnough, G. E. (1996). Life-role salience and values: A review of recent research. *Career Development Quarterly, 45*, 65–86.

Niles, S. G., Herr, E. L., & Hartung, P. J. (2001). *Achieving life balance: Myths, realities, and developmental perspectives*. Columbus, OH: ERIC Clearinghouse on Adult, Career, and Vocational Education.

Niles, S. G., Lewis, D. M., & Hartung, P. J. (1997). Using the Adult Career Concerns Inventory to measure task involvement. *Career Development Quarterly, 46*, 87–97.

Niles, S. G., & Usher, C. H. (1993). Applying the career-development assessment and counseling model to the case of Rosie. *Career Development Quarterly, 42*, 61–65.

Osborne, W. L., Brown, S., Niles, S., & Miner, C. U. (1997). *Career development assessment and counseling: Applications of the Donald E. Super C-DAC approach*. Alexandria, VA: American Counseling Association.

Osipow, S. H. (1983). *Theories of career development* (3rd ed.). Englewood Cliffs, NJ: Prentice-Hall.

Osipow, S. H., & Fitzgerald, L. F. (1996). *Theories of career development* (4th ed.). Needham Heights, MA: Allyn & Bacon.

Parsons, F. (1909). *Choosing a vocation*. Boston, MA: Houghton-Mifflin.

Paul, K. I., & Moser, K. (2009). Unemployment impairs mental health: Meta-analyses. *Journal of Vocational Behavior, 74*, 264–282.

Phillips, S. D. (2011). Implementing self-concept: Matching, developing, and deciding. In P. J. Hartung & L. M. Subich (Eds.), *Developing self in work and career: Concepts, cases, and contexts* (pp. 161–173). Washington, DC: APA.

Richardson, M. S. (1993). Work in people's lives: A location for counseling psychologists. *Journal of Counseling Psychology, 40*, 425–433.

Roe, A. (1956). *The psychology of occupations*. New York, NY: Wiley.

Rogers, C. R. *Client-centered therapy*. Boston, MA: Houghton-Mifflin.

Sargent, L. D., Bataille, C. D., Vough, H. C., & Lee, M. D. (2011). Metaphors for retirement: Unshackled from schedules. *Journal of Vocational Behavior, 79,* 315–324.

Savickas, M. L. (1985). Identity in vocational development. *Journal of Vocational Behavior, 27,* 329–337.

Savickas, M. L. (1994). Donald Edwin Super: The career of a planful explorer. *Career Development Quarterly, 43,* 4–24.

Savickas, M. L. (1997). Career adaptability: An integrative construct for life-span, life-space theory. *Career Development Quarterly, 45,* 247–259.

Savickas, M. L. (2002). Career construction: A developmental theory of vocational behavior. In D. Brown (Ed.), *Career choice and development* (4th ed., pp. 149–205). San Francisco, CA: Jossey-Bass.

Savickas, M. L. (2005). The theory and practice of career construction. In S. Brown & R. Lent (Eds.), *Career development and counseling: Putting theory and research to work* (pp. 42–70). Hoboken, NJ: Wiley.

Savickas, M. L. (2007). Super, Donald Edwin. In F. T. L. Leong (Ed.), *Encyclopedia of counseling, Vol. 4, Career counseling* (pp. 1645–1647). Thousand Oaks, CA: Sage.

Savickas, M. L. (2011a). *Career counseling.* Washington, DC: American Psychological Association.

Savickas, M. L. (2011b). New questions for vocational psychology: Premises, paradigms, and practices. *Journal of Career Assessment, 19,* 251–258.

Savickas, M. L. (2011c). The self in vocational psychology: Object, subject, and project. In P. J. Hartung & L. M. Subich (Eds.), *Developing self in work and career: Concepts, cases, and contexts* (pp. 17–33). Washington, DC: APA.

Savickas, M. L., & Baker, D. B. (2005). The history of vocational psychology: Antecedents, origins, and early development. In W. B. Walsh & M. L. Savickas (Eds.), *Handbook of vocational psychology* (3rd ed., pp. 15–50). Mahwah, NJ: Erlbaum.

Savickas, M. L., & Hartung, P. J. (1996). The Career Development Inventory in review: Psychometric and research findings. *Journal of Career Assessment, 4,* 171–188.

Savickas, M. L., & Porfeli, E. J. (2011). Revision of the Career Maturity Inventory: The adaptability form. *Journal of Career Assessment,* doi:10.1177/1069072711409342.

Savickas, M. L., & Super, D. E. (1993). Can life stages and substages be identified in students? *Man and Work: Journal of Labor Studies, 4,* 71–78.

Shultz, K. S., & Wang, M. (2011). Psychological perspectives on the changing nature of retirement. *American Psychologist, 66,* 170–179.

Super, D. E. (1942). *The dynamics of vocational adjustment.* New York, NY: HarperCollins.

Super, D. E. (1949). *Appraising vocational fitness by means of psychological tests.* New York, NY: HarperCollins.

Super, D. E. (1951). Vocational adjustment: Implementing a self-concept. *Occupations, 30,* 88–92.

Super, D. E. (1953). A theory of vocational development. *American Psychologist, 8,* 185–190.

Super, D. E. (1954). Career patterns as a basis for vocational counseling. *Journal of Counseling Psychology, 1,* 12–20.

Super, D. E. (1955). The dimensions and measurement of vocational maturity. *Teachers College Record, 57,* 151–163.

Super, D. E. (1957). *The psychology of careers.* New York, NY: Harper and Row.

Super, D. E. (1963). Toward making self-concept theory operational. In D. E. Super, R. Starishevsky, N. Matlin, & J. P. Jordaan (Eds.), *Career development: Self-concept theory* (pp. 17–32). New York, NY: College Entrance Examination Board.

Super, D. E. (1969). Vocational development theory: Persons, positions, and processes. *Counseling Psychologist, 1,* 2–30.

Super, D. E. (1970). *Manual for the Work Values Inventory.* New York, NY: Houghton Mifflin.

Super, D. E. (1980). A life-span, life-space approach to career development. *Journal of Vocational Behavior, 16,* 282–298.

Super, D. E. (1983). Assessment in career guidance: Toward truly developmental counseling. *Personnel and Guidance Journal, 61,* 555–562.

Super, D. E. (1985). Coming of age in Middletown: Careers in the making. *American Psychologist, 40,* 405–414.

Super, D. E. (1990). A life-span, life-space approach to career development. In D. Brown & L. Brooks (Eds.), *Career choice and development: Applying contemporary theories to practice* (2nd ed., pp. 197–261). San Francisco, CA: Jossey-Bass.

Super, D. E. (1994). A life-span, life-space perspective on convergence. In M. L. Savickas & R. W. Lent (Eds.), *Convergence in theories of career choice and development: Implications for science and practice* (pp. 63–74). Palo Alto, CA: Consulting Psychologists Press.

Super, D. E., & Knasel, E. G. (1981). Career development in adulthood: Some theoretical problems. *British Journal of Guidance and Counseling, 9,* 194–201.

Super, D. E., & Nevill, D. D. (1985a). *Salience Inventory.* Palo Alto, CA: Consulting Psychologists Press.

Super, D. E., & Nevill, D. D. (1985b). *Values Scale.* Palo Alto, CA: Consulting Psychologists Press.

Super, D. E., Osborne, L., Walsh, D., Brown, S., & Niles, S. G. (1992). Developmental career assessment in counseling: The C-DAC Model. *Journal of Counseling and Development, 71,* 74–80.

Super, D. E., & Overstreet, P. L. (1960). *The vocational maturity of ninth-grade boys.* New York, NY: Teachers College Press, Columbia University.

Super D. E., Savickas, M. L., & Super, C. M. (1996). The life-span, life-space approach to careers. In D. Brown & L. Brooks (Eds.), *Career choice and development: Applying contemporary theories to practice* (3rd ed., pp. 121–178). San Francisco, CA: Jossey-Bass.

Super, D. E., Starishevsky, R., Matlin, N. & Jordaan, J. P. (1963). *Career development: Self-concept theory.* New York, NY: College Entrance Examination Board.

Super, D. E., & Sverko, B. (Eds.). (1995). *Life roles, values, and careers: International findings of the work importance study.* San Francisco, CA: Jossey-Bass.

Super, D. E., & Thompson, A. S. (1981). *The Adult Career Concerns Inventory.* New York, NY: Teachers College, Columbia University.

Super, D. E., Thompson, A. S., Lindeman, R. H., Jordaan, J. P., & Myers, R. A. (1979). *Career Development Inventory: School form*. Palo Alto, CA: Consulting Psychologists Press.

Super, D. E., Thompson, A. S., Lindeman, R. H., Jordaan, J. P., & Myers, R. A. (1988). *Adult Career Concerns Inventory*. Palo Alto, CA: Consulting Psychologists Press.

Taber, B., & Hartung, P. J. (2002). Developmental career assessment and counseling with a multipotentialed client. In S. G. Niles, J. Goodman, & M. Pope (Eds.), *The career counseling casebook: A resource for students, practitioners, and counselor educators* (pp. 171–175). Tulsa, OK: National Career Development Association.

Tan, C. S., & Salomone, P. R. (1994). Understanding career plateauing: Implications for counseling. *Career Development Quarterly, 42,* 291–301.

Vondracek, F. W., Lerner, R. M., & Schulenberg, J. E. (1986). *Career development: A life-span developmental approach*. Hillsdale, NJ: Erlbaum.

Williams, C., & Savickas, M. L. (1990). Developmental tasks of career maintenance. *Journal of Vocational Behavior, 36,* 166–175.

Zhan, Y., Wang, M., Liu, S., & Shultz, K. S. (2009). Bridge employment and retirees' health: A longitudinal investigation. *Journal of Occupational Health Psychology, 14,* 374–389.

Zytowski, D. G. (1994). A Super contribution to vocational theory: Work values. *Career Development Quarterly, 43,* 25–31.

Zytowski, D. (2009). *Super's Work Values Inventory–revised: Technical manual (Version 1.2)*. Ames, IA: Kuder http://www.kuder.com/downloads/SWV-Tech -Manual.pdf

CHAPTER 5

Social Cognitive Career Theory

ROBERT W. LENT

EOPLE'S WORK POSSIBILITIES AND developmental trajectories are affected by many variables, including their personal attributes (e.g., interests, abilities, values), learning and socialization experiences, and the resources, opportunities, and barriers afforded by their environments. Occupational paths are forged not by any one of these forces, but rather by the complex interactions among them. The process of career development plays out over multiple life periods, such as preparation for work (education and training), work entry, adjustment to work, and disengagement from work. Career theories provide systems for explaining how many factors operate together to determine occupational choice and development over the life course. In particular, we rely on theories to assemble the many parts of career development into a plausible whole, to organize existing research and generate new knowledge about how people live their work lives, and to spawn practical methods to promote optimal career-life outcomes.

Social cognitive career theory (SCCT; Lent & Brown, 2006, 2008; Lent, Brown, & Hackett, 1994, 2000) is a relatively recent approach to understanding educational and occupational behavior. It brings together common elements identified by earlier career theorists—especially Super, Holland, Krumboltz, and Lofquist and Dawis—and seeks to create a unifying framework for explaining how people (a) develop vocational interests, (b) make occupational choices, (c) achieve varying levels of career success and stability, and (d) experience satisfaction or well-being in the work environment. An SCCT model of the career self-management process is also under development (Lent & Brown, 2012). This chapter contains three main sections: (a) an overview of SCCT's basic elements and predictions; (b) a brief summary of the theory's research base, including study of diverse populations (e.g., people of color, women, persons with disabilities, gay and lesbian workers); and (c) consideration of developmental and counseling applications for maximizing career options, fostering career choice making, and promoting work success and satisfaction. More comprehensive presentations of SCCT, its research base, conceptual underpinnings, relations to other career theories, practical implications, and applications to particular populations can be found in other sources (e.g., Betz, 2008; Brown & Lent, 1996; Fabian, 2000; Hackett & Byars, 1996; Lent & Brown, 2006, 2008; Lent et al., 1994, 2000; Lent & Hackett, 1994; Morrow, Gore, & Campbell, 1996).

OVERVIEW OF SCCT

This section begins by considering SCCT's connections to other theories of career development. It then introduces SCCT's basic elements and models.

SIMILARITIES AND DIFFERENCES WITH OTHER CAREER THEORIES

Trait–factor (later known as P-E fit) career models, such as Holland's theory (Nauta, Chapter 3, this volume), tend to view people and work environments in trait-oriented terms, emphasizing variables that are relatively global, constant, and enduring across time and situations. These models assume that much of what drives career behavior is based on personal attributes—like interests, abilities, values, and personality dispositions—that are largely molded by genetic endowment and early learning experiences. They also assume that individuals' particular mixes of attributes make them better suited to certain work environments than others. P-E fit models have contributed much to the field's understanding of career behavior and have helped inform career counseling by highlighting relatively stable features of persons and environments that, if appropriately matched, are likely to lead to choices that are both satisfying (from the perspective of the person) and satisfactory (from the perspective of the environment).

Developmental career theories (e.g., Hartung, Chapter 4, this volume) emphasize the more or less predictable tasks and challenges that accompany career development, such as learning about oneself, exploring the world of work, developing a vocational identity, narrowing down career options from the larger fund of possibilities, and establishing and maintaining one's career. Certain developmental theories are also concerned with how the work role relates to other life roles (e.g., parent, leisurite), how contextual factors (e.g., socioeconomic status) affect career trajectories, and—in the case of constructionist-developmental models—how people partly construct, or author, their own career/life stories and experiences (Savickas, Chapter 6, this volume).

SCCT shares certain features with the P-E fit and developmental perspectives. For example, like P-E fit theories, SCCT acknowledges the important roles that interests, abilities, and values can play within the career development process. SCCT shares with the developmental theories a focus on how people negotiate particular tasks and milestones (e.g., career choice). Yet SCCT is also relatively distinctive and designed to complement these other theories. In contrast to P-E fit approaches, SCCT highlights relatively dynamic and domain-specific aspects of both people (e.g., self-views, future expectations, behavior) and their environments (e.g., social supports, financial barriers). Although the relative stability of traits helps in predicting outcomes such as occupational choice, people and environments do not always remain the same; indeed, they sometimes change dramatically. Witness, for example, the huge changes brought about in the workplace by technological advances, corporate downsizing, and economic globalization—and the consequent demands that such changes have placed on workers to update their skills and to cultivate new interests (or find a new home for their old ones).

By focusing on cognitions, behavior, and other factors that, theoretically, are relatively malleable and responsive to particular situations and performance domains, SCCT offers an agenda that complements the P-E fit perspective. An SCCT agenda asks, for example, how are people able to change, develop, and regulate their own behavior? How do interests differentiate and intensify, or shift, over time? What factors, other than traits, promote career choice and change? How can career skills be nurtured and work performances improved? How can work lives be made more satisfying?

Relative to developmental theories, SCCT tends to be less concerned with the specifics of ages and stages, yet more concerned with theoretical elements that may promote or hinder career behavior across developmental tasks and periods. For this reason, SCCT may provide a complementary framework from which to address questions that are relevant to particular developmental theorists, such as how work and other life roles become more or less salient for particular individuals (Super), how individuals' career options become constricted or circumscribed over time (Gottfredson), and how people are able to affect their own developmental progress (Savickas).

BASIC COGNITIVE-PERSON ELEMENTS OF SCCT

The primary foundation for SCCT lies in Bandura's (1986) general social cognitive theory, which emphasizes the complex ways in which people, their behavior, and environments mutually influence one another. As in Bandura's general theory, SCCT assumes that people have the capacity to exercise some degree of *agency* or self-direction and that they also contend with many factors (e.g., environmental supports and barriers) that can strengthen, weaken, or even override personal agency. SCCT highlights the interplay among three cognitive-person variables that partly enable the exercise of agency in career development: self-efficacy beliefs, outcome expectations, and personal goals.

Self-efficacy beliefs refer to "people's judgments of their capabilities to organize and execute courses of action required to attain designated types of performances" (Bandura, 1986, p. 391). These beliefs are among the most important determinants of thought and action in Bandura's (1986) theory. Self-efficacy is not a unitary or global trait, like self-esteem (i.e., general feelings of self-worth), with which it is often confused. Rather, self-efficacy is conceived as a dynamic set of self-beliefs that are linked to particular performance domains and activities. An individual might, for instance, hold strong self-efficacy beliefs regarding his or her ability to play piano or basketball but feel much less competent at social or mechanical tasks.

These beliefs about personal capabilities, which are subject to change based on future experiences and are responsive to environmental conditions (e.g., How supportive is the piano teacher? How tough is the basketball competition?), are acquired and modified via four primary informational sources (or types of learning experience): (1) personal performance accomplishments, (2) vicarious learning, (3) social persuasion, and (4) physiological and affective states (Bandura, 1997). The impact that these experiential sources have on self-efficacy depends on a variety of factors, such as how the individual attends to and interprets them. Prior performance accomplishments often have the greatest influence on self-efficacy. Compelling success experiences with a given task or performance domain (e.g., math) tend to strengthen self-efficacy beliefs in relation to that task or domain; convincing or repeated failures tend to weaken these beliefs.

Outcome expectations refer to beliefs about the consequences or outcomes of performing particular behaviors. Whereas self-efficacy beliefs are concerned with one's capabilities (e.g., "can I do this?"), outcome expectations involve imagined consequences of particular courses of action (e.g., "if I do this, what will happen?"). Bandura (1986) described three types of outcome expectations, including the anticipation of physical, social, and self-evaluative outcomes. He maintained that self-efficacy and outcome expectations both help to determine a number of important aspects of human behavior, such as the activities that people choose to pursue and the ones they avoid. Self-efficacy may be the more influential determinant in many situations that call for complex skills or potentially costly or difficult courses of action (e.g., whether to pursue a medical career). In such situations, people may hold positive outcome expectations (e.g., "a medical career would offer lots of prestige and chances to help others") but avoid a certain choice option if they doubt they have the capabilities required to succeed at it (i.e., "I am not good at science"). However, one can also envision scenarios where self-efficacy is high but outcome expectations are low (e.g., a young woman who is confident in her math-related capabilities but refrains from taking elective math courses because she anticipates negative reactions from her friends).

People develop outcome expectations regarding different academic and career paths from a variety of direct and vicarious learning experiences, such as perceptions of the outcomes they have personally received in relevant past endeavors and the secondhand information they acquire about different career fields (e.g., by observing family and community members or seeing how different forms of work are portrayed in various media). Self-efficacy can also affect outcome expectations, especially in situations where outcomes are closely tied to the quality of one's performance (e.g., strong performance on a classroom test typically results in a high grade and other favorable outcomes). This is because people usually expect to receive positive outcomes (and avoid negative ones) when performing tasks at which they feel competent.

Personal goals may be defined as one's intention to engage in a particular activity or to produce a particular outcome (Bandura, 1986). Goals address the question, "How much and how well do I want to do this?" SCCT distinguishes between *choice-content goals* (or, more simply, choice goals— the type of activity or career one wishes to pursue) and *performance goals* (the level or quality of performance one plans to achieve within a given task or domain). Goals offer an important means by which people exercise agency in their educational and occupational pursuits. By setting personal goals, people help to organize, direct, and sustain their own behavior, even over long intervals without external payoffs. The amount of progress people perceive they are making toward their goals can have important affective consequences (e.g., feelings of satisfaction or dissatisfaction), which may help to reshape future choices.

Social cognitive theory maintains that people's choice and performance goals are affected by their self-efficacy and outcome expectations. For example, strong self-efficacy and positive outcome expectations in relation to musical performance are likely to nurture music-relevant goals, such as the intention to devote time to practice, seek performing opportunities, and perhaps (depending on the nature and strength of one's self-efficacy and outcome expectations in other domains) pursue a career in music. Progress (or lack of progress) in attaining one's goals, in turn, has a reciprocal influence on self-efficacy and outcome expectations. Successful goal pursuit may further strengthen self-efficacy and outcome expectations within a positive cycle.

SCCT's MODELS OF INTEREST, CHOICE, PERFORMANCE, AND SATISFACTION

SCCT currently consists of four conceptually distinct yet overlapping models focusing on (1) the development of interests, (2) the making of choices, (3) the influences on and results of performance, and (4) the experience of satisfaction, or well-being, in educational and occupational spheres. In each model, the basic cognitive-person elements—self-efficacy, outcome expectations, and goals—are seen as operating in concert with other important aspects of persons (e.g., gender, race/ethnicity), their environments, and learning experiences to help shape the contours of academic and career development.

Interest model. Home, educational, and community environments expose children and adolescents to an array of activities—like crafts, sports, math, socializing, and computing—that form the substrate for later career or leisure options. Young people are selectively encouraged by parents, teachers, peers, and important others to pursue, and try to perform well, certain activities from among those that are available to them. By practicing different activities—and by receiving ongoing feedback, both positive and negative, about the quality of their performances—children and adolescents gradually refine their skills, develop personal performance standards, and form self-efficacy and outcome expectations regarding different tasks and domains of behavior. For example, receiving consistent rebuke about one's athletic skills or praise about one's math skills is likely to be reflected in the self-efficacy and outcome expectations that one develops in relation to these two performance domains.

According to SCCT's interest model, illustrated in Figure 5.1, self-efficacy and outcome expectations regarding particular activities help to mold career interests (i.e., each person's particular pattern of likes, dislikes, and

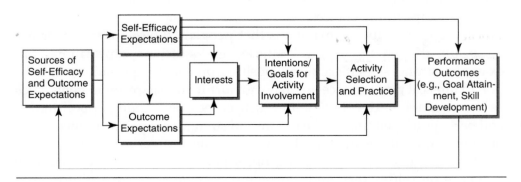

Figure 5.1   Model of How Basic Career Interests Develop Over Time
Copyright 1993 by R. W. Lent, S. D. Brown, and G. Hackett. Reprinted by permission.

indifference in relation to career-relevant tasks). Interest in an activity is likely to blossom and endure when people (a) view themselves as competent (self-efficacious) at the activity and (b) anticipate that performing it will produce valued outcomes (positive outcome expectations). At the same time, people are likely to develop disinterest or even aversion toward activities (such as athletics, in the previous example) in which they doubt their efficacy and expect to receive negative outcomes.

As interests emerge, they—along with self-efficacy and outcome expectations—encourage intentions, or goals, for sustaining or increasing one's involvement in particular activities. Goals, in turn, increase the likelihood of activity practice, and subsequent practice efforts give rise to a particular pattern of performance attainments that, for better or worse, help to revise self-efficacy and outcome expectations within an ongoing feedback loop. This basic process is seen as repeating itself continuously prior to work entry. As recognized by P-E fit theories, career-related interests do tend to stabilize over time and, for many people, are quite stable by late adolescence or early adulthood (see Hansen, Chapter 14, this volume). SCCT assumes that interest stability is largely a function of crystallizing self-efficacy beliefs and outcome expectations, yet that adult interests are not set in stone. Whether interests change or solidify is determined by such factors as whether initially preferred activities become restricted and whether people are exposed (or expose themselves) to compelling learning experiences (e.g., through volunteering, engaging in leadership roles, child rearing, using technological tools) that enable them to rethink or expand their sense of their capabilities and the outcomes offered by different work activities. Thus, SCCT assumes that, when they occur, shifts in interests are largely due to changing self-efficacy beliefs and outcome expectations.

SCCT also takes into account other aspects of people and their environments that affect the acquisition and modification of interests. For example, abilities and values—staples of P-E fit theories—are important in SCCT, too, but their effects on interest are seen as largely funneled through self-efficacy and outcome expectations. That is, rather than determining interests directly, objective ability (as reflected by test scores, trophies, awards, and the like) serves to raise or lower self-efficacy beliefs, which, in turn, influence interests. In other words, self-efficacy functions as an intervening link between ability and interests. Career-related values are contained within SCCT's concept of outcome expectations. Values are traditionally measured as people's preferences for particular work conditions or reinforcers (e.g., status, money, autonomy). Outcome expectations are measured by examining people's beliefs about the extent to which their values would be fulfilled by pursuing particular activities or occupations (e.g., how likely is a career in nursing to provide the work conditions or reinforcers I most value?).

Self-efficacy and outcome expectations do not arise in a social vacuum, nor do they operate alone in shaping interests or other vocational outcomes. Rather, they are forged and function in the context of other aspects of persons and their environments, such as gender, race/ethnicity, genetic endowment, physical health or disability status, and socioeconomic conditions, all of which can play important roles within the career development process. Figure 5.2 offers an overview of how, from the perspective of SCCT, selected person, environment, and learning or experiential variables contribute to interests and other career outcomes. Given space limitations, we focus on the roles that gender and race/ethnicity may play relative to the development of self-efficacy and outcome expectations.

SCCT is concerned more with the psychological and social effects of gender and ethnicity than with the view of sex and race as categorical physical or biological factors. Gender and ethnicity are seen as linked to career development in several key ways, especially through the reactions they evoke from the social-cultural environment and from their relation to the opportunity structure to which individuals are exposed (e.g., one's access to career-relevant models and performance experiences). For example, gender and ethnicity can influence the context in which children acquire self-efficacy and outcome expectations. Gender role socialization processes tend to bias the access that boys and girls receive to experiences necessary for developing strong efficacy beliefs and positive expectations regarding male-typed (e.g., science) and female-typed (e.g., helping) activities. Such processes may help to explain why boys and girls are more likely to develop

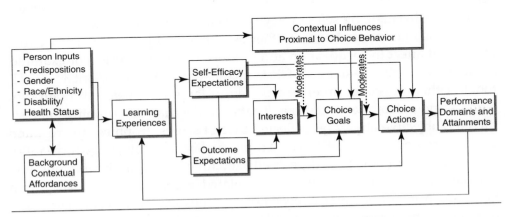

Figure 5.2 Model of Person, Contextual, and Experiential Factors Affecting Career-Related Choice Behavior

Note: Direct relations between variables are indicated with solid lines; moderator effects (where a given variable strengthens or weakens the relation between two other variables) are shown with dashed lines. Copyright 1993 by R. W. Lent, S. D. Brown, and G. Hackett. Reprinted by permission.

skills (along with beneficial self-efficacy and outcome expectations) and, in turn, interests at tasks that are culturally defined as gender-appropriate (Hackett & Betz, 1981). In time, these interests, and the choices they nurture, help to perpetuate well-entrenched patterns of gender segregation in certain fields (see Heppner, Chapter 7, this volume).

To a large extent, then, variables like gender and ethnicity may affect interest development and other career outcomes through socially constructed processes that may appear to operate in the background but that nevertheless can powerfully influence the differential learning experiences that give rise to self-efficacy and outcome expectations—leading, at times, to skewed conclusions about what interests or career options are "right" for certain types of persons. At later stages in the career choice process, gender, ethnicity, culture, socioeconomic status, and disability conditions may, additionally, be linked to the opportunity structure within which people set and implement their career choice goals, as is later discussed.

Choice model. In keeping with developmental theories, choosing a career path is not viewed as a single, static event but, rather, is part of a larger set of dynamic processes. As SCCT's interest model illustrates, career choice is preceded by the development of self-efficacy, outcome expectations, interests, and skills in different performance domains. Over time, these processes make certain choice paths attractive and viable for a given individual and render other options less appealing or likely to be pursued. Moreover, once initial career choices are made, they are subject to future revision because individuals and their environments are dynamic entities. Events and circumstances may well transpire that could not have been foreseen during initial choice making or career entry. New paths (or branches from old paths) may open up; barriers (e.g., glass ceilings) or calamities (e.g., job loss) may arise; value and interest priorities may shift over the course of one's work life. Thus, it seems prudent to think of career selection as an unfolding process with multiple influences and choice points.

For conceptual simplicity, SCCT divides initial choice making into three component parts: (1) the expression of a primary choice (or goal) to enter a particular field, (2) taking actions designed to implement one's goal (e.g., enrolling in a particular training program or academic major), and (3) subsequent performance experiences (e.g., a pattern of successes or failures) that form a feedback loop, affecting the shape of one's future choice options. This conceptual division identifies logical intervention targets for preparing people to make career choices, as well as for helping them to deal with problems in choice making. Throughout the choice process, people do not choose careers unilaterally; environments also choose people. Thus, career choice (and choice stability) is a two-way street that is conditioned, in part, by the environment's receptivity to the individual and judgments about his or her ability to meet training and occupational requirements, both initially and over time. In other words, environmental agents play a "potent role in helping to determine who gets to do what and where, for how long, and with what sorts of rewards" (Lent & Sheu, 2010, p. 692).

Similar to Holland's theory, SCCT assumes that, just as "birds of a feather flock together," people's vocational interests tend to orient them toward certain choice options that, under supportive conditions, might enable them to perform preferred activities and to interact with others who have similar work personalities. For example, a person whose primary interests lie in the social domain is likely to gravitate toward socially oriented occupations, allowing him or her to work with others in a helping or teaching capacity. However, SCCT explicitly recognizes that environments are not always supportive of individuals' preferences and people are not always free to pursue their primary interests. Choice may be constrained, for example, by family wishes, economic realities (e.g., the need to bring in immediate income, lack of funding for training), or the quality of one's prior education. In such situations, as discussed later, personal interests may play little, if any, role in career choice. SCCT, therefore, takes into account variables that, in addition to (or apart from) interests, can influence the choice process.

SCCT's choice model, shown in Figure 5.2, acknowledges the processes that both precede and follow occupational choice. As described earlier, self-efficacy and outcome beliefs are seen as jointly influencing career-related interests, which tend to foster career choice *goals* (i.e., intentions to pursue a particular career path) that are congruent with one's interests. Goals, then, motivate choice *actions*, or efforts to implement one's goals (e.g., seeking relevant training, applying for certain jobs). These actions are, in turn, followed by a particular pattern of performance successes and failures. For instance, after gaining entry to an engineering college, a student may have difficulty completing the required math and physics courses. He or she may also discover that the work conditions and rewards available in engineering suit him or her less well than had been initially anticipated. These learning experiences may prompt the student to revise his or her self-efficacy beliefs and outcome expectations, leading to a shift in interests and goals (e.g., selection of a new major or career path).

Let us also take a closer look at how people's environments affect the choice process. Each person derives certain "affordances" from the environment—for instance, social and material resources or deficits—that help to shape his or her career development (Vondracek, Lerner, & Schulenberg, 1986). In SCCT, these affordances are divided into two general types, based on when they occur within the choice process. The first type includes more *distal, background influences* (e.g., cultural and gender role socialization, types of available career role models, skill development opportunities) that help to shape self-efficacy, outcome expectations, and, hence, interests. We had earlier considered these more distal effects of contextual variables in SCCT's interest model. The second type involves *proximal environmental influences* that come into play during the active phases of choice making. Figure 5.2 includes consideration of these distal (lower left) and proximal (upper right) contextual affordances.

SCCT's choice model highlights two means by which proximal contextual factors may function during the processes of setting and implementing career choice goals. First, SCCT posits that certain conditions may *directly* affect people's choice goals or actions (these direct influences are represented by the solid arrows from contextual variables to goals and actions in Figure 5.2). In certain cultures, for example, one may defer one's career decisions to significant others in the family, even where the others' preferred career path is not all that interesting to the individual. People may also encounter environmental supports or barriers in relation to the options that they, themselves, most prefer. Examples include emotional or financial support for pursuing a particular option, job availability in one's preferred field, and sociostructural barriers, such as discrimination.

Second, contextual variables may affect people's ability or willingness to translate their interests into goals and their goals into actions. According to SCCT, career interests are more likely to blossom into goals (and goals are more likely to be implemented) when people experience strong environmental supports and weak barriers in relation to their preferred career paths. By contrast, nonsupportive or hostile conditions can impede the process of transforming interests into goals and goals into actions. In statistical terms, this implies that contextual supports and barriers can *moderate* the goal transformation process (shown by the dotted paths in Figure 5.2). That is, the relations of interests to goals, and of goals to actions, are expected to be stronger in the presence of favorable versus restrictive environmental conditions.

SCCT explicitly acknowledges that, for a variety of reasons (often economic in nature), many people do not receive support for pursuing their vocational interests; for them, "choice" may mean selecting from among a fairly narrow range of less desirable options. Moreover, as Bandura once observed (personal communication, March 1, 1993), people are not necessarily drawn to work on assembly lines or in coal mines by a consuming interest in the work itself. Their interests may, in essence, be beside the point. Job availability in the context of financial need may be an overriding consideration. In SCCT, self-efficacy and outcome expectations are shown as producing separate paths to goals and goal actions, above and beyond their effects on interests (see Figure 5.2). Thus, when people perceive the need to make work choices that compromise their interests or for reasons other than interests—for instance, because of environmental barriers or limited opportunities—their work-seeking decisions may be influenced less by interests than by pragmatic contextual, self-efficacy, and outcome expectation considerations. For example, a worker might consider such things as what work is available, what my family wants me to do, whether I have the skills to do this work, and whether the payoffs are worth it (i.e., is the option "good enough" to justify its pursuit?).

In sum, SCCT posits that educational and occupational choices are often, but not always, linked to people's interests. Economic, cultural, and other conditions sometimes require a compromise in personal interests. In such instances, choices are determined by what options are available to the individual, the nature of his or her self-efficacy beliefs and outcome expectations, available choice-relevant resources, and the sorts of messages the individual receives from his or her support system. Environmental factors (supports and barriers) may also facilitate or hinder the choice implementation process, regardless of whether people are pursuing preferred or interest-consistent options.

Performance model. SCCT's model of performance focuses both on the level (or quality) of attainment individuals achieve in educational and work tasks (e.g., measures of success or proficiency) and the degree to which they persist at particular tasks or choice paths, especially when they encounter obstacles. Note that SCCT's choice and performance models overlap in their focus on persistence. This is because persistence can be viewed alternatively in terms of choice stability (the decision to endure at a particular course of action) or performance adequacy. From the perspective of the environment, persistence is often considered a sign of performance success because it is assumed that competent performers will persist (and will *be allowed to persist*) longer, resulting in school or college retention and job tenure. However, persistence is an imperfect indicator of performance adequacy because people can shift educational or occupational plans for reasons other than deficient capabilities (e.g., a college student may drop out because of funding problems, a worker may decide voluntarily to pursue attractive options elsewhere or be laid off during corporate downsizing).

As shown in Figure 5.3, SCCT sees educational and vocational performance as involving the interplay among people's ability, self-efficacy, outcome expectations, and performance goals. More specifically, ability—as assessed by indicators of achievement, aptitude, or past performance—affects performance attainments both (a) directly, for instance, via the task knowledge

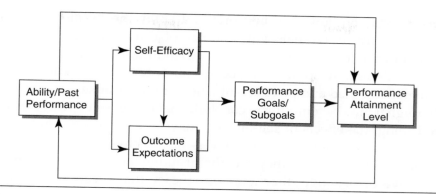

Figure 5.3   Model of Task Performance
Copyright 1993 by R. W. Lent, S. D. Brown, and G. Hackett. Reprinted by permission.

and performance strategies that people develop and (b) indirectly, by serving to inform self-efficacy and outcome expectations. That is, people base their self-efficacy and outcome expectations partly on their perceptions of the skills they currently possess (or can develop), as well as on how well they have performed, and what outcomes they have received, in relevant past performance situations. Self-efficacy and outcome expectations, in turn, influence the level of performance goals that people set for themselves (e.g., aiming for an A in algebra or a certain sales figure at work). Stronger self-efficacy and positive outcome expectations promote more ambitious goals, which help to mobilize and sustain performance efforts.

Consistent with general social cognitive theory (Bandura, 1986), SCCT posits a feedback loop between performance attainments and subsequent behavior. That is, markers of success or failure become part of one's performance history or learning experiences, with the capacity to confirm or revise one's self-efficacy and outcome expectations within a dynamic cycle. Although the performance model focuses on person variables, recall that people develop their talents, self-efficacy, outcome expectations, and goals within a larger sociocultural, educational, and economic context. As shown in Figure 5.2, the learning experiences to which people are exposed and the outcomes they derive from their performances are intimately related to features of their environments, such as educational quality, the nature of available role models, gender role socialization, peer and parental supports, and community and family norms.

It should also be emphasized that, in SCCT's performance model, self-efficacy is seen as complementing—not substituting for—objectively assessed ability. Complex performances draw on requisite abilities yet are also aided by an optimistic sense of efficacy, which helps people organize, orchestrate, and make the most of their talents. What people can accomplish depends partly on how they interpret and apply their skills, which helps to explain why individuals with similar objective abilities can achieve performances that vary greatly in quality (Bandura, 1986). Those who doubt their capabilities may, for instance, be less likely to use their skills effectively or to remain focused and perseverant when problems arise.

Although it may be tempting to conclude that higher self-efficacy is always a good thing, the effects of self-efficacy may, in fact, depend on how high or low it is in relation to current levels of objective ability. People may encounter problems when they greatly misjudge their capabilities in either the positive or negative direction. Self-efficacy that greatly overestimates current capabilities (i.e., overconfidence) may encourage people to attempt tasks for which they are ill prepared, risking failure and discouragement. Self-efficacy beliefs that seriously underestimate documented ability (under-confidence) may interfere with performance by prompting less effort and perseverance, lower goals, greater performance anxiety, and avoidance of realistic challenges (Bandura, 1986). Both types of perceptual bias may hamper skill development. By contrast, self-efficacy that slightly overshoots but is reasonably congruent with current capabilities (slight overconfidence) promotes optimal skill use and motivation for further skill development.

Satisfaction model. SCCT's most recent model focuses on factors that influence people's experience of satisfaction, or well-being, in academic and work settings (Lent & Brown, 2006). Given space constraints and the relative newness of the model, it is outlined only briefly here (a more detailed version of the model, including additional variables, such as work stress and life satisfaction, can be found in Lent & Brown, 2008). As shown in Figure 5.4, satisfaction (i.e., the degree to which one likes or is happy with one's school or work environment) is expected to be influenced by several sets of variables that overlap with the previous SCCT models. In particular, the model posits that people are likely to be happy at school or work to the extent that they are involved in activities they value, see themselves as making progress at personally relevant goals, possess strong self-efficacy at performing necessary tasks and at achieving their goals, and have access to resources in the environment for promoting their self-efficacy and aiding their goal pursuit.

In addition, satisfaction is seen as affected by aspects of one's personality and work conditions. Certain personality traits (e.g., positive and negative affect) have been found to be reliably linked to job satisfaction. Work conditions include a variety of environmental features (e.g., favorable work characteristics, needs-supplies fit, perceived organizational support) that have also been associated with satisfaction. In addition to their direct relations to satisfaction, the model acknowledges several indirect paths by

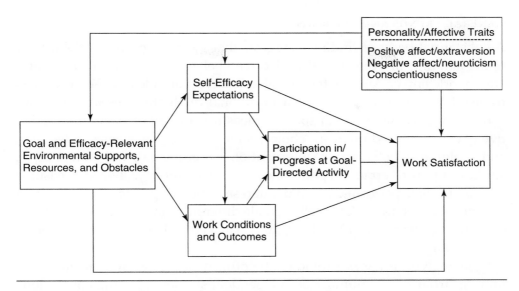

Figure 5.4   A Social Cognitive Model of Work Satisfaction
From Lent and Brown (2006). Copyright 2006 Elsevier. Adapted with permission.

which personality and environmental factors may affect work satisfaction (e.g., certain personality factors may affect perceptions of self-efficacy and environmental support that, in turn, influence satisfaction). Although these indirect paths add complexity to the model, they are necessary to capture the means by which person and situation factors operate together to affect satisfaction. From a counseling perspective, the model emphasizes potentially malleable features of the individual (e.g., self-efficacy, outcome expectations, goal selection and progress) and environment (e.g., supportive supervision, mentoring) that can be harnessed to design satisfaction-promoting interventions.

RESEARCH ON SCCT

SCCT's four models and many of their specific predictions have attracted a good deal of attention from researchers. A full-scale review of research relevant to SCCT is beyond the scope of this chapter, though some of the major research trends and findings can be summarized here. More thorough reviews and meta-analyses of this literature, cited later, may be consulted for in-depth assessments of research linking social cognitive theory to career development processes and outcomes. In this section, I first consider the theory's overall empirical status and then discuss selected applications of SCCT to the career behavior of diverse populations.

GENERAL TRENDS AND FINDINGS

A substantial body of findings suggests that social cognitive variables aid understanding of educational and career behavior prior to, during, and after work entry. Among the social cognitive variables, self-efficacy has received the most attention, with traditional qualitative research reviews concluding that (a) domain-specific measures of self-efficacy are predictive of career-related interests, choice, achievement, persistence, indecision, and exploratory behavior; (b) intervention, experimental, and path analytic studies support certain hypothesized causal relations between measures of self-efficacy, performance, and interests; and (c) gender differences in self-efficacy help to explain male–female differences in occupational consideration (e.g., Bandura, 1997; Betz, 2008; Hackett & Lent, 1992; Swanson & Gore, 2000).

Meta-analytic reviews provide a helpful, quantitative way to integrate findings from a large number of independent studies, allowing conclusions about the strength of relationships across all studies that have addressed particular hypotheses. Several meta-analyses of research, primarily involving late adolescents and young adults, have directly tested a number of SCCT's hypotheses. Meta-analysis of the interest hypotheses, for instance, indicates that self-efficacy and outcome expectations are each good predictors of occupational interests and that, as predicted, the relation of ability to interests appears to operate through (or be mediated by) self-efficacy (Lent et al., 1994) (see Figures 5.1 and 5.2). A meta-analysis of 53 samples, including over 37,000 research participants, reported a strong overall relationship between self-efficacy and career interests ($r = .59$; Rottinghaus, Larson, & Borgen, 2003).

Meta-analysis of SCCT's choice hypotheses has shown that career-related choices are strongly predicted by interests ($r = .60$; Lent et al., 1994). Self-efficacy and outcome expectations also relate to career choice both directly and indirectly, through their linkage to interests (see Figure 5.2) (Lent et al., 1994). In a recent meta-analysis, Sheu et al. (2010) found that interests, self-efficacy, and outcome expectations together strongly predicted choice goals across each of the six Holland themes. Research has also examined the manner in which perceived environmental supports and barriers relate to choice goals. The emerging pattern of findings suggests that, though supports and barriers yield small direct relations to choice outcomes in some Holland themes, their primary role may be to strengthen or weaken self-efficacy and outcome expectations that, in turn, promote interest and choice (Sheu et al., 2010).

Meta-analysis of SCCT's performance model predictions have thus far focused on the relation of self-efficacy to various indicators of performance.

Findings have shown that self-efficacy is a useful predictor of both academic (Multon, Brown, & Lent, 1991) and occupational (Sadri & Robertson, 1993; Stajkovic & Luthans, 1998) performance, and that certain factors affect the strength of the self-efficacy-performance relationship. For instance, Multon et al. (1991) found that self-efficacy was more strongly related to performance in older versus younger students and in low-achieving versus adequately achieving students. Recent meta-analyses have confirmed the utility of self-efficacy in predicting work performance (Brown, Lent, Telander, & Tramayne, 2011) and academic performance and persistence (Brown et al., 2008), although performance goals explained unique variance beyond self-efficacy only in predicting academic persistence. Consistent with hypotheses (see Figure 5.3), ability and past performance success have been linked to future performance outcomes both directly and indirectly, through intervening self-efficacy beliefs (Brown et al., 2008, 2011; Lent et al., 1994).

Tests of the new SCCT model of satisfaction suggest its potential utility, though not enough studies have accrued to warrant a meta-analysis at this point (Sheu & Lent, 2009). Likewise, a number of studies have examined the sources of information, or learning experiences (see Figure 5.2), that are assumed to give rise to self-efficacy beliefs and outcome expectations (e.g., Schaub & Tokar, 2005), though meta-analyses have yet to aggregate their results. Of the four primary sources (performance accomplishments, vicarious learning, social persuasion, physiological and affective states), performance accomplishments (e.g., indicators of one's previous success or failure) typically show the strongest relation to self-efficacy (e.g., Williams & Subich, 2006). Self-efficacy is, in turn, a good predictor of outcome expectations (Lent et al., 1994; Sheu et al., 2010). Such findings offer valuable implications for the design of interventions to promote self-efficacy and outcome expectations and, in turn, subsequent career outcomes.

Collectively, the meta-analyses are consistent with theoretical assumptions that (a) self-efficacy and outcome expectations are good predictors of interests; (b) one's ability or performance accomplishments are likely to lead to interests in a particular domain to the extent that they foster a growing sense of self-efficacy in that domain; (c) self-efficacy and outcome expectations predict career-related choices both directly and indirectly through their linkage to interests; and (d) performance success is enabled both by abilities and self-efficacy, which can aid people to organize their skills and persist despite setbacks.

APPLICATIONS TO DIVERSE POPULATIONS

SCCT was designed to aid understanding of the career development of a diverse array of students and workers, taking into account such factors as race/ethnicity, culture, gender, socioeconomic status, age, and disability status. Hackett and Betz (1981) were the first scholars to extend social cognitive theory to career behavior, focusing on how self-efficacy might illuminate women's career development. They noted that gender role socialization processes tend to provide girls and young women with biased access to the sources of efficacy information (e.g., gender-traditional role models, differential encouragement to pursue culturally prescribed activities). Such experiences nurture self-efficacy for traditionally female activities but may limit self-efficacy in nontraditional career domains. Consistent with their thesis, Betz and Hackett (1981) found that college women reported stronger self-efficacy for performing occupations that are traditionally dominated by women than by men, and that these beliefs were linked to their interests in and consideration of traditional and nontraditional choice options.

Much subsequent research has examined social cognitive variables in relation to gender. For example, Williams and Subich (2006) found that, although occupational self-efficacy beliefs and outcome expectations tended to be associated with the four primary sources of efficacy across Holland themes and gender, women and men reported having received differential exposure to these efficacy sources in particular gender-typed domains (e.g., women reported more Social-type and men more Investigative-type learning experiences). Such findings suggest that gender differences in occupational membership may be partly attributable to gender-based learning/socialization experiences that give rise to self-efficacy and outcome expectations and, ultimately, interests and choices. Although a number of studies have reported gender differences in self-efficacy regarding gender-typed tasks and fields (e.g., mathematics) in general samples of students, such differences are less commonly found in samples of women and men who are likely to have had comparable efficacy-building experiences in particular gender-typed domains (e.g., engineering majors; e.g., Lent et al., 2005). These sorts of findings suggest that women's and men's career pursuits can be constricted or expanded by environmentally guided (and self-sought) learning experiences and, especially, by the types of self-efficacy beliefs and outcome expectations that such experience enables.

Bandura (1997) has observed that "cultural constraints, inequitable incentive systems, and truncated opportunity structures are . . . influential in shaping women's career development" (pp. 436). Although the impact may appear to be less insidious, Heppner (Chapter 7, this volume) has noted that men's career development may also be hemmed in by such sociostructural factors. Social cognitive theory implies several developmental and preventive routes for redressing socially imposed limitations. Such routes include, for example, educating parents and teachers about the implications of gender-typed efficacy development and about ways to foster self-efficacy and support systems, thereby enabling children to acquire (and profit from) performance experiences in as wide a range of activity domains as possible. Indeed, consistent with Gottfredson's theory (2005), encouragement to engage in non-gender-stereotypic activities may need to be provided relatively early in children's lives to preserve the maximum number of options for later educational and career consideration.

Similar social-cognitive dynamics have been discussed in relation to the career development of persons of color. Hackett and Byars (1996) noted, for example, how culturally based exposure to sources of efficacy information (e.g., social encouragement to pursue certain options, experience with racism, role modeling) may differentially affect African American women's career self-efficacy beliefs, outcome expectations, goals, and subsequent career progress. Hackett and Byars suggested theory-based methods, such as developmental interventions, social advocacy, and collective action, to promote the career growth of African American women. Applications of SCCT's basic interest and choice models to Hispanic, African American, and Asian American student samples has found support for the cross-cultural relevance of these models (see Lent & Sheu, 2010, for a review).

SCCT has also been extended to a number of other diverse client populations (see Fabian & Pebdani, Chapter 13, and Fouad & Kantamneni, Chapter 8, this volume). For instance, Szymanski, Enright, Hershenson, and Ettinger (2003) considered self-efficacy and outcome expectations as useful constructs in understanding the career development of persons with disabilities, and Fabian (2000) discussed how SCCT could be used to derive career interventions specifically for adults with psychiatric disabilities. SCCT has also been used to illuminate aspects of career choice and adjustment in lesbian and gay workers (e.g., Morrow et al., 1996). Finally, SCCT hypotheses and models have been found to be viable in emerging cross-cultural and cross-national tests (e.g., see Lent & Sheu, 2010; Lindley, 2006; Sheu & Lent, 2009).

In sum, research provides support for many of SCCT's theoretical assumptions about how cognitive-person variables relate to career interests, choice, performance, and satisfaction. The applications described in this section also convey SCCT's potential utility in understanding and facilitating the career development of persons across a number of diversity dimensions. Despite the promise of these applications, there is need for additional research on how social cognitive variables operate together with culture, ethnicity, socioeconomic status, sexual orientation, and disability status to shape the career development of students and workers. Additional research is also needed on the efficacy of SCCT-based interventions (Gainor, 2006). Nevertheless, currently available findings offer valuable implications for career education and counseling practice. We consider such implications in the next section.

APPLYING SCCT TO PRACTICE

SCCT suggests a variety of ideas for promoting development of academic and career interests and competencies, for preventing or forestalling career-related difficulties, and for helping people remedy existing problems in choosing, finding, or adjusting to work. Suggestions for developmental and preventive applications can be derived from SCCT's basic models, especially from hypotheses about how self-efficacy and the other social cognitive variables develop in childhood and adolescence. In remedial applications, the theory may be used as an organizing framework for adapting existing counseling methods and for developing novel intervention techniques. In this section, we consider ways in which SCCT may be used to address selected developmental and remedial concerns.

PROMOTING ASPIRATIONS AND INTERESTS IN YOUNG PERSONS

Several researchers have used SCCT as a basis for conceptualizing (Prideaux, Patton, & Creed, 2002) or evaluating (McWhirter, Rasheed, & Crothers, 2000) career education programs. Given the typical narrowing of career options over time (Gottfredson, 2005), these school-based applications of SCCT may have particular import in preserving as wide a range of occupational alternatives as possible for later consideration. From the perspective of the theory, several key processes occur during childhood and adolescence—within academic, family, peer, and other settings—that set the stage for later choice making and adjustment. These processes include acquisition of self-efficacy and outcome expectations related to diverse activities, development of career-relevant interests, and formation of career aspirations (i.e., provisional occupational goals or daydreams). They represent prominent developmental tasks of the elementary and middle school years and are continually revisited and refined in high school and beyond (Lent, Hackett, & Brown, 1999).

Young children typically have a very limited grasp of their capabilities, not to mention career activities and paths. Given their limited experience and exposure to career role models, their career-related interests and aspirations are likely to be somewhat stereotypical, narrow, and fluid. Over the course of childhood and adolescence, people typically receive increasing experience with varied performance tasks, as well as direct and vicarious exposure to a widening range of career possibilities. These experiences lead to differentiated beliefs regarding one's capabilities in diverse activity domains and an expanded sense of the working conditions and reinforcers afforded by different career options. Emergent self-efficacy and outcome expectations, in turn, nurture career-relevant interests and goals that tend to become more defined and crystallized over time, yet are still relatively modifiable based on additional learning about the self (e.g., personal capabilities, values) and careers (e.g., skill requirements, available reinforcers). In this way, career aspirations tend to become increasingly responsive to personal interests, capabilities, values, and environmental conditions (e.g., family and cultural expectations, economic realities).

This analysis suggests that self-efficacy and outcome expectations—and the experiences on which they are based—are key to the cultivation of students' academic and career interests and to the range and types of occupational options they are willing to consider. At the same time, students' career aspirations can become constricted either because they acquire inaccurate self-efficacy or outcome expectations or because their environments provide limited or biased exposure to particular efficacy-building experiences (e.g., few opportunities to succeed at scientific pursuits, an absence of gender-similar role models in math). Developmental interventions designed to promote favorable self-efficacy and outcome expectations are likely to be most useful during childhood and adolescence, before interests and aspirations become relatively stable and certain options become prematurely foreclosed.

The four sources of efficacy information can be used as an organizing structure for psychoeducational interventions. Personal performance accomplishments are a particularly valuable intervention target, given their potent effects on self-efficacy. Incrementally graded success experiences can foster a sense of efficacy at particular tasks, yet it is also important to attend to how students interpret the quality of their performances. For example, objective successes may not impact self-efficacy if students attribute their good grades to luck, effort, or task ease. This is a common occurrence in the case of girls' achievements in math, science, and other nontraditional activities (Hackett, 1995). Efforts to modify students' self-efficacy may, therefore, profit from inclusion of cognitive restructuring procedures that encourage students to entertain self-enhancing performance attributions (e.g., crediting one's success to developing personal capabilities, viewing ability as an acquirable attribute rather than a fixed, inborn entity).

Useful intervention elements can also be fashioned from the other three sources of efficacy information. For example, modeling can be used to assist students in exploring academic and career domains that they may not have previously encountered or been encouraged to consider. Students are most likely to identify with role models they perceive as similar to themselves in terms of gender, ethnicity, and other demographic features. Social support and persuasion can be used to encourage students to attempt new tasks, to persist despite initial setbacks, and to interpret their performances favorably, for example, by focusing on skill growth versus ultimate task success. Physiological and affective states may also require attention where, for example, task-related anxiety appears to be diminishing self-efficacy and disrupting performance. Relaxation exercises and other cognitive-behavioral strategies can be used to reduce debilitative anxiety.

Content-specific efficacy beliefs (e.g., in math and other school subjects) need not be the only focus of efficacy-building efforts. It also seems desirable to encourage self-efficacy and skills at larger "career process" domains, such as communication, teamwork, conflict management, leadership, and multicultural sensitivity. Such general skill domains have been seen as integral to students' transition from school to work (Lent et al., 1999). In addition to a focus on self-efficacy enhancement, SCCT would encourage a variety of other developmental intervention targets. In particular, exposure to accurate career information (see Gore, Leuwerke, & Kelly, Chapter 18, this volume) is key to fostering acquisition of realistic outcome expectations (i.e., beliefs about the working conditions and reinforcers available in diverse occupations).

SCCT would also encourage age-appropriate interventions designed to help students explore their emerging interests and the occupational options with which they may be compatible. Such interventions would best be approached with the explicit understanding (communicated to parents, teachers, and students) that interests, goals, values, and skills are fluid attributes that can change and grow with additional experience. Assessment may thus best be viewed as a snapshot at a single point in time, rather than a reflection of immutable qualities. Finally, SCCT would encourage a focus on fostering skills in decision making and goal setting (e.g., breaking larger distal goals into proximal subgoals, locating supports for personal goals). Such self-regulation skills can be taught by using examples from domains, such as studying or friendships, that are meaningful to young people and that can be generalized to career development.

FACILITATING CAREER CHOICE MAKING AND IMPLEMENTATION

In an ideal scenario, people arrive at late adolescence or early adulthood with (a) a good appreciation of their interests, values, and talents; (b) an understanding of how these self-attributes correspond with potential vocational options; (c) clear goals, or choices, that link their self-attributes to suitable occupational paths (i.e., ones that can engage their interests, satisfy their values, and value their talents); (d) adequate skills at making decisions, setting goals, and managing goal pursuit; (e) an environment that provides support for their goals (e.g., social encouragement, mentors, financial resources) and minimal goal-related barriers; and (f) a set of personality traits (e.g., low levels of negative affectivity, high levels of conscientiousness) that can generally aid the process of making and implementing important life decisions by, for example, minimizing chronic indecisiveness and maximizing follow-through with goals and plans.

Those who possess ample amounts of these personal and environmental resources are unlikely to seek the services of a career counselor. Unfortunately, however, problems may occur in any or all of these areas—and various other challenges, such as physical disabilities or difficulties in life domains apart from work/career, may arise as well—that can hamper an individual's efforts at occupational choice making and implementation. Well-prepared career counselors are able to assist with a wide array of these choice-limiting problems. A full-scale discussion of career choice problems and solutions is beyond the scope of this chapter, but here we highlight a few strategies, derived from SCCT, that can aid in navigating certain impasses to choice making and implementation.

Expanding choice options. Like most other approaches to career choice counseling, SCCT aims to help clients select from an array of occupations that correspond reasonably well with important aspects of their work personalities (e.g., interests, values, skills). Some clients are blocked in this effort because their work personalities are not sufficiently differentiated (e.g., measured interests produce a low, flat profile) or because they feel stifled by a constricted range of career options. In such instances, my colleagues and I have found it helpful to explore the social cognitive processes that may underlie choice problems, adapting assessment strategies that are commonly used in career counseling (e.g., Brown & Lent, 1996). An important implication of SCCT's interest model is that people often reject potentially viable options because of inaccurate self-efficacy and outcome expectations (e.g., a person may believe, erroneously, that he or she does not have the skills to perform effectively in a given occupation or that the occupation does not offer the working conditions that he or she values). By revisiting previously discarded options and considering the reasons they have been discarded, career clients can often clarify their interests, skills, and values and also expand the range of potentially satisfying options from which they may choose.

We have used two strategies to explore discarded options. In the first strategy, standardized measures of vocational interests, values/needs, and aptitudes are administered, and the results are examined for discrepancies between the choice options generated by the various measures. We especially look for aptitude–interest and value–interest discrepancies. Instances in which clients appear to have the aptitude to succeed at particular occupations but show relatively low interest may suggest that personal capabilities are being discounted (i.e., that interests may not have developed because one's self-efficacy is unrealistically low). Similarly, instances in which a client's values appear compatible with particular options but the client shows little interest may suggest inaccurate outcome expectations (i.e., he or she may possess limited or biased information about the occupations, resulting in faulty assumptions about their potential to meet his or her needs). Such discrepancies are targeted for further discussion and, possibly, counseling aimed at boosting self-efficacy or instilling accurate outcome expectations.

Our second strategy for exploring foreclosed occupational options uses a modified vocational card sort procedure. We first ask clients to sort a list of occupations into three categories: (1) might choose, (2) would not choose, and (3) in question. We then focus on those occupations that are sorted into the "would not choose" and "in question" categories. The client is encouraged to sort these occupations into more specific categories reflecting self-efficacy beliefs ("might choose if I thought I had the skills"), outcome expectations ("might choose if I thought it could offer things I value"), definite lack of interest ("wouldn't choose under any circumstances"), or other. Occupations sorted into the self-efficacy and outcome expectation subcategories are then explored for accuracy of skill and outcome perceptions. As with the first strategy, further assessment, efficacy building, or information gathering may then be employed to challenge faulty assumptions about self or career and to maximize the range of possible choice options. (See Brown & Lent, 1996, for case examples of the use of each strategy with adult clients.)

Coping with barriers and building supports. A key assumption of SCCT's choice model is that people are more likely to implement career choices (i.e., to translate their goals into actions) if they perceive that their preferred options will be accompanied by minimal barriers and ample supports. Conversely, clients who expect, for example, that their significant others will discourage their favored path, or that they will not be able to access the financial support they need to pursue their choice, may be less willing to follow through with their goals. These assumptions have led us to build consideration of potential supports and barriers directly into the choice counseling process. In particular, we have developed a set of steps to help clients (a) anticipate possible barriers to implementing their choices, (b) analyze the likelihood of encountering these barriers, (c) prepare barrier-coping strategies (i.e., methods for preventing or managing likely barriers), and (d) build supports for their goals within their family, peer, and other social networks.

We have used a modified "decisional balance sheet" procedure to help clients identify potential choice barriers. Specifically, we ask clients to generate both positive and negative consequences in relation to each career option they are seriously considering. We then have them focus on the negative consequences that might prevent them from pursuing each option. Next, the client is asked to estimate the chances that each barrier will actually be encountered, and strategies are developed and rehearsed for preventing or managing the most likely barriers. Brown and Lent (1996) illustrated the use of these barrier-coping methods with a client who had been reluctant to pursue her preferred option because she feared it would jeopardize her romantic relationship. After identifying and analyzing this barrier, the client was helped to neutralize it by negotiating a dual-career strategy with her partner, enabling her to preserve her favored career option.

In addition to anticipating and preparing to deal with barriers, it can be very useful to assist clients in building support systems to sustain their choice efforts (Lent et al., 2000). In fact, support building has been identified as a critical ingredient in successful career choice counseling (see Whiston & James, Chapter 20, this volume). Once clients have identified preferred career goals, they can be encouraged to consider (a) what steps they need to take to implement their goals, (b) what environmental (e.g., social, financial) resources could help them achieve these steps, and (c) what resources they could use to offset any likely choice barriers. Counselors can also help clients consider where and how to access needed supports. In many cases, clients' existing support systems can provide resources useful to their goal pursuit (e.g., access to relevant job contacts). In other cases, resources may be obtained by cultivating new or alternative support systems (e.g., developing friendships with peers who will support, rather than ridicule, one's academic or career aspirations).

Clients' families are often central to their career choice-making and implementation efforts, particularly in collectivist cultures. It is, therefore, useful to build into counseling a consideration of how the client's preferred options mesh with the wishes of his or her family (or significant others). Clients sometimes need assistance in negotiating conflicts between their own goals and others' goals for them. Barrier-coping and support-building strategies in such instances can, for example, include role-play or two-chair dialogues with significant others or, depending on the cultural context and the client's preferences, inviting significant others to participate in a portion of choice counseling.

Goal setting and self-regulation. Some clients need assistance with the processes of setting goals and sustaining goal pursuits, especially if they tend to demonstrate low levels of conscientiousness. These processes involve career self-regulation skills that can help clients achieve their plans, especially in the future, after counseling has been completed. Once a choice goal has been selected, many factors can affect the likelihood that clients will act on it. We have already considered the possible effects of environmental supports and barriers. Another important factor affecting choice implementation is the manner in which people frame their goals. For example, larger, ultimate goals are more likely to be enacted if they are clear, specific, divided into manageable subgoals (e.g., taking preparatory courses, applying to educational programs), set close in time to intended actions, stated publicly, and held with strong commitment (Bandura, 1986). By contrast, vague, amorphous, distal, private, and weakly held goals provide less reliable guides for action. Clients can, therefore, be encouraged to frame their goals in facilitative (e.g., clear, specific, proximal) terms and to consider specific steps and resources needed to implement their goals. Because not all possible barriers to choice implementation can be anticipated and averted, clients can be encouraged to remain flexible and adaptable in their decisional stance, for example, by preparing backup plans.

FACILITATING WORK PERFORMANCE

SCCT offers several implications for efforts to promote academic and career success and optimize performance. The basic hypotheses of SCCT's performance model suggest that self-efficacy beliefs can facilitate attainment in a given academic or career domain as long as an individual possesses at least minimally adequate levels of the skills required in that domain. This does not mean that increased confidence alone will guarantee success, but it does imply, as suggested earlier, that self-efficacy can help people make the most of the skills they have and also facilitate further development of one's skills. Thus, methods designed to boost self-efficacy beliefs may be valuable both in developmentally oriented skill-building programs (discussed earlier in relation to promoting aspirations) and in remedial efforts with persons experiencing performance difficulties.

A basic strategy for improving performance begins with examining possible discrepancies between self-efficacy estimates and data on objectively assessed skills or past performance. Intervention procedures may then be designed that are responsive to the type of discrepancy that is identified. For example, where the client possesses adequate skills but weak self-efficacy beliefs in a given performance domain, the theory would suggest the value of activities designed to help him or her (a) obtain personal mastery experiences with progressively more challenging tasks in that domain, (b) review past success experiences, and (c) interpret past and present successes in ways that promote, rather than discount, perceived competence. Similar to earlier suggestions for promoting self-efficacy beliefs, clients can be encouraged to attribute success experiences at skill development to internal, stable factors, particularly personal ability, rather than to internal, unstable (e.g., effort) or external (luck, task simplicity) factors. As clients succeed at performance tasks or as they review past experiences, they can also be asked for their perceived reasons for task success. Nonadaptive attributions can be challenged, for example, by having clients generate and evaluate alternative interpretations for their performance successes (Brown & Lent, 1996).

This focus on mastery experiences can be augmented by counseling activities that draw on other sources of self-efficacy. For instance, providing exposure to relevant models, verbal support, or assistance with anxiety coping can elevate self-efficacy and, in turn, promote skill development and performance. In addition, SCCT points to outcome expectations and performance goals as operating, along with self-efficacy, as key motivators of performance. Thus, performance-focused counseling might also entail efforts to instill beneficial outcome expectations (e.g., accurate knowledge of work conditions and reinforcers) and realistic, yet challenging performance goals (e.g., ones that are achievable yet stretch and further refine one's skills).

More intensive remedial skill-building efforts, organized around the sources of efficacy information, may be indicated where clients exhibit both weak self-efficacy and deficient skills. There will also be situations where the extent of the skill deficit is very large, the client is unwilling to engage in (or may be unlikely to profit from) remedial activities, or the environment (e.g., college, work organization) is unwilling to support remediation or has decided to terminate the student or employee. In P-E fit terms, such scenarios reflect a serious mismatch between the individual's skills and the skill requirements of the setting. In such cases, educational or career choice (or change) counseling can be offered, with the goal of identifying suitable, alternative academic or occupational options having ability requirements that better correspond with the client's current skills. It should be emphasized that SCCT does not imply that self-efficacy will compensate for a lack of requisite skills or that efforts to boost self-efficacy are always indicated; in fact, such efforts seem unlikely to affect performance (and any gains in self-efficacy may not be sustained) if they ignore seriously deficient skills.

PROMOTING WORK SATISFACTION

The central variables of SCCT's satisfaction model could be used as a structure for assessment as well as for designing interventions to promote satisfaction. Because a variety of person, behavior, and context factors can contribute to work satisfaction, it is important to identify the key factor or set of factors that may be relevant for a particular client. Counseling for work satisfaction would then depend on how the source(s) of satisfaction (or dissatisfaction) are conceptualized. SCCT-based strategies could include, for example, helping clients access desired work conditions, activities, or reinforcers (e.g., via job redesign or skill updating); set and make progress toward valued goals (e.g., by framing clear, proximal, intrinsic, and challenging yet attainable goals); marshal needed supports and resources for goal pursuit and other aspects of career development; enhance task and goal-related self-efficacy; refine skills (e.g., interpersonal, self-regulation, technical) required for work success and the rewards it can bring; cope with negative aspects of one's job (e.g., managing stress); engage in self-advocacy (e.g., in dealing with harsh or uncivil work conditions); or manage the cognitive and behavioral aspects of affective traits that may predispose one toward work dissatisfaction.

Like P-E fit theories, SCCT acknowledges that work dissatisfaction can result from incongruence between personal and environmental attributes and that this displeasure can, therefore, be reduced by improving the fit between P and E. For example, value-reinforcer discorrespondence may be addressed via worker–supervisor negotiation, job restructuring, or skill development. One important difference from traditional P-E fit theories, however, is that SCCT assumes that poor fit can occur along any number of dimensions (e.g., interest, personality, value, skill) that may be salient to the individual. Another difference is the assumption that the subjective perception of P-E fit is often more influential than objectively assessed fit in determining one's satisfaction with the work environment. These differences underline the value of multifaceted fit assessment and counseling strategies that may extend beyond what P-E theories would prescribe. (Brown & Lent, 1996, described examples of SCCT-based counseling that had been initiated by clients experiencing work dissatisfaction due to poor perceived fit between their values or skills and the reinforcers or requirements of their work settings.)

Although focusing on potentially modifiable aspects of work satisfaction, SCCT also acknowledges person and context factors that may limit gains in satisfaction (e.g., nonsupportive organizational leadership or policies). Where work satisfaction cannot be promoted in other ways, job or career change counseling may be considered, assuming that individuals feel free to make such changes and that they have the necessary resources to do so. Where work change options are constrained (as they are for many unhappy workers during the current economic recession), coping and compensatory strategies might be considered, such as pursuing goal-directed activity in other life domains (e.g., leisure, family, community) that offer alternative outlets for satisfaction.

CONCLUSIONS AND PRACTICE IMPLICATIONS

SCCT is an evolving framework that highlights cognitive-person variables, such as self-efficacy, and considers how they function, along with other person and environment factors (e.g., gender, culture, barriers, supports) in shaping people's occupational paths. Although SCCT assumes that people exercise varying degrees of agency in their own career development, it also recognizes conditions that can either limit or strengthen people's ability to influence their school and work lives. The theory consists of models of academic and career interest, choice, performance, and satisfaction. A model of career self-management, designed to complement the current four SCCT models by focusing on the use of adaptive career behaviors, is currently under development.

The following are some practical messages to take away from this chapter:

- Interests are generally a reliable predictor of educational and career choices, but they are not the only such predictor. Especially where people need to compromise their interests in making choices (e.g., due to family or financial considerations), self-efficacy and outcome expectations can augment or surpass interests in directing choices. This underlines the importance of promoting self-efficacy beliefs and outcome expectations that are positive yet realistic.
- The four primary sources of efficacy information can be used to structure interventions designed to promote the development of interests and skills. Efficacy-based interventions can be especially helpful in cases of flat interest profiles or where interests have been constrained by limited or biased exposure to efficacy-building experiences.
- Incrementally graded success experiences, coupled with efforts to ensure favorable interpretation of those experiences, can be especially useful in bolstering self-efficacy and the outcomes to which it can lead.
- Outcome expectations can be fostered by ensuring exposure to accurate sources of educational and occupational information that help clients learn about choice options that can satisfy their values.
- Choice-content and performance goals are important motivators, respectively, of the options that people choose and the levels of performance and persistence they attain in school and work settings. Progress toward personal goals also promotes feelings of work satisfaction. It is important, therefore, that people set and pursue goals in ways that enable them to achieve their own objectives (e.g., by framing clear, specific, proximal subgoals).
- Career development occurs in a social learning context and is facilitated by the presence of supportive environmental conditions (e.g., good-quality education) and the relative absence of barriers (e.g., lack of financial resources for training). Career development can be promoted by exposing children and adolescents, as much as possible, to favorable conditions (e.g., access to diverse coping models) that might offset negative ones (e.g., gender discrimination).

- Support-building and barrier-coping methods can be especially useful adjuncts to educational and career choice counseling. By anticipating and preparing for likely obstacles to their preferred choices and by marshaling needed supports, clients might be enabled to persist toward their goals despite setbacks.
- Adjustment to work, as defined by satisfaction and effective performance, can be facilitated by interventions that attend to self-efficacy, outcome expectations, goals, and behaviors, along with supportive work conditions.

REFERENCES

Bandura, A. (1986). *Social foundations of thought and action: A social cognitive theory.* Englewood Cliffs, NJ: Prentice-Hall.

Bandura, A. (1997). *Self-efficacy: The exercise of control.* New York, NY: Freeman.

Betz, N. E. (2008). Advances in vocational theories. In S. D. Brown & R. W. Lent (Eds.), *Handbook of counseling psychology* (4th ed., pp. 357–374). Hoboken, NJ: Wiley.

Betz, N. E., & Hackett, G. (1981). The relationship of career-related self-efficacy expectations to perceived career options in college women and men. *Journal of Counseling Psychology, 28,* 399–410.

Brown, S. D., & Lent, R. W. (1996). A social cognitive framework for career choice counseling. *Career Development Quarterly, 44,* 354–366.

Brown, S. D., Lent, R. W., Telander, K., & Tramayne, S. (2011). Social cognitive career theory, conscientiousness, and work performance: A meta-analytic path analysis. *Journal of Vocational Behavior, 79,* 81–90.

Brown, S. D., Tramayne, S., Hoxha, D., Telander, K., Fan, X., & Lent, R. W. (2008). Social cognitive predictors of college students' academic performance and persistence: A meta-analytic path analysis. *Journal of Vocational Behavior, 72,* 298–308.

Fabian, E. S. (2000). Social cognitive theory of careers and individuals with serious mental health disorders: Implications for psychiatric rehabilitation programs. *Psychiatric Rehabilitation Journal, 23,* 262–269.

Gainor, K. A. (2006). Twenty-five years of self-efficacy in career assessment and practice. *Journal of Career Assessment, 14,* 161–178.

Gottfredson, L. S. (2005). Applying Gottfredson's theory of circumscription and compromise in career guidance and counseling. In S. D. Brown, & R. W. Lent (Eds.), *Career development and counseling: Putting theory and research to work* (pp. 71–100). Hoboken, NJ: Wiley.

Hackett, G. (1995). Self-efficacy in career choice and development. In A. Bandura (Ed.), *Self-efficacy in changing societies.* Cambridge, UK: Cambridge University Press.

Hackett, G., & Betz, N. E. (1981). A self-efficacy approach to the career development of women. *Journal of Vocational Behavior, 18,* 326–336.

Hackett, G., & Byars, A. M. (1996). Social cognitive theory and the career development of African American women. *Career Development Quarterly, 44,* 322–340.

Hackett, G., & Lent, R. W. (1992). Theoretical advances and current inquiry in career psychology. In S. D. Brown & R. W. Lent (Eds.), *Handbook of counseling psychology* (2nd ed., pp. 419–451). New York, NY: Wiley.

Lent, R. W., & Brown, S. D. (2006). Integrating person and situation perspectives on work satisfaction: A social-cognitive view. *Journal of Vocational Behavior, 69,* 236–247.

Lent, R. W., & Brown, S. D. (2008). Social cognitive career theory and subjective well-being in the context of work. *Journal of Career Assessment, 16,* 6–21.

Lent, R. W., & Brown, S. D. (2012). *A social cognitive model of career self-management.* Unpublished manuscript.

Lent, R. W., Brown, S. D., & Hackett, G. (1994). Toward a unifying social cognitive theory of career and academic interest, choice, and performance [Monograph]. *Journal of Vocational Behavior, 45,* 79–122.

Lent, R. W., Brown, S. D., & Hackett, G. (2000). Contextual supports and barriers to career choice: A social cognitive analysis. *Journal of Counseling Psychology, 47,* 36–49.

Lent, R. W., Brown, S. D., Sheu, H., Schmidt, J., Brenner, B. R., Gloster, C. S., . . . Treistman, D. (2005). Social cognitive predictors of academic interests and goals in engineering: Utility for women and students at historically Black universities. *Journal of Counseling Psychology, 52,* 84–92.

Lent, R. W., & Hackett, G. (1994). Sociocognitive mechanisms of personal agency in career development: Pantheoretical prospects. In M. L. Savickas & R. W. Lent (Eds.), *Convergence in career development theories: Implications for science and practice* (pp. 77–102). Palo Alto, CA: Consulting Psychologists Press.

Lent, R. W., Hackett, G., & Brown, S. D. (1999). A social cognitive view of school-to-work transition. *Career Development Quarterly, 44,* 297–311.

Lent, R. W., & Sheu, H. (2010). Applying social cognitive career theory across cultures: Empirical status. In J. G. Ponterotto, J. M. Casas, L. A. Suzuki, & C. M. Alexander (Eds.), *Handbook of multicultural counseling* (3rd ed., pp. 691–701). Thousand Oaks, CA: Sage.

Lindley, L. D. (2006). The paradox of self-efficacy: Research with diverse populations. *Journal of Career Assessment, 14,* 143–160.

McWhirter, E. H., Rasheed, S., & Crothers, M. (2000). The effects of high school career education on social-cognitive variables. *Journal of Counseling Psychology, 47,* 330–341.

Morrow, S. L., Gore, P. A., & Campbell, B. W. (1996). The application of a sociocognitive framework to the career development of lesbian women and gay men. *Journal of Vocational Behavior, 48,* 136–148.

Multon, K. D., Brown, S. D., & Lent, R. W. (1991). Relation of self-efficacy beliefs to academic outcomes: A meta-analytic investigation. *Journal of Counseling Psychology, 38,* 30–38.

Prideaux, L., Patton, W., & Creed, P. (2002). Development of a theoretically derived school career program: An Australian endeavor. *International Journal for Educational and Vocational Guidance, 2*, 115–130.

Rottinghaus, P. J., Larson, L. M., & Borgen, F. H. (2003). The relation of self-efficacy and interests: A meta-analysis of 60 samples. *Journal of Vocational Behavior, 62*, 221–236.

Sadri, G., & Robertson, I. T. (1993). Self-efficacy and work-related behavior: A review and meta-analysis. *Applied Psychology: An International Review, 42*, 139–152.

Schaub, M., & Tokar, D. M. (2005). The role of personality and learning experiences in social cognitive career theory. *Journal of Vocational Behavior, 66*, 304–325.

Sheu, H., & Lent, R. W. (2009). A social cognitive perspective on well-being in educational and work settings: Cross-cultural considerations. *International Journal for Educational and Vocational Guidance, 9*, 45–60.

Sheu, H., Lent, R. W., Brown, S. D., Miller, M. J., Hennessy, K. D., & Duffy, R. D. (2010). Testing the choice model of social cognitive career theory across Holland themes: A meta-analytic path analysis. *Journal of Vocational Behavior, 76*, 252–264.

Stajkovic, A. D., & Luthans, F. (1998). Self-efficacy and work-related performance: A meta-analysis. *Psychological Bulletin, 124*, 240–261.

Swanson, J. L., & Gore, P. A. (2000). Advances in vocational psychology theory and research. In S. D. Brown & R. W. Lent (Eds.), *Handbook of counseling psychology* (3rd ed., pp. 233–269). New York, NY: Wiley.

Szymanski, E. M., Enright, M. S., Hershenson, D. B., & Ettinger, J. M. (2003). Career development theories, constructs, and research: Implications for people with disabilities. In E. M. Szymanski & R. M. Parker (Eds.), *Work and disability: Issues and strategies in career development and job placement* (2nd ed., pp. 91–153). Austin, TX: Pro-Ed.

Vondracek, F. W., Lerner, R. M., & Schulenberg, J. E. (1986). *Career development: A life-span developmental approach.* Hillsdale, NJ: Erlbaum.

Williams, C. M., & Subich, L. M. (2006). The gendered nature of career related learning experiences: A social cognitive career theory perspective. *Journal of Vocational Behavior, 69*, 262–275.

CHAPTER 6

Career Construction Theory and Practice

MARK L. SAVICKAS

T HE THEORY OF CAREER construction explains the interpretive and interpersonal processes through which individuals construct themselves, impose direction on their vocational behavior, and make meaning of their careers. Intended for use in a multicultural society and global economy, the conceptual framework provides a contemporary explanation of careers and informs a model for career counseling. To accomplish its goals, career construction theory addresses how individuals build careers through personal constructivism and social constructionism. It asserts that individuals construct representations of reality, yet they do not construct reality itself. Furthermore, the theory views careers from a contextualist perspective, one that conceptualizes development as driven by adaptation to an environment rather than by maturation of inner structures. Viewing careers from constructionist and contextual perspectives concentrates attention on self-construction. With self-construction central to the theory, I first consider how people make themselves into who they are and then describe contemporary perspectives on career. This discussion leads to three central perspectives on self that form the foundations of career construction theory: self as actor, self as agent, and self as author. I then elaborate on these three perspectives and explain how they structure a scheme for career intervention and inform a model for career construction counseling. A case study demonstrating the counseling model concludes the chapter.

SELF-MAKING

Making a self and constructing a career involve lifelong projects that evolve in complex phases and multilayered processes (McAdams & Olson, 2010). Individuals compose a self and career by reflecting on experience, using the uniquely human capacity to be conscious of consciousness. This self-conscious reflection uses language to both construct and constitute social realities (Neuman & Nave, 2009). In a sense, we live inside language. Words provide a resource for living that enables thinking and meaning making. Words do not come to adhere to an essential, preexisting self. Rather, language provides the words for the reflexive projects of making a self, shaping an identity, and constructing a career. That is, language enables the subjectivity needed to reflect on our actions and think about who we want to become and what work we want to do. We also use language to hold in place the self-awareness emerging from reflexivity. In a sense, language contains the self, and stories carry the career.

Although we talk our own selves into existence, we need more than language for self-construction. We need experiences on which to reflect, particularly interpersonal experiences, because a self is built from the outside in, not from the inside out. Using language as a tool, we coordinate our actions and social relations. So, a self is not actually self-constructed; it is coconstructed through interpersonal processes. We need each other to make sense of ourselves and the world in which we live. In the process of sense making, the idea of self as a separate person arises. Through self-conscious awareness, the self recognizes itself. This self-consciously created idea of a separate self becomes filled with stories about experience. In a sense, self-conscious reflection through language is the process that makes a self, and the resulting stories are the content that constitutes the self in the form of favored attributes and significant events. In sum, self denotes an emergent awareness that is culturally shaped, socially constituted, and linguistically narrated.

PERSPECTIVES ON SELF-MAKING

The processes of self-making and career construction differ during childhood, adolescence, and adulthood. Individuals begin self-construction as *actors*, later become *agents* that direct the action, and then develop into *authors* who explain the action (McAdams & Olson, 2010). Concentrating on each of these three layers of self-construction has led to theories that privilege distinct perspectives on vocational behavior and career development. To move toward the goal of crafting a comprehensive theory that includes all three views, I use social constructionism as a metatheory. Social constructionism asserts that reality does not exist independent of us. Rather, we construct reality through social processes and interpersonal relationships. From the epistemological position of social constructionism, I then attend to three layers of the self by adapting the tripartite model of personality theories devised by McAdams (1995). Each layer of self as object, subject, or project offers a different and useful way to think about vocational behavior and career construction.

Self as object. The self as actor dominates the objective view of person–environment fit that matches individuals to occupations. This is the first and foundational view of a vocational self that originated early in the 20th century and reached its pinnacle in Holland's (1997) RIASEC model of vocational choices and work environments (see Nauta, Chapter 3, this volume). It serves industrial societies that need to match workers to occupations.

Self as subject. After World War II, a second perspective emerged to supplement the objective view on self. A subjective view on self as agent emerged from humanistic beliefs about self-discovery and self-actualization. Donald Super (1951; see Hartung, Chapter 4, this volume) applied this subjective view of striving toward self-determined goals in his developmental theory of career stages and tasks. Maslow (1954) and Super (1957) articulated a progressive, hierarchical view of self that fit the bureaucratic structure of corporate societies in which individuals set goals, accomplished tasks, and climbed the ladder of success.

Self as project. Concurrent with the digital revolution, a new perspective on self as a project has evolved (Savickas, 2011b). With the move to an information society and a global economy, the corporate structure that sustained career ladders has dissipated. People can no longer count on building a 30-year career in one organization and then retiring with a pension and health care. Although full-time employment remains the dominant form of work, temporary assignments and part-time positions are replacing permanent, full-time jobs. Long-term careers exist for only a minority of workers. For many individuals, work takes the shape of a project with a beginning assignment and an ending product. A quarter of workers have been with their current employer for less than a year. Half of workers have been with their current employer for less than 5 years (Mullins, 2009). Precarious work makes for insecure workers (Kalleberg, 2009). Rather than developing a stable life based on secure employment, today insecure workers must be flexible in maintaining employability through lifelong learning and adapting to occupational transitions. Rather than make plans, individuals must prepare themselves for possibilities.

CAREER CONSTRUCTING

Society's reorganization of work from permanent jobs into temporary assignments prompts a reconceptualization of careers. During the 20th century, career meant a path through work life. Thus, objective career denotes the sequence of positions that an individual occupies from school through retirement. Everyone has an objective career, one that other people may observe across time. Super (1957) portrayed a typical career as a pattern of predictable stages. This career narrative, with its linear trajectory of vocational development tasks during a 30-year tenure in one company, captured the story of work life for many middle-class individuals during the last half of the 20th century. However, today the new social contract between organizations and workers has prompted management and human resource scholars to reconceptualize the meaning of *career*. Super's metanarrative of career stages and tasks dissolves with the loss of the predictable scripts and identifiable paths on which it was based. The story narrated by Super (1957) portrayed career as a value of hierarchical organizations. The company owned the employee's career. Today, individuals own their careers—it is now "me incorporated." Accordingly, management scholars have conceptualized career from a predictable and linear progression through working lives to something that is *boundaryless* (Arthur, 1994) and *protean* (Hall, 1996).

The 21st-century version of boundaryless, protean careers transforms the story from one about maturation in a stable medium to one about adaptation to a changing landscape. This transformation requires a fundamental change in perspective from which vocational psychologists and career counselors may envision careers in a global economy. The 20th-century metaphor of career as a recognizable path through life has now changed to the 21st-century metaphor of career as a carrier of meaning. Today, the metaphor is career as a cart or car that carries the person into uncharted territory. Accordingly, career construction theory views career as a story that individuals tell about their working life, not progress down a path or up a ladder. Without the support of an "organizational career," individuals must construct an individual career that fits their own lives (Beck, 1994). Whereas each person experiences an objective career or path, although not linear and predictable, individuals must construct a subjective career with which to impose meaning and direction on their vocational behavior. Constructing a subjective career resembles the task of making a self. A subjective career emerges from thought or mental activity that constructs a story about one's working life. It is this subjective career story that steers and carries individuals across job changes and occupational transitions. Thus, career construct theory concentrates on composing and using a career narrative about the self as actor, agent, and author.

FOUNDATIONS OF CAREER CONSTRUCTION:
ACTOR, AGENT, AUTHOR

Career construction theory asserts that individuals, through their actions in the family, compose a social role as an actor, then adapt this role for use in the theaters of the school and community, and eventually author an autobiographical story that explains the continuity and coherence in occupational experiences. This progression applies McAdams and Olson's (2010) observation that psychological individuality is rooted in three developmental layers of acting, agency, and authoring. Accordingly, career construction theory attends to an individual's *behaviors* as an actor, *strivings* as an agent, and *explanations* as an author. The objective perspective on the actor delineates a story about the sequence of positions occupied from school through retirement. The subjective perspective on the agent focuses attention on the strivings and adaptations pursued by the occupational plot. The projective perspective on the author examines the autobiographical reflexivity (i.e., individuals' reflections on their own life stories) that patterns work experiences into a meaningful career story. Following this developmental progression, career construction theory begins with actors and their self-construction. It then discusses the two metacompetencies that individuals need for career construction in the 21st century, namely, adaptability and identity (Hall & Mirvis, 1995).

SELF AS ACTOR: COCONSTRUCTING REPUTATION AND PERSON TYPES

Beginning in infancy when they enter the family drama, individuals perform as social actors. Toddlers quickly come to understand the world of the family and also absorb the cultural discourses that surround it. They use their biological endowments and the identity categories presented to them (e.g., gender, race, class, and birth order) to carefully make their places in the family drama. In conjunction with their families and social interactions, individuals craft characters or reputations and then elaborate these distinctive characteristics in the neighborhood and school. The base of the character arc coconstructed in the family of origin will, in due course, help to shape the individual's career theme. The notion of character arc denotes those aspects of a life theme that portray where an individual started, is now, and wants to end up on some essential internal issue.

Introjecting guides and incorporating models. Actors form a character by internalizing the family drama and social world that they experience. An actor constructs a self in an environment of other people, modeling self upon objects in the world, beginning with one's parents. Career construction theory concentrates on two main methods of internalizing models for the self, namely, introjection of guides and incorporation of models. Parents or other familial guides are internalized as introjects or whole objects. Thus, a guide exists in one's inner life as a full representation of the parent, as well as the child's relationship with the guide. The child may easily engage in dialogues with the guides she or he has internalized. All children then must find ways to meet the needs, seek the goals, and resolve the conflicts that they have introjected into their own characters. To make a self that may pursue their goals and solve their problems in growing up, children begin to elaborate the introjected self-structure to accommodate their unique place in the family and then the community.

To resolve problems, troubles, and conflicts that they encounter within their families and with their guides, children look to role models who have solved the same problems in growing up that actors themselves now face. As children, we select role models who portray tentative solutions to our main problems and dominant preoccupations. Role models provide imaginative resources that we first use as children and later as adolescents and adults to inform and shape our identities. Acting as architects of the self, children select role models as their blueprints for self-design. Heroes model a way forward in which children may make lives for themselves by dealing constructively with their problems, preoccupations, and predicaments. We take meaning from our models to make sense of our own lives. We then build a self by adopting and rehearsing the models' characteristics until those characteristics become our own.

In contrast to the influence of introjected guides, role models are incorporated identifications. Incorporation of models is the second core process of self-construction. Although we take in influential guides, they are never accepted as our own choices because we were born to or adopted by those guides. In comparison, we consciously select role models, and in this sense, they represent the first choice we make in constructing our careers. Thus, the choice of role models is indeed a decision about self-construction and the character one prefers to enact in life's drama. Through the incorporation processes of identification and imitation, children shape the self to resemble the model, yet the role model remains external, unlike a guide who becomes an inner other. In a sense, children *take in* guides yet *take on* some characteristics of models with whom they identify. Identification, or the process of producing sameness with some model, occurs as the self incorporates, as a rather permanent part of itself, characteristics of the model.

Reputation. Role-playing, or imitating the model in fantasy and play, mobilizes interests and activities that through repetition and rehearsal develop skills, abilities, and habits. Rehearsing these traits in activities such as household chores, games, hobbies, reading, and studying develops the confidence to address problems in growing up. As these behaviors become increasingly consistent across activities and stable over time, other people come to recognize them as the child's "personality." Thus children develop reputations in their families, neighborhoods, and schools. The term *personality* connotes the view of psychological essentialism that traits compose an identity-determining underlying essence (Rangel & Keller, 2011). Therefore, belief in context-independent essences that reside inside people implies a high cross-situational and temporal stability of traits and behaviors that may be measured with personality and interest inventories.

In contrast to personality as an essence located in the person, career construction theory views *reputation* as residing in the person's social network (Craig, 2009). Reputation is specific to the unique network of people with whom individuals interact. Their reputation, or trait ascription, will eventually be located in the network of coworkers in their occupations. According to Hogan (1983), the primary function of reputation or trait ascription "is to evaluate other people, specifically, to evaluate their potential as resources for the group" (p. 60). Thus, in a group that divides labor among its members, reputation may be used to assign individuals to work roles. For example, according to person–environment fit theory, a conscientious person should make a better banker than a creative person.

Family and friends recognize and discuss personalities by using the cultural categories and folk concepts available to them to distinguish and describe an individual. According to theories of person perception, individuals think of other people in terms of person types that consist of a cluster of causally interconnected traits (Sedikides & Anderson, 1994). These traits seem to have causal connections. For example, someone who is fearful and hesitant to approach other people may be assumed to be shy, and because they are shy, they may be lonely. These person types are implicit social categories that the lay public uses in person perception.

Person types as social categories. In a similar fashion, vocational psychologists and career counselors recognize and discuss personalities by using the categories provided to them by their professions. Rather than implicit person types or social categories, they use explicitly tested person types. Holland and his associates systematically and empirically defined six personality types with a cluster of connected traits, interests, and values. Holland's (1997) RIASEC model, composed of trait complexes organized into types, offers a useful approach for describing and discussing individual actors, as well as a company of actors who populate an occupational group. Formulating these person types or prototypes was a major advance in the science of vocational behavior because the operationally defined explicit RIASEC types replaced the ill-defined implicit types used previously by counselors and researchers. Today, the dominant language or professional jargon for denoting personality or reputation in career studies is that of Holland's (1997) making. His RIASEC prototypes provide a readily comprehensible and broadband tool for organizing vocational phenomena into prototypical categories (see Nauta, Chapter 3, this volume).

The types or trait complexes, although decontextualized and abstract, provide extremely useful comparative dimensions for conducting vocational appraisals of individuals and environments. RIASEC types—including skills, interests, values, and abilities—can be used to summarize an actor's reputation as it relates to work roles. This RIASEC vocabulary enables researchers and counselors to be more efficient and effective in thinking about individuals and the work world, as well as more articulate in communicating their thoughts to each other and to clients. These advantages hold especially true if researchers and counselors understand that the RIASEC language both constructs and constitutes social realities; it does not label preexisting phenomena that have been discovered. Therefore, career construction theory enjoins vocational psychologists and career counselors not to believe the reification fallacy by treating linguistic abstractions as if they were a real thing. In career construction theory, RIASEC types are simply *resemblances* to socially constructed clusters of attitudes and skills; they have no reality or truth value outside themselves. The RIASEC hexagon represents regulated similarities in environments that produce reputational patterns of six types among individuals with heterogeneous potentials.

Self-constructing types. Career construction theory values the RIASEC taxonomy as a remarkable achievement by Holland. Accordingly, it retains the RIASEC language to discuss resemblance to types and the processes of self-making that construct a self-system (Mischel & Morf, 2003). Traditionally, RIASEC personality types are defined by their content, including interests, competencies, and values, rather than by self-constructing processes. Nevertheless, Holland (1997) suggested that RIASEC types may also be viewed as processes shaped by schemas, strategies, and beliefs. Each RIASEC type represents different sets of goals and self-theories. It is a small step to consider RIASEC types as self-constructing types. Relative to this reconceptualization of personality, Mischel and Morf (2003) asserted: "To the degree that individuals share similar goals, interpersonal competencies, and processing dynamics in the self-construction process, they can be studied together as constituting particular self-constructing types" (p. 32). So, while recognizing the usefulness of viewing RIASEC types as personal styles, career construction theory prefers to view them as self-constructing strategies. These strategies are internalized from interpersonal experiences and cultural discourses; that is, they are coconstructed by an individual and society.

Accordingly, this coconstruction perspective asserts that a self is built from the outside in, not from the inside out as personality trait theorists would have it. As Vygotsky (1978) noted, "There is nothing in mind that is not first of all in society" (p. 142). In this regard, Holland (1997) theorized that RIASEC types develop through a child's preferred activities, which in turn lead to long-term interests and competencies. Holland (1997) wrote that "the order of development usually is from activities to dispositions" (p. 19). Holland's hypothesis is certainly compatible with Leontiev's (1983) theorem that the self and other psychological processes originate in activity. For Leontiev, the act is the beginning of self, and the self is a crystallization of activities. As children grow as actors, they develop an internal sense of agency.

Self as Agent: Adapting to Tasks, Transitions, and Traumas

With the development of an internal sense of agency in middle childhood, a second layer of the self begins to take shape (McAdams & Olson, 2010). Having adapted to the family of origin by becoming a recognizable actor in the family drama, the individual must, through agency, extend the self into the community and school. This self-extension requires a formulation of goals to strive for, then projects, and eventually a career. As children progress through grade school, they begin to form goals that serve to direct their adaptation. From this perspective, actors can now also be viewed as self-regulating agents who pursue goals of their own choosing. Career construction theory concentrates on this agency when the self must adapt to transitions. Agency becomes critical when the occupational plot is lost, ruptured, halted, stalled, or silenced. Because agency deals with the processes of resuming movement, it usually is revealed and discussed in the language of action verbs, rather than in the language of nouns used to characterize an actor.

Agency deals with movement into and out of educational and vocational positions, each of which provides a mechanism of social integration. Our goals direct our occupational choices as a preferred strategy for sustaining ourselves in society. In choosing an occupation and participating in a social niche, the actor manifests the self. Super (1963) explained that in expressing occupational preferences, individuals put into occupational terminology their ideas of the kind of people they are; that in entering an occupation, they seek to implement a concept of themselves; and that after stabilizing in an occupation, they seek to realize their potential and preserve self-esteem. At some point, and usually at repeated points, most of us change occupational positions. The move from one position to another is a period of transition during which a person must leave one place, revise goals, choose another place, and enter and establish herself or himself in that unfamiliar space.

Adaptation and developmental tasks. The process of adapting to changing conditions prompts a period of heightened learning and development for the person on the move. Although change fosters personal development, people do not readily initiate large changes themselves because they have grown comfortable where they are and transitions require substantial effort. More often than not, some external event initiates their movement. Career construction theory identifies three major social challenges that prompt change: vocational development tasks, occupational transitions, and work traumas. Vocational development tasks communicate social expectations about age-graded normative transitions. Societies synchronize adolescents and emerging adults to their culture by telling them in advance how to prepare for and enter their work lives. Thus, vocational development tasks provide powerful anticipations with which young people can envision and prepare for occupations congruent with their abilities and interests. Simply stated, the major developmental tasks require that young people, in turn, view work as a salient role, crystallize preferences for vocational fields and levels, specify occupational preferences, enter a fitting job, and progress in that job until moving to the next job. The movement from one job to the next job is called an occupational transition. These transitions may be wanted or unwanted, planned or unexpected, and promotions or demotions. Work traumas, of course, are unpredictable and unwanted. Traumas include painful events such as plant closings, industrial accidents, occupational injuries, and contract violations.

Career construction theory views adapting to these tasks, transitions, and traumas as fostered principally by five sets of behaviors, each named for their adaptive functions: orientation, exploration, establishment, management, and disengagement. These constructive activities form a cycle of adaptive performance that is periodically repeated as an individual must fit into a changing context. Realizing that a new adaptation approaches, individuals can adapt more effectively if they meet changing conditions with growing awareness and information seeking, followed by informed decision making, trial behaviors leading to a stable commitment projected forward for a certain time period, active role management, and eventually forward-looking disengagement. Recycling or reengaging in behaviors associated with the adaptive functions of orientation, exploration, stabilization, management, and disengagement occurs much more frequently in postindustrial economies in which people change jobs about every 5 years (Mullins, 2009). This differs from life in industrial economies, in which people may work 30 years at the same job. Rather than develop biographical certainty about an orderly sequence of tasks in a predictable life course, people now must adapt to an individualized life course (Beck, 1994) with destandardized trajectories consisting of more frequent and less predictable occupational transitions.

Adaptation: readiness, resources, responses, and results. The word *adapt* comes from the Latin, meaning "to fit." It means bringing inner needs and outer opportunities into harmony, with the harmonics of a good adaptation indicated by success, satisfaction, and well-being. Career construction theory characterizes adaptation outcomes as resulting from adaptivity, adaptability, and adapting. These words denote a sequence ranging across adaptive readiness, adaptability resources, adapting responses, and adaptation results. People are more or less prepared to change, differ in their resources to manage change, demonstrate more or less change when change is needed, and as a result, become more or less integrated into life roles over time.

Adaptivity and readiness. In career construction theory, adaptivity denotes the personal characteristic of flexibility or willingness to meet career tasks, transitions, and traumas with fitting responses. We reach the threshold to initiate the interpersonal and intrapersonal processes that guide goal-directed activity when we can no longer assimilate the changes and persevere in routine activities. At that point, we need to accommodate to the disequilibrium by changing the self or circumstances. The required accommodations typically prompt feelings of distress that fuel motivation and bolster the willingness to adapt. However, adaptiveness by itself is insufficient to support adaptive behaviors. Individuals willing to adapt must bring self-regulation resources to bear on changing the situation—what career construction theory calls adaptabilities.

Adaptability and resources. Career adaptability denotes an individual's psychosocial resources for coping with current and anticipated vocational development tasks, occupational transitions, and work traumas that, to some degree large or small, alter their social integration (Savickas, 1997). Individuals draw on these self-regulation resources to solve the unfamiliar, complex, and ill-defined problems presented by the tasks, transitions, and traumas. These resources are considered psychosocial because they reside at the intersection of person-in-environment. Adaptability shapes self-extension into the social environment as individuals connect with society and regulate their own vocational behavior.

As seen in Table 6.1, career construction theory defines four global dimensions of career adaptability and organizes them into a structural model with three levels. At the highest and most abstract level are the four dimensions of career adaptability: concern, control, curiosity, and confidence. These dimensions represent general adaptability resources and strategies that individuals use to manage critical tasks, transitions, and traumas as they construct their careers. At the intermediate level, the model articulates a distinct set of functionally homogeneous variables for each of the four general dimensions. Each set of intermediate variables includes the specific attitudes, beliefs, and competencies—the ABCs of career construction—that shape the concrete adapting behaviors used to master developmental tasks, negotiate occupational transitions, and resolve work traumas. Attitudes are affective variables or feelings that fuel behavior, whereas beliefs are conative variables or inclinations that direct behavior. The attitudes and beliefs dispose individuals to act in certain ways, and thus they form dispositional response tendencies. The competencies, including comprehension and problem-solving abilities, denote the cognitive resources brought to bear on making and implementing career choices.

Dispositional attitudes and beliefs shape the development and use of the competencies. In turn, the cognitive competencies shape the adapting behaviors that actually produce vocational development and construct careers. These coping behaviors constitute the third and most concrete level in the

Table 6.1
Career Adaptability Dimensions

Adaptability Dimension	Attitudes and Beliefs	Competence	Coping Behaviors	Career Problem
Concern	Planful	Planning	Aware Involved Preparing	Indifference
Control	Decisive	Decision making	Assertive Disciplined Willful	Indecision
Curiosity	Inquisitive	Exploring	Experimenting Risk taking Inquiring	Unrealism
Confidence	Efficacious	Problem solving	Persistent Striving Industrious	Inhibition

structural model of career adaptability. Representative behaviors for each dimension appear in Table 6.1. These coping behaviors, along with others, compose the adaptive functions of orientation, exploration, establishment, maintenance, and disengagement. The final column in Table 6.1 lists the likely career problem linked to a deficit in each of the adaptability resources.

Having outlined the structural model of career adaptabilities, let us turn to a detailed explanation of the four dimensions of coping resources. Career construction theory conceptualizes resourceful individuals as (a) becoming *concerned* about their future as a worker, (b) increasing personal *control* over their vocational future, (c) displaying *curiosity* in exploring possible selves and future scenarios, and (d) strengthening the *confidence* to pursue their aspirations. Career adaptability thus increases along the four dimensions of concern, control, curiosity, and confidence.

Career concern. Concern about one's own vocational future is the first and most important dimension of career adaptability. The fundamental function of career concern in constructing careers is reflected by the prime place given to it by prominent theories of vocational development, denoted by names such as Ginzberg's *time perspective*, Super's *planfulness*, Tiedeman's *anticipation*, Crites's *orientation*, and Harren's *awareness* (Savickas, Silling, & Schwartz, 1984). Career concern means essentially a future orientation, a sense that it is important to prepare for tomorrow. Attitudes of planfulness and optimism foster preparedness because they dispose individuals to become aware of the vocational tasks and occupational transitions to be faced and choices to be made in the imminent and distant future. Thinking about one's work life across time is the essence of career because a subjective career is not a behavior; it is an idea. Career construction is fostered by first realizing that one's present vocational situation evolved from past experiences and then connecting these experiences through the present situation to a preferred future. A belief in the continuity of experience allows individuals to connect their present activities to their occupational aspirations and visions of possible selves. This sense of continuity allows individuals to envision how today's effort builds tomorrow's success. Planful attitudes and belief in continuity incline individuals to engage in activities and experiences that promote competencies in planning and preparing for the future. A lack of career concern is called career *indifference*, which reflects apathy, pessimism, and planlessness.

Career control. Control over one's own vocational future is the second most important dimension in career adaptability. The fundamental function of control in constructing careers is reflected by the vast amount of research on topics such as independence, internal locus of control, autonomy, self-determination, effort attributions, and agency (Blustein & Flum, 1999). The dominant culture in the United States, and in those who have assimilated it, leans toward independence in balancing self and society. Consequently, the most popular models and materials for career intervention assume that an individual independently makes career choices. Independence as an interpersonal variable is not part of career construction theory. Career construction theory explicitly acknowledges that, in relation to individualistic and collectivistic contexts, either interdependence or independence may be adaptive. Nevertheless, self-control is important in both contexts.

Career construction theory conceptualizes control as an aspect of intrapersonal processes that foster self-regulation, not interpersonal processes that impact self-regulation (Fitzsimons & Finkel, 2010). Control involves intrapersonal self-discipline and the processes of being conscientious, deliberate, organized, and decisive in performing vocational development tasks and making occupational transitions. Its opposite is confusion, not dependence. Control disposes individuals to engage the vocational development tasks and negotiate occupational transitions, rather than avoid them. Individuals who encounter a narrower range of options, for whatever reasons, exercise career control by exploring the limited number of possibilities to make them personally meaningful and by fine-tuning available choices to enact them uniquely. Conscientious attitudes and belief in personal responsibility incline individuals to intentionally direct vocational actions. A lack of career control is often called career *indecision* and enacted as confusion, procrastination, or impulsivity.

Career curiosity. From a sense of self-control emerges the initiative to learn about the types of work that one might want to do and the occupational opportunities to do it. The fundamental function of curiosity in constructing careers is reflected by the extensive coverage given to it by prominent theories of vocational development under the rubrics of exploration and information-seeking behavior, as well as in their direct products of self-knowledge and occupational information. Career curiosity refers to inquisitiveness about and exploration of the fit between oneself and the work world. When acted upon, curiosity produces a fund of knowledge with which to make choices that fit self to situation. Systematic exploration and reflection on random exploratory experiences move individuals from naive to knowledgeable as they learn how the world works.

Attitudes of inquisitiveness dispose individuals to scan the environment to learn more about self and situations. Belief in the value of being open to new experiences and experimenting with possible selves and various roles prompts individuals to try new things and have adventures. Attitudes and dispositions that favor exploration and openness lead to experiences that increase competence in both self-knowledge and occupational information. Individuals who have explored the world beyond their own neighborhoods have more knowledge about their abilities, interests, and values, as well as about the requirements, routines, and rewards of various occupations. This broader fund of information brings realism and objectivity to subsequent choices that will match self to situations. A lack of career curiosity can lead to *unrealism* about the work world and inaccurate images of the self.

Career confidence. Individuals need confidence to act on their interests. Self-confidence denotes the anticipation of success in encountering challenges and overcoming obstacles (Rosenberg, 1989). In career construction theory, confidence denotes feelings of self-efficacy concerning one's ability to successfully execute a course of action needed to make and implement suitable educational and vocational choices. Career choices require solving complex problems. The fundamental role of confidence in constructing careers is reflected in the extensive scholarship on self-esteem, self-efficacy, and encouragement in theories of vocational development. Career confidence arises from solving problems encountered in daily activities, such as household chores, schoolwork, and hobbies. Moreover, recognizing that one can be useful and productive at these tasks increases feelings of self-acceptance. Broader exploratory experiences reinforce the confidence to try more things. Individuals who have been sheltered or excluded from certain categories of experience (e.g., math and science) find it difficult to be confident in approaching those activities and consequently will be less interested in occupations that require skill at those activities. Mistaken beliefs about gender, race, and social roles often produce internal and external barriers that inhibit the development of confidence.

A lack of career confidence can result in career *inhibition* that thwarts actualizing roles and achieving goals.

Profiles of career adaptability. In theory, individuals should approach tasks, transitions, and trauma with a concern for the future, a sense of control over it, the curiosity to experiment with possible selves and explore social opportunities, and the confidence to engage in designing their occupational future and executing plans to adapt. In reality, development along the four dimensions of adaptability progresses at different rates, with possible fixations and regressions. Delays within or disequilibrium between the four developmental lines produces problems in crystallizing career preferences and specifying occupational choices, problems that career counselors diagnose as indifference, indecision, unrealism, and inhibition. Moderate disharmony in the development of the four dimensions of adaptability produces variant patterns of development. Strong disharmony produces deviant patterns of development. Accordingly, comparing development among the four dimensions is a useful way to understand the antecedents of difficulties in adapting to tasks, transitions, and traumas. Individual differences in the adaptability resources for making and implementing choices may be measured in students with the Career Maturity Inventory-Adaptability Form (Savickas & Porfeli, 2012) and in adults with the Career Adapt-Abilities Scale (Porfeli & Savickas, 2012).

Interplay among adaptiveness, adaptability, adapting, and adaptation. Better outcomes (adaptation results) are achieved by individuals who are willing (adaptive readiness) and able (adaptability resources) to perform coping behaviors that address changing conditions (adapting responses). An analogy to airline travel may sharpen the distinctions between readiness, resources, responses, and results. In preparing to depart, flight attendants ask passengers seated in an exit row whether they are "willing and able" to assist in an emergency. Some people may be willing yet unable; other people may be unwilling yet able. In the language of career construction theory, the attendant is asking the passengers whether they have the willingness and resources that may be needed to act in an emergency. Career construction theory views "willing and able" as "adaptivity and adaptability" or as "readiness and resources." To continue the analogy, the airplane emergency might require some lifesaving actions. In career construction, this adapting or "doing" involves the behaviors that function to accomplish orientation, exploration, establishment, management, and disengagement. The adapting, in turn, leads to some outcome or adaptation that is judged for its goodness of fit as indicated by success and satisfaction.

Adaptation and goals. The process of adaptation is facilitated and directed by a person's goals. In general, the goal is to harmonize inner needs with outer opportunities. In particular, specific inner needs direct one to seek certain goals. Goals are representations of future states that satisfy needs and promise a sense of security (Miller, Galanter, & Pribram, 1960). Goals represent what people want and what they want to avoid. Because clear goals give direction and continuity to behavior, they support the intensified self-regulation needed during periods of transition (Heckhausen, Wrosch, & Schulz, 2010).

Career construction theory views goals as arising from what an individual needs to feel secure. Interests connect personal needs and relevant goals.

From Latin, *inter est* means "to be between." Interests are psychosocial tensional states between an individual's needs and social opportunities to fulfill those needs. The individual looks for interesting objects and activities in the environment that will be useful in meeting goals. The attraction or interest follows from actors evaluating the object of attention as useful in becoming more whole or complete. They believe that engaging in the interesting activity will address the preoccupations and problems that they carry forward from their family of origin and will further their self-construction. People also are attracted to join social environments populated by individuals they resemble. The matching of a person to an occupational group or vocational prototype makes interest inventories possible. However, remember that career construction theory views interests not as essential traits, but as coconstructed beliefs that particular activities or objects may be useful to the actor in furthering self-construction and social adaptation. Of course, many people cannot pursue interests that lead to their goals and meet their need for self-realization. They must take the only employment available to them. This uninteresting work at least fosters adaptation as survival, if not adaptation as self-realization. These individuals must continue to use leisure pursuits to construct and substantiate a self.

Self as Author: Narrating a Career Story

During the elementary school years and into adolescence, the agentic actor portrays a complex amalgam of influences and identifications. When individuals reach late adolescence, society expects them to "get a life" (Habermas & Bluck, 2000), that is, integrate their actions and agency into a unique identity supported by a unified life story. As individuals learn more about themselves as actors and motivated agents, they become ready to pattern their constellation of goals and purposive projects into a coherent and credible story. This identity narrative is not a summing up but a synthesis (Erikson, 1968), a configuration that reconciles multiple abstractions to produce an integrative solution to the problems in making the transition from school to work and from adolescence to adulthood. The identity narrative expresses the uniqueness of an individual in her or his particular context by articulating goals, directing adaptive behavior, and imposing meaning on activities. The individual uses this self-sustaining narrative to evaluate career opportunities and negotiate social constraints.

Identity narratives. As Erikson (1968) noted, career is a central story line in an identity narrative. The essential meaning of career and the dynamics of its construction are revealed in self-defining stories about the tasks, transitions, and traumas that an individual has faced. In career stories that chronicle the recursive interplay between self and society, the actor tells what happened in a job resume, the agent explains why it happened in an occupational plot, and the author interprets what it means with a career theme.

To compose an identity narrative and career story, authors must select and organize incidents and episodes from the micronarratives. At its simplest, the macronarrative sequences occupational positions in a chronological resume. The progression of positions that an individual occupies is an objective career, one publicly observable and documented. Fundamentally, this arrangement of jobs into sequence is a story, yet it is a story without a plot or theme. E. M. Forster (1927) once exemplified the difference between a story and plot this way: "The King died and then the Queen died" is a story because it has a sequence. "The King died, and then the Queen died of grief" adds plot to the story by explaining the action. Emplotment arranges the separate small stories in a sequence directed toward a conclusion (Ricoeur, 1984). It explains why things happened by raising some facts to prominence and adding connections within the occupational sequence. Emplotment also configures the diverse incidents and different episodes into a part-whole structure in which the parts gather meaning in relation to the whole. Emplotment produces a higher-level narrative that incorporates the small stories to illustrate and corroborate the larger grand story of a life.

An occupational plot makes connections that transform the job sequence in the objective career into a subjective career. However, occupational plots explain why an individual changed positions without reference to personal meaning. Plots portray the self as agent, not author. Authoring deeper, private meaning to accompany the public explanation of plot requires a theme. An occupational plot's implicit theme becomes more explicit through its repetition in the accumulating microstories. Cumulating incidents and insights into an abstract theme thickens the plot and amplifies larger meanings. A sense of unity crystallizes as the career theme imposes meaning on the plot parts through their participation in the whole. Autobiographical reasoning seeks to craft some thematic unity, not uniformity, out of contradictory beliefs and baffling behaviors. This unity must be achieved in a properly complicated way that integrates diversity without homogenizing it. Once articulated and authenticated, the career theme provides a unifying idea that, through recurrence, makes a life whole.

The thematic pattern woven by this central idea provides the primary unit of meaning used to understand the facts of a job story and the explanations of the occupational plot. The repeating pattern in a life reveals people to themselves and others. As individuals incorporate new experiences, they use the career theme to impose a pattern of meaning that comprehends the new episodes in the occupational plot. When the plot ruptures, individuals use the recurrent pattern in the macronarrative theme to restore order and direct action.

Career theme. A career theme brings more than unity to a plot; it brings continuity because it traces how a person remains identical with self despite diversity across micronarratives. Even when everything seems to change, the theme remains the same. Recall that in constructing a narrative identity, individuals work out the problem of their sameness across time. A theme grounds the here and now in the there and then. In telling how the self of yesterday became the self of today and will become the self of tomorrow (McAdams & Olson, 2010), an author's identity narrative supports both a stable actor with a continuous story and a flexible agent capable of change. The theme keeps the narrative going by continually integrating events and pulling them into the plot (Giddens, 1991).

In career construction theory, the theme is what matters in the life story. It consists of what is at stake in that person's life, and it brings a perspective to bear on experiences. The theme, clear or complicated, carries to work settings the concerns that constitute the individual and matter most in defining self and expressing identity. A theme articulates a purposive attitude toward life and states the idea that the life serves. The thematic purpose pursued in the occupational plot makes work the outer form of something intensely personal. This can be made clear for a particular person by personalizing the following mapping sentence: "I will become (actor's reputation) so that I can (agent's goal), and in the process (author's theme)." For example, one medical student's mapping sentence was "I will become a psychiatrist so that I may heal families in crisis and in the process reduce my own feelings of helplessness about my own family's suffering." Compare this to a classmate's statement of "I will become a neurosurgeon so that I may perform delicate operations and in the process prove to my father than I am not clumsy." The public meaning in these two statements indicates the social contribution and occupational niche; the private meaning expresses a career theme. Integrative choices allow individuals to actively master what they passively suffered as they turn private preoccupations into public occupations. Readers might complete their own mapping sentence, "I am becoming a counselor to help people (do what), so that I (personal meaning)." For example, one counselor stated that "I became a counselor to do for others what I wish had been done for me when I was hurting."

Character arc. As a carrier of meaning, themes hold the character arc or overarching narrative thread that extends through the entire macronarrative. The character arc portrays where the individual started, is now, and wants to end up on some essential issue. Character begins with an impetus in the family ground that molds and moves the actor. Often stories start with something missing in life, something that individuals need or for which they long. To overcome this limitation, deficiency, or weakness, they seek to attain goals that fulfill the need. They try to fix the flaw at the base of their character arc. As they move from tension to intention, they wrestle with the fear, limitation, block, or wound. In due course, they learn how to overcome the adversity and transform their symptoms into strengths.

The progress from need to goal transforms individuals as they forge a character that addresses their preoccupations and solves their problems. This transformation from tragedy to triumph represents the core of the character, that is, the character arc that defines the person and explains the driving force of the plot. Consider, for example, the following five familiar character arcs: the sickly child who becomes a champion bodybuilder, the stuttering child who becomes a network news anchor, the shy child who becomes an actor, the poor child who grows up to be wealthy, and the cowardly child who becomes a brave fighter. These well-known arcs express cultural scripts that tell how an individual moves from weakness to strength, timidity to confidence, inhibition to expressiveness, poverty to affluence, and fear to fortitude. Applying to practice the perspectives of actor, agent, and author structures an improved scheme for career intervention (Savickas, 1996).

CAREER INTERVENTIONS FOR ACTORS, AGENTS, AND AUTHORS

From the three perspectives on the self as described by career construction theory, three main career interventions assist people to choose and adjust to their work roles. The career services or interventions are vocational guidance for the actor, career education or coaching for the agent, and career counseling for the author (Savickas, 2012). Depending on a client's needs, practitioners may apply vocational guidance to identify occupational fit, career education to foster vocational development and preparedness, or career counseling to shape a vocational identity and design a life. Guidance, education, and counseling are each rooted in a particular paradigm or general pattern of practice, accompanied by their own models, methods, and materials. Kuhn (1996) described a paradigm as a conceptual model with a set of prevailing practices that define a discipline during a certain period of time. The following paragraphs outline fundamental differences among guidance, education, and counseling as distinct paradigms for career intervention.

Vocational guidance meets the needs of individuals moving to cities to work in industrial factories. From the objective perspective of individual differences, guidance views clients as actors who may be characterized by scores on traits and who may be matched to occupations that employ people they resemble. The same principles are applied in academic advising to *guide* students to fitting educational and training niches, to *select* personnel for an organization, and to *classify* armed forces recruits into military positions. The general paradigm for vocational guidance and educational advising is to (a) increase self-knowledge, (b) gather occupational information, and (c) match self to fitting occupations or academic majors. The desired outcome is entering a congruent position leading to success, satisfaction, and stability. Readers interested in learning more about vocational guidance may consult Holland (1997) or Lofquist and Dawis (1991) (also see Chapters 2 and 3 of this volume).

Career education and coaching meets the needs of individuals climbing the corporate ladder of high modernity. From the subjective perspective of individual development, education views clients as agents who may be characterized by their degree of readiness to engage developmental tasks appropriate to their career stages and who may be helped to implement new attitudes, beliefs, and competencies that further their careers. When performed with adults, career education typically is called career coaching. The general paradigm for career education and coaching is to (a) assess developmental status, (b) orient to imminent developmental tasks and occupational transitions, and (c) increase preparedness with relevant coping attitudes, beliefs, and competencies. The outcome for career education and coaching is enhanced adaptability, sometimes called career choice readiness or work adjustment. Those interested in learning more about career education may review career development and assessment counseling (Super, 1983; Chapter 4, this volume) and the social-cognitive framework for career choice and counseling (Brown & Lent, 1996; Chapter 5, this volume).

Career counseling meets the needs of individuals preparing for and participating in the new world of work forged by the digital revolution and global economy (Savickas, 2012). From the project perspective of individual design, counseling views clients as authors who construct their careers by telling autobiographical stories and reflecting on themes that specify their uniqueness. The general paradigm or pattern of practice for career counseling and life designing is (a) construct and deconstruct a career story, (b) reconstruct an occupational plot and career theme, and (c) coconstruct the next episode in the story. The outcome for career designing is an enhanced sense of identity and meaningful vocational action.

The work of guidance entails thinking in terms of resemblance to types and making matches. The work of counseling involves thinking in terms of uniqueness and making meaning. Career counseling does not replace vocational guidance. Rather, career counseling takes its place among the interventions of vocational guidance and career education. Of course, today guidance usually includes some element of career education and career counseling as it addresses questions of choice and adjustment. Nevertheless, the dominant nomothetic discourse of guidance emphasizes generalizations about individuals' belongingness and seeks to inform clients, whereas the dominant idiographic discourse of counseling emphasizes particulars about individuals' uniqueness and seeks to transform clients. Each career intervention—whether guidance, education, or counseling—is valuable and effective for its intended purpose. As counselors select an intervention for a particular student or client, they answer an essential question first posed by Williamson and Bordin (1941, p. 8): What method will produce what types of results with what types of clients? To answer this question, counselors might consider whether they seek to aid the actor, agent, or author.

A COUNSELING MODEL FOR CAREER CONSTRUCTION

The theory of career construction has been applied to practice in a model for career counseling. Although crafted to direct counseling with individuals as authors, counseling for career construction also includes elements to guide actors in choosing work roles and to prepare agents to adapt to transitions. Career construction counseling assumes that individuals begin narrative processing of their biographies (Heinz, 2002) when they are dislocated from the current episode in their career stories or have lost the plot. Some individuals seek counseling to assist them in this identity work, especially if they feel perplexed and confused. The goals of counseling are to have clients tell vocational stories about their work lives and their current transitions and troubles, integrate the vocational stories into an identity narrative about self and work, use that narrative to make meaning of the transition and regulate emotions, script the next scene in the occupational plot, and prompt action to construct a more satisfying life.

Practitioners begin career construction counseling by having clients describe (a) the incident that dislocates them from the current episode in their story, (b) their adaptive readiness and resources, and (c) their goals for a new scenario they want to coconstruct with a counselor. After briefly addressing these three questions and initiating a working alliance, counselors interview clients using a uniform set of questions. The Career Construction Interview (CCI; formerly the career style/story interview; Savickas, 1989, 2011a) has clients tell small stories or micronarratives that reveal how they have constructed self, identity, and career. Storytelling makes the self and crystallizes identity. Career construction counseling concentrates on stories because their language and images are the construction tools that people use to make a self, shape an identity, and build a career.

The English Renaissance poet Ben Jonson wrote, "Language most shows a man; speak that I may see thee." Repeated words and resulting themes are acts of identity through which clients show their selves and search for social roles.

Construction

Five questions in the CCI elicit vocational stories about the actor, agent, author, advice, and arc. First, counselors examine how clients have constructed a self as actor by asking about role models. Second, to assess agentic strivings and goals, counselors ask clients about manifest interests rather than inventoried interests. Interests manifest themselves in conjunction with such things as favorite magazines, television shows, and Web sites. Third, counselors ask clients as authors to describe the script of their current favorite story, whether from a book or a movie. The fourth question requests a favorite saying because a motto usually advises clients about the adaptability resources and adapting actions required to move to the next episode in the occupational plot. The final question inquires about character arc by asking for the earliest recollection (ER) that clients can recall. For most clients, the ER depicts a negative experience that portrays a motif and central conflict (Chae, Goodman, & Edelstein, 2011). Nevertheless, ERs are more about the future in that clients select, elaborate, and reconstruct memories that guide present or future action.

Deconstruction

A client's outward reach has inner boundaries. As a client's vocational stories construct career, the counselor listens for vignettes that require deconstruction. Stories that devitalize a client because of dominating expectations or insidious ideas must be carefully deconstructed to reveal and defeat their self-limiting ideas, confining roles, and cultural barriers. Often, the vignettes that most require deconstruction involve biases regarding gender, race, and social class. Taking apart these mistaken ideas may open pathways not previously seen or possible because clients can only make choices given the world they know.

At the same time, counselors must realize that an individual's stories do not determine the future; instead, storying is an active attempt at making meaning and shaping the future. In telling their stories, individuals are constructing a possible future. They usually tell themselves the stories that they themselves need to hear because, from all their available stories, they narrate those stories that support current goals and inspire action. Rather than remembering, individuals re-member the past so that prior events support current choices and lay the groundwork for future moves

(Josselson, 2000). This is an instance, not of the present taking lessons from the past, but of the past taking lessons from the present, reshaping itself to fit current needs. This narrative truth may, of course, differ from historical fact because it fictionalizes the past. In so doing, it preserves continuity and coherence in the face of change and allows the person to meet that change with the fidelity of the actor and the flexibility of the agent. Having listened closely to a client's vocational stories, and maybe deconstructing some demoralizing ideas and incidents, it comes time to reconstruct the small stories into a large story of career.

RECONSTRUCTION

Reconstruction and emplotment craft a subjective career from client constructions of their work lives. Narrative processing of vocational stories identifies and assembles important incidents into a macronarrative, or a grand story, about the career. The identity narrative tells the story of a person who becomes a character in a world that she or he has coconstructed with significant others. The portrayal bestows personal meaning and social mattering on a life as it tells about pattern and progress. Nevertheless, the portrait does not tell the complete life story; rather, it frames a perspective and illuminates aspects of lived experience relevant to the questions asked by the client. To do this, the identity narrative highlights the occupational plot and career theme in the sequence of vocational stories. The career theme represents the controlling idea served by the plot. The theme also carries the character arc, that is, how the person changes over time relative to preoccupations, puzzlements, and problems. Plot reorganization and theme reconstruction deepen the identity narrative by infusing feeling and broaden it by integrating more vocational stories.

In attempting to discern the career theme while listening to clients' vocational stories, researchers and counselors may become disoriented by the numerous particulars of a life. To prevent becoming confused by a client's complexities and contradictions, counselors listen not to the facts but for the glue that holds the facts together because it is the theme or secret that makes a whole of the life. Recognizing the career theme in the seemingly random actions and incidents explained by an occupational plot can be done in many ways. Career construction theory proposes for this purpose that researchers and counselors listen for the quintessence of a client's vocational stories. They may approach this task by assuming that the archetypal theme of career construction involves turning a personal preoccupation into a public occupation. As Csikszentmihalyi and Beattie (1979) explained, "A life theme consists of a problem or a set of problems which a person wishes to solve above everything else and the means the person finds to achieve a solution" (p. 48). In the work domain, the problem is the preoccupation, and the solution is the occupation. Often, clients' preoccupations are unpleasant, involving difficulty and distress. Yet, some clients' preoccupations are pleasant, involving ease and enjoyment. Thus, the word *problem* means the content of a preoccupation or puzzlement—whether positive or negative—that individuals must address in solving themselves.

Career construction revolves around turning a personal problem into a public strength and then even a social contribution. In counseling for career construction, the essential activity entails articulating the preoccupation and discussing possible solutions in the form of jobs that may extend the occupational plot into the next scene. This often involves helping a client construct interests (Kitson, 1942). Counselors help clients create interest by showing them how a few occupations and avocations directly address their preoccupation and, in so doing, may resolve their problems. The view that interests originate as solutions to problems is not new. In 1940, Carter concluded that interests are "solutions to the problems of growing up" (p. 187). Interest, in proposing a path from preoccupation to occupation, strives to maintain an individual's integrity by charting strategies for survival, integrative adaptation, and optimal development—the very stuff of life themes.

Coconstruction

Having reconstructed an identity narrative about career from the vocational stories, the counselor then presents to a client the draft of her or his life portrait, including the occupational plot, career theme, and character arc. As the client engages and emotionally enters the life portrait, the counselor encourages the client to edit it. This revision involves amendments, adjustments, and alterations. Clients need to modify the life portrait to make it more livable and then extend it into the future. This work by the client is critically important because it is why they came to counseling. Work by the client rather than by the counselor predicts positive outcomes: Clients who find the words and experience the feelings build a scaffold for self-construction and meaning-making that supports scripting the next episode in the occupational plot. Client and counselor join together to candidly craft moves in meaning with which to confront choices relative to tasks, transitions, and traumas. The coconstruction of the life portrait seeks to situate the current dislocation in a way that clarifies priorities, mobilizes central tendencies, and increases the possibility of transformation and development. This occurs as clients access different meanings and knowledge that open new possibilities and restart stalled initiatives. The counselor serves as a witness who validates and authenticates the new story and its intentions. With their intentions more apparent to themselves and their counselors, clients are ready to face challenges and disruptions in their occupational plots, envision the next scene, and begin to act.

ACTION

People need to make their lives happen. Although scripting the next scene brings client experience forward, activity starts clients living ahead of themselves. The necessary action is to turn intentions into behavior infused with meaning (Malrieu, 2003). Client and counselor together craft an action agenda that will move the client from the currently experienced situation to the one currently desired. Through action, not verbal expressions of decidedness, clients engage the world (Krieshok, Black, & McKay, 2009). Going further and deeper into the world answers the questions brought to counseling. Action advances self-making, identity shaping, and career constructing.

In sum, counseling for career construction involves having clients construct their careers by articulating vocational stories, deconstruct demoralizing stories by destabilizing their meanings, reconstruct a life portrait by elaborating the identity narrative, coconstruct the next episode in the occupational plot by transforming the tension into intention, and take actions to create a more satisfying life. Thus, the sequence is articulate, destabilize, elaborate, transform, and act.

CASE STUDY

Live demonstrations of the career construction counseling model show the approach in action (Savickas, 2006, 2009). The following case study demonstrates career constructing by describing the use of this counseling model to help a client coconstruct a viable and suitable identity narrative that enables her to make educational and vocational choices and take actions to lead a more satisfying life.

Meeting Elaine. When the counselor first met Elaine, she was a 20-year-old full-time college student who had just completed the fall semester of her sophomore year. During the spring semester, she must declare her major. She could not decide on a major, although her mother urged her to declare premed. She lived at home and commuted to campus each day. She reported that she had talked about careers with her college counselor yet then felt even more undecided. She guessed she would major in premed and then enter medical school, yet she was unsure about this. She wanted the counselor to help her explore whether medicine was the right choice for her. She sometimes thought engineering would be a better choice, and she took an engineering class during the fall semester. She believed that chemical engineering might be a good choice, yet civil engineering seemed easier. She had requested information from another college where they have better integrated computers into their chemical engineering curriculum. She was attracted by computers and liked the idea that if she transferred to that college she could live in a dormitory. In response to the question of how counseling could be useful to her, Elaine responded that she did not know why she could not choose an academic major, she needed help in making a choice, and wondered whether medicine would be the right choice for her.

Career construction interview (first session). The genius of the counselor is in asking questions, not in finding answers. Clients know the answers, and the counselor's questions help clients acknowledge what they know. The counselor began the story crafting questions of the CCI (Savickas, 2011a) by inquiring about three role models to learn about Elaine as an actor. Elaine stated that *Anne of Green Gables* had spirit and a temper, set goals and went after them, did what she wanted, had integrity, and had fun. The heroine in the book *A Wrinkle in Time* led her friends in a showdown against creatures trying to take over their minds. She thought of ways to stick together and fight the creatures. Laura, in the book *Little House on the Prairie*, had wild ideas of things to do and enjoyed competing with and outdoing others. To assess preferred environments and manifest interests, the counselor asked Elaine about favorite magazines, books, and television shows. She liked *Vogue* because it is about fashion, *BusinessWeek* because it is about advertising campaigns, and *Details* because it is about men's clothing. Her favorite television show was *Laverne and Shirley* because they do things off the norm without getting into trouble. When the counselor asked about her favorite story, Elaine said it was *The Search of Mary Kay Malloy*, the story of an Irish girl's voyage to America by herself. Elaine reported having two favorite sayings. The first, from *Curious George*, was "I am curious about things." The second was "Do it well," which to her meant nearly perfectly. To complete the CCI, Elaine reported the following early recollection: "Going to Disneyland with my grandparents and uncle and his girlfriend. I was in the back of the camper trying to sing and dance for my grandmother. She told me to sit down so I would not get hurt. I got on uncle's girlfriend's nerves by trying to talk to her. I tried to talk but she did not think I should move around at the same time." Elaine gave the story this headline: "Little girl annoyed because she must sit still."

Reconstructing Elaine's story. In responding to the CCI questions, Elaine articulated vocational stories that construct her career. The next task in career construction counseling is to reconstruct these microstories by weaving them into a macronarrative. To begin to make sense of Elaine's stories, the counselor first reviewed how she wanted to use the counseling experience. Her goals framed the perspective from which to view her stories. Elaine wanted the counselor to help her understand why she could not choose, as well as move her closer to making a choice, whether medicine or something else. So in reviewing her career stories, the counselor attended to her sense of career control and experiences with making decisions.

Second, after considering her goals for counseling, the counselor examined the preoccupations at the base of her character arc. This began with finding the first verb in her ER because it indicates a particularly important form of movement for the client. In Elaine's ER, the first verb is *going*. This may mean that she wants to move, be on the go, and travel. The counselor then inspected the remaining stories for evidence to support this idea. The inspection found the phrases "moving around" and "dancing" in the ER and then further support in her favorite story, which tells the story of a girl's journey to another country. "Singing and dancing" seem important to her. She is enthusiastic about life. Also *try* appears three times in the ER, suggesting that Elaine may be industrious and persistent in pursuing difficult goals. *Talking* also appears in the ER, so she likes to communicate and attempts to convince others to change their minds. And finally, in the ER an adult woman tells her to sit down and stop dancing. The counselor recognized a tension in Elaine's life between wanting to be on the go and being told to sit still. It is important to remember that the ER does not cause behavior; rather, she has re-membered it to reflect her current struggle. From the many available stories, clients tell those that they themselves need to hear right now.

Third, the counselor considered the headline that Elaine composed for the ER as a rhetorical compression that expresses the gist of her story. From Elaine's perspective, she is a "little girl" who is annoyed because powerful others stop her from enthusiastically pursuing her dreams. They want her to stay put where they place her. It is worthwhile to read the headline in two ways. On the one hand, it reveals more about a career theme that will shape her occupational plot. On the other hand, it indicates in the here and now the problem she wants to work on during counseling. She wants the counselor to encourage her movement and her gusto for life, as well as teach her how to persuade others to accept her plan rather than steal her life.

Fourth, the counselor attended to Elaine as an actor and the character that she has constructed. How Elaine described her role models reveals core elements in her self-concept and articulates how she wishes to act in the world. Elaine's key figures model spirit, enthusiasm, playfulness, goals, competitiveness, persistence, temper, fighting wrongheaded authority, and enlisting compatriots in these battles. These qualities find expression in her other stories. She is not frightened by wild ideas and doing things off the norm as long as they are fun and do not get her into trouble.

Fifth, the counselor sought to understand how Elaine was attempting to solve her problems in constructing a career and how occupations could help her actively master the problems she faced. To do so, the counselor compared the pain and problems narrated in the ER to the tentative solutions displayed by her role models. In Elaine's case, the ER describes a playful girl being told to sit still and do as she is told. This, of course, resonates with her current dilemma—sitting still as her mother tells her to major in premed. The sitting still might be her metaphor for indecision. The counselor summarized this understanding by drawing a lifeline from the preoccupation with being told to sit still to the effort to build a self that fights for her own independence.

Sixth, the counselor appraised Elaine's vocational preferences by viewing her manifest interests through the lens of Holland's RIASEC hexagon. She shows interest in fashion, clothing design, and advertising campaigns. She likes to do things off the norm without getting into trouble. Looking through the six-sided lens, the counselor sees that Elaine most resembles the Artistic and Enterprising types. Creating and influencing are her two strongest interests. Individuals with this pairing usually show potential for creative leadership and innovative projects yet do not fit easily into occupational niches. They also like to travel, have adventures, and display uniqueness. Enterprising-Artistic types also seem more comfortable being second in command or on a team because the first in command usually resembles the Enterprising-Conventional type. To brainstorm possible jobs, the counselor went to the O*NET to find occupations listed as Enterprising-Artistic and Artistic-Enterprising. The lack of Realistic and Investigative characteristics among Elaine's manifest interests seems atypical for someone in engineering (IRE) or medicine (IRS). If Elaine pursues engineering, it may be in some specialty that emphasizes design work. If she pursues medicine, it might be in an enterprising specialty such as hospital administration or an artistic specialty such as dermatology or plastic surgery.

Seventh, the counselor turned to Elaine's current favored script, which tells of a young girl who travels the country in search of herself. Elaine is living this script in that she must search for herself. She has not yet crystallized an identity; she is fighting off her mother's attempt to confer on her the vocational identity of a physician. Her vocational indecisiveness seems rooted in identity confusion. Career counseling probably should concentrate on identity interventions and occupational exploration in breadth rather than exploration in depth and committing to a specific major. Her advice to herself is the same—be curious and do it right.

Eighth, the counselor profiled Elaine's career adaptability. It is consistent with her indecisiveness and identity ambiguity. She is coping with the vocational development task of crystallizing a vocational identity (not an occupational transition or work trauma) and tentative preferences for occupational fields as a prelude to specifying an academic major and occupational choice. She is deeply concerned about the future, as shown by her entering career counseling for a second time. From her remarks, it is clear that the major deficiency in her adaptabilities is the absence of career control. The counselor will help Elaine view her indecision as a strength, not a weakness. It is her way of fighting powerful creatures who are trying to control her career. She shows some curiosity about possible selves and alternative occupations. For example, she has written to another college for information. She already knows implicitly that exploratory behavior is paramount because her advice to herself is to be curious and do it right. She could use more confidence in her ability to make it happen. With an increased sense of self-control and more information seeking, her career confidence will grow.

Reconstructing a life portrait. Having considered the actor, agent, author, advice, and arc, the counselor then moved to synthesize them into a life portrait (Lawrence-Lightfoot & Davis, 1997). The counselor composed a life portrait to capture Elaine's situation, leaving room to insert and elaborate the finishing touches that the client must add during counseling. The portrait included tentative answers to implicit questions such as "Who am I?" "What is my quest?" and "How can I grow and flourish?" The portrait emphasized and repeated the major career theme, affirming its significance and validity. Then the counselor used the theme with its character arc to unite the meaning of the client's separate career stories into a narrative structure that integrated the diverse vocational stories. The counselor intended to illuminate what is at stake and the choices to be made to enhance the client's ability to decide. After the counselor sketched a portrayal that included the character (innovative leader or leader of innovation) that the client wishes to play, the stage on which she wishes to place the action (travel and adventure), the script she wishes to enact now (self-discovery), the advice she gives herself (be curious yet conscientious), and the arc of her character (struggling to make up her own mind), the counselor was ready to engage Elaine in a conversation about the goals she brought to counseling.

Second session. Good movie directors set up a vista before they take viewers into a scene and then a moment. Thus, the counselor delineated the vista by reviewing Elaine's response to the opening inquiry regarding how she might use counseling. Then the counselor presented the life portrait in a way that highlighted her developmental trajectory, especially her movement from problem to strength, so that she could actually feel her own movement from tension to intention. The counselor presented the portrait as a tentative sketch and invited Elaine to amend and alter it to fit her understanding. In the end, the validity of the coconstructed portrayal is arbitrated by its utility to the client.

The counselor depicted Elaine's current career theme as fighting powerful creatures who are trying to steal her mind or, in this particular instance, her career. She rebels by sitting still and refusing to decide in their favor while she marshals personal resources and social support to make her own choice. Then the counselor paused to get her reaction and revisions. The counselor explored her feelings about the portrait, because affect helps to create meaning. They also looked at her strengths, especially the personal characteristics of which she was proudest. They then discussed how the problems she currently faced were really the best solutions that she could come up with so far. For example, Elaine and her counselor reconstructed her indecision from being a problem to being the best solution she has found for trying to fight off the creatures who are trying to steal her career by making her sit still for what they want. In this way, the counselor attempted to help her use language, especially her own favorite metaphors and verbs, as a means of controlling the situation and increasing feelings of agency. Then the counselor helped Elaine understand how her personal narrative in the ER (singing, dancing, persuading) illuminated her professional interests in Artistic and Enterprising activities. In the end, Elaine and her counselor coconstructed the version of the life portrait that she wanted to use to address the career concerns she brought to counseling.

Coconstruction of her career narrative already had addressed Elaine's first concern—understanding why she did not (rather than cannot) make a decision regarding her academic major. Thus, the counselor moved to her second question—how well a career in medicine would suit her. They considered her manifest interests and how she might wish to position herself in society. They discussed her interests in being a leader, manager, or supervisor who is independent, creative, and on the go. The counselor commented that if she were to become a physician, she would probably be attracted to a specialty such as plastic surgery or dermatology. They talked about exploring majors in computer science (because she mentioned she had written for information about computer majors), advertising, marketing, and business management. They also discussed the importance of her considering being on the move, traveling, and having adventures as she thinks of possible selves and future scenarios. Most of all, they discussed discovering a way in which she could flourish and places where self-definition and self-determination would be possible.

Having addressed, to her satisfaction, the issue of how well medicine suited her and which other fields merited exploration, the counselor turned to her third question, which was how to move forward toward choosing a major. They discussed ways forward from where she now sits, including alternative resolutions and possible selves. The counselor explained that development arises from activity and overcoming difficulties met in the world. They then engaged in a conversation about self-construction activities that might move her closer to being the person she wanted to be, such as working at a summer job away from home, living in a college dormitory, taking a workshop on assertiveness, and meeting with a counselor to discuss family issues. She was encouraged by the conversation and felt that looking back over her life had given her the ability to move forward and the resolve to do so. They agreed to talk on the phone in the middle of the next semester and meet again during the summer.

Follow-up. The next summer when she visited the counselor, Elaine reported that she had taken a continuing education course in assertiveness, worked with a college counselor for five sessions to improve her relationship with her parents and reduce her perfectionism, lived away from home while working a summer job at an amusement park, and completed elective courses in computer science and advertising. She had declared a major in chemical engineering with a minor in computer science yet still wondered if marketing would better fit her.

Epilogue. The counselor next saw Elaine after she graduated with a major in chemical engineering and a minor in computer science. She told the counselor how much she had enjoyed her courses but detested the sexism exhibited by many of her instructors. To combat their bias, she had organized a club for females who were majoring in engineering. She was proud of what they had achieved in combating sexism. She was even more proud of the occupational position that she had recently secured. In two weeks, she would begin a job as a computer systems analyst for a large chemical company. This position required traveling throughout the United States with a team of colleagues to regional branches, where she would solve their computer problems. Furthermore, Elaine told the counselor that she and her mother were now friendly and that her mother was proud of her accomplishments and pleased with her prospects. Elaine looked forward to now becoming a woman on the go, one encouraged by a mother who tells her not to sit still. She glowed as she told me how she had used the things that we had talked about to help her roommates and friends make career choices. Six years later, after obtaining a master's in chemical engineering consulting, she was working as an consultant in chemical product design and enjoyed designing clothing during her leisure time.

CONCLUSIONS AND PRACTICE IMPLICATIONS

Career construction theory explains the interpretive and interpersonal process that individuals as actors, agents, and authors use to make a self, shape an identity, and build a career. The theory highlights the role of two metacompetencies—adaptability and identity—in coping with vocational development tasks, occupational transitions, and work traumas. Adaptability instills the will and skill to direct one's own work life; identity imposes meaning on vocational behavior and work activities. The theory structures a scheme for selecting career interventions and informs a model for career construction counseling. In career construction counseling, practitioners may assist clients to know their reputation as an actor, strivings as an agent, and recurring themes as an author. And more important, counseling for career construction encourages actors to use their adaptability and identity to select and engage in actions that create a more satisfying life.

- *Career construction* counseling concentrates on clients making meaning, forming intentions, and taking purposive action as they design their lives, make vocational choices, negotiate occupational transitions, and cope with troubles at work. Counseling involves collaborative construction, deconstruction, reconstruction, and coconstruction of career narratives that script actions that lead to a more satisfying life and successful career.
- *Opening* career construction counseling finds practitioners asking clients how counseling may be useful to them. Counselors collaborate with each client to craft a shared goal for counseling, one that fosters a working alliance.
- *Constructing* a career narrative begins with counselors eliciting stories from clients about important incidents, recurrent episodes, and self-defining moments. Counselors may prompt such stories by asking clients about their role models, enjoyable magazines and television programs, favorite book and movies, comforting mottoes, and early recollections.
- *Deconstructing* these micronarratives requires counselors to consider whether a client's stories include self-limiting ideas, confining roles, or cultural barriers. If the stories do restrict clients, then counselors help clients to think differently about the stories so as to access new meanings that open possibilities and restart stalled initiatives.

- *Reconstructing* involves integrating the small stories into a macronarrative or large story that concentrates on the occupational plot that binds the stories together and the career theme that invests them with meaning. The resulting life portrait reorganizes experiences to sediment values, emphasize priorities, and highlight recurrent action tendencies.
- *Coconstructing* collaboratively revises the life portrait with new language, fresh perspectives, and expanded vistas that explain what is at stake in the next episode of the career story. This self-clarity enables clients to make their intentions more apparent to themselves and their counselors. With this newfound clarity, clients may envision the next scenes, choose priorities, and form intentions.
- *Performing* the new meanings turns intention into action. Clients need to find courage to enact the next scene and live the new story. If a client hesitates to enact the choice, then practitioners attend to possible barriers and adaptability resources.
- *Closing* career construction counseling involves confirming that clients have accomplished the goals they brought to counseling. Counselors usually end with a few sentences that summarize what has occurred during counseling. In the end, the career problem is resolved, not by giving new information, but by making explicit what the client already knew and encouraging purposive action in light of this knowledge.

REFERENCES

Arthur, M. B. (1994). The boundaryless career [Special issue]. *Journal of Organizational Behavior, 15*(4).

Beck, U. (1994). *Risk society: Towards a new modernity.* London, UK: Sage.

Blustein, D. L., & Flum, H. (1999). A self-determination perspective of interests and exploration in career development. In M. L. Savickas & A. R. Spokane (Eds.), *Vocational interests: Meaning, measurement, and counseling use* (pp. 345–368). Palo Alto, CA: Davies-Black.

Brown, S., & Lent, R. (1996). A social cognitive framework for career choice counseling. *Career Development Quarterly, 44,* 355–367.

Carter, H. D. (1940). The development of vocational attitudes. *Journal of Consulting Psychology, 4,* 185–191.

Chae, Y., Goodman, G. S., & Edelstein, R. S. (2011). Autobiographical memory development from an attachment perspective: The special role of negative events. *Advances in Child Development, 40,* 1–49.

Craig, K. (2009). *Reputation: A network interpretation.* New York, NY: Oxford University Press.

Csikszentmihalyi, M., & Beattie, O. V. (1979). Life themes: A theoretical and empirical exploration of their origins and effects. *Journal of Humanistic Psychology, 19,* 45–63.

Erikson, E. (1968). *Identity: Youth and crisis.* New York, NY: Norton.

Fitzsimons, G. M., & Finkel, E. J. (2010). Interpersonal influences on self-regulation. *Current Directions in Psychological Science, 19,* 101–105.

Forster, E. M. (1927). *Aspects of the novel.* New York, NY: Harcourt Brace.

Giddens, A. (1991). *Modernity and self-identity: Self and society in the late modern age.* Palo Alto, CA: Stanford University Press.

Habermas, T., & Bluck, S. (2000). Getting a life: The emergence of the life story in adolescence. *Psychological Bulletin, 126,* 748–769.

Hall, D. T. (1996). Protean careers of the 21st century. *Academy of Management Executive, 10,* 8–16.

Hall, D. T., & Mirvis, P. H. (1995). The new career contract. *Journal of Vocational Behavior, 47,* 269–289.

Heckhausen, J., Wrosch, C., & Schulz, R. (2010). A motivational theory of life-span development. *Psychological Review, 117*(1), 32–60.

Heinz, W. R. (2002). Transition discontinuities and the biographical shaping of early work careers. *Journal of Vocational Behavior, 60,* 220–240. doi:10.1006/jvbe .2001.1865

Hogan, R. (1983). A socioanalytic theory of personality. In M. Page (Ed.), *Nebraska symposium on motivation 1982* (pp. 55–89). Lincoln: University of Nebraska Press.

Holland, J. L. (1997). *Making vocational choices: A theory of vocational personalities and work environments* (3rd ed.). Odessa, FL: Psychological Assessment Resources.

Josselson, R. (2000). Stability and change in early memories over 22 years: Themes, variations, and cadenzas. *Bulletin of the Menninger Clinic, 64,* 462–481.

Kalleberg, A. L. (2009). Precarious work, insecure workers: Employment relations in transition. *American Sociological Review, 74,* 1–22.

Kitson, H. D. (1942). Creating vocational interests. *Occupations, 20,* 567–571.

Krieshok, T. S., Black, M. D., & McKay, R. A. (2009). Career decision making: The limits of rationality and the abundance of non-conscious processes. *Journal of Vocational Behavior, 75,* 275–290. doi:10.1016/j.jvb.2009.04.006

Kuhn, T. S. (1996). *The structure of scientific revolutions* (3rd ed.). Chicago, IL: University of Chicago Press.

Lawrence-Lightfoot, S., & Davis, J. H. (1997). *The art and science of portraiture.* San Francisco, CA: Jossey-Bass.

Leontiev, A. N. (1983). The deed is the beginning of personality. In V. Davydov, V. Zinchenko, A. A. Leontiev, & A. Petrovskij (Eds.), *A. N. Leontiev. Izbrannie psihologicheskie proizvedija* [A. N. Leontiev. Selected psychological works] (Vol. 1, pp. 381–385). Moscow, Russia: Pedagogika.

Lofquist, L. H., & Dawis, R. V. (1991). *Essentials of person–environment correspondence counseling.* Minneapolis, MN: University of Minnesota Press.

Malrieu, P. (2003). *La question du sens dans les dires autobiographiques* [The issue of meaning in autobiographical narratives]. Toulouse, France: Erès.

Maslow, A. (1954). *Motivation and personality.* New York, NY: Harper.

McAdams, D. P. (1995). What do we know when we know a person? *Journal of Personality, 63,* 365–396.

McAdams, D. P., & Olson, B. D. (2010). Personality development: Continuity and change over the life course. *Annual Review of Psychology, 61,* 517–542. doi:10.1146/annurev.psych.093008.100507

Miller, G. A., Galanter, E., & Pribram, K. H. (1960). *Plans and the structure of behavior.* New York, NY: Holt.

Mischel, W., & Morf, C. C. (2003). The self as a psycho-social dynamic processing system: A meta-perspective on a century of the self in psychology. In M. R. Leary & J. P. Tangney (Eds.), *Handbook of self and identity* (pp. 15–46). New York, NY: Guilford Press.

Mullins, J. (2009). Career planning the second time around. *Occupational Outlook Quarterly, 5,* 12–15.

Neuman, Y., & Nave, O. (2009). Why the brain needs language in order to be self-conscious. *New Ideas in Psychology, 28,* 37–48.

Porfeli, E. J., & Savickas, M. L. (2012). The Career Adapt-Abilities Scale: Construction, reliability, and initial validity of the USA form., *Journal of Vocational Behavior, 80,* 748–753.

Rangel, U., & Keller, J. (2011). Essentialism goes social: Belief in social determinism as a component of psychological essentialism. *Journal of Personality & Social Psychology, 100,* 1056–1078. doi:10.1037/a0022401

Ricoeur, P. (1984). *Time and narrative.* Chicago, IL: University of Chicago Press.

Rosenberg, M. (1989). *Society and the adolescent self-image* (rev. ed.). Middletown, CT: Wesleyan University Press.

Savickas, M. L. (1989). Career-style assessment and counseling. In T. Sweeney (Ed.), *Adlerian counseling: A practical approach for a new decade* (3rd ed., pp. 289–320). Muncie, IN: Accelerated Development Press.

Savickas, M. L. (1996). A framework for linking career theory and practice. In M. L. Savickas & W. B. Walsh (Eds.), *Handbook of career counseling theory and practice.* Palo Alto, CA: Davies-Black.

Savickas, M. L. (1997). Adaptability: An integrative construct for life-span, life-space theory. *Career Development Quarterly, 45,* 247–259.

Savickas, M. L. (2006). *Career counseling* (Specific Treatments for Specific Populations Video Series). Washington, DC: American Psychological Association.

Savickas, M. L. (2009). *Career counseling over time* (Psychotherapy in Six Sessions Video Series). Washington, DC: American Psychological Association.

Savickas, M. L. (2011a). *Career counseling.* Washington, DC: American Psychological Association Press.

Savickas, M. L. (2011b). The self in vocational psychology: Object, subject, and project. In P. J. Hartung & L. M. Subich (Eds.), *Developing self in work and career: Concepts, cases, and contexts* (pp. 17–33). Washington, DC: American Psychological Association Press.

Savickas, M. L. (2012). Life design: A paradigm for career intervention in the 21st century. *Journal of Counseling and Development, 90,* 13–19.

Savickas, M. L., & Porfeli, E. J. (2012). Revision of the Career Maturity Inventory: The adaptability form. *Journal of Vocational Behavior, 80,* 661–673.

Savickas, M. L., Silling, S. M., & Schwartz, S. (1984). Time perspective in career maturity and decision making. *Journal of Vocational Behavior, 25,* 258–269.

Sedikides, C., & Anderson, C. A. (1994). Causal perceptions of inter-trait relations: The glue that holds person types together. *Personality and Social Psychology Bulletin, 20,* 294–302.

Super, D. E. (1951). Vocational adjustment: Implementing a self-concept. *Occupations, 30,* 88–92.

Super, D. E. (1957). *The psychology of careers.* New York, NY: Harper & Row.

Super, D. E. (1963). *Career development: Self-concept theory.* New York, NY: CEEB.

Super, D. E. (1983). Assessment in career guidance: Toward truly developmental counseling. *Personnel and Guidance Journal, 61,* 555–562.

Vygotsky, L. S. (1978). *Mind in society* (M. Cole, Trans.). Cambridge, MA: Harvard University Press.

Williamson, E. G., & Bordin, E. S. (1941). The evaluation of vocational and educational counseling: A critique of the methodology of experiments. *Educational and Psychological Measurement, 1,* 5–24.

THE ROLE OF DIVERSITY, INDIVIDUAL DIFFERENCES, AND SOCIAL FACTORS IN CAREER DEVELOPMENT, CHOICE, AND ADJUSTMENT

CHAPTER 7

Women, Men, and Work: The Long Road to Gender Equity

MARY J. HEPPNER

ORLDWIDE, THROUGHOUT HISTORY, one of the most salient predictors of virtually all aspects of one's work and career development is one's gender. In essence, being born male or female is a powerful predictor of a host of life factors, including whether one works inside or outside the home (or both), the type of jobs one perceives as appropriate, the type of jobs one will be hired to perform, how far one is likely to climb, the level and type of harassment one experiences, the amount of money one will receive, the amount of conflict or enrichment one gets from work and family life, the amount of job satisfaction one reports, and ultimately the quality of one's life (Walsh & Heppner, 2006).

Although recent decades have brought greater gender equity for some men and women, much work remains to be done in most countries around the world, including the United States. For example, a recent United Nations report concludes that (a) women have not achieved equity with men in *any* country; (b) of the world's 1.3 billion poor, nearly 70% are women; (c) between 75% and 80% of the world's 27 million refugees are women and children; (d) out of the world's 1 billion illiterate adults, two-thirds are women; (e) the majority of women earn an average of three-fourths of the pay of men doing the same work in both developing and developed countries; and (f) women are chronically underrepresented in STEM (science, technology, engineering, and math) careers in developed countries around the world (Hausmann, Tyson, & Zahidi, 2010).

Rather than viewing these as "women's problems," it is critical to appreciate the "fundamental transformation" that took place at the fourth Global

Women's Conference in Beijing, where participants saw "the need to shift the focus from *women* to the concept of *gender*, recognizing that the entire structure of society, and all relations between men and women within it, had to be re-evaluated. Only by such a fundamental restructuring of society and its institutions could women be fully empowered to take their rightful place as equal partners with men in all aspects of life.... [This thinking represents] a strong reaffirmation that women's rights are human rights and that gender equity is an issue of universal concern benefiting all" (Division for the Advancement of Women, 2000, p. 1). This position is consistent with that of the fields of counseling and counseling psychology, which have long stressed the mission of social justice (Arredondo & Perez, 2003). There is perhaps no clearer way to achieve social justice than through finding meaningful employment that allows both men and women to have "full and equal participation in a society that is mutually shaped to meet their needs. Social justice includes a vision of society in which the distribution of resources is equitable and all members are physically and psychologically safe and secure" (Bell, 1997, p. 3).

Improving gender equity in countries including the United States not only improves the condition of individual men's and women's lives but also is critical for the functioning of societies. In the UN's earlier programs that were designed for women in countries around the world, women were thought of as passive recipients of support and assistance. This view has changed dramatically, however, to recognize that the development of countries is not possible without the full participation of women. "As the working age population continues to shrink around the world, the mismatch between where talent is available and where it is needed, will inevitably worsen. Solving this conundrum is not easy and means considering untapped and underleveraged talent pools. Unfortunately, women remain chronically underrepresented in the workforce" (Hausmann et al., 2010, p. 10). Thus, to close the gender gap in all work-related areas is of benefit not only to the individual but also to the society as a whole.

It is with this philosophical backdrop that this chapter is written. In essence, the position taken here is that (a) issues of occupational stereotyping, work–family conflict or enrichment, comparable worth, glass ceiling/sticky floors, and disparities in STEM careers are *gender* issues; (b) the problems faced in the United States relevant to equity can be placed within a larger global context; and (c) by placing them in this context, they become issues of universal concern whose resolution benefits everyone. Vocational psychologists and career counselors are in a unique position to help solve these pressing gender-related problems that are literally affecting the health and well-being of countries and peoples around the world. In that sense, we have a very clear mission, to use the rigor of our research and the innovations of our practice to understand and intervene with issues of gender parity that at times seem local but, in fact, are often universal.

The chapter also recognizes that men continue to be victims of gender role stereotyping, and many perceive a highly restricted range of occupational alternatives due to their gender. There is clear evidence that there continues to be discrimination particularly against gay men, men of color, immigrant men, men living in poverty, and men making nontraditional career choices (Heppner & Heppner, 2001; O'Neil, 2008). Perhaps most profoundly, men die earlier than women in almost every country in the world, a fact attributed at least in part to their having more dangerous and stressful occupations (Brooks & Good, 2001).

Work can be a source of enrichment, joy, and meaning for people, but it can also be a source of stress and pain. Some of the stress and pain can be attributed to the differential treatment of men and women in societies around the world and how the social construction of gender causes disparities that can greatly impact the quality of work lives. Thus, it is the purpose of this chapter to review what we currently know about men, women, and work; to offer suggestions for helping clients to examine these issues within an ecological perspective; and to encourage career professionals to work to change systems that perpetuate inequality.

The chapter reviews the literature on three critical areas across the life span related to gender and work: (1) early development and the role of occupational stereotyping in shaping one's occupational choices; (2) gender-related issues in job choice and entry, such as entry into STEM careers, motherhood, gender-related career issues for men, stay-at-home parent roles for men, and men choosing nontraditional occupations; and (3) gender-related experiences once in the workforce, such as salary and gender segregation, gender-based harassment, comparable worth, gender and job satisfaction, and work–family conflict or enhancement. The chapter also provides an analysis of the gender validity of prominent foundational and modern career development theories. Finally, the chapter concludes with specific suggestions for career development practitioners working with men and women.

EARLY DEVELOPMENT AND THE ROLE OF OCCUPATIONAL STEREOTYPING

Gender roles are "socially and culturally defined prescriptions and beliefs about the behavior and emotions of men and women" (Anselmi & Law, 1998, p. 195) that form the basis of gender identity. These stereotypes are shared assumptions that societies have about occupations and are taught both in explicit and highly subtle and nuanced ways (Stangor & Shaller,

1996). Clear and consistent evidence indicates that this social and cultural construction of gender and its impact on the work that men and women eventually obtain starts very early in a child's life. For example, studies indicate that occupational stereotypes develop as early as the preschool years (ages 4–5) (Care, Deans, & Brown, 2007; Gottfredson, 2005), with children indicating stereotypic views of appropriate occupations for each gender, which can severely limit children's perceived range of gender-appropriate occupational alternatives.

Research on occupational stereotyping in adolescents and adults typically asks participants about their explicit beliefs about occupations. For example, participants may be given a list of occupations and asked which occupations require masculine or feminine traits. This type of methodology has been criticized as highly subject to socially desirable responding. For example, individuals who hold stereotypic views of occupations may not express them if they believe that responding in such a manner is either socially unacceptable or illegal (e.g., Civil Rights Act of 1964, Title VII). Researchers have therefore developed more sophisticated methodologies to assess implicit occupational stereotypes. This methodology measures participants' underlying automatic associations and the length of cognitive retrieval time when they are subjected to gender-typical and atypical stimuli. Findings indicate that individuals have implicit stereotypes of occupations that persist even when more explicitly expressed stereotypic views have lessened (White & White, 2006).

Children are frequently exposed to explicit sex role stereotyping of occupations, but a subtler, less conscious form of gender prejudice also has the power to affect the lives of men and women. Dovidio and his colleagues have found evidence of subtle forms of racism and how they may impact the livelihoods of African Americans (Dovidio & Gaertner, 2000). Such subtle manifestations of bias may also impact thoughts, feelings, and, ultimately, actions related to gender. Thus, even well-educated people who perceive themselves to be aware of gender role stereotypes may still respond unconsciously in a stereotypic manner. There is also some evidence that this implicit assessment of one's beliefs and attitudes may predict behavior better than explicit measures of occupational stereotypes (Greenwald & Nosek, 2001). Thus, as children learn occupational stereotypes early in life, these lessons may persist in the unconscious and affect one's perceptions and behaviors, even when contradictory information is provided by later life experiences. This type of internalized sexism and sex-stereotyped beliefs and behaviors affect both men and women and may influence, to a greater degree than realized, the occupations they assume and the mechanisms by which even well-meaning people collude with structures of gender oppression.

These culturally held stereotypes about gender have been shown to bias individuals' assessment of their competence at various career-related tasks, even when controlling for actual ability at doing that task (Correll, 2001). In essence, if a boy or girl comes to believe that he or she is less competent at a task because of gender, this biased perception has been shown to constrain early career-relevant choices. For example, research has found that girls are significantly more likely to report that they are not smart enough or good enough to attain their desired careers (O'Brien, Friedman, Tipton, & Linn, 2000). Furthermore, O'Brien and her colleagues found that over the 5 years of their study, young women chose less prestigious and more traditional careers than those to which they had aspired as high school seniors. In addition, they tended to choose careers that underutilized their abilities (O'Brien et al., 2000).

This gender-based stereotyping of careers is an ongoing phenomenon. As new technologies create new occupations, it is essential to understand how cultural beliefs about the gender appropriateness of occupations emerge and are fostered in societies. For example, a consistent gender gap has been observed both in the use of technology by the young and in the pursuit of technology-related occupations, with boys having a more positive attitude toward computers and more opportunity for mastery of them. This technology gender gap is found in childhood and continues to be reflected in occupational selection later in life (Butler, 2000). Thus, only by understanding the mechanisms of sex role stereotyping can gender inequities start to be addressed so that women and men can perceive themselves as equally competent in the full range of occupations that exist and are being developed.

GENDER-RELATED ISSUES IN JOB CHOICE AND ENTRY

It is important to acknowledge the unspoken privilege of choice. As Blustein (2006, 2011) and Richardson (1993) have poignantly described, the vast majority of women and men in the world have limited volition or choice in what they do to support themselves and their families. Although the fundamental tenets of career counseling as it has developed in the United States emphasizes freedom of choice (Gysbers, Heppner, & Johnston, 2009), the reality is that many people, even within developed countries, do not make career choices based on interest, values, or abilities. The fact that developed countries have more people with the assumed privilege of choice often masks the fact that even in these countries many people do not freely choose a career. Even for people with the privilege of choice, the range of appropriate alternatives may be limited by gender, race, class, ability status, sexual orientation, and a host of other factors (Gottfredson, 2005). A prime example of this is in the long-term disparities between women and men choosing to go into STEM careers.

STEM CAREERS: A GENDER ISSUE

In all developed and developing countries, there is a great need for more individuals who are trained in STEM occupational fields because these fields are critically important to the development of countries and the well-being of citizens around the world. Fully utilizing human resources in this area is seen as a way to improve many aspects of lives in the world community. STEM careers are disproportionally inhabited by males, leading researchers in countries around the globe to ask why we are losing talented women to other fields. Throughout the decades, many hypotheses have been proposed to answer this question, including biological differences, broad contextual influences, and differences in motivation, interests, or attitudes. At the heart of STEM career fields is mathematics, which has been labeled the "critical filter" for women's career development (Betz, 1994, 2006). Researchers have been conducting increasingly sophisticated investigations over the last two decades to understand and remediate the underrepresentation of women in STEM fields. From their work, we are getting a more precise picture of the problem and some possible solutions.

One important part of the problem involves gender stereotypes that perpetuate the myth that girls are not as good at math as boys. Despite the scientific evidence that now clearly disputes this stereotype, it still exists and is at times reinforced by parents, teachers, peers, and the media. The data indicate that math performance for girls and women has steadily increased over the past two decades, leading Boaler and Irving (2007) to conclude: "As we survey the landscape of gender and mathematics relationships in various countries around the world ... in many countries differences in boys and girls mathematics achievement that used to prevail have been eradicated" (p. 287). Various reasons are posited for this equality, such as the possibility that mathematics classrooms are becoming more girl-friendly. However, the continued prevalence of stereotypes concerning females' math inferiority is cause for much concern, given mounting evidence that negative "stereotype threat" can impair the actual performance of girls and women on math-related tasks (Spencer, Steele, & Quinn, 1999).

A recent study by Correll (2001) depicts the mechanisms by which these stereotypes can impact competency beliefs and career choice. In her analyses of a large data set, she found that, even when achieving comparable math grades and test scores, males assessed their own mathematical competence more highly than did females. Furthermore, perceptions of competence in mathematics were found to relate positively to the odds of continuing on a path leading to a quantitative career. Thus, even though males' competency ratings were not based on any indication of greater ability, their higher perceptions of competence led them to pursue the kinds of activities that would allow them to enter a math-related field. Correll noted that "boys do not pursue mathematical activities at a higher rate than girls do because they are better at mathematics. They do so, at least partially, because they *think* they are better" (p. 1724). Thus biased *gender beliefs* regarding self-perceived competence may be one critical mechanism in the process of STEM gender disparity.

Correll (2001) also found that mathematics grades had a significantly more positive effect on girls' than on boys' confidence levels. This may suggest that positive performance experiences are especially important in counteracting strong societal messages about the gender appropriateness of different careers. Identifying mechanisms such as biased gender beliefs is important not only to the STEM fields but also potentially to other fields. For example, if boys feel they are less competent at nurturing or caregiving, they may be less likely to go into nursing or other human service fields where there are critical shortages.

One of the reasons previously given for women's lack of participation in STEM fields is that they have not chosen to pursue advanced training that would qualify them for these positions. However, these figures have changed dramatically over the last decade. For example, by 2001 women were earning almost half (48%) of the bachelor's degrees in mathematics (National Science Foundation, 2007) and also were going on to earn almost a third (29%) of the doctorates (Hill & Johnson, 2004). But even with these advances, women still represent less than one-fourth of the STEM labor force (Fassinger & Asay, 2006).

In a recent study, Else-Quest, Hyde, and Lynn (2010) analyzed data on 493,495 students across 69 counties and found very small gender-related mean differences in math achievement but considerable variability in effect sizes by country. These country differences were found to be predicted by specific domains of gender equity reflecting women's status and welfare. The most powerful predictors were gender equity in school enrollment, women's share of research jobs, and women's parliamentary representation. The authors concluded that "girls will perform at the same level as their male classmates when they are encouraged to succeed, are given the necessary educational tools, and have visible female role models excelling in mathematics" (p. 125). These analyses are a powerful example of how improving gender equity in societies can result in greater participation in critical occupations needed for the development and health of the whole society.

In their development of an evidence-based causal model to explain women's underrepresentation in STEM careers, Ceci, Williams, and Barnett (2009) examined over 400 cross-disciplinary studies, including approximately 20 meta-analyses. They found that math-talented women disproportionately choose nonmath fields and are more likely to leave math-intensive fields. In addition, these math-talented women were more likely to have high verbal competence, which allows for a wider array of attractive occupational choices. Ceci and colleagues also found that more men than women score in the extreme range on gatekeeper tests like the SAT Mathematics or the GRE Quantitative Reasoning test. They concluded from the evidence that these results are based on sociocultural rather than biological factors. This study emphasizes that math-talented women tend to be multitalented and have many career options. Many researchers have pointed to the male environment in STEM fields and the image of the lonely scientist as a factor in women choosing more attractive non-STEM alternatives (Eccles, 2007).

Social cognitive career theory (SCCT; Lent, Brown, & Hackett, 1994; see Chapter 5, this volume) predicts that to develop interest in a particular field, individuals need to have both self-efficacy in their ability to perform the tasks required in that field and positive outcome expectancies about what it would be like to be in that career field. The evidence suggests that women's STEM-related self-efficacy beliefs tend to be lower than men's when ability is held constant, and their STEM-related outcome expectancies are also less positive (Ceci et al., 2009). Although many programs seem to be in place to help develop young women's self-efficacy beliefs regarding their ability to pursue STEM careers (see National Science Foundation, Advance Grants, http://www.nsf.gov), fewer programs seem to be aimed at creating a more woman-friendly work environment, which may lead to more positive outcome expectancies. As Fassinger and Asay (2006) pointed out, much of this work will require systemic change that would benefit all workers, including "developing educational and workplace policies that affirm and support all workers (e.g., equitably distributed benefits, antidiscrimination statements); instituting educational and workplace practices that help to counter discriminatory attitudes (e.g., training in diversity, transparent performance review and reward systems); implementing social policies and laws that support families in all diverse forms (e.g., accessible child care, medical and legal benefits available to all families); and, finally, transforming gender socialization practices so that all individuals have the freedom and support to actualize their best selves" (pp. 450–451).

STEM careers offer perhaps the best example of the damaging impact on societies when mathematics-talented women—who could be making such a difference in the lives of others through their involvement in these critically important occupational sectors—do not enter them. The increasingly sophisticated studies being done in this area offer cross-national, longitudinal, and large-scale representative samples with rigorous designs. They provide much new insight into the problem of lack of gender equity in STEM fields. The evidence suggests that much of the discrepancy between men's and women's entry into STEM fields is associated with (a) social and cultural factors relating to societal messages about appropriate careers for men and women and (b) work environments that are not perceived as attractive to multitalented women. In addition, Lubinski and Benbow's (2006) large-scale longitudinal research on men and women who pursue math and science careers suggests that differences in values (e.g., social/altruistic in women) account for some of the variance in why highly math-talented women (in the top 1% of the distribution of math ability) choose to enter medicine, law, and the social sciences rather than STEM fields. Learning more about the mechanisms underlying these choices can be helpful not only to the STEM fields but also to other fields where men and women enter at different rates.

Gender-Related Career Issues for Men

Much has been written about the societal importance of having men in helping professions such as nursing (which is facing critical shortages) and elementary school teaching (where they are needed as role models) and in stay-at-home parent roles. But if men perceive themselves as less competent at nurturing or caregiving in the same way that women rate themselves as less able at mathematics, similar imbalances may occur in these occupational roles. What makes this imbalance even more likely is the lower wages that accompany female-dominated professions, including the helping professions.

Stay-at-Home Parent Roles for Men

Rochlen, McKelley, Suizzo, and Scaringi (2008) studied a sample of 213 stay-at-home fathers. They found that these men had high levels of relationship and life satisfaction, strong social support, high parenting self-efficacy, and low conformity to traditional male norms. Men who had lower adherence to restrictive male gender norms seemed to be able to be more secure with their identity and able to face the negative views some may still hold regarding their choice. Specifically, parental self-efficacy was a significant predictor of psychological well-being and life satisfaction. In essence, men who were more confident in their parenting reported higher levels of life satisfaction and less psychological distress.

MEN CHOOSING NONTRADITIONAL OCCUPATIONS

Although the scholarly literature base on women going into nontraditional careers is far more extensive than that for men, there are several key studies on men and traditionality of career choice that offer information helpful to career practitioners. Generally, these studies have indicated that men who choose nontraditional career fields tend to have more liberal social attitudes, higher degree aspirations, and higher socioeconomic status than do men who choose more gender-typical career fields (Lease, 2003). In addition, Jome and Tokar (1998) found that men who chose nontraditional careers tend to endorse less antifemininity and toughness norms and have less concern with restricting their emotion and expressing affection toward other men. These men also reported less homophobia. In a follow-up study, Tokar and Jome (1998) found that men's endorsement of masculine gender roles predicted their vocational interests, and those interests, in turn, predicted their career choice traditionality. Thus, it appears that the relationships between gender role constructs and traditional or nontraditional choices may be more complex than earlier thought and may influence interest formation, which, in turn, may predict career choice.

The studies that examine traditional and nontraditional career choices for men have been conducted primarily on White heterosexual men. This reflects the fact that the career development of people of color has, until recently, been understudied by researchers (see Fouad & Kantamneni, Chapter 8, this volume). An exception is a study by Flores, Navarro, Smith, and Ploszaj (2006), who examined the career choice goals of Mexican American adolescent men with an extended version of the SCCT career choice model. Findings from this investigation indicated that Mexican American adolescent men's nontraditional career self-efficacy was predicted by parental support and their acculturation level. They also found that fathers' career nontraditionality predicted their sons' nontraditional career self-efficacy. This kind of theory-based research on the nontraditional choices of diverse men and women is critical to the understanding of gender equity in career choice.

MOTHERHOOD

Perhaps the most profound event affecting women's career development is that of motherhood—specifically, when and if one becomes a mother, how many children she has, her age at first and subsequent births, and how becoming a mother impacts her ability to work outside the home. Although many women around the world work full-time at child rearing, little scholarly research has been conducted on this group of women. As Schultheiss (2009) poignantly describes, many women define motherhood as a career, but our U.S. Census data, our career research and theories, and our common definitions of career do not include this critical job. Moreover, our reward structures favor paid employment outside the home. "This leaves many women who mother or care for others with a disturbing choice: *to mother or to matter*—in the workplace, in society, and in the family where women are often burdened and disregarded in their care giving roles" (Schultheiss, 2009, p. 26). Although the women's movement of the 1960s brought expanded occupational options for women, these options tended to require that women conform to male-dominated hierarchies rather than validating women's unique experiences. As Gysbers and colleagues (2009) discuss, there is a critical need for vocational psychologists and career counselors to work for structural and policy changes that recognize the full range of women's options.

In the United States, women are giving birth at later ages, with births to mothers over the age of 35 increasing by 64% over the time frame 1990 to 2008. This delay in mothering is related to greater educational attainment prior to motherhood. The birthrate among unmarried women is also increasing, particularly in African American and Latina women. The U.S. fertility rate is higher than most other developed nations (e.g., Canada, Asia, most of Europe), though the United States has a poorer parental leave policy than most of these nations (Pew Research Center, 2010). In the United States, mothers continue to have high rates of labor market participation, with approximately 71% working outside the home. Mothers with older children (6–17) are more likely to participate than women with younger children. Unmarried mothers (76%) have higher participation rates than married mothers (69%) (Bureau of Labor Statistics, 2009).

There is a wage gap in the United States and other countries among working mothers versus childfree women. According to a study by the Organisation for Economic Co-operation and Development (OECD, 2002), the monthly earnings of childfree women were higher than that of mothers by an average of 5%. The authors of this report emphasize the variety of possible explanations for this disparity. For example, women with families might prefer jobs that do not require overtime or high work intensity, or there may be discrimination on the part of employers who view women with children as less committed to their work. Budig and England (2001) used the National Longitudinal Survey of Youth to determine that U.S. mothers received a penalty of about 7% of pay per child. About a third of the penalty was explained by years of past experience and seniority. However, the researchers called for further analysis of what accounts for the other two-thirds of penalty not accounted for by experience and seniority. Miller (2010) found for women who had a college degree or a managerial occupation, delaying childbirth improved their career outcomes.

The wage gap related to having children appears to exist for women in other developed countries, such as Austria, Belgium, Germany, Ireland, the United Kingdom, and the Netherlands, as well as the United States. However, "the challenges of meeting work and family obligations are particularly problematic in the United States" (Waldfogel & McLanahan, 2011, p. 5). Specifically, in a study of the world's most competitive economies, the United States was found to be one of the few countries that does not guarantee such benefits as paid maternity and paternity leave or paid leave to care for children who are ill (Earle, Mokomane, & Heymann, 2011). The researchers in this study examined the 20 countries that have been the most competitive over the past 8 to 10 years and added China and India to this list as fast-rising competitors. All of these countries except the United States guaranteed some form of paid leave for new mothers, and the United States was one of two countries to not guarantee paid leave for fathers. Change in such policies is necessary for parents to better balance family and work.

GENDER-RELATED EXPERIENCES IN THE WORKFORCE

SALARY, GENDER SEGREGATION, AND COMPARABLE WORTH

The most recent statistics from the U.S Department of Labor (2010) indicate that women who worked full-time had median earnings that were 80% of those earned by men. These percentages vary by race, with White women having the most disparity compared with same-race men (79%), followed, in order, by Asian American women (82%), Latina women (90%), and African American women (94%). Wages vary by occupational group, and women are employed in predominantly gender-traditional positions that pay considerably less than do gender-nontraditional positions. For example, women currently are over 97% of preschool and elementary school teachers, 96% of dental hygienists, 95% of childcare workers, 92% of typists and word processors, 90% of hairdressers, 91% of receptionists, and 91% of teaching assistants. Conversely, women are less than 2% of carpenters and electricians, 3% of construction workers, 7% of electrical engineers, and 10% of computer engineers.

In nursing, which has made a concerted effort to fill a critical need for more nurses by recruiting men to the profession, men still account for only 8% of registered nurses and 9% of licensed practical nurses. In teaching, where there is a critical need for male role models (especially for young boys in schools, with many households headed by single mothers), men account for 2% of preschool and kindergarten teachers and 8% of elementary and middle school teachers. In addition to the common good that is served by bringing talented men and women to nontraditional fields, for women there is the added advantage that nontraditional fields pay 150% of what traditional fields pay for occupations requiring a similar educational background (U.S. Department of Labor, Bureau of Labor Statistics, 2010). Thus despite some progress in the last few decades regarding both salary disparities and occupational segregation, much remains to be done to achieve occupational integration and parity.

Comparable worth refers to the idea that when traditionally female occupations are judged comparable to jobs filled mostly by men, wages for both positions should be the same. Comparable worth is an effort to examine different job titles and to pay for them based on their inherent value to the employer, regardless of the gender composition of the occupation. Gender-neutral job evaluations have been created to assess the economic value of different jobs. For example, secretarial and janitorial jobs are compared on dimensions such as the (1) education or training required to perform the job, (2) the severity or comfort of the working conditions, and (3) the responsibility involved or the effort required to perform competently in the position. These gender-neutral job evaluations differentiate legitimate wage differences from those that are solely a function of the sex of the jobholder.

One area where there appears to be particularly high wage disparity is care work. England, Budwig, and Folbre (2002) studied occupations that involve caring for others, such as counseling, health professions, teaching, and supervising children. Using panel data from the National Longitudinal Survey of Youth, they found that these occupations paid less than other positions with similar education and employment criteria. As noted earlier, these types of positions are female dominated; thus, this financial devaluing of the caring occupations is felt disproportionately by women.

GENDER-BASED HARASSMENT

Sexual harassment has been identified as "one of the most damaging and ubiquitous barriers to career success and satisfaction of women" (Willness, Steel, & Lee, 2007, p. 127). There are two primary forms of sexual harassment. Quid pro quo harassment is when job-related decisions are based on the worker's acceptance or rejection of unwelcome sexual behavior, such as refusing to go out on a date. The other form is creating a hostile work environment, which is an atmosphere where sexual behavior is offensive, hostile, or intimidating, adversely affecting the employee's ability to do his or her job. An example would be environments where sexist comments and jokes are communicated, even though the worker has indicated these are unwelcome and unwanted.

In their meta-analysis of 41 studies of sexual harassment, Willness and colleagues (2007) found that sexual harassment and its consequences are evident at all socioeconomic and educational levels, across cultures and countries, and in all age groups and professions. Although sexual harassment occurs in both genders, overwhelmingly women are the victims. For example, in 2010 the U.S. Equal Employment Opportunity Commission (EEOC) reported that 84% of the complaints were from women. Studies indicate that sexual harassment occurs in countries around the world, but few countries have specific legislation protecting people from sexual harassment.

Few studies have been conducted on the experiences of men who are sexually harassed in the workplace. Generally, men felt a great deal more in control in the harassment situation and felt they could stop the harassment if needed to a much greater extent than women tend to report. Some men responded that they did not know sexual harassment could happen to men. Some men identified a unique sexual harassment experience that involved the negative stereotyping of men and punishment for deviating from traditional gender roles (Berdahl, Magley, & Walkdo, 1996).

Studies have indicated that sexual harassment leads to a wide range of psychological consequences, such as PTSD, depression, anger, fear, humiliation, and anxiety (Collinsworth, Fitzgerald, & Drasgow, 2009; Willness et al., 2007). The attribution of blame has been found to be the leading factor in predicting level of distress; the more sexual harassment survivors blame themselves, the more distress is felt (Collinsworth et al., 2009). For women of color, there appears to be an additive and interactive effect of sexual harassment and racial harassment. In a study of 91 African American women who had filed lawsuits, researchers found that sexual harassment was associated with psychological withdrawal from work and poorer life satisfaction. Racial harassment accounted for additional variance (above and beyond sexual harassment) in job stress, dissatisfaction with supervisors and coworkers, and PTSD symptoms (Buchanan & Fitzgerald, 2008).

In sum, the impact and psychological consequences of sexual harassment can be quite severe, both at the time of the offense and on a long-term basis. Career counselors and vocational psychologists need to be able to recognize and address harassment when it is relevant to clients' presenting issues or goals in counseling. There are also unique issues of harassment that affect the GLBTQ community in the workplace (see Prince, Chapter 10, this volume).

GENDER AND JOB SATISFACTION

One of the great paradoxes of the career literature over the last few decades is that even though women are paid less for the same work, suffer sexual harassment and discrimination at higher levels than men, and work in positions that are generally considered less attractive, they tend to report greater job satisfaction than men in studies of U.S., Canadian, and European workers (Clark, 1997; Donohue & Heywood, 2004; Sloane & Williams,

2000; Sousa-Poza & Sousa-Poza, 2000). Some have contended that this phenomenon is due to the fact that women have lower expectations regarding what they will gain from work and, thus, are more satisfied with less (Clark, 1997). Others contend that it is the whole bundle of job-related benefits, including coworkers, effort required, job flexibility, fringe benefits, overall working conditions, and intrinsic benefits, that together are appealing enough to overcome the negative aspects of lower salaries (Bender, Donahue, & Heywood, 2005). (See Lent & Brown, Chapter 22, this volume, for added discussion of work satisfaction.)

WORK AND FAMILY: DO THEY CONFLICT WITH OR ENHANCE ONE ANOTHER?

With the majority of women and men now in the workforce, there has been increasing attention to how work and family conflict with or enhance each other. The original focus for this research was on role conflict. A quarter century ago, Greenhaus and Beutell (1985) contributed a seminal paper on how these two separate spheres of life compete for often scarce resources of time and energy. More recently, researchers have begun to study the ways in which work and family can also enrich, complement, or facilitate one another (Barnett & Hyde, 2001; Gareis, Barnett, Ertel, & Berkman, 2009). In essence, aspects of the work role can improve the quality of life in the family role and vice versa. Carlson, Kacmar, Wayne, and Grzywacz (2006) defined work–family enrichment as occurring when resources and experiences gained from one role improve role performance and quality of life in the other role.

A closely related construct is that of family–work balance, which Green-haus, Collins, and Shaw (2009) defined as "the extent to which an individual is equally engaged in—and equally satisfied with—his or her work role and family role" (p. 513). They assessed three work–family balance concepts: time balance, involvement balance, and satisfaction balance. In essence, they found that those who spent more time on family roles than work roles experienced a higher quality of life. How couples balance their work and family roles and how these roles can enrich each other is an important area for future research that could contribute to gender equity and a better quality of life for both women and men.

Social class and level of wages earned may play a powerful role in how work–family conflict or balance is experienced. For example, Richman (2006) found that the constellation of lower wages, more part-time work, lack of benefits, and inflexible work schedules was associated with poorer work–life balance among low-income families and single parents. Richman also found that employers generally had little sympathy for their low-wage earners and did not consider providing a more flexible workplace. Thus, the multiple roles of men and women, the social class group they are from, and their family situation all impact how work and family life are experienced.

GENDER VALIDITY OF CAREER THEORIES

Theory is a critical guide for practice, and yet our traditional career theories have come under increasing criticism for being ethnocentric; blind to culture, gender, and class; and insensitive to changes in the modern occupational world. It can be argued that many of these theories were developed and validated when both gender roles and work roles were much different than they are today. Thus, just as Young, Marshall, and Valach (2007) have argued for culture-specific theory, there may very well be a need for gender-specific theory that also accounts for the vast sociocultural differences of women and men around the world. Perhaps most fundamentally, older theories that focus on person and environment (P-E) fit tend to ignore the dramatically different socialization and lived experience of men and women, which impact barriers and supports, the structure of opportunity, and, ultimately, the choices that men and women feel they have in the occupational world. By not explicitly recognizing and including gender in the building of theory, the explanatory nature of the theory is diminished.

As noted earlier, in much of the world, men and women have relatively little choice in their occupations—they work at whatever job they can get to support themselves and their families. Thus, many individuals in the United States and around the world are taking jobs without the luxury of considering P-E fit. In addition, it can be argued that many career development theories tend to focus more on understanding the lives of middle- and upper-class individuals rather than those with less volition in their vocational lives. As one works with clients across class lines, it is critical to understand the relevance of theories to each individual and her or his circumstances. It is, therefore, crucial that the next generation of researchers and practitioners (including those reading this book) think critically about the adequacy of our theories for girls and boys and men and women around the world. This section considers the gender-related validity of the major theories presented in this text.

MINNESOTA THEORY OF WORK ADJUSTMENT (TWA)

The Minnesota theory of work adjustment (TWA) can be generally helpful to practitioners working with clients who need help with issues of career adjustment, especially performance and satisfaction (see Swanson & Schneider, Chapter 2, this volume). TWA emphasizes that persons exist and behave in an environment. This focus on the context is a critically important element of TWA. In essence, it is the reinforcers of a given work environment—particularly the correspondence between the reinforcers of the environment and what the individual man or woman values—that lead to satisfaction and, ultimately, to longevity in a job, according to TWA.

As we have seen from our review, many women face less than reinforcing circumstances in their work environment, including such issues as sexual harassment, glass ceilings and sticky floors, and salary discrepancies. Non-traditional men, men of color, gay men, and men of lower social classes also experience many issues with work environments that do not explicitly involve their values. TWA can help us help clients of both sexes to clarify the correspondence of their values to the reinforcers in the work environment, their satisfactoriness to their employers, and their likely tenure in the environment. Lyons and colleagues have suggested that the relation of need-reinforcer correspondence to job satisfaction is substantial for African American workers (Lyons & O'Brien, 2006) and LGB individuals (Lyons, Brenner, & Fassinger, 2005). Further, their study of African American workers found that the positive relation of need-reinforcer correspondence and job satisfaction was stronger than the negative relation of racial climate and job satisfaction (Lyons & O'Brien, 2006). Despite these findings, the theory does not explicitly account for factors apart from values and skills that may affect job tenure (e.g., economic downsizing); neither does it consider gender-related barriers and discrimination experiences that can affect work satisfaction and adjustment.

HOLLAND'S THEORY OF VOCATIONAL PERSONALITIES AND WORK ENVIRONMENTS

Holland's theory (see Nauta, Chapter 3, this volume) continues to provide a simple and elegant language for understanding self and career. However, it is critical for practitioners to be aware that raw score inventories, such as the Self-Directed Search (see Hansen, Chapter 14, this volume), may inadvertently encourage gender-stereotypic choices. For example, if a woman has been most able to work in clerical jobs because of the structure of occupational opportunity, she is likely to score high on the conventional activities because that is what she knows. Conventional activities typically are still primarily female dominated and lower paid. As indicated earlier, 92% of typists and word processors are women. Thus, career practitioners need to use care when they interpret this information to clients, help them understand the potential reasons for their Holland code results, and encourage consideration of options that will help them gain skills in areas that may be more reflective of what they can do rather than what they have previously done. Interest inventories that provide gender-based norms can also be used to encourage consideration of nonstereotypic options.

Another critical point from a gender perspective is that women's career development tends (more than men's) to be less directed by sheer passion or interest for an occupation (Spokane & Cruza-Guet, 2005) and to be more constrained by barriers within the occupational structure. Thus, when using Holland theory with girls and women, it is important to look beyond interests alone and to consider the host of other variables that may be influencing occupational preferences (e.g., ability to work in a field that allows greater flexibility for child rearing).

GOTTFREDSON'S THEORY OF CIRCUMSCRIPTION AND COMPROMISE

The theory of circumscription and compromise (Gottfredson, 2005) emphasizes conditions that may constrain career choices, such as the perceived sex appropriateness, context, power differentials, and prestige associated with various choice options. The theory proposes that, from an early age, boys and girls tend to view careers primarily in terms of femininity-masculinity and prestige level. Thus, the self-defined social spaces within the cognitive map of occupations become highly restricted. This theoretical framework can be very helpful in working with boys and girls on career choice issues. Helping young people understand how their choices may have been circumscribed and compromised is an important step in helping them make more authentic choices. Using this information to help young people reconsider and explore occupational options that they have earlier ruled out may also be a valuable activity, especially in cases where they may be constraining their choices to gender-stereotypic options.

SUPER'S DEVELOPMENTAL THEORY AND CAREER CONSTRUCTION THEORY

Super's original theory (Hartung, Chapter 4, this volume) has been modified and expanded in critical ways over a number of decades. Savickas's career construction theory (Chapter 6, this volume) has evolved from Super's developmental theory; thus, both theories are reviewed together in this section. Super's theory is particularly important from a gender perspective in that it recognizes that career development involves more than a choice of occupation and instead a fundamental understanding of how work interacts with different life roles. Thus, issues of motherhood or child-rearing roles can be integrated and understood within this theory. Super's theory has also been influential in helping career counselors and vocational psychologists understand that career development is not a one-time event but rather a process that plays out over time.

Savickas's theory development underscores that our identities are shaped by our social contexts, including culture, gender, and social class. His theory focuses on how one develops one's own life narrative and how that narrative is shaped by the social context. Thus, this theory can be used to help focus the client on the subjective aspects of the career development process. As with other postmodern approaches, career constructivist theory maintains that there is no fixed truth and that individuals construct their own truths and their own realities (Niles & Harris-Bowlsbey, 2005). This places individuals in the position of being active agents in creating their own life stories. How gender helps to shape the life narrative for both men and women is a topic that can aid the field to understand the subjective and culture-bound nature of career development and, more broadly, the role of work in people's lives.

Social Cognitive Career Theory

Perhaps no theory has helped the field of vocational psychology and career counseling understand the vocational development of girls and women as much as social cognitive career theory (SCCT; see Lent, Chapter 5, this volume). SCCT explicitly incorporates gender as a person input and also attends to "background contextual affordances" that affect individuals' learning experiences. These experiences help to shape self-efficacy and outcome expectations, which, in turn, influence interests and goals. This theory has been helpful in guiding research as well as practice. For example, counselors can use the theory to explore how previous learning has affected the client's self-efficacy, outcome expectations, and interests. SCCT can also be used to focus on environmental barriers and supports that can affect women's and men's ability to pursue their preferred choices. Like Gottfredson's theory, SCCT can also be used to help people reexplore occupational options that they might have earlier ruled out on the basis of inaccurate self-efficacy beliefs or outcome expectations. As mentioned earlier, SCCT has been used as the theoretical base for a great deal of research on STEM career fields (e.g., Fouad & Smith, 1996; Lent, Lopez, Lopez, & Sheu, 2008). A portion of this research has specifically examined factors that can affect women's pursuit of STEM careers.

IMPLICATIONS FOR COUNSELORS

It may be concluded that many of our career theories are useful in aiding men and women to find and prosper in satisfying work as long as counselors using these theories incorporate an exploration of gender-related barriers that prevent many people from achieving full labor force participation and work satisfaction. It is also important, as pointed out by Gottfredson's theory of circumscription and compromise and SCCT, to help clients identify and explore occupational options that they may have ruled out on the basis of restricted sex role views, unrealistically low self-efficacy beliefs, or inaccurate outcome expectations. Finally, as shown by research on SCCT and by Brown and Ryan Krane (2000), it is critical to help clients build supports that can facilitate their ability to enter and prosper in satisfying occupations.

However, it also appears clear from the material presented in this chapter that, although some areas of the workplace have experienced greater gender equity, we have a very long way to go. Practitioners can play a key role in promoting discussion of gender equity issues within career counseling. Because many young people hold the belief that gender inequity was resolved in the last century, they are often ill prepared for the realities of today's workplace. Thus, it seems critical to promote discussions of issues such as discrimination against men and women in nontraditional careers, occupational segregation, salary differentials, and the role of implicit gender role socialization in the continuing choices of men and women.

Examining the Implicit and Explicit Biases Shaping Our Work

The first and most important task may be to examine our own biases and ingrained messages about gender and work. The investigations that have examined bias with implicit methodologies make it clear that even very well-educated counselors can still carry implicit messages about men and women that may affect their behavior. It may be difficult to accept that being raised in a society with occupational stereotyping and differential perceptions of competence in men and women can prime us unconsciously to think and act in certain ways. Thus, it takes our constant vigilance to observe and acknowledge how and in what form these unconscious biases present themselves in our work with men and women in our career counseling practices. It is probably the most basic piece of advice: that counselors must know themselves, their own prejudices and biases, the way they hold and use power, and the way they are controlled by others. Counselors must be aware of how racism, sexism, heterosexism, and all the other isms affect their attitudes and behaviors. This deep and sometimes painful learning and reflection is critical to being able to empower others to look at the impact of these forces in their lives.

Empowering Men and Women to Pursue Gender Equity

In working with individual clients for the goal of gender equality, perhaps the most important aspect of the work is empowerment. I use McWhirter and colleagues' definition of empowerment: *The process by which people, organizations or groups who are powerless or marginalized (a) become aware of the power dynamics at work in their life contexts, (b) develop the skills and capacity for gaining some reasonable control over their lives, (c) which they exercise, (d) without infringing on the rights of others, and (e) which coincides with actively supporting the empowerment of others in their community* (Chronister, McWhirter, & Forrest, 2006, p. 170). The model that McWhirter developed in 1994 and refined with her colleagues can be used to help empower marginalized peoples to work for change within their own lives and communities. This "critical feminist" approach can, moreover, be used with diverse people—especially women and men of color, immigrants, lesbians and gay men, people living in poverty, and people with disabilities—and is consistent with the social justice goals of the career counseling profession.

McWhirter's model includes five central tenets, the five C's of collaboration, competence, context, critical consciousness, and community. Collaboration emphasizes that the counselor and client work together to establish the goals of counseling, the tasks that will help to achieve those goals, and the relationship or bond between them. Competence emphasizes the importance of recognizing and using clients' skills and helping them develop new skills. The tenet of competence is rooted in the idea that every client comes with strengths and that we should emphasize these rather than looking for pathology and weakness. Context acknowledges that all vocational behavior is an act in context and as such is intertwined with one's ecological system. Critical consciousness involves the dual processes of power analysis (identifying how power is manifest in a person's life context) and critical self-reflection (generating awareness of how people can transform power dynamics). McWhirter (1994) also emphasizes the importance of counselors developing their own critical consciousness. She suggests this can be done through studying the multicultural literature, having cross-cultural experiences, talking with people from different communities, and engaging in intense self-reflection. Finally, community entails helping people find others with the goal of receiving and providing support.

GENDER MAINSTREAMING: A USEFUL LENS FOR CAREER COUNSELORS

The concept of gender mainstreaming was endorsed by the United Nations (United Nations Office of the Special Adviser on Gender Issues and Advancement of Women, 2002) as a strategy for implementing the goal of gender parity in its programs and services around the world. *Gender mainstreaming* is defined as "planned action, including legislation, policies or programs, in all areas and at all levels. It is a strategy for making women's as well as men's concerns and experiences an integral dimension of the design, implementation, monitoring and evaluation of policies and programs in all political, economic and societal spheres so that women and men benefit equally and inequality is not perpetuated. The ultimate goal is to achieve gender equality" (p. 1).

Although the scope of the work is different, it may be highly useful for career counselors to use this lens of gender mainstreaming to examine all aspects of the work we do, the theories we use, the policies of our agencies, the training of counselors who work in our settings, the resources we use, and the work of our national associations—all with the ultimate goal of providing counseling and other services that promote gender equity.

WORKING FOR BROADER SYSTEMIC CHANGE

Although many of these suggestions have been at the individual level because that is the level at which most career counselors work, it is critical to understand that the systemic changes needed to bring about gender equality go well beyond what can happen with an individual client. However, career development professionals can be part of systemic change through our communities, political structures, lobbying of policy makers, communications with media, and schools and workplaces. Career professionals possess specialized expertise concerning the vocationally related systems-level changes needed to bring about gender equality. In essence, career professionals can serve as advocates of social and policy change that can have sweeping effects far beyond their work with individual clients.

CONCLUSIONS AND PRACTICE IMPLICATIONS

How the role of gender differentially impacts the vocational lives of women and men around the world has been the focus of this chapter. It is critical that career counselors and vocational psychologists not attempt to conduct research, develop theory, or create practice interventions that are gender-blind. The dramatic statistics presented at the beginning of this chapter reflect the disparities in educational and career-related issues in the lives of men and women. The challenge becomes how we can both understand and effectively intervene in the lives of men and women to aid them in seeking the best life quality they can achieve. Our theories can serve as important guides in this process, but as I argue in this chapter, career counselors need to think critically about the gender validity of these theories and use them with prudence and vigilance. Our role as career counselors and vocational scientists is a sacred trust, one in which our sensitivity, theoretical knowledge, and applied expertise can make a critical difference in the lives of women and men as we help them find meaningful work.

This chapter has highlighted the myriad ways that gender impacts career development. Career counselors working with girls and boys and men and women must understand both the blatant and subtle ways that gender bias exists and influences career choice and adjustment. Here are several specific recommendations for practice based on the review of current literature:

- Understand one's own implicit and explicit assumptions about gender that may influence aspects of the career counseling process.
- Understand that, even though much more has been written about the impact of gender on women's career development, both women and men face subtle and blatant discrimination based on gender.
- Help clients understand how their own implicit and explicit assumptions about gender may be influencing their own career development.
- Help clients develop strategies to deal with gender-related bias, prejudice, sexism, and discrimination.
- Help clients understand how the social construction of gender may impact their perceptions about career choice and adjustment, including what careers they deem appropriate.
- Help clients understand the role of math as a critical filter to many career choices.
- Help clients understand that although there has been progress in the area of gender equality, there is still occupational segregation, gender role stereotyping of careers, sexual harassment, and lack of comparable pay for comparable jobs.
- Examine the potential gap men and women have between their aspirations and expectations.
- Recognize which theories are most helpful in guiding gender-aware career counseling.

REFERENCES

Anselmi, D. L., & Law, A. L. (1998). *Questions of gender*. Boston, MA: McGraw-Hill.

Arredondo, P., & Perez, P. (2003). Expanding multicultural competence through social justice leadership. *Counseling Psychologist, 31,* 282–289.

Barnett, R. C., & Hyde, J. S. (2001). Women, men, work, and family: An expansionist theory. *American Psychologist, 56,* 781–796.

Bell, L. A. (1997). Theoretical foundations for social justice education. In M. Adams, L. A. Bell, & P. Griffin (Eds.), *Teaching for diversity and social justice: A sourcebook* (pp. 3–15). New York, NY: Routledge.

Bender, K. A., Donahue, S. M., & Heywood, J. S. (2005). Job satisfaction and gender segregation. *Oxford Economic Papers, 57,* 479–496.

Berdahl, J. L., Magley, V. J., & Walkdo, C. R. (1996). The sexual harassment of men? *Psychology of Women Quarterly, 20,* 527–547.

Betz, N. E. (1994). Career counseling for women in the sciences and engineering. In W. B. Walsh & S. H. Osipow (Eds.), *Career counseling for women* (pp. 237–262). New York, NY: Routledge.

Betz, N. E. (2006). Basic issues and concepts in the career development and counseling women. In W. B. Walsh & M. J. Heppner (Eds.), *Handbook of career counseling for women* (2nd ed., pp. 45–74). Mahwah, NJ: Erlbaum.

Blustein, D. L. (2006). *The psychology of working: A new perspective for career development, counseling, and public policy.* Mahwah, NJ: Erlbaum.

Blustein, D. L (2011). A relational theory of working. *Journal of Vocational Behavior, 79,* 1–17.

Boaler, J., & Irving, T. S. (2007). Mathematics. In B. Banks (Ed.), *Gender and education: An encyclopedia* (pp. 287–293). Westport, CT: Praeger.

Brooks, G. R., & Good, G. E. (2001). *The new handbook of psychotherapy and counseling with men: A comprehensive guide to settings, problems and treatment approaches.* San Francisco, CA: Jossey-Bass.

Brown, S. D., & Ryan Krane, N. E. (2000). Four (or five) sessions and a cloud of dust: Old assumptions and new observations about career counseling. In S. D. Brown & R. W. Lent (Eds.), *Handbook of counseling psychology* (3rd ed., pp. 740–766). New York: Wiley.

Buchanan, N. T., & Fitzgerald, L. F. (2008). Effects of racial and sexual harassment on work and the psychological well-being of African American Women. *Journal of Occupational Health Psychology, 13,* 137–151. doi:10.1037/1076-8998.13.2.137

Budig, M. J., & England, P. (2001). The wage penalty for motherhood. *American Sociological Review, 66*(2), 204–225.

Bureau of Labor Statistics. (2009). *Women in the labor force: A databook.* Retrieved from http://www.bls.gov/cps/wlf-intro-2009.htm

Butler, D. (2000). Gender, girls, and computer technology: What's the status now? *Clearing House, 73*(4), 225.

Care, E., Deans, J., & Brown, R. (2007). The realism and sex type of four- to five-year-old children's occupational aspirations. *Journal of Early Childhood Research, 5,* 155–168. doi:10.1177/1476718X07076681

Carlson, D. S., Kacmar, K. M., Wayne, J. H., & Grzywacz, J. G. (2006). Measuring the positive side of the work–family interface: Development and validation of a work–family enrichment scale. *Journal of Vocational Behavior, 68,* 131–164.

Ceci, S. J., Williams, W. M., & Barnett, S. M. (2009). Women's underrepresentation in science: Sociocultural and biological considerations. *Psychological Bulletin, 135,* 218–261.

Chronister, K. M., McWhirter, E. H., & Forrest, L. (2006). A critical feminist approach to career counseling with women. In W. B. Walsh & M. J. Heppner (Eds.), *Handbook of career counseling for women* (2nd ed., pp. 167–192). Mahwah, NJ: Erlbaum.

Civil Rights Act of 1964, Pub. L. No. 88–352, 78 Stat. 241 (1964).

Clark, A. (1997) Why are women so happy at work? *Labour Economics, 4,* 341–372.

Collinsworth, L. L., Fitzgerald, F. L., & Drasgow, F. (2009) In harm's way: Factors related to psychological distress following sexual harassment. *Psychology of Women Quarterly, 33*(4), 475–490. doi:10.1111/j.1471-6402.2009.01525.x

Correll, S. J. (2001). Gender and the career choice process: The role of biased self-assessments. *American Journal of Sociology, 106,* 1691–1730.

Division for the Advancement of Women. (2000). The four global women's conferences 1975–1995: Historical perspective. Retrieved from http://www.un.org/womenwatch/daw/followup/session/presskit/hist.htm

Donohue, S., & Heywood, J. (2004). Job satisfaction, comparison income and gender: Evidence from the NLSY. *International Journal of Manpower, 25,* 211–234.

Dovidio, J. F., & Gaertner, S. L. (2000). Aversive racism and selection decisions: 1989–1999. *Psychological Sciences, 11,* 315–319.

Earle, A., Mokomane, Z., & Heymann, J. (2011). International perspectives on work–family policies: Lessons from the world's most competitive economies. *The Future of Children, 21,* 191–203.

Eccles, J. S. (2007). Where are all the women? Gender differences in participations in physical sciences and engineering. In S. J. Ceci & W. M. Williams (Eds.), *Why aren't more women in science? Top researchers debate the evidence* (pp. 199–210). Washington, DC: American Psychological Association.

Else-Quest, N. M., Hyde, J. S., & Linn, M. C. (2010). Cross-national patterns of gender differences in mathematics: A meta-analysis. *Psychological Bulletin, 136,* 103–127.

England, P., Budwig, M., & Folbre, N. (2002). Wages of virtue: The relative pay of care work. *Social Problems, 49,* 455–473.

Fassinger, R. E., & Asay, P. A. (2006). Career counseling for women in science, technology, engineering, and mathematics (STEM) fields. In W. B. Walsh & M. J. Heppner (Eds.), *Handbook of career counseling for women* (2nd ed., pp. 427–452). Mahwah, NJ: Erlbaum.

Flores, L. Y., Navarro, R. L., Smith, J., & Plojaz, A. (2006). Testing a model of career choice with Mexican American adolescent boys. *Journal of Career Assessment, 14,* 214–234.

Fouad, N. A., & Smith, P. L. (1996). A test of the social cognitive model for middle school students: Math and science. *Journal of Counseling Psychology, 45,* 403–415.

Gareis, K. C., Barnett, R. C., Ertel, K. A., & Berkman, L. F. (2009). Work–family enrichment and conflict: Additive effects, buffering, or balance? *Journal of Marriage and Family, 71,* 696–707.

Gottfredson, L. S. (2005). Applying Gottfredson's theory of circumscription and compromise in career guidance and counseling. In S. D. Brown & R. W. Lent (Eds.), *Career development and counseling: Putting theory and research to work* (pp. 71–100). Hoboken, NJ: Wiley.

Greenhaus, J. H., & Beutell, N. J. (1985). Sources of conflict between work and family roles. *Academy of Management Review, 10,* 76–88.

Greenhaus, J. H., Collins, K. M., & Shaw, J. D. (2009). The relations between work–family balance and quality of life. *Journal of Vocational Behavior, 63,* 510–531.

Greenwald, A. G., & Nosek, B. A. (2001). Health of the Implicit Association Test at age 3. *Zeitschrift für Experimentelle Psychologie, 48*, 85–93.

Gysbers, N. C., Heppner, M. J., & Johnston, J. A. (2009). *Career counseling: Contexts, process and techniques.* Alexandria, VA: American Counseling Association.

Hausmann, R., Tyson, L. D., & Zahidi, S. (2010). *The global gender gap report.* Geneva, Switzerland: World Economic Forum.

Heppner, M. J., & Heppner, P. P. (2001). The implications of male socialization for career counseling. In G. Brooks & G. Good (Eds.), *A new handbook of counseling and psychotherapy approaches for men.* San Francisco, CA: Jossey-Bass.

Hill, S. T., & Johnson, J. M. (2004). *Science and engineering degrees 1966–2001.* Arlington, VA: National Science Foundation. Retrieved from http://www.nsf.gov /statistics/nsf04311/

Jome, L. M., & Tokar, D. M. (1998). Dimensions of masculinity and major choice traditionality. *Journal of Vocational Behavior, 52*, 120–134.

Lease, S. H. (2003). Testing a model of men's nontraditional occupational choices. *Career Development Quarterly, 51*, 244–258.

Lent, R. W., Brown, S. D., & Hackett, G. (1994). Toward a unifying social cognitive theory of career and academic interest, choice, and performance. *Journal of Vocational Behavior, 45*, 79–122.

Lent, R. W., Lopez, A. M., Lopez, F. G., & Sheu, H. B. (2008). Social cognitive theory and the prediction of interest and choice goals in the computing disciplines. *Journal of Vocational Behavior, 73*, 52–62.

Lubinski, D., & Benbow, C. P. (2006). Math-science expertise study of mathematically precocious youth after 35 years: Uncovering antecedents for the development of math-science expertise. *Perspectives on Psychological Science, 1*, 316–339.

Lyons, H. Z., Brenner, B. R., & Fassinger, R. (2005). A multicultural test of the theory of work adjustment: Investigating the role of heterosexism and fit perceptions in the job satisfaction of lesbian, gay, and bisexual employees. *Journal of Counseling Psychology, 52*, 537–548.

Lyons, H. Z., & O'Brien, K. M. (2006). The role of person–environment fit in the job satisfaction and tenure intentions of African American employees. *Journal of Counseling Psychology, 53*, 387–396.

McWhirter, E. W. (1994). *Counseling for empowerment.* Alexandria, VA: American Counseling Association.

Miller, A. R. (2010). The effects of motherhood timing on career path. *Journal of Population Economics, 24*, 1–30. doi:10.1007/s00148-009-0296-x

National Science Foundation. (2007). *Women, minorities and persons with disabilities in science and engineering: 2007 (NFS 07–315).* Retrieved from http://www.nsf.gov /statistics/women/

Niles, S. G., & Harris-Bowlsbey, J. (2005). *Career development interventions in the 21st century* (2nd ed.). Upper Saddle River, NJ: Pearson Education.

O'Brien, K. M., Friedman S. M., Tipton, L. C., & Linn, S. G. (2000). Attachment, separation and women's vocational development: A longitudinal analysis. *Journal of Counseling Psychology, 47*, 301–315.

O'Neil, J. M. (2008). Summarizing twenty-five years of research on men's gender-role conflict using the Gender Role Conflict Scale: New research paradigms and clinical implications. *Counseling Psychologist, 36*, 358–476.

Organisation for Economic Co-operation and Development. (2002). Women at work: Who are they and how are they faring? In *OECD Employment Outlook 2002* (pp. 61–125). doi:10.1787/empl_outlook-2002-en

Pew Research Center. (2010). The new demography of American motherhood. Retrieved from http://pewsocialtrends.org/files/2010/10/754-new-demography-of-motherhood.pdf

Richardson, M. S. (1993). Work in people's lives: A location for counseling psychologists. *Journal of Counseling Psychology, 40*, 425–433.

Richman, P. (2006). Work stress and health and socioeconomic status. Retrieved from http://www.apa.org/pi/ses/resources/publications/factsheet-wsh.aspx.

Rochlen, A. B., McKelley, R. A., Suizzo, M.-A., & Scaringi, V. (2008). Predictors of relationship satisfaction, psychological well-being and life satisfaction among stay-at-home fathers. *Psychology of Men and Masculinity, 9*(1), 17–28.

Schultheiss, D. E. P. (2009). To mother or to matter: Can women do both? *Journal of Career Development, 36*, 25–48. doi:10.1177/0894845309340795

Sloane, P. J., & Williams, H. (2000). Job satisfaction, comparison earnings and gender. *Labour, 14*, 473–502.

Sousa-Poza, A., & Sousa-Poza, A. (2000). Taking another look at the gender/job satisfaction paradox. *KYKLOS, 53*, 135–152.

Spencer, S. J., Steele, C. M., & Quinn, D. M. (1999). Stereotype threat and women's math performance. *Journal of Experimental Social Psychology, 35*, 4–28.

Spokane, A. R., & Crusa-Guet, M. C. (2005). Holland's theory of vocational personalities in work environments. In S. D. Brown & R. W. Lent (Eds.), *Career development and counseling: Putting theory and research to work* (pp. 24–41). Hoboken, NJ: Wiley.

Stangor, C., & Shaller, M. (1996). Stereotypes as individual and collective representations. In C. Macrae, C. Stangor, & M. Hewstone (Eds.), *Stereotypes and stereotyping* (pp. 3–40). New York, NY: Guilford Press.

Tokar, D. M., & Jome, L. M. (1998). Masculinity, vocational interests, and career choice traditionality: Evidence for a fully mediated model. *Journal of Counseling Psychology, 45*, 424–435.

United Nations, Office of the Special Adviser on Gender Issues and Advancement of Women. (2002). *Gender mainstreaming: An overview*. New York, NY: United Nations.

U.S. Department of Labor, Bureau of Labor Statistics. (2010). *Women in the labor force, a data book*. Washington, DC: Author.

U.S. Equal Employment Opportunity Commission. (2009). Sexual harassment. Retrieved from http://archive.eeoc.gov/types/sexual_harassment.html

Waldfogel, J., & McLanahan, S. (2011). Work and family: Introducing the issue. *The Future of Children, 21*, 3–14.

Walsh, B., & Heppner, M. J. (2006). *Handbook of career counseling of women*. Mahwah, NJ: Erlbaum.

White, M. J., & White, G. B. (2006). Implicit and explicit occupational gender stereotypes. *Sex Roles, 55,* 259–266.

Willness, C. R., Steel, P., & Lee, K. (2007). A meta-analysis of the antecedents and consequences of workplace sexual harassment. *Personnel Psychology, 60,* 127–162.

Young, R. A., Marshall, S. K., & Valach, L. (2007). Making career theories more culturally sensitive: Implications for counseling. *Career Development Quarterly, 56,* 4–18.

CHAPTER 8

The Role of Race and Ethnicity in Career Choice, Development, and Adjustment

NADYA A. FOUAD AND NEETA KANTAMNENI

I N AN IDEAL WORLD, every individual would be free to choose the optimal occupation for himself or herself, have the resources to pursue that occupational dream, and successfully implement that goal. That is, in a nutshell, the American dream, which James Truslow Adams (1931) defined as the "dream of a land in which life should be better and richer and fuller for every [person], with opportunity for each according to ability or achievement" (p. 404). This definition implies that each person's ability should be the sole determinant of his or her success and that opportunity should be available to all to seek that success. Career counseling grew out of efforts at the beginning of the 20th century to help recent immigrants and others with limited resources achieve the American dream (Flores, 2009).

However, then as well as today, the fundamental assumptions underlying this notion of an ideal world may not fit the worldviews of some individuals, may not be available as a dream for other individuals, and may not be possible for still others. Not everyone makes decisions about work based on their abilities. Opportunities available to individuals, and their resources to take advantage of those opportunities, differ dramatically by social class and race/ethnicity. And finally, not everyone's dream to be better and fuller is achieved through work, and not everyone has a dream to be richer. Dreams and expectations about work and career are very much shaped by individuals' cultural expectations and by the society in which they live. It is critical, therefore, for vocational psychologists and career counselors to have an understanding of the role that cultural context plays in helping to form perceptions of work, in the factors that go into decision making about work, and in the ways that counselors can help clients with career- and work-related concerns.

We focus on one aspect of cultural expectations in this chapter, that of racial and ethnic background. Other chapters will provide a review of research and recommendations for other contextual influences, such as gender and social class. It is important to provide a critical lens on specific aspects of culture to help elucidate research and practice due to those specific influences. However, we have argued elsewhere (Fouad & Kantamneni, 2008) that it is important to understand the multiple contextual influences on work- and career-related choices. Thus, we encourage readers to note that although these chapters focus on various aspects of cultural context separately, in reality individuals are influenced by multiple contextual influences simultaneously.

In this chapter, we first provide some background on the role of racial/ethnic disparities in educational and occupational attainment to provide a basis for our argument that it is important to understand the role of racial/ethnic background in understanding influences on individuals' career- and work-related decisions. We then review the available research from the past decade on the cultural validity of many of the major vocational theories, including those presented in Chapters 2 through 6 of this volume. Following this review, we consider recent research on specific culture-relevant factors that have been shown to differ across racial/ethnic groups, such as barriers and supports, the role of racism, acculturation, and the role salience of the worker role. Although some of the research we discuss has been tied to specific theoretical perspectives (e.g., barriers and supports are featured in social cognitive career theory; role salience is a central construct in Super's theory of career development), much of the research on race/ethnicity in relation to career behavior has not been tied to a particular theoretical framework. Finally, we focus on the implications of this research for practitioners and end with recommendations for both researchers and practitioners.

EDUCATIONAL AND OCCUPATIONAL DISPARITIES

A great deal has been written about the large disparities in educational and occupational attainment between White European Americans and individuals from racial/ethnic minority backgrounds. The data clearly indicate that racial/ethnic minority individuals are disproportionately likely to drop out of high school, not complete college, and be overrepresented in lower-paying and lower-skilled occupations (Bureau of Labor Statistics, 2011). There has also been much written about the causes of these educational and occupational disparities. We will not revisit those debates here and instead focus on the consequences of disparities on occupational outcomes.

First, it is important to understand the proportion of various racial/ethnic groups in the United States. The 2010 census contains the most recent data collected on individuals' self-identification of racial/ethnic group membership (Census Bureau, 2011). Individuals could identify as Hispanic/Latino (as an ethnicity) and also could identify as a member of a racial category. This is a recent change in census data collection that recognizes that those of South or Central American descent may belong to many different racial groups. The percentage of individuals identifying as White, non-Hispanic, was 63.7%, continuing a downward trend that has been apparent since the 1970 census (i.e., the percentage of those identifying as White has decreased from 87% in 1970 to 83% in 1980 to 80% in 1990 and 69% in 2000; Gibson & Jung, 2002).

Those identifying as Hispanic/Latino in 2010 grew the most of any racial/ethnic group to 16.3% from 12.6% in 2000 (Census Bureau, 2011). Those identifying as Black/African American, American Indian or Native American, Asian or Pacific Islander, and Other race represented, respectively, 12.6%, 0.9%, 4.8%, and 5.5% of the population. Finally, 2.4% of the population identified as belonging to two or more races. Geographically, racial/ethnic diversity has increased across all regions of the United States, suggesting that career counselors across the country are very likely to be called upon to serve clients who represent racial/ethnic backgrounds different than their own.

We noted earlier that poorer educational and occupational outcomes are disproportionately represented among racial/ethnic minorities relative to their numbers in the population. For example, in 2008, 3,118,000 individuals dropped out of high school; 34% percent of those were African American, and 40% were Hispanic (U.S. Department of Education, Institute on Education Sciences, 2011). There are also racial/ethnic disparities in the numbers of those graduating from high school. In 2009, 87.1% of Whites had completed high school by the time they were 25; these figures were somewhat lower for African Americans (84.1%), about the same (88.2%) for Asian Americans, and substantially lower (61.9%) for Hispanics. These racial/ethnic educational disparities become even more pronounced in considering college completion rates. In 2009, nearly 30% of all Whites and slightly more than 52% of Asian Americans over the age of 25 had completed college, but only slightly more than 19% of African Americans and 13% of Hispanics had completed college (U.S. Department of Education, Institute on Education Sciences, 2011).

As may be expected, these educational disparities also play out in occupational attainment. Although racial/ethnic groups do not differ markedly in their overall participation in the workforce, with about 66% of Whites, 62.4% of African Americans, 66% of Asians, and 68% of Hispanics in the civilian labor force in 2009 (Bureau of Labor Statistics, 2011), they do differ in the types of occupations in which they are employed. African Americans and Hispanics are underrepresented in management and professional occupations and overrepresented in food preparation, building cleaning, transportation, and service occupations (Bureau of Labor Statistics, 2011). Asian Americans are overrepresented in scientific and engineering occupations and underrepresented in many service occupations (Bureau of Labor Statistics, 2011).

Occupational disparities grow exponentially in light of the implications of educational attainment and type of occupation in the recent economic recession. In June 2011, the unemployment rate nationally was 9.2% but only 8.7% for Whites and 7.5% for Asians, yet 16% for African Americans and 11.6% for Hispanics (Bureau of Labor Statistics, 2011). And those in blue-collar positions, in which Hispanics and African Americans are overrepresented, were more likely to lose their jobs than those in white-collar professions (Economic Policy Institute, 2010).

The statistics presented here highlight the differences in educational and occupational outcomes for racial/ethnic minority clients and students. These differences may have resulted from individual choices but may also represent choices constrained by structural barriers to educational and occupational attainment. Each individual's career and work choices are shaped by his or her cultural context, and racial/ethnic background is a large component of that context. Understanding the role of race and ethnicity in work and career decision making is a critically important part of cultural competence for all researchers and practitioners.

CROSS-CULTURAL VALIDITY OF CAREER THEORIES

In this section, we discuss the role that race and ethnicity may play in most of the major career theories and also review research on race and ethnicity that has been conducted in relation to these theoretical perspectives. We acknowledge that some scholars (e.g., Leong & Pearce, 2011; Young, Marshall, & Valach, 2007) have exhorted the field to build theories from within each culture's perspective, rather than trying to make existing theories more culturally relevant. We agree with them, but we also believe it is important to examine the cultural validity of the major career theories.

HOLLAND'S THEORY

Holland's theory (1997) asserts that career choice is an expression of an individual's personality. Holland argues that cultural and personal factors work together to create distinctive personality types; in turn, environments are also characterized by personality types. People and their environments may be described in terms of six basic personality and environment types (Realistic, Investigative, Artistic, Social, Enterprising, and Conventional). The main premise in Holland's theory is to help people understand their personality types in order to find a match with work environments (see Nauta, Chapter 3, this volume). A strong match between an individual's personality and his or her work environment is hypothesized to be related to job satisfaction and job tenure.

Extensive research has examined the cross-cultural validity of Holland's theory. This line of research has examined whether the six vocational personality types exist and correspond to Holland's hypothesized RIASEC pattern in various cultural groups, whether cultural variables predict vocational interests, and whether key tenets proposed by Holland (e.g., congruence) are applicable in cross-cultural populations. Numerous studies have investigated whether vocational interests fall in a RIASEC pattern; several methodologically rigorous studies have found similar structures of the six interest types for the major ethnic groups (e.g., Armstrong, Hubert, & Rounds, 2003; Day & Rounds, 1998; Tracey & Rounds, 1993) with a few exceptions. For example, Flores, Spanierman, Armstrong, and Velez (2006) found that adult Latinos did not have a circular RIASEC ordering, and Kantamneni and Fouad (2011) found that African American females and Latino males did not possess a circular RIASEC ordering, suggesting that the perceived structure of the world of work may be different for these groups.

Research has provided limited evidence that cultural variables predict vocational interests. In an investigation of the vocational interests of South Asian Americans, Kantamneni and Fouad (in press) found that acculturation predicted Realistic interests and that individualistic and collectivistic values predicted Social interests. Participants who identified more strongly with their South Asian cultural background had higher Realistic interests, those who possessed strong individualistic values measured low in Social interests, and those with stronger collectivistic values reported higher Social interests. Similarly, Tang, Fouad, and Smith (1999) found that family influences and acculturation predicted vocational interests for Asian American college students. Asian Americans who were Anglo-acculturated displayed atypical interests.

Relatively little research has examined key tenets proposed by Holland (e.g., congruence, differentiation) within diverse racial/ethnic populations. A meta-analysis conducted by Tsabari, Tziner, and Meir (2005) found that culture moderated the relationship between congruence and job satisfaction; participants from individualistic societies displayed a stronger relationship between interest congruence and satisfaction than did those from collectivist societies. Leong, Austin, Sekaran, and Komarraju (1998) examined the career choices of adult workers in India. They found that congruence, differentiation, and consistency were not predictive of job satisfaction, suggesting cross-cultural limitations for Holland's theory. In studies examining how cultural variables predict congruence for South Asian American college students, Gupta and Tracey (2005) and Kantamneni and Fouad (in press) each found that cultural factors, such as dharma, Asian values, and collectivistic values, did not affect congruence between expressed and measured interests.

Considering the mixed findings as to whether interests fall within Holland's proposed structure and whether key tenets proposed by Holland are applicable to diverse populations, several criticisms of Holland's theory have been offered. First, despite Holland's having listed barriers and lack of resources as among the factors that affect congruence–outcome relations, research on Holland's theory has largely ignored the barriers and limited opportunities faced by many individuals (Hardin, 2007). Second, Holland's theory does not explicitly address the role of culture in developing vocational identities, and the few studies in this area have found contradictory evidence as to how cultural variables affect vocational interests. No research to date has investigated how cultural variables affect vocational interest development. Third, Holland's theory does not pay marked attention to the various societal influences that may affect how an individual perceives his or her environment (Hardin, 2007). Discrimination, barriers, or other forms of prejudice in the workplace may affect how work environments are experienced.

In sum, much of the research examining the cultural validity of Holland's theory has provided evidence for its use with diverse populations. However, some studies (e.g., Flores et al., 2006b; Kantamneni & Fouad, 2011) have not found a circular or hexagonal RIASEC pattern of interests for specific racial/ethnic groups, and the research examining the direct and indirect influence of cultural variables on vocational interests and other important constructs (e.g., congruence, differentiation) in Holland's theory is limited. More research is needed to reach definitive conclusions as to whether Holland's theory is an appropriate and valid theoretical framework for people of color in the United States.

THE THEORY OF WORK ADJUSTMENT

The theory of work adjustment (TWA) is a person–environment fit model that predicts how well individuals will adjust to their job environments (Dawis, 2005). The model focuses on how well individuals' abilities match the abilities required by the job (e.g., individuals' satisfactoriness) and how well individuals' needs and work values are met by the reinforcers in the environment (e.g., individuals' satisfaction). If individuals are both satisfied and satisfactory, they are predicted to stay in the job environment (see Swanson & Schneider, Chapter 2, this volume).

The theory is based on an individual differences perspective, a perspective that Dawis (1994) embraced as viewing "people as individuals and not as members of groups" (p. 41). He noted that focusing on group membership was an inaccurate way to estimate abilities and needs and recommended instead that researchers focus on individuals' reinforcement history. In essence, he predicted that race and ethnicity influence person–environment fit, which in turn influences a person's job satisfaction. Rounds and Hesketh (1994), however, argued the importance of making explicit the effect of race and ethnicity on work adjustment, particularly for variables, such as discrimination, that may moderate an individual's satisfaction.

Lovelace and Rosen (1996) studied the relationship between cultural variables and person–environment fit, hypothesizing that racial/ethnic minority group members may feel less of a fit to their environments than do White managers. They found that African American managers reported lower satisfaction with fit than White or Hispanic managers. However, the effect size was very small (0.03). Lyons and O'Brien (2006) studied racial climate as a moderator of TWA outcome variables (satisfaction) for African American employees. They found that need-reinforcer correspondence was highly related ($r = 0.66$) to satisfaction and that racial climate did not moderate the relationship between satisfaction and intentions to leave the organization. They also found, in qualitative analyses, that participants described TWA reinforcers to explain factors that contributed to their satisfaction, suggesting that TWA work values were relevant for their participants. Their conclusion was that "the TWA has relevance for African American employees" (p. 395). Eggerth and Flynn (in press) also found TWA work values in their study with Latina immigrants. They conducted 10 interviews in two locations in the United States with Latinas who held low-wage jobs. They found that most of the reinforcers were described in the women's narratives about their favorite and least liked jobs, with TWA's compensation and security values noted by each participant.

In sum, the limited research on the role of race/ethnicity in TWA has been shown to support Dawis's (1994) contention that race and ethnicity influence the perception of person–environment fit, which influences TWA outcome variables, such as job satisfaction. The two studies that specifically analyzed TWA constructs have found that the reinforcers proposed by the theory may be used to describe the work values and needs of Latina and African American participants and that need-reinforcer correspondence explained a substantial amount of variance in African American workers' satisfaction.

Clearly, more research is needed to extend these findings to other groups. We also recommend that researchers focus on reinforcers that may be unique to racial/ethnic minority populations, such as working with other minority individuals, or on perceptions of racial fit that may not be applicable to White participants.

GOTTFREDSON'S THEORY OF CIRCUMSCRIPTION AND COMPROMISE

Gottfredson's theory of circumscription and compromise emerged in the 1980s as a theoretical framework to understand the developmental processes that youth undergo in beginning to understand the world of work (Gottfredson, 1981, 2005). Similar to Holland's theory, the theory of circumscription and compromise views vocational choice as a matching process; individuals choose careers that correspond with their interests, goals, skills, and abilities. What makes Gottfredson's theory unique, however, is the close attention it pays to how children and adolescents learn about various occupations and about their identity and sense of self and to how they use this information to determine which occupations fit them (see Gottfredson, 2005).

The circumscription and compromise theory hypothesizes four critical developmental stages that influence the career development process: (1) growth in cognitive abilities, (2) development of self, (3) elimination of least favorite vocational options (circumscription), and (4) development of an understanding of external constraints on vocational choices (compromise). Gottfredson also presents a series of stages in which children, as early as 3 to 5 years of age, begin the career development process. The various stages focus on how children develop their orientation to size, power, and gender (stage 1); understand gender differences in the world of work (stage 2); gain a beginning understanding of social values and varying abilities needed for specific types of jobs (stage 3); and develop an understanding of internal factors (e.g., career interests, needs, values) that may determine their final occupational choice (stage 4).

The focus on development within context, power differentials in the occupational landscape, and social values and prestige associated with various types of work in Gottfredson's theory of circumscription and compromise makes it attractive for understanding the career development of racial/ethnic minorities. However, very little research has empirically examined the applicability of this theory with diverse groups. This may be due to the difficulty in researching career constructs with children at such an early stage; the complexity associated with examining constructs as multifaceted as power, prestige, and social values; or the lack of measurement tools specifically developed within this framework. Regardless, research is needed to fully understand how this theory can be applicable to a broad range of people.

In sum, despite its promise, the dearth of research on the role of race/ethnicity in Gottfredson's theory of circumscription and compromise limits the conclusions that can be drawn about the theory's applicability with persons from diverse racial/ethnic groups. The theory's attention to how people limit the career options they consider has the potential to be very useful for understanding the career development of people of color, particularly in that the occupational landscape of the United States does not make opportunities and access to various types of work equally available to individuals from minority backgrounds. More research is clearly needed to understand the process of circumscription and compromise for individuals from diverse backgrounds.

THE THEORIES OF CAREER DEVELOPMENT AND CAREER CONSTRUCTION

Super's developmental theory is one of the most influential in vocational psychology. As Betz (2008) notes, it revolutionized the field when first introduced in 1953. The theory is summarized by Hartung (Chapter 4, this volume). Savickas's career construction theory (see Chapter 6, this volume) can be seen as an update to Super's theory, one that views career development from a constructionist perspective. The latter emphasizes the view "that individuals actively create their own subjective and personal career realities" (Hartung & Taber, 2008).

Super (Super, Savickas, & Super, 1996) included racial and ethnic background as part of the cultural milieu in which children begin to develop a sense of self-concept that becomes implemented in occupational choices. Super's early work was extensively researched primarily on White, upper-middle-class men, although by the 1980s, researchers examined the applicability of the theory to women and people of color. Early studies examined racial group differences in Super's constructs, such as career maturity (e.g., Westbrook, Buck, Wynne, & Sanford, 1994). More recent research has examined factors related to career adaptability and exploration (e.g., Kenny & Bledsoe, 2005). The latter study defined adaptability as career planning, career outcome expectations, school identification, and perceptions of barriers and found that parents and teachers were significant sources of support for urban youth. Specifically, family support was related to perceptions of barriers and career outcome expectations, and teacher support was related to identifying with school.

Savickas (2011) further defines the self as shaped by culture, noting that "identities are co-constructed by a psychological self and a social context" (p. 18). By definition, the social context is shaped by the individual's cultural group memberships. As the individual grows and develops and expresses his or her identity through narratives, there are many influences on the narrative that will be shaped by cultural messages. Savickas notes that this perspective is influenced by Western cultural values, which assume that the career narrative is composed individually. However, he also notes that individuals are always influenced by others. As he states, "Identity is seldom an individual project" (p. 18), and many others contribute to the construction of identity. Thus, in collectivist societies, individuals' narratives may be highly influenced by the expectations of others because of the importance placed on valuing others' views.

Blustein and colleagues (2010) examined the role of race and ethnicity in a qualitative study based on career construction theory. They found that half of 32 students in their study had incorporated the perception of barriers due to racism into their construction of their careers and future, and half were unaware of the effect of their race or ethnicity. Of those who had incorporated a perspective on racism into their overall career narrative, half had developed mechanisms to counter or be resistant to that racism, and half were more pessimistic about their futures because of racism. The authors concluded with a suggestion that career intervention programs incorporate tools to foster resistance to racism.

In sum, much more research is needed to understand how racial and ethnic group background influences career development across the life span, including the ways in which individuals construct their careers. Future research needs to investigate how career adaptability is shaped by different cultural values and different barriers due to racism and its effects. Blustein and colleagues' (2010) research is a promising beginning, but more research needs to be done to see if career narratives are different in systematic ways across racial/ethnic groups.

SOCIAL COGNITIVE CAREER THEORY

Social cognitive career theory (SCCT) was developed to understand and explain the vocational development of individuals from a broad range of backgrounds (Lent, Brown, & Hackett, 1994, 2000). Briefly stated, the social cognitive career framework asserts that both person inputs (e.g., gender, race/ethnicity, ability status) and background contextual affordances create the learning experiences to which an individual is exposed; these learning experiences influence self-efficacy expectations and outcome expectations, which, in turn, influence interests, goals, and actions. SCCT integrates both individual variables (e.g., interests, values, abilities) and cultural and contextual variables (e.g., environmental factors) to fully understand the career development process (see Lent, Chapter 5, this volume). SCCT operates from an understanding that the environment "plays an undeniable, potent role in helping to determine who gets to do what and where, for how long, and with what sorts of rewards" (Lent & Sheu, 2009, p. 692).

Due to its emphasis on contextual and sociocultural influences on the career development processes, research utilizing SCCT has greatly enhanced our knowledge of how individuals from minority racial/ethnic backgrounds make career decisions. For example, numerous studies have examined how the social cognitive career model is represented within Latino and Mexican American student populations (e.g., Flores, Navarro, & DeWitz, 2008; Flores & O'Brien, 2002), African American student populations (e.g., Gainor & Lent, 1998), and Asian American student populations (e.g., Tang et al., 1999). Additionally, a plethora of research (e.g., Fouad & Smith, 1996; Gainor & Lent, 1998; Lent et al., 2005; Lent, Lopez, Lopez, & Sheu, 2008) has examined the predictive nature of social cognitive career variables (e.g., self-efficacy, outcome expectations) on math- and science-related interests and goals. Much of this research has examined either tests of SCCT's larger models (e.g., interest, choice) or the predictive nature of specific contextual and individual input variables on social cognitive career constructs (e.g., how cultural factors affect career decision-making self-efficacy).

Research has found that self-efficacy and outcome expectations predicted math and science interests and goals in Hispanic and African American high school students (Fouad & Smith, 1996), African American college students (Byars-Winston, 2006; Lent et al., 2005, 2008; Waller, 2006), and Asian American students (Kelly, Gunsalus, & Gunsalus, 2009). For example, in two separate investigations, Lent and his colleagues (Lent et al., 2005, 2008) compared the social cognitive choice model in African American and European American students majoring in engineering. They found that the model accounted for academic interests and choices in both groups of students. Byars-Winston, Estrada, Howard, Davis, and Zalapa (2010) also found support for the social cognitive model in predicting interests and goal commitment among biological science and engineering majors in a diverse samples of African American, Latino(a), Asian American, and Native American college students.

In sum, because of its emphasis on contextual influences in the career development process, SCCT lends itself well to understanding the role of cultural influences on the career development process for racial/ethnic minorities. In fact, it appears that much of the recent research examining the role of cultural influences on career development has utilized a social cognitive framework; as a whole, this research has provided cross-cultural support for the social cognitive career model with various racial/ethnic groups. However, there continues to be a need for additional research that examines how social cognitive career variables operate with other cultural variables, such as ethnic identity, acculturation, and cultural values.

CULTURAL FACTORS RELATED TO CAREER DEVELOPMENT

In the previous section, we briefly reviewed multicultural considerations and applications of the major vocational theories. However, a number of cultural factors deserve attention in their own right, based on the assumption that they have the potential to influence the career behavior of diverse persons. Some of these factors have been studied in relation to particular career theories; others are not currently aligned well with the major theories. This section discusses how these factors—in particular, acculturation, cultural values, role models, perceptions of discrimination, barriers and supports, ethnic identity, and differences between aspirations and expectations—may shape the vocational development of racial/ethnic minority persons.

CULTURAL VALUES

Cultural values can have a meaningful impact on the career choices of racial/ethnic minorities. Take, for example, a Latina college student who comes from a cultural background that emphasizes the values of *familismo* and *colectivismo*; this student may make career decisions that meet cultural or family expectations or that allow her to give back to her community, regardless of her interests, self-efficacy, or outcome expectations. Despite the potentially powerful influence cultural values can have on the career development process, little research to date has fully explicated the relationship between cultural values and career decision making. Only a handful of studies have examined the influence of cultural values on the career development process of racial/ethnic minority populations. As mentioned previously, Tsabsari and colleagues (2005) investigated whether culture moderated the relationship between congruence and job satisfaction and reported that interest congruence was more predictive of job satisfaction in societies that possessed an individualistic value orientation. Although Gupta and Tracey (2005) did not find that the cultural value of dharma predicted congruence, Kantamneni and Fouad (in press) found that the cultural values of individualism and collectivism predicted Social interests in South Asian American college students.

Two studies also examined the influence of cultural values on the process of career counseling. Kim and Atkinson (2002) found that Asian American clients who expressed a strong adherence to Asian cultural values rated Asian American career counselors higher on dimensions of effectiveness than clients with low adherence to Asian cultural values. Clients with low adherence to Asian cultural values rated European American counselors higher on empathic understanding than their Asian American counterparts. Kim, Li, and Liang (2002) investigated the effect of career counseling orientation and cultural values on Asian Americans' perceptions of counselors' effectiveness.

Results indicated that clients with high adherence to Asian cultural values perceived higher empathic understanding and a stronger working alliance with their counselor than did clients with low adherence to Asian cultural values, regardless of the counselor's racial/ethnic background.

A series of qualitative investigations have examined the vocational development of African American (Pearson & Bieschke, 2001), Latina (Gomez et al., 2001), Native American (Juntunen et al., 2001), and Asian American (Fouad et al., 2008) adults. These studies highlighted the influential role that cultural values can have on the vocational development of racial/ethnic minorities. Gomez and colleagues found that cultural variables such as cultural values, gender role messages, and familial career aspirations influenced participants' vocational development. Specifically, participants indicated that cultural values of familism and collectivism influenced how they made career decisions; participants' families were typically oriented toward a collective identity, and participants indicated that they had a responsibility toward the well-being of their family and community. Similarly, Juntunen and colleagues demonstrated that collectivism was strongly related to career development among Native Americans; career success was viewed as a collective experience, and success was often measured by an ability to contribute to the well-being of others within their community. Pearson and Bieschke (2001) investigated the role of cultural factors on persistence in maintaining successful careers for African American women and found that family values had a significant influence on their vocational development; participants received messages about work values from their families, such as messages related to work ethic and altruism.

Finally, Fouad and colleagues (2008) found that cultural values emerged as a typical category in their qualitative analysis of Asian American career development; cultural values were found to influence participants' communication styles at work, their ideas of career and vocational success, their sense of family obligations, and how career exploration was facilitated. Interestingly, Fouad and her colleagues noted that cultural values were primarily transmitted through the families of their participants, and it was often difficult for the participants to delineate between cultural and familial values. As a whole, both qualitative and quantitative investigations highlight the influential role of cultural influences in constructing meaning through work for individuals from racial/ethnic minority backgrounds. Cultural values influence perceptions of the role of work, vocational interests, and how the career counseling process is perceived by individuals from minority backgrounds. Although this research is limited, research has suggested that cultural values may be an essential component of the career development process for racial/ethnic minority group members; further research is needed to fully understand this relationship.

ACCULTURATION

Acculturation has long been hypothesized to play an important role in the career development process of ethnic minorities (Leong & Chou, 1994) and is often linked to educational and career aspirations, vocational interests, career self-efficacy, job satisfaction, and career maturity. Much of the current research has focused on Latino(a)s and Asian Americans. A small number of studies have investigated the relationship between acculturation and educational and career aspirations. In an investigation of the role of acculturation on aspirations, McWhirter, Hackett, and Bandalos (1998) proposed a structural model to predict the educational and career expectations of Mexican American high school girls and found support for acculturation as a predictor of educational aspirations. Similarly, Flores and O'Brien (2002) found that acculturation was significantly correlated with career choice traditionality, career choice prestige, and career aspirations for Mexican American students; women who were more assimilated to mainstream culture chose more gender-traditional and less prestigious occupations than women who were less assimilated to mainstream culture. Rivera, Chen, Flores, Blumberg, and Ponterotto (2007) found that Anglo acculturation significantly predicted self-efficacy regarding female-dominated career options in Hispanic women.

Flores and colleagues (2008), however, found contradictory results in a study of Mexican American high school students. Anglo-oriented acculturation was positively related to educational goal expectations and aspirations in Mexican American high school students; students who were acculturated to mainstream society expressed higher educational aspirations and expectations. Similarly, Flores, Ojeda, Huang, Gee, and Lee (2006) found that Anglo-oriented acculturation emerged as a significant predictor of high educational goals. Mexican American students who indicated high levels of Anglo-oriented acculturation were more likely to have higher educational goals than students who were less acculturated to Anglo culture. Navarro, Flores, and Worthington (2007) found that generation status, Anglo orientation, and Mexican orientation did not significantly predict math and science performance accomplishments; neither did these accomplishments predict math and science outcome expectations or math and science goals. Further investigation is needed to explain these contradictory findings.

Vocational research has also examined the relationship between acculturation and vocational outcomes in Asian Americans. Leong (2001) examined the relationship between acculturation and job satisfaction, occupational stress, and supervisors' performance ratings. He found that acculturation to mainstream culture (Anglo orientation) was found to be positively related to job satisfaction and to supervisors' performance ratings; acculturation was negatively related to occupational stress and strain. Hardin,

Leong, and Osipow (2001) compared the relationships between career maturity, self-construals, and acculturation for Asian Americans and European Americans. Results indicated that low and medium acculturated (medium to high Asian identification) Asian Americans had significantly higher interdependence and lower career maturity scores than European Americans; however, highly acculturated (high Western identification) Asian Americans did not significantly differ from European Americans. Tang and colleagues (1999) investigated the relationship between acculturation and social cognitive variables and reported a significant negative relationship of acculturation to career self-efficacy, vocational interests, and career choice. Self-efficacy was strongly influenced by acculturation, which in turn influenced interests and career choice. Individuals who were more Asian acculturated displayed interests in and chose careers that were more typical and representative of Asian Americans (i.e., science or engineering occupations). Asian Americans who were higher in acculturation (Anglo acculturated) displayed interests and choices in career fields that were less typical and representative for Asian Americans.

On the whole, these studies suggest that acculturation is intimately related to vocational development; many of the studies highlight the important role that acculturation plays in career and educational aspirations, career maturity, and job satisfaction. Yet research in this area is still minimal, and further research is needed to investigate the relationship between acculturation and vocational outcomes. For example, how is acculturation related to the development of vocational interests, perceptions of vocational opportunities, and perceptions of discrimination? Further, the research examining the relationship between acculturation and career development has primarily focused on Asian American and Latino populations, with little research examining other groups (e.g., individuals of African or Middle Eastern descent) in the United States.

ETHNIC IDENTITY

Only a few studies to date have fully examined how racial/ethnic identity and attitudes affect the career development process. Gainor and Lent (1998) investigated the relationship between racial identity attitudes and social cognitive career variables (math self-efficacy, math outcome expectations, math and science interests) for African American college students and found that social cognitive career variables predicted interests across varying levels of racial identity attitudes. Racial identity attitudes were minimally related to social cognitive variables and did not affect the relationship of social cognitive variables to interests and choices in math and science options. These results suggest that the social cognitive career model may be applicable across different racial identity statuses with African American college students. Similarly, Gushue and Whitson (2006) examined how ethnic identity and parent and teacher support were related to career decision self-efficacy and outcome expectations in African American ninth-grade students; they found that ethnic identity was not related to career decision self-efficacy or outcome expectations. Specific to math and science, Kelly, Gunsalus, and Gunsalus (2009) investigated how ethnic identity, self-efficacy, outcome expectations, and career interests predict science and nonscience goal intentions among Korean American college students and found that ethnic identity did not predict goal intentions.

Two studies have found some relationships between ethnic identity and career variables. Byars-Winston and colleagues (2010) found that ethnic identity, other-group orientation, and perceived campus climate were predictive of academic self-efficacy and outcome expectations in a group of African American, Latino, Southeast Asian, and Native American undergraduates majoring in biological science and engineering; other-group orientation was found to significantly predict self-efficacy. Similarly, Byars-Winston (2006) examined how racial ideology (i.e., nationalist, humanist, assimilationist, and oppressed minority) is related to career self-efficacy, career outcome expectations, career interests, and perceived career barriers in African American college students. She found that two racial ideologies (nationalist and assimilationist) were predictive of career self-efficacy, outcome expectations, interests, and barriers. A racial ideology that emphasized the uniqueness of being of African descent (nationalist) and an ideology that emphasized commonalities between African Americans and other Americans (assimilationist) were related to career self-efficacy, outcome expectations, interests, and barriers.

In sum, these studies provide a preliminary understanding of how ethnic identity is related to vocational development. Keep in mind that a majority of the studies that have examined the relationship of ethnic identity to career variables have been conducted using a social cognitive career framework and have provided support for the use of this model with individuals of varying levels of racial/ethnic identity development or racial ideologies. However, more research is needed to fully understand the relationship between ethnic identity and various career constructs, using both the SCCT framework as well as other career theories that are influential in career development.

ROLE MODELS

Role models can act as mentors, provide vocational information, and both directly and indirectly influence career decisions, often playing a critical role in career development (Gibson, 2004). Yet, little empirical research has examined how role models specifically influence the career development process for racial/ethnic minorities. Karunanayake and Nauta (2004) examined differences in role models between Whites and racial/ethnic minorities; they found no differences in the overall number of role models identified by either White or minority students or in the influences of role models on students' career development, although they did find that participants identified role models who were of the same race as their own.

Qualitative investigations have also found that role models are influential in the vocational development of Latinas (Gomez et al., 2001) and Asian Americans (Fouad et al., 2008). In an investigation by Gomez and her colleagues, role models were identified as critical influences in the career development of Latina women. Participants identified their mothers as role models, although several of the participants stated that they lacked Latina professional role models and thus sought role models across professions, ethnicity, race, gender, and age. Fouad and her colleagues also found that role models emerged as an influential contextual influence for Asian Americans' career development. Participants identified models that contributed to their community and reported receiving emotional support from their models. Additionally, family members were most commonly identified as role models for the participants.

Perceptions of Discrimination

Experiences of discrimination can have a lasting impact on the career decisions that individuals from racial/ethnic minority backgrounds make, which may be evidenced in the occupational segregation found in the U.S. labor force. Occupational segregation and differential rates of unemployment between racial/ethnic groups may be due to, in part, restrictions of career and work choices based on bias and prejudice in the hiring process; individuals from racial/ethnic minority backgrounds may experience discrimination that restricts their opportunities for employment. Anticipated discrimination may further restrict vocational choices; for example, individuals may not choose to enter certain types of careers based on fears that they will be discriminated against because of their race/ethnicity or other individual difference factors (e.g., gender, sexual orientation).

Minimal research has been conducted to investigate the role of discrimination empirically. An important investigation by Chung and Harmon (1999) found that ethnic minorities perceived more discrimination in the workplace than did their White counterparts. In a study on urban students' constructions about school, work, race, and ethnicity, Blustein and colleagues (2010) demonstrated that half of their participants had incorporated perceptions of racism into their career construction. Conversely, a study by Evans and Herr (1994) found that perceptions of discrimination were not related to career aspirations in African American college students. These three studies provide a preliminary yet contradictory understanding of the role of discrimination in career development.

PERCEIVED BARRIERS AND SUPPORTS

Perceived barriers (in addition to discrimination) and supports have been identified as important factors in understanding how individuals from diverse backgrounds construct their vocational identity (Lent et al., 1994, 2000; Swanson & Woitke, 1997). Gender and ethnic differences in career and educational barriers have been well documented in the vocational psychology literature (e.g., Luzzo & Hutcheson, 1996; McWhirter, 1997). For example, in two separate studies, McWhirter (1997) and Luzzo and McWhirter (2001) found that ethnic minority college students perceived more educational and career barriers than European American students; ethnic minority college students also perceived themselves to have lower efficacy to cope with their perceived barriers.

Similarly, McWhirter, Torres, Salgado, and Valdez (2007) investigated internal and external educational barriers among Mexican American and White high school students and found ethnic differences in the perception of barriers; Mexican American students expected to encounter more barriers to attaining postsecondary education and experience more difficulty in overcoming their perceived barriers than their White counterparts. Ojeda and Flores (2008) found that perceived educational barriers predicted educational aspirations beyond the influence of gender, generation level, and parents' education in Mexican American high school students. Likewise, Rivera and colleagues (2007) found that perceived barriers were related to the consideration of female-dominated jobs among Hispanic women. Other studies with specific adult populations (e.g., battered women) have found that racial/ethnic minorities may not perceive greater barriers than European Americans (Chronister & McWhirter, 2004).

Research has also investigated supports that can help racial/ethnic minorities overcome institutional obstacles. Constantine, Wallace, and Kindaichi (2005) examined the career decision status of African American adolescents and found that perceived parental support was positively related to career certainty. In a study of inner-city students, mostly of racial/ethnic minority backgrounds, Kenny and her colleagues (2003) found that perceived general support and kinship support was related to school engagement, career aspirations, expectations for future career success, and importance of future work. Similarly, a qualitative investigation by Kenny, Gualdron, Sparks,

Blustein, and Jernigan (2007) examined perceptions of supports and barriers to educational and career attainment among high school students from diverse racial/ethnic backgrounds. Students reported having a number of supports, such as family members, school and/or teachers, and friends. These studies, coupled with the qualitative investigations of racial/ethnic minority women described earlier (e.g., Gomez et al., 2001; Pearson & Bieschke, 2001), provide evidence that supports can be a very positive influence for persons of color. As a whole, studies examining barriers and supports suggest that high school and college students of color may perceive greater educational and career barriers than their White counterparts. However, supports, particularly relational supports, have been found to have a protective influence for students.

OCCUPATIONAL ASPIRATIONS AND EXPECTATIONS

It is important to understand the career aspirations and expectations of individuals from minority racial/ethnic backgrounds. Career aspirations represent vocational preferences or career possibilities if ideal conditions are present, whereas career expectations can be thought of as career pursuits that are realistic and accessible (Metz, Fouad, & Ihle-Helledy, 2009).

Fouad and Byars-Winston (2005) conducted a meta-analysis of 16 studies and found no significant differences in career aspirations based on racial/ethnic identity. However, race and ethnicity were related to perceptions of barriers and opportunities; ethnic minorities perceived fewer opportunities and greater barriers than White Americans. These findings suggest that career aspirations may not be related to ethnic background, but the perception of barriers and opportunities to achieve those aspirations is related to ethnic background. Metz and colleagues (2009) examined discrepancies between occupational aspirations and expectations in over 600 diverse college students and found ethnic differences in the students' aspirations but not in their expectations. The career aspirations and expectations of minority students were more congruent than those of White students; however, career barriers, self-efficacy, and differential status predicted discrepancies between aspirations and expectations for ethnic minority students, but not for White students. Howard and her colleagues (2011) examined the relationship between gender, socioeconomic status (SES), race/ethnicity, and career aspirations in more than 22,000 8th- and 10th-grade students. They found that Native American students reported lower aspirations than students from other racial-ethnic groups, yet these differences were moderated by gender and social class. Native American male students reported aspirations lower than all other males, and Native American and Asian/Pacific Islander students from low-SES backgrounds had lower aspirations than students who were not from low-SES backgrounds. As a whole, these studies suggest that race and ethnicity do indeed affect career aspiration and expectations.

SUMMARY

In sum, empirical investigations (both quantitative and qualitative) have found that cultural influences are indeed related to the vocational development of racial/ethnic minorities. Yet, much of this research is preliminary in nature, and we are just beginning the process of fully understanding how culture affects career development and the meaning that racial/ethnic minorities construct out of their work. In general, vocational researchers have not fully examined cultural factors with specific racial/ethnic populations or subpopulations; neither have they examined the complex ways in which these factors interface with one another. As a result, the field has a very limited understanding of how the career development process may be affected by one's cultural background. Further, much of the research in this section has been conducted with college student samples. Simply attending college is a privilege that many individuals do not have; thus, the findings of these studies may not be generalizable beyond a relatively privileged portion of the racial/ethnic minority population in the United States.

PRACTICAL IMPLICATIONS

So how should career counselors incorporate this information into their practice? How can career counselors be culturally competent when working with racial/ethnic minority clients? We have several suggestions and recommendations for career counselors to consider, including developing foundational knowledge of the cultural values and history of different racial/ethnic groups in the United States. In this section, we briefly review models of career counseling that explicitly incorporate a consideration of culture, offer our recommendations regarding counselors' metacognitions when they work with any client who is culturally different from themselves, and, finally, consider counseling implications related to the specific cultural factors discussed earlier.

CAREER COUNSELING MODELS INCORPORATING CULTURE

Several models have been developed within the past two decades to help counselors integrate and infuse culture into career counseling. They complement each other, each providing some helpful detail on part of the process. Leung's model (1995) concentrates on career interventions. He argues that all career interventions (at the systemic, group, or individual level) need to include a focus on educational outcomes, as well as on occupational outcomes, to help buttress clients against oppression and discrimination. Fouad and Bingham's (1995) culturally appropriate career counseling model emphasizes the effect of racial/ethnic identity on the identification of career issues and the influences of the dominant culture on career processes and decisions.

The most recent model is the cultural formation approach (CFA; Leong, Hardin, & Gupta, 2011). Building on Leong and Hartung's (1997) integrative-sequential conceptual framework for career counseling, CFA identifies five dimensions: (1) cultural identity, (2) cultural conception of career problems, (3) self in cultural context, (4) cultural dynamics in the therapeutic relationship, and (5) overall cultural assessment. The application of the CFA to various racial/ethnic groups was articulated in a series of articles in a June 2010 special issue of the *Journal of Career Development*.

Taking various elements from these models, career counselors are encouraged to consider how culture influences the development of the self, how culture shapes the view of career concerns as a problem, and how culture helps to shape the goals that clients have for counseling. The dominant U.S. culture fosters the sense of self as an independent individual who makes autonomous decisions about his or her life. Other cultures foster the sense of self as someone who is interdependent with others (such as family or clan members), with individuals being expected to achieve group goals, such as pursuing a particular occupational goal to bring honor to the family. Clearly, a client's sense of self as pursuing individual goals versus the goals of his or her family will influence the career counseling process and the career counseling relationship.

Counselors need to understand their own cultural sense of self to ensure that they do not impose their values on their clients. But counselors also need to be prepared to help clients understand when their own sense of self is in flux. As the studies on acculturation point out, many clients navigate two worlds, those of their parents' culture as well as the U.S. dominant culture, with potentially conflicting messages about what is the appropriate path to take as an independent adult. Sometimes clients are confused about which set of expectations to follow, their parents' expectations to adhere to group goals or the larger society's expectations to develop independence. Career choices are part of those expectations, and career counselors can often play an important role in helping clients discover solutions to this dilemma.

COUNSELOR COGNITIONS

Arguing that culturally competent career counseling needs to be an active process that involves career counselors' constant development of insight and monitoring, Byars-Winston and Fouad (2006) proposed a set of metacognitive skills for career counseling. They focused on three processes: developing a plan of action, implementing the plan and self-monitoring, and evaluating the plan. In developing the plan, career counselors need to consider their own cultural identity, their knowledge of the client's racial/ethnic background and identity (or identities), and identify what they do not know about the client's background. Their plan needs to be flexible enough to be readjusted as they learn more about the client. Counselors consider their goals for the client and reflect on the cultural values related to those goals. For example, is the goal focused on achievement, and does this match the client's values? As they plan strategies and interventions, career counselors consider how the strategies were chosen and which strategies might be more appropriate for the client's concerns.

The second process is implementing the plan and developing mechanisms to self-monitor. This process involves actively monitoring what information they are paying attention to and how that may be related to their own (i.e., the counselor's) cultural values. Self-monitoring also includes understanding when some issues or concerns are not addressed because of the counselors' discomfort. Finally, self-monitoring includes being open to information that is not consistent with the cultural assumptions made about the client and that may, therefore, call for modification to the counseling plan.

The final process is evaluating, that is, bringing into conscious thought the question of how effective the counselor has been with interventions. Asking "how effective have I been?" is part of this process, but career counselors are also encouraged to consider what data they will use to assess this. Were the client's goals for counseling met? Did these change over time, and, if so, how might that be related to cultural values and the cultural fit of the interventions? How did the career counselor feel at various stages of career counseling?

PRACTICAL IMPLICATIONS OF RESEARCH ON THE CULTURAL FACTORS

As we noted, several cultural factors have been studied in relation to racial/ethnic minority group individuals. It is critical for career counselors to understand the complex and dynamic ways that cultural variables related to race and ethnicity affect many aspects of career decision making. We have several specific recommendations based on our review of the research:

- Explicitly attend to racism and oppression and the role that they may have played in suppressing options or creating barriers. It is important that counselors create a safe environment to ask about experiences with and perceptions about discrimination.

- Help clients develop strategies to augment resistance to racism.
- Ask clients about the expectations their family or significant others have for their career choices and who have been important positive or negative role models.
- Cultural background may affect the perception that career or work choices are (or are not) exclusively individual choices. In addition to family expectations, there may be cultural assumptions about the desirability (or lack thereof) of some choices. Ask clients whom they will consult on their decision making.
- Culture shapes the perception that career concerns are a problem or that career development is a process. For some individuals, the concept of a career trajectory may be quite foreign. Ask clients how they envision the process of making a decision or a series of decisions about their career or future work.
- Culture will shape career adaptability, including how clients develop resiliency and future orientation. Ask clients how they typically overcome obstacles or barriers. Assess a client's support system and coping skills. Assess whether the client is oriented to future planning or is more focused on the present.
- Cultural values are more influential for some clients than are traditional career planning variables such as interests. Ask clients about the strongest influences in their decisions or choices.
- Ask about both potential barriers and supports, focusing on the client's strengths to facilitate the development of supports and to counter the barriers.
- Determine if the client identifies differences between his or her aspirations (or ideal occupations) and realistic occupational goals. If so, help them to clarify, understand, and address this gap.

SUMMARY

It is critical to understand that all clients belong to one or more cultural groups, that they may adopt (or discount) the cultural values of their groups, and that the cultural values of their different group identities may sometimes conflict. This is true for individuals who identify as European American as well as for members of racial/ethnic minority groups. We argue that culturally competent career counseling is good for all clients because it brings their culture into the center of counseling. However, it also true that career counselors need to understand how racial/ethnic background may influence their clients.

We have discussed research that has investigated various aspects of the major career theories. We agree with Young and colleagues (2007) that, ideally, career theories are best developed emically, from within the cultural framework of racial/ethnic groups. Only then will we fully understand the cultural values that may be influencing work-related decisions. However, the research on how racial/ethnic groups differ on constructs in the major career theories has shown, for the most part, that culturally competent career counseling may be informed by any of the theories, as long as career counselors explicitly use metacognitive skills to culturally adapt the theory. It is clear that cultural values, barriers and supports, acculturation, and perceptions of discrimination must be incorporated, no matter which theoretical perspective a counselor uses. Our overall conclusion is that, at this point, rigorous research is still needed to more fully explain how career choices and adjustment are influenced by racial/ethnic background.

REFERENCES

Adams, J. T. (1931). *Epic of America*. Safety Harbor, FL: Simon.

Armstrong, P. I., Hubert, L., & Rounds, J. (2003). Circular unidimensional scaling: A new look at group differences in interest structure. *Journal of Counseling Psychology*, *50*, 297–308.

Betz, N. E. (2008). Advances in vocational theories. In S. D. Brown & R. W. Lent (Eds.), *Handbook of counseling psychology* (4th ed., pp. 357–374). Hoboken, NJ: Wiley.

Blustein, D. L., Murphy, K. A., Kenny, M. E., Jernigan, M., Pérez-Gualdrón, L., Castañeda, T. . . . Davis, O. (2010). Exploring urban students' constructions about school, work, race, and ethnicity. *Journal of Counseling Psychology*, *57*(2), 248–254. doi:10.1037/a0018939

Bureau of Labor Statistics. (2011). Labor force statistics from the Current Population Survey. Retrieved from http://www.bls.gov/cps/demographics.htm#race

Byars-Winston, A. M. (2006). Racial ideology in predicting social cognitive career variables for Black undergraduates. *Journal of Vocational Behavior*, *69*, 134–148.

Byars-Winston, A., Estrada, Y., Howard, C., Davis, D. & Zalapa, J. (2010). Influence of social cognitive and ethnic variables on academic goals of underrepresented students in science and engineering: A multiple-groups analysis. *Journal of Counseling Psychology*, *57*, 205–218.

Byars-Winston, A. M., & Fouad, N. A. (2006). Metacognition and multicultural competence: Expanding the culturally appropriate career counseling model. *Career Development Quarterly*, *54*, 187–201

Census Bureau. (2011). Census 2010. Retrieved from http://2010.census.gov/2010census/data/index.php

Chronister, K. M., & McWhirter, E. H. (2004). Ethnic differences in career supports and barriers for battered women: A pilot study. *Journal of Career Assessment*, *12*, 169–187.

Chung, Y. B., & Harmon, L. W. (1999). Assessment of perceived occupational opportunity for Black Americans. *Journal of Career Assessment*, *7*, 45–62.

Constantine, M. G., Wallace, B. C., & Kindaichi, M. M. (2005). Examining contextual factors in the career decision path of African American adolescents. *Journal of Career Assessment, 13*, 307–319.

Dawis, R. (1994). The theory of work adjustment as convergent theory. In M. L. Savickas & R. W. Lent (Eds.), *Convergence in career development theories: Implications for science and practice* (pp. 33–43). Palo Alto, CA: CPP.

Dawis, R. V. (2005). The Minnesota theory of work adjustment. In S. D. Brown & R. W. Lent (Eds.), *Career development and counseling: Putting theory and research to work* (pp. 3–23). Hoboken, NJ: Wiley.

Day, S. X., & Rounds, J. (1998). Universality of vocational interest structure among racial and ethnic minorities. *American Psychologist, 53*, 728–736.

Economic Policy Institute. (2010). Depression-like unemployment levels for Hispanics and African-Americans. Retrieved from http://www.epi.org/press/unemployment_rate_for_hispanics_and_african_americans_approaches_depre/

Eggerth, D. E., & Flynn, M. A. (in press). Applying the theory of work adjustment to Latino immigrant workers: An exploratory study. *Journal of Career Development*.

Evans, K. M., & Herr, E. L. (1994). The influence of racial identity and the perception of discrimination on the career aspirations of African American men and women. *Journal of Vocational Behavior, 44*, 173–184.

Flores, L. Y. (2009). Empowering life choices: Career counseling in the contexts of race and social class. In N. C. Gysbers, M. J. Heppner, & J. A Johnston (Eds.), *Career counseling: Contexts, processes, and techniques* (3rd ed., pp. 49–74). Alexandria, VA: American Counseling Association.

Flores, L. Y., Navarro, R. L., & DeWitz, S. (2008). Mexican American high school students' postsecondary educational goals applying social cognitive career theory. *Journal of Career Assessment, 16*, 489–501.

Flores, L. Y., & O'Brien, K. M. (2002). The career development of Mexican American adolescent women: A test of social cognitive career theory. *Journal of Counseling Psychology, 49*, 14–27.

Flores, L. Y., Ojeda, L., Huang, Y., Gee, D., & Lee, S. (2006). The relation of acculturation, problem-solving appraisal, and career decision-making self-efficacy to Mexican American high school students' educational goals. *Journal of Counseling Psychology, 53*, 260–266.

Flores, L. Y., Spanierman, L. B., Amstrong, P. I., & Velez, A. D. (2006). Validity of the Strong Interest Inventory and Skills Confidence Inventory with Mexican American high school students. *Journal of Career Assessment, 14*, 183–202.

Fouad, N. A., & Bingham, R. (1995). Career counseling with racial/ethnic minorities. In W. B. Walsh & S. H. Osipow (Eds.), *Handbook of vocational psychology* (2nd ed., pp. 331–366). Hillsdale, NJ: Erlbaum.

Fouad, N. A., & Byars-Winston, A. M. (2005). Cultural context of career choice: Meta-analysis of race/ethnicity differences. *Career Development Quarterly, 53*, 223–233.

Fouad, N. A., & Kantamneni, N. (2008). Contextual factors in vocational psychology: Intersections of individual, group, and societal dimensions. In S. D. Brown &

R. W. Lent (Eds.), *Handbook of counseling psychology* (4th ed., pp. 408–425). Hoboken, NJ: Wiley.

Fouad, N. A., Kantamneni, N., Smothers, M. K., Chen, Y. L., Fitzpatrick, M. E., & Terry, S. (2008). Asian American career development: A qualitative analysis. *Journal of Vocational Behavior, 72,* 43–59

Fouad, N. A., & Smith, P. L. (1996). A test of social cognitive model for middle school students: Math and science. *Journal of Counseling Psychology, 43,* 338.

Gainor, K. A., & Lent, R. W. (1998). Social cognitive expectations and racial identity attitudes in predicting the math choice. *Journal of Counseling Psychology, 45,* 403.

Gibson, C., & Jung, K. (2002). *Historical census statistics on population totals by race, 1790 to 1990, and by Hispanic origin, 1970 to 1990, for the United States, regions, divisions, and states.* Washington, DC: Census Bureau.

Gibson, D. E. (2004). Role models in career development: New directions for theory and research. *Journal of Vocational Behavior, 65,* 134–156.

Gomez, M. J., Fassinger, R. E., Prosser, J., Cooke, K., Mejia, B., & Luna, J. (2001). Voces abriendo caminos (voices forging paths): A qualitative study of the career development of notable Latinas. *Journal of Counseling Psychology, 48,* 286–300.

Gottfredson, L. S. (1981). Circumscription and compromise: A developmental theory of occupational aspirations. *Journal of Counseling Psychology, 28*(6), 545–579. doi:10.1037/0022-0167.28.6.545

Gottfredson, L. S. (2005). Applying Gottfredson's theory of circumscription and compromise in career guidance and counseling. In S. D. Brown & R. W. Lent (Eds.), *Career development & counseling: Putting theory and research to work* (pp. 71–100). Hoboken, NJ: Wiley.

Gupta, S., & Tracey, T. J. G. (2005). Dharma and interest–occupation congruence in Asian Indian college students. *Journal of Career Assessment, 13,* 320–336.

Gushue, G. V., & Whitson, M. L. (2006). The relationship of ethnic identity and gender role attitudes to the development of career choice goals among black and Latina girls. *Journal of Counseling Psychology, 53,* 379–385.

Hardin, E. E. (2007). Cultural validity of Holland's theory revisited. Paper presented in E. E. Hardin (Chair), *Cultural validity of career theories: A new perspective.* Symposium conducted at the 115th annual convention of the American Psychological Association, San Francisco, CA.

Hardin, E. E., Leong, F. T. L., & Osipow, S. H. (2001). Cultural relativity in the conceptualization of career maturity. *Journal of Vocational Behavior, 58,* 36–52.

Hartung, P. J., & Taber, B. J. (2008). Career construction and subjective well-being. *Journal of Career Assessment, 16,* 75–85.

Holland, J. L. (1997). *Making vocational choices: A theory of vocational personalities and work environments* (3rd ed.). Odessa, FL: Psychological Assessment Resources.

Howard, K. A. S., Carlstrom, A. H., Katz, A. D., Chew, A. Y., Ray, G. C., Lain, L., & Caulum, D. (2011). Career aspirations of youth: Untangling race/ethnicity, SES, and gender. *Journal of Vocational Behavior, 79,* 98–109.

Juntunen, C. L., Barraclough, D. J., Broneck, C. L., Seibel, G. A., Winrow, S. A., & Morin, P. M. (2001). American Indian perspectives on the career journey. *Journal of Counseling Psychology, 48,* 274–285.

Kantamneni, N., & Fouad, N. A. (2011). Structural differences in the 2004 Strong Interest Inventory. *Journal of Vocational Behavior, 78,* 193–201.

Kantamneni, N., & Fouad, N. A. (in press). Contextual factors and vocational interests of South Asian Americans. *Journal of Career Assessment.*

Karunanayake, D., & Nauta, M. M. (2004). The relationship between race and students' identified career role models and perceived role model influence. *Career Development Quarterly, 52,* 225–234.

Kelly, K. R., Gunsalus, A. C., & Gunsalus, R. (2009). Social cognitive predictors of the career goals of Korean American students. *Career Development Quarterly, 58,* 14–28

Kenny, M. E., & Bledsoe, M. (2005). Contributions of the relational context to career adaptability among urban adolescents. *Journal of Vocational Behavior, 66*(2), 257–272. doi:10.1016/j.jvb.2004.10.002

Kenny, M. E., Blustein, D., Chaves, A., Grossman, J., & Gallagher, L. A. (2003). The role of perceived barriers and relational support in the educational and vocational lives of urban high school students. *Journal of Counseling Psychology, 50,* 142–155.

Kenny, M. E., Gualdron, D. S., Sparks, E., Blustein, D. L., & Jernigan, M. (2007). Urban adolescents' constructions of supports and barriers to educational and career attainment. *Journal of Counseling Psychology, 54,* 336–343.

Kim, B. S. K., & Atkinson, D. R. (2002). Asian American client adherence to Asian cultural values, counselor expression of cultural values, counselor ethnicity, and career counseling process. *Journal of Counseling Psychology, 49,* 3–13.

Kim, B. S. K., Li, L. C., & Liang, T. H. (2002). Effects of Asian American client adherence to Asian cultural values, session goal, and counselor emphasis of client expression on career counseling process. *Journal of Counseling Psychology, 49,* 342–354.

Lent, R. W., Brown, S. D., & Hackett, G. (1994). Toward a unifying social cognitive theory of career and academic interest, choice, and performance. *Journal of Vocational Behavior, 45*(1), 79–122. doi:10.1006/jvbe.1994.1027

Lent, R. W., Brown, S. D., & Hackett, G. (2000). Contextual supports and barriers to career choice: A social cognitive analysis. *Journal of Counseling Psychology, 47,* 36–49.

Lent, R. W., Brown, S. D., Sheu, H. B., Schmidt, J., Brenner, B. R., Gloster, C. S., Treistman, D. (2005). Social cognitive predictors of academic interests and goals in engineering: Utility for women and students at historically Black universities. *Journal of Counseling Psychology, 52,* 84–92.

Lent, R. W., Lopez, A. M., Lopez, F. G., & Sheu, H. B. (2008). Social cognitive career theory and the prediction of interests and choice goals in the computing disciplines. *Journal of Vocational Behavior, 73,* 52–62.

Lent, R. W., & Sheu, H. B. (2009). Applying social cognitive career theory across cultures: Empirical status. In J. G. Ponterotto, J. M. Casas, L. A. Suzuki, & C. M. Alexander (Eds.), *Handbook of multicultural counseling* (3rd ed.). Thousand Oaks, CA: Sage.

Leong, F. T. L. (2001). The role of acculturation in the career adjustment of Asian American workers: A test of Leong and Chou's (1994) formulations. *Cultural Diversity and Ethnic Minority Psychology, 7*, 262–273.

Leong, F. T. L., Austin, J. T., Sekaran, U., & Komarraju, M. (1998). An evaluation of the cross-cultural validity of Holland's theory: Career choices by workers in India. *Journal of Vocational Behavior, 52*, 441–455.

Leong, F. T. L., & Chou, E. L. (1994). The role of ethnic identity and acculturation in the vocational behavior of Asian Americans: An integrative review. *Journal of Vocational Behavior, 44*, 155–172.

Leong, F. T. L., Hardin, E. E., & Gupta, A. (2011). Self in vocational psychology: A cultural formulation approach. In P. J. Hartung & L. M. Subich (Eds.), *Developing self in work and career: Concepts, cases, and contexts* (pp. 193–211) Washington, DC: APA. doi:10.1037/12348-012

Leong, F. T. L., & Hartung, P. J. (1997). Career assessment with culturally different clients: Proposing an integrative-sequential conceptual framework for cross-cultural career counseling research and practice. *Journal of Career Assessment, 5*, 183–201.

Leong, F. T. L., & Pearce, M. (2011). Desiderata: Towards indigenous models of vocational psychology. *International Journal for Educational and Vocational Guidance, 11*(2), 65–77. doi:10.1007/s10775-011-9198-z

Leung, S. A. (1995). Career development and counseling: A multicultural perspective. In J. G. Ponterotto, J. M. Casas, L. A. Suzuki, & C. M. Alexander (Eds.), *Handbook of multicultural counseling* (pp. 549–566). Thousand Oaks, CA: Sage.

Lovelace, K., & Rosen, B. (1996). Differences in achieving person–organization fit among diverse groups of managers. *Journal of Management, 22*(5), 703–722. doi:10.1177/014920639602200502

Luzzo, D., & Hutcheson, K. (1996). Causal attributions and sex differences associated with perceptions of occupational barriers. *Journal of Counseling & Development, 75*, 124–130.

Luzzo, D., & McWhirter, E. (2001). Sex and ethnic differences in the perception of educational and career-related barriers and levels of coping efficacy. *Journal of Counseling & Development, 79*, 61.

Lyons, H. Z., & O'Brien, K. M. (2006). The role of person–environment fit in the job satisfaction and tenure intentions of African American employees. *Journal of Counseling Psychology, 53*(4), 387–396. doi:10.1037/0022-0167.53.4.387

McWhirter, E. H. (1997). Perceived barriers to education and career: Ethnic and gender differences. *Journal of Vocational Behavior, 50*, 124–140.

McWhirter, E. H., Hackett, G., & Bandalos, D. L. (1998). A causal model of the educational plans and career expectations of Mexican American high school girls. *Journal of Counseling Psychology, 45*, 166–181.

McWhirter, E. H., Torres, D. M., Salgado, S., & Valdez, M. (2007). Perceived barriers and postsecondary plans in Mexican American and White adolescents. *Journal of Career Assessment, 15*, 119–138.

Metz, A. J., Fouad, N., & Ihle-Helledy, K. (2009). Career aspirations and expectations of college students. *Journal of Career Assessment, 17*, 155–171.

Navarro, R. L., Flores, L. Y., & Worthington, R. L. (2007). Mexican American middle school students' goal intentions in mathematics and science: A test of social cognitive career theory. *Journal of Counseling Psychology, 54*, 320–335.

Ojeda, L., & Flores, L. Y. (2008). The influence of gender, generation level, parent's education level, and perceived barriers on the educational aspirations of Mexican American high school students. *Career Development Quarterly, 57*, 84–95.

Pearson, S. M., & Bieschke, K. J. (2001). Succeeding against the odds: An examination of familial influences on the career development of professional African American women. *Journal of Counseling Psychology, 48*, 301–309.

Rivera, L. M., Chen, E. C., Flores, L. Y., Blumberg, F., & Ponterotto, J. G. (2007). The effects of perceived barriers, role models, and acculturation on the career self-efficacy and career consideration of Hispanic women. *Career Development Quarterly, 56*, 47–61.

Rounds, J., & Hesketh, B. (1994). The theory of work adjustment: Unifying principles and concepts. In M. L. Savikas & R. W. Lent (Eds.), *Convergence in career development theories: Implications for science and practice* (pp. 177–186). Palo Alto, CA: CPP.

Savickas, M. L. (2011). *Theories of psychotherapy series. Career counseling.* Washington, DC: American Psychological Association.

Super, D. E., Savickas, M. L., & Super, C. M. (1996). The life-span, life-space approach to careers. In D. Brown, L. Brooks, & Associates (Eds.), *Career choice and development* (3rd ed., pp. 121–178). San Francisco, CA: Jossey-Bass.

Swanson, J. L., & Woitke, M. B. (1997). Theory into practice in career assessment for women: Assessment and interventions regarding perceived career barriers. *Journal of Career Assessment, 5*, 443–462.

Tang, M., Fouad, N. A., & Smith, P. L. (1999). Asian Americans' career choices: A path model to examine factors influencing their career choices. *Journal of Vocational Behavior, 54*, 142–157.

Tracey, T. J., & Rounds, J. (1993). Evaluating Holland's and Gati's vocational-interest models: A structural meta-analysis. *Psychological Bulletin, 113*, 229

Tsabari, O., Tziner, A., & Meir, E. I. (2005). Updated meta-analysis on the relationship between congruence and satisfaction. *Journal of Career Assessment, 13*, 216–232.

U.S. Department of Education, Institute on Education Sciences. (2011). National Center on Education Statistics. Retrieved from http://nces.ed.gov/

Waller, B. (2006). Math interest and choice intentions of non-traditional African-American college students. *Journal of Vocational Behavior, 68*, 538–547.

Westbrook, B. W., Buck, R. W., Jr., Wynne, D. C., & Sanford, E. (1994). Career maturity in adolescence: Reliability and validity of self-ratings of abilities by gender and ethnicity. *Journal of Career Assessment, 2*(2), 125–161. doi:10.1177/106907279400200203

Young, R. A., Marshall, S. K., & Valach, L. (2007). Making career theories more culturally sensitive: Implications for counseling. *Career Development Quarterly, 56*(1), 4–18.

CHAPTER 9

Social Class, Poverty, and Career Development

CINDY L. JUNTUNEN, SABA RASHEED ALI, AND KIPP R. PIETRANTONIO

THE CALL FOR CAREER specialists to attend more fully to the needs of people living with limited financial or social means has been made repeatedly (Blustein, 2006; Blustein, McWhirter, & Perry, 2005; Diemer & Ali, 2009; Fouad & Brown, 2000; Sloan, 2005). In the current climate of economic downturn in the United States and around the world, the need for career counselors to grapple with poverty and class issues is starkly apparent. For example, the U.S. Census Bureau reported that the number of Americans living in poverty in 2010 exceeded 46 million (or 15%), the largest number since poverty estimates have been reported (DeNavas-Walt, Proctor, & Smith, 2011). In 2010, 10.4 million Americans were identified as "working poor," meaning that their income was below the federal poverty level even though they spent at least 27 weeks of the year working or looking for work (U.S. Department of Labor, Bureau of Labor Statistics, 2011a). In fact, current trends suggest that poverty is now more likely to be experienced as working poverty than as nonworking poverty (Caputo, 2007).

Despite such acute conditions and the underlying chronic nature of differential social class and wealth distribution in the United States, the influence of social class and poverty in career development continues to be understudied relative to other social identity factors such as race, gender, and sexual orientation. In this way, career development theory has been consistent with the broader domains of psychology and the counseling literature. Scholars have suggested that limited progress in examining social class in the larger fields of psychology and counseling may be related to numerous factors, including the American taboo against discussing social class

(Liu, 2011), unexamined social class biases among providers (Smith, 2005, 2010; Smith & Mao, 2012), and distancing from the poor through cognitions, behaviors, and institutional policies (Lott, 2002). Through these and related mechanisms, career counselors and vocational psychologists may recapitulate the invisibility of the working poor in American society (Shipler, 2005).

Fortunately, career scholars are beginning to challenge the status quo by actively addressing social class and poverty in career counseling interventions and research. Social class influences preparation for and entrance into the labor market, making it inextricably linked with career development (Diemer & Ali, 2009). Further, access to work and its resulting resources are important components of social mobility in the United States (Fouad & Fitzpatrick, 2009). Career counselors are therefore in a unique position to have a positive impact on the lives of individuals and families living with limited resources, but only if they are able to effectively integrate social class issues into their treatment planning and interventions.

The integration of social class into career counseling can be challenging because of the lack of clarity in identifying what is actually meant by social class (Liu, 2011; Liu, Ali, et al., 2004). Social class is frequently equated with socioeconomic status (SES), which can be assessed as a function of income, education, and occupation (Hollingshead, 1975). More complex considerations of social class include the experience of class as a worldview (Liu, Soleck, Hopps, Dunston & Pickett, 2004), access to resources and education (Blustein, Juntunen, & Worthington, 2000), and complex interactions of multiple indicators of social status (Brown et al., 2002). A full discussion of social class must include groups with sufficient and even significant resources, and there is some evidence that individuals who are identified as privileged (i.e., wealthy, upper or upper-middle class) may also confront important issues that limit their career options (Lapour & Heppner, 2009). However, people with limited incomes are both more likely to be in need of vocational resources and less likely to have them. Given that reality, this chapter focuses primarily on working with clients living with lower social status, fewer economic resources, and less job security, including the working poor and the unemployed.

Given the profound link between social class, poverty, and career development (Diemer & Ali, 2009), it is critical that career specialists develop a foundational understanding of the influence of social class on access to and achievement in the world of work. Further, it is necessary to assess the tools already at our disposal to work effectively with clients from less privileged backgrounds and to improve our ability by adding new and relevant knowledge and skills. The major career theories presented in the first chapters of this text have attended to social class to varying degrees. This chapter presents a brief critique of each theory's consideration of social class and offers suggestions for theory development that can improve applicability to clients of varying social class status. For career counselors to work effectively with social class issues, they need to have some familiarity with the sociological and social work perspectives related to social class, as well as vocational and career development perspectives. To that end, this chapter offers a discussion of different perspectives on social class, drawing from sociological and psychological theories. We then review the existing empirical literature relevant to the influence of class issues on work and vocational behavior across the life span, including literature from social work that is directly relevant to working with career counseling clients living with limited means. The chapter concludes with specific suggestions for practitioners, designed to increase both understanding of class and poverty issues and the usefulness and relevance of career interventions.

CONSIDERATION OF SOCIAL CLASS AND POVERTY IN MAJOR CAREER DEVELOPMENT THEORIES

Extant career theory has paid limited explicit attention to the life and struggles of working-class people. From 2005 to 2009, over 6 million jobs were lost in the United States alone. Tragically, the state of career development theory may not be prepared for this type of economic shift, which results in significant personal distress and potential for subsequent mental health concerns. Socioeconomic issues are generally an afterthought or considered a "frictional factor" (Dawis, 2005, p. 15) to psychological theory, including vocational psychology theory. Blustein (2006), in contrast, argues that not only are SES issues relevant but also they are the inherent cornerstone of why individuals work. He describes work as a means of survival and a method of acquiring power within a culture. This description bears a striking resemblance to what it means to participate in social class mobility, in that Blustein is positing that people work to obtain the resources necessary for moving from lower to higher social status.

Some aspects of career counseling theory may actually serve as a barrier to meeting the needs of clients from a lower social status. That is, they are inherently designed to help people find work that is satisfying based on various factors such as personality variables, interests, skills, abilities, level of ambition, past achievements, work experience, and developmental goals. These are important career development issues, but they may not be adequate for addressing the unique concerns of people living in poverty or lower socioeconomic status. Rarely does a career theory elaborate on relevant issues such as preparing for employment with limited resources, transitioning lifestyles, decreasing quality of life, vocational oppression and discrimination, or working with little hope of promotion or long-term employment. The expansion of career development theory to be inclusive of real-life SES factors, and to stretch the continuum of career counseling practices to address the relevant contextual factors related to socioeconomic resources, is crucial to meeting the needs of people in the immediate and long-term future.

PERSON–ENVIRONMENT FIT THEORIES

The first and possibly most widely employed approach to career counseling is person–environment (P-E) fit theory, which posits the importance of matching an individual's values, abilities, and interests with characteristics of a particular work environment. Both Holland's (1997) RIASEC model (see Nauta, Chapter 3, this volume) and the Minnesota theory of work adjustment (TWA; Dawis, 2005; Swanson & Schneider, Chapter 2, this volume) focus on the fit between the individual and the work environment. The RIASEC model has been subject to significant research, and its tenets have been generally corroborated across cultures (Day & Rounds, 1998; Nauta, 2010). Many assessments and measures that are used daily in college counseling centers, high school guidance offices, and government work agencies are drawn from Holland's theory.

TWA is also a widely used and empirically supported career theory. Dawis (2005) outlined some of the underlying assumptions of the model. Advocates of this theory believe that people have needs that have to be met and that they will attempt to meet them through the work environment. Many of the behaviors people engage in are an effort to meet these requirements. Simultaneously, work environments also have needs, and if the person's skill set can satisfy the work environment's needs, this will result in a state of satisfactoriness. If the environment also meets the individual's needs, this will result in satisfaction for the employee.

Both Holland's RIASEC model and TWA provide important information about obtaining work that is likely to be satisfactory, based on individual and work environment characteristics. Dawis and Lofquist (1984) have also outlined the use of TWA for on-the-job adjustment and counseling for career change. Further, Dawis (2005) outlined adjustment styles that individuals apply when they feel their satisfaction is threatened. These are important aspects of TWA and potentially have applicability for social class and poverty issues, via averting the risk of unemployment. However, even within this context, it is assumed that individuals will be given an opportunity to react in order to improve their satisfactoriness or will at least be aware that their employment may be in jeopardy. Although people do lose jobs as a result of a lack of "fit" or satisfactoriness, for an increasing number of employees the risk of job loss is tied to external factors (e.g., organizational downsizing). This economic reality creates a disconnect between theory and the experience of employees. The assessments, interventions, and tools of P-E fit theories can be useful for clients with limited means and reduced opportunities for employment, if wielded by counselors with a solid understanding of and appreciation for the social context experienced by clients.

DEVELOPMENTAL CAREER THEORIES

The career theory approaches of Donald Super (1990; Super, Savickas, & Super, 1996; Hartung, Chapter 4, this volume), Mark Savickas (Chapter 6, this volume), Linda Gottfredson (2005), and Vondracek, Lerner, and Schulenberg (1983) all address career development as an inherent part of human development. They vary importantly in their attention to the social context of career development and specifically to the influence of social class and poverty.

The field of career counseling owes a debt of gratitude to Super (1990) for his innovative ideas about career activities across the life span, which shifted the focus from vocational guidance to career counseling and contributed to important counseling skills. Nonetheless, his conceptual framework was ensconced in the experience of White, male, middle-class individuals who represented the dominant culture. Over time, Super (1990) began to integrate a broader spectrum of life experiences, including those of women and international populations. He also adjusted important constructs in his theory to address social influences, particularly through attending to the need to be prepared to recycle in careers. Despite these adjustments, neither Super nor his colleagues directly addressed the needs of low-income individuals.

Career construction theory has also attended only minimally to social class issues, although it, too, has the potential to address specific concerns with its emphasis on career adaptability (Savickas, Chapter 6). Within career construction theory, there is a fundamental assumption that individuals are making active choices that create a career narrative. Savickas (2005) states: "Careers do not unfold, they are constructed as individuals make choices that express their self-concepts and substantiate their goals in the social reality of work roles" (p. 43). Unfortunately, careers in the lives of low-income people often do "unfold," but are reactions of necessity rather than choice. The fundamental belief that people have the choice to construct a narrative as opposed to having a narrative imposed on them is a major oversight of career construction theory. This is not to say that individuals lack agency as a personal characteristic, but that the choices that lead to the construction of the narrative may be much more forced than is assumed by the notion that individuals constructing a career narrative are seeking to express their identity.

Savickas (2005) also asserts that, regardless of SES, most people can find opportunities in their work to both express themselves and make a contribution. However, previous research (Halle, 1984) has indicated that working-class jobs are distant from the decision-making process, which suggests that self-expression may have less influence for those employed in the working class. This undoubtedly has an effect on an individual's ability to construct meaning and purposefulness around their vocational identity. The concern here is that the level of agency, or volition, within this expression may differ dramatically as a function of SES (Blustein, 2006). Simply looking at a work wardrobe can express this clear difference. A middle-class individual working a white-collar office job may be able to pick out various professional outfits that express who they are, select a different one each day depending on their mood or the tasks ahead, and display them as a competent professional. In contrast, individuals who work in low-income service jobs may only be able to express individuality through the color of undershirt beneath their uniforms, the choice of their full or shortened name on their nametag, or their choice of which black nonslip shoes they choose to purchase. This speaks to an individual's self-determination of the decision-making power around career construction and the degree of control a worker has in everyday life.

Gottfredson (2005) proposed that career interests develop through critical advances in the understanding of social space that occurs throughout childhood. She explicitly addressed social class through her attention to the role of social valuation in the process of circumscription and compromise. Specifically, she hypothesized that children start to rule out work opportunities based on their social value by the ages of 9 to early teens. Interestingly, this is approached from the perspective of setting the floor on possible job options (i.e., those that are "too low") by ruling out work that is "unacceptably low in social standing" (2005, p. 79). Gottfredson does clearly link this to community norms and reference groups, acknowledging, for example, that youth from working-class families are going to have a different perspective than those from middle-class families. The upper boundary of possible job options is assumed to be determined by the effort one is willing to invest, such that the decision about whether to pursue jobs of great social value revolves around whether that pursuit is too hard. This assumption may allow a counselor to overlook the possibility that a client of lower social status may actually be ruling out higher-valued jobs because they seem too high in social standing (i.e., no one in the client's reference group has ever had that job), rather than too hard to obtain (i.e., capable of doing the work).

Finally, Vondracek and colleagues (1986) proposed a career life span development model that explicitly examines the interaction of the individual and his or her social context. A basic assumption of this approach is that the individual and the environment in which he or she exists are viewed as changing *interdependently* over time (Vondracek & Lerner, 1982), which has interesting implications for thinking about clients dealing with the external forces of the labor market and national and global economies. Career life span development is heavily influenced by the ecological human development theory proposed by Bronfenbrenner (1993). Bronfenbrenner conceptualized an ecological system consisting of four major subsystems, which interact to influence human development. These subsystems include (a) the microsystem, which consists of the interpersonal interactions that occur in a given setting, such as home, school, work, or social group; (b) the mesosystem, in which two or more microsystem environments interact, such as the relationship between work and home; (c) the exosystem, the social structures and linkages that indirectly impact individuals, such as community resources or neighborhood characteristics; and (d) the macrosystem, which is most distal from the individual and includes the norms and values of the larger society.

This approach to development can easily be transferred to career development for lower-income and poor individuals, who are often in the situation of having to respond and adapt to numerous forces outside their control. Several vocational scholars (Brown et al., 1996; Heppner & O'Brien, 2006; Young, 1983) have argued that the ecological framework is a valid tool for addressing the vocational issues presented by social class and poverty.

SOCIAL LEARNING THEORIES

Career counseling theories that specifically address the influence of social factors are, not surprisingly, more likely to have included considerations of social class and poverty, and they also address the systems and settings identified in the ecological approach. Two specific theories worthy of note in this arena are social learning theory (Krumboltz, 1979) and social cognitive career theory (SCCT; Lent, Brown, & Hackett, 1994; Lent, Chapter 5, this volume). Krumboltz (1979) identified four variables that contributed to identifying and making decisions about vocational goals: genetic endowments and special abilities, environmental situations and events, associative and instrumental learning experiences, and task approach skills. The explicit attention to genetic endowments, including sex, race, and special abilities, provided a framework for examining differences in vocational attainment across sex, racial/ethnic, and other biologically identified groups of career decision makers. It is the inclusion of social and cultural factors, such as geography, legislation, labor market forces, family factors, and educational settings that both sets social learning theory apart from previous vocational theories and makes it theoretically useful for considering social class and poverty issues.

Social learning theory explicitly recognizes that individual interests or choices are not the only determinants of vocational attainment. This set the stage both for understanding factors that contribute to self-efficacy, which has become a critical consideration in understanding social class influence on vocational behavior, and for addressing the systems of the ecological development theory (Bronfenbrenner, 1993). Social learning theory did not address specific counseling goals. But more recently, in presenting happenstance learning theory (HLT), Krumboltz (2009) proposed: "The goal of career counseling is to help clients learn to take actions to achieve more satisfying career and personal lives—not to make a single career decision" (p. 135). This focus on helping clients learn to take action, combined with an understanding of social determinants, can contribute to developing effective interventions.

SCCT is a theory that takes into account many of the issues discussed throughout the chapter so far and does so in the form of distal, proximal, and background factors that may influence individuals' career choices (Lent, Chapter 5, this volume). As of yet, social class factors appear to be underexamined in SCCT theory and research (Lent, Brown & Hackett, 2000), at least relative to other contextual factors. Further, the focus on vocational interests as contributing to goals and actions does not fully address the reality of individuals who either do not have the option of making decisions based on their interests or do not have the resources to explore interests. However, the potential for SCCT theory to be inclusive of social class and poverty factors has been clearly articulated (Diemer & Ali, 2009; Fouad & Fitzpatrick, 2009).

SCCT does explicitly acknowledge that the expression of interests is not the only avenue by which career goals are set and work-seeking behaviors are initiated. In fact, the constructs of self-efficacy and outcome expectations may directly predict goals and behaviors. For example, an individual whose primary concern is survival may identify work that he or she feels capable of doing and that will result in a livable wage, regardless of whether the nature of that work is inherently interesting or rewarding. As is demonstrated in the upcoming section of this chapter focused on career development milestones research, both SCCT and the core construct of self-efficacy have played important roles in understanding the influence of social class on academic and vocational achievement. Additional and intensive focus on individuals living in poverty or at lower levels of social class may allow adjustments to the theory that will make the SCCT model more inclusive and relevant across social status.

Summary of Career Theory and Social Class

The attention to social class and poverty clearly varies across career theories. The effects of outsourcing, globalization, and global recession are largely overlooked in career theory but are very relevant in career counseling. This requires that career counselors integrate knowledge and perspectives outside of vocational theory to be as effective as possible in their work with clients. To that end, the next section of this chapter addresses perspectives on social class and poverty that have been developed both inside and outside of career theory but can be brought to bear on these critical questions.

ADDITIONAL PERSPECTIVES ON SOCIAL CLASS AND POVERTY

There are numerous ways to consider social class, social status, and socioeconomic status (Diemer & Ali, 2009). We begin with a discussion of sociological perspectives that anchor an understanding of socioeconomic status and social class. This is followed by an emerging vocationally informed perspective, the measurement of differential status identity (DSI; Brown et al., 2002; Fouad & Brown, 2000). Blustein's psychology of working perspective, which infuses social class into vocational theory, is then explored. Both DSI and the psychology of working perspective highlight the importance of understanding individual worldviews, which is addressed more fully through the social class worldview model (Liu, Soleck, et al., 2004). The section concludes with a discussion of the factors that can limit career counseling with poor populations.

Sociological Perspectives

Sociologists and economists generally focus on the macrolevel underpinnings of poverty and its relationship to work (Blustein, 2006; Corcoran, 1995). These perspectives help to elucidate the systemic factors that contribute to poverty. In particular, sociologists tend to stress the importance of "previous generations of wealth and neighborhood characteristics" (Diemer & Ali, 2009, p. 254) and strongly argue that these have more influence in occupational attainment than is considered by more individualistic models of career development.

The importance of past generation, neighborhood, and sociocultural influences was identified in a review of four sociological models (Corcoran, 1995): the resources model, the correlated disadvantages model, the welfare culture model, and the underclass model. The resources model views the transmission of poverty as being largely influenced by parental resources; poor parents need to decide between putting resources into education and other strategies for increasing social capital for their children versus pure survival needs such as food and shelter. The correlated disadvantages model is closely related, noting that poor parents are not just poor; they also have less access to education and other resources themselves. The welfare culture model posits that the government welfare system nurtures values, attitudes, and behaviors that support a life in poverty. Finally, the underclass model proposes that poor neighborhoods isolate their inhabitants from access to other resources and that this is particularly influenced by joblessness.

Reviewing the empirical support for these models generated by a flurry of research attention in the late 1980s and early 1990s, Corcoran (1995) concluded that the economic resources model was the most likely to contribute to generational poverty and that parental resources would predict the social and economic capital of the next generation. This conclusion was supported by multiple studies using large longitudinal data sets that demonstrated that poor children, across racial groups (primarily African American and White), had lower adult economic status and fewer educational and occupational opportunities. Corcoran also noted that African American children were more likely to live in families with lower economic resources and, even when economic backgrounds were similar, were eventually less likely to do well economically because of race-based employment discrimination.

There is contemporary evidence that generational wealth continues to contribute to the disparities between Whites and African Americans (Oliver & Shapiro, 2006). Shapiro, Meschede, and Sullivan (2010) conducted research and policy analysis on these discrepancies across decades and described the "broken chain of achievement" (p. 2) that contributes to higher poverty rates among African Americans. These authors concluded that the data demonstrate very large disparities in accumulation of wealth between White Americans and their African American counterparts within the same income categories (i.e., comparing those in the same jobs). As a result of a history of unequal opportunity structures, African Americans cannot rely on past generations to assist them with financial needs, provide academic or extracurricular experiences for their children, or assist them in times of familial crisis. Further, in an economic crisis, African American families have fewer resources to draw on if they are impacted by unemployment or disability (Ali, in press; Shapiro et al., 2010). This lack of generational wealth has an aggregate impact over generations. Thus, despite traditional expectations (e.g., that higher education leads to better-paying jobs), it is more difficult for African Americans to achieve the same wealth as their White counterparts because of the cumulative effect of prior economic disadvantage.

Within the current career development literature, there has been little attention to how economic factors such as generational wealth relate to occupational attainment. Integrating sociological perspectives with career development theories can provide a richer source of information that attends to both the person aspects and the structural aspects of poverty and its relationship to occupational attainment and work. Attending to family economic resources as a key contextual factor that influences the development of self-efficacy, goals, and interests, as well as understanding of self and the world of work, could help to inform career counseling. The following perspectives provide some guidance on how to integrate social status issues into vocational perspectives.

DIFFERENTIAL STATUS IDENTITY

Recognizing the complex interaction between external, objective measures of socioeconomic status and the internalized perceptions of social status, Fouad and Brown (2000) proposed the concept of differential status identity (DSI) to assess individuals' perceptions of their own access to economic resources, access to social power, and access to prestige, relative to others in society. DSI therefore considers internalized perceptions of one's gender, ethnicity, socioeconomic resources, and other social identities and how these perceptions influence psychological and social well-being (Thompson & Subich, 2006). The constructs of DSI have been used to develop the Differential Status Identity Scale (Brown et al., 2002), allowing some initial research on this construct.

Preliminary research on DSI suggests that it might provide a promising lens for understanding the impact of social class and poverty on career development. For example, individuals raised in families with lower access to economic resources reported experiencing more direct and systemic classism during their lifetimes than those raised in middle- and upper-class families (Thompson & Subich, 2011). Further, DSI was directly related to career decision self-efficacy and career indecisiveness; specifically, individuals who perceived themselves as having less access to social power and economic resources had higher levels of career indecision and lower levels of self-efficacy. Interestingly, institutional classism (i.e, the ways in which social institutions, such as school, work, and government, treat individuals differently based on real or perceived social class as reflected in norms, regulations, and policies) was more likely to have a negative effect on DSI than direct interpersonal classism (i.e., being treated differently by another person due to real or perceived social class status), suggesting that it is the systemic macrosystem influence of class that may be most deleterious.

PSYCHOLOGY OF WORKING

The psychology of working (Blustein, 2006) is a multidisciplinary perspective that attempts to integrate working as a life domain within the realm of human development. Within this perspective, Blustein articulates the importance of working for survival, relates this directly to issues of poverty, and argues that a common theme among individuals "without grand career narratives" (or those living in poverty) is that work is viewed primarily as a means of survival. Further, he draws from sociological literature to underscore the importance of work as a means of providing structure for communities and draws on Wilson's (1996) work to illustrate the structural demise that occurs in communities that lose major sources of employment, such as manufacturing plants.

In line with his conclusions, Blustein (2006) issued a challenge to vocational psychologists and career development theorists that more research is needed on the experience of working for those who have the fewest economic resources. Implicit within this discussion is the need to consider the structural changes that are occurring in the current workforce that are contributing to poverty rates. For example, recently the Center for Labor Market Studies issued a policy brief that highlights the discrepancies between the affluent and those with limited economic resources as a result of the current economic climate. Sum and Khatiwada (2010) reported that while individuals living in the bottom of the income distribution in the United States faced a true labor market depression, those within the top deciles of the income distribution experienced full employment.

Social class discrepancies are an important consideration in the discussion of the relationship between poverty and work. Blustein (2006) asserts that classism often operates as a barrier to occupational attainment and deserves more attention within the vocational psychology and career counseling literature. Blustein notes that the social class worldview model (SCWM; Liu, Soleck, et al., 2004) offers promise in expanding the psychology of working perspective by integrating classism as a form of oppression.

SOCIAL CLASS WORLDVIEW MODEL

Although not a vocational theory, SCWM (Liu, Soleck, et al., 2004) has broad implications for understanding how social class and poverty affect access to occupational opportunities. SCWM focuses on the meaning and importance of individuals' subjective experiences and definitions of social class and classism. SWCM also posits that all people belong to an economic culture and experience pressure to meet the expectations placed on them by their economic culture, through behaving in certain ways or having certain possessions (Liu, Soleck, et al., 2004).

Classism, which is central to SCWM, is defined as prejudice and discrimination directed at people engaged in behaviors not congruent with the values and expectations of their economic culture. Classism can be directed:

(a) upward (negative feelings toward those perceived to be snobs and elitists), (b) downward (negative feelings toward those perceived as worse off), (c) laterally (classism directed at people perceived as similar to oneself, for example, keeping up with the Joneses), and (d) internally as internalized classism (emotional and cognitive difficulty experienced by individuals when they fail to meet the demands of their economic culture). Individuals tend to unconsciously internalize class-related messages (Liu, Soleck, et al., 2004), which can subsequently impact their work expectations or beliefs.

Liu and Ali (2008) outlined a four-step model that can facilitate exploration of class experiences for individuals living in poverty. Ali, Fall, and Hoffman (in press) applied this model to working with individuals who are unemployed and experience social status changes. The four-step model (Liu & Ali, 2008) proposes the following: (a) assist the client to identify and understand his or her economic culture and the types of messages received about working or losing one's job; (b) assist the client to explore how these messages may have affected current occupational choices; (c) identify the client's experiences with classism (e.g., internal, lateral, downward) and encourage developing adaptive, realistic, and healthy expectations about himself or herself by reviewing the client's belief system regarding occupational choices; and (d) help the client challenge his or her experiences with classism by reflecting on strong messages she or he received about work and discussing how these messages impact current job search processes or educational planning.

This four-step model can be used in conjunction with other theoretical interventions, such as those based in SCCT. For example, it is common with SCCT school-based career interventions to explore career barriers and their impact on self-efficacy beliefs and outcome expectations. Using the current model with students living in poverty to explore the types of classism they experienced and to identify messages about work might be useful in helping them make plans and identify support systems to overcome internal and external class-related barriers. This model can be extended to help clients understand how classist messages they have received related to work or institutionalized experiences may have affected their work histories (Ali et al., in press). Further, the model can also assist counselors to identify their own social class biases related to working with individuals living in poverty. We turn next to a discussion of how classism often operates as a barrier to working with individuals living in poverty.

BARRIERS TO WORKING WITH THE POOR

Recently, several scholars have discussed the general lack of attention to issues of poverty in the psychological literature (Lott, 2002; Smith &

Mao, 2012). Lott (2002) noted that when psychologists do write about or research those living in poverty, they often conceptualize individuals' concerns and problems from a distanced perspective that starkly contrasts the experiences of those living in poverty with those of the middle-class norm, resulting in a form of classism that excludes and discounts the experiences of those living in poverty. Heppner and O'Brien (2006) argued that one of the major barriers to providing services to this population is classism that results from cognitive distancing, as described by Lott (2002). Often, this classism is subtle and manifests itself in avoidance of individuals living in poverty.

Another barrier to providing vocational counseling for individuals living in poverty is quite simply physical access to services. Smith (2010) argued that if we want to help individuals living in poverty, then we need to provide services in locations that are convenient to these clients. Further, Lott and Bullock (2007) recommended that psychologists become more involved in public policy efforts to rectify broken governmental systems such as TANF (Temporary Assistance for Needy Families), commonly referred to as welfare to work. By first working with poor clients and conducting research that delineates their needs, career counselors and vocational psychologists may be in a better position to contribute to policy efforts.

The goal of contributing to policy efforts is daunting, given the myriad issues that have to be addressed. For example, Haley-Lock and Shah (2007) articulated the numerous ways that government and private-sector policies support the structure of low-wage employment that keeps up to 25% of the working population living in poverty. To effect policy change, they suggest the need to (a) change public policies to better match job and worker characteristics (e.g., expanding criteria for unemployment insurance so that leaving work for a valid reason does not make a worker ineligible or extending the definition of dependents qualifying for Family and Medical Leave Act), (b) reduce the vulnerabilities that accompany minimum wage policies (e.g., by expanding the benefits of the earned income tax credit), and (c) expand the opportunities available to workers in lower-wage work (e.g., by increasing access to child care or health care or encouraging skill development of lower-wage workers). Although individual career counselors may not be able to effect these changes, they can inform and contribute through collective advocacy with local, state, and national policy makers and employers.

THE INFLUENCE OF SOCIAL CLASS AND POVERTY ON CAREER DEVELOPMENT MILESTONES

Following a brief flurry of research in the 1970s and 1980s on the relationship of SES to such career factors as vocational maturity (Dillard, 1976), work task complexity (MacKay & Miller, 1982), and occupational choice (Hannah & Khan, 1989), vocational research on SES and social class diminished. A resurgence occurred in the early 2000s, likely in response to increased awareness of SES and poverty issues following the Personal Responsibility and Work Opportunity Reconciliation Act (welfare-to-work legislation) of 1996. There has since been increasing research on the influence of social class, or at least socioeconomic status, on academic achievement and aspirations, career aspirations and expectations, access to employment, and work satisfaction and performance.

CAREER ASPIRATIONS AND EXPECTATIONS IN YOUTH

In 2009, 31 million children in the United States (42% of the child population) lived in low-income families (Annie E. Casey Foundation, 2011), and the proportion of children of color living in poverty is even greater (Edelman & Jones, 2004). The influence of childhood poverty is persistent, as children raised in low-income families are more likely to earn less as adults (Holzer, Schanzenbach, Duncan, & Ludwig, 2007) and less likely than children in higher-SES families to advance economically relative to their parents (Isaacs, Sawhill, & Haskins, 2008). Shipler (2005) eloquently described the educational and work experiences of children living in working-poor families, noting that the lack of financial resources can exacerbate other concerns and interrupt educational opportunities. "Money may not always cure, but it can often insulate one problem from another" (p. 76). Children without the insulation offered by financial safety are more likely to have health concerns and less likely to flourish in school.

The impact on future college or work readiness can be seen as early as entrance to elementary school, as children from lower-income families have weaker math skills at the point of entrance to kindergarten and demonstrate less growth in math skills than do children from middle-income families (Jordan & Levine, 2009). Similarly, lower-income children demonstrate lower reading abilities both at entrance to school and at the end of third grade, which is associated with a greater likelihood of dropout from high school (Annie E. Casey Foundation, 2010). Among undergraduate college students, stereotype threat (i.e., the risk of confirming a negative stereotype about the social group to which one belongs; Steele & Aronson, 1995) has also been identified as a source of decreased performance on tests presented as diagnostic of ability for students of lower SES backgrounds (Croizet & Claire, 1998). In other words, students of lower SES backgrounds performed more poorly when the test was presented as a test of intellectual ability in which they might represent their social group but equally well when the same test was presented as nondiagnostic.

SES has also been identified as having a complex effect on adolescent aspirations and expectations for work and education. Consistent with an ecological approach to adolescent vocational development (Young, 1983), the findings of this body of research suggest that it is difficult to separate SES effects from parental influences, which are in turn influenced by school and other social influences. For example, in a qualitative study of work perspectives among urban youth (Chaves et al., 2004), the authors posited that "there may be a deep connection between how work is viewed in one's family and by the adolescent themselves" (p. 284). They found that the ninth-grade youth in their study often had relatively bleak perspectives on work based on family messages and saw work as a pathway to survival rather than a means of personal satisfaction or self-expression, as is often assumed in career theory.

In a large ($N > 9,000$) longitudinal study in Great Britain, socioeconomic disadvantage was identified as a significant deterrent to academic potential, but this effect was moderated by teacher expectations, as well as parental involvement and aspirations of the parent for the child (Schoon, Parsons, & Sacker, 2004). That is, the relation between disadvantage and academic potential was substantially lower among children whose teachers and parents expected them to succeed and whose parents were educationally involved and had high aspirations for their children. In another study of 272 adolescents (ages 11–15) in Rome, mothers' aspirations for their children and self-efficacy beliefs, regardless of SES, were most predictive of academic aspirations and occupational choices of the children (Bandura, Barbaranelli, Caprara, & Pastorelli, 2001).

Mixed findings have emerged from research in a different cultural context, that of the rural Appalachian region of the United States (Ali & McWhirter, 2006; Ali & Saunders, 2006). In one study (Ali & Saunders, 2006), student self-efficacy and parental support predicted expectations to attend college after high school, more so than socioeconomic status as measured by parental education and occupation. In another study, students from lower-SES backgrounds perceived more barriers to attending college, had lower self-efficacy about attending college, and expected to work full-time upon completion of high school (Ali & McWhirter). The authors noted that these students may have had limited encouragement to attend college, as well as little information about opportunities for financial aid and other barrier-reducing resources.

Across these diverse studies, self-efficacy of mothers (beliefs that they can help their children academically) and students (beliefs that they can accomplish necessary educational tasks) emerges as a construct that is core to shaping the aspirations of low-income youth. Researchers have also examined other facilitative factors, specifically sociopolitical development and hope. Diemer and his colleagues (Diemer, 2009; Deimer & Hsieh, 2008; Diemer, Hsieh, & Pan, 2009; Diemer et al., 2010) have examined the ways in which critical consciousness and sociopolitical development (SPD) might augment career exploration and aspirations among poor youth of color by fostering increased self-determination and agency. Critical consciousness refers to "the capacity to recognize and overcome sociopolitical barriers" (Diemer & Blustein, 2006, p. 220), such as oppression and discrimination. SPD includes being conscious of sociopolitical oppression and being motivated to engage in social action to change it (Watts, Griffith, & Abdul-Adil, 1999). Although inquiry in this area is relatively new, there are indications that critical consciousness can contribute to greater commitment to pursuing a career in the future and to clearer vocational identity among urban adolescents (Diemer & Blustein, 2006). Other findings suggest that SPD contributes to both work salience and vocational expectations among high school students (Diemer et al., 2010) and may contribute to reducing the disparity between vocational aspirations (ideal career) and expectations (expected career) among lower-SES adolescents of color (Diemer & Hsieh, 2008).

Work hope (Juntunen & Wettersten, 2006) and vocational hope (Diemer & Blustein, 2007) have been the focus of a small number of investigations. In the development of the Work Hope Scale, work hope was shown to detect differences between populations with differential access to financial resources, leading the authors to conclude that it may contribute to a unique understanding of the internal factors contributing to work behaviors among economically disenfranchised youth and adults (Juntunen & Wettersten, 2006). Subsequent use of the Work Hope Scale has suggested that work hope contributes uniquely and significantly to achievement-related beliefs among high school students (Kenny, Walsh-Blair, Blustein, Bempechat, & Seltzer, 2010) and career decision making among Ukrainian college students, which the authors posited may reflect a positive relationship between self-esteem and personal agency (Yakushko & Sokolova, 2010).

OBTAINING EMPLOYMENT

Career theory and research tend to focus more heavily on the processes by which people prepare for, select, and maintain careers and attend less to the actual steps involved in obtaining work or looking for a job. Two exceptions to this are examination of the school-to-work transition and the welfare-to-work transition, which has also been studied by social work researchers. The salience of social class in the transition from welfare to work is readily apparent, as is the lack of economic resources that necessitated the original receipt of welfare. The school-to-work transition is arguably a transition that most young adults experience but in the context of the current chapter represents the transition from high school to work navigated by youth who are not bound for college, which is often associated with limited economic resources (Blustein et al., 2000).

In a qualitative study of young adults making the transition from school to work, Blustein et al. (2002) found that low-SES youth experienced more educational barriers and had fewer educational resources than did high-SES youth. Low-SES youth also had less career guidance from parents, were less likely to engage in career self-exploration, and were less likely to actively plan for their future. The authors concluded that social class "affects the context of the STW transition and also influences how people feel about themselves and their work lives" (p. 322). In another qualitative study exploring the relationship between sociocultural factors and college attendance, Lehmann (2004) found that working-class youth planning to attend college perceived the experience as riskier and more tenuous than youth whose parents had attended college. In contrast, working-class youth who were pursuing work through apprenticeship expressed greater enthusiasm about their planned work experience. The author concluded that the school-to-work transition might replicate preexisting social inequalities but cautioned that this need not be seen as purely a limitation if the individual is intentional and self-aware in the process, offering an opportunity for career counseling interventions to address such inequality.

In a longitudinal study drawn from the Youth Development Study (Mortimer, 2003), the job search activity, employment status, and hourly wages of more than 1,000 youth were assessed over a 13-year period that included the school-to-work transition (Vuolo, Staff, & Mortimer, 2011). Socioeconomic factors were not found to predict employment status or income. However, parental education, which is an indicator of family social class, was related to higher levels of agency in the job pursuit process, and high agency was in turn related to higher hourly salary and less unemployment. The authors suggest that agency, or agentic striving, may foster resiliency that supports the school-to-work transition even in times of economic difficulty.

The job search for recipients of welfare (TANF) is complicated by numerous barriers. In one longitudinal study of more than 1,000 TANF recipients in a metropolitan area, 89% of the sample endorsed at least one of a set of 10 potential barriers identified by the researchers (Dworsky & Courtney, 2007): lack of high school diploma or GED (57%), met diagnostic criteria for depression (47%), health concerns (25%), mental health concerns during the past year (22%), disability (21%), having an infant under 1 year old (20%), being in an abusive relationship in the past year (15%), never held a previous job (9%), caring for family member with a disability (8%), and substance abuse within last year (6%). Further, 80% of the sample reported having two or more barriers. Note that the researchers did not assess potential access barriers, such as having transportation or child care available, which have also been identified as common concerns (Haley-Lock & Shah, 2007; Juntunen et al., 2006) and could make other barriers even more challenging to navigate. Dworsky and Courtney (2007) found that participants who endorsed barriers were less likely to be employed than those without barriers and were also more likely to earn a lower wage when they did work; these effects were increased as barriers multiplied.

To support the transition from welfare to work, federal and state dollars finance a variety of employment services agencies. The outcomes of the interventions provided by such agencies are mixed and can vary significantly in response to state and local labor market issues. Beimers and Fischer (2007) found that the services provided to TANF recipients had little effect on either entrance to employment or salary, with the exception of job development activities. Getting leads to specific jobs, which was supported by strong relationships between the service agency and employers, was the best contributor to obtaining and maintaining employment. The authors also noted that it is important to tailor services to the individual needs of TANF recipients. This echoes findings from a large evaluation of TANF programs (Gueron & Hamilton, 2002), in which the authors concluded that adopting a rigid one-size-fits-all approach was less successful than programs that included a mix of training and job search activities that best fit the needs of individual participants.

Of particular importance to career counselors, Gueron and Hamilton (2002) concluded that there is a clear need for welfare-to-work transition programs to include skills-enhancing activities and for programs that foster career advancement, in addition to meeting the goal of obtaining initial employment. Such recommendations clearly anchor welfare-to-work interventions within the realm of career counseling, although relatively few such programs have been developed. One example of a community-based welfare-to-work career intervention was developed by Juntunen and colleagues (2006). The program, called Project HOPE, was designed around interventions for families that targeted self-exploration and goal setting, increased self-efficacy, and specific job search skills. Parents and children met in parallel groups, and both participated in career-relevant activities. Adult participants demonstrated a decrease in depression following participation. No direct effect was found for vocational identity, but depression was negatively correlated with vocational identity, suggesting that there may have been an indirect effect.

WORK ROLE SALIENCE, SATISFACTION, AND PERFORMANCE

Limited research examines the correlation between social class and the experience of work obtained, but some relationships have been identified.

In a review of the literature on career development and social class in the early 1990s (Brown et al., 1996), the authors concluded that workers of lower social class saw the work role as less salient or central to their self-concept; experienced fewer psychological, financial, or physical rewards from work; and were more likely to have higher rates of absenteeism and turnover. The authors were very cautious, however, in overgeneralizing from these findings, given the small numbers of studies that examined each issue.

Following the transition from welfare to work among 434 workers in Illinois, Scott (2006) identified high levels of job satisfaction, as approximately 80% of respondents reported being satisfied or very satisfied with work. Interestingly, participants who had received TANF assistance for longer periods of time reported higher levels of satisfaction. Employment in a professional or technical area and higher wages were also important predictors of satisfaction.

Performance in secondary education has also been linked to adult work adjustment among individuals from lower social class backgrounds (Schoon et al., 2004), leading the authors to suggest that disadvantaged youth who "prove themselves" in secondary education attain lasting benefits that support their work adjustment and health as adults.

IMPLICATIONS FOR PRACTICE

The variety of considerations contributing to the complex relationships between SES and vocational outcomes highlights the need to continue to pursue scholarship that increases our understanding in this area. Nonetheless, together the studies reviewed here provide some implications for practice that may be particularly useful for counselors and psychologists addressing career aspirations and expectations. As part of the ecological context in which career goals emerge, SES has the potential to serve as a barrier, and appropriate interventions can alleviate the impact of this barrier.

INTERVENTIONS WITH YOUTH

Given that youth from lower-income homes are less likely to have full exposure to educational and career opportunities, career counseling interventions such as assessment and exploration of interests, values, and goals are likely to prove very helpful. Such interventions need to be carefully balanced with the counselor's awareness of relevant social pressures experienced by the client, including the potential for family financial needs to outweigh individual interests or choices.

Interventions should address specific barriers, such as having limited knowledge of financial aid and other resources that support higher education. Relatedly, barriers can be addressed by exposing youth to adults from similar backgrounds who have gone to college and still maintained meaningful ties to their home communities (Ali & McWhirter, 2006), providing a potent vicarious source of self-efficacy.

Interventions that are designed to increase academic coping self-efficacy, work hope, and sociopolitical development among lower-income youth are all likely to positively influence career attainment. These might include increasing exposure to work through job-shadowing and supervised work experiences, identifying goals and the steps necessary to navigate the pathways to those goals, engaging in critical analyses of social structures, and developing strategies that empower youth to see themselves as agents of change for both themselves and the larger social structure. Finally, interventions that include both parents and children may be particularly useful, given the evidence that parental support is an important predictor of self-efficacy and career aspirations (Ali & Saunders, 2006; Bandura et al., 2001; Chaves et al., 2004). The Annie E. Casey Foundation (2011) heavily emphasizes a multigenerational response to preparing the next generation to move out of poverty, noting that the entire family needs increased support to foster children's socioeconomic upward mobility.

JOB-SEEKING ASSISTANCE

Career counselors often assist individual clients in the job search process, providing guidance through career assessment, understanding P-E fit, and identifying local resources for finding available jobs. The issues encountered by individuals of lower social class status may feel distinctly different, and as the previous literature has addressed, the career counselor may need to help clients with fewer economic resources manage a more complex set of barriers. However, several suggestions for practice emerge from these findings. First, it is important to identify the unique set of barriers faced by the individual client (Dworsky & Courtney, 2007), including barriers that are likely to be overlooked by counselors who work primarily with middle-class clients, such as transportation, money for food and shelter, and access to child care. Second, it is important for counselors to be familiar with the local employment services agencies and to collaborate with them in identifying resources for clients. Further, career counselors and psychologists can serve as consultants to help employment services agencies infuse career development activities into their services (Juntunen & Bailey, in press). Finally, interventions that focus on developing increased agency and self-efficacy are again relevant for the job search process and have the potential to increase resiliency in the face of economic stressors.

HELP WITH WORK ADJUSTMENT

The very limited exploration of social class and attitudes toward work among working adults offers few practice implications. However, the psychology of working perspective (Blustein, 2006) provides useful principles for addressing issues related to survival and power, social connectedness, and self-determination for workers. By addressing work as a central part of the lived experience, counselors and psychologists are more able to provide integrated and holistic interventions with all clients. Such an approach would consider attitudes toward work, satisfaction gained from work, and the salience of work as part of career counseling. In providing services to women living in poverty, Heppner and O'Brien (2006) described the need to foster resiliency. Specifically, they encouraged counselors to work on a set of five skills and attitudes presented by Bernard (1995) as central to resiliency: social competence, problem-solving skills, critical consciousness, autonomy, and sense of purpose.

CONCLUSIONS

Social class and poverty present significant challenges to career counselors and psychologists, yet the research demonstrates that numerous points of leverage can be used to intervene in the multigenerational pattern of sustained poverty. The following is a list of suggestions that career counselors can implement to increase their ability to meet the needs of low-income and poor families and to ensure that the profession does not overlook this significant and unfortunately growing population of clients.

1. Engage in self-awareness and reflectivity.
   a. Career counselors need to examine their own classist beliefs.
   b. Career counselors need to examine the tendency to distance or protect themselves from poverty, as well as other barriers that might be keeping them from working with the poor.
   c. Career counselors need to increase their competency in social class and poverty issues by reading broadly from the sociological and social work literatures, in addition to the vocational literature.
2. Microsystem interventions for individuals, families, and groups.
   a. Career counselors need to examine how clients perceive social class, attending to the importance of perception as identified in

the differential status identity (Fouad & Brown, 2000) or social class worldview (Liu, Soleck, et al., 2004) models.

b. Career counselors need to be prepared to intervene with family systems, given the evidence of generational influence regarding social class and poverty. Specifically, career counselors can work with parents to help them identify ways to support the self-efficacy of their children.

c. Career counselors need to be prepared to assess individual barriers (Dworsky & Courtney, 2007) to develop appropriately personalized interventions.

d. Career counselors need to use validated career interventions, including assessments of interests, values, and goals, while attending to the important influence of the contextual factors of social class and poverty on client choices and options. Models such as that proposed by Liu and Ali (2008) can be particularly helpful in integrating social class issues into theory-driven career interventions.

e. Career counselors need to help clients explore resources such as work hope (Juntunen & Wettersten, 2006) and resiliency to support active engagement with career-seeking activities and goal setting.

f. Career counselors need to engage clients in sociopolitical development (Diemer et al., 2010) to help them to identify and think critically about social factors and to understand ways in which they can challenge sociocultural barriers, such as classism and oppression.

3. Exosystem interventions—community and regional systems.

   a. Career counselors need to be familiar with, and preferably have collaborative relationships with, job service and employment services training agencies in their community. Through these relationships, counselors can promote the use of individualized approaches to obtaining work, which have been demonstrated to be more successful than standardized government interventions (Gueron & Hamilton, 2002).

   b. Career counselors need to be willing to advocate with local employers to support programs and policies that facilitate employment opportunities for clients.

   c. Career counselors need to be prepared to work with local schools to support and implement training programs that will promote employment options for youth and young adults.

4. Macrosystem intervention—policy and governmental systems.

   a. Career counselors need to advocate for policies, programs, and resources that will support high-quality work for youth (Mortimer, 2003).

b. Career counselors need to get involved in government advocacy that supports appropriate social services and living wages for workers.

c. Career counselors need to contribute to interventions and research that can be shared with policy makers to demonstrate effective programs that support sustainable employment for all.

REFERENCES

Ali, S. R. (in press). Poverty, social class, and working. In D. Blustein (Ed)., *Handbook of the psychology of working*.

Ali, S. R., Fall, K., & Hoffman, T. D. (in press). Life without work: Understanding social class changes and unemployment through theoretical integration. *Journal of Career Assessment*.

Ali, S. R., & McWhirter, E. H. (2006). Rural Appalachian youth's vocational/ educational post-secondary aspirations: Applying social cognitive career theory. *Journal of Career Development, 33*, 87–111. doi:2006-21280-00110.1177/089484 5306293347

Ali, S. R., & Saunders, J. L. (2006). College expectations of rural Appalachian youth: An exploration of social cognitive career theory factors. *Career Development Quarterly, 55*(1), 38–51.

Annie E. Casey Foundation. (2010). *Early warning! Why reading by the end of third grade matters*. KIDS COUNT Special Report. Baltimore, MD: Author. Retrieved from http://www.aecf.org/~/media/Pubs/Initiatives/KIDS%20COUNT/123 /2010KCSpecReport/Special%20Report%20Executive%20Summary.pdf

Annie E. Casey Foundation. (2011). *America's children, America's challenge: Promoting opportunity for the next generation*. Baltimore, MD: Author. Retrieved from http:// www.aecf.org/KnowledgeCenter/~/media/Pubs/Initiatives/KIDS%20COUNT /123/2011KIDSCOUNTDataBook/2011KCDB_FINAL_essay.pdf

Bandura, A., Barbaranelli, C., Caprara, G. V., & Pastorelli, C. (2001). Self-efficacy beliefs as shapers of children's aspirations and career trajectories. *Child Development, 72*(1), 187–206. doi:10.1111/1467-8624.00273

Beimers, D., & Fischer, R. L. (2007). Pathways to employment: The experiences of TANF recipients with employment services. *Families in Society, 88*(3), 391–400.

Bernard, B. (1995). *Fostering resilience in children* (Report No. EDO-PS-95-9). Champaign, IL: ERIC Clearinghouse on Elementary and Childhood Education.

Blustein, D. L. (2006). *The psychology of working: A new perspective for career development, counseling, and public policy*. Mahwah, NJ: Erlbaum.

Blustein, D. L., Chaves, A. P., Diemer, M. A., Gallagher, L. A., Marshall, K. G., Sirin, S., & Bhati, K. S. (2002). Voices of the forgotten half: The role of social class in the school-to-work transition. *Journal of Counseling Psychology, 49*, 311–323. doi:10.1037/0022-0167.49.3.31110.1037/0022-0167.49.3.3112002-01965-004

Blustein, D. L., Juntunen, C. L., & Worthington, R. L. (2000). The school-to-work transition: Adjustment challenges of the forgotten half. In S. D. Brown & R. W.

Lent (Eds.), *Handbook of counseling psychology* (3rd ed., pp. 435–470). New York, NY: Wiley.

Blustein, D. L., McWhirter, E. W., & Perry, J. C. (2005). An emancipator communitarian approach to vocational development theory, research, and practice. *Counseling Psychologist, 33*(2), 141–179. doi:10.1177/0011000042722682005-02090-001

Bronfenbrenner, U. (1993). The ecology of cognitive development: Research models and fugitive findings. In R. H. Wozniak & K. Fischer (Eds.), *Scientific environments* (pp. 3–44). Hillsdale, NJ: Erlbaum.

Brown, M. T., D'Agruma, H., Brown, A., Sia, A., Yamini-Diouf, Y., Porter, S., & Ruiz de Exparza, C. et al. (2002, August). *Differential status identity: Construct, measurement, and initial validation.* Symposium presented during the annual convention of the American Psychological Association, Chicago.

Brown, M. T., Fukunaga, C., Umemoto, D., & Wicker, L. (1996). Annual review, 1990–1996: Social class, work, and retirement behavior. *Journal of Vocational Behavior, 49,* 159–189.

Caputo, R. K. (2007). Working and poor: A panel study of maturing adults in the U.S. *Families in Society, 88*(3), 351–359.

Chaves, A., Diemer, M., Blustein, D., Gallagher, L., DeVoy, J., Casares, M., & Perry, J. (2004). Conceptions of work: The view from urban youth. *Journal of Counseling Psychology, 51,* 275–286. doi:10.1037/0022-0167.51.3.275

Corcoran, M. (1995). Rags to rags: Poverty and mobility in the United States. *Annual Review of Sociology, 21,* 237–267. doi:21.080195.001321

Croizet, J. C., & Claire, T. (1998). Extending the concept of stereotype threat to social class: The intellectual underperformance of students from low socioeconomic backgrounds. *Personality and Social Psychology Bulletin, 24,* 588–594.

Dawis, R. V. (2005). The Minnesota Theory of Work Adjustment. In S. D. Brown, R. W. Lent (Eds.), *Career development and counseling: Putting theory and research to work* (pp. 3–23). Hoboken, NJ: Wiley.

Dawis, R. V., & Lofquist, L. H. (1984). *A psychological theory of work adjustment.* Minneapolis: University of Minnesota Press.

Day, S. X., & Rounds, J. (1998). Universality of vocational interest structure among racial and ethnic minorities. *American Psychologist, 53*(7), 728–736. doi:10.1037/0003-066X.53.7.728

DeNavas-Walt, C., Proctor, B. D., & Smith, J. C. (2011). Income, poverty, and health insurance coverage in the United States: 2010. *U.S. Census Bureau, Current Population Reports,* P60-239 (RV). Washington, DC: U.S. Government Printing Office.

Diemer, M. A. (2009). Pathways to occupational attainment among poor youth of color: The role of sociopolitical development. *The Counseling Psychologist, 37*(1), 6–35. doi:10.1177/0011000007309858

Diemer, M. A., & Ali, S. (2009). Integrating social class into vocational psychology: Theory and practice implications. *Journal of Career Assessment, 17*(3), 247–265. doi:10.1177/1069072708330462

Diemer, M. A., & Blustein, D. L. (2006). Critical consciousness and career development among urban youth. *Journal of Vocational Behavior*, 68(2), 220–232. doi:10.1016/j.jvb.2005.07.001

Diemer, M. A., & Blustein, D. L. (2007). Vocational hope and vocational identity: Urban adolescents career development. *Journal of Career Assessment*, 15(1), 98–118. doi:10.1177/1069072706294528

Diemer, M. A., & Hsieh, C. (2008). Sociopolitical development and vocational expectations among lower socioeconomic status adolescents of color. *Career Development Quarterly*, 56(3), 257–267.

Diemer, M. A., Hsieh, C., & Pan, T. (2009). School and parental influences on sociopolitical development among poor adolescents of color. *The Counseling Psychologist*, 37(2), 317–344. doi:10.1177/0011000008315971

Diemer, M. A., Wang, Q., Moore, T., Gregory, S. R., Hatcher, K. M., & Voight, A. M. (2010). Sociopolitical development, work salience, and vocational expectations among low socioeconomic status African American, Latin American, and Asian American youth. *Developmental Psychology*, 46(3), 619–635. doi:10.1037/a0017049

Dillard, J. M. (1976). Relationship between career maturity and self-concepts of suburban and urban middle- and urban lower-class preadolescent Black males. *Journal of Vocational Behavior*, 9(3), 311–320. doi:10.1016/0001-8791(76)90058-0

Dworsky, A., & Courtney, M. E. (2007). Barriers to employment among TANF applicants and their consequences for self-sufficiency. *Families in Society*, 88(3), 379–389.

Edelman, M. W., & Jones, J. M. (2004). Separate and unequal: America's children, race, and poverty. *Future of Children*, 14(2), 134–137. doi:2004-20083-00910.2307/1602800.

Fouad, N. A., & Brown, M. T. (2000). The role of race and social class in development: Implications for counseling psychology. In S. D. Brown & R. W. Lent (Eds.), *Handbook of counseling psychology* (3rd ed., pp. 379–408). New York, NY: Wiley.

Fouad, N. A., & Fitzpatrick, M. E. (2009). Social class and work-related decisions: Measurement, theory, and social mobility. *Journal of Career Assessment*, 17(3), 266–270. doi:10.1177/1069072708330677

Gottfredson, L. S. (2005). Applying Gottfredson's theory of circumscription and compromise in career guidance and counseling. In S. D. Brown & R. W. Lent (Eds.), *Career development and counseling: Putting theory and research to work* (pp. 71–100). Hoboken, NJ: Wiley.

Gueron, I. M., & Hamilton, G. (2002). *The role of education and training in welfare reform*. Washington, DC: Brookings Institution.

Haley-Lock, A., & Shah, M. (2007). Protecting vulnerable workers: How public policy and private employers shape the contemporary low-wage work experience. *Families in Society*, 88(3), 485–495.

Halle, D. (1984). *America's working man: Work, home, and politics among blue collar property owners*. Chicago, IL: University of Chicago Press.

Hannah, J. S., & Kahn, S. E. (1989). The relationship of socioeconomic status and gender to the occupational choices of grade 12 students. *Journal of Vocational Behavior*, 34(2), 161–178. doi:10.1016/0001-8791(89)90012-2

Heppner, M. J., & O'Brien, K. M. (2006). Women and poverty: A holistic approach to vocational interventions. In W. Walsh & M. J. Heppner (Eds.), *Handbook of career counseling for women* (2nd ed., pp. 75–102). Mahwah, NJ: Erlbaum.

Holland, J. L. (1997). *Making vocational choices: A theory of vocational personalities and work environments* (3rd ed.). Odessa, FL US: Psychological Assessment Resources.

Hollingshead, A. A. (1975). *Four-factor index of social status.* Unpublished manuscript, Yale University, New Haven, CT.

Holzer, H. J., Schanzenbach, D. W., Duncan, G. J., & Ludwig, J. (2007). The economic costs of poverty in the United States: Subsequent effects of children growing up poor. *National Poverty Center Working Paper Series, 07*(04), 1–4.

Isaacs, J., Sawhill, I., & Haskins, R. (2008). *Getting ahead or losing ground: Economic mobility in America.* Economic Mobility Project, Pew Charitable Trusts. Retrieved from   http://www.brookings.edu/~/media/research/files/reports/2008/2 /economic%20mobility%20sawhill/02_economic_mobility_sawhill.pdf

Jordan, N. C., & Levine, S. C. (2009). Socioeconomic variation, number competence, and mathematics learning difficulties in young children. *Developmental Disabilities Research Reviews, 15*(1), 60–68. doi:10.1002/ddrr.46

Juntunen, C. L., & Bailey, T.-K. M. (in press). Training and employment services for adult workers. In D. Blustein (Ed.), *Handbook of the psychology of working.*

Juntunen, C. L., Cavett, A. M., Clow, R. B., Rempel, V., Darrow, R. E., & Guilmino, A. (2006). Social justice through self-sufficiency: Vocational psychology and the transition from welfare to work. In R. L. Toporek, L. H. Gerstein, N. A. Foud, G. Roysircar, & T. Israel (Eds.), *Handbook for social justice in counseling psychology* (pp. 294–309). Thousand Oaks, CA: Sage.

Juntunen, C. L., & Wettersten, K. B. (2006). Work hope: Development and initial validation of a measure. *Journal of Counseling Psychology, 53,* 94–106. doi:10.1037/0022-0167.53.1.94

Kenny, M. E., Walsh-Blair, L. Y., Blustein, D. L., Bempechat, J., & Seltzer, J. (2010). Achievement motivation among urban adolescents: Work hope, autonomy support, and achievement-related beliefs. *Journal of Vocational Behavior, 77*(2), 205–212. doi:10.1016/j.jvb.2010.02.005

Krumboltz, J. D. (1979). A social learning theory of career decision making. In A. M. Mitchell, G. B. Jones, & J. D. Krumboltz (Eds.), *Social learning and career decision making* (pp. 19–49). Cranston, RI: Carroll.

Krumboltz, J. D. (2009). The happenstance learning theory. *Journal of Career Assessment, 17,* 135–154.

Lapour, A., & Heppner, M. J. (2009). Social class privilege and adolescent women's perceived career options. *Journal of Counseling Psychology, 56*(4), 477–494. doi: 10.1037/a0017268

Lehmann, W. (2004). ''For some reason, I get a little scared'': Structure, agency, and risk in school-work transitions. *Journal of Youth Studies, 7*(4), 379–396. doi:10.1080 /1367626042000315185

Lent, R., Brown, S. D., & Hackett, G. (1994). Toward a unifying social cognitive theory of career and academic interest, choice, and performance. *Journal Of Vocational Behavior, 45*(1), 79–122. doi:10.1006/jvbe.1994.1027

Lent, R. W., Brown, S. D., & Hackett, G. (2000). Contextual supports and barriers to career choice: A social cognitive analysis. *Journal of Counseling Psychology, 47,* 36–49.

Liu, W. M. (2011). *Social class and classism in the helping professions: Research, theory and practice.* Los Angeles, CA: Sage.

Liu, W., & Ali, S. (2008). Social class and classism: Understanding the psychological impact of poverty and inequality. In S. D. Brown & R. W. Lent (Eds.), *Handbook of counseling psychology* (4th ed., pp. 159–175). Hoboken, NJ: Wiley.

Liu, W. M., Ali, S. R., Soleck, G., Hopps, J., Dunston, K., & Pickett, T., Jr,. (2004). Using social class in counseling psychology research. *Journal of Counseling Psychology, 51*(1), 3–18. doi:10.1037/0022-0167.51.1.32003-11100-001

Liu, W. M., Soleck, G., Hopps, J., Dunston, K., & Pickett, T. (2004). A new framework to understand social class in counseling: The social class worldview and modern classism theory. *Journal of Multicultural Counseling and Development, 32,* 95–122. doi:2004-13339-003

Lott, B. (2002). Cognitive and behavioral distancing from the poor. *American Psychologist, 57,* 100–110. doi:1189955310.1037/0003-066X.57.2.1002002-10716-002

Lott, B., & Bullock, H. E. (2007). *Psychology and economic injustice: Personal, professional, and political intersections.* Washington, DC: American Psychological Association. doi:10.1037/11501-000

MacKay, W. R., & Miller, C. A. (1982). Relations of socioeconomic status and sex variables to the complexity of worker functions in the occupational choices of elementary school children. *Journal of Vocational Behavior, 20*(1), 31–39. doi:10.1016/0001-8791(82)90061-6

Mortimer, J. T. (2003). *Working and growing up in America.* Cambridge, MA: Harvard University Press.

Nauta, M. M. (2010). The development, evolution, and status of Holland's theory of vocational personalities: Reflections and future directions for counseling psychology. *Journal of Counseling Psychology, 57*(1), 11–22. doi:10.1037/a0018213

Oliver, M., & Shapiro, T. (2006). *Black wealth/White wealth: A new perspective on racial inequality.* New York, NY: Routledge.

Savickas, M. L. (2005). The theory and practice of career construction. In S. D. Brown, R. W. Lent (Eds.), *Career development and counseling: Putting theory and research to work* (pp. 42–70). Hoboken, NJ: Wiley.

Schoon, I., Parsons, S., & Sacker, A. (2004). Socioeconomic adversity, educational, resilience, and subsequent levels of adult adaptation. *Journal of Adolescent Research, 19,* 383–404.

Scott, J. (2006). Job satisfaction among TANF leavers. *Journal of Sociology and Social Welfare, 33*(3), 127–149.

Shapiro, T. M., Meschede, T., & Sullivan, L. (2010). *The racial wealth gap increases fourfold.* (Research and Policy Brief). Waltham, MA: Institute on Assets and Social Policy. Retrieved from http://iasp.brandeis.edu/pdfs/Racial-Wealth-Gap-Brief.pdf

Shipler, D. K. (2005). *The working poor: Invisible in America.* New York, NY: Vintage.

Sloan, T. (2005). Global work-related suffering as a priority for vocational psychology: Comment. *Counseling Psychologist, 33*(2), 207–214. doi:10.1177/001100 0004272721

Smith, L. (2005). Psychotherapy, classism, and the poor: Conspicuous by their absence. *American Psychologist, 60,* 687–697. doi:2005-11834-00210.1037/0003-066X .60.7.687

Smith, L. (2010). *Psychology, poverty, and the end of social exclusion: Putting our practice to work.* New York, NY: Teachers College Press.

Smith, L., & Mao, S. (2012). Social class and psychology. In N. A. Fouad, J. A. Carter, & L. M. Subich (Eds.) , *APA handbook of counseling psychology, vol. 1: Theories, research, and methods* (pp. 523–540). Washington, DC: American Psychological Association. doi:10.1037/13754-020

Steele, C. M., & Aronson, J. (1995). Stereotype threat and the intellectual test performance of African Americans. *Journal of Personality and Social Psychology, 65*(5), 797–811.

Sum, A., & Khatiwada, I. (2010). *Labour underutilization problems of U.S. workers across household income groups at the end of the Great Recession: A truly Great Depression among the nation's low income workers amidst full employment among the most affluent.* Paper prepared for the C. S. Mott Foundation, February 2010.

Super, D. E. (1990). A life-span, life-space approach to career development. In D. Brown, L. Brooks, & Associates (Eds.), *Career choice and development: Applying contemporary theories to practice* (2nd ed., pp. 197–261). San Francisco, CA: Jossey-Bass.

Super, D. E., Savickas, M. L., & Super, C. M. (1996). The life-span, life-space approach to careers. In D. Brown, L. Brooks, & Associates (Eds.), *Career choice and development* (pp. 121–178). San Francisco: Jossey-Bass.

Thompson, M. N., & Subich, L. M. (2006). The relation of social status to the career decision-making process. *Journal of Vocational Behavior, 69,* 289–301 doi:10.1016/j.jvb.2006.04.008.

Thompson, M. N., & Subich, L. M. (2011). Social status identity: Antecedents and vocational outcomes. *Counseling Psychologist, 39*(5), 735–763. doi:10.1177 /0011000010389828

U.S. Department of Labor, Bureau of Labor Statistics. (2011a). A profile of the working poor, 2009. Report 1027. Retrieved from http://www.bls.gov/cps /cpswp2009.pdf

Vondracek, F. W., & Lerner, R. M. (1982). Vocational role development in adolescence. In B. B. Wolman (Ed.), *Handbook of developmental psychology* (pp. 602–614). Englewood Cliffs, NJ: Prentice Hall.

Vondracek, F. W., Lerner, R. M., & Schulenberg, J. E. (1983). The concept of development in vocational theory and intervention. *Journal of Vocational Behavior, 23,* 179–202.

Vondracek, F. W., Lerner, R. M., & Schulenberg, J. E. (1986). *Career development A life-span developmental perspective.* Hillsdale, NJ: Erlbaum.

Vuolo, M., Staff, J., & Mortimer, J. T. (2011). Weathering the great recession: Psychological and behavioral trajectories in the transition from school to work. *Developmental Psychology*. Advance Online Publication. doi:10.1037/a0026047

Watts, R., Griffith, D., & Abdul-Adil, J. (1999). Sociopolitical development as an antidote for oppression: Theory and action. *American Journal of Community Psychology, 27*, 255–272.

Wilson, W. J. (1996). *When work disappears: The world of the new urban poor*. New York, NY: Knopf.

Yakushko, O., & Sokolova, O. (2010). Work hope and influences of the career development among Ukrainian college students. *Journal of Career Development, 36*(4), 310–323. doi:10.1177/0894845309345670

Young, R. A. (1983). Career development of adolescents: An ecological perspective. *Journal of Youth and Adolescence, 12*(5), 401–417. doi:10.1007/BF02088723

CHAPTER 10

Career Development of Lesbian, Gay, Bisexual, and Transgender Individuals

JEFFREY P. PRINCE

THE CAREER LITERATURE PERTAINING to lesbian, gay, bisexual, and transgender (LGBT) individuals has grown dramatically in recent years (Chung, Williams, & Dispenza, 2009). The first conceptual and practical articles emerged in the late 1980s and early 1990s (Elliott, 1993; Hetherington, Hillerbrand, & Etringer, 1989), and increasingly sophisticated, empirical investigations began to follow within a decade (Bieschke & Matthews, 1996; Chung, 2001). Today, lesbian and gay issues appear increasingly in the counseling literature (Croteau, Bieschke, Fassinger, & Manning, 2008), and scholarly efforts in this domain represent one of the most significant recent advances in vocational psychology (Chung, in press). Nevertheless, the literature focusing on the array of theoretical and practical career issues encountered by the diversity of LGBT populations remains limited. There is no literature specifically relating to the career development or career counseling of bisexual individuals, and very little devoted to that of transgender populations. Consequently, although many scholarly works, including this one, contain the term *LGBT* in their titles, the content of most has been focused primarily on lesbian and gay concerns, with limited attention to career issues specific to bisexual and transgender individuals (O'Neil, McWhirter, & Cerezo, 2008; Phillips, Ingram, Smith, & Mindes, 2003).

This chapter highlights findings from the range of scholarly contributions that have informed our understanding and practice of career development and career counseling with LGBT individuals. First, major vocational theories are evaluated for their applicability to sexual minority populations; this is followed by a discussion of additional issues unique to the career development and career counseling of LGBT individuals. The intention of this chapter is to bring together theoretical and empirical work with practical recommendations to enable career professionals to work more effectively with sexual minority clients.

Before turning to the literature in this domain, it might be helpful to clarify terminology. *Sexual orientation* and *sexual identity* are terms that are frequently used when discussing LGBT individuals; these terms are not interchangeable. Simply put, sexual orientation refers to a person's attraction (emotional, sexual, spiritual) toward an individual of the same or opposite sex (Pepper & Lorah, 2008). Sexual orientations can be described along a continuum of multiple dimensions of behaviors and preferences rather than as fitting into four limiting categories of lesbian, gay, bisexual, and heterosexual (Chung & Katayama, 1996). Fully defining sexual orientation is beyond the scope of this chapter, and there does not appear to be consensus on its definition in the literature (Chung, in press).

Sexual identity, by contrast, refers to the way in which a person identifies and represents herself or himself in a social context in reference to her or his sexual orientation (e.g., identifying as lesbian, gay, bisexual, queer, questioning, or heterosexual). Identities are fluid and socially constructed, according to most models. For example, most people have some degree of bisexuality in terms of sexual orientation, yet those who identify as bisexual comprise distinct subgroups and may differ in significant ways from those who identify as lesbian and gay (Worthington & Reynolds, 2009). For simplicity, the term *LGB* will be used in this chapter to represent the range of sexual identities that are typically referenced in the career literature because most studies have used these categories rather than more complex terms.

Both sexual orientation and sexual identity are separate from gender identity, which refers to a person's internal identification as male or female. An individual's gender identity may or may not be the person's assigned biological sex at birth. *Transgender* is an inclusive term that applies to a range of people who do not conform to a male–female dichotomy (Law, Martinez, Ruggs, Hebl, & Akers, 2011). Transgender populations also include individuals with a range of sexual orientations. The developmental and career concerns specific to transgender individuals can be quite different from those specific to LGB individuals; at the same time, LGBT populations as a group have a number of career experiences in common due to their shared sexual minority status in a heterosexually dominant culture. Consequently, this chapter uses the terms *LGB* or *LGBT*, depending on the groups being referenced, and includes a section that reviews the limited but growing vocational literature that speaks directly to transgender career development and counseling.

Definitions aside, all LGBT individuals share experiences of stigma and marginalization that impact their career development in a variety of ways. At the same time, LGBT individuals develop strengths and experiences that enhance career development as a result of going through life with sexual minority status. The important question is, what factors have emerged in the literature to help us understand and work more effectively to promote the career development of LGBT individuals?

CAREER THEORIES

Over the past 20 years, scholarly contributions that apply theories of vocational psychology to LGBT populations have steadily increased. This section draws attention to these writings, evaluates the relevance and usefulness of a number of current theories, and clusters this work into three theoretical categories: person–environment fit, developmental, and social learning/social cognitive theories. The extent of this literature remains limited, however, and significant future research in this domain is needed to fully evaluate the validity of using any extant career theory with sexual minority populations.

PERSON–ENVIRONMENT FIT THEORIES

The earliest publication to examine a theory of person–environment (P-E) fit for its relevance to sexual minority populations was an empirical study by Chung and Harmon (1994). This investigation was stimulated by the earlier work of C. Hetherington (1991), who proposed that influences on the career decision making of lesbians and gay men may be quite different than those for heterosexuals. Chung and Harmon used Holland's *The Self-Directed Search* (Holland, 1985) to evaluate how an individual's sexual orientation might impact measured interest patterns. They compared the interests of gay men with heterosexual men for each of Holland's six types and found that gay men demonstrated lower Realistic and Investigative interests and higher Artistic and Social interests. Their study highlighted the importance for counselors to consider the career aspirations and interest patterns of gay men, not only with respect to measured interests but also relative to environmental forces, such as stereotyping and homophobia, that influence expressed career goals and choices.

Another early contribution by Mobley and Slaney (1996) challenged the adequacy of Holland's theoretical assumptions (Holland, 1997; Nauta, Chapter 3, this volume) in accounting for the career behaviors of lesbians and gay men. They suggested expanding the working assumptions and principles of Holland's theory with Cass's (1979) model of lesbian and gay identity development to incorporate the dual, developmental identity challenges faced by lesbian and gay individuals, that is, the development of both a career identity and a sexual minority identity. They described how vocational measures that assess Holland's constructs are influenced not only by the level of one's career identity but also by the stage of one's sexual identity. For example, they postulated that younger lesbian and gay individuals may experience greater career indecision and lack of clarity in their career interests and values because of the simultaneous challenge of recognizing and integrating a minority sexual identity. Furthermore, they suggested that assessing Holland's construct of congruence for lesbian and gay clients, compared to heterosexual clients, requires counselors to address not only the role of vocational interests but also the significant influence of workplace climate (i.e., discrimination or support based on one's sexual minority status).

Early contributions such as these laid the groundwork for more sophisticated empirical investigations into the environmental and personal factors specific to LGBT populations that influence P-E fit. In fact, more recent work (Lyons, Brenner, & Fassinger, 2005; Lyons & O'Brien, 2006) indicates that theories of P-E fit may better account for the career behaviors and workplace experiences of sexual minority and other marginalized populations than of nonmarginalized populations. In particular, the variable of workplace environment (whether discriminatory or supportive) appears to be a critical factor in assessing fit. Croteau (1996), for example, reviewed studies showing that up to 66% of LGB employees experience workplace discrimination.

An individual's decision to identify as LGBT in the workplace and the environmental response to this decision highlight important aspects of workplace characteristics. Disclosure—being out to their supervisors, colleagues, and clients—may result in increased physical and mental health (Croteau, Bieschke, et al., 2008; Waldo, 1999). At the same time, disclosure comes with the risks of overt and covert prejudice and homophobia, such as limited job advancement and stigmatization (Croteau, Anderson, Distefano, & Kampa-Kokesch, 2000).

Waldo (1999) developed a measure of workplace heterosexist experiences to assess the impact of two forms of heterosexism: direct (e.g., antigay jokes) and indirect (e.g., assumptions of heterosexuality). He found that being out in the workplace was positively related to experiencing direct heterosexism and that heterosexism overall was associated with adverse psychological well-being, health, job satisfaction, and other job-related outcomes. Similarly, Ragins, Singh, and Cornwell (2007) found that those individuals who reported greater fear of negative consequences of disclosure received fewer promotions and reported more stress-related symptoms than those who reported less fear. These findings highlight the importance of assessing contextual factors in the workplace. Interestingly, they are in contrast to the view that disclosure is uniformly a positive step for LGBT individuals; concealment actually may be a necessary and adaptive decision for individuals in hostile environments.

The theory of work adjustment (TWA; Dawis & Lofquist, 1984), a classic P-E fit theory, has been widely researched in relation to career choice and work adjustment (see Swanson & Schneider, Chapter 2, this volume). The basic tenets of the theory hold that P-E fit (in terms of person values–environment reinforcers and person abilities–environment ability requirements) influences work adjustment. Although TWA was not designed to explain LGBT career development, researchers have extended it to this context. The line of reasoning has been that group-specific cultural variables, such as those relevant to LGBT populations, influence P-E fit, which, in turn, influences job satisfaction, performance, and tenure. For example, workplace contextual variables related to LGBT status could be expected to produce different work experiences (e.g., encountering heterosexism versus LGBT supportive climates); such experiences could lead to individuals being more or less in correspondence with their environments and more or less satisfied with their jobs. Thus, when counseling LGBT clients on job/career choice and adjustment, a TWA approach might focus both on traditional (value, ability) fit dimensions and on the workplace climate specifically for LGBT workers. Counselors then can help clients identify aspects of work environments that are affirming or harmful to clients' job functioning and well-being.

Research evaluating the usefulness of this theory with LGBT individuals, however, has only begun. Some authors have predicted that P-E fit would play a minimal role in influencing workplace satisfaction and tenure of marginalized populations because of significant structural barriers to job opportunities and choices (Fassinger, 2001). In other words, because marginalized individuals have limited access to the full array of employment options, they may not leave a job that is a bad fit for them due to their limited alternatives. However, recent research evaluating TWA with marginalized populations has demonstrated the opposite (Lyons et al., 2005; Lyons & O'Brien, 2006). Lyons and colleagues (2005), for example, found that the importance of P-E fit for LGB workers was not overshadowed by discrimination. Instead, LGB workers' perceptions of P-E fit took on greater significance, compared to workers in general. They found that almost half of the variance in LGB employees' job satisfaction was attributable to how well they perceived fitting their current work environment. The authors suggested that P-E fit may take on greater importance because the nature of LGB employees' stigmatized status may lead them to be more highly attuned to the culture of their work environments when making workplace decisions.

DEVELOPMENTAL THEORIES

Developmental theories have historically viewed career development as occurring within a broader social context in which a person's vocational identity and self-concept develop over time as an individual interacts with the environment (Hartung, Chapter 4, this volume; Savickas, Chapter 6, this volume; Super, 1990; Tiedeman & O'Hara, 1963). For LGBT individuals, the development of a vocational identity co-occurs with the development of a sexual identity, and both of these processes take place within a larger environmental context that is pervasively heterosexist and homophobic. Consequently, from a developmental perspective, an LGBT individual's implementation of a vocational self-concept should be greatly influenced by her or his awareness and integration of sexual identity and by the levels of social acceptance and discrimination present in his or her social and occupational environment.

Dunkle (1996) contributed an early publication that examined the use of Super's (1990) career development theory with LGB individuals. He hypothesized that the sexual identity development of LGB individuals has a significant influence on their career development. He outlined Super's stages of career development, along with the career implications for gay and lesbian individuals at each stage. For example, he hypothesized that gay and lesbian adolescents and young adults in Super's exploration stage might be managing early stages of sexual identity confusion at the same time and, consequently, experiencing high levels of psychological distress. This, in turn, might interfere with achieving vocational maturity. As another example, men and women who begin the coming out process in their 30s and 40s face the challenge of managing their sexual identity during Super's establishment stage. During this stage, individuals typically develop greater stability, commitment, and mastery of their careers. However, individuals who come out later in life, during the establishment stage, are confronted with the challenge of managing their sexual identity on the job. This might lead to changing careers and recycling (reexploring both self and environments) to find a different career that allows fuller expression of one's identity.

Other authors (Belz, 1993; C. Hetherington, 1991; Prince, 1995) have also described how the coming-out process can disrupt the typical course of career development. For example, C. Hetherington (1991) hypothesized a bottleneck effect wherein LGB individuals in the early stages of coming out might approach career developmental tasks at a slower pace because of the need to deal with competing demands associated with sexual identity development.

Similarly, Gonsiorek (1988) and colleagues (Gonsiorek & Rudolph, 1991) proposed that many gay and lesbian adolescents develop a "false identity" based on the lack of nurturing support from peers and others for all aspects of their identity, instead of a true identity based on trust in their own self-evaluations of their needs, values, and interests.

Gottfredson's (2005) developmental theory of circumscription and compromise is another useful theory that might be applied to understanding how LGB individuals develop career aspirations—in particular, how these aspirations may be shaped by perceptions of obstacles, such as discrimination and heterosexism. Croteau and colleagues (2000), for example, proposed that gender role socialization influences the career development and occupational aspirations of gay and lesbian children differently than heterosexual children. They suggested that gay and lesbian children may internalize vocational stereotypes about gay men and lesbians that, in turn, constrict their perceptions about appropriate career options. Schneider and Dimito (2010) provided some empirical support for this assertion. They found that individuals who had experienced the highest level of anti-LGBT discrimination reported less satisfaction with their career choices, and they perceived fewer work options. They found that gay men and visible minorities were especially likely to be negatively affected by prior discrimination. Interestingly, they also found that lesbians were more likely than gay men to report that their sexual orientation was a positive force in opening up academic and career possibilities for them. The authors hypothesized that coming out as a lesbian may remove restrictive social expectations around gender, thereby freeing lesbian women to consider less traditional career paths.

A number of investigations have identified social support as an important contextual variable that positively contributes to both sexual identity and career development of LGB individuals (Jordan & Deluty, 1998; Nauta et al., 2001; Schmidt & Nilsson, 2006). In particular, these studies have found family and community support to be especially useful career development resources for LGB persons (Boatwright, Gilbert, Forrest, & Ketzenberger, 1996; Tomlinson & Fassinger, 2003). For example, in a study of college students, Schmidt, Miles, and Welsh (2011) found that social support served as a buffer against the negative impact of perceived discrimination on vocational decision making and college adjustment. They recommended that career counselors of college students focus on their clients' support network as a central consideration in counseling.

Over the past decade, a number of scholars have advanced our understanding of the complexity of sexual identity development (Chung, in press; D'Augelli, 2006; Rosario, Schrimshaw, & Hunter, 2004). They have stressed the importance of cultural differences in the formation of an LGB identity.

They have also questioned a basic assumption of earlier sexual identity models: that achieving an integrated and healthy identity is dependent on coming out socially and in the workplace. Fukuyama and Ferguson (2000) stressed that this is particularly pertinent for LGB individuals who are from cultures in which homosexuality is especially stigmatized. Clients from underrepresented populations, they argue, delicately balance multiple identities when evaluating when and if to come out and to whom. For example, LGB people of color may choose different levels of disclosure to family members, friends, or colleagues to maintain harmony across a range of communities.

Similarly, there is an increasing trend among younger LGBT individuals to avoid labeling themselves in any setting because of the potential stigmatization and oversimplification such labels place on definitions of sexual identity (Diamond, 2003). Fassinger and Arseneau (2007) expanded on this more complex conceptualization by drawing attention to the myriad between-group and within-group differences that exist among LGBT populations. For example, there are important between-group differences in experiences that shape the work trajectories of these four sexual minority groups. In addition, these influences are filtered through within-group differences, such as class, race, and age. Furthermore, individual characteristics, such as personality, add an influence that is unique to each person. Fassinger and Arseneau (2007) suggest that counselors attend to all of these differences to avoid oversimplification and to sharpen the focus of counseling. More empirical work is clearly needed to support and refine current models of sexual identity development and to provide clearer guidance on the complex reciprocal influences of career and sexual identity development.

SOCIAL LEARNING THEORIES

Several authors have advocated applying the constructs of Krumboltz's (1979) social learning theory of career decision making and social cognitive career theory (SCCT; Lent, Brown, & Hackett, 1994) to LGB populations (Datti, 2009; Fassinger, 1996; Morrow, Gore, & Campbell, 1996). Datti (2009), for example, presented a detailed map for using Krumboltz's theory to conceptualize the unique career-related challenges of LGBT individuals. Krumboltz outlined four factors that influence individuals' career decisions: genetics, environmental conditions, learning experiences, and task approach skills. Datti emphasized that many of the environmental conditions and events that Krumboltz described as common contextual factors for heterosexual individuals may more intensely impact LGBT individuals. For example, geographic location and political climate affect all people, but these environmental conditions are particularly influential factors for sexual minority individuals. Federal, state, and local laws in the United

States and most other countries deny LGBT individuals fundamental human rights such as job protection, health insurance, pensions, and marriage licenses. Furthermore, protections from workplace discrimination in hiring and promotion on the basis of sexual or gender orientation are lacking in most work environments. He recommended that counselors help LGB clients weigh these factors when making decisions about employers and job location.

Several authors have emphasized that SCCT is a particularly useful theory for understanding the process of career development and decision making for individuals from marginalized groups who encounter workplace and societal discrimination (Byars & Hackett, 1998; Lent, Brown, & Hackett, 2000). Morrow and colleagues (1996) were among the first to demonstrate the value of applying SCCT to the career development of lesbian women and gay men. They described how societal influences such as stereotyping, nonsupport for emerging interests, and peer pressure can shape and truncate the range of academic and career interests of lesbian and gay individuals by influencing their self-efficacy and outcome expectations. They also stressed how barriers such as prejudice and discrimination based on sexual orientation impede the translation of interests into academic and career goals and choices. They suggested, for example, that lesbian women and gay men, when anticipating oppression or discrimination in a particular domain, are less likely to develop an enduring interest in that domain, despite having high self-efficacy. To put it simply, they wrote: "The crucial issue may not be, 'Can I do it?' but 'What will happen if I do?'" (p. 141).

More recently, scholars have used the constructs of SCCT to describe how LGB workers choose sexual identity management strategies (Chung 2001; Chung, Williams, & Dispenza, 2009; Lidderdale, Croteau, Anderson, Tovar-Murray, & Davis, 2007). Sexual identity management refers to whether and how LGB individuals disclose their sexual identity at work. Chung (2001) developed a model of sexual identity management based on an earlier model that outlined strategies that LGB persons might use, depending on the level of risk and potential consequences of a workplace situation (Griffen, 1992). Chung's five strategies, ranging along a continuum from most discreet to most transparent, include (1) *acting* (engaging in a heterosexual relationship to appear heterosexual), (2) *passing* (fabricating information to give the impression of being heterosexual), (3) *covering* (censuring information that would reveal an LGB identity, (4) *implicitly out* (behaving honestly without labeling oneself as LGB), and (5) *explicitly out* (openly stating that one is LGB).

Lidderdale and colleagues (2007) proposed using SCCT as a framework for understanding how LGB individuals learn about and choose among such approaches for managing identity in the workplace. Their model describes how socially learned self-efficacy beliefs and outcome expectations interact with workplace contextual factors to determine which sexual identity management strategy an individual will choose to use at any particular time. For example, an individual would likely develop strong, positive self-efficacy beliefs and outcome expectations regarding being out if he or she has a history of exposure to the value of diversity and to LGB role models who manage their identities openly. This individual would then be more likely to choose identity management strategies that are open. Conversely, adverse learning experiences about being out may produce weaker self-efficacy beliefs and strong negative outcome expectations (e.g., anticipated ridicule or discrimination), prompting choice of more cautious identity management strategies.

Models of sexual identity management draw attention to the prevalence of various forms of formal and informal workplace discrimination and provide an understanding of the ways in which LGB individuals may cope with them. These models stress the ongoing daily choices that LGB individuals make to reveal or conceal sexual identity in response to potential discrimination in the workplace. They take into account the individual's other social and cultural identities and stress the variability of individual and cultural needs. They do not assume or promote one coping strategy as more desirable than another. Instead, they encourage exploration of the risks and benefits of various coping strategies that correspond with a particular individual's identity development and needs; they focus on the unique psychological processes and learning experiences of the individual. For example, choosing to be out in the workplace is not always an optimal choice (Chen-Hayes, 2005); workers from cultures that are more group than individually focused and workers struggling with poverty may be less likely to experience high self-efficacy or to anticipate positive outcomes from being out at work (Croteau, Anderson, & VanderWal, 2008).

An emerging body of literature has expanded the study of sexual identity management and workplace discrimination to the experiences and challenges facing LGBT individuals in leadership positions (Fassinger, Shullman, & Stevenson, 2010; Goodman, Schell, Alexander, & Eidelman, 2008). Fassinger and colleagues (2010), for example, proposed an innovative multidimensional model of LGBT leadership that addresses the interaction of identity disclosure, gender conformity, and workplace contextual factors. This model emphasizes the strengths that LGBT leaders often bring to organizations, such as tolerance of ambiguity, sensitivity to diverse employees, understanding of oppression, creativity, and willingness to take risks. At the same time, they point out how easily a hostile workplace climate can result from negative stereotypes or derogatory comments about LGB leaders from coworkers.

Lehavot and Lambert (2007), for example, found that participants rated lesbian and gay leaders most negatively when they behaved in ways that confirmed sexual identity stereotypes (gay men acting feminine, lesbians behaving in masculine ways). Thus, lesbian and gay leaders may be at greater risk for negative perceptions by followers when they behave in ways considered inappropriate for their gender. Research with lesbian and gay leaders has focused on individuals who are out in the workplace. It is quite reasonable to assume, however, that many LGBT individuals who choose not to disclose their sexual identity at work also may avoid taking on leadership roles due to the risk and scrutiny that that such visibility brings. Research on the leadership career paths of LGBT workers, whether out or not, is an exciting new area of the career development literature.

USING CAREER ASSESSMENT TOOLS

Although the literature addressing career development and counseling of LGB persons has grown significantly, few publications have focused on using career assessment tools with LGB individuals. *Measurement and Evaluation in Counseling and Development* (Hansen, 1997) devoted a special issue to the topic of heterosexism and homophobia in psychological assessment, and the *Journal of Career Assessment* has published two articles on LGB career assessment (Chung, 2003b; Prince, 1997b). Several book chapters also have incorporated case studies and practical guidelines for using career assessments with sexual minority clients (Pope, 1992; Pope, Prince, & Mitchell, 2000; Prince & Potoczniak, 2012). Otherwise, this topic has largely been ignored. It is also noteworthy that the *Standards for Educational and Psychological Testing* (American Educational Research Association, American Psychological Association, & National Council on Measurement in Education, 1999) address other dimensions of diversity but are silent on the development and use of tests with LGBT persons. Nevertheless, as research has shown with members of other socially oppressed groups, career assessments with questionable validity for LGB populations can be misleading and even harmful when inappropriately used (Walsh & Betz, 1995).

Sound career assessment requires assessment skills that are rooted in the counselor's self-awareness and knowledge of the psychological, cultural, and environmental concerns that are specific to LGB individuals (Chung, 2003b; Prince, 1997b). For example, Chung (2003b) emphasized the need for counselors to consider how their worldview, particularly their attitudes and possible biases regarding homosexuality and bisexuality, might influence their selection and use of assessments. For example, a counselor with biased attitudes toward LGB individuals might use assessment results to inappropriately direct some LGB clients to more gender-traditional careers by discounting scores on scales that are counter to gender expectations. He pointed out the need for counselors to increase their knowledge in a number of domains, such as sexual identity development, workplace discrimination, LGB relationships, and diversity within the LGB community, and to seek out consultation when needed.

Furthermore, it is critical to evaluate each potential assessment tool for bias before using it with LGBT clients. Widely used career assessment instruments do not include item content relevant to the specific career development experiences of LGB populations, and they have not been designed to assess theoretical constructs that speak to LGB career concerns (Prince, 1997a, 1997b). Effective assessment therefore requires counselors to use supplemental strategies to address influences such as sexual identity development, identity management, workplace discrimination, and heterosexism. Regrettably, effectively adapting the assessment process to meet LGB client needs is not always easy to do, given that clients' sexual identity status is often invisible. Counselors need to routinely assume at first that all clients may be lesbian, gay, or bisexual. Furthermore, counselors need to consider routinely collecting intake information from clients regarding their sexual identity so that relevant historical material (such as experiences with discrimination and stigma) can be explored and integrated into the assessment process.

Although some counselors may find it awkward to raise the question of sexual identity status in the first interview, it is nevertheless important to gather this information. It is good practice, for example, to include an item relating to sexual identity on written intake forms that clients complete prior to the first interview. These forms routinely collect other demographic and historical information, such as gender, ethnicity, and education, that allow the counselor to form first impressions and guide the first interview. The absence of an item on sexual identity reinforces the invisibility of sexual minorities; by omission, the form can relay the message that heterosexuality is assumed.

TRANSGENDER INDIVIDUALS

The literature addressing the work and career concerns of transgender individuals has increased over the past few years, helping to inform both researchers and practitioners. Nevertheless, scholarly contributions continue to rely heavily on extrapolations from findings with lesbian and gay populations and to use informal sources of information such as websites of transgender organizations (Brown & Rounsley, 1996; O'Neil et al., 2008). Pepper and Lorah (2008) were among the first to summarize common career and workplace issues faced by transgender individuals and to provide recommendations for career counselors. They emphasized the numerous and significant workplace challenges that transgender individuals confront, such as deciding whether to transition (i.e., begin dressing, behaving, or living as the new gender) in their current job and choosing how to deal with coworkers' prejudice and discrimination. Additional challenges include managing social isolation at work and facing high rates of underemployment (Schilt, 2006).

There has been growing recognition of the different work experiences specific to persons within the larger transgender category. For example, some of the workplace experiences and prejudices faced by male-to-female (MTF) transgender persons differ from those of female-to-male (FTM) transgender persons because of gender role expectations. MTF persons may confront the loss of societal and workplace privileges of living as a man, whereas FTM persons may encounter very different experiences and conflicts (Pepper & Lorah, 2008). It is not surprising, therefore, that research findings indicate that workplace conflicts are a primary reason for transgender individuals to seek counseling (Rachlin, 2002).

Only recently have researchers begun to gather data to support previous theoretical work in this area. Budge, Tebbe, and Howard (2010) used a qualitative case study approach to better understand the career decision-making processes and workplace experiences of transgender people. They identified a number of themes across their interviews that described the transition process at work, such as: preparing for the transition, coming out at work, appearance at work, coworker reactions, and coping experiences at work. They also identified a number of themes related to individuals' career decision making, such as occupational barriers and occupational opportunities. For example, all participants described barriers that related to prejudice and discrimination. They included overt discrimination, job loss due to gender identity, bathroom discrimination, and needing to work harder to compensate for transgender status. Occupational opportunities for a number of participants included the discovery of interests in teaching and social justice as a result of helping coworkers understand transgender issues.

Similarly, Law and colleagues (2011) examined individual experiences and organizational characteristics to understand the work experiences of transgender individuals. They found less stigmatization toward women transitioning to men than toward men transitioning to women. They also found that coworkers and organizational support played essential roles in influencing the experiences of transgender individuals. Specifically, their results indicated that individuals had greater job satisfaction and organizational commitment when they had supportive coworkers who reacted positively to their workplace disclosure. In addition, they found that participants were more likely to disclose at work if there were individuals outside of work to whom they could disclose their identity.

These studies highlight a number of factors that can inform career counselors working with transgender clients, particularly those who are considering whether to disclose their gender identity. Career counselors need to engage in realistic yet sensitive conversations with transgender clients about prejudice and discrimination and focus on helping them to build strong support networks. Counselors also need to obtain training or supervision to learn more about the legal and medical issues that influence the lives of transgender people. Finally, the growing literature in this area emphasizes the important role of workplace environment and the need for career professionals to advocate for strengthening laws and policies that support the recruitment and retention of qualified transgender workers.

CONCLUSIONS AND PRACTICE IMPLICATIONS

The foundations of counselor competence with LGB clients are in many ways similar to those that are recommended for other nonmajority clients who endure stereotyping and stigmatization (Israel & Selvedge, 2003). For example, the multicultural counseling literature emphasizes the need for counselors to examine the stereotypes and biases they hold about various ethnic groups and to acquire knowledge about the acculturation, worldview, and identity development of their clients (Sue, Arredondo, & McDavis, 1992). Competent career counseling with LGB clients requires these same efforts.

In addition, there are factors unique to working with LGB populations that need to be incorporated. For instance, addressing sexual orientation requires discussing sexuality, a particularly difficult topic for many people and one that polarizes religious groups and political parties. A counselor needs to determine for each client to what degree sexual orientation needs to become a primary or secondary focus of counseling and to examine whose needs are driving that decision, the counselor's or the client's. For example, a lesbian college sophomore who presents with career indecision may or may not need or want to talk about her sexual orientation. On the one hand, a counselor needs to provide an affirmative environment for exploring the influence of sexual orientation so that the topic is not ignored due to discomfort. On the other hand, overemphasis and an exclusive focus on sexual orientation might lead to early termination if a client feels that her or his presenting career needs are being discounted or deferred.

Fortunately, a number of professional practice guidelines provide counselors with a valuable framework for working effectively and responsibly with LGB clients. "Guidelines for Psychological Practice with Lesbian, Gay and Bisexual Clients" (APA, 2012), for example, integrates information in areas such as assessment, identity, and diversity to help practitioners engage in affirmative practice. Similarly, the Association for Lesbian, Gay, Bisexual and Transgender Issues in Counseling (2003) has published competencies for counseling LGBT clients, and these have been adopted by the American Counseling Association. These competencies assist counselors in examining their personal biases and values regarding LGBT clients and provide guidance in applying appropriate and effective interventions. Included among these competencies are several that are specific to career development. They suggest that competent counselors need to pursue the following four strategies: (1) counter occupational stereotypes that restrict LGBT clients' career development and career decision making, (2) explore ways in which government statutes do not protect LGBT workers from discrimination, (3) help LGBT clients make career choices that facilitate both identity formation and job satisfaction, and (4) connect LGBT clients with sexual minority role models who can increase awareness of viable career options.

A social justice approach offers an additional framework that is useful for career counselors. This approach highlights the ways in which the social and political contexts of LGBT persons' lives (e.g., heterosexism, societal disapproval, and deprivation of fundamental human rights) interfere with healthy development (Meyer, 2003). The American Counseling Association's *Advocacy Competencies* (Ratts, Toporek, & Lewis, 2010) provide a detailed framework for counselors wanting to infuse social justice work into their counseling practice. These competencies identify ways in which counselors can engage in both individual counseling and community-based work to help clients achieve optimal results. Along these lines, Whitcomb and Loewy (2006) provided specific suggestions for engaging in social justice work on behalf of LGB people. They recommended that counselors become involved in local and national politics and advocacy efforts to influence public opinion, policies, and laws that are harmful to the career development of LGBT persons.

A recurring theme throughout the scholarly literature of LGBT career development is the need for counselors to implement an LGBT-affirmative approach to counseling—one that emphasizes the strengths and benefits of LGBT identities and that supports an individual's flourishing in all areas of life (Rostosky & Riggle, 2011). One example is Shultheiss's (2003) relational approach to career counseling with sexual minority women. She advocated that counselors focus on strengthening clients' interpersonal support systems and examine how partners, friends, and family can facilitate career development and career aspirations. Connecting LGBT clients with supportive communities is critical to combating the isolation that is typical for LGBT individuals who grow up in families that do not share their minority status and in cultures that are heterosexually defined.

One important source of support for many LGBT clients is a romantic partner or spouse who may play a particularly significant role in reducing the stress and isolation that result from workplace discrimination and heterosexism. At the same time, integrating a same-sex relationship into one's work life presents unique challenges to lesbian and gay couples—an important one being whether to come out in the workplace together. For example, lesbian and gay couples often struggle in deciding when and if to bring a partner to work-related social events or whether to mention a partner when negotiating benefits for a new job. O'Ryan and McFarland (2010) identified several themes that can assist counselors with couples trying to successfully blend their relationship and careers. They found, for example, that it was important for couples to engage in discussions together to plan and weigh the options of coming out in the workplace. Similarly, they found that couples who made efforts to create lesbian- and gay-positive social networks increased their sense of well-being and empowerment.

Another essential recommendation for career counselors is to become knowledgeable about the specific issues that are the context of LGBT clients' lives (e.g., sexual identity development, sexual identity management in the workplace, the impact of stigma, heterosexism, discrimination). Counselors need to be informed so they can work with each client to understand and address how these factors have influenced career development and decision making and how they may continue to do so in the future. The invisibility of sexual identity can complicate such exploration. Bieschke and Matthews (1996) noted, for example, that often an LGB client will choose not to disclose sexual identity status to a counselor, particularly when a client is unsure of the degree to which the counselor is LGB-affirmative. Clients may look for clues in the counselor's office or in the counselor's words or behaviors to determine if he or she is knowledgeable and supportive. Thus, it is incumbent on career counselors to demonstrate LGB-supportive behaviors, such as avoiding heterosexist language in communications with all clients, and to create an LGB-affirmative physical environment. For example, counselors might display office artwork or periodicals that are LGB-affirmative. Similarly, many organizations create affirmative office climates by placing decals or signs on office doors or in waiting rooms to indicate the office is an LGB "safe space."

It is also essential for counselors to use relevant career resources to help clients explore jobs and careers. Most traditional career resources and career libraries do not feature LGBT-related material; this absence contributes to the stigmatization, invisibility, and isolation of LGB individuals. Proactive efforts are required to ensure that career resources are expanded to include occupational data, job listings, and career information from LGB-positive sources such as local and national LGBT organizations and from employers that offer LGBT-affirmative policies. For example, the Human Rights Campaign (http://www.hrc.org), the National Gay and Lesbian

Chamber of Commerce (http://www.nglcc.org), and Out and Equal Workplace Advocates (http://www.outandequal.org) produce an array of career resources specific to LGB populations. Using resources such as these not only provide LGBT clients with relevant information but also ensure that career counselors remain up-to-date on current work issues that impact the lives of LGB clients.

Over the past 20 years, there have been important advances in understanding the unique career concerns of LGBT individuals. There have also been important societal changes, such as increasing recognition of domestic partnerships by employers and, in some locations, the legalization of marriage of same-sex couples. Nevertheless, LGBT individuals continue to deal with contextual factors inherent in living and working in a heterosexual society, and we have yet to expand or develop career theories that adequately speak to these complexities. Still, the incredible diversity of cultural groups that make up LGBT populations presents unlimited opportunities; both scholars and career practitioners are in an ideal position to develop more effective interventions, to empower LGBT individuals to thrive at school and work, and to advocate for a more just society.

REFERENCES

American Educational Research Association, American Psychological Association, National Council on Measurement in Education, Joint Committee on Standards for Educational & Psychological Testing (US). (1999). *Standards for educational and psychological testing*. Washington, DC: American Educational Research Association.

American Psychological Association. (2012). Guidelines for psychological practice with lesbian, gay, and bisexual clients. *American Psychologist, 67*(1), 10–42. doi:10.1037/a0024659

Association for Lesbian, Gay, Bisexual and Transgender Issues in Counseling. (2003). *Competencies for counseling gay, lesbian, and bisexual (LGB) clients*. Retrieved from http://www.algbtic.org/resources/competencies.html

Belz, J. R. (1993). Sexual orientation as a factor in career development. *Career Development Quarterly, 41*(3), 197–200.

Bieschke, K. J., & Matthews, C. (1996). Career counselor attitudes and behaviors toward gay, lesbian, and bisexual clients [Special issue: Vocational Issues of Lesbian Women and Gay Men]. *Journal of Vocational Behavior, 48*(2), 243–255. doi:10.1006/jvbe.1996.0021

Boatwright, K. J., Gilbert, M. S., Forrest, L., & Ketzenberger, K. (1996). Impact of identity development upon career trajectory: Listening to the voices of lesbian women [Special issue: Vocational Issues of Lesbian Women and Gay Men]. *Journal of Vocational Behavior, 48*(2), 210–228. doi:10.1006/jvbe.1996.0019

Bohan, J. S. (1996). *Psychology and sexual orientation: Coming to terms*. Florence, KY: Taylor & Francis/Routledge.

Brown, M. L., & Rounsley, C. A. (1996). *True selves: Understanding transsexualism—for families, friends, coworkers, and helping professionals*. San Francisco, CA: Jossey-Bass.

Budge, S. L., Tebbe, E. N., & Howard, K. A. S. (2010). The work experiences of transgender individuals: Negotiating the transition and career decision-making processes. *Journal of Counseling Psychology, 57*(4), 377–393. doi:10.1037/a0020472

Byars, A. M., & Hackett, G. (1998). Applications of social cognitive theory to the career development of women of color. *Applied & Preventive Psychology, 7*(4), 255–267. doi:10.1016/S0962-1849(98)80029-2

Cass, V. C. (1979). Homosexual identity formation: A theoretical model. *Journal of Homosexuality, 4*(3), 219–235.

Chen-Hayes, S. F. (2005). Challenging multiple oppressions in counselor education. In J. M. Croteau, J. S. Lark, M. A. Lidderdale, & Y. B. Chung (Eds.), *Deconstructing heterosexism in the counseling professions: A narrative approach* (pp. 53–57). Thousand Oaks, CA: Sage.

Chung, Y. B. (2001). Work discrimination and coping strategies: Conceptual frameworks for counseling lesbian, gay, and bisexual clients. *Career Development Quarterly, 50*(1), 33–44.

Chung, Y. B. (2003a). Career counseling with lesbian, gay, bisexual, and transgendered persons: The next decade [Special issue: Career Counseling in the Next Decade]. *Career Development Quarterly, 52*(1), 78–85.

Chung, Y. B. (2003b). Ethical and professional issues in career assessment with lesbian, gay, and bisexual persons. *Journal of Career Assessment, 11*(1), 96–112. doi:10.1177/106907202237462

Chung, Y. B. (in press). Sexual orientation and sexual identity: Theory, research and practice. In *APA handbook of counseling psychology*. Washington, DC: American Psychological Association.

Chung, Y. B., & Harmon, L. W. (1994). The career interests and aspirations of gay men: How sex-role orientation is related. *Journal of Vocational Behavior, 45*(2), 223–239. doi:10.1006/jvbe.1994.1033

Chung, Y. B., & Katayama, M. (1996). Assessment of sexual orientation in lesbian/gay/bisexual studies. *Journal of Homosexuality, 30*(4), 49–62. doi:10.1300/J082v30n04_03

Chung, Y. B., Williams, W., & Dispenza, F. (2009). Validating work discrimination and coping strategy models for sexual minorities. *Career Development Quarterly, 58*(2), 162–170.

Committee on Lesbian and Gay Concerns. (1991). Avoiding heterosexual bias in language. *American Psychologist, 46*(9), 973–974. doi:10.1037/0003-066X.46.9.973

Croteau, J. M. (1996). Research on the work experiences of lesbian, gay and bisexual people: An integrative review of methodology and content. *Journal of Vocational Behavior, 48*, 195–209.

Croteau, J. M., Anderson, M. Z., Distefano, T. M., & Kampa-Kokesch, S. (2000). Lesbian, gay, and bisexual vocational psychology: Reviewing foundations and planning construction. In R. M. Perez, K. A. DeBord, & K. J. Bieschke (Eds.), *Handbook of counseling and psychotherapy with lesbian, gay, and bisexual clients* (pp. 383–408).Washington, DC: American Psychological Association. doi:10.1037/10339-016

Croteau, J. M., Anderson, M. Z., & VanderWal, B. L. (2008). Models of workplace sexual identity disclosure and management: Reviewing and extending concepts. [Special issue: Offering New Insights into GLBT Workplace Experiences]. *Group & Organization Management, 33*(5), 532–565. doi:10.1177/1059601108321828

Croteau, J. M., Bieschke, K. J., Fassinger, R. E., & Manning, J. L. (2008). Counseling psychology and sexual orientation: History, selective trends, and future directions. In S. D. Brown & R. W. Lent (Eds.), *Handbook of counseling psychology* (pp. 194–211). Hoboken, NJ: Wiley.

Datti, P. A. (2009). Applying social learning theory of career decision making to gay, lesbian, bisexual, transgender, and questioning young adults. *Career Development Quarterly, 58*(1), 54–64.

D'Augelli, A. R. (2006). Developmental and contextual factors and mental health among lesbian, gay, and bisexual youths. In A. M. Omoto, H. S. Kurtzman (Eds.), *Sexual orientation and mental health: Examining identity and development in lesbian, gay, and bisexual people* (pp. 37–53). Washington, DC: American Psychological Association. doi:10.1037/11261-002

Dawis, R. V., & Lofquist, L. H. (1984). *A psychological theory of work adjustment: An individual-differences model and its applications*. Minneapolis: University of Minnesota Press.

Diamond, L. M. (2003). Was it a phase? Young women's relinquishment of lesbian/bisexual identities over a 5-year period. *Journal of Personality and Social Psychology, 84*(2), 352–364. doi:10.1037/0022-3514.84.2.352

Dunkle, J. H. (1996). Toward an integration of gay and lesbian identity development and Super's life-span approach [Special issue: Vocational Issues of Lesbian Women and Gay Men]. *Journal of Vocational Behavior, 48*(2), 149–159. doi:10.1006/jvbe.1996.0015

Elliott, J. E. (1993). Career development with lesbian and gay clients. *Career Development Quarterly, 41*(3), 210–226.

Fassinger, R. E. (1996). Notes from the margins: Integrating lesbian experience into the vocational psychology of women [Special issue: Vocational Issues of Lesbian Women and Gay Men]. *Journal of Vocational Behavior, 48*(2), 160–175. doi:10.1006/jvbe.1996.0016

Fassinger, R. E. (2001). Diversity at work: Research issues in vocational development. In D. B. Pope-Davis & H. L. K. Coleman (Eds.), *The intersection of race, class, and gender in multicultural counseling* (pp. 267–288). Thousand Oaks, CA: Sage.

Fassinger, R. E., & Arseneau, J. R. (2007). "I'd rather get wet than be under that umbrella": Differentiating the experiences and identities of lesbian, gay, bisexual, and transgender people. In K. J. Bieschke, R. M. Perez, & K. A DeBord (Eds.), *Handbook of counseling and psychotherapy with lesbian, gay, and bisexual clients* (pp. 19–49). Washington, DC: American Psychological Association.

Fassinger, R. E., Shullman, S. L., & Stevenson, M. R. (2010). Toward an affirmative lesbian, gay, bisexual, and transgender leadership paradigm. *American Psychologist, 65*(3), 201–215. doi:10.1037/a0018597

Fukuyama, M. A., & Ferguson, A. D. (2000). Lesbian, gay, and bisexual people of color: Understanding cultural complexity and managing multiple oppressions. In R. M. Perez, K. A. DeBord, & K. J. Bieschke (Eds.), *Handbook of counseling and psychotherapy with lesbian, gay, and bisexual clients* (pp. 81–105). Washington, DC: American Psychological Association. doi:10.1037/10339-004

Gonsiorek, J. C. (1988). Mental health issues of gay and lesbian adolescents. *Journal of Adolescent Health Care, 9*(2), 114–122. doi:10.1016/0197-0070(88)90057-5

Gonsiorek, J. C., & Rudolph, J. R. (1991). Homosexual identity: Coming out and other developmental events. In J. C. Gonsiorek, J. D. Weinrich, J. C. Gonsiorek, & J. D. Weinrich (Eds.), *Homosexuality: Research implications for public policy* (pp. 161–176). Thousand Oaks, CA: Sage.

Goodman, J. A., Schell, J., Alexander, M. G., & Eidelman, S. (2008). The impact of a derogatory remark on prejudice toward a gay male leader. *Journal of Applied Social Psychology, 38*(2), 542–555.

Gottfredson, L. S. (2005). Applying Gottfredson's theory of circumscription and compromise in career guidance and counseling. In S. D. Brown & R. W. Lent (Eds.), *Career development and counseling: Putting theory and research to work* (pp. 71–100). Hoboken, NJ: Wiley.

Griffin, P. (1992). From hiding out to coming out: Empowering lesbian and gay educators. In K. M. Harbeck (Ed.), *Coming out of the classroom closet: Gay and lesbian students, teachers, and curricula* (pp. 167–196). Binghamton, NY: Harrington Park Press.

Hansen, J. C. (1997). Heterosexism and homophobia: Potential cultural biases in assessment. *Measurement and Evaluation in Counseling and Development, 30*(2), 66–67.

Hetherington, C. (1991). Life planning and career counseling with gay and lesbian students. In N. J. Evans & V. A. Wall (Eds.), *Beyond tolerance: Gays, lesbians and bisexuals on campus* (pp. 131–146). Alexandria, VA: American College Personnel Association.

Hetherington, C., Hillerbrand, E., & Etringer, B. D. (1989). Career counseling with gay men: Issues and recommendations for research. *Journal of Counseling & Development, 67*(8), 452–454.

Hetherington, E. M. (1991). The role of individual differences and family relationships in children's coping with divorce and remarriage. In P. A. Cowan & E. M. Hetherington (Eds.), *Family transitions* (pp. 165–194). Hillsdale, NJ: Erlbaum.

Holland, J. L. (1985). *The self-directed search: A guide to educational and vocational planning*. Odessa, FL: Psychological Assessment Resources.

Holland, J. L. (1997). *Making vocational choices* (3rd ed.). Odessa, FL: Psychological Assessment Resources, Inc.

Israel, T., & Selvidge, M. M. D. (2003). Contributions of multicultural counseling to counselor competence with lesbian, gay and bisexual clients. *Journal of Multicultural Counseling and Development, 31*(2), 84–98.

Jordan, K. M., & Deluty, R. H. (1998). Coming out for lesbian women: Its relation to anxiety, positive affectivity, self-esteem and social support. *Journal of Homosexuality, 35*(2), 41–63. doi:10.1300/J082v35n02_03

Krumboltz, J. D. (1979). A social learning theory of career decision making. In A. M. Mitchell, G. B. Jones, & J. D. Krumboltz (Eds.), *Social learning and career decision making* (pp. 19–49). Cranston, RI: Caroll.

Krumboltz, J. D., Mitchell, A. M., & Jones, G. B. (1976). A social learning theory of career selection. *Counseling Psychologist*, 6(1), 71–81. doi:10.1177 /001100007600600117

Law, C. L., Martinez, L. R., Ruggs, E. N., Hebl, M. R., & Akers, E. (2011). Trans-parency in the workplace: How the experiences of transsexual employees can be improved. *Journal of Vocational Behavior*, 79(3), 710–723. doi:10.1016 /j.jvb.2011.03.018

Lehavot, K., & Lambert, A. J. (2007). Toward a greater understanding of antigay prejudice: On the role of sexual orientation and gender role violation. *Basic and Applied Social Psychology*, 29(3), 279–292.

Lent, R. W., Brown, S. D., & Hackett, G. (1994). Toward a unifying social cognitive theory of career and academic interest, choice, and performance. *Journal of Vocational Behavior*, 45(1), 79–122. doi:10.1006/jvbe.1994.1027

Lent, R. W., Brown, S. D., & Hackett, G. (2000). Contextual supports and barriers to career choice: A social cognitive analysis. *Journal of Counseling Psychology*, 47(1), 36–49. doi:10.1037/0022-0167.47.1.36

Lidderdale, M. A., Croteau, J. M., Anderson, M. Z., Tovar-Murray, D., & Davis, J. M. (2007). Building lesbian, gay, and bisexual vocational psychology: A theoretical model of workplace sexual identity management. In K. J. Bieschke, R. M. Perez, & K. A. DeBord (Eds.), *Handbook of counseling and psychotherapy with lesbian, gay, and bisexual clients* (pp. 245–270). Washington, DC: American Psychological Association.

Lyons, H. Z., Brenner, B. R., & Fassinger, R. E. (2005). A multicultural test of the theory of work adjustment: Investigating the role of heterosexism and fit perceptions in the job satisfaction of lesbian, gay, and bisexual employees. *Journal of Counseling Psychology*, 52(4), 537–548. doi:10.1037/0022-0167.52.4.537

Lyons, H. Z., & O'Brien, K. M. (2006). The role of person–environment fit in the job satisfaction and tenure intentions of African American employees. *Journal of Counseling Psychology*, 53(4), 387–396. doi:10.1037/0022-0167.53.4.387

Meyer, I. H. (2003). Prejudice, social stress, and mental health in lesbian, gay, and bisexual populations: Conceptual issues and research evidence. *Psychological Bulletin*, 129, 674–697.

Mobley, M., & Slaney, R. B. (1996). Holland's theory: Its relevance for lesbian women and gay men [Special issue: Vocational Issues of Lesbian Women and Gay Men]. *Journal of Vocational Behavior*, 48(2), 125–135. doi:10.1006/jvbe.1996 .0013

Morrow, S. L., Gore, P. A., & Campbell, B. W. (1996). The application of a sociocognitive framework to the career development of lesbian women and gay men [Special issue: Vocational Issues of Lesbian Women and Gay Men]. *Journal of Vocational Behavior*, 48(2), 136–148. doi:10.1006/jvbe.1996.0014

Nauta, M. M., Saucier, A. M., & Woodard, L. E. (2001). Interpersonal influences on students' academic and career decisions: The impact of sexual orientation. *Career Development Quarterly*, 49(4), 352–362.

O'Neil, M. E., McWhirter, E. H., & Cerezo, A. (2008). Transgender identities and gender variance in vocational psychology: Recommendations for practice, social advocacy, and research. *Journal of Career Development, 34*(3), 286–308. doi:10.1177/0894845307311251

O'Ryan, L. W., & McFarland, W. P. (2010). A phenomenological exploration of the experiences of dual-career lesbian and gay couples. *Journal of Counseling & Development, 88*(1), 71–79.

Pepper, S. M., & Lorah, P. (2008). Career issues and workplace considerations for the transsexual community: Bridging a gap of knowledge for career counselors and mental health care providers. *Career Development Quarterly, 56*(4), 330–343.

Phillips, J. C., Ingram, K. M., Smith, N. G., & Mindes, E. J. (2003). Methodological and content review of lesbian-, gay-, and bisexual-related articles in counseling journals: 1990–1999. *Counseling Psychologist, 31*(1), 25–62. doi:10.1177/0011000002239398

Pope, M. (1992). Bias in the interpretation of psychological tests. In S. H. Dwarkin & F. Gutierrez (Eds.), *Counseling gay men and lesbians: Journey to the end of the rainbow* (pp. 456–462). Alexandria, VA: American Counseling Association.

Pope, M. S., Prince, J. P., & Mitchell, K. (2000). Responsible career counseling with lesbian and gay students. In D. A. Luzzo (Ed.), *Career counseling of college students: An empirical guide to strategies that work* (pp. 267–282). Washington, DC: American Psychological Association. doi:10.1037/10362-015

Prince, J. P. (1995). Influences on the career development of gay men. *Career Development Quarterly, 44*(2), 168–177.

Prince, J. P. (1997a). Assessment bias affecting lesbian, gay male and bisexual individuals. *Measurement and Evaluation in Counseling and Development, 30*(2), 82–87.

Prince, J. P. (1997b). Career assessment with lesbian, gay, and bisexual individuals. *Journal of Career Assessment, 5*(2), 225–238. doi:10.1177/106907279700500208

Prince, J. P., & Potoczniak, M. J. (2012). Using psychological assessment tools with lesbian, gay, bisexual and transgender clients. In S. H. Dwarkin & M. Pope (Eds.), *Casebook for counseling lesbian, gay, bisexual, and transgender persons and their families* (pp. 319–328). Alexandria, VA: American Counseling Association.

Rachlin, K. (2002). Transgender individuals' experiences of psychotherapy. *International Journal of Transgenderism, 6*(1).

Ragins, B. R., Singh, R., & Cornwell, J. M. (2007). Making the invisible visible: Fear and disclosure of sexual orientation at work. *Journal of Applied Psychology 92*(4), 1103–1118.

Ratts, M. J., Toporek, R. L., & Lewis, J. A. (Eds.). (2010). *ACA advocacy competencies: A social justice framework for counselors.* Alexandria, VA: American Counseling Association.

Rosario, M., Schrimshaw, E. W., & Hunter, J. (2004). Ethnic/racial differences in the coming-out process of lesbian, gay, and bisexual youths: A comparison of sexual identity development over time [Special issue: Lesbian, Gay, and Bisexual Racial and Ethnic Minority Individuals: Empirical Explorations]. *Cultural Diversity and Ethnic Minority Psychology, 10*(3), 215–228. doi:10.1037/1099-9809.10.3.215

Rostosky, S. S., & Riggle, E. D. B. (2011). Marriage equality for same-sex couples: Counseling psychologists as social change agents. *Counseling Psychologist, 39*(7), 956–972. doi:10.1177/0011000011398398

Schilt, K. (2006). Just one of the guys? How transmen make gender visible at work. *Gender & Society, 20*(4), 465–490. doi:10.1177/0891243206288077

Schmidt, C. K., Miles, J. R., & Welsh, A. C. (2011). Perceived discrimination and social support: The influences on career development and college adjustment of LGBT college students. *Journal of Career Development, 38*(4), 293–309. doi:10.1177/0894845310372615

Schmidt, C. K., & Nilsson, J. E. (2006). The effects of simultaneous developmental processes: Factors relating to the career development of lesbian, gay, and bisexual youth. *Career Development Quarterly, 55*(1), 22–37.

Schneider, M. S., & Dimito, A. (2010). Factors influencing the career and academic choices of lesbian, gay, bisexual, and transgender people. *Journal of Homosexuality, 57*(10), 1355–1369. doi:10.1080/00918369.2010.517080

Schultheiss, D. E. P. (2003). A relational approach to career counseling: Theoretical integration and practical application. *Journal of Counseling & Development, 81*, 301–310.

Sue, D. W., Arredondo, P., & McDavis, R. J. (1992). Multicultural counseling competencies and standards: A call to the profession. *Journal of Multicultural Counseling and Development, 20*(2), 64–88.

Super, D. E. (1990). A life-span, life-space approach to career development. In D. Brown & L. Brooks (Eds.), *Career choice and development: Applying contemporary theories to practice* (2nd ed., pp. 197–261). San Francisco, CA: Jossey-Bass.

Tiedeman, D. V., & O'Hara, R. P. (1963). *Career development: Choice and adjustment.* New York, NY: College Entrance Examination Board.

Tomlinson, M. J., & Fassinger, R. E. (2003). Career development, lesbian identity development, and campus climate among lesbian college students. *Journal of College Student Development, 44*(6), 845–860. doi:10.1353/csd.2003.0078

Waldo, C. R. (1999). Working in a majority context: A structural model of heterosexism as minority stress in the workplace. *Journal of Counseling Psychology, 46*(2), 218–232. doi:10.1037/0022-0167.46.2.218

Walsh, W. B., & Betz, N. E. (1995). *Tests and assessment* (3rd ed.). Englewood Cliffs, NJ: Prentice-Hall.

Whitcomb, D. H., & Loewy, M. I. (2006). Diving into the hornet's nest: Situating counseling psychologists in LGB social justice work. In R. L. Toporek, L. H. Gerstein, N. A. Fouad, G. Roysircar, & T. Israel (Eds.), *Handbook for social justice in counseling psychology: Leadership, vision and action* (pp. 215–230). Thousand Oaks, CA: Sage.

Worthington, R. L., & Reynolds, A. L. (2009). Within-group differences in sexual orientation and identity. *Journal of Counseling Psychology, 56*(1), 44–55. doi:10.1037/a0013498

CHAPTER 11

Personality, Career Development, and Occupational Attainment

STEVEN D. BROWN AND ANDREAS HIRSCHI

R ESEARCH ON PERSONALITY AND its relation to life outcomes is a vibrant
field of inquiry with important implications for career development
practice. An increasing number of studies have shown that people's
relatively enduring personality traits relate to a variety of career and work-
related outcomes. In a meta-analytic review, Roberts, Kuncel, Shiner, Caspi,
and Goldberg (2007) found that personality traits explained unique variance
in both long-term unemployment rates and occupational stability over and
above intelligence and socioeconomic status, both of which had already been
found to be important predictors of these work outcomes. In another meta-
analysis of predictors of career success, Ng, Eby, Sorensen, and Feldman
(2005) found that personality traits predicted other indices of occupational
attainment as well, including salary, number of promotions, and career
satisfaction. Although current research (e.g., Roberts et al., 2007) also suggests
that personality traits explain only a small percentage of variance in these
career outcomes, their contributions are still substantial enough (alone and
when compared to the variance accounted for by other factors) to warrant
consideration in career development and counseling.

This chapter discusses what we currently know about normal personality and its role in career development, choice making, and occupational
attainment. We begin by providing an overview of different perspectives
on the role of personality in career development and then discuss the
structure of normal personality, focusing specifically on five major personality traits (known as the Big 5) that have been studied extensively in
the literature. We then review research that has linked the Big 5 personality traits with career outcomes across the life span and conclude with

a set of counseling and preventive implications that can be derived from the research.

PERSPECTIVES ON THE RELATION OF PERSONALITY AND LIFE OUTCOMES

There are two basic models of how to explain relations between personality and career and life outcomes. The *trait* perspective (McCrae et al., 2000) focuses on the stability of traits and posits that traits represent endogenous basic tendencies of thinking, feeling, and acting that are shaped largely by biology and lead to characteristic ways of adapting to the different environmental settings in which individuals interact. Thus, extraversion, as a trait that is largely inherited and biologically determined, leads people to think, feel, and act in particular ways in their natural environments (e.g., to feel comfortable in and approach social situations versus feeling uncomfortable and avoiding them). This perspective is supported by research showing significant genetic and limited environmental (e.g., parental) influences on traits, similar manifestations of traits across cultures, and temporal stability of traits (McCrae et al., 2000).

A different perspective is proposed by the *plasticity* model of personality change, which posits that traits are fairly stable aspects of people's personalities but that personality change is possible and, indeed, probable. According to this view, personality is completely shaped neither by biology nor by the environment. Rather, personality development is a by-product of a dynamic interaction between persons and their environments that results in both trait stability and change (Caspi, Roberts, & Shiner, 2005). According to this perspective, much of the stability in adult personality can indeed be explained by genetic factors. However, personality traits also show significant stability over time due to niche-building processes; people are passive victims of neither their environments nor their genes and actively create, seek out, and remain in environments that are congruent with their traits. Thus, trait stability (more on this later in the chapter) is a function of both biology and niche building.

However, as we will also see later, traits are not entirely stable because not only do people select environments that are correspondent with their personalities (niche building) but also environments, once entered, have an impact on people's personalities. This perspective is supported by meta-analytic research showing significant normative changes in personality until about the age of 50, with major changes seeming to occur in early adulthood rather than in adolescence (Roberts & Del Vecchio, 2000; Roberts, Walton, & Viechtbauer, 2006). Other research has shown that occupational attainment among men is associated with increases in dependability, responsibility, independence, and success motivation (Elder, 1969). Among women, it has been found that participation in the labor force is associated with increases in dominance, independence, and self-confidence (Clausen & Gilens, 1990; Roberts, 1997).

In sum, it is likely that personality traits play several roles in the career development process. In particular, (a) traits represent specific biological temperaments that affect how people think, feel, and act in their careers and work lives; (b) people actively seek out educational and work environments that correspond to and reinforce their personalities; (c) people shape their environments to better fit their personality traits; and (d) people react to and change their traits based on environmental experiences.

THE STRUCTURE AND STABILITY OF NORMAL PERSONALITY

Although research on personality has a long history dating back to at least World War I with the development of the Woodworth Personal Data Sheet, this history has been quite checkered until the past 30 or so years. A major problem that beset early personality research was the lack of a clear theoretical structure that could parsimoniously account for the covariation found among a large and ever growing number of personality traits. Looking back at past personality research in industrial and organizational psychology, Hogan and Roberts (2000) concluded: "There are thousands of personality measures in the published literature" (p. 6) and that the research was "in conceptual disarray, with no overarching theoretical paradigm" (p. 7).

Fortunately, findings have converged over the past 30 or so years to suggest that five major personality constructs or traits, referred to as the Big 5, may be sufficient to describe the basic dimensions of normal personality (Mount & Barrick, 1995). These five traits (commonly labeled *neuroticism* or *emotional stability, extraversion, openness, agreeableness,* and *conscientiousness*) have been found via factor analyses of nearly every major personality inventory (e.g., Costa & McCrae, 1985, 1986) and through study of trait adjectives in a variety of languages (Goldberg, 1990). They also emerge in both self-reports and in observer ratings (e.g., spouses, peers, teachers, and guidance counselors) (e.g., Costa & McCrae, 1985). Finally, large-scale meta-analyses have shown that these five traits may also generalize across cultures (e.g., Salgado, 1997) and predict many important life outcomes, including work choice, performance and satisfaction, and occupational attainment and success. In the remainder of this section, we first define each of the five traits. We then summarize data on the stability of these traits and the implications of stability data for practice.

NEUROTICISM OR EMOTIONAL STABILITY

Neuroticism generally refers to a lack of positive adjustment and emotional stability and is associated with the experience of a wide variety of negative emotions (e.g., sadness, anxiety, guilt). People high in neuroticism (or low on emotional stability) tend also to report themselves to be self-conscious and vulnerable and may respond impulsively in their lives (Costa & McCrae, 1992). Evidence suggests that neurotic individuals are especially attentive to the negative consequences of their (and others') actions and choices, are especially affected by negative events, perceive events as more negative than do people lower on this trait, and often display less satisfaction with their lives and more indecision than those who score lower on this dimension (e.g., Suls & Martin, 2005). By contrast, those who score low on measures of neuroticism tend to be emotionally stable, calm, relaxed, and capable of facing stressful situations without becoming rattled (Costa & McCrae, 1992).

EXTRAVERSION

Extraverts tend to be socially oriented (e.g., warm and gregarious), active (e.g., adventuresome and assertive), and surgent (e.g., dominant and ambitious). Additionally, extraverts tend to report greater levels of positive emotionality (e.g., happiness, joy) and to have larger friendship networks than introverts (e.g., Watson & Clark, 1997). Some investigators (e.g., Roberts et al., 2006) have suggested that extraversion is defined primarily by two lower-order trait complexes having to do with social dominance (e.g., dominance, assertiveness, and self-confidence in social contexts) and social vitality (e.g., sociability, gregariousness, energy level, and positive affect). Regardless of how lower-order traits (i.e., facets) are clustered, most conceptions of extraversion include warmth, gregariousness, assertiveness, activeness, excitement seeking, and positive emotionality as core facets (Costa & McCrae, 1992). Introverts (i.e., those scoring low on a measure of extraversion) tend to be reserved (but not necessarily unfriendly), lack the energy that more extraverted individuals display, and prefer being alone to being with others (Costa & McCrae, 1992).

It is important to note at this juncture that neuroticism and extraversion both contain affective dimensions: For neuroticism, it is a tendency to experience negative emotion across time and situations; for extraversion, it is the tendency to experience positive emotions. Parallel research on the structure of human emotions has suggested that two dimensions (positive affectivity and negative affectivity) provide a comprehensive way to understand human temperament (Watson & Tellegen, 1985). Individuals predisposed to display high levels of positive affectivity (PA) generally report experiencing a variety of positive emotions (e.g., joy, happiness, excitement, enthusiasm), and those predisposed to negative affectivity (NA) report experiencing a variety of negative emotions (e.g., anxiety, guilt, fear, anger). These two dimensions of affective temperament have also been found to be mostly independent (Watson & Tellegen, 1985), with the low end of PA being associated with feelings of boredom, lack of excitement, and dullness (rather than negative emotion). Those low on NA tend to report being calm and relaxed (but not necessarily happy or elated). NA has been found to correlate highly with neuroticism and may represent the affective dimension of this trait, while PA may represent the affective dimension of extraversion.

Openness

Open individuals tend to be imaginative and curious, original and flexible in their thinking, broadminded and liberal, receptive to their feelings and emotions, appreciative of art and beauty, and often see themselves as non-conformists (Costa & McCrae, 1992). They actively seek out new experiences, see such experiences as opportunities for growth (rather than as challenges to their self-esteem), and are comfortable in ambiguous situations. There is also evidence (DeNeve & Cooper, 1998) that those high in openness experience emotions (whether positive or negative) more intensely than those who are less open. Those scoring low on measures of openness tend to be more conventional and conservative, prefer familiar to novel situations, and experience their emotions less intensely than do more open individuals (Costa & McCrae, 1992).

Agreeableness

Agreeable individuals tend to be cooperative versus competitive with others and trusting versus cynical about the motives of others. They tend to be straightforward and deferent in their interactions with others and describe themselves (and are described by others) as caring, empathic, good-natured, forgiving, and tolerant (Costa & McCrae, 1992). Agreeableness also seems to be defined by a high motivation to achieve interpersonal intimacy (McCrae & Costa, 1991) and to get along with others in pleasant and satisfying relationships (Organ & Lingl, 1995). Agreeable individuals are also altruistic and willing to assist others in need of help versus being self-centered and reluctant to get involved in the problems of others (Costa & McCrae, 1992).

Conscientiousness

Conscientiousness seems to be described by three primary facets: achievement orientation (e.g., being goal directed, hardworking, and persistent), dependability (e.g., being responsible and self-disciplined), and orderliness (e.g., being planful and organized). Conscientious persons also think carefully before acting and are often considered cautious and deliberate (Costa & McCrae, 1992). Thus, persons scoring high on conscientiousness tend to display high levels of self-control and a will to achieve, in addition to being dependable, planful, deliberate, and organized in various domains of their lives (e.g., at work and in relationships). Those scoring low tend to be more undependable and less reliable, lack ambition, procrastinate in completing tasks, and are more easily discouraged than those scoring higher on this trait (Costa & McCrae, 1992).

Stability of the Big 5

Does personality change over the life course? The answer, as we implied in an earlier section of this chapter, is no, yes, and it depends. There are three different ways to conceptualize and measure personality change (or its opposite—stability). The first is via correlating scores obtained from a single group of persons assessed at two different times, with the time intervals between the two testing sessions ranging from as short as a few weeks to as long as 30 years. This method yields an index of rank-order stability and addresses the degree to which individuals maintain their rank order with same-age peers across testing intervals. A high correlation suggests that individuals largely maintain their rank orders across testing periods. Thus, a correlation obtained on a measure of extraversion of, say, .70 (a rather high correlation) over a 20-year test-retest period would suggest that persons who were the most extraverted among their peers at 18 are also among the most extraverted at 38.

The second method tracks the mean scores obtained by cohorts of people over time. This method yields an index of mean score stability or change and provides an index of normative change. For example, if the mean scores obtained on a measure of extraversion show longitudinal increases over testing periods, it is assumed that people as a group become more extraverted over time. The third method tracks changes in individuals' scores (or personality profiles) over time and addresses questions of individual change or stability.

The current evidence suggests that the Big 5 traits show very high levels of rank-order stability (correlations in the .70 to .80 range), even over 20- to 30-year testing windows (e.g., McCrae & Costa, 1999). Thus, it appears that personality is quite stable—that highly neurotic, extraverted, open, agreeable, or conscientious people, when compared to their lower-scoring peers, remain among the most neurotic, extraverted, open, agreeable, or conscientious at other periods in their lives. This level of stability is probably due to the combination of heredity and niche-building experiences that we noted earlier.

A different picture, however, emerges when one looks at the data on mean or normative change. These data suggest that personality does change over the life course. For example, Roberts and colleagues (2006) conducted a meta-analysis of normative personality change and found that all five personality traits (especially emotional stability, conscientiousness, and the social dominance aspect of extraversion) showed changes over the life course, with changes being most pronounced in early adulthood between the ages of 22 and 30. In other words, people in general tend to become more emotionally stable, conscientious, assertive, socially dominant, and socially self-confident during their early adult years. Roberts and colleagues (2006) hypothesized that age-graded experiences organized around normative developmental tasks in young adulthood (e.g., finding work, establishing relationships, entering into marriage, raising a family, becoming involved in a community) may propel people to become more emotionally stable, conscientious, and socially dominant and confident during the early adult years. They also suggested that more attention should be given to understanding the early adult years in addition to the adolescent years.

These two sources of stability data are not incompatible. They simply suggest that although people may collectively show age-graded changes in their personalities, individuals themselves seem to maintain their standing within their age cohorts. For example, people may become more emotionally stable during their early adult years, but the most stable at 22 are likely to remain among the most stable at 30.

The third type of research that tracks individual stability and change has shown that some people do make substantial personality changes over their life course. Emerging evidence has also begun to provide some potential explanations for changes in personality, where such changes occur. Roberts, Caspi, and Moffitt (2003) studied an educationally and occupationally diverse sample of young adults at 18 and again at 26. Two important sets of findings emerged from this study. First, traits associated with neuroticism, extraversion (both sociability and dominance), and conscientiousness at 18 years of age predicted a variety of positive work outcomes at the age of 26. For example, adolescents who scored high on negative emotionality (a component of neuroticism) at 18 occupied less prestigious jobs, were less satisfied with their jobs (regardless of where they were working), achieved fewer promotions at work, and had experienced more financial difficulties at age 26 than did those scoring lower on this trait. On the flip side, adolescents who were more emotionally stable, conscientious, sociable, and dominant at 18 were more likely than their lower-scoring counterparts to report higher levels of job satisfaction (again regardless of occupation) and career success at 26 and to report greater financial solvency. These findings provide support for other data we discuss later in the chapter (and have already mentioned) that personality is an important predictor of a variety of different work outcomes.

The second set of findings, however, points to possible mechanisms for personality change, namely, that occupational attainment, job satisfaction, and financial security may be sources of personality change. This study replicated the types of normative changes that we discussed earlier: that traits associated with emotional stability, extraversion, and conscientiousness tended to increase over the course of the study. However, occupational attainment, job satisfaction, and financial security seemed to accelerate these changes. In other words, young adults who had achieved occupational success and satisfaction and financial security showed more pronounced increases in emotional stability, extraversion, and conscientiousness than did those who had not achieved the same types of occupational and financial success at 26.

These findings suggest to us that helping adolescents and young adults achieve occupationally and find satisfying jobs may affect their personality development. It is true that certain personality traits have the potential to set people on a course for a less than satisfying occupational future. However, it might also be true that effective career counseling can, to some degree, help people fit their personalities more seamlessly into their work (i.e., find their niches) and, in the long run, change their life courses and grow their personalities. This is an important topic for further research, and many chapters in this book provide readers with excellent suggestions for improving career intervention effectiveness. We turn next to a discussion of the role of personality in career development across the life span.

THE RELATIONS OF PERSONALITY TO CAREER OUTCOMES ACROSS THE LIFE SPAN

Most theories of career development (see Hartung, Chapter 4; Savickas, Chapter 6, this volume) suggest that the ability to implement a sound vocational choice (find one's niche, as it were) and subsequently adjust to one's work is a developmental process that begins in childhood and accelerates during the adolescent and young adult years. Major developmental tasks of adolescence and young adulthood involve (a) exploring one's self and the occupational world, (b) crystallizing interests and forming a vocational identity, (c) developing educational and occupational aspirations, (d) engaging in career planning, and (e) specifying an initial occupational choice. In addition, engagement in these developmental tasks seems to require that people possess the confidence as well as the skills to accomplish them successfully. Tasks of subsequent developmental periods involve implementing a choice (i.e., finding a job or completing necessary education) and achieving satisfaction and success at work. In this section, we review research relevant to each of these major developmental tasks, starting with tasks involved in the exploration stage of career development. We also review research on the relationship between personality and career confidence (i.e., self-efficacy beliefs in being able to accomplish these developmental tasks). We then review research on the role of personality in later development periods, including job finding, work satisfaction and performance, and occupational attainment.

PERSONALITY AND CAREER EXPLORATION

Personality traits are related to the degree to which adolescents engage in career exploration activities. The most consistent findings reveal that conscientiousness, extraversion, and emotional stability are implicated in the career exploration process among high school and college students, with the strongest effects attributed to conscientiousness (Reed, Bruch, & Haase, 2004; Rogers & Creed, 2011; Rogers, Creed, & Ian Glendon, 2008). In particular, it appears that students who are more goal directed, achievement oriented, organized, and planful tend to engage more actively in career exploration activities than do those who are less conscientious. In addition, the relation of extraversion to exploration may be due to the fact that extraverts tend to have more energy and tend to be more proactive in their lives than those who are less extraverted (McCrae & Costa, 1999). Extraverted students may also feel more comfortable seeking information from others as part of career exploration than do less extraverted students. Finally, career exploration entails self-reflection and environmental exploration (Zikic & Hall, 2009) that might be anxiety provoking to less emotionally stable youngsters. Research also suggests that more versus less neurotic individuals tend to use a variety of avoidance strategies to cope with anxiety (e.g., Brown et al., 2012). Thus, avoiding exploration activities, although less adaptive in the long run, might in the short run allow less emotionally stable students to cope with the anxiety elicited by the exploration process.

PERSONALITY AND VOCATIONAL INTERESTS

Personality seems to be related to the types of interests that people develop, as well as to their overall levels of vocational interests. Many empirical studies have established that vocational interest types, as represented by Holland's RIASEC model (Nauta, Chapter 3, this volume), are distinct from, but meaningfully related to, basic personality traits (Mount, Barrick, Scullen, & Rounds, 2005). For example, two meta-analyses have found consistent relationships among several Big 5 personality traits and RIASEC interest types (Barrick, Mount, & Gupta, 2003; Larson, Rottinghaus, & Borgen, 2002). Both studies found that extraversion was related to Social and Enterprising interests and that openness was related to Artistic and Investigative interests. Somewhat less consistent were findings linking agreeableness with Social interests and conscientious with Conventional interests. There is some evidence, however, that agreeableness might serve to differentiate between those with Social versus Enterprising interests (Costa, McCrae, & Holland, 1984). That is, although both Enterprising and Social types (in Holland's schema) tend to score above average on various measures of extraversion, Social individuals (e.g., counselors, teachers) tend to score higher on measures of agreeableness than do more Enterprising types (e.g., salespeople and politicians). Meanwhile, Sullivan and Hansen (2004) found that different facets of openness may distinguish between those having Artistic and Investigative interests. Investigative interests were related positively to openness to ideas (and negatively to openness to feelings), and Artistic interests showed the strongest associations with an openness facet reflecting a deep appreciation for art and beauty (aesthetics).

In addition to the content of individuals' interests (i.e., the fields in which people express their interests), personality also tends to be related to the absolute levels of interests that people display (i.e., their interest profile elevation; Bullock & Reardon, 2005; Darcy & Tracey, 2003). The most consistent finding is that openness is positively related to profile elevation (Ackerman & Heggestad, 1997; Costa et al., 1984; De Fruyt & Mervielde, 1997; Fuller, Holland, & Johnston, 1999; Gottfredson & Jones, 1993; Hirschi, 2009; Holland, Johnston, & Asama, 1994). Other studies have found that neuroticism relates negatively to interest profile elevation (Ackerman & Heggestad, 1997; De Fruyt & Mervielde, 1997; Fuller et al., 1999; Holland et al., 1994).

In other words, adolescents' level of openness to new experiences and ideas may be reflected in their vocational interests—more open individuals report higher levels of interest in all RIASEC areas than do persons who are less open. There are also data to suggest that such profile elevation provides people with greater flexibility in their choices because of their interest and comfort in a variety of different types of occupational settings (Darcy & Tracey, 2003). A high level of neuroticism may have the opposite effect; it may result in lower levels of interest across interest areas and less flexibility in arriving at a satisfying career choice.

Personality and Vocational Identity Development

Vocational identity is a central construct of several extant theories (see Nauta, Chapter 3; Hartung, Chapter 4; and Savickas, Chapter 6, this volume) and can be defined as the development of a coherent view of oneself as a worker. Achieving a clearly defined vocational identity involves understanding how important work is vis-à-vis other roles; developing a clear perception of one's vocational interests, abilities, goals, and values; and linking this self-knowledge with career roles. A well-developed vocational identity is commonly assumed to be a cornerstone of successful career development and to be essential to mastering other career development tasks (see Skorikov & Vondracek, 2007, for a review).

A number of studies have revealed that vocational identity achievement is related to personality traits. For example, high school and college students who have achieved a clear and coherent vocational identity report lower levels of neuroticism and higher levels in conscientiousness, extraversion, openness, and agreeableness (e.g., Clancy & Dollinger, 1993; Luyckx, Soenens, & Goossens, 2006). In an exemplary longitudinal study of female Belgian undergraduates, Luyckx and colleagues (2006) showed that personality traits and identity development were reciprocally related with traits having an effect on identity development and also that success in identity development affected subsequent personality traits. Consistent with other research that we have already reviewed, conscientiousness predicted an increase in identity achievement, and identity achievement, in turn, predicted increases in conscientiousness. This study, like those discussed earlier in the chapter, suggests another avenue for personality change—by helping students and young adults in the identity development process.

Personality and Educational and Career Aspirations

Educational and career aspirations are important components of career development and are stressed in Super's theory of career development (Hartung, Chapter 4, this volume) and social cognitive career theory (Lent, Chapter 5, this volume). Longitudinal studies have also shown that educational and career aspirations relate to later educational and career attainment (Schoon & Parsons, 2002). Moreover, research indicates that the educational and career aspirations of high school and college students may be meaningfully related to certain personality traits.

One trait that has been repeatedly shown to relate to higher educational aspirations is openness. Several studies with college students (Gasser, Larson, & Borgen, 2004; Rottinghaus, Lindley, Green, & Borgen, 2002) and secondary students (Salami, 2008) have reported that students with higher levels of openness (i.e., those who tend to be insightful, intellectual, and open-minded) have higher educational goals than their classmates who are lower on this trait. Hirschi (2010) investigated career aspirations in relation to traits from a different perspective by coding aspirations of Swiss adolescents according to the content dimensions of things versus people and data versus ideas (Prediger, 1982). The results of this 1-year longitudinal study showed that extraversion related negatively to the development of career goals involving dealing with things (e.g., mechanic) and positively to the development of goals involving dealing with people (e.g., retail sales). Openness related negatively to the development of goals dealing with data (e.g., office clerk) and positively to goals involving working with ideas (e.g., graphic designer). In sum, although more research is needed to establish how traits are related to career aspirations, students' personalities seem to be related to both the level and content of their aspirations. Openness seems to relate to the levels of aspirations reported by both high school and college students, and other personality traits relate more to the content of students' aspirations.

PERSONALITY AND CAREER PLANNING

Only a few studies have investigated the relation of personality traits to the degree to which students engage in career planning (e.g., set short- and long-term goals for themselves and develop coherent plans for acquiring necessary education and training and entering occupations of choice). Rogers and Creed (2011) and Hirschi, Niles, and Akos (2011) showed that neuroticism was negatively related to career planning among groups of Australian high school and Swiss secondary students, respectively. It has also been found that high school and college students higher in extraversion, conscientiousness, and openness (e.g., Rogers & Creed, 2011) report engaging in more career planning, with conscientiousness once again emerging as the strongest predictor. These findings seem to suggest that less emotionally stable students may avoid career planning activities like they avoid earlier career exploration activities. These findings also suggest, similar to the findings for career exploration, that more organized, achievement-oriented, goal-directed (conscientious), open, and extraverted students are more likely to engage actively in the developmental task of planning for their future careers than students who are less conscientious, open, and extraverted.

PERSONALITY AND CAREER DECIDEDNESS

The relation of personality to career decidedness has been frequently studied in the vocational psychology and career development literatures. One of the most consistent findings is that neuroticism and its related traits (i.e., trait negative affectivity, trait anxiety, depression, dysfunctional thinking) are negatively related to levels of career decidedness (Feldman, 2003; Hirschi et al., 2011; Lounsbury, Hutchens, & Loveland, 2005; Lucas & Wanberg, 1995; Saunders, Peterson, Sampson, & Reardon, 2000). In a meta-analysis, Brown and Rector (2008) also showed that these traits correlated highly with indices of chronic indecision (i.e., the degree to which persons report long-term difficulties with making decisions). It therefore appears that people who report low emotional stability and related traits have more difficulties in reaching a career decision and may also have difficulties making a variety of other types of decisions as well (e.g., which school to attend, whether to make a romantic commitment).

Other personality traits, although less frequently investigated, have also been found to relate to career decidedness. Several studies have reported that conscientiousness, agreeableness, and extraversion all relate positively to career decidedness among high school and college students (Jin, Watkins, & Yuen, 2009; Lounsbury et al., 2005; Wang, Jome, Hasse, & Bruch, 2006), with the effect sizes obtained for conscientiousness rivaling those obtained for neuroticism. Hence, it appears that adolescents and young adults who are generally more reliable, careful, organized, self-disciplined, open, and extraverted are not only likely to explore and plan more than their less conscientious, extraverted, and open peers but are also more likely to arrive at a career decision more efficiently.

Although more research is needed before we can make strong inferences about the relation of Big 5 traits to career development tasks, evidence seems to be emerging that a core set of traits seems to facilitate adolescents' and young adults' career development. Specifically, emotional stability, extraversion, and conscientiousness seem to be associated with more active career exploration and planning, more coherent vocational identities, higher levels of educational and vocational aspirations, and greater levels of career decidedness. In addition, openness seems to relate to career choice flexibility (i.e., breadth of interests), career exploration, and career planning. These traits, it will be recalled, were also identified as core traits related to occupational attainment and financial success by Roberts and colleagues (2003) and therefore have important implications for promoting career success across the life course.

PERSONALITY AND CAREER CONFIDENCE

Research has also shown that successful completion of career development tasks requires that people not only have the skills to complete them but also the confidence (or self-efficacy beliefs) that they are personally capable of doing what is required to be successful (see Lent, Chapter 5, this volume).

One of the most frequently studied types of self-efficacy beliefs that have been associated with personality are career decision-making self-efficacy beliefs (i.e., the confidence that one can do what is necessary to make successful vocational decisions). Neuroticism has been found to be negatively related to career decision-making self-efficacy among high school (Rogers et al., 2008) and college students (Hartman & Betz, 2007; Wang et al., 2006). Cross-sectional (Schyns & von Collani, 2002), longitudinal (Spurk & Abele, 2011), and meta-analytic (Judge & Ilies, 2002) studies have also found that neuroticism is related negatively to work self-efficacy, that is, the confidence in successfully mastering a variety of work-related tasks and challenges. Neuroticism seems also to be negatively related to confidence in successful performance across different occupational areas (Hartman & Betz, 2007; Nauta, 2004; Schaub & Tokar, 2005). Collectively, these findings suggest that less emotionally stable individuals not only may question their abilities to make career decisions but also may display less confidence than more emotionally stable individuals in their abilities to be successful in a variety of different occupations.

Besides neuroticism, conscientiousness has also been found to predict career confidence. Meta-analyses (e.g., Judge & Ilies, 2002) have found significant positive relations between conscientiousness and both work and academic self-efficacy beliefs, even after controlling for the positive effects of general cognitive ability on self-efficacy beliefs. Other studies have reported positive relations between conscientiousness and career decision-making self-efficacy among undergraduate (Hartman & Betz, 2007), graduate (Jin et al., 2009), and high school students (Rogers et al., 2008). Finally, several studies have found that extraversion also is a positive predictor of career and academic self-efficacy. More extraverted students and working adults have shown more work and academic self-efficacy in a meta-analysis (Judge & Ilies, 2002), more vocational self-efficacy in a 2-year longitudinal study among German university graduates (Spurk & Abele, 2011), and more career decision-making self-efficacy among U.S. college students (Hartman & Betz, 2007; Wang et al., 2006). Once again, we find that the core constellation of emotional stability, extraversion, and conscientiousness relates not only to career development task success but also to the confidence that students and young adults have in their abilities to complete these tasks.

PERSONALITY, JOB FINDING, WORK ADJUSTMENT, AND OCCUPATIONAL ATTAINMENT

The relationships of the Big 5 personality traits to job-finding success, work satisfaction, and job satisfactoriness (performance) are reviewed in other chapters (see Jome & Phillips, Chapter 21; Lent & Brown, Chapter 22, this volume) and therefore are only summarized briefly in this section. We also discuss some of the research cited earlier on the role of personality in occupational attainment.

Personality and job-finding success. In general, research reveals that two of the Big 5 personality traits—extraversion and conscientiousness—seem to be related to job-finding success (see Jome & Phillips, Chapter 21). In addition, meta-analyses (e.g., Kanfer, Wanberg, & Kantrowitz, 2001) have suggested that these two personality traits may affect job search success via two avenues. First, both extraversion and conscientiousness seem to have direct effects on success at finding a job, perhaps because conscientious and extraverted people tend to perform better in employment interviews than their less conscientious and more introverted peers (more conscientious job seekers also probably submit more well-developed resumes and other materials). Second, these traits also seem to affect job-finding success via their influences on the intensity and effort that job seekers put into the job search process. Conscientious job seekers are organized and planful, tend to set goals for their job search efforts, and persevere in the face of setbacks, and more extraverted persons tend to be more comfortable (and self-efficacious) in using their social networks as sources of job leads. Thus, conscientiousness and extraversion may give persons a competitive advantage when they are seeking jobs. People displaying higher levels of these two traits tend to work harder in the job search process, organize their efforts better, develop goals to direct their job search efforts, and make use of more resources in the job search process (especially interpersonal resources in the case of extraverts). They may also feel more comfortable and efficacious in job interviews and may display in the interview characteristics that employers seek from potential employees.

Personality and job satisfaction and satisfactoriness. Lent and Brown (Chapter 22, this volume) reviewed findings on the relationships between personality traits and job satisfaction and satisfactoriness. The former (job satisfaction) represents employees' satisfaction with (liking of) their jobs. The latter (job satisfactoriness) reflects employers' satisfaction with their employees. Job satisfaction is typically assessed via employee self-reports, and job satisfactoriness is typically measured by supervisor performance appraisals. Meta-analyses (e.g., Heller, Watson, & Illies, 2004; Judge, Heller, & Mount, 2002) have suggested that emotional stability, extraversion, and conscientiousness yield small (conscientiousness) to moderate (emotional stability and extraversion) correlations with job satisfaction.

In terms of job satisfactoriness, supervisor performance appraisals seem to be influenced by at least three different types of employee behaviors: task performance, organizational citizenship behaviors, and counterproductive work behaviors (see Lent & Brown, Chapter 22, this volume). Task performance represents how well employees perform the job duties prescribed by their job descriptions; organizational citizenship behaviors refer to extra-role behaviors that contribute to organizational goals (e.g., helping and cooperating with others, showing commitment to the organization; see Borman, 2004). Organizational citizenship behavior also includes behaviors that challenge the status quo and offer innovative suggestions for organizational improvement (see Van Dyne & LePine, 1998). Counterproductive work behaviors (as the name implies) detract from the organization's goals and mission and can include gossiping and spreading rumors about coworkers, engaging in actions that harass or harm others, taking extra-long breaks, and violating security procedures (see Rotundo & Sackett, 2002).

Meta-analytic investigations have shown that conscientiousness is related to various indices of task performance (e.g., Barrick & Mount, 1991) as well as to organizational citizenship and counterproductive work behaviors (e.g., Chiaburu, Oh, Berry, Li, & Gardner, 2011). Others of the Big 5 personality traits have also been implicated in organizational citizenship and counterproductive work behaviors. For example, Chiaburu and colleagues (2011) found that openness and agreeableness (and conscientiousness) were related to cooperative types of organizational citizenship behavior, and extraversion and openness (and conscientiousness) related to status quo–challenging types of organizational citizenship behaviors. Thus, as Lent and Brown (Chapter 22, this volume) summarized, it appears that employees who are dispositionally cooperative (agreeable) and open to new experiences and ideas (open) may be more likely to engage in the cooperative types of citizenship behaviors that are valued during performance appraisals. Persons who are outgoing and assertive (extraversion) and open to change (openness) may be more likely than less extraverted and open employees to effectively challenge the status quo when such behavior is called for. Conscientious employees (those who are goal directed, organized, planful, and achievement oriented) seem to have an advantage over less conscientious employees in all major performance domains that are considered by supervisors in employee appraisals.

Personality and occupational attainment. Large-scale prospective studies suggest that personality traits are not only related to employees' satisfaction and performance but also to their long-range occupational attainments (e.g., Roberts et al., 2003, 2007). The results of Roberts and colleagues' (2003) study, presented earlier in the section on the stability of the Big 5, suggested that levels of emotional stability, extraversion, and conscientiousness displayed at age 18 predicted participants' subsequent (at age 26) levels of job satisfaction, employment success, and financial stability.

Roberts and colleagues (2007) meta-analytically combined the results of large-scale longitudinal studies on the relationships between the Big 5 personality traits and success in three important domains of human functioning: work, relationships, and health. Their analyses suggested that childhood levels of emotional stability, extraversion, agreeableness, and conscientiousness predicted attained occupational status 46 years later, even after controlling for childhood intelligence (Judge, Higgins, Thoresen, & Barrick, 1999). Further, Roberts and colleagues (2007) found that these Big 5 traits collectively accounted for as much variance in occupational attainment as intelligence and socioeconomic status.

Roberts and colleagues (2007) cited several processes that might explain how personality relates to occupational attainment. These processes include (a) niche finding (i.e., successful people find jobs that fit with their dispositions and personalities), (b) recruitment effects (e.g., people are selected into jobs and given preferential treatment on the basis of their personality characteristics), (c) environmental shaping (e.g., successful people change their work environments to better fit their personalities), (d) attrition effects (i.e., less well-fitting employees leave, or are asked to leave, the work setting), and (e) direct effects of personality on performance (e.g., certain personality characteristics like conscientiousness naturally give rise to higher levels of achievement via goal setting, self-efficacy, and perseverance, and people who possess these characteristics will achieve more at school and at work). The reader is referred to Roberts and colleagues (2007) for a more complete discussion of these processes. However, these findings clearly suggest that the Big 5 traits (especially emotional stability, extraversion, and conscientiousness and in certain conditions openness and agreeableness) relate in important ways to career development, choice, adjustment, and attainment across the life span. We next turn to the counseling, developmental, and preventive implications of these findings.

COUNSELING, DEVELOPMENTAL, AND PREVENTIVE IMPLICATIONS

It should be clear from our review that personality traits can influence, to some degree, persons' success at negotiating major tasks of career development and in finding satisfaction and success in their work environments. These data indicate that people's levels of emotional stability, extraversion, and conscientiousness are related positively to nearly every career-related outcome, including (a) engagement in career exploration and planning activities; (b) development of a vocational identity; (c) facility at, and perceived efficacy in, making career decisions; and (d) subsequent levels of job satisfaction and occupational attainment. Neuroticism is also related negatively to the breadth of interests that adolescents and young adults display, and openness seems to have the opposite effect, that is, to broaden interests. Conscientiousness (along with extraversion) is also implicated in individuals' job-finding success, as well as in their work performance (i.e., task performance, organizational citizenship behaviors, and counterproductive work behaviors). Finally, several personality traits are also related to the content of persons' interests. Extraverted versus less extraverted people tend to display social and enterprising interests, and openness is associated with interests in artistic and investigative occupations. Agreeableness may serve to differentiate between interests in social versus enterprising occupations, and certain facets of openness may differentiate interests in artistic versus investigative occupations.

Although research (e.g., Roberts et al., 2007) also shows that personality traits account for only small amounts of variance in career outcomes (other aspects of the person and his or her context are also important), we find the data sufficiently compelling that we typically ask clients early in counseling (before or after the first session) to complete a measure of the Big 5 personality traits like the NEO-Five Factor Inventory (NEO-FFI; Costa & McCrae, 1992; see Rottinghaus & Hauser, Chapter 17, this volume). We then use the information provided by this assessment in two ways. First, we use personality information as another source of data to understand clients' presenting problems and help them, if necessary, find good-fitting occupations (i.e., help them find their niches). Second, we use the data to help us structure counseling to be most useful for clients.

ENHANCING UNDERSTANDING OF CLIENTS' PRESENTING CONCERNS AND NICHE FINDING

Research on career counseling applications of personality data is amazingly sparse and often not entirely helpful. We cite available research whenever possible in this section but mainly rely on our clinical experiences when drawing counseling implications. We have found that personality data can be useful by enabling career counselors to gain a fuller understanding of clients' presenting concerns (e.g., needing to make or remake a choice, find a job, achieve greater satisfaction or satisfactoriness at work). Information on clients' personalities, we think, may also provide a vehicle for incorporating preventive goals into career counseling.

In relation to establishing preventive goals, we have found it helpful to provide clients with opportunities to learn strategies to manage the effects of their personalities on their lives. To accomplish such preventive tasks, we prefer, despite the data on trait stability, to view traits as a set of specific behaviors that, like most other behaviors, can be broken down into smaller segments and altered through observation and practice (see also Lent & Brown, Chapter 22, this volume). In other words, our experiences suggest that persons can learn to behave in trait-inconsistent ways when called for by the demands of their environments if counseling (a) helps them gain insights into how their personalities can affect the types of decisions they make and the experiences they have and (b) provides a safe environment in which to learn and practice trait-inconsistent behaviors. Although we have no empirical data to support this position, we illustrate in the remainder of this section strategies that we have used to promote the acquisition and use of trait-inconsistent behaviors. The reader is referred to Brown, Ryan, and McPartland (1996) and Lent and Brown (Chapter 22, this volume) for additional strategies.

Using personality data to gain a fuller understanding of clients' presenting concerns. Neuroticism, conscientiousness, and openness represent traits that can affect clients' abilities to make decisions and achieve satisfaction and success at work. They thus represent three good examples of how an understanding of clients' personalities can inform career counseling practice. They also provide examples of our prevention focus, that is, how we work to help clients learn to manage their personalities in their everyday interactions with their work and nonwork environments.

Although the exact mechanisms by which neuroticism influences decision-making abilities and job satisfaction are not fully understood, two central paths of influence that we have already discussed may be via the tendencies of more versus less neurotic individuals to (a) focus on the negative aspects of themselves, their choices, and environments and (b) use various avoidance strategies to cope with the anxiety and other negative feelings occasioned by such a style (see Brown et al., 2012). Thus, clients who score high (e.g., one standard deviation or more above the mean) on a measure of neuroticism may have trouble deciding on an educational or career option and see more negative than positive consequences associated with most options they have considered. As a result, such clients may have considered only a small number of occupational options and may even have settled on a less than optimal option as an avoidance strategy. Similarly, clients who are seeking help for problems of job satisfaction may, if they also score high on a neuroticism scale, view the conditions of their work environments (e.g., the amount of work required of them, the support they receive from supervisors and fellow workers, the clarity of their work roles) to be more troublesome than do less neurotic clients (see Lent & Brown, Chapter 22, this volume).

If assessment and interview results converge to confirm that neuroticism contributes to clients' choice-making problems, we typically discuss this with them and help them consider and weigh more carefully the positive consequences of various choice options. We also have them consider options they might have eliminated from consideration earlier in their lives and discuss with them their reasons for eliminating these options. We employ similar strategies with job-dissatisfied clients—help them consider the degree to which their negative cognitive style may color perceptions at work, evaluate the validity of these perceptions, and consider the validity of alternative ways of viewing their work environments (see Lent & Brown, Chapter 22, this volume).

For both types of clients (those seeking to make a choice and those experiencing work dissatisfaction), we also try to help them understand how their natural tendencies to focus on and magnify the negative aspects of their choices, jobs, and other aspects of life might have caused them difficulties in the past. We then suggest that this cognitive style can be managed by learning how to use these tendencies as cues to refocus their attention on more positive possibilities. We also assign homework between sessions to practice this set of skills to resolve the problem that brought clients to counseling (choice or dissatisfaction problems) and in other situations (e.g., relationships) they encounter. Although these strategies are unlikely to change clients' personalities substantially, they can provide clients with a set of skills they can use to manage the negative consequences of their personality traits (e.g., neuroticism) in the future (see Brown et al., 1996).

Conscientiousness is another personality trait that can influence the decision-making process. It can also influence clients' success in finding jobs and their performance appraisals at work. Clients who enter with decision-making problems and concomitant low levels of conscientiousness often need more help from counselors than others in gathering and processing information that will inform their decisions. They will also probably need more help and support in carrying out these tasks than more conscientious clients. Counselors working with clients experiencing performance problems at work and low levels of conscientiousness may need first to explore with clients the degree to which specific aspects of conscientiousness (e.g., lack of goal directedness or organization, poor time management or follow-through) may be contributing to unsatisfactory performance appraisals. We then help clients consider how they might alter these behaviors at work and whether their level of conscientiousness has contributed to other difficulties they have experienced in their lives. One focus of counseling becomes helping clients set goals to behave in more conscientious ways at work and in other areas of their lives. Although motivation to engage in such counter-trait behavior may be low for less conscientious clients, reframing such behavior as alterable with practice may increase clients' motivation to enact such behaviors in work settings and elsewhere.

Clients with problems in the job search process may also need special assistance from counselors if they also display low levels of conscientiousness or extraversion. Specifically, they may need help (a) setting job search goals and actively pursuing these goals (conscientiousness) and (b) acquiring the self-efficacy beliefs, skills, and comfort required to access and make effective use of their social networks (extraversion). Such clients may also need more help in preparing for employment interviews than will more conscientious and extraverted clients. In these cases, too, we try to help clients consider how their levels of conscientiousness and introversion might have affected other areas of their lives and to develop strategies to manage trait-driven tendencies in the future.

Finally, clients scoring high on measures of openness may also seek help from career counselors, especially for issues involved in making or remaking career decisions. Although openness can provide people with greater decision-making flexibility because of their rather wide-ranging interests, it can also lead to decision-making confusion precisely for the same reason (i.e., wide-ranging interests). Thus, we have occasionally seen clients exhibiting high levels of openness who were seeking help to choose from a large number of occupational possibilities. We typically take a two-pronged approach in working with these clients. We first try to normalize their decision-making confusion by discussing with them how their levels of openness probably contribute to their current predicament, but that being highly open also has a number of more positive consequences (e.g., excitement about exploring new ideas, enthusiasm for trying on new roles and experiences, and heightened flexibility). We then provide assistance in decision making by supplementing vocational interest data with other sources of information (e.g., needs and values, abilities, role salience, lifestyle considerations, avocational interests). The outcome is often the identification of a best-fitting set of occupations for further exploration and a discussion about how clients can implement their wide-ranging interests in leisure and volunteer pursuits.

Using personality data to enrich niche-finding efforts. Clients' levels of extraversion and conscientiousness, as well as their openness and agreeableness, may also provide diagnostic information for helping clients identify good-fitting occupational possibilities. Extraversion, as we have previously discussed, is related to interest in social and enterprising activities and occupations. Thus, clients who display above-average levels of extraversion may be directed to consider these more people-oriented occupations. Their level of agreeableness may then allow them to distinguish among people-oriented occupations. Persons displaying above-average levels of agreeableness may prefer social occupations (i.e., occupations involving helping and teaching that typically attract cooperative, sympathetic, and empathic individuals), while those scoring lower on a measure of agreeableness may find enterprising occupations more satisfying (i.e., occupations involving selling and persuading that attract more competitive individuals).

Openness, as we previously discussed, seems also to be related to client interests. Open individuals seem to be attracted to investigative and artistic occupations that allow for creativity, intellectual stimulation, and autonomy; those who are less open may prefer more conventional occupations that involve concrete work tasks. There is also evidence that different facets of openness differentiate investigative and artistic occupations: People with investigative interests (e.g., scientists) may be more open to new ideas than to feelings, and those with artistic interests seem especially to have high levels of aesthetic appreciation. Thus, personality information can complement interest, value, and ability data and enable clients to more readily identify their niches in the world of work.

Personality data can also be used in niche-finding efforts with persons who are experiencing adjustment problems due to incongruence between their personality traits and the requirements of their work environments. For example, agreeable persons working in competitive, enterprising work environments may find more satisfaction in a social environment that encourages cooperation and is more congruent with their personalities. Similarly, more introverted clients may find occupations that require substantial levels of social interactions or assertiveness less than satisfying places to work. A less than open person may find that working in occupations that require creativity, intellectual stimulation, and autonomy (investigative and artistic) to be a poor fit and a source of dissatisfaction. Finally, investigative occupations may be more appealing to people whose openness is primarily defined by openness to ideas rather than feelings, whereas artistic occupations may be better niches for those scoring highest on an aesthetics facet of openness.

For those who find themselves in environments that are not congruent with their personality traits, counseling can be directed at exploring ways to (a) modify the current work environment (e.g., find ways to be of service to others instead of competing with them) or (b) change to jobs or occupations that may offer a better fit with their personalities. Where neither of these options is viable, counseling may entail exploring nonwork outlets that better allow one to express one's personality than does the current work setting (see Lent & Brown, Chapter 22, this volume).

USING PERSONALITY DATA TO STRUCTURE SESSIONS AND IMPROVE EFFECTIVENESS

Personality data may also allow counselors to plan their sessions and work with clients more effectively. For example, counselors might anticipate that clients scoring high versus low on measures of neuroticism may have chronic problems in making important life decisions (Brown & Rector, 2008) and may bring with them a constellation of other characteristics (e.g., tendency to experience negative emotions and focus on negative outcome expectations) that require individual (rather than group) counseling of a longer than typical duration (see Brown & Ryan Krane, 2000). Some research has also suggested that high levels of neuroticism might cause people to settle prematurely (as an avoidance strategy) on a less than satisfying career choice (see Brown et al., 2012).

There are meta-analytic data suggesting that many clients respond well to four or five sessions of career counseling and that individual and group forms of counseling may be equally effective for many clients (e.g., Brown & Ryan Krane, 2000; Whiston, Brecheisen, & Stephens, 2003). However, our clinical experiences suggest that these data might not hold well for clients entering counseling with high levels of neuroticism and chronic indecisiveness (Brown & Ryan Krane, 2000). The first author, for example, once saw a client who displayed rather high levels of neuroticism (scored two standard deviations above the mean on the NEO-FFI Neuroticism scale) for 35 sessions of individual counseling that lasted approximately a year and a half. She also scored rather high on the NEO-FFI Conscientiousness scale and in the average ranges on the other three NEO-FFI scales. This client indicated early in counseling that she frequently felt a good deal of anxiety in making important decisions in her life and usually opted for the least threatening option in these situations. She had chosen her current career field because she had little doubt that she had the skills to perform adequately in it but was now seeking counseling because she was bored with her work and found it to be exceptionally unchallenging.

Interest, value, and ability data had converged by the fifth counseling session to suggest several more challenging occupational options; the client specifically noted that one of the options generated from these assessment data was one that she had fantasized about for a number of years. She chose as one goal in counseling to see if she could pursue this option. The next 30 sessions focused, in part, on (a) helping her develop goals for entry into this occupational field (e.g., acquiring the necessary education and persevering in these educational pursuits, generating support from her family and social networks), (b) supporting her as she implemented her goals, and (c) challenging her when she downplayed her accomplishments and successes. Counseling also involved helping her learn to challenge her negative cognitive style. By the end of counseling, she had successfully completed her first semester of full-time graduate study, acquired a mentor in her field, and seemed to be making progress in managing her personality tendencies in school and other areas of her life.

Clients' levels of conscientiousness may also have implications for how counselors work with them. For example, clients displaying low levels of conscientiousness may not follow through on between-session activities as consistently as more conscientious clients. They might also fail to keep counseling appointments as frequently as their more conscientious peers (Costa & McCrae, 1992). The client discussed in the previous paragraphs who had also scored high on the NEO-FFI Conscientiousness scale attended every scheduled session over the 18 months of counseling and worked very diligently to establish and accomplish between-session (and long-term) goals. Thus, despite her high level of neuroticism, her conscientiousness seemed to facilitate substantially the successes she achieved in counseling. Others of the authors' clients who seemed to be less conscientious, however, have not fared as well and have required more strenuous efforts to keep them on track (even for those with other personality traits that would have suggested an easier course of counseling).

IMPLICATIONS FOR PREVENTIVE AND DEVELOPMENTAL INTERVENTIONS

As we have previously suggested, there appears to be a core set of personality traits (e.g., emotional stability, extraversion, and conscientiousness) that can have long-range effects on career development and occupational attainment. These core traits seem to be related to the amount of career exploration and planning undertaken by adolescents and young adults, as well as to their confidence in their abilities to make career decisions and to arrive at a satisfying career choice. These traits have also been shown to relate to different indices of career success in adulthood (e.g., work performance and satisfaction, occupational attainment, and financial stability). Openness has also been implicated in career exploration and planning success.

These data suggest to us that the behaviors and attitudes associated with these core traits may be important targets for early intervention efforts. It is not clear whether early intervention efforts will result in substantial personality changes (although they might, because traits seem to be more malleable in youth than in adults). However, the personality data do suggest that if we can help children and adolescents acquire more conscientious and extraverted ways of behaving, as well as more positive ways of viewing themselves and their futures, such efforts, if successful, might have long-term benefits for their work and personal lives and help them find their niches and grow their personalities.

CONCLUSIONS AND PRACTICE IMPLICATIONS

In summary, we have attempted to show how an understanding of clients' personalities (especially their levels of emotional stability, extraversion, openness, agreeableness, and conscientiousness) has implications for career counseling practice. The most important points that we tried to make in this chapter include the following:

- There appears to be a core set of traits (i.e., emotional stability, extraversion, and conscientiousness) that seem to be related to all major career development tasks and later occupational attainment. Openness also seems to be related to several outcomes, including vocational identity development, level of educational and career aspirations, involvement in career planning, decision-making flexibility, and willingness and ability to engage in organizational citizenship behavior at work.
- Although personality traits (including all of the Big 5 traits) show high levels of individual stability in adulthood, change is possible, especially if persons engage in, or are helped to engage in, trait-congruent experiences. Helping adolescents and young adults find their occupational niches may not only improve their lives but also help them develop their personalities in adaptive ways.
- Personality data might be collected routinely in counseling (at least as routinely as information on interests, values, and abilities are collected).
- Personality data, if routinely collected, can enrich the counseling process by providing important diagnostic information, facilitating clients' niche finding, and enabling counselors to better tailor counseling to the uniqueness of each client.
- Personality, though related to a variety of important career outcomes, accounts for only a small proportion of the variance in these outcomes. There are, therefore, a variety of other personal and contextual variables that influence career development and adjustment. However, helping clients find (at whatever age) their occupational niches (those places where their personalities, interests, values, and abilities can find a good-fitting home) may start them on the road to a more satisfying life, regardless of where they started out.

REFERENCES

Ackerman, P. L., & Heggestad, E. D. (1997). Intelligence, personality, and interests: Evidence for overlapping traits. *Psychological Bulletin, 121,* 219–245.

Barrick, M. R., & Mount, M. K. (1991). The big five personality dimensions and job performance: A meta-analysis. *Personnel Psychology, 44,* 1–26.

Barrick, M. R., Mount, M. K., & Gupta, R. (2003). Meta-analysis of the relationship between the Five-Factor model of personality and Holland's occupational types. *Personnel Psychology, 56,* 45–74.

Borman, W. C. (2004). The concept of organizational citizenship behavior. *Current Directions in Psychological Science, 13*, 238–241.

Brown, S. D., Hacker, J., Abrams, M., Carr, A., Rector, C., Lamp, K., Telander, K., & Siena, A. (2012). Validation of a four factor model of career indecision. *Journal of Career Assessment, 20*, 3–21.

Brown, S. D., & Rector, C. C. (2008). Conceptualizing and diagnosing problems in vocational decision-making. In S. D. Brown & R. W. Lent (Eds.), *Handbook of counseling psychology* (vol. 4, pp. 392–407). Hoboken, NJ: Wiley.

Brown, S. D., Ryan, N. E., & McPartland, E. B. (1996). Why are so many people happy and what do we do with those who aren't? *Counseling Psychologist, 24*, 751–757.

Brown, S. D., & Ryan Krane, N. E. (2000). Four (or five) sessions and a cloud of dust: Old assumptions and new observations about career counseling. In S. D. Brown & R. W. Lent (Eds.), *Handbook of counseling psychology* (3rd ed., pp. 740–766). New York, NY: Wiley.

Bullock, E. E., & Reardon, R. C. (2005). Using profile elevation to increase the usefulness of the Self-Directed Search and other inventories. *Career Development Quarterly, 54*(2), 175–183.

Caspi, A., Roberts, B. W., & Shiner, R. L. (2005). Personality development: Stability and change. *Annual Review of Psychology, 56*, 453–484.

Chiaburu, D. S., Oh, I. S., Berry, C. M., Li, N., & Gardner, R. G. (2011). The five-factor model personality traits and organizational citizenship behavior. *Journal of Applied Psychology, 96*, 1140–1166.

Clancy, S. M., & Dollinger, S. J. (1993). Identity, self, and personality: I. Identity status and the five-factor model of personality. *Journal of Research on Adolescence, 3*(3), 227–245.

Clausen, J. A., & Gilens, M. (1990). Personality and labor force participation across the life-course: A longitudinal study of women's careers. *Sociological Forum, 5*, 595–618.

Costa, P. T., Jr., & McCrae, R. R. (1985). *The NEO Personality Inventory manual*. Odessa, FL: Psychological Assessment Resources.

Costa, P. T., Jr., & McCrae, R. R. (1986). Personality stability and its implications for clinical psychology. *Clinical Psychology Review, 6*, 407–423.

Costa, P. T., Jr., & McCrae, R. R. (1992). *Professional manual for the revised NEO Personality Inventory (NEO-PI-R) and the NEO Five-Factor Inventory (NEO-FFI)*. Odessa, FL: Psychological Assessment Resources.

Costa, P. T. J., McCrae, R. R., & Holland, J. L. (1984). Personality and vocational interests in an adult sample. *Journal of Applied Psychology: An International Review, 69*, 390–400.

Darcy, M., & Tracey, T. J. G. (2003). Integrating abilities and interests in career choice: Maximal versus typical assessment. *Journal of Career Assessment, 11*, 219–237.

De Fruyt, F., & Mervielde, I. (1997). The five-factor model of personality and Holland's RIASEC interest types. *Personality and Individual Differences, 23*(1), 87–103.

DeNeve, K. M., & Cooper, H. (1998). The happy personality: A meta-analysis of 137 personality traits and subjective well-being. *Psychological Bulletin, 124*, 179–229.

Elder, G. H. (1969). Occupational mobility, life patterns, and personality. *Journal of Health and Social Behavior, 10,* 308–323.

Feldman, D. C. (2003). The antecedents and consequences of early career indecision among young adults. *Human Resource Management Review, 13*(3), 499–499.

Fuller, B. E., Holland, J. L., & Johnston, J. A. (1999). The relation of profile elevation in the Self-Directed Search to personality variables. *Journal of Career Assessment, 7,* 111–123.

Gasser, C. E., Larson, L. M., & Borgen, F. H. (2004). Contributions of personality and interests to explaining the educational aspirations of college students. *Journal of Career Assessment, 12*(4), 347–365. doi:10.1177/1069072704266644

Goldberg, L. R. (1990). An alternative "description of personality": The Big 5 factor structure. *Journal of Personality and Social Psychology, 59,* 1216–1229.

Gottfredson, G. D., & Jones, E. M. (1993). Psychological meaning of profile elevation in the Vocational Preference Inventory. *Journal of Career Assessment, 1,* 35–48.

Hartman, R. O., & Betz, N. E. (2007). The five-factor model and career self-efficacy: General and domain-specific relationships. *Journal of Career Assessment, 15*(2), 145–161. doi:10.1177/1069072706298011

Heller, D., Watson, D., & Illies, R. (2004). The role of person versus situation in life satisfaction: A critical examination. *Psychological Bulletin, 130,* 574–600.

Hirschi, A. (2009). Development and criterion validity of differentiated and elevated interests in adolescence. *Journal of Career Assessment, 17*(4), 384–401. doi:10.1177/1069072709334237

Hirschi, A. (2010). Vocational interests and career goals: Development and relations to personality in middle adolescence. *Journal of Career Assessment, 18*(3), 223–238. doi:10.1177/1069072710364789

Hirschi, A., Niles, S. G., & Akos, P. (2011). Engagement in adolescent career preparation: Social support, personality and the development of choice decidedness and congruence. *Journal of Adolescence, 34*(1), 173–182. doi:10.1016/j.adolescence.2009.12.009

Hogan, R. T., & Roberts, B. W. (2000). A socioanalytic perspective on person/environment interactions. In W. B. Walsh, K. H. Craik, & R. H. Price (Eds.), *New directions in person-environment psychology* (pp. 1–24). Mahwah, NJ: Erlbaum.

Holland, J. L., Johnston, J. A., & Asama, N. F. (1994). More evidence for the relationship between Holland's personality types and personality variables. *Journal of Career Assessment, 2,* 331–340.

Jin, L., Watkins, D., & Yuen, M. (2009). Personality, career decision self-efficacy and commitment to the career choices process among Chinese graduate students. *Journal of Vocational Behavior, 74*(1), 47–52.

Judge, T. A., Heller, D., & Mount, M. K. (2002). Five-factor model of personality and job satisfaction: A meta-analysis. *Journal of Applied Psychology, 87,* 530–541.

Judge, T. A., Higgins, C. A., Thoresen, C. J., & Barrick, M. R. (1999). The big five personality traits, general mental ability, and career success across the life span. *Personnel Psychology, 52,* 621–652.

Judge, T. A., & Ilies, R. (2002). Relationship of personality to performance motivation: A meta-analytic review. *Journal of Applied Psychology, 87*(4), 797–807. doi:10.1037/0021-9010.87.4.797

Kanfer, R., Wanberg, C. R., & Kantrowitz, T. M. (2001). Job search and employment: A personality-motivational analysis and meta-analytic review. *Journal of Applied Psychology, 86,* 847–855.

Larson, L. M., Rottinghaus, P. J., & Borgen, F. H. (2002). Meta-analyses of Big Six interests and big five personality factors. *Journal of Vocational Behavior, 61*(2), 217–239.

Lounsbury, J. W., Hutchens, T., & Loveland, J. M. (2005). An investigation of big five personality traits and career decidedness among early and middle adolescents. *Journal of Career Assessment, 13*(1), 25–39. doi:10.1177/106907270427027

Lucas, J. L., & Wanberg, C. R. (1995). Personality correlates of Jones' three-dimensional model of career indecision. *Journal of Career Assessment, 3*(3), 315–329. doi:10.1177/106907279500300405

Luyckx, K., Soenens, B., & Goossens, L. (2006). The personality-identity interplay in emerging adult women: Convergent findings from complementary analyses. *European Journal of Personality, 20*(3), 195–215. doi:10.1002/per.579

McCrae, R. R., & Costa, P. T., Jr. (1991). Adding liebe und arbeit: The full five-factor model of personality. *Personality and Social Psychology Bulletin, 17,* 227–232.

McCrae, R. R., & Costa, P. T., Jr. (1999). A five-factor theory of personality. In L. A. Pervin & O. P. John (Eds.), *Handbook of personality: Theory and research* (vol. 2, pp. 139–153). New York, NY: Guilford Press.

McCrae, R. R., Costa, P. T., Ostendorf, F., Angleitner, A., Hrebickova, M., Avia, M. D., ... Smith, P. B. (2000). Nature over nurture: Temperament, personality, and life span development. *Journal of Personality and Social Psychology, 78*(1), 173–186.

Mount, M. K., & Barrick, M. R. (1995). The Big 5 personality dimensions: Implications for research and practice in human resource management. In G. Ferris (Ed.), *Research in personnel and human resources* (Vol. 13, pp. 153–200). Greenwich, CT: JAI Press.

Mount, M. K., Barrick, M. R., Scullen, S. M., & Rounds, J. (2005). Higher-order dimensions of the big five personality traits and the big six vocational interest types. *Personnel Psychology, 58*(2), 447–478.

Nauta, M. M. (2004). Self-efficacy as a mediator of the relationships between personality factors and career interests. *Journal of Career Assessment, 12*(4), 381–394. doi:10.1177/1069072704266653

Ng, T. W. H., Eby, L. T., Sorensen, K. L., & Feldman, D. C. (2005). Predictors of objective and subjective career success. *A meta-analysis. Personnel Psychology, 58*(2), 367–408.

Organ, D. W., & Lingl, A. (1995). Personality, satisfaction, and organizational citizenship behavior. *Journal of Social Psychology, 135,* 339–350.

Prediger, D. J. (1982). Dimensions underlying Holland's hexagon: Missing link between interests and occupations? *Journal of Vocational Behavior, 21,* 259–287.

Reed, M. B., Bruch, M. A., & Haase, R. F. (2004). Five-factor model of personality and career exploration. *Journal of Career Assessment, 12,* 223–238. doi:10.1177/1069072703261524

Roberts, B. W. (1997). Plaster or plasticity: Are adult work experiences associated with personality change in women? *Journal of Personality, 65*(2), 205–232.

Roberts, B. W., Caspi, A., & Moffitt, T. E. (2003). Work experiences and personality development in young adulthood. *Journal of Personality and Social Psychology, 84,* 582–593.

Roberts, B. W., & Del Vecchio, W. F. (2000). The rank-order consistency of personality traits from childhood to old age: A quantitative review of longitudinal studies. *Psychological Bulletin, 126*(1), 3–25.

Roberts, B. W., Kuncel, N. R., Shiner, R., Caspi, A., & Goldberg, L. R. (2007). The power of personality: The comparative validity of personality traits, socioeconomic status, and cognitive ability for predicting important life outcomes. *Perspectives on Psychological Science, 2*(4), 313–345.

Roberts, B. W., Walton, K. E., & Viechtbauer, W. (2006). Patterns of mean-level change in personality traits across the life course: A meta-analysis of longitudinal studies. *Psychological Bulletin, 132*(1), 1–25.

Rogers, M. E., & Creed, P. A. (2011). A longitudinal examination of adolescent career planning and exploration using a social cognitive career theory framework. *Journal of Adolescence, 34*(1), 163–172. doi:10.1016/j.adolescence.2009.12.010

Rogers, M. E., Creed, P. A., & Ian Glendon, A. (2008). The role of personality in adolescent career planning and exploration: A social cognitive perspective. *Journal of Vocational Behavior, 73*(1), 132–142. doi:10.1016/j.jvb.2008.02.002

Rottinghaus, P. J., Lindley, L. D., Green, M. A., & Borgen, F. H. (2002). Educational aspirations: The contribution of personality, self-efficacy, and interests. *Journal of Vocational Behavior, 61*(1), 1–19.

Rotundo, M., & Sackett, P. R. (2002). The relative importance of task, citizenship, and counterproductive performance to global ratings of job performance: A policy-capturing analysis. *Journal of Applied Psychology, 87,* 66–80.

Salami, S. O. (2008). Roles of personality, vocational interests, academic achievement and socio-cultural factors in educational aspirations of secondary school adolescents in southwestern Nigeria. *Career Development International, 13*(7), 630–647. doi:10.1108/13620430810911092

Salgado, J. F. (1997). The five factor model of personality and job performance in the European community. *Journal of Applied Psychology, 82,* 30–43.

Saunders, D. E., Peterson, G. W., Sampson, J. P., Jr., & Reardon, R. C. (2000). Relation of depression and dysfunctional career thinking to career indecision. *Journal of Vocational Behavior, 56*(2), 288–298. doi:10.1006/jvbe.1999.1715

Schaub, M., & Tokar, D. M. (2005). The role of personality and learning experiences in social cognitive career theory. *Journal of Vocational Behavior, 66*(2), 304–325. doi:10.1016/j.jvb.2004.09.005

Schoon, I., & Parsons, S. (2002). Teenage aspirations for future careers and occupational outcomes. *Journal of Vocational Behavior, 60,* 262–288.

Schyns, B., & von Collani, G. (2002). A new occupational self-efficacy scale and its relation to personality constructs and organizational variables. *European Journal of Work and Organizational Psychology, 11*(2), 219–241. doi:10.1080 /13594320244000148

Skorikov, V. B., & Vondracek, F. W. (2007). Vocational identity. In B. Skorikov & W. Patton (Eds.), *Career development in childhood and adolescence* (pp. 143–168). Rotterdam, The Netherlands: Sense.

Spurk, D., & Abele, A. E. (2011). Who earns more and why? A multiple mediation model from personality to salary. *Journal of Business and Psychology, 26*(1), 87–103. doi:10.1007/s10869-010-9184-3.

Sullivan, B. A., & Hansen, J. C. (2004). Mapping the associations between interests and personality: Toward a conceptual understanding of individual differences in vocational behavior. *Journal of Counseling Psychology, 51*, 287–298.

Suls, J., & Martin, R. (2005). The daily life of the garden-variety neurotic: Reactivity, stressor exposure, mood spill-over, and maladaptive coping. *Journal of Personality, 73*, 1485–1509.

Van Dyne, L., & LePine, J. A. (1998). Helping and extra-role behaviors: Evidence of construct and predictive validity. *Academy of Management Journal, 41*, 108–119.

Wang, N., Jome, L.-M., Haase, R.-F., & Bruch, M.-A. (2006). The role of personality and career decision-making self-efficacy in the career choice commitment of college students. *Journal of Career Assessment, 14*(3), 312–332. doi:10.1177 /1069072706286474

Watson, D., & Clark, L. A. (1997). Extraversion and its positive emotional core. In R. Hogan, J. A. Johnson, & S. R. Briggs (Eds.), *Handbook of personality psychology* (pp. 767–793). San Diego, CA: Academic Press.

Watson, D., & Tellegen, A. (1985). Toward a consensual structure of mood. *Psychological Bulletin, 98*, 219–235.

Whiston, S. C., Brecheisen, B. K., & Stephens, J. (2003). Does treatment modality affect career counseling effectiveness? *Journal of Vocational Behavior, 62*, 150–165.

Zikic, J., & Hall, D. T. (2009). Toward a more complex view of career exploration. *Career Development Quarterly, 58*(2), 181–191.

CHAPTER 12

Relational Influences on Career Development

MAUREEN E. KENNY AND MARY BETH MEDVIDE

RECOGNITION OF THE IMPORTANCE of relationships in career development theory and practice is expanding in the literature (Blustein, 2011). Traditionally, career development was conceptualized as an individual process, largely independent of the vast array of relationships that are integral to our lives. Super's (1957) notion that optimal career choice involves the implementation of the self-concept grew out of the American ethos of individual autonomy and choice.

Over the past three decades, several theoretical perspectives have given attention to the role of contextual factors, including environmental supports and barriers, in career development. Super's original stage theory (1957) was broadened to encompass the life-space, recognizing the overlap between career and relational contexts (Super, 1980; see Hartung, Chapter 4, this volume). Social cognitive career theory (SCCT; Lent, Brown, & Hackett, 2000; see Lent, Chapter 5, this volume) focuses heavily on the role of contextual factors in the development of vocational interests, career decision making, and satisfaction with career choices. Support from family, peers, teachers, and other adults in school and community settings, for example, is conceptualized as environmental supports, which bolster the development of self-efficacy beliefs and positive outcome expectations and the transformation of interests into goals and actions. Developmental contextual metatheory has also been applied to understanding the career development process (Vondracek, Lerner, & Schulenberg, 1986). According to this framework, individual development takes place within the context of multiple interacting spheres of influence at the proximal and distal levels of the social context. Family, peers, teachers, and other significant persons represent important influences at the proximal level, which are inevitably impacted by more distal influences exerted through the social, political, and economic contexts.

Recent theoretical work, including relational cultural theory (Schultheiss, 2003), career construction theory (Savickas, 2005; see Savickas, Chapter 6, this volume), and psychology of working (Blustein, 2006), has conceptualized relationships as essential to the fabric of work and life. These scholars (Blustein, 2006; Savickas, 2005) have critiqued traditional theories for assuming a level of autonomy and life choice that is not experienced by many persons, especially those in positions of diminished economic and political power, across the United States and the globe. The need for social connection is recognized, however, as central to the lives of all people and can be found through work experiences (Blustein, 2011). Social connections can take positive and negative forms, with social support, in its varied dimensions, offering positive connection. Social support is multifaceted and includes providing a sense of belonging or social integration; bolstering self-esteem or confidence through emotional support; setting expectations; offering specific advice, guidance, or knowledge through information support; and lending tangible assistance, such as financial support, child care, or transportation (Kenny et al., 2007; Schultheiss, Kress, Manzi, & Glasscock, 2001). Relationships can also provide access to what has long been referred to as social capital—the system of privileged social connections and associated knowledge that is needed to effectively negotiate and advance through society (Coleman, 1990).

This chapter examines theory and research on the role of relationships in the career development process. We review existing research, identify strengths and limitations of current knowledge, and discuss implications for career development interventions at the individual, family, school, and broader contextual levels. Although proximal relationships, including family, peers, and mentors, have garnered the most attention in the career development literature (Richardson, 2012), distal social structures and culture inevitably shape proximal relationships and exert indirect and direct effects on career development pathways and outcomes (Schultheiss, 2003). Relationships cannot be accurately understood outside of the social and cultural contexts in which they are embedded (Schultheiss, 2006). Therefore, our discussion of proximal relationships includes references to a broad array of social and cultural factors. In describing research findings, we identify, when reported in the research, sample characteristics, such as gender, social class, sexual orientation, race, and ethnicity, that interplay with broader contextual influences. We discuss relationships both as facilitators and hindrances to career development across the life span. Although relationships can offer protective functions in the context of economic and psychological distress, they can also present barriers and add to life stress when they are negative or conflictual (Kenny et al., 2007). Because the literature is relatively distinct by age range, we begin with a discussion of childhood and adolescence through college age and then move to a discussion of adulthood.

RELATIONAL INFLUENCES FROM CHILDHOOD THROUGH YOUNG ADULTHOOD

Among children and adolescents, the influence of proximal relationships, including family, peers, and teachers, has been examined in relation to varied indices of career progress. Adults in the family, community, and school offer varied types of social support and serve as role models for academic and career attainment (Kenny, Blustein, Chaves, Grossman, & Gallagher, 2003). To the extent that academic success is a precursor to career development (Lapan, 2004), the important roles of family, peers, and teachers in school achievement are also relevant to understanding career development. Although significant attention has been given to the role of relational factors in the development of educational and career aspirations (e.g., Kenny & Bledsoe, 2005), recent research suggests that aspirations are now high among most youth in the United States, although the prerequisite academic skills and knowledge of the educational and career pathways for realizing these aspirations may be lacking (Kenny & Walsh-Blair, 2012). Consequently, literature relevant to enhancing the career options, choices, and attainment of young people draws from the work of scholars in education and developmental and counseling psychology.

Following the work of Roe (1957) and Super (1957, 1980), scholars and clinicians have long recognized that interests in career and work start at a young age. Indeed, developing meaningful relationships with family and other adult role models was identified by Super (1980) as a key developmental task of childhood, with important consequences for fostering career awareness. Although research on the career development of elementary school children remains sparse (Schultheiss, Palma, & Manzi, 2005), existing scholarly work reveals that children's social and academic experiences as early as first grade can mark a trajectory that influences school engagement, academic progress, and ultimately career choice and attainment (Entwisle, Alexander, & Olson, 2005). Howard and Walsh (2010) found that elementary school children benefit from developmentally appropriate discussions about academic achievement and career attainment, suggesting the need to enhance relational factors that impact academic and career development before school disengagement emerges (Lapan, 2004).

Career development across the adolescent years is of great consequence because educational and social decisions made at this age can have lasting effects on opportunities for academic and career advancement (Perry, Liu, & Pabian, 2010). Unfortunately, the adolescent years are a period of declining school engagement for some youth, leading to school dropout in ninth grade for the most disengaged (Balfanz, Herzog, & MacIver, 2007). These who leave school lack the requisite skills and training needed for entry into well-paid employment and earn substantially less over their lifetimes than peers who successfully complete postsecondary education (Kenny & Walsh-Blair, 2012). Research has found that students who recognize the importance of school for their vocational futures are likely to engage in school and achieve academically (Kenny et al., 2007). In light of the financial, social, and emotional costs of school disengagement, researchers have given attention to the varied sources of social support associated with academic achievement across the school years and into postsecondary education or the workforce (Kenny et al., 2003; Kenny & Walsh-Blair, 2012).

FAMILY RELATIONSHIPS

Review of the career development literature across the child and adolescent years identifies family as a consistent, yet modestly significant, factor in academic achievement and career development (Keller & Whiston, 2008). Hargrove, Creagh, and Burgess (2002), for example, found among an ethnically diverse group of college students that perceived family support for school and work achievement had a small but significant relationship with involvement in career planning. The modest effect of family suggests that a range of individual and contextual factors, both proximal and distal, add to and interact with family factors in influencing academic and career development outcomes (Kenny et al., 2003).

A number of theoretical models, including Bowlby's (1982) construct of attachment, have been applied in understanding the mechanisms through which families influence academic and career development. A number of studies among high school and college students in the United States (e.g., Blustein, Prezioso, & Schultheiss, 1995; Kenny & Rice, 1995) and international settings (e.g., Emmanuelle, 2009; Vignoli, Croity-Belz, Chapeland, de Fillipis, & Garcia, 2005) support the theoretical premise that secure attachment fosters career exploration, thereby advancing career maturity and the formation of a vocational identity. Attachment theory highlights the capacity of adaptive relationships to offer a secure base of emotional support that facilitates growth in autonomy and individual identity (Kenny & Rice, 1995). Wright and Perrone (2008) theorize, additionally, that the quality of internalized working models of attachment developed in early experiences impact individuals' levels of self-efficacy and outcome expectations, which, according to SCCT, are central in career development (Lent et al., 2000).

Although much research focuses on predominantly White, affluent samples (Keller & Whiston, 2008), Kenny, Gallagher, Alvarez-Salvat, and Silsby (2002) found that secure attachment was positively related to academic grade point average among a multiethnic sample of urban high school students from low-income families.

The construct of social support has also been highlighted as a mechanism by which parents and other family members influence the academic achievement and career development of youth, including the formation of career interests, career planning, decision making, and the value placed on work roles. Keller and Whiston (2008) described two forms of support provided by parents with regard to career development: constructive, pragmatic support related to career planning and more general support, such as encouragement and praise. Among middle school students in urban and rural areas of the Midwest, instrumental and relational supports were associated with student career decision-making self-efficacy, although parent encouragement and praise was a stronger predictor than career-focused support (Keller & Whiston, 2008). Among racial and ethnic minority adolescents, perceived relational support from family members has been positively associated with school engagement, educational and career planning, and student comfort and certainty regarding their career choices (e.g., Perry et al., 2010). Diemer (2007) analyzed longitudinal data from the National Educational Longitudinal Study (NELS) following poor youth of color for 2 years after high school graduation and found that instrumental and relational support from parents was associated with the view that work is an important aspect of one's future. Diemer and colleagues (2010) found, furthermore, that parental instrumental and relational support was positively associated with career expectations when accompanied by discussions of how discrimination and racism may impact future academic and career attainment. This suggests that the benefits of parental support to career development among racial and ethnic minority adolescents might be enhanced when parents also provide a space to discuss inequality and ways to cope with injustices.

Parent expectations, academic interests, attitudes, and school involvement have also been related to the academic and career outcomes of their children. In a study of working and middle-class White families, Dotterer, McHale, and Crouter (2009) found that parental interest in academic subjects and their positive expectations about education were associated with academic achievement in middle childhood through adolescence. Research with low-income urban adolescents has suggested that family attitudes and expectations may also influence children's career aspirations and engagement in goal-directed behaviors (Kenny et al., 2007). Hill and Tyson (2009) examined 50 studies and found that parent efforts to help their early adolescent children understand the relationships between school and their future aspirations for work were more strongly related to their academic performance than was direct help with homework.

As children grow older, parents' capacity or willingness to be involved in school may decline if they are unfamiliar with the subject areas or lack the skills needed to provide help (Keller & Whiston, 2008). Bartel (2010) found that African American parents living in poverty wanted to provide relational, instrumental, and financial support for their children but were limited by their own educational status and contextual barriers, such as working full-time, being in limited contact with their child's teacher, and having few opportunities to be involved in school events. Income and social class of family of origin have been linked across a large body of research with academic and career attainment (Diemer, 2007), with recent scholarship seeking to elucidate the mechanisms that explain and buffer these effects. For example, families of first-generation college students may lack the social capital and financial resources enjoyed by college-educated families that pay for college visits and SAT preparation. Nevertheless, family support and encouragement can be instrumental in whether low-income and first-generation students do attend college (Tierney & Auerbach, 2005).

Whereas family support has generally positive effects, some parents may become overinvolved and interfering, which can have negative effects on academic and career development. This notion is consistent with family systems theory, which specifies enmeshment as a dysfunctional pattern of family interaction (Minuchin, 1974), and with attachment theory, which specifies optimal attachment behavior as promoting autonomy and offering support as needed (Kenny & Rice, 1995). A study of German high school students revealed that while parental support was positively related with career exploration, both parental disengagement and interference were associated with career decision-making difficulties (Dietrich & Kracke, 2009). The concept of the helicopter parent popularized by the media also emphasizes the ways in which overinvolved parents, primarily from middle and upper social classes, can stifle the development of their adolescent and young adult offspring. Among low-income families in the United States, the phenomenon of the helicopter parent is rare (Wartman & Savage, 2008).

Research on family influence has been limited by an overemphasis on mothers and traditional nuclear families. Although mother–child dyads have been the focus of most studies, research suggests that support and guidance from father figures are also crucial in career development of youth (Keller & Whiston, 2008). Beyond the nuclear family, extended family and community members can also be important sources of support, especially among youth of color who may benefit from added support in confronting the effects of racism and discrimination on career progress (Kenny et al., 2003). In efforts to encourage research that assesses the influence of extended family on career development, Fouad and colleagues (2010) developed a measure of family influence in career decision making that assesses informational and financial support from family, as well as family expectations, values, and beliefs, and is intended to be relevant across all family structures. Preliminary research with a socioeconomically diverse sample of college and technical school students revealed significant relationships between family influence and career decision-making style, self-efficacy, and adaptability (Kies, Fouad, Liu, & Figueiredo, 2011). For career counselors, this measure has potential for use with clients in exploring the interrelationships of family support, values, and expectations with career decision making.

Despite the limitations of existing research, the importance of family in academic and career development cannot be disputed. Family interest, expectations, and involvement in their children's academic development are consistently associated with school and career attainment. Research is needed, however, to more clearly delineate which parenting behaviors impact which specific aspects of career development and to understand variations by culture and social class.

Families are a source of both emotional and instrumental support, although parental capacity to offer guidance concerning specific academic and career goals may vary, based on parent education and experience (Perna et al., 2008). When families have less access to social capital related to academic and career development, this type of support may be accessed from other caring adults in school and community settings.

Teacher Relationships

Given that education occurs in the school setting, it is not surprising that perceived support and guidance from teachers on academic and social issues is consistently associated with academic motivation, achievement, and school engagement. In elementary school, children who perceive positive support from teachers are likely to engage in positive classroom interactions, demonstrate motivation and persistence in completing tasks, and develop mastery-oriented goals (Wentzel, Battle, Russell, & Loony, 2010). Although support is also crucial across adolescence, secondary school students are typically taught by a group of teachers, which can make it difficult to form close student–teacher relationships (Danielsen, Wiium, Wilhelmsen, & Wold, 2010).

Although teacher influence has been studied most in relation to academic outcomes, teacher support also benefits career development outcomes for students. Perceived teacher support, including teacher investment in helping students to be successful, positive regard and caring toward students, high expectations for educational success, and accessibility as a source of support and career information, has been positively related to career decision making self-efficacy and vocational outcome expectations among European American high school seniors attending an urban public high school in the Midwest (Metheny, McWhirter, & O'Neil, 2008). By creating an accepting class environment, showing care for students, setting expectations, and offering guidance, teachers can also facilitate career planning and adaptability and foster positive achievement-related beliefs and hope for the future among low-income students of color (Kenny & Bledsoe, 2005; Kenny, Walsh-Blair, Blustein, Bempechat, & Seltzer, 2010).

Teacher–student interactions are not always positive and can have negative effects on student academic and social development beginning in the early grades. This is unfortunate, as student work-readiness skills, including social competence, positive work habits, and personal management skills, are learned at school, as well as among family and peers (Lapan, 2004). Mercer and DeRosier (2008) found that teacher disapproval of students in third grade was associated with peer rejection, low academic performance, and reported symptoms of depression across the elementary school years. At the high school level, Bae, Holloway, Li, and Bempechat (2008) found that Mexican American students, especially those who were not high academic achievers, began to disengage from school when they perceived that teacher expectations for their classroom behavior and performance were low.

Research has also focused on how the ethnic and racial attitudes of teachers relate to their expectations of students and of themselves as teachers. Cammarota (2004), for example, found that teacher misperceptions about Latino culture negatively impacted student–teacher relationships and undermined teacher expectations for student success. As a result, Latino high school students felt isolated in their school and disengaged as a way to cope with negative experiences. Research by Ferguson (2003) revealed further that teachers who held stereotypical views of economically disadvantaged African American students did not hold themselves responsible for their students' academic progress.

Teachers have a significant impact across the school years in facilitating or hampering academic and career development through their level of student support, their racial attitudes, and their beliefs and expectations of specific students or student groups. Because of their focus on academic instruction, the role of teachers in academic attainment is more robust than for career guidance, which appears to be small yet significant (Metheny et al., 2008). Research suggests that the relationship between support from parents and teachers on adolescents' attitudes about school and planning for the future is complex. In a study of urban high school youth, Kenny and Bledsoe (2005), for example, found that support from teachers was a stronger predictor of students' school attitudes than parent support, but that parent support was a stronger predictor of student career outcome expectations. Perry and colleagues (2010) found among a diverse sample of urban youth that both parent and teacher support contributed to student career planning and decision-making self-efficacy, which in turn explained student school engagement. In efforts to more fully understand the relative value of family and teachers in school and career planning, further research is needed to examine the mechanisms by which both teachers and families influence career development across race, culture, and social class.

Peer Relationships

In addition to family members, peers represent an important and often-studied relational influence across childhood and adolescence. Peers have been found to be influential in the classroom setting, where classmate acceptance is associated with a positive academic self-concept (Flook, Repetti, & Ullman, 2005). During adolescence, youth spend increasing amounts of time with peers and look to them for advice and guidance (Flook et al., 2005). When peers say positive things about school and value academic success, adolescents are likely to internalize these attitudes and identify positively with school (Kenny & Bledsoe, 2005).

Considerable attention has also been given to the negative effects of peer relationships. Youth who lack supportive peer relationships appear to be at risk both academically and emotionally. For example, low-income Latino middle school students who perceive little support from classmates were found to report negative school attitudes and symptoms of psychological distress, which persisted as they transitioned into high school (Demaray, Malecki, Davidson, Hodgson, & Rebus, 2005). In research among low-income urban high school students, Kenny and colleagues (2007) found that although most students identified friends who support them in doing well in school and preparing for their future vocational lives, they also describe peers with negative school attitudes as barriers to their own academic progress. Some research (e.g., Fordham & Ogbu, 1986) suggests that low-income minority youth are particularly likely to be surrounded by peers who devalue school and associate doing well with "acting White." Other findings suggest that peer norms across racial and ethnic groups in the United States associate school success with being a "nerd" (Tyson, Darity, & Castellino, 2005). Because "having the right friends" can be important for academic success and for career planning (Kenny et al., 2007), establishing those types of friendships can be a crucial challenge.

Overall, a limited body of research has examined the role of peer relationships on career development. When social, behavioral, and academic development are recognized as integral to career preparation, the importance of peers is substantial. Adolescents describe their peers as both supports and barriers for educational and career development. Although friends are rarely cited as a source of specific career guidance, they can be highly influential as sources of emotional support and in shaping attitudes and behavior toward school and career (Kenny et al., 2007).

MENTORING RELATIONSHIPS

Research has found that the presence of a mentor, typically identified as a supportive nonparental adult, can play a significant role in fostering positive psychosocial development and academic progress (Herrera, Grossman, Kauh, & McMaken, 2011). Mentors can be formed naturally with caring adults in the school, community, workplace, or other settings or can be established through formal mentoring programs. Hanlon, Simon, O'Grady, Carswell, and Callaman (2009) found that middle school African American students who were matched to an adult through a school-based mentoring program earned higher grades and better ratings from teachers than counterparts who did not participate in the program. Similarly, the presence of natural mentoring relationships with adults and older peers in the school and the community has been associated with greater school engagement, positive academic expectations, and a sense of belonging in the school among Latino high school students (Sanchez, Esparza, & Colon, 2008). Adult mentors in the workplace are considered an important element of successful work experience for adolescents but have been largely neglected in research (Zimmer-Gembeck & Mortimer, 2006). Kenny and colleagues (2010), however, found among ethnically diverse high school students that perceived support and autonomy from mentors in work-based learning programs were related to positive student attitudes toward school and career planning.

Mentoring has also been studied among college undergraduates, with an emphasis on college persistence among students of color. Campbell and Campbell (2007) found that racial and ethnic minority students who were matched with a faculty mentor earned higher GPAs, completed more classes, and were more likely to return to college the following year. College women planning to enter male-dominated fields, such as science and engineering, may also benefit from academic and career mentoring (Liang, Spencer, Brogan, & Corral, 2008).

RELATIONAL VIOLENCE AMONG YOUTH

With regard to the potential negative impact of relationships, many youth are exposed to interpersonal violence in the home or in the community, with negative repercussions for academic achievement. The effects of domestic violence and childhood abuse have been studied, with research indicating that witnessing or experiencing violence in the home is related to negative mental health, psychosocial, and academic outcomes (Thompson & Whimper, 2010). In addition to violence within the family, youth may be exposed to violence in the community or school, which can lead to ongoing and residual effects that interfere with academic achievement (Holt, Finkelhor, & Kaufman Kantor, 2007). Peer bullying has negative academic and psychosocial effects for both victims and perpetrators (Nakamoto & Schwartz, 2010). As a result of increased awareness of the academic and psychological costs of bullying, school laws regarding bullying have been strengthened in some states.

Implications for Practice With Children and Adolescents

In work with children and adolescents, intervention is often carried out within school settings to promote academic development, career progress, and work readiness behaviors (Lapan, 2004). In recognition of the relation of emotional support among youth to a variety of important social, psychological, academic, and career outcomes, interventions should strive to promote positive and supportive relationships with adults in the home, school, workplace, and community. This entails a broad view of educational and career counseling, which defines the counselor role, consistent with the national model of the American School Counselor Association (2005), as influencing factors that shape school culture and climate and advocating for underserved youth who are at risk for academic and psychological difficulties.

Because all relationships are embedded in a social and cultural context, counselors and educators who seek to enhance supportive relationships must do so with awareness and sensitivity to the diversity in their community. Seeking to promote teacher and counselor sensitivity and responsiveness to students across race, ethnicity, social class, and sexual orientation can be important in fostering positive relationships. Research affirms that diverse youth often experience feelings of alienation in the school and community when significant adults communicate disinterest or disregard for them and their futures (Cammarota, 2004). Counselors need to be attentive to the overall school climate, which includes reducing discrimination and bullying as practiced by students and faculty (Kenny & Walsh-Blair, 2012). Among students, attention should be directed toward building a culture of personal respect and high expectations for academic and vocational achievement. Such efforts are needed to protect youth from those negative peers who serve as a distraction from educational and career goals (Kenny et al., 2007).

Counselors and teachers are a primary conduit for information and guidance regarding future educational and vocational opportunities and play a critical role in communicating expectations and vocational hope for the future to youth and their families. Counselors can bolster the capacity of families to use their cultural strengths in support of the academic and career development of their young people. In addition, quality college counseling that begins at the middle school level can help to make students and their families aware of the coursework needed for college entry and success and assist students and their families in the college application and financial aid process (Perna et al., 2008). Outreach to families, employers, and other community members can increase access for youth across social class and ethnic backgrounds to career guidance and support, including awareness of higher education pathways and professional work opportunities. Mentors in community and work-based learning sites can be influential in offering emotional support and specific career and educational guidance for young people and their families.

Research highlighting the importance of adult support has been incorporated in some educational reform and career planning efforts. Career academies, for example, have demonstrated positive results in enhancing academic achievement and reducing school dropout among those youth most vulnerable to leaving school (Kemple, 2008). Although career academies vary in their specific theme and structure, all are designed to integrate academic and vocational coursework around a career theme and to increase feelings of school belonging by arranging for students and teachers in the same career theme area to have several classes together each day (Hooker & Brand, 2009).

In addition, some schools have sought to increase teacher–student interaction by structuring advisory sessions, which increase teacher involvement in student mentoring and guidance and help teachers interact with the students they teach on a more personal level. The Career Institute, a public school in New York City, was designed to foster academic attainment and develop career competencies among academically at-risk students by integrating academic and career development programming across the middle school and high school years (Rivera & Schaefer, 2009). The curriculum is designed jointly by teachers and school counselors, and students work with the same teacher in advisory sessions over 7 years of school, allowing close and supportive relationships to develop among students and school faculty. Preliminary evaluation of the advisory model suggests promising results (Fleischman & Heppen, 2009).

In individual and group work with youth, career counselors need to attend to the interrelationships among the academic, social, psychological, and vocational domains of development, recognizing how social and psychological factors impact academic attainment and career choice. Career guidance can assist youth in exploring how peers, teachers, and family have impacted educational and career development, and in identifying strategies and resources for accessing additional sources of emotional and instrumental support. The Choices Program (Vera et al., 2007) was designed as a culturally relevant and responsive classroom intervention for Latino youth and includes units that examine social barriers to academic and career progress and build student efficacy in responding adaptively to peer pressure. Jackson, Kacanski, Rust, and Beck (2006) developed workshops for low-income urban Black and Latino eighth- and ninth-grade students to increase awareness of the personal and contextual supports that can be used to reach their school and career goals. Short-term evaluation revealed that this intervention was successful in increasing student awareness of relational supports, although the longer-term impact of this change was not assessed.

ADULT CAREER DEVELOPMENT IN A RELATIONAL CONTEXT

For adults, work and relationships are conceptualized as interfacing in numerous ways. Richardson (2012), for example, describes how personal relationships, relationships in the workplace (i.e., market work), caregiving relationships (i.e., care work), and the demands of market work and care work interrelate and ultimately influence both personal and vocational decisions. Blustein (2011) explains that work is an important site for meaningful social relationships, that relationships can give meaning and purpose to work, and that relationships both at the work site and in the personal arena can help persons cope with work-based challenges. The social connection offered through work can also be devastated when employment is lost, which is unfortunately a frequent event during times of economic distress. At the same time, relationships from multiple sources may be turned to for support in coping with unemployment or as a source of gratification for persons who invest their energies in unpaid work in caring for others.

Globalization, advances in technology, and increasing job instability are radically impacting the workforce in the United States and across the globe (Blustein, 2006). As a consequence, the traditional linear career trajectory has been replaced by the protean career, characterized by numerous job changes, nonlinear progressions, and more frequent periods of unemployment. In this work landscape, tensions among career interests, goals, and external realities increase, and relational support and social emotional skills become increasingly important for career decision making and advancement (Di Fabio & Kenny, 2012). The 21st-century workplace values communication, collaboration, and team building, as well as innovation and problem solving (Partnership for 21st Century Skills, 2008). Across the protean career, personal identity and satisfaction are derived from relational fulfillment as well as from individual achievement. Taken as a whole, an inclusive understanding of the work lives of individuals is emerging that recognizes the varied and dynamic roles of relationships in both paid and unpaid labor.

Our review of existing research highlights a variety of intersections between relationships and work across adult life. Relevant literature draws from sociology, marriage and family counseling, industrial psychology, and occupational health psychology. Vocational choices, adjustment, and advances in the world of work are also widely understood as a product of individual and contextual factors. Workplace mentors, along with organizational and broader social policies, inevitably impact career attainment. Whereas much research has focused on the positive aspects of workplace relationships, such as mentoring, the effects of negative workplace relationships, such as discrimination and bullying, also deserve attention. We begin with a discussion of the work–family interface, which has been a focus of extensive study, and then consider domestic violence and different types of workplace relationships.

WORK–FAMILY INTERFACE

As the number of women in the labor market increased across the late 20th and into the 21st century, there was a surge of research on the relationship between work and family (Schultheiss, 2003). Super's (1957) original theory was revised to consider how multiple roles across vocational and personal domains can converge to foster a healthy vocational identity and a high quality of life (Super, 1980). Consistent with this notion, occupational health research indicates that psychological well-being often improves as people take on multiple roles across life domains (van Steenbergen, Ellemers, & Mooijaart, 2007). This positive spillover across life roles can lead to enhanced work performance, increased organizational commitment, and higher levels of satisfaction in the workplace (Grzywacz & Marks, 2000), as well as increased commitment to home responsibilities and higher levels of family satisfaction (van Steenbergen et al., 2007).

Although this research suggests that family and work obligations can be successfully combined and enhance one another, research also suggests that individuals do not always have enough time, energy, or resources to function successfully across all life roles (Grzywacz & Marks, 2000). In these circumstances, job satisfaction and commitment to work may decline, and burnout may increase (Amstad, Meier, Fasel, Elfering, & Semmer, 2011). Conflict between the demands of work and family can also contribute to marital discord, family dissatisfaction (van Steenbergen et al., 2007), and psychological distress (Amstad et al., 2011).

Research has also examined gender differences in the benefits and challenges of balancing work and family. Work–family conflict and stress, for example, may be greater for women when they take on more household and familial responsibilities than their male partners. This can lead to family stress and negatively impact work productivity (van Steenbergen et al., 2007). There is some indication that a more egalitarian division of responsibilities has emerged among U.S. couples (Bureau of Labor Statistics, 2011), and findings related to gender differences in work–family conflict may be changing as a result. Nevertheless, data suggest that women remain more likely than their male partners to change their career paths and to forgo workplace opportunities because of family responsibilities (Schultheiss, 2009).

Career development research has typically focused on married heterosexual couples with children; the applicability of this research to other family constellations, such as single parents, unmarried couples, extended kin networks, and same-sex partners is, therefore, unclear. Consequently, Schultheiss (2003) has argued for increased attention to other family types that may have unique needs arising from a variety of socially constructed barriers in the school, community, and workplace, such as prejudice and discrimination. Several authors (Schultheiss, 2009; Richardson, 2012) have also critiqued theory and research on the work–family interface for valuing paid market work over unpaid care work, such as caring for children, aging parents, and other loved ones. Work is traditionally understood in relation to economic productivity, with caregiving conceptualized as a family responsibility that can interfere with paid responsibilities in the workplace (Schultheiss, 2009). Richardson (2012) maintains that caregiving should be given equal respect in relation to work in the public domain and recognized as a form of work practice and career choice. However, this viewpoint has not been fully embraced in scholarship or career counseling practice.

Domestic Violence

Domestic and other types of interpersonal violence are examples of negative relational qualities that can also impede career development among adults. The barriers associated with domestic and other forms of interpersonal violence can interface with career barriers related to gender, poverty, and minority status. Women are four times more likely than men to be victims of intimate partner violence (United States Department of Justice, 2011). Those women living in households making under $7,500 per year are 6 times more likely than women in households with an annual income above $50,000 to experience domestic violence (Catalano, 2006).

Career interventions can be beneficial in helping survivors of domestic violence to develop the vocational skills needed to leave an abusive relationship, enter the workforce, and gain financial independence (Chronister & McWhirter, 2006). In addition to vocational skills, effective career interventions often focus on building support networks with friends and family that can foster self-efficacy about work abilities and enhance optimism about the future (Chronister et al., 2009). A burgeoning line of research (Chronister et al., 2009; Chronister & McWhirter, 2006) focuses on working with domestic violence survivors to develop a critical perspective on oppression in their lives related to race, social class, and gender (Chronister & McWhirter, 2006). This approach has the potential to augment traditional career interventions by reducing self-blame among survivors of domestic violence. A study by Chronister and McWhirter (2006) found that women who participated in an intervention that included traditional career components and discussions on the impact of domestic violence made more progress toward their goals than women who did not have the opportunity to discuss those experiences.

RELATIONSHIPS IN THE WORKPLACE

Within the workplace, relationships can also have positive benefits or serve as impediments. Mentoring represents one workplace factor that can facilitate career development; discrimination and bullying represent relational factors that often have negative effects.

Mentoring. Applied psychology research suggests that mentoring in the workplace is beneficial for persons hoping to advance within their organizations and expand their array of vocational skills. The emotional support from a mentoring relationship can foster self-efficacy and a positive vocational identity, which are essential for skill building and goal setting (Allen, Eby, Poteet, Lentz, & Lima, 2004). Despite these beneficial positive effects, mentoring relationships can also be characterized by negative feelings. Protégés, for example, may criticize their mentors for inadequate support or insufficient feedback, and mentors may question their protégés' commitment to learning (Allen et al., 2004). Mentoring relationships can also breed a sense of entitlement among some protégés who believe they are more deserving of preferential treatment than their peers, which can lead to resentment in the organization toward mentors and mentees (Allen et al., 2004).

Research suggests that mentoring may be particularly important for women, racial and ethnic minorities, and gays and lesbians, who may face sexism, racism, homophobia, and discrimination. In addition to traditional mentoring functions, mentoring can offer members of these marginalized groups a safe place to discuss socially constructed barriers that limit opportunities for workplace advancement (Benishek, Bieschke, Park, & Slattery, 2004). Perceptions of prejudice and discrimination across the organization can, however, limit workers' willingness to seek out informal mentoring relationships (Brenner, Lyons, & Fassinger, 2010).

Workplace discrimination. For some racial and ethnic minority workers, relationships in the workplace can be characterized by experiences with prejudice and discrimination. Although the federal government protects racial minorities against overt acts of discrimination at work, subtle forms of discrimination and prejudice persist, have negative effects, and are often difficult to eradicate (King et al., 2011). Kern and Grandey (2009), for example, found that racial minority service workers who experienced microaggressions by White customers reported increased stress levels and decreased feelings of well-being. As defined by Sue and colleagues (2007), racial microaggressions are commonplace, hostile, or derogatory comments and behaviors that are directed intentionally and unintentionally toward persons of color. By analyzing 219 court cases where complaints of racial discrimination were brought against employers, King and colleagues (2011) found that microaggressions were often dismissed by judges because of subjective interpretations of what constitutes serious harassment and difficulty by the plaintiffs in demonstrating the intentionality of these acts. King and colleagues (2011) concluded that legal definitions of discrimination make it difficult to demonstrate that experiences of microaggression are damaging to plaintiffs' personal and professional lives.

Experiences of workplace discrimination among gays and lesbians are complicated by the fact that these workers may have few formal interpersonal or organizational resources to seek remediation. Currently, there is a federal statute to protect gay and lesbian workers against workplace discrimination in the public sector, but private corporations are not legally obligated to protect their workers from discriminatory practices (Human Rights Campaign, 2011). The effects of federal and state laws within workplaces that do not abide by antidiscrimination policies have been a growing area of research. Mercier (2008) found that lesbian participants' perceptions of their relationships with coworkers were impacted by fears of and actual experiences with discrimination and homophobic responses to self-disclosures about partners and children. There were also financial costs to discriminatory work practices because partners and children were not eligible for health care benefits. Participants reported that the stress of working in a homophobic environment and the pressure to conform to heteronormative attitudes about work and family created strain that seeped into their relationships with partners and children.

Workplace bullying. Bullying, which is often associated with school outcomes in children and adolescents, is also a concern for adult workers. Workplace bullying can take the form of ongoing physical or verbal aggression or attempts to exclude and isolate certain workers (Einarsen, 2000). Bullying can contribute to stress and negative mental health outcomes (Rodríguez-Muñoz, Moreno-Jiménez, Sanz Vergel, & Garrosa Hernández, 2010) and often has negative effects on work productivity, organizational commitment, and job satisfaction (Einarsen, 2000). Based on the results of their meta-analysis, Neilsen, Matthiesen, and Einarsen (2010) concluded that bullying is a common and significant problem in the workplace and suggested that it should be addressed at individual, interpersonal, organizational, and policy levels.

Clearly, organizations and the persons who lead them need to devise policies that support worker satisfaction and realization of career potential. Rhoades and Eisenberger (2002) argue that organizations with these policies are likely to have employees who perceive their work environment to be caring and committed to their well-being. When employees perceive little or no organizational support, they are likely to report diminished competence and be less productive and committed than are those who perceive sufficient organizational support (Rhoades & Eisenberger, 2002).

IMPLICATIONS FOR PRACTICE WITH ADULTS

Awareness of the critical role of social relationships across the life span and as factors that interrelate with career development has important implications for career assessment and intervention. Although the specific ways in which knowledge of relationships is integrated will vary based on the counselor's theoretical perspective, we recommend a holistic approach to assessment and intervention that recognizes the reciprocal relationships among the social, emotional, academic, and vocational dimensions of life. By appreciating the numerous connections among work life and relationships across the personal, work, and caregiving contexts, the distinctions between psychotherapy and career counseling break down (Schultheiss, 2009). As a result, an integrative approach that combines psychotherapy and career counseling is advantageous (Blustein, 2011).

In working with individuals, career counselors can address the importance and influence of relationships from a variety of theoretical perspectives. From the life design perspective (Savickas et al., 2009), for example, a counselor might conduct a life story interview that assists clients in exploring their current life across vocational, familial, interpersonal, and spiritual contexts. From the SCCT perspective (Lent et al., 2000), the counselor might work with a client to identify relational resources and barriers in the present, anticipate future obstacles, and develop proactive strategies that will maximize activities and relational supports to reach work goals. A key tenet of SCCT is that people will take action to reach goals if they believe that there are ample supports in place and few barriers. Counselors can assist clients in examining social networks to identify supportive family members, peers, and work colleagues and to develop strategies for accessing relational resources to overcome barriers. The relational cultural perspective (Schultheiss, 2003) also includes an in-depth exploration of influential relationships. Clients might be assisted in examining positive and negative relationships across work, personal, and family contexts, with attention to resolving conflicts across these spheres and locating and accessing alternate sources of support, if needed. Schultheiss (2003) suggests the discussion of a difficult work situation as a tool in counseling for identifying influential relationships, conflict, and support. Counselors can guide clients in exploring the interface between work and family life and the importance of market and care work for client life meaning, psychological well-being, and career advancement (Schultheiss, 2006). The counseling relationship provides an immediate source of support, through which the client can gain confidence and skills for confronting and negotiating difficult relationships and building supportive and mutually enhancing relationships.

Counselors can also work directly with clients in developing the kind of social and emotional skills needed to engage in adaptive relationships in the workplace and across personal life domains (Blustein, 2006). Knowing how to access social support, negotiate conflict, and effectively express one's needs can be critical for numerous career development processes, including career decision making, seeking employment, coping with job loss, adjusting to and advancing in the workplace, and responding to domestic or workplace violence, bullying, or discrimination.

As with youth, assessment and intervention should focus not only on individuals but also on the proximal and distal social contexts in which they are embedded. Counselors need to be aware of the ways in which local and federal laws impact family leave policies, workplace discrimination, and bullying. Counselors can work with clients to become more aware of these and other sociopolitical factors that affect work relationships, job performance, and work satisfaction. They may also strive to increase client awareness concerning the impact of institutional policies and support and their rights as they relate to personal and career development decisions. Counselors might also assist clients in devising ways to effect change in the contexts in which they are embedded, such as the family and the workplace. Counselors can work with clients to gain skills in self and group advocacy for changing community, organizational, and governmental policies. For clients who experience microaggressions in the workplace, counselors might assist them in critically examining these incidents, possible responses, and their rights as employees (Richardson, 2012). Counseling can also empower clients to mobilize personal and professional resources in confronting the microaggressions and evaluating the effectiveness of change efforts.

Counselors and vocational psychologists can play a vital role in shaping practices and policies that enhance the kinds of healthy and just relationships that promote optimal career development for all groups. These professionals may also choose to engage in social and political advocacy to change policies at the community, state, and federal levels that undermine healthy relationships and restrict the career choice and advancement of disenfranchised groups. Schultheiss (2009), for example, argues that psychologists should advocate for legislation that is more just in distributing resources to full-time caregivers or helping caregivers who want to transition back into market work.

CONCLUSIONS AND PRACTICE IMPLICATIONS

Existing research reveals a complex interface among relationships in the personal life domain, workplace relationships, and educational and career development. Across the life span, family, friends, coworkers, supervisors, and others interrelate in important and complex ways with career development processes. Although more research is needed to understand how characteristics of specific relationships contribute to specific educational and career development outcomes, career counseling practice cannot ignore both the positive and negative impacts of relationships. Existing research provides several broad implications for the preparation of career counselors and the practice of career counseling and other interventions at multiple contextual levels to support career development. More specific implications for work with children, adolescents, and adults were discussed earlier in this chapter.

As emphasized throughout this chapter, the practice of career counseling inevitably intersects with psychotherapy across a variety of life domains. The interrelationship of work and relationships in paid work and care work domains has implications for the knowledge and skills needed by the career counselor. In addition to a command of career theory and practice, the career counselor should have a sound grasp of theory and research regarding the development of healthy relationships across the life span and how the academic, social, psychological, and vocational dimensions of individual development are interrelated. In addition, knowledge of how these developmental trajectories interface with broader contextual factors, such as the structure of organizations, race relations, culture, gender, and social class is vital. Career counselors should thus possess broad developmental and contextual knowledge and exercise competence in career, personal, and multicultural counseling.

With regard to practice, career counseling entails a focus on individuals as well as the contexts in which they are embedded. Career counseling with individuals and groups should attend to the roles of relational supports and barriers in career exploration, decision making, work adjustment, career advancement, and job loss and their relation to client psychological well-being. Counselors can assist clients in exploring the interface of work and relationships, the ways in which relationships serve as resources and barriers in navigating one's career path, and how to best negotiate these relationships. In addition to a focus on academic and career skill development, counseling can aid clients in developing the social and emotional skills that will contribute to positive and successful relationships and psychological well-being both within and outside of the workplace. Some clients may also benefit from assistance in developing skills needed for negotiating and overcoming contextual barriers they may encounter. Clients can be supported in social change efforts as individuals or as part of a larger social action effort. Assisting clients, such as youth living in poverty or low-income women who are victims of domestic violence, to gain a critical understanding of the social conditions that have contributed to their social status is an emerging area of career counseling research and practice.

Career counselors may also strive to enhance the relational contexts that support academic and career development. For youth, increasing the capacities of teachers and school administrators to support the academic and career attainment for all students is important. Counselors can assist clients or significant others in the social network, such as family, teachers, or mentors, to gain an appreciation of how relational assets and barriers are shaped by broader contextual factors. Following from this awareness, counselors, teachers, mentors, and employers can be guided in creating environments that reduce oppression, including bullying and microaggressions. Counselors who are employed by work organizations may be involved in developing mentoring programs and other workplace policies and support systems that foster employee work productivity, satisfaction, and career advancement. Work and relational issues intersect for youth, couples, and families in many ways, as we have described in this chapter. As a result, marriage and family counselors as well as career counselors often address concerns regarding care work and paid work, the balance of work and family responsibilities for couples, and the impact of job stress or job loss on family interactions.

Related to their knowledge of the ways in which distal contextual factors, such as poverty, racism, classism, ageism, ableism, and heterosexism, impact relational quality and academic and career outcomes, some career counselors may also choose to influence social, educational, political, and economic policy by taking on advocacy roles. Counselors can, for example, advocate for and promote policies within the context of K-12 classrooms, universities, workplaces, community organizations, or the society at large to support healthy relationships and career development for all persons. Career counselors can use their expertise in career and personal development to inform the voting public through contributions to local print and broadcast media or may contribute to policy briefs directed toward local and national legislatures. Although these functions go beyond the traditional role of the career counselor, the effect of broader social policy on relational well-being and academic and workplace development are propelling a growing number of counselors to engage in social and political advocacy roles.

REFERENCES

Allen, T. D., Eby, L. T., Poteet, M. L., Lentz, E., & Lima, L. (2004). Career benefits associated with mentoring for protégés: A meta-analysis. *Journal of Applied Psychology, 89*(1), 127–136. doi:10.1037/0021-9010.89.1.127

American School Counselor Association. (2005). *The ASCA national model: A framework for school counseling programs* (2nd ed.). Alexandria, VA: Author.

Amstad, F. T., Meier, L. L., Fasel, U., Elfering, A., & Semmer, N. K. (2011). A meta-analysis of work–family conflict and various outcomes with a special emphasis on cross-domain versus matching-domain relations. *Journal of Occupational Health Psychology, 16,* 151–169. doi:10.1037/a0022170

Bae, S., Holloway, S. D., Li, J., & Bempechat, J. (2008). Mexican American students' perceptions of teacher expectations: Do perceptions differ depending on student achievement levels? *Urban Review, 40,* 210–225. doi:10.1007/s11256-007-0070-x

Balfanz, R., Herzog, L., & MacIver, D. (2007). Preventing student disengagement and keeping students on the graduation path in urban middle-grades schools: Early identification and effective interventions. *Educational Psychologist, 42*(4), 223–235.

Bartel, V. B. (2010). Home and school factors impacting parental involvement in a Title I elementary school. *Journal of Research in Childhood Education, 24,* 209–228. doi:10.1080/02568543.2010.487401

Benishek, L. A., Bieschke, K. J., Park, J., & Slattery, S. M. (2004). A multicultural feminist model of mentoring. *Journal of Multicultural Counseling and Development, 32,* 428–442. doi:2005–00106-016

Blustein, D. L. (2006). *The psychology of working: A new perspective for career development, counseling, and public policy.* Mahwah, NJ: Erlbaum.

Blustein, D. L. (2011). A relational perspective of careers and working: A social constructionist analysis. *Journal of Vocational Behavior, 79,* 1–17. doi:10.1016/j.jvb.2010.10.004

Blustein, D. L., Prezioso, M. S., & Schultheiss, D. P. (1995). Attachment theory and career development: Current status and future directions. *Counseling Psychologist, 23,* 416–432. doi:1996–91454-001

Bowlby, J. (1982). *Attachment and loss: Vol. 1. Attachment.* New York, NY: Basic Books.

Brenner, B. R., Lyons, H. Z., & Fassinger, R. (2010). Can heterosexism harm organizations? Predicting the perceived organizational citizenship behaviors of gay and lesbian employees. *Career Development Quarterly, 28,* 321–355.

Bureau of Labor Statistics. (2011). *American time use survey—2010 results.* Washington, DC: Department of Labor. Retrieved from http://www.bls.gov/tus/data.htm

Cammarota, J. (2004), The gendered and racialized pathways of Latina and Latino youth: Different struggles, different resistances in the urban context. *Anthropology & Education Quarterly, 35,* 53–74. doi:10.1525/aeq.2004.35.1.53

Campbell, T. A., & Campbell, D. E. (2007). Outcomes of mentoring at-risk college students: Gender and ethnic matching effects. *Mentoring & Tutoring, 15*(2), 135–148. doi:10.1080/13611260601086287

Catalano, S. (2006). *Intimate partner violence in the U.S.* Washington, DC: United States Department of Justice. Retrieved from http://bjs.ojp.usdoj.gov/content/pub/pdf/ipvus.pdf

Chronister, K. M., Brown, C., O'Brien, K. M., Wettersten, V. B., Burt, M., & Shahane, A. (2009). Domestic violence survivors: Perceived vocational supports and barriers. *Journal of Career Assessment, 17,* 116–131. doi:2009–00743-00710.1177/1069072708325858

Chronister, K. M., & McWhirter, E. H. (2006). An experimental examination of two career interventions for battered women. *Journal of Counseling Psychology, 53,* 151–164. doi:2006–04241-00110.1037/0022-0167.53.2.151

Coleman, J. S. (1990). *Foundations of social theory.* Cambridge, MA: Harvard University Press.

Danielsen, A. G., Wiium, N., Wilhelmsen, B. U., & Wold, B. (2010). Perceived support provided by teachers and classmates and students' self-reported academic initiative. *Journal of School Psychology, 48,* 247–267. doi:2038094910.1016/j.jsp.2010.02.0022010-07246-00

Demaray, M. K., Malecki, C. K., Davidson, L. M., Hodgson, K. K., & Rebus, P. J. (2005). The relationship between social support and student adjustment: A longitudinal analysis. *Psychology in the Schools, 42,* 691–706. doi:2005–11036-00210.1002/pits.20120

Di Fabio, A., & Kenny, M. E. (2012). Emotional intelligence and perceived support among Italian high school students. *Journal of Career Development,* first published on October 5, 2011 as doi:10.1177/0894845311421005

Diemer, M. A. (2007). Parental and school influences upon the career development of youth of color. *Journal of Vocational Psychology, 70,* 502–524. doi:10.1016/j.jvb.2007.02.003

Diemer, M. A., Wang, Q., Moore, T., Gregory, S. R., Hatcher, K. M., & Voight, A. M. (2010). Sociopolitical development, work salience, and vocational expectations among low socioeconomic status African American, Latin American, and Asian American youth. *Developmental Psychology, 46,* 619–635. doi:0.1037/a0017049

Dietrich, J., & Kracke, B. (2009). Career-specific parental behaviors in adolescents' development. *Journal of Vocational Behavior, 75,* 109–119. doi:2009–1304900410.1016/j.jvb.2009.03.005

Dotterer, A. M., McHale, S. M., & Crouter, A. C. (2009). The development and correlates of academic interests from childhood through adolescence. *Journal of Educational Psychology, 101,* 509–519. doi:2009–04640-02110.1037/a0013987

Einarsen, S. (2000). Harassment and bullying at work: A review of the Scandinavian approach. *Aggression and Violent Behavior, 4,* 371–401. doi:2000–15622-00310.1016/S1359-1789(98)00043-3

Emmanuelle, V. (2009). Inter-relationships among attachment to mother and father, self-esteem, and career indecision. *Journal of Vocational Behavior, 75,* 91–99. doi:2009–13049-00210.1016/j.jvb.2009.04.007

Entwisle, D. R., Alexander, K. L., & Olson, L. S. (2005). First grade and educational attainment by age 22: A new story. *American Journal of Sociology, 110,* 1458–1502. doi:2005-05833-00510.1086/428444

Ferguson, R. F. (2003). Teachers' perception and expectations and the Black-White test score gap. *Urban Education, 38,* 460–507. doi:10.1177/0042085903038004006

Fleischman, S., & Heppen, J. (2009). Improving low-performing high schools: Searching for evidence of promise. *The Future of Children, 19,* 105–133. doi:10.1353/foc.0.0021

Flook, L., Repetti, R. L., & Ullman, J. B. (2005). Classroom social experiences as predictors of academic performance. *Developmental Psychology, 41,* 319–327. doi:2005-02477-00410.1037/0012-1649.41.2.319

Fordham, S., & Ogbu, J. (1986). Black students' school success: Coping with the burden of "acting White." *Urban Review, 18,* 176–206. doi:1988–12135-001

Fouad, N. A., Cotter, E. W., Fitzpatrick, M. E., Kantamneni, N., Carter, L., & Bernfeld, S. (2010). Development and validation of the Family Influence Scale. *Journal of Career Assessment, 18,* 276–291. doi:10.1177/1069072710364793

Grzywacz, J. G., & Marks, N. F. (2000). Reconceptualizing the work–family interface: An ecological perspective on the correlates of positive and negative spillover between work and family. *Journal of Occupational Health Psychology, 5,* 111–126. doi:1999-15533-01010.1037//1076-8998.5.1.111

Hanlon, T. E., Simon, B. D., O'Grady, K. E., Carswell, S. B., & Callaman, J. M. (2009). The effectiveness of an after-school program targeting urban African American youth. *Education & Urban Society, 42*(1), 96–118. doi:2009–20514-00510.1177/0013124509343144

Hargrove, B. K., Creagh, M. G., & Burgess, B. L. (2002).Family interaction patterns as predictors of vocational identity and career decision-making self-efficacy. *Journal of Vocational Behavior, 61,* 185–201. doi:2002–18408-00110.1006/jvbe.2001.1848

Herrera, C., Grossman, J. B., Kauh, T. J., & McMaken, J. (2011). Mentoring in schools: An impact study of Big Brothers Big Sisters school-based mentoring. *Child Development, 82,* 346–361. doi:10.1111/j.1467-8624.2010.01559.x

Hill, N. E., & Tyson, D. F. (2009). Parental involvement in middle school: A meta-analytic assessment of the strategies that promote achievement. *Developmental Psychology, 45,* 740–763. doi:2009-05916-011

Holt, M. K., Finkelhor, D., & Kaufman Kantor, G. (2007). Multiple victimization experiences of urban elementary school students: Associations with psychosocial functioning and academic performance. *Child Abuse and Neglect, 31,* 503–515. doi:2007–08408-00410.1016/j.chiabu.2006.12.006

Hooker, S., & Brand, B. (2009). *Success at every step: How 23 programs support youth on the path to college and beyond.* Retrieved from http://www.aypf.org/wp-content/uploads/2012/03/SuccessAtEveryStep.pdf

Howard, K., & Walsh, M. E. (2010). Conceptions of career choice and attainment: Developmental levels in how children think about careers. *Journal of Vocational Behavior, 76,* 143–152. doi:10.1016/j.jvb.2009.10.0102010-05279-002

Human Rights Campaign. (2011). *Corporate equality index: Rating American workplaces on lesbians, gay, bisexual, and transgendered equality.* Washington, DC: Author.

Jackson, M. A., Kacanski, J. M., Rust, J. P., & Beck, S. E. (2006). Constructively challenging diverse inner-city youth's beliefs about educational and career barriers and supports. *Journal of Career Development, 32,* 203–218. doi:10.1177 /0894845305279161

Keller, B. K., & Whiston, S. C. (2008). The role of parental influences on young adolescents' career development. *Journal of Career Assessment, 16,* 198–217. doi:2008-04718-00410.1177/1069072707313206

Kemple, J. J. (2008). *Career academies: Long-term impacts on labor market outcomes, educational attainment, and transitions to adulthood.* New York, NY: Manpower Demonstration Research Corporation.

Kenny, M. E., & Bledsoe, M. (2005). Contributions of the relational context to career adaptability among urban adolescents. *Journal of Vocational Behavior, 66,* 257–272. doi:10.1016/j.jvb.2004.10.002

Kenny, M. E., Blustein, D. L., Chaves, A., Grossman, J. M., & Gallagher, L. A. (2003). The role of perceived barriers and relational support in the educational and vocational lives of urban high school students. *Journal of Counseling Psychology, 50,* 142–155. doi:2003–03644-00410.1037/0022-0167.50.2.142

Kenny, M. E., Gallagher, L. A., Alvarez-Salvat, R., & Silsby, J. (2002). Sources of support and psychological distress among academically successful inner-city youth. *Adolescence, 37,* 161–182. doi:2002-13255-011

Kenny, M. E., Gualdron, L., Scanlon, D., Sparks, E., Blustein, D., & Jernigan, M. (2007). Urban adolescents' construction of supports and barriers to their educational and career attainment. *Journal of Counseling Psychology, 54,* 336–343. doi:10.1037/0022-0167.54.3.3362007-09249-01110.1037/0022-0167.54.3.336

Kenny, M. E., & Rice, K. G. (1995) Attachment to parents and adjustment in late adolescent college students: Current status, applications, and future considerations. *Counseling Psychologist, 23,* 433–456. doi:1996–06509-001

Kenny, M. E., & Walsh-Blair, L. Y. (2012). Educational development: Applications. In N. Fouad (Ed.), *APA handbook of counseling psychology, vol. 2: Practice, interventions, and applications* (pp. 29–55). Washington, DC: American Psychological Association.

Kenny, M. E., Walsh-Blair, L. Y., Blustein, D. L., Bempechat, J., & Seltzer, J. (2010). Achievement motivation among urban adolescents: Work hope, autonomy support, and achievement- related beliefs. *Journal of Vocational Behavior, 77,* 205–212. doi:10.1016/j.jvb.2010.02.005

Kern, J. H., & Grandey, A. A. (2009). Customer incivility as a social stressor: The role of race and racial identity for service employees. *Journal of Occupational Health Psychology, 14,* 46–57. doi:2008-19186-00510.1037/a0012684

Kies, A. L., Fouad, N. A., Liu, J. P., & Figueiredo, C. M. (2011). *Convergent validity of the Family-Influence Scale on Career Decision Making.* Poster presented at the 119th annual convention of the American Psychological Association, Washington, DC.

King, E. B., Dunleavy, D. G., Dunleavy, E. M., Jaffer, S., Morgan, W. B., Elder, K., & Graebner, R. (2011). Discrimination in the 21st century: Are science and the law aligned? *Psychology, Public Policy, and Law, 17*(1), 54–75. doi:10.1037 /a0021673

Lapan, R. (2004). *Career development across the K-16 years: Bridging the present to satisfying and successful futures*. Alexandria, VA: American Counseling Association.

Lent, R. W., Brown, S. D., & Hackett, G. (2000). Contextual supports and barriers to career choice: A social cognitive analysis. *Journal of Counseling Psychology, 47*, 36–49. doi:.2000-13659-00410.1037//0022-0167.47.1.36

Liang, B., Spencer, R., Brogan, D., & Corral, M. (2008). Mentoring relationships from early adolescence through emerging adulthood: A qualitative analysis. *Journal of Vocational Behavior, 72*, 168–182. doi:2008-03620-00310.1016/j.jvb.2007.11.005

Mercer, S. H., & DeRosier, M. E. (2008). Teacher preference, peer rejection, and student aggression: A prospective study of transactional influence and independent contributions to emotional adjustment and grades. *Journal of School Psychology, 46*(6), 661–685. doi:2008-15618-00510.1016/j.jsp.2008.06.006

Mercier, L. R. (2008). Lesbian parents and work: Stressors and supports for the work–family interface. *Journal of Gay and Lesbian Social Services: Issues in Practice, Policy, & Research, 19*, 25–47. doi:10.1080/10538720802131675

Metheny, J., McWhirter, E. H., & O'Neil, M. E. (2008). Measuring perceived teacher support and its influence on adolescent career development. *Journal of Career Assessment, 16*, 218–237. doi:2008–04718-00510.1177/1069072707313198

Minuchin, S. (1974). *Families and family therapy*. Cambridge, MA: Harvard University Press.

Nakamoto, J., & Schwartz, D. (2010). Is peer victimization association with academic achievement? A meta-analytic review. *Social Development, 19*, 221–242. doi:10.1111/j.1467-9507.2009.00539.x

Nielsen, M. B., Matthiesen, S. B., & Einarsen, S. (2010), The impact of methodological moderators on prevalence rates of workplace bullying. A meta-analysis. *Journal of Occupational and Organizational Psychology, 83*, 955–979. doi:10.1348/096317909X481256

Partnership for 21st Century Skills. (2008). *21st Century Skills, Education & Competitiveness*. Tucson, AZ: Author. Retrieved from: http://www.p21.org/storage /documents/21st_century_skills_education_and_competitiveness_guide.pdf

Perna, L., Rowan-Kenyon, H., Thomas, S., Bell, A., Anderson, R., & Chunyan, L. (2008). The role of college counseling in shaping college opportunity: Variations across high schools. *Review of Higher Education, 31*(2), 131–159.

Perry, J. C., Liu, Z., & Pabian, Y. (2010). School engagement as a mediator of academic performance among urban youth: Parental career support and teacher support. *Counseling Psychologist, 38*, 269–295. doi:10.1177/0011000009349272

Rhoades, L., & Eisenberger, R. (2002). Perceived organizational support: A review of the literature. *Journal of Applied Psychology, 8*, 698–714. doi:10.1037/0021 -9010.87.4.698

Richardson, M. S. (1993). Work in people's lives: A location for counseling psychologists. *Journal of Counseling Psychology, 40*, 425–433. doi:10.1037/0022-0167.40.4.425

Richardson, M. S. (2012). Counseling for work and relationship. *Counseling Psychologist, 40*, 190–242. doi:10.1177/0011000011406452

Rivera, L. M., & Schaefer, M. B. (2009). The Career Institute: A collaborative career development program for traditionally underserved secondary (6–12) school students. *Journal of Career Development, 35,* 406–426. doi:10.1177/0894845308327737

Rodríguez-Muñoz, A., Moreno-Jiménez, B., Sanz Vergel, A. I., & Garrosa Hernández, E. (2010). Post-traumatic symptoms among victims of workplace bullying: Exploring gender differences and shattered assumptions. *Journal of Applied Social Psychology, 40,* 2616–2635. doi:10.1111/j.1559-1816.2010.00673.x

Roe, A. (1957). Early determinants of vocational choice. *Journal of Counseling Psychology, 4,* 212–217.

Sanchez, B., Esparza, P., & Colon, Y. (2008). Natural mentoring under the microscope: An investigation of mentoring relationships and Latino adolescents' academic performance. *Journal of Community Psychology, 36,* 468–482. doi:2008–05377-00510.1002/jcop.20250

Savickas, M. (2005). The theory and practice of career construction. In S. Brown & R. Lent (Eds.), *Career development and counseling: Putting theory and research to work* (pp. 42–70). Hoboken, NJ: Wiley.

Savickas, M. L., Nota, L., Rossier, J., Dauwalder, J. P., Duarte, M. E., Guichard, J., & Vianen, van A. E. M. (2009). Life designing: A paradigm for career construction in the 21st century. *Journal of Vocational Behavior, 75,* 239–250. doi:10.1016/j.jvb.2009.04.0042009-13571-001

Schultheiss, D. (2003). A relational approach to career counseling: Theoretical integration and practical application. *Journal of Counseling and Development, 81,* 301–310.

Schultheiss, D. E. P. (2006). The interface of work and family life. *Professional Psychology: Research and Practice, 37,* 334–341. doi:2006-09259-00210.1037/0735-7028.37.4.334

Schultheiss, D. E. P. (2009). To mother or matter: Can women do both? *Journal of Career Development, 36,* 25–47. doi:10.1177/08948453093407952009-12455-003

Schultheiss, D. E. P., Kress, H. M., Manzi, A. J., & Glasscock, J. M. (2001). Relational influences in career development: A qualitative inquiry. *Counseling Psychologist, 29,* 214–239. doi:2001-00036-002

Schultheiss, D. E. P., Palma, T., & Manzi, A. (2005). Career development in middle childhood: A qualitative inquiry. *Career Development Quarterly, 53,* 246–262. doi:2005-02922-005

Sue, D. W., Capodilupo, C. M., Torino, G., Bucceri, J. M., Holder, A. Nadal, K., & Esquilin, M. (2007). Racial microaggressions in everyday life: Implications for clinical practice. *American Psychologist, 62,* 271–286. doi:10.1037/0003-066X.62.4.271

Super, D. E. (1957). *The psychology of careers.* New York, NY: Harper & Row.

Super, D. E. (1980). A life-span, life-space, approach to career development. *Journal of Vocational Behavior, 13,* 282–298.

Thompson, R., & Whimper, L. A. (2010). Exposure to family violence and reading level of early adolescents. *Journal of Aggression, Maltreatment, & Trauma, 19,* 721–733. doi:10.1080/10926771003781347

Tierney, W. G., & Auerbach, S. (2005). Toward developing an untapped resource: The role of families in college preparation. In W. G. Tierney, Z. Corwin, & J. E. Colyar (Eds.), *Preparing for college: Nine elements of effective outreach* (pp. 29–48). Albany: State University of New York Press.

Tyson, K., Darity, W., & Castellino, D. (2005). It's not a "Black thing": Understanding the burden of acting White and other dilemmas of high achievement. *American Sociological Review, 70*, 582–605. doi:10.1177/0003122405070004031

United States Department of Justice. (2011). *Criminal victimization 2010.* Washington, DC: Author.

van Steenbergen, E. F., Ellemers, N., & Mooijaart, A. (2007). How work and family can facilitate each other: Distinct types of work–family facilitation and outcomes for women and men. *Journal of Occupational Health Psychology, 12*, 279–300. doi:10.1037/1076-8998.12.3.279

Vera, E. M., Caldwell, J., Clarke, M., Gonzales, R., Morgan, M., & West, M. (2007). The Choices program: Multisystemic interventions for enhancing the personal and academic effectiveness of urban adolescents of color. *Counseling Psychologist, 35*, 779–796. doi:10.1177/0011000007304590

Vignoli, E., Croity-Belz, S., Chapeland, V., de Fillipis, A., & Garcia, M. (2005). Career exploration in adolescents: The role of anxiety, attachment, and parenting style. *Journal of Vocational Behavior, 67*, 153–168. doi:2005–11536-00310.1016/j.jvb.2004.08.006

Vondracek, F. W., Lerner, R. M., & Schulenberg, J. W. (1986). *Career development: A life-span developmental approach.* Hillsdale, NJ: Erlbaum.

Wartman, K. L., & Savage, M. (2008). *Parent involvement in higher education: The relationship among students, parents, and the institution.* San Francisco, CA: Jossey-Bass.

Wentzel, K. R., Battle, A., Russell, S. L., & Loony, L. B. (2010). Social supports from teachers and peers as predictors of academic and social motivation. *Contemporary Educational Psychology, 35*, 193–210. doi:10.1016/j.cedpsych.2010.03.002

Wright, S. L., & Perrone, K. M. (2008). The impact of attachment on career-related variables: A review of the literature and proposed theoretical framework to guide future research. *Journal of Career Development, 35*, 87–106. doi:2009–01080-00110.1177/0894845308325643

Zimmer-Gembeck, M. J., & Mortimer, J. T. (2006). Adolescent work, vocational development, and education. *Review of Educational Research, 76*, 537–566. doi:10.3102/00346543076004537

CHAPTER 13

The Career Development of Youth and Young Adults With Disabilities

ELLEN S. FABIAN AND ROXANNA PEBDANI

U NDERSTANDING THE CAREER development of youth and young adults with disabilities requires knowledge of both individual and environmental factors. One of the challenges of trying to conceptualize the impact of disability on career development is the enormous heterogeneity among individuals with disabilities, suggesting that no theory can be fully applicable or nonapplicable to this group (Szymanski, Enright, Hershenson, & Ettinger, 2010). As a result, disability is best viewed not as a static construct that has a similar effect on all individuals, but as a socially defined construct that can be a risk factor to the achievement of career and social participation (Pledger, 2003). From this perspective, one can understand that although the career development of individuals with disabilities follows the same processes and is impacted by the same factors as the career development of nondisabled individuals, having a disability exposes individuals to unique experiences that may influence their career development.

Despite decades of advances in special education and disability law and policy, the postschool outcomes for many youth with disabilities exiting from special education programs remain dismal and considerably below those of their peers without disabilities (Newman, Wagner, Cameto, & Knokey, 2009). This state of affairs not only limits opportunities to these youth but also guarantees that the financial and social costs of their unfulfilled potential will be ones that the entire country continues to pay for well into this century. For example, recent information from the Social Security Administration indicates that about 350,000 youth ages 18 to 25 are receiving disability-related social security income supports rather than working. This alone costs taxpayers more than $10 billion annually (Social Security Administration [SSA], 2011).

School reform initiatives popularized at the turn of the 20th century may have limited impact on the more than 2.2 million special education students in America today, less than 30% of whom earn a high school diploma (Wittenburg & Maag, 2002). In general, students who receive special education certificates are more likely to be unemployed, more likely to earn less money when they eventually secure work, and more likely to receive public assistance than they would if they had obtained a high school diploma (Newman et al., 2009).

Unfortunately, the bleak future encountered by these youth is not improved upon their entering adulthood. The economic and labor force achievements associated with working-age adults with disabilities significantly lags behind that of adults without disabilities in America. Recent data from the Bureau of Labor Statistics (2011) reports that 23% of youth with disabilities participated in the labor force compared to 35% of those without disabilities. As these youths age, the disparities increase. For example, 45% of young adults with disabilities ages 20 to 24 participate in the labor force compared to 72% of young adults without disabilities. In general, estimates are that 66% of the working-age population of individuals with disabilities are not participating in the labor force (U.S. BLS, 2011).

Finally, the National Longitudinal Transition Study (NLTS), the largest study of school-to-adult life transition of students leaving secondary special education programs, found that only 20% of these students achieved what they (i.e., the students themselves) considered successful adult adjustment by 5 years after graduation. Successful adult adjustment was defined as independent functioning in the following three domains: (1) employment, (2) residential, and (3) social activities (Wagner, Newman, Cameto, Garza, & Levine, 2005).

The barriers to work participation for youth and young adults with disabilities have been addressed by federal legislation, policy initiatives, and vocational program advances. Still, employment and educational data associated with this group suggest that they continue to fare worse than any other group in America. The purpose of this chapter is to review the context and issues confronted by youth and young adults with disabilities as they manage their careers and work lives. Specifically, we describe characteristics of the population, review significant legislative and policy issues that influence career and employment, summarize effective career programmatic interventions, and recommend best practices.

DEFINITIONS OF DISABILITY

According to the 2010 United States Census, approximately 49.7 million Americans report some type of disability. Recent data from the American Community Survey indicate that about 5.6% of youth ages 16 to 20 report having one or more disabilities (Erickson, Lee, & von Schrader, 2010). It requires little imagination to see the enormous heterogeneity of abilities, limitations, and experiences within this large group. There are multiple types of disabilities (e.g., spinal cord injuries, developmental disabilities, psychiatric disorders, sensory disorders, AIDS), all of which exist along a continuum of severity in terms of their impact on the functional capacities of the individual. In addition, myriad factors influence an individual's reaction to disability, including personality, age, intelligence, educational level, family factors, gender, and exposure to discrimination and prejudice (e.g., Lidal, Huynh, & Biering-Sørensen, 2007; Wewiorski & Fabian, 2004; Xu & Martz, 2010). All of these factors, in turn, influence careers and employment (Patterson, DeLa-Garza, & Scaller, 1997). Given these issues, it is clear that any definition of disability needs to be broad enough to encompass them and to take into account the interaction of the functional attributes of the disability with the environment.

Although there is no one accepted or universal definition of disability, today disability is understood as a multifaceted experience representing an interaction of the person and the environment. Older definitions of disability equated the idea of having an impairment or a pathology with having a handicap (Hahn, 1993). This medical model definition attributed the barriers that individuals with a disability encountered to the impairment or health condition, thus locating the "problem" within the individual. The medical model solution to vocational training was either to change the person, by ameliorating the condition to the extent possible, or, where not possible, to compensate for the disability by training the person to function in an alternative way.

Disability advocates in the 1960s argued against this medical model, proposing that disability could be understood as a barrier in the environment, not in the individual, and that removing obstacles meant modifying the physical and the social environment, not changing the person. The person-in-environment conception that has emerged today not only reflects federal definitions of disability but also provides a framework for rehabilitation and career interventions (Szymanski et al., 2010). Recently, definitions describing disability as a positive attribute have emerged (e.g., Davis, 2010). These new definitions challenge the idea that persons need to develop the skills and have opportunities to succeed *despite* their disability and present the perspective that persons can succeed with and because of their disability, if the social-political environment is changed.

Being aware of emerging disability definitions is important because they affect the attitudes and behaviors of both persons with disabilities and the professionals who provide services to them (Hershenson, 1992). Understanding the meaning of disability to the individual is crucial to understanding the impact of the disability on his or her career development (Beveridge, Craddock, Liesener, Stapleton, & Hershenson, 2002). Understanding how professionals define disability facilitates selection of interventions that do not unintentionally impede career and social participation outcomes of youth and young adults with disabilities.

Although there is consensus today regarding the multifaceted approach to understanding disability, there are still more than 20 different federal definitions of disability written into various laws (National Institute on Disability and Rehabilitation Research, 1995). The most relevant laws—those that would encompass the majority of youth and young adults—include special education, vocational rehabilitation, and the Americans With Disabilities Act.

The definition of disability within special education is codified in the Individuals With Disabilities Education Improvement Act of 2004 (IDEIA; PL 108–446). IDEIA defines a child with a disability as a child "with mental retardation, hearing impairments (including deafness), speech or language impairments, visual impairments (including blindness), serious emotional disturbance (hereinafter referred to as emotional disturbance), orthopedic impairments, autism, traumatic brain injury, other health impairments, or specific learning disabilities, and who, by reason thereof, needs special education and related services." The definition of disability under IDEIA does not presume that the nature or extent of the disability needs to interfere with functioning in a life domain, as stipulated in other laws, such as those that authorize adult services through the public vocational rehabilitation services program. This situation can create difficulties and confusion for many students as they leave school and come under the adult system of services.

The definition of disability in the federal vocational rehabilitation program (codified in the Workforce Investment Act of 1998) is a physical, mental, or emotional impairment that needs to present a "substantial impediment to employment." Similarly, the Americans With Disabilities Act (P.L. 101–336) definition of disability includes a physical, mental, or emotional impairment that substantially limits functioning in a major life activity, such as walking, learning, or working. Finally, disability is defined by the Social Security Administration as a physical or mental condition that is "marked and severe" and that can be expected to last not less than 12 months or that may result in death. Although the Social Security Administration does not provide services, it does provide income to some 13 million beneficiaries under its disability income support programs (SSA, 2011).

To an extent, the various definitions of disability have created confusion for people with disabilities and their families. For example, as of 2009, about 6.6 million children met the special education definition of disability, with the largest disability category being learning disability (about 39%) (National Center for Educational Statistics, 2009). However, not all of these children meet the vocational rehabilitation definition of disability, a status that limits their eligibility for certain types of services. This situation has created an "aging out" phenomenon for youth with disabilities who graduate or leave secondary schools (where they have qualified for special services) and then enter an adult system where their condition no longer meets more stringent criteria (Certo et al., 2003).

The person-in-environment approach, as reflected in some federal definitions, has important implications for career planning and vocational interventions. First, it is equally important for counselors to have knowledge of working and work environments as it is to have knowledge about specific disabilities. This means that counselors must pay attention to how the physical and attitudinal environment creates career barriers for persons with disabilities. Second, it provides a foundation for understanding that an impairment (and the symptoms associated with it) is less relevant to vocational planning than is the functional manifestations of the impairment in a specific environmental context. For example, the fact that an individual has schizophrenia with its characteristic symptoms is less important than how these symptoms are functionally relevant (such as attenuated concentration) in a particular job context. Functional definitions of impairments enable counselors and clients to develop strategies that reduce their effect on performance. Third, this approach emphasizes the importance of counselor knowledge regarding disability law and policy issues to effectively assist youth and young adults in preparing for and securing jobs.

BARRIERS TO WORK

In American culture, work is understood to encompass both a sense of identity and the primary means of attaining the economic and social benefits that contribute to overall quality of life. Because of this, employment has traditionally been among the most critical measures of the status and progress of various groups in American society, including, for example, women, ethnic minorities, and people with disabilities. It has also provided a general yardstick against which the quality of various systems, whether educational, vocational, or social in nature, has been measured.

For people with disabilities in America, employment has long represented a significant challenge to full participation in society. For example, national polls of individuals with disabilities consistently find that even though two-thirds of working-age people with disabilities are not employed, most want to work (Houtenville, 2000). Interestingly, these discrepancies in employment participation tend to persist through economic cycles; in other words, whether the rest of the economy is doing well or poorly, unemployment among people with disabilities remains stuck at 30% to 40% (Bjelland, Burkhauser, von Schrader, & Houtenville, 2010). This suggests a complex array of factors, both intrinsic and extrinsic, contributing to this generally bleak picture. It is important for career counselors to be familiar with the common obstacles to employment; those that have received the most attention in the literature are described here.

FEDERAL POLICY REGARDING DISABILITY BENEFITS AND ACCESS TO HEALTH INSURANCE

People with disabilities who qualify for income support programs through the Social Security Administration (about 13 million) may be discouraged from considering employment because they fear loss of benefits, particularly health insurance (Orszag, 2010, December 9). This issue has been cited as one of the most severe in terms of discouraging people with disabilities to return to work or to leave benefits rolls and enter employment.

EMPLOYER ATTITUDES AND DISCRIMINATION

Despite the more positive media depiction of individuals with disabilities, and despite legislative advances such as the Americans With Disabilities Act, there have been only modest improvements noted in the attitudes and practices of employers (Dozmal, Houtenville, & Sharma, 2008; Hernandez, Keys, & Balcazar, 2000). This is a particularly salient barrier for individuals with certain highly stigmatized conditions, such as emotional and mental disabilities, as well as chronic diseases such as AIDS. Negative employment attitudes influence hiring, tenure, and promotion for persons with disabilities (Dozmal et al., 2008). More important, negative social attitudes, or stigma, may affect vocational identity development for youth, thus interfering with several important career processes described later.

LACK OF ADEQUATE PREPARATION FOR THE WORKPLACE

The majority of young people with disabilities continue to lag behind their peers in postsecondary school training and education (Loprest & Maag,

2007). Young people with severe disabilities, such as mental and emotional disabilities, or multiple ones tend to receive inadequate preparation for jobs and/or leave school prior to attaining employment. Inadequate preparation also affects persons with mild disabilities. For example, the results of several studies on the career and employment outcomes of adolescents with disabilities found that they experienced (a) limitations in early career exploratory experiences, (b) limited opportunities to develop decision-making abilities, and (c) poorer vocational well-being (Loprest & Maag, 2007; Moore, Konrad, Yang, Ng, & Doherty, 2011).

PROFESSIONAL ATTITUDES TOWARD EMPLOYMENT

People with disabilities who need services the most are frequently the least likely to be served because of the perceived difficulties in providing these services, as well as the intensity and duration of services required (Certo et al., 2003; Wehman, Brooke, & Revell, 2007). Moreover, people with severe disabilities are often not provided with career or vocational choices; instead, they are frequently "placed" in entry-level jobs that they leave because of lack of interest and choice in the matter (Fabian, 1999). What Szymanski and Trueba (1994) wrote nearly two decades ago still applies to individuals with significant disabilities: "at least some of the difficulties faced by persons with disabilities are not the result of functional impairments, but rather are the result of a castification process embedded in societal institutions for rehabilitation and education and enforced by well-meaning professionals" (p. 195).

LEGISLATION AND DISABILITY

A long federal tradition of laws has provided access to educational and vocational opportunities for people with disabilities. Knowledge of federal legislation that affects disability benefits and services is a critical matter for those who provide career services to people with disabilities. This section describes the major disability-related legislation with particular relevance to practice and to the specific barriers to employment described earlier.

Vocational and career-related support for people with disabilities in the United States has grown over the past century, partly as a result of federal legislation. In the early 20th century, services for people with disabilities were few and far between. In the early 1900s, vocational programs became more common, and in 1918 the Soldiers Rehabilitation Act provided services for veterans with disabilities, which were then extended to the civilian population in 1920. Still, it was not until the mid-1950s that funding for vocational services for civilians was increased. The Vocational Rehabilitation

Amendments of 1954 expanded the types of services that could be offered with federal funds and also authorized funding for rehabilitation counselor graduate programs to increase the numbers and quality of counselors staffing these programs. However, it was not until the Education of All Handicapped Children Act in 1976 that children with disabilities were guaranteed a free and appropriate public education.

More recently, a number of laws have been passed improving workplace access for people with disabilities. These laws include the Individuals With Disabilities Education Act, the Americans With Disabilities Act, the Ticket to Work Incentives Improvement Act, and the Workforce Investment Act of 1998. These laws are reviewed in this section.

The Individuals With Disabilities Education Improvement Act (IDEIA; PL 101–476)

The IDEIA established specific federal regulations for youth with disabilities who are transitioning from school to adult life. Although special education legislation has existed since the landmark 1976 Education of All Handicapped Children (EAHC) Act, it was not until this act was amended in 1990, 1997, and 2004 and renamed the Individuals With Disabilities Education Act that it addressed the issue of special education youth as they prepare to leave secondary school for adult life. Prior to this, the act referred mainly to the rights of children with disabilities to a "free and appropriate public education." In 1990, when the act was renamed, it required that students with disabilities include transition planning in their individualized education programs (IEPs). Another important policy shift in this law was to mandate that children with disabilities be educated in the "least restricted environment," a policy shift that had significant implications for school-based inclusion in both academic and career settings. The most recent amendments to IDEIA, passed in 2004, created the new name, The Individuals With Disabilities Education Improvement Act (IDEIA), and mandated collaborative transition planning to ensure a seamless exit from high school to college or careers. The transition objectives covered under IDEIA included (a) postsecondary education and vocational training, (b) employment, (c) independent living, and (d) social and community participation.

IDEIA has spawned considerable federal investment in devising more effective vocational interventions for special education youth who exit or graduate from high school (Sitlington, Neubert, & Clark, 2010). That these programs are achieving some measure of success is reflected in some of the positive indicators that are attributed to them. For example, according to the 2004 *Digest of Education Statistics*, 11% of college students reported having some type of disability (Horn & Nevill, 2006), a considerable increase over enrollment figures in the 1990s. However, as discussed earlier in the chapter, youth receiving special education services (particularly minority youth) still lag considerably behind their nondisabled peers on most postschool outcomes (Fabian, 2007; National Council on Disability [NCD], 2007). It is clear that despite some progress, IDEIA and its mandates have still not significantly improved the overall integration of youth with disabilities into adult life. Several of the persisting barriers to inclusion have been discussed earlier in the chapter, and some are described in later sections on career counseling and development approaches.

THE AMERICANS WITH DISABILITIES ACT (ADA; PL 101–336)

The ADA, enacted in 1990, represented a major shift in disability policy in America (Miller, 2000). Its provisions prohibit discrimination against people with disabilities in all facets of life: employment, public services, private businesses, telecommunications, and transportation. For career and employment-related counselors, the major interest is in two key areas of the ADA: Title I, which covers employment, and the definition of the protected individual (i.e., *who* is an individual with a disability).

The latter definitional issue has received a great deal of attention in policy and legal circles since the act first passed. The ADA defines disability as a "physical, mental or emotional impairment" that substantially limits functioning in a major life activity. Major life activities are defined broadly and include walking, speaking, breathing, seeing, learning, caring for self, and working, among others. Over the years, the courts increasingly limited the definition of disability under the act, determining that a disability is no longer covered when it can be mitigated by devices or equipment (such as eyeglasses) or medication (such as antidepressants) (NCD, 2003). Although such a change may seem minor, it had major implications for employees, who, for example, may have a psychiatric condition that is controlled by medication but still would benefit from accommodations in the workplace that would otherwise be offered under the protections of the act. In response to this narrowing definition of disability, the Americans With Disabilities Act was amended by the ADA Amendments Act of 2009, in part to address some of the legal issues arising from the narrowed definition of who is protected under the act.

Another key area under the employment provisions of Title I is the requirement for employers to provide reasonable accommodations. The law states that employers must provide "reasonable accommodations" that would enable a qualified individual with a disability to perform the essential functions of a job. What is important here is the legal word *qualified*, meaning that an applicant or employee must have the requisite background, credentials, education, or experience to perform the essential functions of the job with or without an accommodation. Thus, a clerical employee who demonstrates requisite typing speed and accuracy and who uses a wheelchair might need a computer keyboard hand rest that would allow him or her to type more easily. Typically, reasonable accommodations are modifications to the physical space, equipment, workplace procedures, policies, or practices. When effective, reasonable accommodations have been found to improve the job satisfaction, retention, and productivity of people with disabilities (MacDonald-Wilson, Fabian, & Dong, 2008). However, requesting a reasonable accommodation requires the applicant or employee with a disability to disclose their condition to the employer. Many individuals with nonobvious disability conditions (e.g., HIV/AIDS, psychiatric illnesses) may fail to invoke this right because of a fear of evoking negative stereotypes.

TICKET TO WORK AND WORK INCENTIVES IMPROVEMENT ACT (TWIIA; PL 106–170)

In 1999, Congress enacted the Ticket to Work and Work Incentives Improvement Act as a means of addressing conflicting federal policies that acted as barriers in the decision to either enter or return to work for people with disabilities who are beneficiaries of one of the Social Security Administration's income transfer programs (Social Security Disability Insurance or Supplemental Security Income). The act was designed to extend the health care coverage (Medicare or Medicaid) that SSA beneficiaries are entitled to even after they make a decision to enter or return to work. The "ticket" portion of the act gives the individual with a disability the choice of vocational service providers by allowing them to "purchase" these services from eligible providers. This approach was viewed as one way to motivate beneficiaries in the decision to enter or return to work. Although the voucher system represents a sweeping policy shift in vocational service provision, the Ticket to Work has been severely underused since it was enacted. For example, as of 2011, only 3% of eligible beneficiaries were using their ticket to purchase vocational services (SSA, 2011). Explanations for this severe underuse have to do with systems barriers (there are not enough eligible vocational providers), the complexity of the federal law and policies (individuals still fear losing their benefits), and insufficient attention to the meaning of work and vocational choices for people with disabilities (a topic addressed later in this chapter).

WORKFORCE INVESTMENT ACT (WIA; PL 105–220)

The Workforce Investment Act (WIA) of 1998 was enacted to consolidate and improve employment, training, literacy, and vocational rehabilitation programs for people with disabilities. Under this act, states are required to write workforce development plans that specifically address how they will meet the vocational and employment-related needs of diverse populations requiring services, including transitioning youth, adults with disabilities, unemployed and underemployed workers, and various other constituents with poor employment histories and high unmet needs. Although states vary in how they implement the WIA, most have established One Stop Career Centers, where people who require various services to support employment, such as vocational rehabilitation, counseling, or employment training, can access them in one setting (Gervey, Gao, Tillman, Dickel, & Kneubuehl, 2009).

Title IV of the WIA covers the reauthorization of the Rehabilitation Act of 1973. Important provisions have implications for career planning for persons with disabilities. For example, self-determination and vocational choice have been mandated within the act, insofar as its provisions apply to the state-federal system of vocational rehabilitation services. This aspect of the act reflects the changes in laws over the past several decades that have emphasized equitable treatment for individuals with disabilities across educational and work settings.

As is evident, there is a long and complicated history of efforts on the part of the federal government to offer vocational services and improve employment outcomes for people with disabilities. Overall, the effect of this legislation has probably had more to do with improving social attitudes, community access, and participation of people with disabilities than it has improved employment outcomes. Although there are a number of complex reasons for the persisting poor employment rates for youth and young adults with disabilities, one underlying issue may be improving career and vocational interventions.

CAREER DEVELOPMENT FOR INDIVIDUALS WITH DISABILITIES

Before describing career theories and interventions that may be relevant to improving employment outcomes for youth and young adults with disabilities, it is important to establish the context for career development for these persons. Career counseling and career development are actually relatively new concepts in disability studies, even though vocational rehabilitation programs specifically designed to assist with job finding have existed for about a century. Historically, conceptions of disability that focused on individual deficits tended to severely limit, if not disregard, career choice activities; they simply emphasized getting a job, any job. Despite numerous studies supporting the benefits of paid employment for people with disabilities (Dunn, Wewiorski, & Rogers, 2008; Provencher, Gregg, Mead, & Meuser, 2002), there have been too few efforts to develop theoretically based and empirically supported interventions for youth and young adults with disabilities (Hershenson, 2005; Szymanski et al., 2010). This section reviews some of the widely used theories of career development, including some that have not been specifically applied to people with disabilities but that might have some relevance in addressing their unique needs. Specifically, we review (a) trait and factor theories, (b) social cognitive and learning theories, and (c) developmental approaches.

TRAIT AND FACTOR THEORIES

Early vocational rehabilitation approaches to career development relied heavily on two approaches: (1) trait-factor theories and (2) theories of work adjustment. The trait and factor or matching approaches (Parsons, 1909) used in rehabilitation settings emphasized assessing an individual's traits (e.g., intelligence), academic or occupational skills, and physical-neurological capacities (e.g., communication, self-care) in order to predict or match people to occupations or jobs. During the first part of the 20th century (the growth and expansion years of vocational rehabilitation services in the United States), people with disabilities were sometimes matched to jobs based on their skills, but also their impairments. Hence, people who were deaf were referred to positions in production departments of publishing companies, where the excessive noise of printing presses were presumed not to be a barrier to work. While matching people to jobs based on impairments is not advocated today, the trait and factor approach to career counseling is still the most widely used in vocational rehabilitation service delivery (Szymanski et al., 2010), despite problems such as questions about the validity of various assessment tools, the inattention to career choice, and the focus on the individual rather than the environment.

The Minnesota theory of work adjustment (Lofquist & Dawis, 1969; see Swanson & Schneider, Chapter 2, this volume) and Hershenson's (1981) theory are trait and factor or person-environment fit approaches that have been used widely with individuals with later-onset disabilities. The unique aspect of these theories is that they were developed to understand work choice and retention issues for people with disabilities and to suggest applications to practice. Despite the early attention to work adjustment theory in the rehabilitation literature, there are few contemporary examples of their applicability, particularly in relation to youth and young adults (Szymanski et al., 2010).

SOCIAL LEARNING AND COGNITIVE THEORIES

Both social cognitive career theory (SCCT; see Lent, Chapter 5, this volume) and self-determination theory have garnered significant contemporary attention as promising approaches to improving employment outcomes for youth and young adults with disabilities.

SCCT. Interest in self-efficacy as a potentially useful construct in explaining career behavior emerges from studies that have examined this construct in other special populations, such as women (Hackett & Betz, 1981) and racial-ethnic minorities (Hackett & Byars, 1996). In the disability literature, self-efficacy has also been studied as a predictor of work status among samples of individuals with a variety of impairments. For example, several authors have examined the relation of self-efficacy beliefs to career interests and behavior of students with learning and emotional disabilities, suggesting that not only do such students have lower efficacy beliefs than their nondisabled peers (Ochs & Roessler, 2001; Slemon & Shafir, 1997) but also that self-efficacy beliefs play an important role in understanding their career choice and interests.

Paganos and DuBois (1999) investigated the relationship between self-efficacy beliefs and career interests in high school students with learning disabilities and found that self-efficacy was the strongest contributor to career interests for these students, beyond the contribution of outcome expectancies. Similarly, Ochs and Roessler (2001) found significantly lower career self-efficacy beliefs among high school students with learning disabilities than among their nondisabled peers. In a study of students with serious emotional disturbance, Willis (2002) found work self-efficacy beliefs to be a significant predictor of postschool employment.

Studies have also examined the utility of social cognitive predictors of employment outcomes for other disabled groups. For example, Regenold, Sherman, and Fenzel (1999) found that higher work self-efficacy beliefs predicted employment status for a sample of individuals with psychiatric disorders. In another study of predictors of vocational outcome among adults with psychiatric disorders, Mowbray, Bybee, Harris, and McCrohan (1995) found that positive outcome expectations regarding return to work were predictive of work status. Altmaier, Russell, Kao, Lehmann, and Weinstein (1993) found confidence in the ability to perform various activities of daily living were related to positive rehabilitation outcomes for clients with low back pain. Barlow, Wright, and Cullen (2002) found that higher job-seeking self-efficacy beliefs were associated with the ability to manage disability issues during job interviews among a heterogeneous group of people with disabilities. Finally, Hutton (2006) found that work-related self-efficacy was positively related to individuals with arthritis requesting job accommodations.

Several studies have also been designed to enhance self-efficacy beliefs (Strauser, Lustig, & Ciftci, 2008). Conyers and Szymanski (1998) found that a brief career intervention was effective in improving career self-efficacy for college students with and without disabilities. Enright (1997) evaluated a short-term career intervention designed to improve career decision-making self-efficacy and self-esteem among a heterogeneous group of adults with disabilities. Although the experimental group did not gain higher levels of career decision-making self-efficacy, they did show an increase in life decision-making self-efficacy. Finally, Fabian, Beveridge, and Ethridge (2009) found that the SCCT construct of career barriers was applicable to a sample of clients in a state vocational rehabilitation system; they also found that personal and social support factors potentially mitigated the influence of these barriers on clients' intentions to work.

Self-determination theory. Self-determination has been a guiding principle or philosophy in the delivery of vocational and rehabilitation services to people with significant disabilities since the early 1970s (Nirje, 1980). Although initially self-determination for people with disabilities was defined more as a philosophy or policy, later efforts have sought to define the theory and its constructs to develop appropriate interventions. Philosophically, self-determination refers to the rights of people with disabilities to exercise choice. Conceptually, self-determination is a theory of motivation that "highlights the importance of three fundamental psychological needs—autonomy, competence, and relatedness" (Guay, Senecal, Gauthier, & Fernet, 2003, p. 165).

In special education and rehabilitation, self-determination has been broadly defined as the combination of skills, knowledge, and beliefs that enable a person to engage in goal-directed, self-regulated, and autonomous behavior (Algozinne, Browder, Karvonen, Test, & Wood, 2001). This broad definition has led to a lack of consistency in efforts to apply SDT to the career-related needs of people with disabilities. Algozzine and colleagues noted this difficulty in their meta-analysis of the effect of self-determination skills training on academic and career-related outcomes for people with disabilities. They concluded that studies defined and operationalized self-determination variously as informed choice, decision-making skills, and self-advocacy skills, among others. For example, Wehmeyer and Kelchner (1995) developed an instrument, the ARC Self-Determination Scale, to measure what they referred to as "functional" self-determination, which included such diverse elements as problem solving, decision making, planning, self-advocacy, self-efficacy, and outcome expectations.

Wehmeyer and Schwartz (1998) found that higher levels of self-determination related to better jobs and longer job retention for a sample of young adults with intellectual disabilities, a finding replicated in a follow-up study (Wehmeyer & Palmer, 2003). Benitez, Lattimore, and Weymeyer (2005) used a case study design to evaluate the effects of a self-determination career development model on involvement of students with emotional and behavioral disorders in vocational planning. Wehmeyer and colleagues (2009) developed a career intervention model to improve career planning and decision making for young women with intellectual disabilities.

DEVELOPMENTAL THEORIES

Two developmental theories that are particularly applicable to people with disabilities include Super's (1990) life-span, life-space theory (see Hartung, Chapter 4, this volume) and Gottfredson's (2005) theory of circumscription and compromise.

Super's theory. Career maturity, a construct emerging from Super's career development theory (Super, Savickas, & Super, 1996) has been studied in the disability literature. In this research, the timing of the disability during a person's career development is important to consider, and three subgroups of persons with disabilities have been identified and hypothesized to undergo different career development processes: those with precareer-onset disabilities, those with midcareer-onset disabilities, and those with progressive or episodic disabilities (Beveridge et al., 2002).

Persons with precareer disabilities progress through their career develop-ment with a disability. Research on the lack of workplace preparation for persons with disabilities (especially those with developmental and learning disabilities) is most applicable to this group. Individuals with midcareer disabilities acquire or are diagnosed with a disability at some point during their career development. According to Hershenson (1996), if the impair-ments (perceived or actual) associated with the disability affect the person's work competencies, they will result in subsequent changes in their work personality and work goals. Super (1990) referred to this as a "minicycle," involving the recycling of new growth, exploration, and establishment tasks. Depending on the age of initial onset or diagnosis, the effects of progressive or episodic disabilities can be similar to those of precareer or midcareer dis-abilities. An important difference is that each significant functional change in an individual's disability has the potential to have a similar effect to that of acquiring a midcareer disability, as well as a potential cumulative effect. It is necessary to understand the effect of each episode or change in functional abilities on the individual's attitudes about both work and disability.

Several studies have suggested that individuals with disabilities manifest lower levels of career maturity than their nondisabled peers (e.g., Hitchings, Luzzo, Retish, Horvath, & Ristow, 1998). Mori (1982) found that special education students were significantly less knowledgeable about job duties than were general education students. Rojewski (1993) found that learning-disabled high school students scored lower in career maturity than did their nondisabled peers. Ochs and Roessler (2001) similarly found lower levels of career maturity and career information among disabled high school students. Although the number of studies exploring career maturity and other developmental constructs among youth and young adults with disabilities is small, there is empirical support for its utility in the disability context (Lindstrom & Benz, 2002). For example, the sequence of developmental tasks and stages is applicable to understanding and promoting career progression of those with congenital disabilities. In addition, as Szymanski and colleagues (2010) explain, developmental constructs can be useful for exploring and intervening when certain types of traumatic disabilities may create "career regression," that is, when the extent of the impairments requires reconsideration of career goals.

Gottfredson's theory of circumscription and compromise. Children with early-onset or congenital impairments often lack exposure to or participation in early career activities (such as role-playing or fantasies) due to poor educational settings, parental overprotection, and social stigmatization (Cohen, Nabors, & Pierce, 1993; Fleitas, 2000; Macharey & von Suchodoletz, 2008). According to Gottfredson's theory (2005), lack of participation or exposure to age-appropriate career activities puts children at risk for restrictions in later career or vocational options or prematurely ruling out career possibilities. This hypothesis may help explain, for example, why youth with disabilities frequently exit high school lacking a career goal (Fabian, 2007) or even perceiving the possibility of a vocational future. Studies have shown that even when children with early-onset disabilities are mainstreamed into regular academic settings, social isolation and stigmatization can limit their active participation in meaningful career and academic development activities (Loprest & Maag, 2007).

Moreover, Gottfredson (2005) suggests that individual developmental processes, such as cognitive ability, are important considerations in deciding whether children are "ready" for and can benefit from career activities. For example, she posits that the way career information is presented (in terms of complexity and comprehensibility) to school-age children will be differentially useful, depending on a child's cognitive development stage. Thus, the fact that children with early-onset disabilities may be socially or cognitively prevented from benefiting from school-based career activities may restrict their exploration, increase the likelihood that they will prematurely foreclose on career possibilities, and interfere with goal setting and achievement. One recent study of the vocational well-being of adults who had early-onset or congenital disabilities found that they expressed lower overall well-being and more employment discrimination than those with later-onset disabilities (Moore et al., 2011). Gottfredson's theory, although not widely used in the disability career-related literature, may shed some light on the persistently poor postschool employment outcomes for youth with disabilities.

IMPLICATIONS FOR CAREER COUNSELING

Traditional career counseling approaches for individuals with disabilities have relied on trait and factor approaches, where the emphasis was on matching capacities to job demands. Although there is nothing inherently wrong with this approach, the manner in which practices evolved proved problematic in terms of assisting individuals with disabilities to secure jobs based on choice. One problem is that vocational evaluations tended to emphasize deficits, which can severely constrain choice. Second, even within a "strengths-based" assessment approach, various problems have been noted in the application of standardized tests and instruments for people with disabilities (Parker & Schaller, 2003), raising questions about their predictive usefulness with several disabled populations. Specific problems include nonrepresentative norms, inexperienced test takers, inappropriate and/or inadequate modifications to standardization protocols, and poorly trained examiners (Parker & Schaller, 2003).

Traditional career assessments have sometimes been modified by, for example, including informal interviews and observational techniques (Power, 2000), having family members or significant others participate in helping the individual identify interests and skills (Hagner & DiLeo, 1993), and relying more on contextual assessment methods, where observations and ratings occur in a specific environmental context. In this manner, career assessment can become an intervention, particularly from a "strengths-based" perspective, that helps motivate the individual toward an employment orientation.

Another type of intervention that has received some attention is improving career- and work-related self-efficacy. In this regard, it is particularly important to note that individuals with disabilities tend to have lower efficacy beliefs and outcome expectations regarding career- and work-related factors than their nondisabled peers (e.g., Szymanski et al., 2010). This finding is not surprising, as they may have less exposure to the types of experiences and activities that contribute to building efficacy, such as volunteer and work experiences, exposure to role models, and reinforcing feedback (Benz & Halpern, 1993). In addressing these barriers, it is important to note that the studies that have used interventions to improve career self-efficacy beliefs have shown positive results in terms of mitigating the effects of negative feedback and/or environmental inadequacies that have limited vocational development (Conyers & Szymanski, 1998). For example, Breeding (2008) demonstrated that an expanded, collaborative career assessment approach in vocational rehabilitation settings improved career decision-making self-efficacy among a sample of disabled participants. Allaire, Niu, and LaValley (2005) explored the effects of a job retention intervention designed to improve participants' beliefs in their capacity to work. They found that those in the treatment group experienced almost a 50% reduction in job termination compared to the control group. This suggests that career counselors need to assess—either formally or informally—the work-related efficacy beliefs and outcome expectations of their clients with disabilities and be aware of how these beliefs may have compromised their interests, goals, and future expectations.

Direct interventions designed to bolster self-efficacy can be incorporated into career counseling programs using strategies that help clients anticipate and shape a vocational future (Fabian, 2000; Strauser et al., 2008). Counselors can ensure that clients are exposed to a diverse array of vocational options, as well as peers who have achieved success in different jobs and settings. More intensive coaching or support, both individually and in groups, may assist clients with disabilities to persist in achieving their goals. These types of interventions would apply to individuals in all stages of career development.

Because young adults with disabilities have been found to exhibit lower levels of career maturity than their peers, counselors may need to incorporate developmentally oriented strategies as much as possible into career education programs. For example, one of the strongest predictors of successful postsecondary adjustment for youth with disabilities is having a paid employment experience prior to leaving high school (Luecking & Fabian, 2000). Unlike their nondisabled counterparts, youth with disabilities may not have had the types of volunteer and entry-level job experiences (such as babysitting or delivering newspapers) that contribute to developing work attitudes and interests. Assisting high school students to acquire paid work experiences, similar to their nondisabled peers, promotes the development of a vocational self-concept, as these experiences provide opportunities for exploration, as well as personal feedback regarding vocational preferences and aptitudes. At the same time, paid work experiences set the stage for identifying longer-term career goals. These developmental issues are even more important for children with early-onset disabilities, whose social isolation and family overprotectiveness may impede their participation in career development tasks, such as role-playing and career fantasies. Such limited exposure constrains opportunities by prematurely foreclosing career options.

The purpose of career counseling activities is to assist the individual in identifying and pursuing career goals. The shift in disability policy from a deficit model to an empowerment model has also affected rehabilitation planning and goal setting by encouraging individuals to consider a wider array of vocational choices (Koscuilek, 1998). At the same time, the Americans With Disabilities Act improved opportunity structures for people with disabilities by reducing environmental barriers that may have circumscribed career goals. Reasonable accommodations that are mandated under the ADA enable individuals with disabilities to perform a much wider variety of jobs than were possible prior to its enactment, for example, allowing hearing-impaired young adults to have interpreters on the job or mobility-impaired individuals to request adaptive equipment. At the same time, technological advances have made many work settings and jobs more accessible to people with disabilities, for instance, e-mail communication as a means of accessibility for people who are deaf or hearing impaired and talking software for people who are blind.

As indicated earlier, motivation and outcome expectations are particularly important for individuals with disabilities, where a paucity of previous experience, lack of access to role models, and negative social attitudes may have severely impeded career decision making and goal setting. Self-determination training interventions designed to improve autonomy, decision making, and planning skills can contribute to identification and articulation of career goals. Encouraging a perspective on career goals and future planning may also involve career constructivist interventions that assist clients to view a career as an "unfolding story" (Krieshok, Hastings, Ebberwein, Wettersten, & Owen, 1999). Career narratives encourage clients to make meaning of their vocational selves as they work toward shaping a vocational future (see Savickas, Chapter 6, this volume). The potential value of constructivist counseling for this population is its focus on agency and control—helping the individual trace his or her past and narrate a future.

Another important task for counselors lies in helping clients clarify the meaning of work in their lives (Blustein, 2008). Particularly for people with disabilities who encounter significant policy, systemic, and attitudinal barriers to work, discovering reasons or motivators to work need to be considered in any career development plan. Counselors may need to alter their assumptions regarding work as a primary life activity to viewing work as an option that clients may or may not incorporate into their life planning, similar to the life stage considerations of parents taking time away from work to raise children or adult children reducing job or career commitments to care for aging parents.

For some people with disabilities, the need to move seamlessly in and out of the labor market, depending on health status and other issues, is more empowering than a one-size-fits-all approach to work (Baron & Salzer, 2002). Career counselors may need to regard long-term attachment to the labor market as a necessary and sufficient goal for many but not all individuals and encourage people to map a vocational future that allows for individual differences in the amount of energy expended toward work. This is a particularly important stance for young adults with remitting-relapsing disabilities (e.g., depression, diabetes, AIDS, multiple sclerosis). For example, a young woman who experiences severe depressive episodes who wants a career in health care administration may need to look at occupational alternatives that more easily accommodate rapid reentry to the job market if she requires time off. Even persons with stabler disabilities may need to reflect on the meaning and value of work in their lives, as well as prepare to cope with the types of barriers described earlier.

Generally speaking, career counseling tends to taper off when counselor and client have identified career goals and specific steps to achieve them. However, career counselors may need to be more actively engaged in the job search and adjustment process with individuals with disabilities, based on the issues raised earlier in the chapter, such as inadequate preparation for the job market, disability disclosure issues, negative social attitudes, and fear of loss of insurance benefits. In the rehabilitation field, job search and subsequent job placement have received a great deal of attention—much more than general career development or career counseling. As a result, there are a number of different approaches described in the literature for helping an individual to secure a job, including job-seeking skills groups (Azrin, Flores, & Kaplan, 1975), supported employment (Wehman, Revell, & Kregel, 1998), and marketing applicants to employers using job development methods (Gilbride, Stensrud, & Johnson, 1994).

The fundamental practices of all of these approaches are similar. They include careful preparation of individuals with disabilities for job interviews (including discussing legal rights and disclosure of disability), customizing jobs based on their essential tasks or demands, helping employers identify workplace accommodation solutions, and maintaining relationships to support work retention and career advancement (Hagner, 2003). Work retention or job support groups help employees manage possible negative attitudes, navigate the complex issues regarding Social Security benefits, and provide connections for future employment. Some of these services, such as job placement, postemployment support, or benefits counseling, may be provided through various federal and state groups, including the state's vocational rehabilitation agency, One Stop Career Centers, and Social Security Administration field offices. Career counselors may want to maintain linkages with all of these resources in their local communities.

A final thought regarding career counseling for individuals with disabilities is that taking disability into account is frequently not much different than considering other individual difference variables, such as race, sex, or age, in devising effective strategies. Mainstream career development theorists and practices have tended to ignore the application of concepts and services to people with disabilities, even as the research in applying these same constructs to other diverse groups continues to grow. Such theory extensions were also hampered by traditional practices in vocational rehabilitation that focused on individual impairments and deficits, rather than on the individual's functional attributes or the environment. As we continue to shift from a deficit to an empowerment model, it is expected that more attention will be directed toward understanding the career behavior of and career practices for individuals with disabilities. Additional research studies that can assist in extending career theories and practices to individuals with disabilities are clearly needed.

CONCLUSIONS

- View disability as a characteristic, not an essential personal attribute, that might need to be considered in understanding career issues and designing interventions. In other words, youth with disabilities are more similar to than different from their nondisabled peers. The differences are more likely shaped by background experiences and social or environmental issues than by individual impairment or health condition.
- It is primarily the differences, usually inequalities, arising from background experiences and social or environmental barriers that create the greatest need for career counseling and interventions. Make sure that career intervention approaches include strategies (from any theoretical approach) that address these social and environmental barriers.
- Understanding and encouraging young adults with disabilities to invoke their legal rights under the Americans With Disabilities Act is essential in the career counseling process. Assisting them considering the costs and benefits involved in disclosing disability in the workplace to invoke these rights promotes a proactive and timely approach to the identification and request of reasonable accommodations.
- Some particularly worthwhile approaches to improving career outcomes for youth with disabilities include focusing on social cognitive constructs, particularly interventions designed to boost varied aspects of career-related self-efficacy. Addressing the complex affective issues involved in career choice for youth with disabilities, such as adjustment to disability, and exploring how career choices are affected by negative social attitudes might be particularly amenable to developmental and constructivist career counseling approaches.

REFERENCES

Algozinne, B., Browder, D., Karvonen, M., Test, D. W., & Wood, W. M. (2001). Effects of interventions to promote self-determination for individuals with disabilities. *Review of Educational Research, 71*(2), 219–277.

Allaire, S. H., Niu, J., & LaValley, M. P. (2005). Employment and satisfaction outcomes from a job retention intervention delivered to persons with chronic diseases. *Rehabilitation Counseling Bulletin, 48*, 100–109.

Altmaier, E. M., Russell, D. W., Kao, C. F., Lehmann, T., & Weinstein (1993). The role of self-efficacy in rehabilitation outcome among chronic low back pain patients. *Journal of Counseling Psychology, 40*(3), 335–359.

Americans With Disabilities Act (ADA). 1990. U.S. Code. Vol. 42, secs 12101–213.

Americans With Disabilities Act Amendments Act (ADAAA) of 2008, Public Law 110–325, 42 U.S.C., 12101–12210.

Azrin, N., Flores, T., & Kaplan, S. (1975). Job finding club: A group-assisted program of obtaining employment. *Behavioral Research and Therapy, 13*(1), 17–27.

Barlow, J., Wright, C., & Cullen, L. (2002). A job-seeking self-efficacy scale for people with physical disabilities: Preliminary development and psychometric testing. *British Journal of Guidance & Counseling, 30*, 37–53.

Baron, R. C., & Salzer, M. S. (2002). Accounting for unemployment among people with mental illness. *Behavioral Sciences & the Law (20)*6, 585–599.

Benitez, D. T., Lattimore, J., & Weymeyer, M. (2005). Promoting the involvement of students with emotional/behavioral disorders in career and vocational planning and decision-making: The Self-Determined Career Development Model. *Behavioral Disorders, 30*(4), 431–447.

Benz, M. R., & Halpern, A. S. (1993). Vocational and transition services needed and received by students with disabilities during their last year of high school. *Career Development for Exceptional Individuals, 16*, 197–211.

Beveridge, S., Craddock, S., Liesener, J., Stapleton, M., & Hershenson, D. (2002). INCOME: A framework for conceptualizing the career development of persons with disabilities. *Rehabilitation Counseling Bulletin, 45*, 195–206.

Bjelland, M. J., Burkhauser, R. V., von Schrader, S., & Houtenville, A. J. (2010). *Progress report on the economic well-being of working age people with disabilities.* Rehabilitation Research and Training Center on Employment Policy for Persons With Disabilities, Employment & Disability Institute, Cornell University.

Blustein, D. L. (2008). The role of work in psychological health and well being: A conceptual, historical and public policy perspective. *American Psychologist, 63*, 228–240.

Breeding, R. R. (2008). The effect of work interest profiling on career decision self-efficacy and work locus of control. *Rehabilitation Counseling Bulletin, 51*(2), 96–106.

Certo, N. J., Mautz, D., Smalley, K., Wade, H. A., Luecking, R., Pumpian, I., Batterman, N., (2003). Review and discussion of a model for seamless transition to adulthood. *Education and Training in Developmental Disabilities, 38*(1), 3–17.

Cohen, R., Nabors, L. A., & Pierce, K. A. (1993). Preschooler's evaluations of physical disabilities: A consideration of attitudes and behavior. *Journal of Pediatric Psychology, 19*(1), 103–111.

Conyers, L., & Szymanski, E. M. (1998). The effectiveness of an integrated career intervention on college students with and without disabilities. *Journal of Postsecondary Education and Disability, 13*(1), 23–34.

Davis, L. (2010). The end of identity politics: On disability as an unstable category. In L. J. David (Ed.), *The disability studies reader* (pp. 301–315). New York, NY: Routledge.

Domzal, C., Houtenville, A., & Sharma, R. (2008). Survey of employer perspectives on employment of people with disabilities: Technical report. (Prepared under contract to the Office of Disability and Employment Policy, U.S. Department of Labor). McLean, VA: CESSI.

Dunn, E. C., Wewiorski, N. J., & Rogers, E. S. (2008). The meaning and importance of employment to people in recovery from serious mental illness: Results of a qualitative study. *Psychiatric Rehabilitation Journal 32*(1), 59–62.

Enright, M. S. (1997). The impact of short-term career development program on people with disabilities. *Rehabilitation Counseling Bulletin, 40,* 285–301.

Erickson, W., Lee, C., & von Schrader, S. (2010). *Disability statistics from the 2008 American Community Survey (ACS).* Ithaca, NY: Cornell University Rehabilitation Research Training Center on Disability Demographics and Statistics (STATSR-RTC).

Fabian, E. (1999). Re-thinking work: The example of consumers with serious mental health disorders. *Rehabilitation Counseling Bulletin, 42,* 302–316.

Fabian, E. (2000). Applying social cognitive career theory to individuals with psychiatric disorders. *Psychiatric Rehabilitation Journal, 23,* 262–269.

Fabian, E. S. (2007). Urban youth with disabilities: Factors affecting transition employment. *Rehabilitation Counseling Bulletin, 50*(3), 130–138.

Fabian, E. S., Beveridge, S., & Ethridge, G. (2009). Differences in perceptions of career barriers and supports for people with disabilities by demographic background and case status factors. *Journal of Rehabilitation 75*(1), 41–49.

Fleitas, J. (2000). Sticks, stones, and the stigmata of childhood illness and disability. *Reclaiming Children and Youth, 9*(3), 146–150.

Gervey, R., Gao, N., Tillman, D., Dickel, K., & Kneubuehl, J. (2009). Person-centered employment planning teams: A pilot study to enhance employment and training outcomes for persons with disabilities accessing the One-Stop. *Journal of Rehabilitation, 75*(2), 43–49.

Gilbride, D. D., Stensrud, R., & Johnson, M. (1994). Current models of job placement and employer development: Research, competencies and educational considerations. *Rehabilitation Education, 7,* 215–239.

Gottfredson, L. S. (2005). Applying Gottfredson's theory of circumscription and compromise in career guidance and counseling. In S. D. Brown & R. W. Lent (Eds.), *Career development and counseling* (pp. 71–100). Hoboken, NJ: Wiley.

Guay, F., Senecal, C., Gauthier, L., & Fernet, C. (2003). Predicting career indecision: A self-determination theory perspective. *Journal of Counseling Psychology, 50,* 165–177.

Hackett, G., & Betz, N. E. (1981). A self-efficacy approach to the career development of women. *Journal of Vocational Behavior, 18,* 326–339.

Hackett, G., & Byars, A. M. (1996). Social cognitive theory and the career development of African American women. *Career Development Quarterly, 44,* 322–340.

Hagner, D. (2003). Job development and job search assistance. In E. Szymanski & R. M. Parker (Eds.), *Work and disability: Issues and strategies in career development and job placement* (pp. 343–372). Austin, TX: PRO-ED.

Hagner, D., & DiLeo, D. (1993). *Working together: Workplace culture, supported employment, and persons with disabilities.* Cambridge, MA: Brookline.

Hahn, H. (1993). The political implications of disability definitions and data. *Journal of Disability Policy Studies, 4,* 41–52.

Hernandez, B., Keys, C., & Balcazar, F. (2000) Employer attitudes toward workers with disabilities and their ADA employment rights: A literature review. *Journal of Rehabilitation, 66*(4), 4–16.

Hershenson, D. B. (1981). Work adjustment, disability, and the three r's of vocational rehabilitation: A concept model. *Rehabilitation Counseling Bulletin, 25,* 91–97.

Hershenson, D. B. (1992). Conceptions of disability: Implications for rehabilitation. *Rehabilitation Counseling Bulletin, 35*(3), 154–160.

Hershenson, D. B. (1996). Work adjustment: A neglected area in career counseling. *Journal of Counseling & Development, 74,* 442–446.

Hershenson, D. B. (2005). INCOME: A culturally inclusive and disability-sensitive framework for organizing career development concepts and interventions. *Career Development Quarterly, 54,* 150–161.

Hitchings, W. E., Luzzo, D. A., Retish, P., Horvath, M., & Ristow, R. S. (1998). Identifying the career development needs of college students with disabilities. *Journal of College Student Development, 39*(1), 23–32.

Horn, L., & Nevill, S. (2006), *Profile of undergraduates in U.S. postsecondary education institutions: 2003–04: With a special analysis of community college students.* U.S. Department of Education. Washington, DC: National Center for Education Statistics.

Houtenville, A. (2000). *Economics of disability research report #2: Estimates of employment rates for persons with disabilities in the United States by state, 1980–1998.* Ithaca, NY: Research and Rehabilitation Training Center for Economic Research on Employment Policy for Persons with Disabilities, Cornell University.

Hutton, C. C. (2006). The role of work self-efficacy in sustaining employment among individuals with arthritis. *Dissertation Abstracts International: Section B: Sciences and Engineering, 67* 2B.

Individuals With Disabilities Education Act, 20 U.S.C. §1401 *et seq.*

Individuals With Disabilities Education Act Regulations, 34 C.F.R. §300 *et seq.*

Individuals With Disabilities Education Improvement Act of 2004 (IDEIA; PL 108–446).

Koscuilek, J. (1998). Empowering the life choices of people with disabilities through career counseling. In N. C. Gysbers, M. J. Heppner, & J. A. Johnson (Eds.), *Career counseling: Process, issues and techniques* (pp. 109–121). Needham Heights, MA: Allyn & Bacon.

Krieshok, T. S., Hastings, S., Ebberwein, C., Wettersten, K., & Owen, A. (1999). Telling a good story: Using narratives in vocational rehabilitation with veterans. *Career Development Quarterly, 46*(7), 204–214.

Lidal, I. B., Huynh, T. K., & Biering-Sørensen, F. (2007). Return to work following spinal cord injury: A review. *Disability and Rehabilitation 29*(17), 1341–1375.

Lindstrom, L. E., & Benz, M. R. (2002). Phases of career development: Case studies of young women with learning disabilities. *Exceptional Children, 69*(1), 67–83.

Lofquist, L. H., & Dawis, R. V. (1969). *Adjustment to work.* New York, NY: Appleton-Century-Crofts.

Loprest, P., & Maag, E. (2007). The relationship between early disability onset and education and employment. *Journal of Vocational Rehabilitation, 26*(1), 49–62.

Luecking, R., & Fabian, E. (2000). Paid internships and employment success for youth in transition. *Career Development for Exceptional Individuals, 23,* 205–221.

MacDonald-Wilson, K., Fabian, E., & Dong, S. (2008). Best practices in reasonable accommodations: Findings based on the research literature. *The Rehabilitation Professional,* 221–232.

Macharey, G., & von Suchodoletz, W. (2008). Perceived stigmatization of children with speech-language impairment and their parents. *Folia Phoniatricia et Logopaedica, 60,* 256–263.

Miller, P. S. (2000). The evolving ADA. In P. D. Blanck (Ed.), *Employment, disability, and the Americans With Disabilities Act* (pp. 3–18). Evanston, IL: Northwestern University Press.

Moore, M. E., Konrad, A. M., Yang, Y., Ng, E. S. W., & Doherty, A. (2011). The vocational well-being of workers with childhood onset of disability: Life satisfaction and perceived workplace discrimination. *Journal of Vocational Behavior, 79,* 681–698.

Mori, A. A. (1982). Career attitudes and job knowledge among junior high school regular, special, and academically talented students. *Career Development for Exceptional Individuals, 5,* 62–69.

Mowbray, C. T., Bybee, D., Harris, S. N., & McCrohan, N. (1995). Predictors of work status and future work orientation in people with psychiatric disability. *Psychiatric Rehabilitation Journal, 53,* 31–42.

National Center for Educational Statistics. (2009). Digest of Education Statistics: 2009. Retrieved from http://nces.ed.gov/programs/digest/d09/tables/dt09_050.asp?referrer=list.

National Council on Disability. (2003). The Americans With Disabilities Act policy brief: Righting the ADA. Retrieved from http://www.ncd.gov/publications.

National Council on Disability. (2007). *Empowerment for Americans with disabilities: Breaking barriers to careers and full employment*. Washington, DC: Author.

National Institute on Disability and Rehabilitation Research. (1995). *Federal statutory definitions of disability*. Falls Church, VA: Conwal. (ERIC Document Reproduction Service No. ED 427 472).

Newman, L., Wagner, M., Cameto, R., & Knokey, A. (2009). *The post high-school outcomes of youth with disabilities up to 4 years after high school. A report from the National Longitudinal Transition Study-2 (NTLS-2)*. Menlo Park, CA: SRI International.

Nirje, B. (1980). The normalization principle. In R. J. Flynn & K. E. Nitsch (Eds.), *Normalization, social integration and community services* (pp. 31–49). Baltimore, MD: University Park Press.

Ochs, L. A., & Roessler, R. T. (2001). Students with disabilities: How ready are they for the 21st century? *Rehabilitation Counseling Bulletin, 44*, 170–176.

Orszag, P. (2010, December 9). *Making disability work*. Op-ed, *The New York Times*.

Paganos, R. J., & DuBois, D. C. (1999). Career self-efficacy development and students with learning disabilities. *Learning Disabilities Research and Practice 4(1)*, 25–34.

Parker, R., & Schaller, J. L. (2003). Vocational assessment and disability. In E. M. Szymanski & R. M. Parker (Eds.), *Work and disability: Issues and strategies in career development and job placement* (2nd ed., pp. 155–200). Austin, TX: Pro-Ed.

Parsons, F. (1909). *Choosing a vocation*. Boston, MA: Houghton-Mifflin.

Patterson, J., DeLaGarza, D., & Schaller, J. (1997). Rehabilitation counseling practice: Considerations and interventions. In R. Parker & E. Szymanki (Eds.), *Rehabilitation counseling: Basics and beyond* (3rd ed., pp. 269–302). Austin, TX: Pro Ed.

Pledger, C. (2003). Discourse on disability and rehabilitation issues: Opportunities for psychology. *American Psychologist, 58*, 279–285.

Power, P. (2000). *A guide to vocational assessment* (3rd ed.). Austin, TX: Pro Ed.

Provencher, H. L, Gregg, R., Mead, S., & Meuser, K. T. (2002). The role of work in the recovery of persons with psychiatric disabilities. *Psychiatric Rehabilitation Journal, 26(2)*, 132–144.

Regenold, M., Sherman, M. F., & Fenzel, M. (1999). Getting back to work: Self efficacy as a predictor of employment outcome. *Psychiatric Rehabilitation Journal, 22*, 361–367.

Rojewski, J. W. (1993). Theoretical structure of career maturity for rural adolescents with learning disabilities. *Career Development for Exceptional Individuals, 16*, 39–52.

Sitlington, P., Neubert, D. A., & Clark, G. (2010). *Transition education and services for adolescents with disabilities* (5th ed.). Boston, MA: Pearson.

Slemon, J. C., & Shafir, U. (1997, March). *Academic self-efficacy of post-secondary students with and without learning disabilities*. Paper presented at the annual meeting of the American Educational Research Association, Chicago, IL.

Social Security Administration. (2011). *Monthly statistical snapshot, August, 2011*. Retrieved from http://www.ssa.gov/policy/docs/quickfacts/stat_snapshot/

Social Security Administration. (2011). *The work site ticket tracker*. Retrieved from http://www.socialsecurity.gov/work/tickettracker.html.

Strauser, D., Lustig, D., & Ciftci, A. (2008). Psychological well-being: Its relation to work personality, vocational identity, and career thoughts. *Journal of Psychology* 142(1), 21–35.

Super, D. (1990). A life-span, life-space approach to career development. In D. Brown & L. Brooks (Eds.), *Career choice and development: Applying contemporary theories to practice* (2nd ed., pp. 197–261). San Francisco, CA: Jossey-Bass.

Super, D. E., Savickas, M. L., & Super, C. M. (1996). The life-span, life-space approach to careers. In D. Brown, L. Brooks, & Associates (Eds.) *Career choice and development* (3rd ed., pp. 121–178), San Francisco, CA: Jossey-Bass.

Szymanski, E. M., Enright, M. S., Hershenson, D. B., & Ettinger, M. J. (2010). Career development theories, constructs and research: Implications for people with disabilities. In E. M. Szymanski & R. M. Parker (Eds.), *Work and disability: Issues and strategies in career development and job placement* (pp. 87–132). Austin, TX: Pro-Ed.

Szymanski, E. M. & Trueba, H. (1994). Castification of people with disabilities: Potential disempowering aspects of castification in disability services. *Journal of Rehabilitation, 60*, 12–20.

United States Census Bureau. (2010). Disability among the working age population. Retrieved from http://www.census.gov/prod/2010pubs/acsbr09-12.pdf.

United States Department of Education. (2001). *Office of Special Education Programs, State and local implementation of IDEA.* Washington, DC: Author.

U.S. Department of Labor, Bureau of Labor Statistics. (2011). Persons with a disability: Labor force characteristics summary. Retrieved from http://www.bls.gov/news.release/disabl.nr0.htm

Wagner, M. M., Newman, L., Cameto, R., Garza, N., & Levine, P. (2005). *After high school: A first look at the postschool experiences of youth with disabilities.* Menlo Park, CA: SRI International.

Wehman, P., Brooke, V. A., & Revell, W. G. (2007). Inclusive employment: Rolling back segregation of people with disabilities. In P. Wehman, K. Inge, W. G. Revel, & V. A. Brooke (Eds.), *Real work for real pay* (pp. 3–18). Baltimore, MD: Paul H. Brookes.

Wehman, P., Revell, W. G., & Kregel, J. (1998). Supported employment: A decade of rapid growth and impact. *American Rehabilitation, 24*(1), 31–43.

Wehmeyer, M. L., & Kelchner, K. (1995). *The Arc's Self- Determination Scale.* Arlington, TX: Arc National Headquarters.

Wehmeyer, M. L., & Palmer, S. B. (2003). Adult outcomes for students with cognitive disabilities three years after high school: The impact of self-determination. *Education and Training in Developmental Disabilities, 38*, 131–144.

Wehmeyer, M. L., Parent, W., Lattimore, J., Obremski, S., Poston, D., & Rousso, H. (2009). Promoting self-determination and self-directed employment planning for young women with disabilities. *Journal of Social Work and Disability Rehabilitation, 8*(3–4), 117–131.

Wehmeyer, M. L., & Schwartz, M. (1998). The relationship between self-determination and quality of life for adults with mental retardation. *Education and Training in Mental Retardation and Developmental Disabilities, 33*, 3–12.

Wewiorski, N., & Fabian, E. F. (2004). Association between demographic and diagnostic factors and employment outcomes for people with psychiatric disabilities: A synthesis of recent research. *Mental Health Services Research, 6*(1), 9–21.

Willis, S. (2002). *The relationship of social cognitive variables to outcomes among young adults with emotional disturbance.* Unpublished dissertation, University of Maryland, College Park.

Wittenburg, D., & Maag, E. (2002). School to where? A literature review on economic outcomes of youth with disabilities. *Journal of Vocational Rehabilitation, 17,* 265–280.

Workforce Investment Act of 1998, WIA, 112 Stat. 936, Public Law 105–220.

Xu, Y. J., & Martz, E. (2010). Predictors of employment among individuals with disabilities: A Bayesian analysis of the Longitudinal Study of the Vocational Rehabilitation Services Program. *Journal of Vocational Rehabilitation, 32*(1), 35–45.

SECTION THREE

ASSESSMENT AND OCCUPATIONAL INFORMATION

CHAPTER 14

Nature, Importance, and Assessment of Interests

JO-IDA C. HANSEN

RESEARCH HAS PROVIDED SUBSTANTIAL information about the properties of interests but has not provided an answer to the basic question: What *are* interests? Identifying the essence and origin of interests and developing precise definitions of interests have been elusive tasks. Extant theories of career development and vocational interests that describe the function of interests hint at but do not directly address the more fundamental question of what interests are. Early interest theories generally included both *components* and *determinants* in their definitions of interests. Although many components of interests have been proposed, three major components have been identified most often: personality, motivation and drive, and self-concept. The two most widely cited determinants of interests are nature, which emphasizes the heritability of interests, and nurture, which emphasizes socialization and learning and includes numerous environmental and psychological influences hypothesized to shape interests. Nonetheless, the construct of interests has become, in many ways, synonymous with scores presented on interest inventory profiles. Interests, in other words, frequently are regarded simply as "what the test measures." Within the context of this chapter, interests are defined as a preference for activities expressed as likes and dislikes (e.g., "I like dancing" or "I dislike text messaging").

INTERESTS AND VOCATIONAL THEORIES

Vocational interests are one of many variables included in most theories of career development. Interests also are candidates for inclusion in emerging perspectives on the biological bases of behavior.

387

INTERESTS IN MAJOR THEORIES OF CAREER DEVELOPMENT

Among all vocational theories, Holland's (1997) theory of vocational personality types focuses most explicitly on interests (Nauta, Chapter 3, this volume). Holland proposed that interest personalities can be summarized as six types: Realistic, Investigative, Artistic, Social, Enterprising, and Conventional. He also postulated that the relationship among these six types can be illustrated as an irregular hexagon, with the types adjacent to one another on the hexagon having more characteristics in common than types farther apart on the hexagon. Holland's theory features interests as a reflection of personality. The notion that interests and personality share common variance (i.e., are correlated) has been a popular hypothesis for decades. Holland's theory of vocational personality types (Holland, 1997), which provides a comprehensive model of vocational interests and their relationship to career decision making, satisfaction, and performance, has driven much of the research that examines the relationship between interests and personality. His theory also has been used to organize the profiles of all major interest inventories and to develop interpretive materials to accompany the profiles; to provide a framework for integrating higher-order abilities, personality, values, interests, and needs; and to describe interests relative to people, work environments, and job tasks.

The extent to which interests play a role in other theories of career development varies. For example, as described by Swanson and Schneider (Chapter 2, this volume), the theory of work adjustment (TWA; Dawis & Lofquist, 1984) focuses on the way in which abilities and values and their correspondence with an environment's requirements and reinforcers predicts work outcomes (e.g., satisfaction, performance, tenure). Although TWA postulates do not specify the role of interests in work adjustment, Dawis and Lofquist, the primary architects of TWA, do acknowledge that vocational interests also predict satisfaction, performance, and tenure.

Super's theory of vocational development, as described by Hartung (Chapter 4, this volume), includes interests among those constructs that "form a personality" and "yield an occupational or vocational identity." Super's career-development and assessment counseling (C-DAC) model also includes interests as one of several constructs he recommended assessing to help clients explore their life roles. Super's model assumes that readiness to make decisions must be established before the assessment of interests, abilities, or values can contribute to the career exploration process. Although Super acknowledged the assessment of interests in the C-DAC career counseling model, the model pays little attention to interests except during the growth stage. Gottfredson's (2005) theory of circumscription and compromise, another developmental theory, views social class, sex, and intelligence as influences on a person's self-concept as well as on the compromises people make in choosing their careers. Interests are viewed within this theory as just one of several vocationally relevant elements that compose the self-concept. The theory suggests that, under certain conditions, people may sacrifice pursuit of career options that match their interests rather than compromise on other dimensions (e.g., occupational prestige).

In career construction theory (see Savickas, Chapter 6, this volume), interests play a role in the development of children's reputations in their families, neighborhood, and schools. Career construction theory acknowledges Holland's typology as an operational definition of vocational personality and views RIASEC types as self-constructing strategies. In career construction theory, interests are not assessed with the help of an interest inventory. Rather, interests are explored and identified when "counselors ask clients about manifest interests...Interests manifest themselves in conjunction with such things as favorite magazines, television shows, or websites."

Social cognitive career theory (SCCT; Lent, Chapter 5, this volume) also emphasizes the impact that external forces (e.g., home, schools, peers) have on the development of interests. However, SCCT places more emphasis on the mechanisms involved in shaping or molding interests than does Super's theory of career development or career construction theory. As individuals try activities and receive feedback on their performance, they develop both self-efficacy and outcome expectations about the activities. If as a result of feedback or self-evaluation they view themselves as becoming competent, then the "interest in the activity is likely to blossom and endure." Empirical support for the precise ordering of interests and self-efficacy in the SCCT model is mixed, but research shows that both interests and self-efficacy contribute to decisions to pursue activities (see Lent, Chapter 5).

EMERGING PERSPECTIVES: THE ROLE OF NATURE IN INTEREST DEVELOPMENT

Most career theories, then, focus on the role that nurture plays in shaping and developing interests. Although none of the career theories explicitly denies that nature (i. e., genes) plays a role in the origin of a person's interests, they also do not directly address the degree to which interests are determined by heritability of interests. Behavior genetics studies, using twins as well as participants with other kinships, allow research designs that tease apart genetic and nongenetic effects. Especially informative research using twins reared together and apart supports a combination of nature and nurture determinants of interests. One study, which controlled for gender and age and used a large sample that included eight kinships, showed a genetic effect of 36% (Betsworth et al., 1994). This same study identified 9% shared environmental effects (e.g., living in the same home) and an additional 55% nonshared environmental effects (e.g., having different friends) and measurement error. This proportion of genetic and environmental effects is typical of the results reported in other studies. Such findings are consistent with the early appearance of interest choices in young children and the great stability of interests over the life span.

A social neuroscientific model of the processes underlying interests is a new approach that offers some promise for a biological understanding of the basis for interests (Hansen, Sullivan, & Luciana, 2011). This model is based on individual differences in the tendency to exhibit positive emotions as described in behavioral approach systems research. Personality research has linked the approach system with various individual differences, such as motivation, positive emotionality, and affiliation-communion. In this stream of research (e.g., Depue & Collins, 1999), approach motivation is conceptualized as having two components: *agency* (e.g., gregariousness, dominance in social hierarchies, potency, assertiveness, achievement, activity) and *affiliative/communal* tendencies (e.g., warmth, affection, and social bonding). Agency (e.g., pleasure from Enterprising activities such as leading, persuading, and selling) and communion (e.g., enjoyment from activities such as helping and teaching) have been shown to reflect distinct neurobiological processes and have been theorized to shape personality. Given the relations between interests and personality, agency and communion also may shape vocational and leisure interests.

The neuroscientific model can be interpreted in the context of work that has examined the relations between interests, personality, and abilities and has shown that Social and Enterprising interests and personality areas are not clearly associated with abilities. Taken together, these two lines of research (Ackerman & Heggestad, 1997; Hansen et al., 2011) suggest that people with low approach motivation (and consequently less interest in Social and Enterprising activities) are likely to have interests associated with specific abilities (e.g., visual perception and math reasoning with Realistic and Investigative interests, perceptual speed with Conventional interests, ideational fluency with Artistic interests). In contrast, people with high approach motivation are more likely to have interests that involve working with people. In both instances, the likelihood of positive reinforcement increases as individuals identify meaningful patterns and consistencies in types of activities, and these patterns coalesce into vocational interests. Pursuing research that integrates the approach motivation system and interests may contribute to understanding the neurobiology that predisposes people to pursue or avoid vocational and leisure activities.

INTERESTS, PERSONALITY, AND ABILITIES

The relations between interests and personality and abilities have been studied extensively. The broad brush conclusion from this line of research is that the three constructs share a small amount of variance but are not redundant.

INTERESTS AND PERSONALITY

Many attempts have been made to understand the relation of interests and personality. Much of this research has focused on Holland's six types and the five factor model (FFM) of personality, also known as the Big Five (Barrick, Mount, & Gupta, 2003). Some research also has examined the relationship between either Holland types or basic interests and the 11 personality traits of Tellegen's big three (Staggs, Larson, & Borgen, 2007; Tellegen, 2000). The general conclusion that can be drawn from these lines of research is that two or three personality and interest variables share a modest amount of variance: Openness and Holland's Investigative and Artistic interests, Extraversion and Enterprising and Social interests, and to a lesser extent, Agreeableness and Holland's Social interests. However, research examining the relations among lower-order personality facets (i.e., 30 NEO-PR-I facets), Holland's six personality types, and lower-order interests (i.e., basic interest scales of the Strong Interest Inventory) suggests that once the associations between interests and personality facets are accounted for, correlations between higher-order personality factors such as the Big Five and interest types are negligible (Sullivan & Hansen, 2004b). Thus, the vast majority of the relations between interests and personality that have been examined, at both higher-order levels (e.g., Holland types and the Big Five) and lower-order levels (e.g., basic interest scales and the 30 NEO Personality Inventory facets), are relatively weak, and the evidence leads to the conclusion that, for prediction and career counseling purposes, interests and personality should not be treated as interchangeable constructs. Research that has explored the incremental increase in prediction when personality, interests, and self-efficacy are allowed to make independent contributions supports this contention (Rottinghaus, Lindley, Green, & Borgen, 2002; also see Brown & Hirschi, Chapter 11, this volume).

INTERESTS AND ABILITIES

Early models of career counseling typically attempted to match the abilities of the client with the requirements of the job. Later, vocational assessment was expanded from concentrating on the measurement of abilities to include assessment of interests. E. K. Strong Jr. (1943), one of the early proponents of assessing interests in addition to abilities, suggested that "the relationship among abilities, interests, and achievements may be likened to a boat with a motor and a rudder. The motor (abilities) determines how fast the boat can go, the rudder (interests) determines which way the boat goes" (p. 17). Research supports Strong's contention that interests add incremental validity beyond ability to the prediction of educational and occupational choices and other outcomes (Lubinski, 2000). As Strong (1927a) noted, "The majority of [people] are practically equally fitted to enter a considerable number of occupations" (p. 297). He later concluded: "Interests supply something that is not disclosed by ability and achievement.... Counseling that considers both abilities and interests is distinctly superior to that based on either alone, for it is in a position to establish both what the [person] can do and what [she or he] wants to do" (Strong, 1943, p. 19).

INTEGRATIVE MODELS

Research examining the overlap of interests, personality, and cognitive abilities has led to integrative models of the role of individual differences in career counseling. Four trait complexes appear in several integrative models: (1) Science/Math, which includes Realistic and Investigative interests and math reasoning and visual perception abilities; (2) Intellectual/Cultural, which includes Investigative and Artistic interests, general mental ability, ideational fluency, and intellectual engagement and openness to experience; (3) Social, which includes Social and Enterprising interests, extroversion, social potency, and well-being; and (4) Clerical/Conventional, which includes Conventional interests, perceptual speed, and control, conscientiousness, and traditionalism (Ackerman & Heggestad, 1997). Research that combines cognitive abilities, interests, and personality offers a more complete understanding of a client's potential career choices and also suggests that the resulting trait complexes may be more predictive of individual's choices than any one construct used in isolation (Armstrong & Rounds, 2008). Integrative models (e.g., Ackerman and Heggestad's trait complexes) also provide an empirical foundation to guide the counselor's development of hypotheses about the client and a framework for interpreting results from vocational and psychological tests (Armstrong & Rounds, 2010).

STABILITY OF INTERESTS

Construct stability is an important prerequisite for any variable incorporated into decision-making exercises, such as those used in career counseling. This is especially true for interests because the stability of the construct is intertwined with the reliability of the scores on the tests used to assess interests. If interests are not stable, then interest inventories have no chance of predicting occupational or educational choices, even over short time spans. Based on the early work of E. K. Strong Jr. (1935, 1943) and on decades of research since Strong's early work, we know that interests are very stable over time. In fact, interests may be the most stable of all psychological constructs. We also know that the stability of interests depends on the age at Time 1 testing (the younger the participants, the less stable the interests) and the length of the interval between Time 1 and Time 2 testing (the longer the interval, the less stable the interests). On average, for example, the stability coefficients for individuals tested at age 18 and again at age 22 (4 years) and age 30 (12 years) are about .80 and .70, respectively (Hansen & Swanson, 1983; Swanson & Hansen, 1988). Thus, by age 20, interests are quite stable, even over periods of 5 to 10 years, and by age 25, interests are very stable. This evidence of the stability of interests for individuals, combined with evidence of test–retest reliability for an instrument, allows test users to have confidence in test scores that are used to predict future behaviors, such as job or college major choice.

Occasionally, efforts also are made to look at the stability of an *individual's* interests. This approach typically correlates an individual's profile scores for Time 1 with profile scores for Time 2. Generally, about 50% of individuals have Time 1 and Time 2 interest profiles that are substantially similar, and for many individuals, the rank order correlations are in the high .90s over relatively long time periods (e.g., 15 years) (Hansen & Swanson, 1983; Swanson & Hansen, 1988). However, these same studies illustrate that individual differences in interest stability do occur. The intraperson correlations for a sample often range from lows in the $-.20$s to highs in the $+.90$s, illustrating that for some individuals, dramatic changes in interests do occur over time.

Research also has explored the extent to which the interests of people in specific occupations or people in general change or remain stable over the decades. Even in times of a quickly changing society and technology, studies show that interests of people within a particular occupation (e.g., bankers, lawyers, foresters, psychologists, engineers, reporters) are virtually identical over 40 or 50 years (Hansen, 1988). Nonetheless, a cross-temporal meta-analysis covering the time periods of 1976–2004, which used a birth cohort design, showed a statistically significant increase in Enterprising interests for female college students and smaller yet still significant decreases in Realistic, Investigative, and Artistic interests for male college students. Gender differences in Conventional and Investigative interests also decreased significantly from older to younger cohorts (Bubany & Hansen, 2011). Consistent with both SCCT and the theory of circumscription and compromise, these results support the hypothesis that, over time, sociocultural factors may influence the development of interests.

WHY MEASURE INTERESTS?

Within the counseling intervention framework, interests may be assessed for a number of reasons with the goal of helping individuals make informed occupational and educational choices. First and foremost, measured interests can be used by counselors to guide the development of hypotheses about clients. These hypotheses, in turn, may be used to guide career exploration and to provide clients with a fresh perspective and new information. For clients, the profile scores promote self-understanding by various means: identifying previously unknown interests, broadening occupational possibilities for some people and narrowing choices for others, or simply confirming career choices. Although expressed and inventoried interests show similar evidence of predictive validity for occupation and college major choices, many individuals who must make career and educational choices are undecided. For these clients, the scores on interest inventories can serve as powerful stimuli to jump-start the exploration process and develop career ideas and possibilities.

Interest inventories also are used for selection in employment settings to help employers determine those job candidates who will be most likely to complete training, stay with the company, and be successful. Some employers also use interest inventories for placement to help workers find the right position within the company, especially when exceptional employees become dissatisfied with their current positions but wish to remain with the company in another role. Conversely, career counseling that incorporates the use of an interest inventory can be very helpful with displaced employees who have been downsized, terminated, or disabled. In sum, exploration that includes interest assessment can be valuable throughout the life span: first for educational and job decisions, then again as people seek more challenging work, then perhaps at some point if they question an initial decision, and once again, if they experience career plateaus. As people approach retirement, they may repeat the process of exploring their interests, focusing on ways to make the transition from actualizing their vocational interests to engaging in activities that reflect their leisure interests (Hansen, in press; Hansen & Scullard, 2002).

P-E INTEREST CONGRUENCE AND SATISFACTION
AND PERFORMANCE

Research on job satisfaction has shown that a plethora of variables contribute to the prediction of a satisfied outcome (see Lent & Brown, Chapter 22, this volume). The role that interests play in job satisfaction usually is studied by examining the congruence or match between an individual's measured interests and the interest requirements of the environment in which she or he works. Typically, these studies look at higher-order interests such as Holland's six types. The results from these studies, even those using meta-analysis, are mixed, but generally the correlation between person–environment interest congruence and satisfaction is about .25 to .30 (Hansen, in press).

Intuitively, one expects the correlations between P-E interest congruence and satisfaction to be larger. One popular explanation for the smaller than expected relation is the restricted range (which can decrease correlations) in people's job satisfaction (Dik & Hansen, 2008). Another explanation is that moderator variables, such as occupational level, career stage, Holland type, personality type, values, group importance, job involvement, and career salience, play a role in reducing the correlation (Dik & Hansen, 2011). A third explanation focuses on the measurement of the satisfaction criterion. Multifactor or facet measures of job satisfaction seem better suited to tease apart the relation between P-E congruence than are global measures. For example, correlations around .40 have been found between congruence and satisfaction with more specific job facets, such as pay, coworkers, and promotions (Hansen, in press).

A fourth explanation centers on the level at which interests are assessed in most congruence-satisfaction studies. Often in studies showing relatively modest correlations, interests are measured and work environments are coded using Holland's six types, which represent higher-order interests. However, studies conducted at a lower-order level of interest assessment (e.g., occupational scales) suggest that a large proportion of people (e.g., 70% to 80%) who are satisfied with their jobs score high on occupational scales that match their chosen occupations or college majors (Hansen & Dik, 2005; Holland, 1997; Pendergrass, Hansen, Neuman, & Nutter, 2003). Finally, the way in which congruence is operationalized also may affect the congruence satisfaction relation (Dik, Hu, & Hansen, 2007).

Well-being criteria, other than work satisfaction, shown to be positively related to P-E congruence include life satisfaction, meaningfulness, happiness, self-image, and self-esteem (Dik & Hansen, 2008; Hansen & Ton, 2001). Criteria negatively related to P-E congruence include somatic complaints, burnout, and anxiety. P-E congruence also is related to persistence (i.e., tenure), educational and vocational stability, adjustment, and achievement (Harms, Roberts, & Winter, 2006; Porter & Umbach, 2006). However, combining interests and abilities or aptitudes appears to improve predictions of achievement in work and academic settings beyond the levels that can be achieved using either construct alone (Wise, McHenry, & Campbell, 1990). The data support Strong's early contention that people will do well in an occupation if they have both the necessary interest and ability but that people with only ability and no interest can do well but may not (Strong,

1943). In the same way that the combination of interests and abilities predicts success and performance better than either does alone, incorporating values also can improve the prediction of work outcomes, especially job satisfaction (Rounds, 1990).

METHODS OF INTEREST INVENTORY SCALE CONSTRUCTION

Historically, three methods have dominated the development of interest inventories: rational-theoretical, the empirical method of contrast groups, and item clustering. In the course of interest inventory development, all three methods or combinations of these methods may ultimately be employed. The rational-theoretical approach begins with a well-defined construct. Ideally, this approach relies on theory for the definition of the construct to be measured and for item development and selection. The definition of the measured construct, the item content, and the use of psychometric data to relate scores to measures of other theoretical constructs contribute to the interpretation of the scales. The empirical method of contrast groups is based on the assumption that individuals postulated to differ on the construct also will differ in their responses to test items. Items are selected for inclusion in the test because they discriminate significantly between two or more groups hypothesized to differ on a criterion or construct.

The empirical method of clustering relies most heavily on statistical analyses (e.g., factor or cluster analysis) to identify underlying dimensions in a large pool of items. The dimensions then become the basis for the scales used to measure the constructs, which, in turn, contribute to the interpretation of the scores. In practice, the various approaches to test development often are used in a logical sequence. Theory is used initially to generate the item pool. Empirical relationships (i.e., contrast groups or clustering) may then be used to retain, reject, or modify items. Interpretation of scores from the scales derived by this process have the advantage of a theoretical and empirical foundation for the underlying dimensions represented by the test.

ASSESSMENT OF INTERESTS

Three of the most frequently used interest inventories are the Self-Directed Search (SDS; Holland, 1994), Strong Interest Inventory (Donnay et al., 2005), and the Campbell Interest and Skill Survey (CISS; Campbell, Hyne, & Nilsen, 1992). All three of these instruments include scales to measure Holland's six types. However, the SII and the CISS measure interests at three levels of specificity, whereas the SDS focuses only on the broad Holland types. Although the SII and the CISS profiles include sets of scales that resemble one another, their approaches to norming and standardizing the instruments differ. Another notable difference between the SII and the CISS is the inclusion of Skill scales on the CISS that parallel the Interest scales. The Skill scales are designed to provide an estimate of the individual's ability to do tasks related to the interests measured by the Orientations Scales, Basic Interest Scales, and Occupational Scales. The SII does have a companion instrument, the Skills Confidence Inventory (Betz, Borgen, & Harmon, 1996), that provides skill estimates for the six Holland types, but the CISS has Skill scales that match all of the Interest scales reported on the CISS profile.

SELF-DIRECTED SEARCH

Holland developed the Self-Directed Search, first published in 1971, as a vehicle for assessing a person's resemblance to each of his six vocational personality types (Holland, 1994). Holland selected items for the SDS using his theoretical model, which is based on "voluminous data about people in different jobs" (Holland, 1985, p. 3). The six scales are Realistic (works with things, practical and concrete), Investigative (works with ideas, analytical and scientific), Artistic (works with ideas, creative and imaginative), Social (works with people, empathetic and warm), Enterprising (works with people, ambitious and domineering), and Conventional (works with data, detail oriented and conscientious). Although any combination of types is possible, the closer the types are on the hexagon, the more likely they are to appear together as a person's pattern of interests or as the pattern of activities that occur in a work environment (see Nauta, Chapter 3, this volume).

The SDS item pool is composed of 228 items dispersed over four sections: work activities (66 items), self-estimated competencies (66 items), occupations (84 items), and self-estimates of abilities that represent each of the six types (12 items). The reading level of the items is estimated at the seventh- or eighth-grade level, and a Form Easy (E) is available for individuals who read at about the fourth-grade level (Holland, 1994). The SDS most often is given as a self-administered, self-scored, and even self-interpreted interest inventory. However, a computer-administered and -scored version is available. A scoring key is used to compute raw scores on the six scales that can be interpreted directly for a client, or scores can be compared to various norm groups provided in the manual (e.g., high school girls and boys, college women and men). The three highest raw scores are used to form a summary code, which is used to identify vocational and educational opportunities that incorporate similar interests represented in the individual's summary code. Holland and his colleagues developed an array of interpretive materials to be used with the inventory results, including a *Dictionary of Holland Occupational Codes* (Gottfredson & Holland, 1996) and the *Educational Opportunities*

Finder (Rosen, Holmberg, & Holland, 1997) that provide Holland codes for occupations and educational programs. These resources are very useful for matching scores on the six broad types to possible occupations and majors for a client to consider.

The SDS has been used extensively in vocational psychology research for the past 30 years. As a result, a wealth of evidence for the validity and reliability of the SDS has been aggregated. Over 4- to 12-week test–retest intervals, the median scale score reliability coefficients range from .76 to .89, respectively. Studies examining evidence of the concurrent validity of the SDS suggest that adults enter occupations that match their high point code about 60% of the time. The evidence for predictive validity for SDS scores is more variable and depends on the length of time between initial testing and the follow-up assessment, age at initial testing, and educational level. Generally, studies show that between 40% and 80% of college students and adults are in majors and occupations that match their summary code's first letter.

STRONG INTEREST INVENTORY

The Strong Interest Inventory (SII) was first published in 1927 under the title Vocational Interest Blank (Strong, 1927b). The item pool for the SII (Consulting Psychologists Press, 2004) currently includes 291 items divided into six content areas: occupational titles, school subjects, work activities, leisure activities, self characteristics, and preferences in the world of work. The reading level is estimated to be at about the eighth grade. The SII is a comprehensive survey that provides several levels of analysis of an individual's interests. At the highest order and broadest level are the six general occupational themes (GOT) developed to measure the six RIASEC vocational types proposed by Holland. Within career counseling, these scales address the question, "What am I like?"

The original GOTs were developed using a sequential method of scale construction. First, items were selected that represent the definitions and descriptions that Holland proposed for each of the six types. Then, item statistics (i.e., intercorrelations) were used to select those items that con- tributed to the homogeneity of the scales. The GOTs were modified as part of the 2004 revision of the SII; Cronbach's alphas range from .90 to .95. Test–retest stability over intervals less than 8 months range from .84 (Artistic) to .89 (Realistic). Over intervals of 8 to 23 months, the stability coefficients range from .80 (Artistic) to .92 (Realistic). Evidence of validity for the GOT scores includes large correlations between same-named scales on Holland's Vocational Preference Inventory (VPI; Holland, 1975) and the SII and evidence of the power of the GOT to separate occupational groups over about 3 standard deviations of scores in a logical way (e.g., engineers and electricians score high and mental health workers and reporters score low on the Realistic theme) (Hansen & Campbell, 1985).

The 30 Basic Interest Scales (BIS) represent the next level of specificity, and scores on these scales help the client to answer the question, "What do I like?" They include scales such as Mechanics and Construction, Medical Science, Visual Arts & Design, Counseling & Helping, Entrepreneurship, and Office Management. The original BISs were developed using the empirical method of clustering. Subsequent versions of the BIS have relied on factor analysis. As one would expect based on these methods of scale construction, the item content of each scale is homogeneous, with alpha coefficients ranging from .80 (Social Services) to .92 (Computer Hardware & Electronics). Similar to the GOT, evidence of validity for the BIS scores consists of studies examining the extent to which the scales differentiate occupations in a logical manner (e.g., auto dealers and life insurance agents score high and psychologists and physicists score low on the Sales BIS) (Hansen & Campbell, 1985).

The Occupational Scales provide the greatest level of specificity of interest measurement on the SII and answer the question, "Who am I like?" They compare the interests of the respondent directly to those of people employed in the occupation who are satisfied with their work. A total of 122 occupations are represented on the profile; about 30% of the scales represent occupations that typically can be entered without a college degree (e.g., carpenter, cosmetologist, florist, optician, travel consultant), and the remainder represent occupations of a more professional nature (e.g., architect, nurse, psychologist, social science teacher, executive).

The Occupational Scales are constructed using the empirical method of contrast groups. This technique identifies about 25 to 35 items for each Occupational Scale that differentiate the likes and dislikes of women or men in the occupation from women in general or men in general (called the General Representative Sample). The item content of the Occupational Scales is heterogeneous, and, therefore, internal consistency measures of reliability are not meaningful. However, because the scales are used to make decisions about college majors and careers, the concept of scale score stability is very important for this set of scales. The median test–retest correlation for the Occupational Scales is .86, with a range of .71 to .93 over an interval of 2 to 23 months (Donnay et al., 2005). Evidence of the validity of the Occupational Scales was a major research focus of early authors of the SII (e.g., Hansen & Campbell, 1985; Strong, 1943). One study has shown evidence of concurrent validity for the GOT, BIS, and Personal Styles Scales on the 2004 SII (Gasser, Larson, & Borgen, 2007). However, no such evidence has been reported for the 2004 Occupational Scales. Therefore, much of the evidence of validity for the 2004 version of the SII relies on generalizing from earlier studies.

Two studies (Savickas, Taber, & Spokane, 2002; Sullivan & Hansen, 2004a) have demonstrated that scores on the SII correlate substantially with scores on same-named scales on other interest inventories (e.g., the CISS, the SDS, the KOIS, and the UNIACT). These same studies have shown that SII scale scores have small correlations with scores on other interest inventory scales that are unrelated. For example, the median correlation reported for same-named scale scores for the SII and CISS was .62 and .66 for samples of women and men college students, respectively. For the same samples, the median correlations between nonmatching scales (e.g., Conventional and Creating) were .05 and .06 (Sullivan & Hansen, 2004a).

The extent to which the Occupational Scales predict educational and occupational choices is a line of evidence of validity for SII scores that has been developed throughout the history of the inventory. The typical method for examining concurrent and predictive validity (collectively labeled *criterion validity*) involves comparing scores on the Occupational Scales to declared choices. In the case of concurrent validity, the research participants complete the SII and provide information about their current occupations or educational choices at the same time. In the case of predictive validity, the research participants complete the SII at Time 1; then, at some time in the future (usually after several years have passed), they are contacted to participate in a follow-up study to determine their educational choice or occupation at Time 2. The summary statistic reported in these studies simply provides the percent of participants who scored high on Occupational Scales that match their choices (e.g., a participant who scored high on the Reporter scale and is majoring in journalism or who scored high on Financial Analyst and works in that field). The results from these studies are quite stable from one study to the next and from one version of the SII to another. Generally, the concurrent studies show matches for about 75% of the sample, and the predictive studies show matches of about 70% to 75% over Time 1–Time 2 intervals of 4 years and about 60% to 65% over Time 1–Time 2 intervals of 12 years (Hansen & Dik, 2005; Hansen & Swanson, 1983).

The fourth set of scales presented on the SII profile is five Personal Style Scales (PSS). The Learning Environment (LE) scale measures the extent to which an individual has interests similar to others who persist in academic environments. People who score high on the scale often are interested in learning for learning's sake and often aspire to complete graduate degrees. People with average scores on the LE scale have academic interests similar to people who have completed undergraduate college degrees, and people with low scores are similar to those who do not pursue college degrees. Studies examining evidence of validity for the LE scale indicate that the scores are not related to ability. Rather, interests of those who score low on the scale tend to reflect an interest in education for the practical knowledge that can be gained and directly applied to the work setting. The Cronbach alpha for the LE scale is .76, and test–retest stability over 2 to 23 months is .88 (Donnay et al., 2005).

The Work Style (WS) scale on the current SII reflects interests of those who enjoy spending time with and working with people (high scores), as well as those interested in activities that allow them to work with ideas, data, and things (low scores). For example, child care providers, flight attendants, and life insurance agents score high and biologists, computer programmers, and physicists score low on WS. Cronbach alpha for the WS Scale is .86, and test–retest over 2 to 23 months is .91. The third scale is the Risk Taking (RT) scale, which measures a willingness to try new things and to take social, financial, and physical risks (high scores). Electricians and police officers score high, and dental assistants and mathematicians score low. Cronbach alpha for the RT Scale is .82, and test–retest over 2 to 23 months is .86.

The Leadership Style (LS) scale correlates with introversion-extroversion. High scores reflect an interest in leading and managing others, whereas low scores reflect the interests of people who prefer to work alone. Corporate trainers and public administrators score high; auto mechanics and farmers score low on LS. Cronbach alpha for the LS Scale is .87, and test–retest over 2 to 23 months is .86. The most recently developed Personal Style Scale is the Team Orientation (TO) scale, which correlates .55 with the Leadership Style Scale (Donney et al., 2005). The TO scale has two poles that range from an interest in accomplishing tasks independently to an interest in accomplishing tasks collectively. The Cronbach alpha for TO is .86, and the test–retest coefficient over 2 to 23 months is .74.

The five Personal Style Scales are normed on a sample of adult women and men drawn from a large number of occupations. The mean for this people-in-general sample is set equal to 50, and the standard deviation is set at 10. Generally, scores on the Personal Style Scales that are above 55 are considered high, and scores below 45 are considered low.

Campbell Interest and Skill Survey

The Campbell Interest and Skill Survey (CISS; Campbell et al., 1992) is a 320-item instrument that assesses vocational interests (200 items) and self-estimates of skills (120 items) in parallel fashion. Thus, the profile reports two scores (i.e., interest and skill) for each of the 98 scales. Combining self-estimates of interests and skills into one inventory was a unique approach at the time of publication of the CISS in 1992. The reading level is estimated at the sixth-grade level. All of the scales on the CISS are normed and standardized on combined samples of women and men drawn from a large variety of occupations. The mean for this sample is set equal to 50 with a standard deviation of 10. The profile provides interpretive comments, based on the respondent's interest and skill scores on each scale, that advise a course of action for the individual to consider: "pursue" (high interest and high skill), "develop" (high interest and low skill), "explore" (low interest and high skill), and "avoid" (low interest and low skill).

The types of scales presented on the CISS profile are similar to those on the Strong Interest Inventory. At the most general level, the CISS features seven Orientation Scales. Six of the seven scales measure Holland's six types: the Producing, aNalyzing, Creating, Helping, Influencing, and Organizing scales measure, respectively, realistic, investigative, artistic, social, enterprising, and conventional interests. The seventh Orientation scale is Adventuring, which measures an interest in physical and competitive activities and risk taking. Evidence of construct validity for the Orientation Scales suggests that, with the exception of the Adventuring scale, the Orientation Scales are good representatives of Holland's six types (Sullivan & Hansen, 2004a). The median correlation between matching CISS and SII GOT scales is about .70. For nonmatching scales, the median correlation is about .16. The correlation between CISS Adventuring and SII Risk Taking scale scores is large ($r = .65$), indicating that the CISS scale, similar to the SII scale, is a measure of willingness to take risks, try new activities, and be spontaneous. Like the SII GOTs, the CISS Orientation Scales have homogeneous item content, large alpha coefficients (ranging from .82 to .93), and robust test–retest correlations (median $r = .87$ for interests and .81 for skills over 90 days) (Campbell et al., 1992).

The 29 Basic Interest Scales measure more specific interests than do the Orientation Scales and include some interests not represented among the BIS on the SII, including Adult Development, Child Development, International Activities, Fashion, Woodworking, and Animal Care. Conversely, the SII includes Basic Interest Scales that measure interests not represented on the CISS profile: Healthcare Services, and Programming & Information Systems. The alpha coefficients for the Basic Interest Scales range from .69 to .92, with a median of .86 for the Interest scales, and from .62 to .87 with a median of .79 on the Skill scales. The median test–retest coefficient over a period of 90 days is .83 for the Interest scales and .79 for the Skill scales (Campbell et al., 1992). Evidence of validity for the Basic Interest Scales includes (a) large correlations with SII scales that measure similar interests (e.g., correlations of .86 between SII and CISS Science scales and .77 between SII Teaching and CISS Adult Development) (Sullivan & Hansen, 2004a) and (b) the ability of the Interest and Skill scales to differentiate samples of people from various occupations in a meaningful way. For example, occupations that have high mean interest scores on CISS Mechanical Crafts include airline mechanics, test pilots, and carpenters; occupations that have low mean scores on this scale include secretaries, social workers, and nursing administrators (Campbell et al., 1992).

The 60 Occupational Scales on the CISS were constructed using the empirical method of contrast groups that also is used to construct SII Occupational Scales. The CISS and SII Occupational Scales do differ in several important ways, however. First, the SII OS are separate sex scales; in other words, for each occupation, one scale was developed based on women in the occupation contrasted with women in general, and another scale was developed based on men in the occupation contrasted with men in general. The CISS scales, by contrast, are combined-sex scales that used criterion (i.e., occupations) and contrast (i.e., people in general) samples composed of women and men to develop the scales. Another difference is the way in which the scales are normed and standardized. The SII scales are normed on the occupational criterion sample with the mean set equal to 50. Therefore, a score of 50 on the SII OS indicates strong similarity in interests between the individual taking the inventory and the people in the occupation. However, the OS on the CISS are normed on a people-in-general sample such that a score of 50 indicates little similarity with people in the occupation; rather, scores on the CISS suggesting strong similarity in interests between the individual and the people in a particular occupation are in the range of 65 to 70.

The *CISS Manual* (Campbell et al., 1992) reports the power of each Interest and Skill scale to discriminate between people in the general population and those in specific occupations using Tilton's overlap statistic. Generally, the mean score for people in general on the Skill scales is about 1.8 standard deviations below the mean score for the occupational criterion samples (range from .9 to 3.5 standard deviations). For the Interest scales, the mean for the people in general is about 2 standard deviations below the mean for people in the occupation (range from 1.2 to 2.9 standard deviations). In addition, two studies demonstrated evidence of convergent and discriminant validity of scores on the Interest scales with Kuder and SII occupational scale scores (Savickas et al., 2002; Sullivan & Hansen, 2004a).

Evidence of validity for the Skill Scale scores shows convergence and discrimination for the Skill Scale scores and the CISS Interest Scales, Strong Interest Inventory, and self-reported Minnesota Ability Estimates Questionnaire (MAEQ) scores (Hansen & Leuty, 2007). The relations between same-name CISS Interest and Skill Scale scores range from .46 (Helping) to .71 (aNalyzing) for females and from .62 (Advertising) to .72 (Helping) for males. Relations between the CISS Skill Scale scores and MAEQ scores were in the expected directions. For example, influencing scores correlated .40 with verbal aptitude, and the correlation between aNalyzing and numerical aptitude was .49. The correlations between CISS Interest Scale scores and the MAEQ were lower. For example, the correlation between Influencing interest scores and verbal aptitude scores was .25 and between aNalyzing and numerical scores was .41.

Three studies have looked at the concurrent validity of the CISS to predict college majors. The first two studies examined the use of the Interest and Skill scales with college students from a variety of majors (Hansen & Leuty, 2007; Hansen & Neuman, 1999). The results of these studies showed that 69% to 72% of the women and 76% to 80% of the men scored high on Interest scales that matched their declared college majors. The hit rates for the Skill Scales scores were slightly lower; 58% to 61% of the women and 61% to 69% of the men scored high on Skill scales that matched their majors. The third study (Pendergrass et al., 2003) examined the extent to which men student athletes chose college majors that agreed with their measured interests. Among the student athletes in nonrevenue sports (e.g., tennis, golf, cross country, swimming), 74% scored high on Interest scales matching their declared majors. Seventy-one percent of the comparison sample of nonathlete students and 63% of the athletes participating in revenue sports (e.g., basketball, football) scored high on Interest scales matching their declared majors.

Another set of scales on the CISS includes the Academic Focus Scale (AF), which measures interests and skills related to academic pursuits, and the Extraversion Scale (ES), which measures interests and skills related to social interactions. The Academic Focus scale was constructed using the empirical method of contrast groups that selected items that differentiated people in general from individuals with high levels of education. The items on the Extraversion Scale are ones that have large correlations with a composite extraversion scale from the Campbell Leadership Index (CLI; Campbell, 1991). The 90-day test–retest coefficients for the AF Interest and Skill scales are .87 and .77, respectively. For the ES, the stability coefficients are .85 for the Interest scale and .82 for the Skill scale (Campbell et al., 1992).

As expected, high-scoring occupations on the Academic Focus Interest and Skill scales include those that require college and graduate degrees and have an interest in science and academic topics such as medical researchers, physicians, and math/science teachers. Low-scoring occupations include those in business fields such as financial planners, insurance agents, and Realtors. High-scoring occupations on the Extraversion Interest and Skill scales include those who work closely with others, such as guidance counselors and corporate trainers; occupations scoring low include those where people tend to work alone or with things rather than people, such as chemists and carpenters (Campbell et al., 1992).

USING INTEREST INVENTORIES IN CAREER COUNSELING

The use of interest inventories in career counseling evolved out of career guidance programs that emerged in the 1930s to ease unemployment during the Great Depression. World War II served as another catalyst, as programs were developed, especially through the Veterans Administration, to help returning veterans take advantage of educational opportunities offered through the G.I. Bill to choose new occupations. The University of Minnesota's Department of Psychology, with its emphasis on individual differences, assessment, and applied psychology, became a major research and counseling center with close ties to the Minneapolis VA Hospital. From this work emerged the trait-and-factor Minnesota Point of View of counseling, a model that is very directive and involves providing clients with information and suggestions to guide their decision making. The assessment of abilities and interests was an important ingredient in early applications of trait and factor counseling; later, assessment of needs, values, and personality also was incorporated into the model. Most current models of career counseling still include assessment of interests as an important component. However, fewer models emphasize the need to objectively measure abilities, values, and personality.

"Three Sessions and a Cloud of Dust": Assessment and Intervention

Therapeutic assessment (TA) advocated by Finn and his colleagues (Finn & Martin, in press) has been shown to meet standards of evidence-based interventions (Morey, Lowmaster, & Hopwood, 2010) and to result in positive personal change (Ougrin, Ng, Low, 2008; Poston & Hanson, 2010). Much of the empirical work in this area has been done with clients whose diagnoses include anxiety disorders, oppositional defiant disorder, and borderline personality disorder. Many of the 17 studies included in one meta-analysis (Poston & Hanson, 2010) involved only test administration and feedback, in other words as little as two sessions, as the therapeutic intervention. Yet, the results indicated an overall effect size of .42. The ingredients in TA that may explain why brief interventions that include assessment can have therapeutic effects include using test results to change the client's self-narrative or the way people view themselves, using TA techniques to involve clients in setting goals for the assessment process, and the power of psychological tests to be "empathy magnifiers" (Finn, 2007).

Although TA may conjure images of the Minnesota Point of View, models of career counseling have expanded beyond the old "test 'em and tell 'em" approach. As counselors needed better intervention skills to deal with both personal and vocational concerns, they turned to Carl Rogers's nondirective approach. Currently, counselors often augment trait-and-factor interpretation methods with attention to (a) the working alliance, (b) contextual and cultural factors and individual differences that have an impact on decision making, (c) developmental stages, (d) economic and social realities, and (e) personal issues. Although career counseling has evolved and changed, the philosophy of the Minnesota Point of View—assessment of client strengths and weaknesses and the use of test results to make predictions that will garner satisfaction and success for the client—remains relevant.

Career counseling approaches that incorporate assessment of multiple constructs allow counselors to more fully understand the client than do approaches that incorporate only interest assessment. Comparing results from ability and personality tests with results from interest and value/needs measures allows the counselor to better understand what motivates the client (interests and values), how the client interacts with others (personality), and the level of complexity at which the client is able to function (abilities). Also, once clients have examined their scores on an interest inventory, they may find it difficult to make a decision because the possibilities, based on interests alone, are many and varied. Clients often find it helpful at this point to have additional information to help them begin to narrow their choices. Having data on abilities, personality, and values provides additional information to determine the best P-E fit for the client.

In terms of refining choices, a consideration of abilities helps to determine the level of occupational and educational complexity that the individual will be able to successfully pursue. Understanding personality can provide direction within an organization. For example, a person who scores low on measures of responsibility and assertiveness probably will not make a good manager. In the same way, understanding needs and values can help persons understand how they fit into a work environment. A person scoring high on the need for independence may not appreciate a job with close supervision from a superior. Likewise, those who value achievement will probably want to work in a challenging job.

Unfortunately, financial and time constraints often limit assessment to vocational interests. In those instances, counselors will find it useful to use past behaviors to help them understand the client more fully. For example, counselors can gather information on performance in coursework and on achievement tests to estimate abilities. They can inquire about what is important for an individual to have in a job, an employer, a work setting, and coworkers to estimate values, and they can ask clients to describe how they interact with others on the job, within their family, and with friends and strangers to better understand their clients' personality and the environments in which they excel.

SELECTING AN INTEREST INVENTORY

Which inventory to use in career counseling depends to some extent on the age of the client and the resources of the counseling agency. Younger clients' (e.g., freshmen and sophomores in high school) interests may not be developed sufficiently to have differentiated scores on occupation-specific scales such as those that appear on the SII or CISS. For younger clients, then, the most useful information probably will come from higher-order scales such as those found on Holland's SDS, the Orientation Scales of the CISS, or General Occupational Themes of the SII. For older high school students, college students, and adults, scales that measure interests relative to specific occupations (i.e., Occupational Scales) are useful.

The SDS is one of the more economical interest inventories available to consumers primarily because the instrument can be self-scored. Instruments like the CISS and SII, which have a multitude of scores as well as interpretive comments presented on the profile, must be machine-scored, which increases the price of these instruments. The trade-off, then, is the reasonable cost of the SDS versus the more detailed information provided by the CISS and SII. Where cost and access are important considerations, the Interest Profiler, available free on the O*NET website (http://www.onetcenter.org/IP.html) is another possibility. The Interest Profiler is a relatively brief, rudimentary interest measure that provides a summary of the test taker's Holland types.

PREPARING TO USE INTEREST INVENTORIES

To prepare to use interest inventories, counselors should study the inventory's manual. Typically, test manuals include information on the purpose of the inventory and provide an overview of the testing materials. Most manuals describe the way in which the scales were constructed, normed, and standardized; report evidence of reliability and validity; note inventory limitations; and offer suggestions for the use and interpretation of the scale scores. The manual also will provide information that helps the counselor know what the scale names mean and what scores are considered high, average, or low.

ADMINISTERING AN INTEREST INVENTORY

Interest inventories may be administered either individually or in group settings. The traditional paper-and-pencil interest inventory format still is available, but computer-administered versions are increasingly popular. Regardless of the administration format or setting, a standardized introduction should be given to orient the client to the testing expectations. Also, for clients who may have difficulty understanding the items, it generally is permissible to provide them with definitions or explanations to ensure that they understand the items.

Preparing to Interpret an Interest Inventory

Prior to meeting with the client to interpret the test results, counselors should review the profile. This review should include checking validity indices that may indicate some problem with test administration or the client's responses and examining the profile for patterns of interests that emerge across various sets of scales. In addition to providing an assessment of work-related interests, interest inventories also often tap leisure interests and preferences for various types of work, recreational activities, and living environments. Therefore, as the counselor prepares for the interpretation session, it is useful to think broadly about how the client may satisfy the interests that are reported on the interest inventory profile. During the session, clients then can be encouraged to think about ways in which they can satisfy their interests across the many roles in their lives (e.g., worker, family member, leisurite, friend, volunteer) (Hansen, 2000).

Interpreting an Interest Inventory

Interest inventories help clients identify their interests in an efficient manner, and during the interpretation session, the scores are used to stimulate discussion about occupations and activities that match their interests. The results also provide a framework for stimulating discussion about options that clients may not have considered in the past and about ways in which some interests may be better satisfied through leisure or volunteer activities than through the world of work. The client–counselor exchange, in turn, is used to verify working hypotheses.

Although it may be tempting to view test interpretation as a discrete activity within career counseling, research has shown that college student clients tend to recall very little about the specific profile results reported to them 1 year earlier (Hansen, Kozberg, & Goranson, 1994). Therefore, the interpretation of test results should be integrated into the overall counseling process. Also, regardless of the interest inventory that has been administered, the exploration of occupational and educational options can be enhanced by using materials tied to Holland's RIASEC coding scheme (e.g., Gottfredson & Holland, 1996; Rosen, Holmberg, & Holland, 1994). A set of specific steps for interpreting interest inventories appears at the end of this chapter.

The counselor needs to be knowledgeable about the meaning of scale scores to provide the client with accurate information about the results and to convey the nuances of the results. Understanding the nuts and bolts of test construction and knowing the evidence of reliability and validity for an instrument provide a necessary foundation for proper test interpretation. However, counseling skills also are required for interpreting test results, and common intervention techniques such as establishing rapport, developing a positive working alliance, and providing a safe and supportive atmosphere are just as important during test interpretation as during any other counseling session. Communication skills also are important. Throughout the process, the counselor is striving to facilitate the client's active involvement in understanding the results and relating them to the goals of counseling. In subsequent counseling sessions, clients often find it useful to return to their profiles to refresh their memory, clarify results, and integrate the test scores with the exploration process and their counseling goals.

RESPONSIBLE USE OF TESTS

Most test publishers require test purchasers to verify their educational background, training, and experience and will sell interest inventories only to those who are qualified. Generally, a master's degree, including coursework in psychological testing and measurement, is the minimum requirement. Effective use and interpretation of interest inventories also requires training in current testing issues, such as the effect of gender differences on interest scores and interpretation and the fair use of interest inventories with diverse racial, ethnic, and cultural groups. Most test publishers have made concerted efforts to ensure that the basic elements of interest inventories—the items—are relevant for most test takers. These efforts include revising items so that the wording does not suggest in any way that some activities or occupations are not appropriate for all groups and constructing scales that reflect activities that appeal to multiple groups. Also, efforts have been made to collect evidence of validity for test scores for diverse populations and to better understand the nature of differences in interests between women and men and among various cultural groups. Nonetheless, counselors still need to be aware that cultural background and contextual variables may have an impact on test results.

Gender Differences in Interests

Gender differences in interests have been studied throughout the history of interest measurement, and the results of these studies have guided inventory development. Women and men do report differential levels of interests in some areas—most notably, women express more artistic and social interests, and men express more realistic and investigative interests (Su, Rounds, &

Armstrong, 2009). Numerous studies have pointed to these gender differences in interests as an explanation for the underrepresentation of girls and women in STEM (science, technology, engineering, and mathematics) fields (Ceci, Williams, & Barnett, 2009; Schmidt, 2011; Su et al., 2009).

Some have suggested that the differences in interests between women and men will disappear as the barriers to occupational entry in nontraditional occupations fall. Yet, studies that have examined gender differences in interests at both the item and scale score level over a 50-year period suggest that gender differences in interests are quite stable and robust (Hansen, 1988). However, a recent study (Bubany & Hansen, 2011) that used cross-temporal meta-analysis to examine interest stability across birth cohorts suggests some convergence in the interests of female and male college students over the past 30 years. Specifically, gender differences in Investigative, Enterprising, and Conventional interests decreased significantly. However, gender differences in Realistic, Artistic, and Social interests did not decrease. E. K. Strong (1943) was among the first to attempt to develop combined-gender occupational scales. However, he concluded (as have many researchers following in his footsteps) that separate-gender scales were more effective for counseling. This conclusion is especially true for the use of interest inventories with women or men who have interests that are nontraditional for their gender (e.g., women who are interested in farming and men who are interested in clerical work). Nonetheless, some interest inventories do report scores that are based only on combined-gender samples.

Another strategy used by test publishers to reduce gender bias in interest inventories occurs at the item level. Language that infers that a job or activity is appropriate for only one gender or the other has been eliminated from extant inventory items (as well as interpretive materials). For some interest inventories, new items have been developed that have similar appeal to women and men to replace items that were more stereotypic for one gender or the other. In spite of efforts to develop gender-fair interest inventories, within the broad career counseling context, women and men still may feel restricted in their occupational and educational choices and, therefore, may need support and encouragement from their counselors to explore broadly (see Heppner, Chapter 7, this volume).

CULTURAL DIFFERENCES IN INTERESTS

The relevance of interests across cultures has been examined most often by looking statistically at the relations among Holland's interest types across racial or ethnic groups. Often this focus intersects with social class, but relatively little work has focused specifically on interests and social class. Several large-scale studies using the SII and the UNIACT show that the intercorrelations among the six types fit Holland's circular model for African American, Asian American, Native American, Mexican American, and European American participants (Fouad, Harmon, & Borgen, 1997). This suggests that inventories based on Holland's RIASEC model have validity for diverse populations. Nonetheless, the use of interest inventories with racial, ethnic, and culturally diverse clients may be enhanced if counselors strive to understand the values and attitudes of other cultures and also are aware of their own values and possible biases and stereotypes.

Most of the research exploring the usefulness of interest inventories with ethnic and racial groups has been concurrent validity studies used to assess the extent to which scores on the profiles predict occupational entry or choice of a college major. Generally, American Indian, African American, Asian American, and Latina/Latino students score high on scales representing the occupations or college majors they have chosen at about the same rate as Anglo American students (about 55% to 75%), and the hit rates substantially exceed chance hit rates (about 20% to 25%) (Hansen & Lee, 2007; Haviland & Hansen, 1987; Holland, 1997). Studies using multiple regression (Diemer, Wang, & Smith, 2010) and multidimensional scaling (Tang, 2009) also have shown that interests significantly predict college major choices for American Indian/Alaska Native, Asian Hawaiian/Pacific Islander, Black/African American, and Latina/Latino youth who attended high school in low-income neighborhoods and for students from the northeast areas of China.

One concern with most interest inventories is that the scales are constructed using samples composed primarily of Anglo Americans. Ideally, then, normative data would be made available by the publisher for various racial, ethnic, and cultural groups. The reality, however, is that this goal is rarely achieved. In lieu of these data, good counseling practice is essential. Another concern is that most interest inventories are administered in English. Clients who do not speak English, or for whom English may be a second language, may not understand the meanings or nuances of some items or the labels for some scales. The best practice for counselors is to collaborate with clients to gain an understanding of cultural influences and at the same time to be aware of individual differences that may have an impact on the career decision-making process (see Fouad & Kantamneni, Chapter 8, this volume).

TAKE-HOME MESSAGE: STEPS FOR INTERPRETING
AN INTEREST INVENTORY

Although counselors will want to develop their own style for interpreting interest inventories—one that blends test interpretation with their theoretical approach to counseling interventions and to career development and decision making—several basic steps can be incorporated into most interpretations. The order certainly can be changed to individualize the counseling process, but the steps outlined here offer one format frequently used by counselors.

- Review the purpose for taking the inventory and looking at the results.
- Ask for any reactions the client may have had to taking the inventory.
- Remind the client that interest inventories do not measure abilities.
- Ask if the client can predict two or three high scores—usually for the scales that measure the Holland types.
- Briefly describe how the scale scores were derived.
- Explain the way in which the scales are normed and standardized, and describe the sample to which the client is being compared.
- Explain the meaning of numerical scores and interpretive comments.
- Describe what the scales mean, and give an example of one or two items on the scale.
- Ask the client for reactions to the scores (i.e., how accurate is the picture that the scores paint for the client).
- Ask clients to clarify how they satisfy each of their interests (e.g., work, recreation, social activities), and encourage integration of the results with past and current activities to help understand the results.
- Look for patterns across the profile and ponder ways in which interests in various activities might be combined into a job or career.
- Identify additional related educational or occupational possibilities not reported on the profile that might also satisfy the client's interests.
- Develop a plan with the client for the next steps to take in the career exploration process.
- Ask the client to summarize the results at the end of the session, and allow time to discuss any misunderstandings.

CONCLUSIONS

Longitudinal outcome research has shown that students who receive a basic interest inventory interpretation tend to participate more in career exploration activities than do students who have not taken an interest inventory and had it interpreted (Randahl, Hansen, & Haverkamp, 1993). Incorporating interest inventories into career counseling models provides clients and counselors with information that will assist clients to develop their potential. This is true in career counseling as well as in selection and placement uses of interest inventories. Whether the goal is to enhance an individual's satisfaction with the job or the organization's satisfaction with the individual, knowledge of interests is one component in career counseling that can help meet both of these goals.

REFERENCES

Ackerman, P. L., & Heggestad, E. D. (1997). Intelligence, personality, and interests. Evidence for overlapping traits. *Psychological Bulletin, 121*, 219–245.

Armstrong, P. I., & Rounds, J. B. (2008). Vocational psychology and individual differences. In S. D. Brown & R. W. Lent (Eds.), *Handbook of counseling psychology* (pp. 375–391). Hoboken, NJ: Wiley.

Armstrong, P. I., & Rounds, J. B. (2010). Integrating individual differences in career measurement: The Atlas Model of Individual Differences and the Strong Ring. *Career Development Quarterly, 59*, 143–153.

Barrick, M. R., Mount, M. K., & Gupta, R. (2003). Meta-analysis of the relationship between the five-factor model of personality and Holland's occupational types. *Personnel Psychology, 56*, 45–74.

Betsworth, D. G., Bouchard, T. J., Jr., Cooper, C. R., Grotevant, H. D., Hansen, J. C., Scarr, S., & Weinberg, R. A. (1994). Genetic and environmental influences on vocational interests assessed using adoptive and biological families and twins reared apart and together. *Journal of Vocational Behavior, 44*, 263–278.

Betz, N. E., Borgen, F. H., & Harmon, L. W. (1996). *Skills Confidence Inventory: Applications and technical guide.* Palo Alto, CA: Consulting Psychologists Press.

Bubany, S. T., & Hansen, J. C. (2011). Birth cohort change in the vocational interests of female and male college students. *Journal of Vocational Behavior, 78*, 59–67.

Campbell, D. P. (1991). *Manual for the Campbell Leadership index.* Minneapolis, MN: Pearson Assessments.

Campbell, D. P., Hyne, S. A., & Nilsen, D. L. (1992). *Manual for the Campbell Interest and Skill Survey.* Minneapolis, MN: Pearson Assessments.

Ceci, S. J., Williams, W. M., & Barnett, S. M. (2009). Women's under-representation in science: Sociocultural and biological considerations. *Psychological Bulletin, 135*, 218–261.

Consulting Psychologists Press. (2004). *Strong Interest Inventory.* Palo Alto, CA: Author.

Dawis, R. V., & Lofquist, L. H. (1984). *A psychological theory of work adjustment.* Minneapolis: University of Minnesota Press.

Depue, R. A., & Collins, P. F. (1999). Neurobiology of the structure of personality. Dopamine facilitation of incentive motivation and extraversion. *Behavioral and Brain Sciences, 28*, 313–395.

Diemer, M. A., Wang, Q., & Smith, A. V. (2010). Vocational interests and prospective college majors among youth of color and poverty. *Journal of Career Assessment, 18*, 97–110.

Dik, B. J., & Hansen, J. C. (2008). Following passionate interests to well-being. *Journal of Career Assessment, 16*, 86–100.

Dik, B. J., & Hansen, J. C. (2011). Moderation of P-E fit: Job satisfaction relations. *Journal of Career Assessment, 19*, 35–50.

Dik, B. J., Hu, R. S. C., & Hansen, J. C. (2007). An empirical test of the Modified C Index and SII, O*NET, and DHOC occupational code classifications. *Journal of Career Assessment, 15,* 279–300.

Donnay, D. A. C., Morris, M., Schaubut, N., Thompson, R., Harmon, L. W., Hansen, J. C., ... Hammer, A. L. (2005). *Strong Interest Inventory manual: Research, development, and strategies for interpretation.* Palo Alto, CA: Consulting Psychologists.

Finn, S. E. (2007). *In our clients' shoes: Theory and techniques of therapeutic assessment.* Mahwah, NJ: Erlbaum.

Finn, S. E., & Martin, H. (in press). Therapeutic assessment: Using psychological testing as brief therapy. In K. Geisinger and Associates (Eds.), *Handbook of testing and assessment in psychology.* Washington, DC: American Psychological Association.

Fouad, N. A., Harmon, L. W., & Borgen, F. H. (1997). The structure of interests in employed male and female members of U.S. racial/ethnic minority and non-minority groups. *Journal of Counseling Psychology, 44,* 339–345.

Gasser, C. E., Larson, L. M., & Borgen, F. H. (2007). Concurrent validity of the 2005 Strong Interest Inventory: An examination of gender and major field of study. *Journal of Career Assessment, 15,* 23–43.

Gottfredson, G. D., & Holland, J. L. (1996). *Dictionary of Holland occupational codes.* Odessa, FL: Psychological Assessment Resources.

Gottfredson, L. S. (2005). Applying Gottfredson's theory of circumscription and compromise in career guidance and counseling. In S. D. Brown & R. W. Lent (Eds.), *Career development and counseling: Putting theory and research to work* (pp. 71–100). Hoboken, NJ: Wiley.

Hansen, J. C. (1988). Changing interests: Myth or reality? *Applied Psychology: An International Review, 37,* 137–150.

Hansen, J. C. (2000). Interpretation of the Strong Interest Inventory. In C. E. Watkins Jr., & V. L. Campbell (Eds.), *Testing and assessment in counseling practice* (pp. 227–262). Mahwah, NJ: Erlbaum.

Hansen, J. C. (in press). Person–environment fit approach to cultivating meaning. In B. J. Dik, Z. S. Byrne, & M. F. Steger (Eds.), *Purpose and meaning in the work place.* Washington, DC: American Psychological Association.

Hansen, J. C., & Campbell, D. P. (1985). *Manual for the SVIB-SCII* (4th ed.). Stanford, CA: Stanford University Press.

Hansen, J. C., & Dik, B. J. (2005). Evidence of 12-year predictive and concurrent validity for SII Occupational Scale scores. *Journal of Vocational Behavior, 67,* 365–378.

Hansen, J. C., Kozberg, J. G., & Goranson, D. (1994). Accuracy of student recall of Strong Interest Inventory results 1 year after interpretation. *Measurement and Evaluation in Counseling and Development, 26,* 235–242.

Hansen, J. C., & Lee, W. V. (2007). Evidence of concurrent validity of SII scores for Asian American college students. *Journal of Career Assessment, 15,* 1–11.

Hansen, J. C., & Leuty, M. E. (2007). Evidence of validity for the Skill Scale scores of the Campbell Interest and Skill Survey. *Journal of Vocational Behavior, 71,* 23–44.

Hansen, J. C., & Neuman, J. L. (1999). Evidence of concurrent prediction of the Campbell Interest and Skill Survey (CISS) for college major selection. *Journal of Career Assessment, 7,* 239–247.

Hansen, J. C., & Scullard, M. G. (2002). Psychometric evidence for the Leisure Interest Questionnaire and analyses of the structure of leisure interests. *Journal of Counseling Psychology, 49,* 331–341.

Hansen, J. C., Sullivan, B. A., & Luciana, M. (2011). A social neuroscientific model of vocational behavior. *Journal of Career Assessment, 19,* 216–227.

Hansen, J. C., & Swanson, J. (1983). The effect of stability of interests on the predictive and concurrent validity of the SCII for college majors. *Journal of Counseling Psychology, 30,* 194–201.

Hansen, J. C., & Ton, M. (2001). Using a person–environment fit framework to predict satisfaction and motivation in work and marital roles. *Journal of Career Assessment, 9,* 315–331.

Harms, P. D., Roberts, B. W., & Winter, D. (2006). Becoming the Harvard man: Person–environment fit, personality development, and academic success. *Personality and Social Psychology Bulletin, 32,* 851–865.

Haviland, M. L., & Hansen, J. C. (1987). Criterion validity of the Strong-Campbell Interest Inventory for American Indian college students. *Measurement and Evaluation in Counseling and Development, 19,* 196–201.

Holland, J. L. (1975). *Manual for the Vocational Preference Inventory.* Palo Alto, CA: Consulting Psychologists.

Holland, J. L. (1985). *Self-Directed Search professional manual.* Odessa, FL: Psychological Assessment Resources.

Holland, J. L. (1994). *Self-Directed Search user's guide.* Lutz, FL: Psychological Assessment Resources.

Holland, J. L. (1997). *Making vocational choices: A theory of vocational personalities and work environments* (3rd ed.). Odessa, FL: Psychological Assessment Resources.

Lubinski, D. (2000). Scientific and social significance of assessing individual differences: "Sinking shafts at a few critical points." In S. T. Fiske (Ed.), *Annual review of psychology 51* (pp. 405–444). Palo Alto, CA: Annual Reviews.

Morey, L. C., Lowmaster, S. E., & Hopwood, C. J. (2010). A pilot study of manual assisted cognitive therapy with a therapeutic assessment augmentation for borderline personality disorder. *Psychiatry Research, 178,* 531–535.

Ougrin, D., Ng, A. V., & Low, J. (2008). Therapeutic assessment based on cognitive-analytic therapy for young people presenting with self-harm: Pilot study. *Psychiatric Bulletin, 32,* 423–426.

Pendergrass, L. A., Hansen, J. C., Neuman, J. L., & Nutter, K. J. (2003). Examination of the concurrent validity of the scores from the CISS for student-athlete college major selection: A brief report. *Measurement and Evaluation in Counseling and Development, 35,* 212–218.

Porter, S. R., & Umbach, P. D. (2006). College major choice: An analysis of P-E fit. *Research in Higher Education, 47,* 429–449.

Poston, J. M., & Hanson, W. M. (2010). Meta-analysis of psychological assessment as a therapeutic intervention. *Psychological Assessment, 22,* 203–212.

Randahl, G. J., Hansen, J. C., & Haverkamp, B. E. (1993). Instrumental behaviors following test administration and interpretation. Exploration validity of the Strong Interest Inventory. *Journal of Counseling and Development, 71,* 435–439.

Rosen, D., Holmberg, K., & Holland, J. L. (1994). *The educational opportunities finder.* Odessa, FL: Psychological Assessment Resources.

Rottinghaus, P. J., Lindley, L. D., Green, M. A., & Borgen, F. H. (2002). Educational aspirations: The contribution of personality, self-efficacy and interests. *Journal of Vocational Behavior, 61,* 1–19.

Rounds, J. B. (1990). The comparative and combined ability of work value and interest data in career counseling with adults. *Journal of Vocational Behavior, 37,* 32–45.

Savickas, M. L., Tabor, B. J., & Spokane, A. R. (2002). Convergent and discriminant validity of five interest inventories. *Journal of Vocational Behavior, 61,* 139–184.

Schmidt, F. L. (2011). A theory of sex differences in technical aptitude and some supporting evidence. *Perspectives on Psychological Science, 6,* 560–573.

Staggs, G. D., Larson, L. M., & Borgen, F. H. (2007). Convergence of personality and interests: Meta-analysis of the Multidimensional Personality Questionnaire and the Strong Interest Inventory. *Journal of Career Assessment, 15,* 423–445.

Strong, E. K., Jr., (1927a). Vocational guidance of engineers. *Industrial Psychology Monthly, 11,* 291–298.

Strong, E. K., Jr., (1927b). *Vocational Interest Blank.* Stanford, CA: Stanford University Press.

Strong, E. K., Jr., (1935). Permanence of vocational interests. *Journal of Educational Psychology, 25,* 336–344.

Strong, E. K., Jr., (1943). *Vocational interests of men and women.* Stanford, CA: Stanford University Press.

Su, R., Rounds, J., & Armstrong, P. I. (2009). Men and things, women and people: A meta-analysis of sex differences in interests. *Psychological Bulletin, 135,* 859–884.

Sullivan, B. A., & Hansen, J. C. (2004a). Evidence of construct validity of the interest scales on the Campbell Interest and Skill Survey. *Journal of Vocational Behavior, 65,* 179–202.

Sullivan, B. A., & Hansen, J. C. (2004b). Mapping associations between interests and personality: Toward a conceptual understanding of individual differences in vocational behavior. *Journal of Counseling Psychology, 51,* 287–298.

Swanson, J. L., & Hansen, J. C. (1988). Stability of vocational interests over four-year, eight-year, and twelve-year intervals. *Journal of Vocational Behavior, 33,* 185–202.

Tellegen, A. (2000). *Manual for the Multidimensional Personality Questionnaire.* Minneapolis: University of Minnesota Press.

Tang, M. (2009). Examining the application of Holland's Theory to vocational interests and choices of Chinese college students. *Journal of Career Assessment, 17,* 86–98.

Wise, L. L., McHenry, J. J., & Campbell, J. P. (1990). Identifying optimal predictor composites and testing from generalizability across jobs and performance factors. *Personnel Psychology, 43,* 355–366.

CHAPTER 15

Nature, Importance, and Assessment of Needs and Values

JAMES ROUNDS AND JING JIN

WORK VALUES ARE SHARED interpretations of what people want and expect from work (Nord, Brief, Atieh, & Doherty, 1990). As such, values are central to our understanding of both the meaning of work and the reasons why people work. This shared social reality influences the type of work people design for others to do and how people are socialized for work. Values are central to human motivation and have a long history in psychology. Research on values can be found in many fields in psychology, with much of the theory and research coming from personality and social psychology and the more applied research coming from organizational and counseling psychology. The development of work value measures for career counseling comes from the traditional vocational psychology emphasis on occupational choice and adjustment (Dawis, 1991).

It is generally assumed that values are related to an individual's choice of a career and work behavior outcomes. Values assessment represents an opportunity to frame a client's career-related decisions in the context of underlying motivations. The comparisons between an individual's values and the rewards offered by different occupations can provide information on what kinds of occupations to explore (see Swanson & Schneider, Chapter 2, this volume). How well an individual's values fit with an organization has implications for career management strategies. Value–organization fit may influence early career success by contributing to mentoring relations, challenging career assignments, and fast-track promotion ladders (Bretz & Judge, 1994). Values assessments can have benefits for both the individual and organization, as individuals can identify work values that are not sufficiently rewarded and organizations can recruit employees with a close values fit.

Although work values offer potentially important information, value measures have received less research attention than measures of other individual differences characteristics, such as interests. Few papers have been published on work values since the 1990s, and the topic of work values in many career development and assessment textbooks is an afterthought. But this situation is not confined to career counseling and vocational psychology. Rohan (2000), in a review of introductory social psychology and personality textbooks, found no discussion of value theory in the 1990s. There are few work value measures commercially available and fewer still with sufficient reliability and validity to be recommended for use with clients. There are several reasons for this state of affairs. Vocational psychology from a counseling psychology perspective has historically focused on vocational choice for high school and college students, a population for which the assessment emphasis has been on vocational interests (Rounds, 1990). Work values are considered to be most applicable to individuals who have had some experience in the workplace, an adult clientele not frequently seen at college counseling centers. The critical loss of the work value research programs of Super and of Dawis and Lofquist has probably also played an important role in the decline in empirical research.

Several developments have, however, revitalized research on work values. One development is the study of values from a social-cultural approach (Fischer, Vauclair, Fontaine, & Schwartz, 2010; Hofstede, 2001). A second development has been the Occupational Information Network's (O*NET; Peterson, Mumford, Borman, Jeanneret, & Fleishman, 1999) adoption of the Minnesota work adjustment assessment model for needs and values (Dawis & Lofquist, 1984), providing the potential to link need and value scores to the wide range of career-relevant information to all occupations in the U.S. Department of Labor's O*NET database. Finally, industrial and organizational psychology researchers have continued to advance the study of values within work settings. This chapter highlights these recent developments and focuses on major contributions to the study of values, the importance of work values in career development, work value assessment strategies, and the major work value measures used in career and organizations.

We begin with a review of the concept of needs and values, laying a conceptual foundation for the use of value measures in career and organizational interventions. Second, we survey and define the content domain of work values (i.e., the kinds of work values that have been studied). Because work values have typically been studied within a person-environment fit tradition, we then describe the variety of research coming from this tradition that supports the ways that values are applied in vocational and organizational interventions. This research includes the relations of values to work outcomes, change and stability of work values from middle school to early adulthood, and gender, race, and ethnic differences. We end this chapter with a review of work value measures and suggestions for practical use of work values in career and organizational interventions.

CONCEPTUAL ISSUES

Several conceptual distinctions can be made between needs and values, but a close reading of the literature leads us to question some of these distinctions when applied to the practice of career counseling. Similarly, distinctions are made between general or life values and work values, but few studies have examined the relations between these two types of values (Roe & Ester, 1999). This lack of research leaves open a number of important questions. Do work values emerge from general values as individuals interact with work? Alternatively, do work values influence general values? These questions are similar to the issue of multiple roles and values: Do different values become salient as a person moves from one role to another? Should general value measures such as the Study of Values (Allport, Vernon, & Lindzey, 1970) be used in career assessment, or is it best to use work-specific value measures such as the Minnesota Importance Questionnaire? Answers to these questions have practical implications for assessment. Similar questions arise from attempts to distinguish work values and vocational interests. An understanding of the relations between them and their connection to occupations would influence many assessment practices. What is the best way to link the assessment of interests and values? In many cases, the literature has no clear answers to these conceptual and practical concerns.

NEEDS

The concept of psychological needs in modern psychology can be traced to Henry Murray's (1938) person-environment, need-press theory. Murray proposed a list of psychological needs that were important to human behavior. *Needs* refer to how the individual feels, behaves, or reacts. *Press* is defined as what the environment can do to facilitate or hinder the fulfillment of needs. The combination of individual needs and environmental press can be used to explain a wide variety of behaviors. The impact of Murray's theory can be seen on more recent person–environment conceptualizations of needs and values.

Many writers have regarded needs and values as equivalent. For example, Maslow (1954, 1959) viewed needs and values as similar, and at times he used these terms interchangeably. Rokeach (1973), however, saw needs as biologically derived and values as cognitive representations of those needs subject to influence by social and institutional demands. The need for sex, for example, is cognitively transformed such that love or intimacy is valued as a result. Super (1962, 1995) saw needs as the manifestation of physiological conditions related to survival. Super, like Rokeach (1973), viewed needs as refined through interactions with the environment, leading to the development of values. The resulting values are objectives used to satisfy needs through interest in certain activities. Super (1995) described the needs-value–interests link as such: Valuing material things may lead individuals to seek wealth, and people generally seek wealth through an interest in managerial and remunerative occupations. In Super's example, value attainment is also linked to occupational choice, as individuals tend to choose occupations that provide opportunities to fulfill values.

Much of the research on needs comes from theories of work motivation in organizational psychology. Work motivation theories attempt to explain the context and processes that account for an individual's energy, direction of effort, and maintenance of that effort in a work setting. One group of work motivation theories is based directly on the concept of needs, appropriately called *need theories*. The need theories that are most prominent in work motivation are Herzberg, Mausner, and Snyderman's (1959) hygienes-motivators theory, Maslow's (1954, 1959) self-actualization theory, and Alderfer's (1969) existence–relatedness–growth theory. Need theories propose that needs energize and direct an individual's behavior toward satisfaction of those needs. Therefore, an assessment of needs may provide important insight into the motivational forces underlying career-related decisions.

An important contribution of need theories is the identification and classification of needs. These need theories are often viewed as taxonomies of motivational variables. For example, Maslow classified needs into five categories: physiological, security, social, self-esteem, and self-actualization. Need theories were popular during the 1960s and 1970s, but interest in these models eventually declined, probably due to a failure to obtain empirical support (see Campbell & Pritchard, 1976). In reviewing work motivation theories, Kanfer (1991; also see Kanfer, Chen, & Pritchard, 2008) classified need and expectancy theories together because intrinsic motives, needs, and values are hypothesized to activate and direct behavior. Expectancy/valence theories introduced a cognitive mediation role for needs and values to explain the process of work motivation. Kanfer criticized these approaches for "not specifying the mediating processes by which motivational energy is transformed and/or directed toward specific behaviors or patterns of action" (p. 83). These criticisms are also applicable to life value models (e.g., Brown, 1996; Super, 1995).

VALUES

Essential to understanding work values is knowledge of value theory and thought in social psychology. The development of values can be traced to the philosopher Spranger's (1928) six basic types of individuality: theoretical, economic, aesthetic, social, political, and religious. Allport and Vernon's (1931) *Study of Values*, the first systematic attempt to measure values, was based on Spranger's theory and his six basic values. For Allport, values are "propriate" functioning, meaning that people are motivated to act in a manner that is expressive of the self. A value is "a belief upon which a man [*sic*] acts by preference" (Allport, 1961, p. 454). Much of the early research and practice used broad value measures such as the *Study of Values* to assess work-relevant values.

Since Allport, many other researchers have contributed to the broad study of values, including concepts that are important to our current understanding of work values. One such contribution is Rokeach's (1973) theoretical writing and his Value Survey, both of which renewed interest in the study of values. As with Allport, for Rokeach values are beliefs with some means or end of action that are judged to be desirable or undesirable. Because values are beliefs, they can have cognitive, affective, and behavioral components. Rokeach saw values as enduring but less stable than traits and identified two kinds of values: instrumental and terminal. *Instrumental values* are beliefs concerning desirable modes of conduct (e.g., ambitious, obedient). *Terminal values* are beliefs concerning desirable end states of existence (e.g., comfortable life, equality). Rokeach (1973) believed that values are central to understanding behavior. Although not taking such a broad view of values, Brown (1996; Brown & Crace, 1996) proposed a value model to account for human motivation that outlines the function of values in decision making and the impact that values have on the outcome of life choices. Similar to Rokeach, Brown and Crace defined values as cognitive representations, transformations of needs, providing standards, orienting people to desired end states, and enduring. Compared to other definitions, they emphasized an internal, cognitively mediated function of values as the basis of human motivation.

Needs and values are rarely the central components of theories in vocational counseling and psychology. An exception is the theory of work adjustment (Dawis & Lofquist, 1984; Swanson & Schneider, Chapter 2, this volume), which uses needs and values as explanatory constructs. Values in the theory of work adjustment are part of the work personality that also includes abilities and needs. Vocational needs are reinforcing conditions that have been found to be important to job satisfaction. Values are defined in terms of vocational needs as "second-order needs" or "underlying common elements of needs" (see Dawis & Lofquist, 1984, pp. 83–86; Dawis, 2001). Essentially, values are reference dimensions for needs, primarily defined by data reduction techniques such as factor analysis. Values can also be described in terms of work environment reinforcer systems, reflecting the kinds of work reinforcers that are important for an individual.

Super (1995) argued that vocational needs in the theory of work adjustment are similar to his values (see also Macnab & Fitzsimmons, 1987). Operationally, this is true. The measures developed by Super (1970) and Dawis and Lofquist (1984) use similar constructs to describe either needs or values. When examined closely, it is evident that need items in the Minnesota Importance Questionnaire (MIQ; Rounds, Henly, Dawis, Lofquist & Weiss, 1981) and value items in Work Values Inventory (Super, 1970) both assess the relative importance of work outcomes to the person. The difference in terminology is due to the origins of the theory of work adjustment. Dawis and Lofquist drew their ideas from Schaffer's (1953) research on job satisfaction and the behavioral tradition of Skinner (1938) with its emphasis on reinforcement (Lofquist & Dawis, 1991), whereas Super drew his ideas from the developmental work of Buehler (1933) and Ginzberg, Ginsburg, Axelrad, and Herma (1951).

Schwartz (1992) provides an up-to-date summary of how values have been conceptualized in psychology (see also Rohan, 2000). Schwartz reported that five features of values are frequently discussed in the value literature. Values (1) are beliefs, (2) pertain to desirable end states of behaviors, (3) guide selection or evaluation of behaviors and events, (4) remain stable across context and time, and (5) are ordered in terms of relative importance. Values, therefore, are stable motivational constructs that represent broad goals and, like traits, apply across context and time (Schwartz, 1994). Among value researchers, Schwartz currently has the most active research program. He has studied the structural relations of values across cultures (Fischer et al., 2010) and the relations of values and behaviors (Bardi & Schwartz, 2003) and has applied his theory of cultural values to work (Schwartz, 1999).

DISTINCTIONS FROM RELATED CONCEPTS

Researchers have grappled with several conceptual issues surrounding the definition of values, the first of which involves the distinction between life values and work values. Research into life values has tended to ignore developments in the field of work values. For example, two attempts to apply Schwartz's model of cultural values to the world of work fall short in their understanding of work values (Ros, Schwartz, & Surkiss, 1999; Schwartz, 1999). Ros and colleagues (1999) used Schwartz's 10 cultural values to derive only four work values (intrinsic, extrinsic, social, and mixed), a number that is far smaller than what is found in most work value taxonomies.

Work value research, however, has clearly been influenced by mainstream studies on life values (Dawis, 1991; Ronen, 1994). Elizur and Sagie (1999), for example, began with a multifaceted definition of life and work values and then generated both life and work value items. They reported that the structure within work and life domains was similar but that life and work values occupied two distinct regions in a three-dimensional conical structure. Life values were located at the base of the cone and work values at the top, suggesting that context is important for values assessment. One interesting issue that emerges from this research is the notion of compensatory models: Can fulfillment of a value through work compensate for its nonfulfillment in other life situations, or vice versa? Such value compensation has potentially important implications for career counseling, as clients may choose from different roles and environments to achieve a sense of value fulfillment in their lives. Research that is applicable to the life and work role distinction involves conflicts between work and family demands. Perrewe and Hochwarter (2001), for example, have proposed a model to capture work and family values as they relate to work–family conflict and outcomes. Studies examining the interrelations between work and life values are an emerging area of research, leaving this topic open for additional research and the emergence of new approaches.

The second issue, especially important to career counseling, is how needs, values, and interests are distinct but interrelated concepts. Super (1995) defined *interests* as preferences for activities in which individuals expect to attain or satisfy their needs and values. An interest, then, is one of the many manifestations of a value. For example, altruism (the value of helping others) leads a person to prefer social occupations (i.e., an interest in work where there will be an opportunity to help others). However, pairing values and interests is rarely this simple because values can often be linked to several different interest areas. For example, the value of achievement can be linked to investigative, artistic, and enterprising interests. A more sophisticated application would link a pattern of values and needs to different interest areas (Armstrong, Day, McVay, & Rounds, 2008). Therefore, a critical issue in the use of values and other assessment measures in career counseling is the ability to link together information from different sources to create a multifaceted picture of the individual and relevant career choices.

Dawis (1991) reviewed the conceptual definitions of interest and values and concluded that distinguishing between values and interests is difficult at the conceptual level, leading applied psychologists to prefer operational definitions. From an operational point of view, interests involve liking and disliking, and values involve importance and unimportance. This perspective makes it easy to distinguish between value and interest measures: Value measures ask individuals to rate the importance of items, whereas interest measures ask individuals to rate their liking of items. However, from a counseling standpoint, the lack of a clear conceptual distinction suggests that values and interests may be intertwined for many clients who are making career-related decisions.

CONTENT DOMAIN OF VALUES

A key to the study and assessment of values is to decide what values to measure and how these values are interrelated. To develop a measure of values or to evaluate an existing measure, researchers need to address three questions: What are the substantive contents (definition) of values? How comprehensive is the sample of values generated by the definition? How are the relations among values structured? We review three research programs and describe how these programs address these questions. The research programs reviewed are Dawis and Lofquist (1984), Super (Super & Sverko, 1995), and Schwartz (1992).

DAWIS AND LOFQUIST'S THEORY OF WORK ADJUSTMENT

In the theory of work adjustment, the vocational needs measured by the Minnesota Importance Questionnaire (MIQ; Rounds et al., 1981) are grouped into six work values, creating a hierarchical taxonomy (see Table 15.1). In this model, values are conceptualized as reference dimensions and latent variables for the description of needs. Studies of the factor structure of the 20 vocational needs in the MIQ have yielded a six-dimensional structure of work values. The six values can also be described in terms of work rewards that can satisfy the cluster of needs. The work environment descriptions for the six values are:

Achievement—an environment that encourages accomplishment.
Comfort—an environment that is comfortable and nonstressful.
Status—an environment that provides recognition and prestige.
Altruism—an environment that fosters harmony with and service to others.
Safety—an environment that is predictable.
Autonomy—an environment that stimulates initiative.

Dawis and Lofquist have also conceptualized three bipolar value dimensions: Achievement versus Comfort, Altruism versus Status, and Safety versus Autonomy. These dimensions are crossed with three types of rewards: self (achievement, autonomy), social (altruism, status), and environment (comfort, safety). The resulting structure graphically represents these opposing sets of values and three major classes of rewards.

This six-value structure was first identified in factor analyses of MIQ data in separate samples of 3,033 employed workers, 1,621 vocational rehabilitation

Table 15.1
Dawis and Lofquist (1984) 6 Work Values and 21 Needs

Work Value	Need	Item
Achievement	Ability utilization	I could do something that makes use of my abilities
	Achievement	The job could give me a feeling of accomplishment
Comfort	Activity	I could be busy all the time
	Independence	I could work alone on the job
	Variety	I could do something different each day
	Compensation	My pay would compare well with that of other workers
	Security	The job could provide for steady employment
	Working conditions	The job would have good working conditions
Status	Advancement	The job would provide an opportunity for advancement
	Recognition	I could get the recognition for the work I do
	Authority	I could tell people what to do
	Social status	I could be "somebody" in the community
Altruism	Co-workers	My co-workers would be easy to make friends with
	Social service	I could do things for other people
	Moral values	I could do the work without feeling that it is morally wrong
Safety	Company policies	The company would administer its policies fairly
	Supervision-human	My boss would back up the workers with top management
	Supervision-tech	My boss would train the workers well
Autonomy	Autonomy	I could plan my work with little supervision
	Creativity	I could try out some of my own ideas
	Responsibility	I could make decisions on my own

Source: A Psychological Theory of Work Adjustment, by R. V. Dawis and L. H. Lofquist, 1984, Minneapolis: University of Minnesota Press.

clients, 419 college students, and 285 vocational-technical students (Gay, Weiss, Hendel, Dawis, & Lofquist, 1971). This same six-factor structure was replicated across eight sex-by-age samples of 9,377 vocational rehabilitation clients (Lofquist & Dawis, 1978). Recently, the MIQ was revised for the O*NET (see Gore, Leuwerke, & Kelly, Chapter 18, this volume), producing the Work Importance Profiler and Work Importance Locator (WIP and WIL; McCloy et al., 1999b, 1999c). In the development of the computerized form of the WIP, exploratory and confirmatory factor analyses were conducted to evaluate the six-factor work values model. Results provided moderate support for Dawis and Lofquist's model, although the MIQ and WIP fit a seven-factor model better than the six-factor model. The seven-factor structure is similar to the six-factor structure, with the critical difference being that the Comfort value splits into Internal Comfort (Activity, Independence, and Variety) and External Comfort (Compensation, Security, and Working Conditions). In practice, the six-factor work value model (with a single Comfort value) continues to be used when presenting results to career counseling clients.

SUPER'S THEORY OF CAREER DEVELOPMENT

Much of Super's final research on work values came from the Work Importance Study (WIS; Super & Sverko, 1995). One objective of the WIS was to investigate the relative importance of work compared to other activities and to study the rewards that youth and adults seek in their major life roles across cultures. In a series of studies (see Ferreira-Marques & Miranda, 1995), decisions were made about the kinds of life and work values to assess and how to assess them. The items composing these values scales, with the exception of the Working Conditions Value scale, had both work- and non-work-related items. The list of values used in the WIS is shown in Table 15.2. As expected, many of the values (e.g., ability utilization, aesthetics, creativity) could be attained in multiple roles and situations. Other values are tied more specifically to work roles (e.g., economics, working conditions, advancement) or to nonwork roles (personal development, lifestyle).

Also shown in Table 15.2 are the five value orientations identified in a principal components analysis of 18,318 participants from 10 countries: Australia, Belgium (Flanders), Canada, Croatia, Italy, Japan, Poland, Portugal, South Africa, and the United States (Sverko, 1995). Many of the participants were students from secondary schools. The five Value Orientations (Sverko, 1995, p. 228) are:

Utilitarian Orientation—the importance of economic conditions and material career progress.

Individualistic Orientation—the importance of an autonomous way of living.

Orientation Toward Self-Actualization—the importance of inner-oriented goals for personal development and self-realization.

Social Orientation—the importance of social interaction.

Adventurous Orientation—the importance of risk.

In studies of the factor congruence across samples, only the Utilitarian and Individualistic value orientations showed generalizability. Sverko (1995) speculated that the lack of generalizability for the Self-Actualization, Social, and Adventurous orientations may be due to intergroup differences and

Table 15.2
5 Value Orientations, 18 Work Values, and Sample Items

Orientation	Value	Sample Item
Utilitarian	Economics	Have a high standard of living
	Advancement	Get ahead
	Prestige	Be admired for my knowledge and skills
	Authority	Tell others what to do
	Achievement	Have results which show that I have done well
Individualistic	Life-style	Living according to my ideas
	Autonomy	Act on my own
	(Creativity)	Discover, develop, or design new things
	(Variety)	Have every day different in some way from the one before it
Self-actualization	Ability utilization	Use my skill and knowledge
	Personal development	Develop as a person
	Altruism	Help people with problems
	(Achievement)	Have results which show that I have done well
	(Aesthetics)	Make life more beautiful
	(Creativity)	Discover, develop, or design new things
Social	Social Interaction	Do things with other people
	Social Relations	Be with friends
	(Variety)	Have every day different in some way from the one before it
	(Altruism)	Help people with problems
Adventurous	Risk	Do risky things
	(Physical activity)	Get a lot of exercise
	(Authority)	Tell others what to do

Note. Work values in parentheses have salient loading on more than one Orientation or do not load on this Orientation for all samples examined. The value of Working Conditions did not have salient loadings on the Orientations. Cultural Identity and Physical Prowess values were not included in the cross-cultural analyses.

Source: "The Structure and Hierarchy of Values Viewed Cross-Nationally," pp. 225–240, by B. Sverko, in *Life Roles, Values, and Careers: International Findings of the Work Importance Study*, D. E. Super and B. Sverko, eds., 1995, San Francisco: Jossey-Bass.

sampling errors. Another possible reason is that the structure of values may differ across secondary students, college students, and adults.

SCHWARTZ'S CIRCUMPLEX MODEL OF VALUES

Schwartz (1992) grouped value types according to common goals, reasoning that basic human values in all cultures would represent biological needs, social interaction, and group functioning. Informed by values identified by previous researchers and discussed in philosophical and religious writing, Schwartz developed and classified values into 10 motivational types, assumed to represent the range of values found across cultures:

Power—social status, prestige, control or dominance

Achievement—personal success through competence according to social standards

Hedonism—pleasure or sensuous gratification for oneself

Stimulation—excitement, novelty, challenge

Self-direction—independence of thought and action, creating, exploring

Universalism—understanding, tolerance, protection of all people and nature

Benevolence—preserving and enhancing the welfare of people

Tradition—respect and commitment to cultural or religious customs

Conformity—restraint of actions and impulses that may upset or harm others or violate social norms

Security—safety and stability of society, relationships, and self

A key aspect of Schwartz's value theory is the structural relations among values. The 10 values are organized according to the idea that the pursuit of a value has consequences that can be congruent with, or in conflict with, other values. For example, the pursuit of conformity may conflict with the pursuit of self-direction in cases where both values are important to the individual. The values are arranged in a circular fashion, beginning with Power and ending with Security, portraying the patterns of congruency and conflict. Conflicting values are opposite on the circle and congruent values are adjacent. Along the perimeter, the distance between any two values is a measure of the similarity of the motivations expressed by the value; those that are closer are more similar in motivation. Schwartz's model, with its emphasis on the properties of a circumplex, is similar to Holland's (1997) vocational interest circle and may eventually have important implications for counseling.

COMPARISON OF VALUE CLASSIFICATIONS

How comprehensive and similar are the value taxonomies? To answer this question, we inspected the need and value definitions and items of two classifications—Dawis and Lofquist, and Super—and then matched similar values. The results of this evaluation lead to the taxonomy shown in Table 15.3, which illustrates their similarity to one another. For example, both classifications have a value that emphasizes the importance of an environment that provides recognition and prestige. Dawis and Lofquist's label for the value is Status, and Super's label is Utilitarian.

Table 15.3

Comparison of Similar Categories in Dawis and Lofquist's (1984)
Work Values/Needs and Super's (Super & Sverko, 1995) Work
Orientations/Values

Dawis/Lofquist	Super
Achievement	Self-actualization
Ability utilization	Ability utilization
Achievement	
Autonomy	Individualistic
Creativity	Creativity
Responsibility	
Autonomy	Autonomy
	Personal development
	Life-style
	Aesthetics
	Variety
Status	Utilitarian
Advancement	Advancement
Recognition	Achievement
Authority	Authority
Social status	Prestige
	Economics
Altruism	Social
Co-workers	Social relations
Social service	Altruism
Moral values	
	Social interaction
Comfort	
Security	
Compensation	
Working conditions	Working conditions
Activity	
Independence	
Variety	
Safety	
Company policies and practices	
Supervision—human resources	
Supervision—technical	
	Adventurous
	Risk
	Physical activity

There is considerable overlap among value classifications listed in Table 15.3, with Dawis and Lofquist having the most comprehensive work value system. Super does not include organizational values similar to Dawis and Lofquist's Safety value. It is surprising that Super's classification includes only one value—working conditions—in the category that Dawis and Lofquist label Comfort. Super's classification, however, contains general values (e.g., Personal Development) that are not necessarily tied to a work setting but that do allow for a values assessment across other environments. But a comparison with Schwartz's model indicates that several life values are missing from Super's system, such as Hedonism, Universalism, Benevolence, Tradition, and Conformity.

Nord and colleagues (1990) suggested that models of work values are deficient because they omit several critical elements individuals might want from work (also see, Lyons, Higgins, & Duxbury, 2010). These include spiritual dimensions, the relationship between producers and customers, and the nature of the product relative to its ability to satisfy important human needs. It might be noted, however, that Dawis and Lofquist's Moral Values, in the Altruism category, partially addresses the spiritual dimension and the nature of the product dimension. Super's Altruism, contained in the Social category, may partially represent the producer and customer relationship dimension. Similarly, several of the values identified by Schwartz (1996) seem to fit in Nord and colleagues' omitted categories, including Universalism, Benevolence, and Tradition.

The question of which taxonomy is most representative of the domain of values depends partly on the area of research interest or clinical application. Schwartz (1992) has the most comprehensive set of life values, making this taxonomy an appropriate choice for use in general investigations. Dawis and Lofquist's taxonomy seems to be the best available description of work values and would be the most appropriate for exploring career development issues or other aspects of the world of work. Nevertheless, more study of the domain of work values is necessary before researchers and practitioners can claim to be measuring the full spectrum of values relevant to people's work lives. Additional research is also needed to clarify the relations between work and life values.

INDIVIDUAL DIFFERENCES

PERSON–ENVIRONMENT FIT PERSPECTIVE

Research has been concerned with how work values and work environments are related to outcomes. These relations are usually studied from a person-environment fit (P-E) perspective, in which various forms of P-E fit have been studied, including person-vocation, person-job, person-organization, and person-group (Kristof-Brown & Guay, 2010). A large body of research has found that the correspondence or compatibility between individual attributes (such as needs and values) and characteristics of the environment (such as job demands or organizational culture) is related to a variety of work-related outcomes (Ostroff & Judge, 2007; Kristof-Brown & Guay,

2010). Work value measures are designed to measure the importance of work outcomes expected to be related to satisfaction. It is not surprising, then, that work values and value-environment fit have been consistently found to predict job satisfaction (Dawis, 1991; Kristof, 1996; Locke, 1976; Ronen, 1994). Research has expanded beyond the traditional work outcome of job satisfaction. Studies have linked value-environment fit with several other outcomes as well, such as career choice (Judge & Bretz, 1992; Young & Hurlic, 2007), career satisfaction and occupational commitment (Cable & DeRue, 2002), and career success (Ballout, 2007; Bretz & Judge, 1994).

Recently, researchers have used meta-analysis to summarize various forms of P-E value congruence and work outcomes. Meta-analytic studies have shown that value correspondence relates positively to organizational commitment and negatively to turnover intentions. These meta-analyses have also reported positive relations between value congruence and job performance, and negative relations with work withdrawal behaviors and turnover decisions (Arthur, Bell, Villado, & Doverspike, 2006; Kristof-Brown, Zimmerman, & Johnson, 2005; Verquer, Beehr, & Wagner, 2003). Edwards and Cable (2009) explored why value correspondence is linked to work outcomes in a large representative sample of employed adults. According to their results, shared values between employees and organizations promote the development of trust, mutual liking, friendship, enhanced communication, and information exchange within the organization, which lead to positive work outcomes.

STABILITY AND CHANGE

Studies of work value stability and change usually adopt two approaches: rank-order stability and mean-level change. Rank-order stability refers to the relative standing of individuals within a group over time (De Fruyt et al., 2006) and is usually operationalized as a test–retest correlation. Mean-level change refers to whether a group of people as a whole increases or decreases on certain work value dimensions over time; it is also referred to as absolute or normative change (Caspi & Roberts, 1999) and is measured by mean differences. The existence of rank-order stability does not rule out the possibility of mean-level change. In fact, both have been shown to provide unique information in understanding stability and change.

Information on the rank-order stability of work values across the life span comes from a meta-analysis of longitudinal studies (Jin & Rounds, 2012). Results indicated that rank-order stability (i.e., test–retest correlation) of values remains relatively high ($\rho = .62$) across four age periods (12–17.9, 18–21.9, 22–25.9, and 26–after years). The age period between 18 and 22 is a time when work values appear to be least stable; many individuals are in college or engaged in postsecondary training, which is characterized as information gathering and exploring various career directions (Twenge, Campbell, Hoffman, & Lance, 2010). The college years (between 18 and 22) are a time when work values appear to be least stable, and the level of stability increases as individuals age, plateauing in young adulthood (after age 22). This is consistent with arguments that values are less stable during young adulthood, such as high school and college, when individuals are still exploring various career directions (Twenge et al., 2010). After age 22, when the majority of individuals have entered into the workplace, their position in the population with respect to different values tends to stabilize and plateau, as indicated by highest rank-order stability after 22 years old. That is, a person with high achievement values compared to his or her age group at 22 will tend to have high achievement values when compared to same-age peers later in life (e.g., at 30).

Although there are few longitudinal studies conducted on value stability and change beyond the age of 26, some researchers argue that values should fluctuate with added work experience. Mortimer and Lorence (1979) proposed two possible models: the occupational-selection model and the occupational-socialization model. In the occupational-selection model, central values and motives are formed mainly in childhood and adolescence; people choose their jobs based on their existing traits, values, and interests; and change during adulthood is relatively minor and superficial. In the occupational-socialization model, work experience is seen as promoting value changes over time and as molding values in the transition to adulthood. Mortimer and Lorence found support for both models. On one hand, they found the persistence of "self-selection"—that work values during the college years predict the attainment of valued occupational rewards 10 years later; on the other hand, rewarding occupational experiences were also able to significantly change the salience of values over time. With a national longitudinal sample, Lindsay and Knox (1984) also found support for both selection and socialization effects.

Mean-level change in values is often thought to be a consequence of the maturation process and of societal or historical changes shared by a population (Helson & Moane, 1987). A normative value change toward expanding the self and gaining more information is found during adolescence and early adulthood, when individuals are primarily engaged in schooling. Jin and Rounds's (2012) meta-analysis found that intrinsic values increase and extrinsic and status values decrease during the college (18–22) years. Sheldon (2005) has suggested that the liberal environment and the opportunity to explore new identities in college are particularly promotive of the development of intrinsic values. Later on in adulthood (after age 22), extrinsic and status values increase dramatically (Jin & Rounds, 2012). One possible explanation for this shift in values is that adults take on added responsibilities related to work, family, and civic involvement (Costa & McCrae, 2006). Such responsibilities may prompt less ideological and more pragmatic values.

In summary, it appears that an individual's standing within the population is least stable during college years. During college, the population as a whole attaches more importance to intrinsic values while de-emphasizing all the remaining values; during the initial entry into the workforce (22–26 years old), only extrinsic values show an increase in importance; later on, after early adulthood years (26 years and beyond), besides the continuous increase of extrinsic values, there was also a dramatic increase in status values. It is important that practitioners take into account stability and change in work values when assessing values and developing interventions across the life span.

GENDER DIFFERENCES

Numerous studies have investigated gender differences in work values with mixed and conflicting empirical findings. Differences in sample composition and size may account for the conflicting findings (Rowe & Snizek, 1995). To overcome these shortcomings, researchers have more recently conducted national surveys or meta-analyses and reported their results in terms of effect sizes, representing the magnitude of the differences in values between men and women. The typical effect size index used in these studies is the standardized mean difference (d), which is interpreted as the difference between the mean of men and women in standard deviations. Thus, a d of .50 suggests that the one group (e.g., men) scores about a half a standard deviation higher than the other (e.g., women) on a particular value. A d of 0.00 indicates that there is no difference between the scores of men and women. In most reviews, d is calculated in such a way that a positive d indicates that men score higher than women on that value, and a negative d indicates that women score higher than men. Many researchers use Cohen's (1988) suggestions for interpreting the magnitude of the effect (i.e., small $d = .20$, medium $d = .50$, large $d = .80$). In sum, the results of these national surveys (Konrad, Ritchie, Lieb, & Corrigall, 2000; Rowe & Snizek, 1995) and meta-analyses (Konrad et al., 2000) have found mostly small gender differences in values except for communal values. Women report stronger values for helping others and working with people than do men, with effect sizes in the medium range for these values ($d = -.36$ to $-.45$).

RACE AND ETHNIC DIFFERENCES

Similar to the gender-difference literature on work values, much of the early research, although in this case drawn from national samples, was based on small numbers of ethnic/minority participants. Most of the research has explored value differences between Whites and African Americans (Brenner, Blanzini, & Greenhaus, 1988; Kashefi, 2011; Martin & Tuch, 1993; Ransford & Miller, 1983; Shapiro, 1977). In general, this body of research suggests that African Americans report stronger values for extrinsic rewards (e.g., income and job security) and lesser values for such intrinsic rewards such as job accomplishments than do Whites, although these differences reduce considerably (but not completely) when social class (i.e., education, occupation, and income) and family background variables are controlled (Martin & Tuch, 1993; Shapiro, 1977). Similar patterns of differences were found in more recent studies. For example, Kashefi (2011) found that Whites preferred intrinsic rewards ($d = .29$), and African Americans preferred extrinsic ($d = .31$) rewards, although, as in earlier results, these differences disappeared among Whites and African Americans holding professional and managerial occupations. African Americans also preferred relational ($d = .11$) and enhancement ($d = .29$) rewards (e.g., status and prestige) more than did Whites in this study. Finally, some studies (e.g., Ransford & Miller, 1983) have found that gender differences in values may be more profound for Whites ($d = .66$) than for African Americans ($d = .11$).

Studies of Asians, American Indians, or Hispanics are few, and explanations of those racial differences typically take an Individual-Collectivism perspective (Triandis, McCusker, & Hui, 1990). Individualist cultures emphasize personal needs and goals, thus promoting values such as autonomy, independence, and personal growth. Collectivistic cultures, on the contrary, place the needs and goals of the group over those of the individual, promoting communal values such as relationship with others and conformity with norms and traditions. Despite this theoretical connection, empirical results in regard to individualism and collectivism and work values of different racial and ethnic groups are mixed and unclear (e.g., Hartung, Fouad, Leong, & Hardin, 2010; Robinson & Betz, 2008). These mixed findings may be due to the small samples of convenience or the need to develop more elaborate models to explain the relations of individualism and collectivism and work values (e.g., Oyserman, Coon, & Kemmelmeier, 2002). Future studies are encouraged to collect more representative and larger samples.

APPLICATION OF VALUES MEASURES IN CAREER COUNSELING

THEORY OF WORK ADJUSTMENT: MINNESOTA IMPORTANCE QUESTIONNAIRE

We begin the discussion of work value measures with the Minnesota Importance Questionnaire (MIQ; Gay, Weiss, Hendel, Dawis, & Lofquist, 1971; Rounds et al., 1981) because the MIQ lays the foundation for the recent development of the O*NET values measures. Most of the research and the counseling applications that come from the MIQ are applicable to the O*NET value measures as well. The MIQ is a rationally derived measure of 20 vocational needs organized under six work-related values based on the theory of work adjustment (Dawis & Lofquist, 1984; Swanson & Schneider, Chapter 2, this volume). This measure was developed as part of the work adjustment project at the University of Minnesota. The MIQ reflects a P-E fit approach to career counseling (Rounds & Tracey, 1990), which assumes that individuals will seek a work environment that matches their behavioral dispositions, including both needs and abilities.

Vocational needs are viewed as a subset of a larger set of personality needs and are especially important for understanding how individuals can identify career choices that will lead to satisfaction through reinforcement. Work-related reinforcers are rewards that are associated with the performance of work-related behaviors, and vocational needs are preferences for different reinforcers. The purpose of the MIQ is to help individuals identify the relative importance of each reinforcer and link these preferences to different occupational choices. In a counseling setting, the MIQ can be used to help identify the needs that are most important to the individual and then identify work environments that offer corresponding reinforcers. Comparisons between an individual's needs and the reinforcer patterns of different occupations provide a systematic way to explore the world of work and identify career choices that are most likely to be satisfying.

There are two forms available for the MIQ. One is a 210-item paired-comparison form that includes 190 forced-choice items where respondents are asked to choose between two need statements, and 20 absolute scale rating items, where respondents are asked to indicate the importance of each of the needs. The second form is a multiple rank-order measure where the forced-choice items are replaced by a series of items asking respondents to rank the relative importance of sets of five needs. Both versions are pencil-and-paper measures that need to be sent to the publisher for scoring. As noted in its manual (Rounds et al., 1981), the MIQ has excellent psychometric characteristics, including good internal consistency and test–retest reliability, which suggests that the MIQ is a reliable measure that assesses individual characteristics that tend to remain stable over time. Data collected as part of the University of Minnesota Work Adjustment Project also demonstrate that MIQ scores are predictive of job satisfaction (see Dawis & Lofquist, 1984).

The MIQ and career counseling. Strategies for using MIQ results in counseling are outlined in the MIQ manual (Rounds et al., 1981). The first step in interpretation is to examine the logically consistent triad (LCT) score, an index of the nonrandomness of the client's response pattern. A number of factors can contribute to random responding, in which case results may reflect the individual's inability to choose among different options or may reflect some problem in the assessment process, including poor understanding of the task, low motivation, carelessness, a response set, an attempt to fake results, or too low a reading ability. In cases where the LCT score indicates a valid profile, there are a number of interpretation strategies recommended. One method of interpretation is to use the scores on each scale to create an individual's hierarchy of needs and then use this hierarchy as a starting point for exploring career-related options. MIQ scores can also be interpreted with reference to the norms that have been developed for the measure, and scores can be used to predict satisfaction in different occupations, both at the individual occupation level (Stewart et al., 1986) and based on clusters of occupations from the Minnesota Occupational Classification System (MOCS III; Dawis et al., 1987). Additional strategies include having the client interpret the meaning of each need statement or having the client do a self-estimation of needs.

The MIQ has many characteristics that make it useful for career counseling. Its development is rooted in an empirically supported psychological theory of career development. The MIQ has a hierarchical structure of needs and values that allows for a discussion of results at different levels of specificity to reflect the varying developmental levels of career counseling clients. More specifically, clients who are in the early stages of career development may benefit more from a general discussion of values, whereas clients who are further along in the process of making career-related decisions may benefit from a more detailed discussion of specific needs. The needs and values measured by the MIQ can be linked to occupational outcomes, although the MIQ offers information on only a limited number of occupations that are not grouped by level of educational requirements. It should be noted that the MIQ, the research data that supported its development, and the information it provides in counseling are becoming progressively more dated. Fortunately, both of these concerns have been addressed by the development of the MIQ-based O*NET value measures.

O*NET VALUE MEASURES

Two values measures, developed as part of the O*NET (see Gore et al., Chapter 18, this volume), update and expand the information available from the MIQ. Linking results to the O*NET increases the number of occupations that can be matched to an individual's needs and values and allows for the organization of occupations based on job zones, a series of hierarchical categories based on the required level of education and training. The Work Importance Profiler (WIP; U.S. Department of Labor, 2000b) is a computerized assessment program that uses the multiple-rank order format from the MIQ. On completion of the WIP, a report can be generated that includes a list of occupations from the O*NET database that match the individual's profile, sorted into categories reflecting different levels of educational requirements. Interpretation of WIP results and their application in career counseling is otherwise the same as for the MIQ.

The Work Importance Locator (WIL; U.S. Department of Labor, 2000a) is a self-scoring measure that uses a card-sorting task to determine the relative importance of the MIQ needs. Value scores are calculated by hand using a workbook that also lists a number of occupations that are associated with each value by job zone. Details of the development of these measures are presented in technical reports by McCloy and colleagues (1999a, 1999b). Overall, the reliability for the computerized WIP is comparable to the reliability for the MIQ, but the reliability for the WIL is less impressive, perhaps reflecting the limitations of using a card-sorting technique.

*O*NET value measures and career counseling.* A critical issue with the use of assessment instruments in the career counseling process is being able to link results to occupational choices. In general, the use of a values measure can lead to insights about what is important to the client, serving as a catalyst for personal growth. However, a values measure that can be linked to occupations offers the critical advantage of a second level of discourse—an examination of how values are related to satisfaction. It is this advantage that separates the MIQ and its O*NET offspring from the other value taxonomies and measures discussed in this chapter. The data used to connect O*NET value profiles to occupations are more extensive and up-to-date than what is available for the MIQ (Rounds, Armstrong, Liao, Lewis, & Rivkin, 2008). These data and the measures themselves can be downloaded free at the U.S. Department of Labor's O*NET website, http://www.onetcenter.org. The O*NET presents an impressive and unprecedented opportunity to combine different types of information on occupations to create a cohesive picture of how individuals can be matched to work environments. A battery of assessment instruments has been developed for the O*NET, including an ability measure, computerized and pencil-and-paper Holland-based interest measures, and the MIQ-based value measures. Results can be linked to information on the more than 800 occupations in the O*NET database, including generalized work activities, work and organizational contexts, skill and ability requirements, knowledge areas and requirements for occupational preparation, and occupational interests and values.

Of the two O*NET-based values measures, the computerized WIP offers more sophisticated methods for matching results to occupational information and can be used to generate a detailed report for review by the counselor and client. The self-scoring WIL version is useful in cases where there is limited access to computers or for group administrations. The WIL can also be used within a counseling session where the client can talk through the meaning of the need statements, for example, while sorting the need statements according to their importance.

MEASURES BASED ON SUPER'S THEORY: VALUES SCALE AND WORK VALUES INVENTORY–REVISED

Super (1957) initially developed the Work Values Inventory for his Career Pattern Study. Over the past 50 years, Super's prototype value measure has been revised many times and has been in and out of print. Currently, the best versions of Super's measures are the Values Scale (Nevill & Super, 1986) and Super's Work Values Inventory–Revised (Zytowski, 2006). The Values Scale is based on Super's (1980) career development theory and was initially developed in several languages for the cross-cultural study of the career development process, the results of which are detailed in Super and Sverko (1995). Nevill and Kruse (1996) have reviewed the empirical support for the Values Scale and discussed its use in career assessment and counseling. Super's Work Values Inventory–Revised is a commercially available measure within the Kuder Career Planning System.

The Values Scale is a 105-item instrument measuring the importance of 21 values, using 21 five-item scales with a 4-point response format. Nevill and Super (1986) suggest that this assessment method allows for both ipsative and normative interpretations of the results of the Values Scale. By ranking values according to the relative scores obtained on each scale, it is possible to create a values hierarchy for an individual. However, given the social desirability of many values (see Rokeach, 1973), most instrument designers have opted for a forced-choice format to create a values hierarchy. With the rating method used in the Values Scale, it is possible for a client who is having difficulty making career-related decisions to indicate that all of the values are "very important" to him or her, making the results meaningless. In other cases, variability in the range of responses may reflect only measurement error instead of substantive differences in the importance of each value. Apart from the values hierarchy, it is possible to provide a normative interpretation of the results, which would compare an individual's scores to a set of norms obtained from a representative sample of the population to which the individual belongs. Unfortunately, such an application is not yet possible. Although the Values Scale was used in the multinational WIS, the data from that project have yet to be presented in a form that would permit this type of normative interpretation. The Values Scale is currently out of print.

Zytowski (2006) has developed a commercially available form of Super's work values, called Super's Work Value Inventory–Revised (SWVI-R). The SWVI-R is a revision of Super's 1970 Work Values Inventory. The SWVI-R consists of 12 scales of 6 items each, for a total of 72 items. The scales consist of the following work values: Achievement, Coworkers, Creativity, Income, Independence, Lifestyle, Mental Challenge, Prestige, Security, Supervision, Work Environment, and Variety. Clients respond to the items using a 5-point response format reflecting the degree of importance of each value. Zytowski (2006) recommended creating a values hierarchy for clients based on a ranking of their values on each scale. Because of the possibility that clients will rate all values as important, normative interpretations are not recommended. To link the SWVI-R values with occupations, Zytowski (2006) matched the 12 SWVI-R work values with the 20 O*NET work values. From this matching, a list of O*NET occupations are generated. Because of value mismatches (e.g., WIP Activity with SWVI-R Independence), we recommend that counselors not use this section of the SWVI-R report.

Initial research shows that, with the exception of the Independence scale, the SWVI-R scales are reliable (Robinson & Betz, 2008). Structural studies have yet to converge on a common framework for the SWVI-R scales (cf., Robinson & Betz, 2008; Zytowski, 2006). Norms have been developed but the representativeness of the norm sample is unclear from the technical manual (Zytowski, 2006). Although these issues are a drawback to practical use, a major concern similar to the development of the Value Scale is that the coverage of values is limited when compared to other inventories. Research is needed to expand the coverage of the SWVI-R work-value domain.

Use of work value inventories in career counseling. Many of the articles and manuals on the use of work values in counseling focus on specific inventories. But most of the advice and recommendations in these articles and manuals are applicable to any assessment of work values. The application of the Values Scale in career counseling has been linked to Super's (1983) career development assessment and counseling (C-DAC) model by Nevill and Kruse (1996) (see Hartung, Chapter 4, this volume). In this model, there are three important issues to address: The first issue is to determine values the client would like to realize through work; the second, to assess the relative importance of work to the client relative to other life roles; and the third, to assess the client's readiness to make career-related decisions.

According to Nevill and Kruse (1996), the Values Scale addresses the first issue by assessing the values of the individual and identifying those that will be important to him or her in the work domain. Understanding the importance of the work role relative to other life roles has important implications for the career counseling process because clients who do not see work as important may not be in the best position to work with the results of career-related assessment measures. Nevill and Kruse recommend discussing with the client the relative importance of different life roles. For clients who do not view the work role as important, Nevill and Kruse recommend using interventions designed to increase awareness of the importance of work, as these clients may not be ready to engage in a detailed analysis of assessment results. In comparison, clients who view the worker role as important would not need this type of intervention before attempting to make critical educational and career-related decisions.

The primary limitation of using the Values Scale in career counseling is the limited data available linking results to career-related outcomes. The comparisons are the MIQ and WIP, the results of which can be linked to meaningful vocational outcomes based on empirical data. For example, if a person scores high on the MIQ or WIP measures of Achievement or Ability Utilization, a database of occupational information can be used to identify potential career choices where these values will be reinforced. In comparison, if a person scores high on the Values Scale measures of Achievement or Ability Utilization, there is no equivalent database of information for interpreting results. Furthermore, the Values Scale assesses a limited range of work values, lacking the organizational values measured by the MIQ and WIP.

OTHER VALUE MEASURES

In addition to the MIQ, its O*NET-based variations, and Super's Values Scale and Zytowski's revised Work Values Inventory, there are a number of values measures available, varying in psychometric robustness, that correspond to the various taxonomies and models previously discussed in this chapter. Included in this category are Rokeach's (1973) classic values measure; Kopelman, Rovenpor, and Guan's (2003) update of the Allport-Vernon-Lindzey Study of Values; the circumplex measure of values proposed by Schwartz (1992; see Struch, Schwartz, & van der Kloot, 2002); the values measure used by Hofstede (1980, 2001) in his cross-cultural research; and any number of idiosyncratic value measures developed by researchers in the industrial-organizational area, a review of which is beyond the scope of this chapter. The use of these measures in career counseling could lead to interesting discussions and an increased understanding of the relative importance of different values to a client, but the inability to reliably link these results to occupational outcomes limits the range of their clinical application.

CONCLUSIONS AND PRACTICE IMPLICATIONS

Values represent an important source of information that can be used to facilitate the career development process. Work values are embedded in Dawis and Lofquist's theory of work adjustment and Super's discussions of career development. A critical reason to assess work values in career counseling is that value correspondence (fit between person values and work outcomes) is related to occupation and job choice and to satisfaction with work environments. Furthermore, when individuals enter the work force, value congruence is related to job performance, organizational commitment, and turnover. A possible reason for why value congruence is related to satisfaction and performance is that shared values between employees and organizations promote the development of trust, mutual liking, friendship, enhanced communication, and information exchange within the work setting.

Intrinsic values increase after high school (18–22 years), when many young adults leave their families and engage in further training or schooling. During early adulthood (age 22 and beyond), adults place more importance on extrinsic and status values. These findings indicate that counselors need to assist high school and college students in understanding possible value changes across early adulthood when exploring careers. There are small gender, ethnic, and racial differences in work values, with the most prominent difference being gender differences in work values that involve communion. Women value communion, the tendency to work with or help people, more than do men.

The use of a values measure in career counseling should be part of an integrative strategy combining different sources of information and perspectives to help individuals make informed career-related decisions. Among the measures that represent the different value taxonomies and models presented in this chapter, the O*NET-based WIP and WIL offer the best strategy for linking values to occupations. The other values measures we reviewed cannot link results to the range of career-related information available in the O*NET. As the U.S. Department of Labor continues to develop and update the O*NET database, the discrepancy between the range of information available through the WIP and other measures will continue to grow. In short, other value measures may be a starting point for a discussion of what is important to a client but cannot provide an answer to the potentially more interesting question of how to link these values to work.

REFERENCES

Alderfer, C. P. (1969). An empirical test of a new theory of human needs. *Organizational Behavior and Human Performance, 4,* 142–175.

Allport, G. W. (1961). *Pattern and growth in personality*. New York, NY: Holt, Rinehart and Winston.

Allport, G. W., & Vernon, P. E. (1931). *A study of values*. Cambridge, MA: Houghton-Mifflin.

Allport, G. W., Vernon, P. E., & Lindzey, G. (1970). *Study of values* (rev. 3rd ed.). Chicago, IL: Riverside.

Armstrong, P. I., Day, S. X, McVay, J. P., & Rounds, J. (2008). Holland's RIASEC model as an integrative framework for individual differences. *Journal of Counseling Psychology, 55*, 1–18.

Arthur, W., Bell, S. T., Villado, A. J., & Doverspike, D. (2006). The use of person–organization fit in employment decision making: An assessment of its criterion-related validity. *Journal of Applied Psychology, 91*, 786–801.

Ballout, H. I. (2007). Career success: The effects of human capital, person–environment fit and organizational support. *Journal of Managerial Psychology, 22*, 745–761.

Bardi, A., & Schwartz, S. H. (2003). Values and behavior: Strength and structure of relations. *Personality and Social Psychology Bulletin, 29*, 1207–1220.

Brenner, O. C., Blazini, A. P., & Greenhaus, J. H. (1988). An examination of race and sex differences in managerial work values. *Journal of Vocational Behavior, 32*, 336–344.

Bretz, R. D., Jr., & Judge, T. A. (1994). Person–organization fit and the theory of work adjustment: Implications for satisfaction, tenure, and career success. *Journal of Vocational Behavior, 44*, 32–54.

Brown, D. (1996). Brown's value-based, holistic model of career and life-role choices and satisfaction. In D. Brown, L. Brooks, & Associates (Eds.), *Career choices and development* (3rd ed., pp. 337–372). San Francisco, CA: Jossey-Bass.

Brown, D., & Crace, R. K. (1996). Values in life role choices and outcomes: A conceptual model. *Career Development Quarterly, 44*, 211–224.

Buehler, C. (1933). *Der menschilch lebenslauf als psychologisches problem* (The human life course as a psychological subject). Leipzig, Germany: Hirzel.

Cable, D. M., & DeRue, D. S. (2002). The convergent and discriminant validity of subjective fit perceptions. *Journal of Applied Psychology, 87*, 875–884.

Campbell, J. P., & Pritchard, R. D. (1976). Motivation theory in industrial and organizational psychology. In M. D. Dunnette (Ed.), *Handbook of industrial and organizational psychology* (pp. 63–130). Chicago, IL: Rand Mc Nally.

Caspi, A., & Roberts, B. W. (1999). Personality change and continuity across the life course. In L. A. Pervin & O. P. John (Eds.), *Handbook of personality theory and research* (pp. 300–326). New York, NY: Guilford.

Cohen, J. (1988). *Statistical power analysis for the behavioral sciences* (2nd ed.). Hillsdale, NJ: Erlbaum.

Costa, P. T., Jr., & McCrae, R. R. (2006). Age changes in personality and their origins: Comment on Roberts, Walton, and Viechtbauer (2006). *Psychological Bulletin, 132*, 26–28.

Dawis, R. V. (1991). Vocational interests, values, and preferences. In M. D. Dunnette & L. M. Hough (Eds.), *Handbook of industrial and organizational psychology* (2nd ed., vol. 2, pp. 833–871). Palo Alto, CA: Consulting Psychologists.

Dawis, R. V. (2001). Toward a psychology of values. *Counseling Psychologist, 29,* 458–465.

Dawis, R. V., Dohm, T. E., Lofquist, L. H., Chartrand, J. M., & Due, A. M. (1987). *Minnesota Occupational Classification System III.* Minneapolis: Vocational Psychology Research, Department of Psychology, University of Minnesota.

Dawis, R. V., & Lofquist, L. H. (1984). *A psychological theory of work adjustment.* Minneapolis, MN: University of Minnesota Press.

De Fruyt, F., Bartels, M., Van Leeuwen, K. G., De Clercq, B., Decuyper, M., & Mervielde, I. (2006). Five types of personality continuity in childhood and adolescence. *Journal of Personality and Social Psychology, 91,* 538–552.

Edwards, J. R., & Cable, D. M. (2009). The value of value congruence. *Journal of Applied Psychology, 94,* 654–677.

Elizur, D., & Sagie, A. (1999). Facets of personal values: A structural analysis of life and work values. *Applied Psychology: An International Review, 17,* 501–514.

Ferreira-Marques, J., & Miranda, M. J. (1995). Developing the work importance study. In D. E. Super & B. Sverko (Eds.), *Life roles, values, and careers: International findings of the work importance study* (pp. 62–74). San Francisco, CA: Jossey-Bass.

Fischer, R., Vauclair, C., Fontaine, J. R. J., & Schwartz, S. H. (2010). Are individual-level and country-level value structures different? Testing Hofstede's legacy with the Schwartz Value Survey. *Journal of Cross-Cultural Psychology, 41,* 135–151.

Gay, E. G., Weiss, D. J., Hendel, D. D., Dawis, R. V., & Lofquist, L. H. (1971). Manual for the Minnesota Importance Questionnaire. *Minnesota Studies in Vocational Rehabilitation, 28,* 1–83. Minneapolis: University of Minnesota, Industrial Relations Center.

Ginzberg, E., Ginsburg, S. W., Axelrad, S., & Herma, J. (1951). *Occupational choice: An approach to a general theory.* New York, NY: Columbia University Press.

Hartung, P. J., Fouad, N. A., Leong, F. T. L., & Hardin, E. E. (2010). Individualism-collectivism: Links to occupational plans and work values. *Journal of Career Assessment, 18,* 34–45.

Helson, R., & Moane, G. (1987). Personality change in women from college to midlife. *Journal of Personality and Social Psychology, 53,* 176–186.

Herzberg, F., Mausner, B., & Snyderman, B. (1959). *The motivation to work* (2nd ed.). New York, NY: Wiley.

Hofstede, G. (1980). *Culture's consequences: International differences in work-related values.* Beverly Hills, CA: Sage.

Hofstede, G. (2001). *Cultural consequences: Comparing values, behaviors, institutions and organizations across nations.* Thousand Oaks, CA: Sage.

Holland, J. L. (1997). *Making vocational choices: A theory of vocational personalities and work environments* (3rd ed.). Odessa, FL: Psychological Assessment Resources.

Jin, J., & Rounds, J. (2012). Stability and change in work values: A meta-analysis of longitudinal studies. *Journal of Vocational Behavior, 80,* 326–339.

Judge, T. A., & Bretz, R. D. (1992). Effects of work values on job choice decisions. *Journal of Applied Psychology, 77,* 261–271.

Kanfer, R. (1991). Motivation theory and industrial and organizational psychology. In M. D. Dunnette & L. M. Hough (Eds.), *Handbook of industrial and organizational psychology* (vol. 1, pp. 75–170). Palo Alto, CA: Consulting Psychologists Press.

Kanfer, R., Chen, G., & Pritchard, R. D. (2008). The three C's of work motivation: Content, context, and change. In R. Kanfer, G. Chen, & R. D. Pritchard (Eds.), *Work motivation: Past, present, and future* (pp. 1–16). New York, NY: Routledge.

Kashefi, M. (2011). Structure and/or culture: Explaining racial differences in work values. *Journal of Black Studies, 42,* 638–664.

Konrad, A. M., Ritchie, J. E., Lieb, P., & Corrigall, E. (2000). Sex differences and similarities in job attributes preferences: A meta-analysis. *Psychological Bulletin, 126,* 593–641.

Kopelman, R. E., Rovenpor, J. L., & Guan, M. (2003). The study of values: Construction of the fourth edition. *Journal of Vocational Behavior, 62,* 203–220.

Kristof, A. (1996). Person–organization fit: An integrative review of its conceptualizations, measurement, and implications. *Personnel Psychology, 49,* 1–48.

Kristof-Brown, A. L., & Guay, R. P. (2010). Person–environment fit. In S. Zedeck (Ed.), *APA handbook of industrial and organizational psychology* (vol. 3, pp.3–50). Washington, DC: American Psychological Association.

Kristof-Brown, A. L., Zimmerman, R. D., & Johnson, E. C. (2005). Consequences of individual's fit at work: A meta-analysis of person-job, person-organization, person-group, and person-supervisor fit. *Personnel Psychology, 58,* 281–342.

Lindsay, P., & Knox, W. E. (1984). Continuity and change in work values among young adults: A longitudinal study. *American Journal of Sociology, 89,* 918–931.

Locke, E. A. (1976). The nature and causes of job satisfaction. In M. D. Dunnette (Ed.), *Handbook of industrial and organizational psychology* (pp. 1297–1349). Chicago, IL: Rand McNally.

Lofquist, L. H., & Dawis, R. V. (1978). Values as second-order needs in the theory of work adjustment. *Journal of Vocational Behavior, 13,* 12–19.

Lofquist, L. H., & Dawis, R. V. (1991). *Essentials of person environment correspondence counseling.* Minneapolis: University of Minnesota Press.

Lyons, S., Higgins, C. A., & Duxbury, L. (2010). Work values: Development of a new three-dimensional structure based on confirmatory smallest space analysis. *Journal of Organizational Behavior, 31,* 969–1002.

Macnab, D., & Fitzsimmons, G. W. (1987). A multitrait–multimethod study of work-related needs, values and preferences. *Journal of Vocational Behavior, 30,* 1–15.

Martin, J. K., & Tuch, S. A. (1993). Black-White differences in the value of job rewards revisited. *Social Science Quarterly, 74,* 884–901.

Maslow, A. H. (1954). *Motivation and personality.* New York, NY: Harper & Row.

Maslow, A. H. (1959). *New knowledge in human values.* New York, NY: Harper & Row.

McCloy, R. A., Waugh, G., Medsker, G., Wall, J., Rivkin, D., & Lewis, P. (1999a). *Determining the Occupational Reinforcer Patterns for O*NET occupational units* (2 vols.). Raleigh, NC: National Center for O*NET Development.

McCloy, R., Waugh, G., Medsker, G., Wall, J., Rivkin, D., & Lewis P. (1999b). *Development of the Computerized Work Importance Profiler.* Raleigh, NC: National Center for O*NET Development.

McCloy, R., Waugh, G., Medsker, G., Wall, J., Rivkin, D., & Lewis P. (1999c). *Development of the Paper-and-Pencil Work Importance Locator*. Raleigh, NC: National Center for O*NET Development.

Mortimer, J. T., & Lorence, J. (1979). Work experience and occupational value socialization: A longitudinal study. *American Journal of Sociology, 84*, 1361–1385.

Murray, H. A. (1938). *Explorations in personality*. New York, NY: Oxford University Press.

Nevill, D. D., & Kruse, S. J. (1996). Career assessment and the values scale. *Journal of Career Assessment, 4*, 383–397.

Nevill, D. D., & Super, D. E. (1986). *The Value Scale: Theory, application, and research*. Palo Alto, CA: Consulting Psychologists Press.

Nord, W. R., Brief, A. P., Atieh, J. M., & Doherty, E. M. (1990). Studying meaning of work: The case of work values. In A. P. Brief & W. R. Nord (Eds.), *Meanings of occupational work* (pp. 21–64). Lexington, MA: Lexington.

Ostroff, C., & Judge, T. A. (Eds.). (2007). *Perspectives on organizational fit*. Mahwah, NJ: Erlbaum.

Oyserman, D., Coon, H. M., & Kemmelmeier, M. (2002). Rethinking individualism and collectivism: Evaluation of theoretical assumptions and meta-analysis. *Psychological Bulletin, 128*, 3–72.

Perrewe, P. L., & Hochwarter, W. A. (2001). Can we really have it all? The attainment of work and family values. *Current Directions in Psychological Science, 10*, 29–33.

Peterson, N. G., Mumford, M. D., Borman, W. C., Jeanneret, E. A., & Fleishman, P. R. (1999). *An occupational information system for the 21st century: The development of the O*NET*. Washington, DC: American Psychological Association.

Ransford, H. E., & Miller, J. (1983). Race, sex, and feminist outlooks. *American Sociological Review, 48*, 46–59.

Robinson, C. H., & Betz, N. E. (2008). A psychometric evaluation of Super's Work Values Inventory–Revised. *Journal of Career Assessment, 16*, 456–473.

Roe, R. A., & Ester, P. (1999). Values and work: Empirical findings and theoretical perspective. *Applied Psychology: An International Review, 48*, 1–21.

Rohan, M. J. (2000). A rose by any name? The values construct. *Personality and Social Psychology Review, 4*, 255–277.

Rokeach, M. (1973). *The nature of human values*. New York, NY: Free Press.

Ronen, S. (1994). An underlying structure of motivational need taxonomies: A cross-cultural confirmation. In H. C. Triandis, M. D. Dunnette, & L. M. Hough (Eds.), *Handbook of industrial and organizational psychology* (vol. 4, pp. 241–270). Palo Alto, CA: Consulting Psychologist Press.

Ros, M., Schwartz, S. H., & Surkiss, S. (1999). Basic individual values, work values, and the meaning of work. *Applied Psychology: An International Review, 48*, 49–71.

Rounds, J. B. (1990). The comparative and combined utility of work-value and interest data in career counseling with adults. *Journal of Vocational Behavior, 37*, 32–45.

Rounds, J., Armstrong, P. I., Liao, H.-Y., Lewis, P., & Rivkin, D. (2008). *Second generation occupational value profiles for the O*NET system*. Raleigh, NC:

National Center for O*NET Development. Retrieved from http://www.onetcenter .org/reports/SecondOVP_Summary.html

Rounds, J. B., Henly, G. A., Dawis, R. V., Lofquist, L. H., & Weiss, D. J. (1981). *Manual for the Minnesota Importance Questionnaire: A measure of needs and values.* Minneapolis, MN: University of Minnesota Department of Psychology.

Rounds, J. B., & Tracey, T. J. (1990). From trait-and-factor to person–environment fit counseling: Theory and process. In W. B. Walsh & S. H. Osipow (Eds.), *Career counseling* (pp. 1–44). Hillsdale, NJ: Erlbaum.

Rowe, R., & Snizek, W. E. (1995). Gender differences in work values: Perpetuating the myth. *Work and Occupations, 22,* 215–229.

Schaffer, R. H. (1953). Job satisfaction as related to need satisfaction in work. *Psychological Monographs, 67,* (Whole Serial Number 364).

Schwartz, S. H. (1992). Universals in the content and structure of values: Theoretical advances and empirical tests in 20 countries. In M. P. Zanna (Ed.), *Advances in experimental social psychology* (vol. 24, pp. 1–65). San Diego, CA: Academic Press.

Schwartz, S. (1994). Are there universal aspects in the structure and contents of human values? *Journal of Social Issues, 50,* 19–45.

Schwartz, S. (1996). Value priorities and behavior: Applying a theory of integrated value systems. In C. Seligman, J. M. Olson, & M. P. Zanna (Eds.), *Values: The Ontario symposium* (vol. 8, pp. 1–24). Hillsdale, NJ: Erlbaum.

Schwartz, S. H. (1999). A theory of cultural values and some implications for work. *Applied Psychology: An International Review, 48,* 23–47.

Shapiro, E. G. (1977). Racial differences in the value of job rewards. *Social Forces, 56,* 21–30.

Sheldon, K. M. (2005). Positive value change during college: Normative trends and individual differences. *Journal of Research in Personality, 39,* 209–223.

Skinner, B. F. (1938). *The behavior of organisms.* New York, NY: Appleton-Century-Crofts.

Spranger, E. (1928). *Types of men: The psychology and ethics of personality* (Paul J. W. Pigors, Trans.). Halle, Germany: Max Niemeyer Verlag.

Stewart, E. S., Greenstein, S. M., Holt, N. C., Henly, G. A., Engdahl, B. E., Dawis, R. V., . . . Weiss, D. J. (1986). *Occupational reinforcer patterns.* Minneapolis: Vocational Psychology Research, University of Minnesota Department of Psychology.

Struch, N., Schwartz, S. H., & van der Kloot, W. A. (2002). Meanings of basic values for women and men: A cross-cultural analysis. *Personality and Social Psychology Bulletin, 28,* 16–28.

Super, D. E. (1957). *The psychology of careers.* New York, NY: Harper and Bros.

Super, D. E. (1962). The structure of work values in relation to status, achievement, interest, and adjustment. *Journal of Applied Psychology, 46,* 227–239.

Super, D. E. (1970). *Work Values Inventory.* Boston, MA: Houghton Mifflin.

Super, D. E. (1980). A life-span, life-space approach to career development. *Journal of Vocational Behavior, 16,* 282–298.

Super, D. E. (1983). Assessment in career guidance: Toward truly developmental counseling. *Personnel and Guidance Journal, 61,* 555–562.

Super, D. E. (1995). Values: Their nature, assessment, and practical use. In D. E. Super & B. Sverko (Eds.), *Life roles, values, and careers: International findings of the work importance study* (pp. 54–61). San Francisco, CA: Jossey-Bass.

Super, D. E., & Sverko, B. (Eds.). (1995). *Life roles, values, and careers: International findings of the work importance study*. San Francisco, CA: Jossey-Bass.

Sverko, B. (1995). The structure and hierarchy of values viewed cross-nationally. In D. E. Super & B. Sverko (Eds.), *Life roles, values, and careers: International findings of the work importance study* (pp. 225–240). San Francisco, CA: Jossey-Bass.

Triandis, H. C., McCusker, C., & Hui, C. H. (1990). Multimethod probes of individualism and collectivism. *Journal of Personality and Social Psychology, 59,* 1006–1020.

Twenge, J. M., Campbell, S. M., Hoffman, B. J., & Lance, C. E. (2010). Generational differences in work values: Leisure and extrinsic values increasing, social and intrinsic values decreasing. *Journal of Management, 36,* 1117–1142.

U.S. Department of Labor. (2000a). *Work Importance Locator: User's guide*. Washington, DC: Employment and Training Administration.

U.S. Department of Labor. (2000b). *Work Importance Profiler: User's guide*. Washington, DC: Employment and Training Administration.

Verquer, M. L., Beehr, T. A., & Wagner, S. H. (2003). A meta-analysis of relations between person–organization fit and work attitudes. *Journal of Vocational Behavior, 63,* 473–489.

Williams, J. E., & Best, D. L. (1990). *Measuring sex stereotypes: A multination study*. Newbury Park, CA: Sage.

Young, A. M., & Hurlic, D. (2007). Gender enactment at work: The importance of gender and gender-related behavior to person-organizational fit and career decisions. *Journal of Managerial Psychology, 22,* 168–187.

Zytowski, D. (2006). *Super Work Values Inventory–Revised: Technical manual* (Version 1.0). Retrieved from http://www.kuder.com/solutions/kuder-assessments.aspx #supers_work_values_inventory

CHAPTER 16

Ability and Aptitude Assessment in Career Counseling

A. J. METZ AND JANICE E. JONES

T HIS CHAPTER HIGHLIGHTS THE use of abilities, aptitudes, and skills in expanding career options, narrowing options, making a career decision, and managing one's career. First, we examine some of the historical milestones associated with ability assessment. Then we define important constructs and review the structure and stability of these constructs, with special attention to gender and cultural differences. Assessment strategies, methods, and tools are also explored, with the primary goal of promoting effective, scientifically informed career practices in high school, college, and the workforce.

HISTORICAL MILESTONES IN ABILITY ASSESSMENT

The measurement of human capacity has a long tradition dating back to at least the fourth century BC, when Greek physicians and philosophers like Hippocrates and Plato began to make connections between the brain and cognitive functioning, suggesting that the brain contributed to motivation, feelings, sensations, wisdom, and knowledge and was the site of all knowledge (Crivellato & Ribatti, 2007). The first written account demonstrating the use of ability assessment, in fact, appeared as long ago as during the Han Dynasty in China (206 BC to 220 AD), when competitive exams were used for civil service selection, allowing persons, regardless of background and wealth, to attain high-ranking positions in the government (Miyazaki, 1981). The first theory of intelligence appeared in the 16th-century writings of Spanish philosopher Juan Huarte de San Juan and described individual variations in memory, learning, and imagination (Hunt, 2005). Despite the long history of interest in the assessment of human capacity, the modern history of the study of individual differences in human traits is attributed to the work of Sir Francis Galton (Jensen, 2002). Galton initially studied the heredity of human ability by examining the pedigrees of high-achieving individuals. He later studied monozygotic twins and from this research concluded that general mental ability, or what he referred to as intelligence, is inherited in much the same way as many physical traits (Jensen, 2002). Galton believed that the speed of information processing was the basis for general ability and therefore measured intelligence using reaction time to simple tests of visual and auditory stimuli (Acton & Schroeder, 2001).

Galton conceived general ability as the sum of an individual's scores on various tests of mental ability. Charles Spearman refined Galton's ideas and introduced a two-factor theory of intelligence that comprised a general factor (g)—which instead of being the sum of scores on various tests, is distilled from the correlations between them—and a specific factor (s), which reflects a factor that is specific to a particular test. Thus, for example, the score that a student receives on a vocabulary test is influenced by his or her general learning ability (g) and factors specific to performing well on a vocabulary test (e.g., size of parents' vocabulary, number of books in the home). To determine the degree to which a test measured g (the common factor) within the context of other tests, Spearman pioneered a new statistical method, factor analysis (Jensen, 2002). Since 1904, factor analytic methods have supported g as a common factor inherent in the psychometric structure of abilities as measured by a diverse array of cognitive tests.

Alfred Binet and Theodore Simon have been credited with developing the first IQ test. In the early 1900s, the French government passed a law requiring all children to attend school. They sought help in identifying children who were likely to need specialized assistance in their education. The Binet-Simon Scale included questions assessing attention, memory, and problem-solving skills. Based on his observations about how children answered questions on the test, Binet proposed a measure of intelligence based on the average abilities of children of a particular age group. He called this concept "mental age." An American psychologist at Stanford University, Lewis Terman, adapted Binet's original test for use in the United States. This test was published in 1916 and called the Stanford-Binet Intelligence Scale. Terman proposed that an IQ could be calculated by dividing the individual's mental age by his or her chronological age and multiplying by 100. Although IQ scores are calculated differently today, an IQ of 100 still represents an average level of intelligence. The military developed two additional intelligence tests during World War I—the Army Alpha (verbal tests for literate recruits) and the Army Beta (nonverbal) tests of intelligence. Understanding and measuring intelligence became a major focus of research after World War I.

Another avenue of research on ability assessment during the post–World War I era is illustrated by research conducted at the University of Minnesota that sought to analyze the types of abilities required in different jobs and develop tests of these job-specific abilities. For example, their efforts resulted in the publication of the Minnesota Mechanical Ability Tests (MMAT; Anderson, Elliott, Paterson, Toops, & Heidbreder, 1930). Tests of abilities such as the MMAT attempted to match an individual with a job based on specific job-related abilities instead of intelligence. Thus, instead of focusing only on overall differences in *g*, abilities were conceptualized more specifically to include multiple individual-difference factors that were thought to influence learning and performance in different jobs. That is, different jobs require different abilities, and the assessment of job-specific abilities provides a more effective way to select employees than by simply assessing *g*. This view (that the assessment of work-specific abilities enables better job matching than intelligence) led to the development of a variety of multiaptitude test batteries and underlies most ability assessment in career counseling today.

Three major multiaptitude test batteries developed in the post–World War I period are still used today. The United States Armed Forces revised the Army Alpha and Beta intelligence tests to create the Armed Services Vocational Aptitude Test Battery (ASVAB) used for selection and assignment purposes. The U.S. Department of Labor designed the General Aptitude Test Battery (GATB) to predict job performance and later revised the GATB to provide a multiaptitude test battery to be used in conjunction with the O*NET (see Gore, Leuwerke, & Kelly, Chapter 18, this volume). This test battery (called the Ability Profiler) is discussed along with the ASVAB later in this chapter.

DEFINING ABILITIES, SKILLS, AND APTITUDES

Abilities, aptitudes, and skills are separate but highly related constructs. Ability is the physical or mental capacity (learned or innate) to complete a specific act or task (Snow, 1994). Ability assessments consist of a series of timed tasks or work samples and measure the relative ease with which an individual can perform the task. Results indicate strengths and weaknesses in specific abilities or what the person can do now and will be potentially able to do in the future (Betz, Fitzgerald, & Hill, 1989). Thus, for example, a person with strong mechanical abilities has already acquired a high level of proficiency with mechanical activities (compared to his or her peers) and has the potential to acquire even more proficiency with appropriate experience.

Skills represent proficiency, competence, or dexterity that has been acquired through practice and repeated use. Skills can be domain-general (e.g., interpersonal communication, leadership) or domain-specific (e.g., ability to analyze blueprints). In an employment context, workplace skills may be assessed through educational credentialing, observation of task performance, or task performance outcome. In a career counseling context, self-estimates of skill may be useful in the consideration of alternate careers, appraisal of occupational requirements, self-promotion (e.g., resume development, employment interviews), training needs, and educational planning. Skills are similar to abilities in that they provide self-knowledge and can be used to assess fit between a potential employee and the specific requirements of a job. The Minnesota theory of work adjustment (TWA; see Swanson & Schneider, Chapter 2, this volume) describes how abilities and skills differ. According to TWA, abilities are broader than skills and represent "reference dimensions" for skills (i.e., contain a group of skills). For example, math abilities are composed of a number of skills, including arithmetic computation and reasoning skills. Most measures of abilities that we focus on in this chapter use a number of skills tests to measure a smaller set of abilities. One example, the Ability Profiler available via O*NET uses 11 skills tests to measure nine higher-order work-related abilities. Because skills are dependent on learning or training, they are thought to be more easily manipulated than abilities (Fleishman, Costanza, & Marshall-Mies, 1999).

Snow (1996) defines *aptitude* as "learning to learn, learning to reason, learning to find and solve problems, learning to be interested and industrious, to persevere, to achieve in the face of novelty, complexity, adversity, and change" (p. 537). He further suggests that "the term aptitude is intended to signify preparedness—an aspect of the present state of a person that is propaedeutic; that is, needed as preparation for future achievement in some particular situation" (p. 537). In a career counseling context, aptitude can be viewed as the "likelihood of learning or acquiring the skills required by the occupation" (p. 457; Dawis, Goldman, & Sung, 1992). Most measures used in counseling are both ability and aptitude tests in that they provide scores to estimate a person's current level of performance and potential (ability) as well as potential for future success in different occupations (aptitude). Unless specified otherwise, we use abilities and aptitudes interchangeably in this chapter because assessment goals in counseling are both diagnostic (i.e., assess current level of ability and potential) and predictive (i.e., identify occupations in which a person will be successful in the future).

ISSUES IN UNDERSTANDING AND ASSESSING ABILITIES

The effective use of ability assessment requires knowledge in a number of important domains. This section begins with an introduction to the organization of modern hierarchical ability models and presents empirical evidence for the stability of abilities. Next, gender differences and cultural differences in cognitive abilities are examined through contemporary empirical sources. Finally, attention is turned to the role of self-estimates of ability and their impact on career decision-making and performance.

STRUCTURE OF ABILITIES

Numerous theories of intelligence offer insight into the structure of abilities. A comprehensive review of all theories of intelligence is not within the purview of this chapter. For an overview of major theories of intelligence (psychometric, cognitive, cognitive-contextual, and biological), readers are directed to Gardner (2011). The following is a brief review of psychometric and cognitive-contextual theories of intelligence. Psychometric theories of intelligence are reviewed, as they have received strong empirical support; cognitive-contextual theories are included, given their relevance to career counseling.

Psychometric theories of intelligence are based on the examination of individual differences in performance on tests that measure more specific cognitive abilities. As noted earlier, Spearman (1927) was the first to use factor analysis to reveal two underlying dimensions of cognitive ability: *g*, or general intelligence, and *s*, representing any number of specific abilities related to particular tasks. Thurstone (1938) used Spearman's factor analytic methods to identify seven primary mental abilities: vocabulary, math reasoning, spatial ability, memory, reasoning, word fluency, and perceptual speed. Horn and Cattell (1996) introduced a hierarchical ability model. Their factor analysis of ability tests yielded 30 to 40 first-order factors. These were then factor analyzed to produce 5 to 9 second-order factors.

Two second-order factors that bear mention are fluid intelligence and crystallized intelligence. Fluid intelligence is associated with the capacity to learn and includes tasks such as inductive reasoning, deductive reasoning, and drawing inferences. Crystallized intelligence is the knowledge gained from exposure to one's environment (e.g., school, culture). Fluid and crystallized intelligence are correlated (Brody & Brody, 1976) yet exhibit differential patterns of growth and decline over time (Gardner, 2011). Horn and Hofner (1992) suggest that fluid intelligence crests in the early to mid-20s and then declines, whereas crystallized intelligence does not peak until the early 40s and may remain stable into late adulthood.

Carroll (1993) conducted an exploratory factor analysis of over 460 cognitive ability data sets and provided the first comprehensive, systematic organization of the structure of human cognitive abilities (McGrew, 2009). Specifically, Carroll obtained a three-strata hierarchical structure of cognitive abilities. At the top of the hierarchy (Stratum III) is *g*, or general cognitive ability. Stratum II, the second level of the hierarchy, includes eight broad ability factors: Fluid Intelligence, Crystallized Intelligence, General Memory and Learning, Broad Visual Perception, Broad Auditory Perception, Broad Retrieval Ability, Broad Cognitive Speediness, and Processing Speed. Stratum I, the bottom of the hierarchy, represents 68 very specific abilities. The Cattell-Horn and Carroll three-strata models have gone through updates and revisions but remain standard models for understanding the structure of human intelligence. Although they differ, the two models have more recently been integrated into a single theory of intelligence, the Cattell-Horn-Carroll (CHC) model (McGrew, 2005, 2009). The three models are graphically depicted in Figure 16.1. As we will see later in this chapter in our discussion of multiaptitude test batteries, most ability assessment in career counseling focuses on job-related Stratum II and Stratum III-like abilities.

Cognitive abilities are important in career counseling because they predict job performance. Citing meta-analytic research, Gottfredson (2003) affirmed that g, or general intelligence, predicts performance to some degree in all jobs, and best in the most cognitively complex jobs. The addition of Stratum II

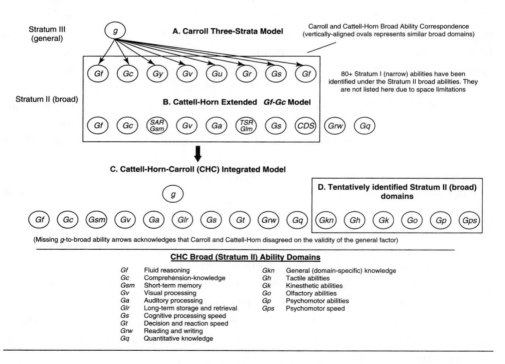

Figure 16.1 Schematic Representation and Comparisons of Carroll's Three-Strata, Cattell-Horn's Extended Gf-Gc, and the integrated Cattell-Horn-Carroll Models of Human Cognitive Abilities

abilities adds little to the prediction equation and then only for certain types of jobs (e.g., spatial ability for architects). Gottfredson cautioned counselors not to ignore specific abilities, but to understand the utility of general cognitive ability across work tasks and settings.

Psychometric theories focus on the structure of cognitive abilities and try to identify those that contribute to overall intelligence. In the context of career counseling, cognitive abilities are necessary but not sufficient to predict occupational or educational success and performance. Clients will also need practical and social skills to succeed in the workplace. Thus, the cognitive-contextual theories of intelligence bear mention. Sternberg, Kaufman, and Grigorenko (2009) recently provided a componential subtheory of intelligence (i.e., "successful intelligence"), defined as "the ability to achieve success in life, given one's personal standards, within one's sociocultural context" (p. 72). Included in this model is the ability to capitalize on strengths and remediate weaknesses. In their model, intelligence is viewed as adapting to, selecting, and shaping one's environment (e.g., solving conflicts at work, integrating feedback, collaborating with others).

Gardner (1983, 1999) also proposed a contextual theory of intelligence that highlights seven relatively independent intelligences: linguistic, logical-mathematical, musical, bodily-kinesthetic, spatial, interpersonal, and intra-personal. More recently, Gardner (1999) supplemented this list with three additional intelligences: naturalistic, spiritual, and existential. Finally, theories of emotional intelligence have been proffered to emphasize the importance of perceiving, integrating, understanding, and regulating emotions. More specifically, emotions are sources of information that can be used to navigate social contexts. Although contextual theories of intelligence do not yield easily testable claims (Gardner, 2011), they offer worthy discussion points with clients as additional information to use in considering occupational options and diagnosing sources of work-performance problems.

STABILITY OF ABILITIES

Large-scale, longitudinal studies have demonstrated that cognitive abilities tend to be highly stable over time. Honzik, MacFarlane, and Allen (1948) assessed intelligence at ages 8 and 18 and found the test–retest correlation to be .70. In another study, an intelligence test was given at ages 4, 14, and 29. The test–retest correlation at age 14 was .64; at adulthood, it was .80 (Bradway & Thompson, 1962). Mortensen and Kleven (1993) found very high stability quotients from middle to late adulthood ($r = .90$). Finally, raw stability coefficients calculated for intelligence tests administered between ages 11–70, 11–79, and 11–87 were .67, .66, and .51, respectively (Gow et al., 2011). This body of research suggests that at least 50% of the variance in late-life cognitive performance can be attributed to childhood cognitive ability (p. 237) and that people who score high in comparison to same-age peers on a particular ability will remain among the highest scorers compared to same-age peers on that ability 10, 20, and 30 years later. These data provide support for the use of ability assessments in career counseling because they suggest that abilities assessed at one point in a client's life can be used to make predictions about the types of occupations in which a person might be successful later in life.

GENDER DIFFERENCES

Questions regarding gender differences in abilities cannot be easily answered (Williams & Ceci, 2007). The long-standing notion that men excel on quantitative measures and women on verbal measures is an oversimplification of findings. In fact, observed differences are dependent on a number of factors, such as age, ethnicity, nationality, being tested on familiar or novel material, and historical time period (Priess & Hyde, 2010). Many different abilities comprise quantitative ability (e.g., computations, arithmetic reasoning) and verbal ability (e.g., vocabulary, verbal reasoning), and although relatively stable, abilities can be fostered and new skills learned. Further, it is important to examine participants' location in the distribution of scores; larger gender differences are frequently observed in extremely bright or talented individuals and may be washed out in a group of average-performing individuals. Moreover, careful attention has been paid in the design of intelligence and aptitude tests to eliminate or balance questions that demonstrate gender bias (Priess & Hyde, 2010).

In samples representative of the general population, gender differences in overall IQ scores tend to be small or nonsignificant (Dreary, Thorpe, Wilson, Starr, & Whalley, 2003; Priess & Hyde, 2010). There are however, gender differences in performance on subtests. For example, on commonly used intelligence tests, boys and men tend to perform better than girls and women on tests of spatial ability, girls and women perform slightly better in verbal ability, and boys and men perform slightly better in quantitative ability. However, taking a closer look at the data may blur these notions. When "quantitative ability" is further broken down, there is evidence that girls excel at quantitative computation at a very early age, and boys excel at mathematical reasoning in adolescence (Fennema, 1974; Halpern, 1986).

Meta-analytic studies can also shed light on gender differences and similarities. Using 100 studies, Hyde, Fennema, and Lamon (1990) conducted a meta-analytic investigation of gender differences in math ability. They found that in a general population, women had slightly better mathematics performance than men. They replicated previous work that showed girls and women are slightly better at computation and boys and men at problem solving. With respect to gender differences across racial/ethnic groups, these researchers found no gender differences in African American or Hispanic populations, but in Asian American samples, girls and women performed slightly better than boys and men. Note that all of these gender differences are quite small in a practical sense. Although there is evidence that gender differences in average mathematical performance have decreased over time (Hyde, Lindberg, Linn, Ellis, & Williams, 2008), there remains considerable variation in the ratio of boys to girls in the tails of the distribution, with boys being more highly represented in the top 10% and 5%. With respect to verbal ability, the gender differences are small, consistent internationally, and apparently shrinking over time (Hyde & Linn, 1988). Girls continue to be overrepresented in the top 10% and 5% of verbal ability distributions as compared to boys.

CULTURAL DIFFERENCES

Addressing cultural differences in ability assessment is no easy task. The study of differences in cognitive ability has spanned the fields of psychology, anthropology, biology, and sociology, with no universally accepted definition or measurement tools (Eysenck, 1998). Scholars continue to passionately debate the nature, origins, and practical implications of differences according to group membership. For example, some have used claims of group differences in cognitive ability to rationalize racial discrimination; others have made policy recommendations and sought legislation to provide specific groups with resources (Neisser et al., 1996).

Ethnic group differences in ability have been studied by examining mean scores on intelligence tests, mostly at the level of *g* (Neisser et al., 1996). Although some differences exist, Neisser and colleagues (1996) suggest that in working with a client, the individual's score is more important than the mean score of a client's reference group. At the same time, because measures of cognitive ability are used to make high-stakes decisions, it is also important to know the validity of inferences made from these tests and whether test scores relate to performance criteria equally well for each racial/ethnic subgroup (Jencks & Phillips, 1998). A conventional method for examining these potential differences is to compare the slopes and intercepts of regression lines across groups. With respect to children in the school system, studies have demonstrated no differences in validity coefficients or intercepts for racial/ethnic subgroups in predicting academic achievement (e.g., Canivez & Watkins, 1998; Weiss & Prifitera, 1995; Weiss, Prifitera, & Roid, 1993). Thus, cognitive ability tests given in early childhood seemed to predict subsequent academic achievement equally well for European

Americans, African Americans, Latinos, and Asian Americans. These findings are consistent in the workforce as well—there seems to be no predictive bias (slope and intercept differences) between cognitive ability tests in common use in practice and work performance (Rotundo & Sackett, 1999; Schmidt, Pearlman, & Hunter, 1980).

There is evidence that schooling can impact intelligence test scores (Ceci, 1991). For example, attendance at school can promote learning that leads to higher test scores, promotion from one grade to the next, and academic persistence (Neisser et al., 1996). Therefore, the quality of a client's school experience may be salient. Clients from low socioeconomic backgrounds may have attended poorer school systems and, subsequently, may have had fewer educational opportunities and resources than those who attended school systems in wealthier neighborhoods with a higher tax base. Although race/ethnicity is not directly linked to socioeconomic status, economically disadvantaged schools tend to have larger populations of ethnic minority students.

SELF-ESTIMATED ABILITIES

Theories of career development highlight the important role of self-concept (Super, Savickas, & Super, 1996) and individual perceptions of abilities (Lent, Brown, & Hackett, 1994) in career decision making and performance. Thus, objective measures of ability assessment (on which much of the research we have discussed so far is based) may be considered incomplete, as they do not address self-perceptions and tap only a limited number of abilities (e.g., they do not assess social abilities). Self-estimates of ability may provide a systematic and efficient way to complete the picture.

Ability self-estimates may be assessed through an interview, checklist, or card sort. The most straightforward way to find out about clients' perceptions of their abilities is to ask them directly (expressed abilities). One can also get information about abilities clients have demonstrated in the past (manifested abilities) by asking questions such as, "What subjects did you excel in at school?" "If I asked your former boss to list your strengths, what would she say?" "What skills do you think are needed for this job?" and "How would I know you had this skill?" In some cases, clients have had numerous educational and work experiences that provided them with feedback on their strengths and liabilities. In other cases, clients may struggle to list more than three skills.

Another self-assessment tool that may be slightly more helpful is a skills checklist. A skills checklist can be downloaded from many online sources such as State job centers (e.g., http://www.wisconsinjobcenter.org/publications/8961), college career centers (e.g., http://owl.english.purdue.edu/owl/resource/626/01) or comprehensive online career guidance systems (e.g., http://www.onetonline.org/find/descriptor/browse/skills). Clients can be shown a list of skills and asked to identify the ones they currently possess. Counselors can then engage clients in a conversation about skills they have (e.g., how they demonstrate these skills, how they can incorporate them into their resume, how they can talk about their skills with employers) and skills they need to develop. A skill deficit may point to a need for additional education or training.

In addition to an interview or checklist, a card-sort activity can be used to help clients examine their skills. There are several commercially available card sorts (e.g., Motivated Skills Card Sort–Revised; Knowdell, 1990), but counselors can also create their own card sort by writing each skill from a skills checklist on separate index cards. Clients can then be instructed to go through the deck of cards and make three piles: one to designate skills they feel highly proficient in, one to designate adequate competence, and a third to designate little or no skill. The results should then be discussed with the client. For example, the client may be asked about relationships between skills they are proficient in and those they enjoy using, if they are able to use these skills in their current job, or if it would be important to them to seek a job in which they could use these skills. Card sorts can also be used to explore the accuracy of ability percepts by asking clients about the bases for their assessment and asking them to share their results with, and gain feedback from, others who know them (e.g., Brown & Lent, 1996; Lent, Chapter 5, this volume).

Finally, more formal, standardized ability self-estimate measures have been developed, including the Ability Explorer (Harrington & Harrington, 1996), Inventory of Work Relevant Abilities (IWRA; ACT, 1998), Self-Directed Search (SDS; Holland, Powell, & Fritzsche, 1994), and the Campbell Interest and Skills Survey (Campbell, Hyne, & Nilsen, 1992). One advantage of using these measures of ability self-estimates versus interviews, skills checklists, and card sorts is that these measures have been designed to generate occupational and educational options for clients, many of which the client might not have previously known about or considered. Thus, objective tests and these formal ability self-estimates may expand career options for clients, especially among those with limited knowledge about and experience in the occupational world.

However, there are challenges to using self-estimates of ability. Self-estimates may not correlate strongly with objective ability scores (Gati, Fishman-Nadav, & Shiloh, 2006; Mabe & West, 1982). Ability self-estimates may also be subject to distortion due to inadequate or limited experience, response style, intentional self-promotion, and cheating (Prediger, 2002). Women may underestimate their abilities, and men may overestimate them (Betsworth, 1999). Further, those who have lower measured intelligence may overestimate their abilities (Gati et al., 2006). At the same time, self-perceived ability is important in career counseling as it may determine career interests, expected success, and anticipated satisfaction (Barak, 1981; Barak, Librowsky, & Shiloh, 1989). Barak, Shiloh, and Haushner (1992) found that interests could be modified by altering perceived ability. For instance, a client with low and inaccurate ability estimates could be confronted with objective evidence disconfirming these perceptions (e.g., grades, test scores). Lent and Brown (1996) describe strategies for challenging clients' self-efficacy belief estimates (see Lent, Chapter 5, this volume).

The advantages to using informal ability assessments are that they may be free or low-cost, easy and quick to administer, and less stressful for clients than formal assessments (Niles & Harris-Bowlsbey, 2009). However, major disadvantages to informal ability assessments include a lack of scientific rigor and the inability to generate occupational and educational options for further exploration. Thus, more formal assessments (be they objective tests or ability self-estimates) may be especially helpful for clients with limited knowledge about work. Formal assessments for these clients may generate options that they never heard about or previously considered. Niles and Harris-Bowlsbey (2009) described additional reasons for implementing formal career assessments. First, formal assessments are supported by data and provide evidence of validity and reliability. Second, there is a standard way to interpret the results. This allows the counselor to compare a client's results with a norm reference group. Third, because formal assessments report the populations for which the instrument has been tested and normed, counselors can determine the appropriateness of the instrument for their clients.

Prior to selecting any of these assessment tools, counselors are encouraged to review assessment and counseling competencies and responsibilities (see Krieshok & Black, 2009). Minimally, counselors should have coursework in psychological measurement and assessment, as well as training or experience with the specific instrument they intend to use. It is also necessary for counselors to consult the test's manual to examine the development of the measure; recommended uses and possible misuses; evidence of validity, reliability, and fairness; and the composition of norm groups. Instructions for administration, scoring, and interpretation are also included in the test manual or user's guide. In addition to information provided in the test manual, counselors can consult independently published test reviews to determine if the instrument is suitable for the intended use (e.g., Maddox, 2008; Murphy, Plake, Impara, & Spies, 2001; Spies, Carlson, & Geisinger, 2010).

DEVELOPMENTALLY APPROPRIATE ABILITY ASSESSMENT

Abilities, aptitudes, and skills have been associated with career counseling since the inception of Parson's (1909) trait-and-factor approach. As reviewed by Swanson and Schneider (Chapter 2, this volume), trait-and-factor approaches assume that abilities can be objectively measured and correlated with job requirements to predict success. Early approaches to career counseling focused on assessing an individual's strengths and weaknesses to determine potential for specific types of work. Currently, this information is viewed as one component of self-knowledge that can be used in vocational exploration, decision making, self-promotion, and career management.

The following sections describe how counselors can use ability assessment with their clients. In high school settings, ability assessment is used to provide an accurate appraisal of strengths and weaknesses and promote a connection between this self-knowledge and the world of work. Ability assessment is further used to help students set educational goals, select appropriate coursework, and prepare for transitions to college or the workforce. In college settings, ability assessment is used to make admissions decisions, place students in remedial and accelerated classes, facilitate major-choice and occupational decisions, and prepare students for transition to the workforce. Similarly, ability assessment can help adults explore careers, make decisions, and prepare for the workforce. For those already in the workforce, ability assessment may be used to aid career transitions, self-promotion, and career management.

STRATEGIES, METHODS, AND TOOLS FOR WORKING WITH HIGH SCHOOL STUDENTS

Barton and Coley (2011) suggest that there are unprecedented challenges to preparing high school students for higher education and the world of work. For example, there is debate as to the purpose and mission of public education. In 1893, the consensus was that all high school students should receive a college-focused curriculum irrespective of postgraduation aspirations. The pendulum then swung toward a choice-based model in which students could identify different curricular pathways based on the desire to attend college or immediately enter the workforce. Unfortunately, assignment replaced choice, and subgroups of students were rigidly tracked into college-bound or workforce-bound paths. As a response, the school system promoted choice through the proliferation of course offerings. Students were now able to choose between multiple courses that would meet educational requirements. Reactions spurred the phrase "the shopping mall high school" (Powell, Farrar, & Cohen, 1985). Educational reform efforts then began to emphasize the "new basics" (English, science, math, social studies, and computer science) and proficiency standards that led to the test-based accountability movement (e.g., No Child Left Behind Act of 2001).

A more recent strategy to promote educational achievement can be seen in a growing emphasis on college and career readiness. The Race to the Top legislation, along with widespread state efforts to link primary, secondary, and postsecondary education systems, are intended to promote college and workforce readiness for all students (Education Week, 2011). For example, ACT defines college and career readiness through a system of assessment and curricular support. This system includes the EXPLORE, PLAN, and ACT tests.

EXPLORE. The EXPLORE test (ACT, 2011) was designed for use with eighth- and ninth-grade students. It includes two components. The first is related to career and education planning and incorporates an interest inventory and a needs assessment. The second component is a curriculum-based achievement test that includes four 30-minute multiple-choice sections measuring knowledge and skills in English (usage/mechanics and rhetoric), math (prealgebra, algebra, geometry, and statistics/probability), reading (comprehension), and science (reasoning). The EXPLORE test is developmentally and conceptually linked to the PLAN and ACT tests such that scores on one can be used to predict scores on another. The technical characteristics of the EXPLORE test can be found in the technical manual (ACT, 2011).

The EXPLORE test is a paper-and-pencil test that takes approximately 2 to 3 hours. It can be administered year-round, but schools typically identify a testing window. ACT provides test preparation materials and sample test questions in addition to a technical manual and interpretive guide. Individualized score reports are divided into four sections. The *Your Scores* section provides (a) individual scores for English, Math, Reading, and Science; (b) a composite score; (c) percentile ranks for each score; and (d) an estimate PLAN composite score range. The *Your Plans* section highlights reported academic plans, career cluster preferences, planning needs, and estimated college readiness as demonstrated by a comparison to appropriate grade-level benchmark scores. A section titled *Your Career Possibilities* shows how specific career interests map onto the *World-of-Work Map* (see Gore et al., Chapter 18, this volume). Finally, *Your Skills* is a section that offers recommendations for developing skills in each of the tested competency areas. Counselors can use EXPLORE results to help students understand their strengths and weaknesses, develop educational goals, explore occupational possibilities, and ensure a college-ready trajectory.

PLAN. The PLAN test (ACT, 2007b) was designed for use with 10th-grade students. It mirrors the EXPLORE test with respect to content, test administration, individualized score reports, and how to use the results. The technical characteristics of the PLAN test can be found in the technical manual (ACT, 2007b).

ACT. The ACT (ACT, 2007a) is a 215-item, multiple-choice achievement test designed for use with 11th- and 12th-grade students. It is similar to EXPLORE and PLAN in that it is comprised of a career and educational planning component and a curricular-based test that measures learning in four content domains: English (usage/mechanics, rhetoric), Math (prealgebra, algebra, intermediate algebra, geometry/plane geometry, trigonometry), Reading (social studies, natural sciences, prose fiction, humanities), and Science (data representation, research summaries, conflicting viewpoints). There is an optional writing component. The technical characteristics of the ACT test can be found in the technical manual (ACT, 2007a).

The ACT test is a paper-and-pencil test that takes approximately 4 to 5 hours. It is administered only at registered test sites on specific test dates. ACT provides numerous test preparation materials on its Web site (e.g., a downloadable brochure, an ACT question of the day, and an online test preparation program.). ACT score reports display individual test scores for the four primary domains (English, Math, Reading, Science), seven subscales within these domains, and the writing component. A composite score is calculated from the average of scores on the four primary domains. This score ranges from 1 to 36 and is used by colleges to make high-stakes admissions decisions. National and state percentile ranks for the primary domains, subscales, composite, and writing score are provided to numerically represent the percentage of recent high school graduates that scored at or below the test taker. Counselors can help students compare their ACT scores to the national or state norms, match them to the requirements of colleges, and assess strengths and weaknesses. Further, scores can be used to determine college readiness. ACT has created benchmark scores for the four primary domains. These scores represent the minimum score needed to obtain a 50% chance of obtaining a B or higher in a first-year college course. Counselors can help students compare their scores to the benchmarks and suggest additional coursework or remediation. The last page of the ACT score report lists interest inventory results and can be used to help students explore careers and college majors.

SAT. The SAT (College Board, 2011) is a 171-item aptitude test designed for use with 11th- and 12th-grade students. The purpose of the SAT test is to demonstrate a student's potential to succeed in college, and it is therefore used for high-stakes admissions decisions. As described previously, an aptitude test measures how well a student can process verbal and quantitative information, solve problems, and think critically. Aptitude tests capture a student's capacity for learning; achievement tests measure knowledge associated with a specific curriculum. Questions on the SAT measure three domains: Critical Reading, Writing, and Math. The reading component assesses a student's ability to understand vocabulary, synthesize information, and draw inferences from short and long passages. The writing component is divided into two sections: multiple-choice questions (identifying errors in grammar and usage) and a short essay. The math component measures a student's ability to apply mathematical concepts to solve problems and interpret tables, charts, and graphs. Students can also choose to take hour-long subject tests. There are 20 subject tests in all that cover five general areas: English (e.g., literature), history, languages (e.g., German, German With Listening), math, and science (e.g., biology). Kobrin, Patterson, Shaw, Mattern, and Barbuti (2008) provide evidence of predictive validity for the newest version of the SAT.

The SAT test is a paper-and-pencil test that takes approximately 3 to 4 hours. It is administered only at registered test sites on specific test dates. The College Board provides numerous test preparation materials on their Web site (e.g., a study guide, question of the day, full practice test, and an online test preparation program). Students receive a score report that provides detailed information about their performance. The Score Report Summary outlines their results for each of the three primary domains. Scores range from 200 to 800. Thus, an SAT composite score (all three primary domains combined) ranges from 600 to 2400. Students are also able to see how many questions they answered correctly, incorrectly, and omitted for each of the primary domains and the corresponding subscales. Further, students are shown how their scores compare to other students in their school, state, and the nation.

STRATEGIES, METHODS, AND TOOLS FOR WORKING WITH COLLEGE STUDENTS

Ability assessment does not end once a student is accepted into college. A number of states have a placement assessment policy requiring their colleges to assess the academic skills of incoming students and place them in developmentally appropriate courses. Other states allow colleges to set their own policies regarding placement tests. ACCUPLACER and COMPASS are the two most commonly used standardized placement tests. ACCUPLACER (College Board) is a computer-adaptive test that measures knowledge and skills in math, English, reading, and writing. Similar to ACCUPLACER, COMPASS (ACT) is an untimed, computerized test that evaluates the same four areas of development. Neither test has a passing score. Rather, scores indicate areas of strength and weakness and help admissions counselors or academic advisors schedule appropriate coursework.

In college, ability assessment may be used to help students navigate various stages of career development (e.g., developing self-knowledge, obtaining educational and occupational information, exploring occupational possibilities, making decisions, developing job search skills, gaining relevant experience, applying to graduate school, networking, and securing employment). Formal or informal ability assessment may take place in a variety of contexts, such as credit-bearing career courses; first-year experience seminars; individual or group counseling settings; academic advising; special programs for minorities, women, or individuals with disabilities; programming in residence life; leadership development programs; or computer-assisted career guidance. In this section, two ability assessments will be described. Readers are also directed to the following section on ability assessment with adults for tools that are also useful for college students and work-bound youth.

Campbell Interest and Skill Survey. The Campbell Interest and Skill Survey (CISS; Campbell, Hyne, & Nilsen, 1992) is an assessment tool that is frequently used with college-age persons to help them identify their skills and interests and to make future educational and occupational plans. The CISS is described in detail in Chapter 14 of this volume, and the reader is referred to this chapter for detailed information on the CISS. With information on both interest level and skills confidence, counselors can help students explore additional career options or narrow their occupational alternatives. Counselors should analyze discrepancies between scores on interest and skill ratings to ensure the clients are not underestimating their self-efficacy beliefs and possibly foreclosing on occupations that may be rewarding. For example, there is a solid literature base implicating low self-efficacy beliefs and perceived barriers in the underrepresentation of women in science, technology, engineering, and math (STEM) disciplines.

Graduate Record Exam. The Graduate Record Exam (GRE; Educational Testing Service, 2011) is an aptitude test that measures an individual's ability to perform graduate-level work. Thus, it is typically required by graduate programs as part of the admissions application. The three sections include Verbal Reasoning (analyzing, synthesizing, understanding relationships), Quantitative Reasoning (problem solving related to mathematical operations), and Analytical Writing (critical thinking and writing skills). The test format may be computer based or paper based, depending on the test location. The GRE takes approximately 3 hours and 45 minutes to complete.

In August 2011, the GRE introduced new questions and score scales. The Verbal Reasoning and Quantitative Reasoning scores are now reported on a scale of 130–170, in 1-point increments; the Analytical Writing score is reported on a 0–6 score scale with half-point increments. Validity evidence indicates the GRE measures appropriate content, has minimal adverse consequences, and predicts success in graduate school (e.g., Bridgeman, Burton, & Cline, 2008). Employing meta-analytic strategies to combine the results of multiple individual studies, Kuncel, Hezlett, & Ones (2001) found small to moderate correlations between GRE scale scores and important graduate academic outcomes. Specifically, the Verbal, Quantitative, and Analytic subtests were all positively correlated with graduate school GPA (ρ = .34, .32, and .36, respectively) and faculty ratings of research ability, professional work, potential, and overall performance (ρ = .42, .47, and .35, respectively). The Verbal subtest was the strongest predictor of scores on the comprehensive exam (ρ = .44) and time to completion (ρ = .28). Counselors may need to help students interpret their results and determine if their score is strong enough to apply for specific graduate programs. Discussion may incorporate management of test-taking anxiety, helpful study strategies, the location of study materials, or ways to strengthen other aspects of the graduate school application (e.g., personal statement, letters of recommendation).

STRATEGIES, METHODS, AND TOOLS FOR WORKING WITH ADULTS

Formal or informal ability assessment can be used in conjunction with other assessment tools (e.g., interests, values) to help adult clients explore career possibilities and make effective career decisions or transitions. They can also be used to help adolescents and young adults identify their primary skills and abilities and to generate occupational possibilities. As indicated earlier, a major advantage of formal ability assessment is that it can help clients expand their knowledge of the occupational world and generate occupational possibilities they may not have previously thought about. Thus, formal ability assessments may be particularly helpful for persons with a limited knowledge of and exposure to the occupational world or those who have been outside the paid work force for an extended period of time (e.g., homemakers, prisoners, those on religious missions). Ability assessment can also be essential in identifying transferable skills and can be used to identify congruent occupational titles for those wanting to remain within their field but in a different setting (e.g., geographic move, layoff, dismissal) or to identify alternate occupations for those seeking to leave their field. Further, ability assessment can be used to determine the capacity to perform essential job functions and to identify workplace accommodations. Finally, ability assessment can corroborate or dispute self-appraisals and be used to enhance work performance. Three formal ability assessment instruments are described here. Readers are directed to Whitfield, Feller, and Wood (2009) for additional measures.

O*NET Ability Profiler. The Occupational Information Network (O*NET) Ability Profiler (U.S. Department of Labor, 2009; see http://www.onetcenter .org) is a multiple-aptitude battery that supplanted earlier Department of Labor instruments such as the General Aptitude Test Battery (GATB, U.S. Department of Labor, 1970). It provides a series of 11 separately timed tests that measure nine basic abilities important in the workforce: verbal ability, arithmetic reasoning, computation, spatial ability, form perception, clerical perception, motor coordination, manual dexterity, and finger dexterity. Six sections are administered in paper-and-pencil format (e.g., arithmetic reasoning, vocabulary, three-dimensional space, computation, name comparison, and object matching) and five sections include psychomotor exercises (mark making, place, turn, assemble, and disassemble). The O*NET Ability Profiler was designed for clients who are at least 16 years old and able to read English at a sixth-grade level or higher.

All of the materials needed to administer the Ability Profiler can be downloaded free from the Web site (i.e., instrument packet, administration manual, training manual, computer scoring program, and scoring guide). Certification and/or training is not required to administer the Ability Profiler, but to ensure successful administration, counselors should read and study the training manual. Training seminars are also available through the O*NET Academy. Administering all 11 timed sections takes approximately 2½ hours. If the client is not seeking a job requiring manual dexterity, one can omit those sections of the test.

The computerized scoring software produces a score report that displays the client's summary of scores and percentile ranks compared to a norm reference sample of over 5,000 individuals representing diversity in terms of gender, ethnicity, age, education level, and employment status. The score report may provide valuable information about a client's strengths and weaknesses and how these compare to a nationwide sample. The score report also provides a list of occupations that fit the client's ability profile according to job zone. Job zones designate the amount of education, experience, and training that specific occupations require. For example, occupations in Job Zone 1 require little or no preparation, while occupations in Job Zone 5 require extensive preparation. All occupations in the O*NET database have been coded according to job zone. The client's ability profile will also produce a job zone classification. This allows clients to search for occupations within their specific job zone or explore occupations based on their anticipated level of education or training. Once clients have a list of occupations they would like to explore, they can be directed to the O*NET OnLine, a detailed database of over 800 occupations (see Gore et al., Chapter 18, this volume). The O*NET Ability Profiler can be used in conjunction with the O*NET Interest Profiler and the O*NET Work Importance Profiler, a measure of work values (see Rounds & Jin, Chapter 15, this volume).

CAPS. The Career Ability Placement Survey (CAPS; Knapp, Knapp, & Knapp-Lee, 2003) is a multidimensional ability assessment tool designed to measure eight vocationally relevant abilities: mechanical reasoning, spatial relations, verbal reasoning, numerical ability, language usage, word knowledge, perceptual speed and accuracy, and manual speed and dexterity. This measure was normed on middle, high school, and college students and therefore may be appropriate for individuals ranging from sixth grade through adulthood. The technical manual, examiner's guide, self-scoring booklets, self-interpretation profiles, and administration tape or CD can be purchased from the Educational and Industrial Testing Service (EdITS) Web site (http://www.edits.net). Data on the psychometric properties of the measure are found in the technical manual.

The CAPS is administered in a paper-and-pencil format and takes approximately 50 minutes to complete. The test-taking materials are available in English or Spanish. The test can be self-scored or machine scored by the company. Summary scores and percentile ranks are provided for each of the eight test sections, allowing clients to examine their abilities in relation to others at their same educational level. Further, scores can be interpreted with respect to the 14 COPSystem Career Clusters (e.g., Technology, Science, Arts, Communication). This allows clients to explore occupational areas that correspond to their present abilities and areas for which they may require additional education or training. The CAPS is part of a comprehensive system that includes a vocational interest inventory (Career Occupational Preference System, COPS) and a personal values inventory (Career Orientation Placement and Evaluation Survey, COPES).

ASVAB. The Armed Services Vocational Aptitude Test Battery (ASVAB; U.S. Department of Defense, 2005) is a multiaptitude 200-item test battery that was originally designed to predict job performance in the military and subsequently make enlistment decisions. Since that time, the Department of Defense has supplemented the original ASVAB by designing the ASVAB Career Exploration Program, a comprehensive career exploration and planning program aimed at connecting high school and college students with satisfying employment in civilian or military occupations. Hence, there are three versions of the ASVAB: (1) CAT-ASVAB, (2) MET-site ASVAB, and (3) Student ASVAB. The first two are specifically used for enlistment purposes (Department of Defense, 2011). The CAT-ASVAB is a computer adaptive test given at military entrance processing stations. The MET-site ASVAB is a paper-and-pencil test given at mobile examination test sites. Each exam is timed, employs a multiple-choice response format, and includes nine subtests: General Science, Arithmetic Reasoning, Word Knowledge, Paragraph Comprehension, Mathematics Knowledge, Electronics Information, Auto Information, Shop Information, and Mechanical Comprehension.

Score reports provide individual subtest scores, composite scores, and the Armed Forces Qualification Test (AFQT) score, which is a percentile score based on a composite of the Arithmetic Reasoning, Math Knowledge, Word Knowledge, and Paragraph Comprehension scores. Each of the service branches sets minimum AFQT scores for enlistment. Other composite scores on the ASVAB determine eligibility for specific career fields or military occupations. A client who plans to enter a branch of the U.S. Armed Forces or Coast Guard may want to take an ASVAB practice test and read about ASVAB study techniques (see http://www.military.com/ASVAB).

The Student ASVAB is a paper-and-pencil test administered by Department of Defense test proctors or school counselors in participating high schools, colleges, or vocational schools. It has the same nine subtests as the other ASVAB tests but also includes a separate interest inventory. The ASVAB Summary Results displays grade-specific standard scores, score bands, and percentile ranks for each of the nine subtests as well as three composites: verbal ability, math ability, and academic ability. The academic ability composite assesses potential for postsecondary education. Similar to the other versions of the ASVAB, test takers receive an AFQT score. Results can be used to search both military and civilian occupations. Test scores may be used by the Department of Defense for recruiting and research purposes for up to 2 years. However, taking the Student ASVAB does not necessitate entrance into the military. There are numerous advantages to using this version of the ASVAB with student and adult clients. For example, taking the measure is free for clients taking classes at a participating school. Further, there are supplemental web-based and printed materials to help clients use their test results to explore career possibilities and plan their coursework. Moreover, the ASVAB has solid psychometric properties in terms of reliability (Moore, Pedlow, Krishnamurty, & Wolter, 2000), validity (Welsh, Kucinkas, & Curran, 1990), and test fairness (Wise et al., 1992).

CAREER MANAGEMENT

The work tasks carried out by the American labor force have drastically changed since the introduction of computers. Occupations using complex communications, critical thinking, and problem solving have grown exponentially while occupations requiring routine cognitive tasks and manual labor have declined (Levy & Murname, 2004). Trilling (2009) suggests that we are in the midst of a "21st Century skills gap" that is financially burdensome to our economy as employers search worldwide to find and hire new employees who have the requisite skill set and do not require extra training or development. He suggests that we need to start early to educate and train our future workforce. Specifically, he identifies work skills that will be essential to demonstrate in the 21st century: (a) Learning and Innovation (critical thinking and problem solving, communication, and creativity), (b) Digital Literacy (information, media, and technical computer skills), and (c) Life and Career Skills (flexibility, adaptability, self-direction, productivity, accountability, leadership, responsibility, and social and cross-cultural interaction skills). The value placed on these skills can be seen through educational legislation, national standards for school counselors (ASCA 2004), state models of comprehensive guidance programming, and more recently, competency-based instruction and assessment in the school systems. Thus, ability assessment can help bridge the 21st-century skills gap by ensuring that clients enter the job market with the necessary skills to succeed.

Blustein (2006) describes how the psychological contract between employee and employer has been transformed. Instead of expecting a long-term relationship in which responsibilities and pay increase over time (i.e., the corporate ladder), careers are being redefined as protean, boundaryless, and portfolio-based (Hall, 2002). Career transitions are not only possible but also probable. Because career management is no longer an organizational responsibility, it is imperative that counselors help their clients understand the need to be proactive in their personal work trajectories. To maintain marketability, workers can assess their abilities, needs, and preferences on a regular basis, identify skill deficits, and plan strategies to overcome these gaps. Twenty-first-century workers will want to remain flexible, adaptable, and willing to upgrade their skill sets. Ongoing ability assessment may assist in career management.

CONCLUSIONS AND PRACTICE IMPLICATIONS

Ability assessment may be used to expand career options, narrow options, inform career decision making, and maintain employability. A few final thoughts that bear mention:

- Ability assessment can be used in conjunction with other measures of individual differences (e.g., interests, values, personality) to provide a more complete picture of the client. Abilities predict occupational performance and success; interests and values predict occupational satisfaction. Thus, counselors should help clients assess all three of these important characteristics because a goal of career counseling is to help clients enter work that they will find satisfying and in which they will perform adequately.

- Substandard work performance may be due, in part, to mismatching abilities (see Swanson & Schneider, Chapter 2, this volume). Thus, it is important to help clients match their abilities with the ability requirements of their jobs and to help them, if necessary, acquire additional proficiency in their current jobs or find jobs that are more ability correspondent.

- Self-perceived abilities are important to consider in counseling because they provide estimates of abilities that may not be measured by objective ability tests. Formal self-estimate tools, like objective ability tests, have the advantage of generating occupational possibilities for clients that informal ability assessments (e.g., expressed or manifested abilities, checklists, and card sorts) do not. However, people may not be able to accurately estimate their abilities. Thus, counselors need to help clients evaluate the accuracy of their ability self-estimates. Several authors (e.g., Tracey & Hopkins, 2001) have suggested that ability self-estimates administered early in counseling may stimulate more complete occupational exploration than objective ability tests. The latter, if employed, may be more useful in later stages of counseling when clients are narrowing options.

- Contextual variables such as age, gender, ethnicity, ability status, and SES should be addressed in the selection, interpretation, and use of formal objective or ability self-estimate measures. Counselors should review the test manual to determine the psychometric properties of the test and appropriateness for specific clients (test fairness, potential for adverse impact, etc.). Test interpretation should include a discussion of cultural influences, as they may have influenced prior learning, educational experiences, and current ability estimates. Further, cultural influences may affect the career decision-making process, occupational choices, goal setting, and goal-related behavior.

- Finally, ability assessment can foster career management through the identification of strengths and weaknesses and transferable skills. Counselors can help clients compare current abilities with the requirements of a targeted position and make recommendations for amending skill deficits or promoting strengths.

REFERENCES

ACT. (1998). *Career Planning Survey technical manual.* Iowa City, IA: Author.

ACT. (2007a). ACT: Technical manual. Retrieved from http://www.act/org/aap /pdf/ACT_Technical_Manual.pdf

ACT. (2007b). PLAN: Technical manual. Retrieved from http://www.act/org/plan /downloads.html

ACT. (2011). EXPLORE: Technical manual. Retrieved from http://www.act.org /explore/pdf/TechManual.pdf

Acton, G. S., & Schroeder, D. H. (2001). Sensory discrimination as related to general intelligence. *Intelligence, 29*(3), 263–271.

American School Counselor Association. (2004). *ASCA national standards for students.* Alexandria, VA: Author.

Anderson, D., Elliott, R., Paterson, D., Toops, H., & Heidbreder, E. (1930). *Minnesota Mechanical Ability Tests: The report of a research investigation subsidized by the Committee on Human Migrations of the National Research Council and conducted in the Department of Psychology of the University of Minnesota.* Minneapolis: University of Minnesota Press.

Barak, A. (1981). Vocational interests: A cognitive view. *Journal of Vocational Behavior, 19,* 1–14.

Barak, A., Librowsky, I., & Shiloh, S. (1989). Cognitive determinants of interests: An extension of a theoretical model and initial empirical examinations. *Journal of Vocational Behavior, 34,* 318–334.

Barak, A., Shiloh, S., & Haushner, O. (1992). Modification of interests through cognitive restructuring: Test of a theoretical model in preschool children. *Journal of Counseling Psychology, 39,* 490–497.

Barton, P., & Coley, R. (2011). *The mission of the high school: A new consensus of the purposes of publish education?* Princeton, NJ: Educational Testing Services.

Betsworth, D. (1999). Accuracy of self-estimated abilities and the relationship between self-estimated abilities and realism for women. *Journal of Career Assessment, 7*(1), 35–43.

Betz, N., Fitzgerald, L., & Hill, R. (1989). Trait-factor theories: Traditional cornerstone of career theory. In M. Arthur, D. Hall, & B. Lawrence (Eds.), *Handbook of career theory* (pp. 26–40). Cambridge, UK: Cambridge University Press.

Blustein, D. L. (2006). The changing nature of work in the 21st century. In D. L. Blustein (Ed.), *The psychology of working: A new perspective for career development, counseling and public policy.* New York, NY: Erlbaum.

Bradway, K., & Thompson, C. (1962). Intelligence at adulthood: A twenty-five year follow-up. *Journal of Educational Psychology, 53,* 1–14.

Bridgeman, B., Burton, N., & Cline, F. (2008). Understanding what the numbers mean: A straightforward approach to GRE predictive validity. (Report No. GREB 04-03ETS RR-08-46). Princeton, NJ: ETS.

Brody, E., & Brody, N. (1976). *Intelligence: Nature, determinants, and consequences.* New York, NY: Academic Press.

Brown, S. D., & Lent, R. W. (1996). A social cognitive framework for career choice counseling. *Career Development Quarterly, 44*(4), 354–366.

Campbell, D. P., Hyne, S. A., & Nilsen, D. C. (1992). *Manual for the Campbell Interest and Skill Survey*. Minneapolis, MN: National Computer Systems.

Canivez, G., & Watkins, M. (1998). Long-term stability of the Wechsler Intelligence Scale for Children–third edition. *Psychological Assessment, 10*(3), 285–291.

Carroll, J. (1993). *Human cognitive abilities: A survey of factor-analytic studies*. Cambridge, England: Cambridge University Press.

Ceci, S. (1991). How much does schooling influence general intelligence and its cognitive components? A reassessment of the evidence. *Developmental Psychology, 27*(5), 703–722.

College Board. (2011). *Educator's handbook for the SAT and the SAT subject tests*. Princeton, NJ: Author.

Crivellato, E., & Ribatti, D. (2007). Soul, mind, brain: Greek philosophy and the birth of neuroscience. *Brain Research Bulletin, 71*(4), 327–336.

Dawis, R., Goldman, S., & Sung, Y. (1992). Stability and change in abilities for a sample of young adults. *Educational and Psychological Measurement, 52*, 457–465.

Dreary, I., Thorpe, G., Wilson, V., Starr, J., & Whalley, L. (2003). Population sex differences in IQ at age 11: The Scottish Mental Survey 1932. *Intelligence, 31*, 533–542.

Education Week. (2011). Uncertain forecast: Education adjusts to a new economic reality. *Quality Counts, 30*(16), 1–70.

Educational Testing Service. (2011). GRE information and registration bulletin. Princeton, NJ: Author. Retrieved from http://www.ets.org/s/gre/pdf/gre_info _reg_bulletin.pdf

Eysenck, H. (1998). *Intelligence: A new look*. New Brunswick, NJ: Transaction.

Fennema, E. (1974). Mathematics learning and the sexes: A review. *Journal for Research in Mathematics Education, 5*(3), 126–139. doi:10.2307/748949

Fleishman, E., Costanza, D., & Marshall-Mies, J. (1999). Abilities. In N. Peterson, M. Mumford, W. Borman, P. Jeanneret, & E. Fleishman (Eds.), *An occupational information system for the 21st century: The development of the O*NET* (pp. 49–69). Washington, DC: American Psychological Association.

Gardner, H. (1983). *Frames of mind: The theory of multiple intelligences*. New York, NY: Basic Books.

Gardner, H. (1999). *Intelligence reframed: Multiple intelligences for the 21st century*. New York, NY: Basic Books.

Gardner, M. K. (2011). Theories of intelligence. In M. Bray & T. Kehle (Eds.), *The Oxford handbook of school psychology* (pp. 79–100). New York, NY: Oxford University Press.

Gati, I., Fishman-Nadav, Y., & Shiloh, S. (2006). The relations between preferences for using abilities, self-estimated abilities, and measured abilities among career counseling clients. *Journal of Vocational Behavior, 68*, 24–38.

Gottfredson, L. (2003). The challenge and promise of cognitive career assessment. *Journal of Career Assessment, 11*(2), 115–135.

Gow, A., Johnson, W., Pattie, A., Brett, C., Roberts, B., Starr, J., & Deary, I. (2011). Stability and change in intelligence from age 11 to ages 70, 79, and 87: The Lothian birth cohorts of 1921 and 1936. *Psychology and Aging, 26*(1), 232–240.

Hall, D. (2002). *Careers in and out of organizations*. Thousand Oaks, CA: Sage.

Halpern, D. F. (1986). *Sex differences in cognitive abilities*. Hillsdale, NJ: Erlbaum.

Harrington, J., & Harrington, T. (1996). *Ability explorer:* Preliminary technical manual. Chicago, IL: Riverside.

Holland, J., Powell, A., & Fritzsche, B. (1994). *The self-directed search professional user's guide*. Odessa, FL: Psychological Assessment Resources.

Honzik, M., MacFarlane, J., & Allen, L. (1948). The stability of mental test performance between two and eighteen years. *Journal of Experimental Education, 17,* 309–324.

Horn, J., & Cattell, R. (1996). Refinement and test of the theory of fluid and crystallized general intelligences. *Journal of Educational Psychology, 57,* 253–270.

Horn, J., & Hofner, S. (1992). Major abilities and development in the adult period. In R. Sternberg & C. Berg (Eds.), *Intellectual development* (pp. 44–49). New York, NY: Cambridge University Press.

Hunt, E. (2005). Information processing and intelligence: Where we are and where we are going? In R. J. Sternberg & J. E. Pretz (Eds.), *Cognition and intelligence: Identifying the mechanisms of the mind* (pp. 1–25). New York, NY: Cambridge University Press.

Hyde, J. S., Fennema, E., & Lamon, S. J. (1990). Gender differences in mathematics performance: A meta-analysis, *Psychological Bulletin, 107,* 139–155.

Hyde, J. S., Lindberg, S., Linn, M., Ellis, A., & Williams, C. (2008). Gender similarities characterize contemporary state assessments of mathematics performance. *Science, 321,* 494–495.

Hyde, J. S., & Linn, M. C. (1988). Gender differences in verbal ability: A meta-analysis. *Psychological Bulletin, 104,* 53–69.

Jencks, C., & Phillips, M. (1998). *The Black-White test score gap*. Washington, DC: Brookings Institution.

Jensen, A. R. (2002). Galton's legacy to research on intelligence. *Journal of Biosocial Science, 34*(2), 145–172.

Knapp, L., Knapp, R., & Knapp-Lee, L. (2003). *Career Ability Placement Survey: Directions for administering and interpreting the CAPS*. San Diego, CA: EdITS.

Knowdell, R. (1990). *Motivated Skills Card Sort–revised*. Camberwell, Australia: Career Research & Testing.

Kobrin, J., Patterson, B., Shaw, E., Mattern, K., & Barbuti, S. (2008). *Validity of the SAT for predicting first-year college grade point average* (Report No. 2008–5). New York, NY: College Board.

Krieshok, T., & Black, M. (2009). Assessment and counseling competencies and responsibilities: A checklist for counselors. In E. Whitfield, R. Feller, & C. Wood (Eds.), *A counselor's guide to career assessment instruments* (5th ed., pp. 61–68). Broken Arrow, OK: National Career Development Association.

Kuncel, N., Hezlett, S., & Ones, D. (2001). A comprehensive meta-analysis of the predictive validity of the Graduate Record Examination: Implications for graduate school selection and performance. *Psychological Bulletin, 127*(1), 162–181.

Lent, R. W., & Brown, S. D. (1996). A social cognitive framework for career choice counseling. *Career Development Quarterly, 44*(4), 354–366.

Lent, R. W., Brown, S. D., & Hackett, G. (1994). Toward a unifying social cognitive theory of career and academic interest, choice, and performance. *Journal of Vocational Behavior, 45,* 79–122.

Levy, F., & Murnane, R. (2004). *The new division of labor: How computers are creating the next job market.* Princeton, NJ: Princeton University Press.

Mabe, P., III, & West, S. (1982). Validity of self-evaluation ability: A review and meta-analysis. *Journal of Applied Psychology, 67,* 280–296.

Maddox, T. (2008). *Tests* (6th ed.). Austin, Texas: Pro-ED.

McGrew, K. (2005). The Cattell-Horn-Carroll theory of cognitive abilities. In D. Flanagan & P. Harrison (Eds.), *Contemporary intellectual assessment: Theories, tests, and issues* (2nd ed., pp. 136–181). New York, NY: Guilford Press.

McGrew, K. (2009). CHC theory and the human cognitive abilities project: Standing on the shoulders of the giants of psychometric intelligence research. *Intelligence, 37,* 1–10.

Miyazaki, I. (1981). *China's examination hell: The civil service examinations of imperial China.* New Haven, CT: Yale University Press.

Moore, W., Pedlow, S., Krishnamurty, P., & Wolter, K. (2000). *National longitudinal survey of youth 1997 (NLSY97): Technical sampling report.* Chicago, IL: National Opinion Research Center.

Mortensen, E., & Kleven, M. (1993). A WAIS longitudinal study of cognitive development during the life span from ages 50 to 70. *Developmental Neuropsychology, 9,* 115–130.

Murphy, L., Plake, B., Impara, J., & Spies, R. (2002). Tests in print IV. Lincoln, NE: Buros Institute of Mental Measurements.

Neisser, U., Boodoo, G., Bouchard, T., Boykin, A., Brody, N., Ceci, S., . . . Urbina, S. (1996). Intelligence: Knowns and unknowns. *American Psychologist, 51,* 77–101.

Niles, S., & Harris-Bowlsbey, J. (2009). *Career development interventions in the 21st century.* Upper Saddle River, NJ: Pearson.

Parsons, F. (1909). *Choosing a vocation.* Boston, MA: Houghton, Mifflin.

Powell, A., Farrar, E., & Cohen, D. (1985). *The shopping mall high school: Winners and losers in the educational marketplace.* Boston, MA: Houghton Mifflin.

Prediger, D. (2002). Abilities, interests, and values: Their assessment and their integration via the World-of-Work Map. *Journal of Career Assessment, 10*(2), 209–232.

Priess, H. A., & Hyde, J. S. (2010). Gender and academic abilities and preferences. In J. C. Chrisler & D. R. McCreary (Eds.), *Handbook of gender research in psychology* (pp. 297–316). New York, NY: Springer.

Rotundo, M., & Sackett, P. (1999). Effect of rater race on conclusions regarding differential prediction in cognitive ability tests. *Journal of Applied Psychology, 84*(5), 815–822.

Schmidt, F., Pearlman, K., & Hunter, J. (1980). The validity and fairness of employment and educational tests for Hispanic Americans: A review and analysis. *Personnel Psychology, 33,* 705–724.

Snow, R. (1994). Abilities and aptitudes. In R. Sternberg (Ed.), *Encyclopedia of human intelligence* (vol. 1, pp. 3–5). New York, NY: Macmillan.

Snow, R. (1996). Aptitude development and education. *Psychology, Public Policy, and Law, 2*(3–4), 536–560.

Spearman, C. (1927). *The abilities of man.* New York, NY: Macmillan.

Spies, R., Carlson, J., & Geisinger, K. (Eds.). (2010). *The eighteenth mental measurement yearbook.* Lincoln, NE: Buros Institute of Mental Measurements.

Sternberg, R., Kaufman, J., & Grigorenko, E. (2009). *The essential Sternberg: Essays on intelligence, psychology, and education.* New York, NY: Springer.

Super, D., Savickas, M., & Super, C. (1996). The life-span, life-space approach to careers. In D. Brown & L. Brooks (Eds.), *Career choice and development* (3rd ed., pp. 121–178). San Francisco, CA: Jossey-Bass.

Thurstone, L. (1938). *Primary mental abilities.* Chicago, IL: University of Chicago Press.

Tracey, T., & Hopkins, N. (2001). Correspondence of interests and abilities with occupational choice. *Journal of Counseling Psychology, 48*(2), 178–189.

Trilling, B., & Fadel, C. (2009). *21st century skills: Learning for life in our times.* San Francisco, CA: Jossey-Bass.

U.S. Department of Defense. (2005). *ASVAB career exploration program: Counselor manual.* Washington, DC: Author.

U.S. Department of Labor. (1970). *Manual for the USES General Aptitude Test Battery.* Washington, DC: Author.

U.S. Department of Labor. (2009). *Ability profiler user's guide.* Washington, DC: U.S. Department of Labor, Employment and Training Administration.

Weiss, L., & Prifitera, A. (1995). An evaluation of differential prediction of WIAT achievement scores from WISC-III FSIQ across ethnic and gender groups. *Journal of School Psychology, 33*(4), 297–304.

Weiss, L., Prifitera, A., & Roid, G. (1993). The WISC-III and the fairness of predicting achievement across ethnic and gender groups. In B. Bracken & R. McCallum (Eds.), *Wechsler Intelligence Scale for Children* (3rd ed., pp. 35–42). Brandon, VT: Clinical Psychology Publishing.

Welsh, J. R., Kucinkas, S. K., & Curran, L. T. (1990). Armed Services Vocational Battery (ASVAB): Integrative review of validity studies (Technical Report No. 90–22). Brooks Air Force Base, TX: Air Force Systems Command.

Whitfield, E., Feller, R., & Wood, C. (2009). *A counselor's guide to career assessment instruments* (5th ed., pp. 61–68). Broken Arrow, OK: National Career Development Association.

Williams, W., & Ceci, S. (2007). Introduction: Striving for perspective in the debate on women in science. In S. J. Ceci & W. M. Williams (Eds.), *Why aren't more women in science? Top researchers debate the evidence* (pp. 3–23). Washington, DC: American Psychological Association.

Wise, L., Welsh, J., Grafton, F., Foley, P., Earles, J., Sawin, L., & Divgi, D. R. (1992). *Sensitivity and fairness of the Armed Services Vocational Aptitude Battery (ASVAB) technical composites.* Seaside, CA: Defense Manpower Data Center.

CHAPTER 17

Assessing Additional Constructs Affecting Career Choice and Development

PATRICK J. ROTTINGHAUS AND P. MAGGIE HAUSER

C AREER COUNSELING CLIENTS OFTEN face tumultuous changes or seemingly more mundane decision points with varying degrees of awareness about themselves and the road ahead. Indeed, career choice and development behaviors are influenced by complex sets of traits (Ackerman & Heggestad, 1997), motives (Rottinghaus & Van Esbroeck, 2011), and developmental tasks, all occurring within an ever-changing economy and multicultural context. Previous chapters have elaborated on the importance of abilities, vocational interests, and work values. These constructs are central to most career theories and career interventions. However, the rich theory and research traditions in vocational psychology offer a broader scope of additional factors critical to career-related behavior that provide enhanced understanding of unique career challenges.

The present chapter extends the focus of career assessment to additional client characteristics to which practitioners can attend as they seek a more complete understanding of how clients adjust to changing circumstances over time and across various transition points. In the first edition of this text, Swanson and D'Achiardi (2005) outlined factors beyond the "big three" (i.e., abilities, interests, needs/values), and we are charged to address the same open-ended task. Guided by their work, we complement the topics they covered by elaborating on certain constructs that received less attention (e.g., career adaptability) and provide updates on career assessment research and practice since 2005. Moreover, we reference earlier theory chapters in this text to highlight measures and assessment systems affiliated with major theories (e.g., social cognitive career theory [SCCT], career construction theory) and topics (e.g., diversity, social factors) that are crucial for career counseling practice. The majority of this chapter elaborates on key domains that have been well researched and have achieved established measures. Throughout this chapter, we focus on specific measures and assessment strategies that have received empirical support and that can enhance career counseling practice. Finally, the chapter is organized into three major sections. In the first section, we use the major theories discussed in the first section of this book as an organizing scheme but focus specifically on constructs that are not covered in the other assessment chapters. For example, in relation to Donald Super's theory of career development (see Hartung, Chapter 4, this volume), we discuss the assessment of career maturity, adaptability, and role salience. We also cover the assessment of vocational identity as a central component of Holland's theory (see Nauta, Chapter 3, this volume) and self-efficacy beliefs, outcome expectations, goals, supports, and barriers in relation to SCCT (see Lent, Chapter 5, this volume).

The second section of our chapter focuses on the assessment of constructs that are used often in career counseling but are not necessarily aligned with any specific theory. Included in this section are brief discussions of the assessment of personality and decision-making difficulties. The third section summarizes the chapter by providing a set of take-home messages to practitioners on the choice and use of the assessment tools discussed in the two prior sections. In all cases, we discuss only relatively psychometrically sound measures and limit our discussion further to a few measures that are relatively widely used in career research and counseling.

THEORY-DERIVED MEASURES

Unlike the atheoretical programs of research that led to prominent measures of individual differences (e.g., interests, abilities), many career assessments have been developed based on career development theories. We focus on the assessment of a broad array of constructs, including career maturity, career adaptability, self-efficacy, outcome expectations, goals, and social roles that relate to how people navigate the ever-changing occupational world.

CAREER MATURITY AND CAREER ADAPTABILITY

Whereas interests, abilities, and values are important characteristics related to career planning, developmental theorists emphasize the process of career development, or *how* careers evolve over time. Career maturity and career adaptability generally incorporate the developmental tasks and strategies involved in exploring, committing to, and executing career plans. *Career maturity* involves readiness for planning one's career and focuses on how well adolescents meet developmental tasks involved in educational and vocational decisions. Super's (1955) research on processes involved in career decision making highlighted the importance of attitudinal (i.e., planfulness, exploration) and cognitive (i.e., decision-making, occupational knowledge) dimensions of career maturity. Assessing these aspects of career development can inform practitioners about how well prepared, or ready, a student is to make occupational choices. Traditional measures of these dimensions include the Career Maturity Inventory (Crites & Savickas, 1996; Savickas & Porfeli, 2011) and the Career Development Inventory (Savickas & Hartung, 1996).

In 1979, Super and colleagues introduced the term *career adaptability* to incorporate concerns of adult workers (Super & Kidd, 1979; Super & Knasel, 1979). Super and Knasel (1981) defined *career adaptability* as the "readiness to cope with changing work and working conditions" (p. 195). Given the challenges presented by unstable occupational structures, individuals must continually monitor and modify their ongoing career management strategies, which entail adaptations. Therefore, researchers and practitioners now emphasize how people cope with the challenges of navigating careers in contemporary society. In addition to summarizing historical highlights of career adaptability, this section features specific measures based on emerging theory and research.

Building on the work of Donald Super, Savickas (1997) suggested that career adaptability should replace career maturity as an integrative construct that connects disparate segments of career development and avoids the limitations of a maturational framework while encompassing the major components of "planful attitudes, self and environmental exploration, and informed decision making" (p. 254). Savickas (2005) defined *career adaptability* as "a psychosocial construct that denotes an individual's readiness and resources for coping with current and imminent vocational development tasks, occupational transitions, and personal traumas" (p. 51). This self-regulatory process of attitudes, beliefs, and competencies encompasses individual dimensions of concern, control, curiosity, and confidence (Savickas, 2005), which informed the development of the Career Adapt-Abilities measure explained later. Adaptive individuals embrace these qualities as they navigate educational and career transitions. Each dimension encompasses a set of more specific attitudes, beliefs, competencies, and affiliated coping behaviors that reflect adaptability (see Savickas, Chapter 6, this volume).

Savickas (2011) uses his life story interview to identify themes drawn from stories. However, the lack of agreed-upon operational definitions of career adaptability has limited the applicability of this construct in research and practice. In an attempt to address this concern, Creed, Fallon, and Hood (2009) tested a model of career adaptability that was informed by extant definitions emphasizing career planning, self-exploration, career exploration, and decision making, conceptualized as self-regulatory mechanisms, in a large sample of college students. This research yielded a good fit for the model comprising these components, which can inform the development of quantitative career adaptability measures.

Bandura's (2001, 2006b) scholarship on human agency relates to career adaptability (Rottinghaus, Buelow, Matyja, & Schneider, 2012). Agency involves a complex of four features: intentionality, forethought, self-reactiveness, and self-reflectiveness (Bandura, 2001). Career-related agency reflects the internal motivation clients have to control and manage behaviors necessary to achieve favorable outcomes such as career transitions (Rottinghaus et al., 2012). Bandura (2006b) captured important connections between human agency and adaptability: "People who develop their competencies, self-regulatory skills, and enabling beliefs in their efficacy can generate a wider array of options that expand their freedom of action, and are more successful in realizing desired futures" (p. 165). The Career Futures Inventory–Revised (CFI-R; Rottinghaus et al., 2012) emphasizes agency within the context of career adaptability. Additional details on various career maturity and adaptability measures follow.

Career Development Inventory. Growing out of the career pattern study and first published in 1979, the Career Development Inventory (CDI; Super, Thompson, Lindeman, Jordaan, & Myers, 1981; Thompson & Lindeman, 1981) is a 120-item standardized measure of Super's (1955) attitudinal and cognitive dimensions of career maturity: Career Planning, Career Exploration, Decision Making, and World-of-Work Information. A fifth scale, Knowledge of Preferred Occupation, measures one's knowledge regarding typical duties and qualities of work for one of 20 occupational groups selected by the respondent. Savickas and Hartung (1996) provide a thorough analysis of the CDI, including a history of the development of the CDI's versions and a review of research.

Career Maturity Inventory. Crites (1961, 1973) developed the Career Maturity Inventory (CMI; originally called the Vocational Development Inventory) from his ongoing longitudinal research program in the 1960s examining readiness attitudes and career planning competencies involved in making informed career plans. The CMI was revised in 1973, 1978, 1995, and most recently in 2011 (Crites & Savickas, 2011; available at http://www.vocopher.com) to incorporate three of the four career adaptability dimensions from career construction theory (i.e., Concern, Curiosity, and Confidence), as well as relational style in making occupational decisions for students in grades 5–12. This new 24-item version, CMI (Form C) includes five scores: A Total score comprising the three six-item career adaptability measures, and a separate six-item Consultation Scale, which measures relational style, or the degree to which clients seek information and assistance related to career decision-making, ranging from independent to interdependent. A supplemental guide explains the logic behind each correct answer, which enables practitioners to "teach the test" to clients. Savickas and Porfeli (2011) presented initial reliability and validity evidence for the CMI (Form C) through confirmatory factor analyses and relationships with the Vocational Identity Scale (Holland & Holland, 1977). A 10-item Screening Form version of the CMI is also available to obtain a "general level of career choice readiness and decisional adaptability" (Savickas & Porfeli, 2011, p. 367) in large group settings. Savickas and Porfeli (2011) recommend that individuals with lower scores should engage in broad exploration activities (e.g., identity and values clarification interventions), whereas those with higher scores should proceed with in-depth occupational exploration (e.g., interest inventory interpretations).

Career Adapt-Abilities. The Career Adapt-Abilities Scale (CAAS; Savickas, 2011; Savickas & Porfeli, 2012) is a 24-item measure, comprised of 6 items assessing perceptions of competence across four dimensions of career adaptability: concern, control, curiosity, and confidence. *Concern* is "the extent to which an individual is oriented to and involved in preparing for the future"; *Control* is "the extent of self-discipline as shown by being conscientious and responsible in making decisions"; *Curiosity* is "the extent to which an individual explores circumstances and seeks information about opportunities"; and *Confidence* is "the extent of certitude that one has the ability to solve problems and do what needs to be done to overcome obstacles" (Savickas & Porfeli, 2012, p. 664). Clients rate the degree to which they have developed each of the 24 abilities, using a response scale ranging from Strongest (5) to Not Strong (1). The four scales demonstrated acceptable internal consistency reliability, ranging from .74 (Control) to .85 (Confidence). A series of confirmatory factor analyses supported the factor structure of the measure. In addition, evidence suggests that the four scales may be useful in countries beyond the United States: Research has confirmed the four-factor structure of the CAAS in 13 countries. Upon examining the structure and between-factor relationships, the authors have also concluded that scores on the four factors can be combined to yield an overall adaptability score.

Career Futures Inventory–Revised. Rottinghaus, Day, and Borgen (2005) developed the original 25-item Career Futures Inventory (CFI) to assess favorable views of the future and adaptability, yielding a three-factor measure that provides scores for career adaptability, career optimism, and perceived knowledge of the job market. The authors define *career adaptability* as "a tendency affecting the way an individual views his or her capacity to plan and adjust to changing career plans and work responsibilities, especially in the face of unforeseen events" (p. 5). The 28-item Career Futures Inventory–Revised (CFI-R; Rottinghaus et al., 2012) expanded the original measure by incorporating components of Bandura's (1986) personal agency construct (i.e., self-awareness, control, and career transition self-efficacy) and relational aspects of career development. Thus, the revised Career Futures Inventory provides scores on five scales measuring Career Agency, Occupational Awareness, Support, Work–Life Balance, and Negative Career Outlook. Cronbach's alpha internal consistency estimates for these scales ranged from .78 (Work–Life Balance) to .90 (Career Agency). The CFI-R may serve as an intake assessment tool to highlight clients' needs and inform counseling objectives. Researchers and administrators can use the CFI-R to measure outcomes of individual or group career counseling or to evaluate class interventions.

VOCATIONAL IDENTITY

Next we examine the role of the self-concept or vocational identity as an important aspect of career development. Super (1955) used the term *self-concept* to refer to the views that individuals develop of themselves (e.g., their interests, needs, goals, values, and salience of the work versus other roles) that they attempt to implement in choosing occupational paths. Holland (1997) used the term *vocational identity* to refer to the coherence of persons' views of themselves. Both theorists hypothesized that these (self-concept and vocational identity) views of the self are critical in promoting optimum career development and aid in the career choice and adjustment process (see Hartung, Chapter 4, and Nauta, Chapter 3, this volume).

Vocational identity has been widely researched and has yielded at least one useful scale. Holland (1997) defined *vocational identity* as "the possession of a clear and stable picture of one's goals, interests, and talents" (p. 5). The Vocational Identity Subscale of Holland, Daiger, and Power's (1980) My Vocational Situation (MVS) is a sound measure of vocational identity. The MVS Vocational Identity (VI) scale includes 18 true-false items addressing how well clients have established a clear sense of various aspects of their career plans. The MVS includes two additional items assessing need for occupational information and potential barriers. The MVS can be used as a needs assessment at intake to identify appropriate interventions. For example, some clients may have developed a coherent vocational identity (as revealed by their scores on the VI scale) but report significant barriers in response to the Barriers items. This pattern of responses suggests that a focus on identifying and overcoming barriers would be a central focus for counseling. By contrast, counselors would help clients with low VI scores to better understand and integrate their interests, values, abilities, and goals into a coherent self-understanding.

Social Cognitive Career Theory Constructs

Building on insights from Bandura's (1977, 1986) social cognitive theory, Lent, Brown, and Hackett's (1994) SCCT offers an array of well-researched factors involved in interest development, career choices, academic and career-related performance, and work satisfaction (see Lent, Chapter 5, this volume). This section summarizes three interconnected constructs especially emphasized from the SCCT perspective that are pivotal to assessment and career counseling interventions: self-efficacy, outcome expectations, and goals.

Self-efficacy. *Self-efficacy* is defined as one's perceived ability to organize and execute courses of action to accomplish specific tasks (Bandura, 1977, 1986). First applied to the career domain by Betz and Hackett (1981; Hackett & Betz, 1981) and serving as a central feature in SCCT (Lent et al., 1994), self-efficacy is among the most widely studied career constructs. Numerous specialized career self-efficacy measures have been developed to assess clients' beliefs in their capacities to execute courses of action related to career decision making (e.g., Career Decision Self-Efficacy Scale, CDSE; Betz & Taylor, 2001) and the career search process (Solberg, 1998). In addition, self-efficacy for specific occupationally relevant content, typically organized by Holland's RIASEC themes or more specific dimensions (e.g., mathematics), can be used by counselors to help clients gauge their perceived skills and inform interventions to increase self-efficacy through the framework of Bandura's (1977) four sources of self-efficacy (e.g., Betz & Schifano, 2000).

For example, the Skills Confidence Inventory (SCI; Betz, Borgen, & Harmon, 1996) includes self-efficacy measures of the six Holland themes and was developed as a companion to the Strong Interest Inventory (SII; Harmon, Hansen, Borgen, & Hammer, 1994; Hansen, Chapter 14, this volume). Betz and her colleagues also developed the Expanded Skills Confidence Inventory (ESCI; Betz et al., 2003) to assess more specific content analogous to the Basic Interest Scales (e.g., Mathematics, Science, Teaching) of the SII. The ESCI has been incorporated into the Career and Personality Assessments (CAPA) system as the Career Confidence Inventory (CCI; Betz & Borgen, 2010) and now covers 27 specific dimensions for which self-efficacy can be assessed. Using a similar format, the Kuder Skills Assessment (KSA; Zytowski, Rottinghaus, & D'Achiardi, 2007) includes 16 10-item measures, representing content organized by the U.S. Department of Education's Career Clusters (e.g., Manufacturing, Marketing). The KSA has separate versions for adolescents and adults, incorporating appropriate degrees of item difficulty. Rottinghaus (2009) reported that scores on the scales of the KSA– College and Adult version demonstrated high reliability and concurrent validity by demonstrating that relevant scales (i.e., Finance, Marketing & Sales, and Business Operations) distinguished between groups of business majors specializing in accounting, management, finance, and marketing.

Self-efficacy measures are meant to be used for specified content domains (Bandura, 2006a). Therefore, researchers have developed measures for relevant content domains expressly for specific populations. For example, Fouad, Smith, and Enochs (1997) developed the Middle School Self-Efficacy Scale, which includes age-appropriate content and measures of career decision-making self-efficacy, outcome expectations, and intentions-goals. Smith and Fouad (1999) developed a separate series of measures addressing self-efficacy, outcome expectations, interests, and goals for content involving art, social studies, math/science, and English, targeting a university population.

Practitioners should be aware that nuanced interpretations can be made, depending on the precise language of the directions and item stems (Betz & Rottinghaus, 2006). The traditional item format asks clients if they "can do" a specific task, based on a scale ranging from 0% to 100%, without comparative judgments to peers. Most career self-efficacy measures instruct clients to rate the degree to which they can perform a specified task using a 5-point Likert rating scale. However, many related measures use slightly different formats, which affect the interpretation of clients' scores. For example, The Campbell Interest and Skill Survey (CISS; Campbell, Hyne & Nilsen, 1992; Hansen, Chapter 14, this volume) is commonly included within the literature examining self-efficacy for career-relevant content, although the item format reflects ability self-estimates (e.g., expert, slightly below average in comparison to one's peers) versus an individual frame of reference distinctive of self-efficacy. Brown, Lent, and Gore (2000) found that the two formats were somewhat distinct, with ability self-estimates measured by peer comparison instruments (CISS) informing self-efficacy beliefs (perceptions of what one can do). Nonetheless, both formats seem to be useful in counseling, and no research to date has suggested that one format yields more useful information than the other in counseling. Counselors might be aware though that ability self-estimates are but one (albeit important) influence on self-efficacy beliefs.

Outcome expectations. According to SCCT, an individual's self-efficacy beliefs, as well as beliefs about consequences associated with a particular action, can influence interest development, goal selection, and actions. Lent and colleagues (1994) defined *outcome expectations* as "personal beliefs about probable response outcomes" (p. 83), essentially what will happen if I pursue X. For example, Jamie may not pursue a biology major, even though she has high science self-efficacy, if she does not think a science major would provide satisfying career options for her. Bandura (1986) noted that the content of outcomes may be physical, social, or personal. Outcome expectations, together with self-efficacy beliefs, guide behaviors (Fouad & Guillen, 2006) by affecting individuals' approach or avoidance behaviors and persistence in the face of obstacles. Thus, a person with strong self-efficacy and positive outcome expectations for a specific career pursuit (e.g., science) will be more likely to pursue career-relevant tasks (e.g., take science courses, select a science major) and persist in the face of obstacles than those with low self-efficacy beliefs and less positive outcome expectations. Knowledge of a client's outcome expectations especially provides important information to identify why a person with high self-efficacy in an area may not report strong interest. For example, many math- and science-talented women may choose not to pursue a science, technology, engineering, and mathematics (STEM) career because they perceive that STEM work environments might not be especially welcoming to women (see Betz, 1989, for a discussion of the null environment).

Outcome expectations typically are assessed using an adapted version of Vroom's (1964) expectancy-value model of work motivation. Such scales typically ask participants to indicate the degree of importance they place on various values. Then, for each value, participants are asked to indicate how likely it would be satisfied if they were to take a specific action (e.g., pursue a career in engineering). Practitioners then must combine the importance ratings with the likelihood ratings to yield an overall index of outcome expectations (see Brooks & Betz, 1990, for a good example of such a measure).

This two-step process of collecting separate ratings for importance and likelihood has often been reduced to a single step, essentially asking participants to respond to various statements containing positive outcomes (e.g., satisfaction with salary) that may result from taking a particular action (Bieschke, 2000). For example, participants may be asked how satisfied they would be with their salary if they entered the field of chemistry. Thus, different values (e.g., monetary compensation) are implicit in the outcomes. Participants are asked to rate their agreement that each outcome will occur or how likely each is to occur, assuming they were to take the action or achieve a designated level of performance. Gore and Leuwerke (2000) introduced a variation of the single-step process in which participants essentially generate their own personal weighting scheme. Participants are presented with a list of various work values and asked to rate the degree to which they would fulfill those most important to them, given the selection of various careers.

There are a variety of other formats that counselors can use when working with clients. For example, Lent and Brown (2006) suggest asking how likely each of a variety of outcomes are for different career fields, ranging from *highly unlikely* to *highly likely*. Alternatively, one may ask the extent to which favored outcomes would be available (*not very much* to *very much*; e.g., Gore & Leuwerke, 2000). Regardless of format, the basic goal of outcome expectations assessment is to gather data on the types of outcomes clients expect from different career or educational pursuits. These data can then be used to gather occupational information to ascertain the accuracy of these outcome expectations. For example, a client may drastically underestimate the income potential from a specific occupational pursuit for which he or she has high self-efficacy beliefs (see Lent, Chapter 5, this volume).

Recent research has focused on positive outcome expectations (or affirmatively worded values); however, it is also important to assess negative outcome expectations (Fouad & Guillen, 2006; Lent & Brown, 2006). Counselors can assess for negative consequences that clients are expecting, such as discrimination, loneliness, social disapproval, and work–family conflict, that may then help explain their avoidance of certain career options. For example, a client may avoid a career that seems gender-typed for the opposite sex (e.g., a male avoiding a career in cosmetology).

Goals. Personal goals reflect individuals' plans to engage in a particular task or achieve a certain outcome. SCCT incorporates two primary forms of personal goals: choice content goals and performance goals (Lent & Brown, 2006). Choice content goals refer to what sort of activities one hopes to pursue, whereas performance goals refer to the degree and quality of achievement one hopes to demonstrate in a given domain. Choice content goals function to motivate individuals to pursue preferred options in their educational or vocational field (Lent et al., 2003), whereas performance goals reflect the level of success individuals hope to attain for a given task (Phillips & Gully, 1997).

The assessment of goals tends to be relatively straightforward. In social cognitive career studies, choice goals are usually assessed by asking participants to indicate their intent to select or perform a particular activity (e.g., choosing a college major). Participants are typically asked to rate their likelihood of selecting or persisting in a particular the activity. For example, Lent and Brown (2006) suggest presenting a set of aspirational statements, such as "I intend to take a math course next semester," to which participants respond by rating their level of agreement, ranging from *strongly disagree* to *strongly agree*. Choice goals often help provide a prediction of eventual actions, particularly if goals are stated clearly, are set proximally to the behavior, and refer to actions that are within the individuals' control (Ajzen, 1988). In an assessment of performance goals, instead of the counselor asking about intent to select or persist at the activity, a participant indicates how well he or she intends to perform the activity. For example, clients may indicate the productivity level they plan to attain in a given work environment (Locke & Latham, 1990).

SOCIAL ROLES AND RELATIONAL PATTERNS

Although many believe that vocational psychology has focused entirely on the individual perspective (Richardson, 2012), there are now a variety of theoretical models that explicitly consider the role of social and contextual issues in career development (e.g., Lent, Brown, & Hackett, 1994, 2000; Lent, Chapter 5, this volume). Lent (2012) asserted that foundational vocational psychology theories have always incorporated attention to work issues within the context of multiple life roles (Super et al., 1996) and have inherently attended to the contextual factors. For example, person–environment fit models (e.g., Dawis, 2005; Holland, 1997) emphasized the influence of factors within educational and work environments. However, changes in society and the workplace are driving renewed emphasis on relational factors in career development (Blustein, 2001, 2011; Richardson, 2012; Schultheiss, 2003), including work–family interface, role salience, and support (see Heppner, Chapter 7, and Kenny & Medvide, Chapter 12, this volume). We next briefly examine the importance of life role salience and supports.

Life role salience. Today, men and women often hold commitments at both home (e.g., parental, housework) and the workplace, and it can be difficult to balance the various roles associated with those commitments. Various terms, such as *role scarcity, resource drain, conflict*, and *negative spillover* (see Edwards & Rothbard, 2000, for an overview), have been used to describe the limited and fixed amounts of resources for each role (e.g., time and energy) that one may experience. Managing multiple roles between home and work can be problematic because they draw on the same scarce resources. It is particularly important in counseling to ascertain how salient the work role is for the client vis-à-vis other life roles and to incorporate this information when considering the desirability and feasibility of different career pursuits. Role salience assessment also provides useful information in working with clients experiencing dissatisfaction with their current jobs. For example, a client may experience job dissatisfaction because the job interferes with the pursuit of other roles (e.g., parent, spouse, leisurite) that are more important (salient) to the client.

The Salience Inventory (SI; Neville & Super, 1986) is a 170-item self-report instrument that measures three different salience variables (i.e., participation, commitment, and value expectations) assessed across five life roles (i.e., study, work, community service, home, and leisure activities). *Participation* items assess amount of time and energy a client has invested in each of the life roles. *Commitment* items inquire about the respondents' emotional attachment toward the five life roles, and the *value expectations* items address the likelihood of clients having opportunities to express their values in a given role. Assessing life-role salience early in the career counseling process can provide the counselor with information about the client's readiness to explore his or her interests, abilities, and values (Nevill & Calvert, 1996). Nevill and Calvert specifically suggested using the SI to gather information about the importance the client places on work in comparison to other roles. Assessing for the client's degree of involvement in work and home life roles, and possible conflicts between them, can inform counseling objectives. For example, if a client perceives the worker role as unimportant, then the client may have little motivation to explore career options. For these clients, Nevill and Calvert suggest using interventions that enhance the client's awareness and interest in various career fields (e.g., job shadowing, relevant readings). When examining the relative ranking of salience across various roles, it is important to explore how societal expectations (e.g., gender, culture) may affect clients' perceptions of career and lifestyle concerns.

Supports.   Identifying and engaging various support systems can help clients overcome challenges, thereby enhancing career development. From the perspective of SCCT, supports are considered "environmental variables that can facilitate the formation and pursuit of individuals' career choices" (Lent et al., 2000, p. 42). In line with the counseling profession's focus on client strengths, it is essential to assess not only barriers that one may face in the career development process but also variables that may facilitate the process as well. Two measures that can be helpful in assessing clients' levels of support around career development concerns are the Social Support

Behaviors (SS-B) measure (Vaux, Riedel, & Stewart, 1987) and the Support scale from the Career Futures Inventory–Revised (Rottinghaus et al., 2012). The SS-B emphasizes five modes of social support (i.e., emotional support, socializing, practical assistance, financial assistance, and advice/guidance) from specific individuals for respondents facing a particular stressor. The Support scale of the CFI-R identifies clients' perceptions of emotional and instrumental support from others in their life related to pursuing career goals. These measures can be used to help a client recognize specific sources of support (e.g., mentors, family members) in his or her life and identify potential needs to enhance weak support systems. Clients may benefit from a discussion of how to build professional networks and use existing formal resources in the community settings (e.g., career services, alumni). Regardless, it is important for clients to recognize how to foster relationships and ask for help when necessary.

This section presented an overview of various career constructs derived from prominent career development theories, including career maturity, career adaptability, self-efficacy, outcome expectations, goals, role salience, and social supports. Attending to these aspects of the career decision-making process can supplement information gathered through the assessment of the Big Three (interests, needs/values, and abilities). In the next section, we examine several important factors that are used in career counseling that traditionally have not been linked to specific career development theories.

ADDITIONAL FACTORS RELEVANT TO CAREER DEVELOPMENT

An integrative and comprehensive approach to assessment requires attention to additional factors that may influence career decisions. For example, personality assessment can provide information regarding how clients generally think, feel, and respond to situations within various occupational and social settings. In addition, this section summarizes career decision-making difficulties, including various sources of indecision and barriers that potentially hinder career development.

ASSESSMENT OF PERSONALITY

Personality traits reflect a relatively enduring set of tendencies or overall styles of thinking and feeling and are often represented by the Big Five traits of Neuroticism, Extraversion, Openness to Experience, Agreeableness, and Conscientiousness (Digman, 1990). As discussed by Brown and Hirschi (Chapter 11, this volume), personality traits are related to vocational interests; choice of occupations; confidence in performing tasks; work performance, satisfaction, and tenure; and even how clients approach the process of learning. Personality traits also relate to how people conduct job searches and how they respond to different forms of counseling.

Although Holland (1997) considered his six RIASEC types as constituting vocational personality dimensions, and meta-analyses have demonstrated substantial shared variance between the Big Five personality traits and Holland's vocational interest types (Larson, Rottinghaus, & Borgen, 2002), these two sets of constructs are largely empirically distinct. Practitioners commonly assess the Big Five personality traits through such measures as the NEO Personality Inventory–Revised (NEO PI-R; Costa & McCrae, 1992) and its variants (see later). The Myers-Briggs Type Indicator–3rd Edition (MBTI; Myers, McCaulley, Quenk, & Hammer, 1998) is also often used in career counseling to assess other dimensions of personality. In addition, the personal style scales of the Strong Interest Inventory (Donnay, Morris, Schaubhut, & Thompson, 2005) can provide useful insights into clients' typical ways of interacting with the world related to career choice and development. Additional personality measures that are used less frequently by career practitioners include the 16 PF–5th Edition (Cattell, Cattell, & Cattell, 1993) and California Psychological Inventory (Gough & Bradley, 1996).

NEO Personality Inventory–Revised (NEO PI-R; Costa & McCrae, 1992). The 240-item NEO PI-R (Costa & McCrae, 1992) is the most widely researched measure of the Big Five personality factors, and it includes six more specific facets within each general factor (e.g., Warmth and Assertiveness are two of the facets of Extraversion). Several versions of the NEO are available, including the NEO-FFI, a 60-item measure assessing the Big Five only (i.e., it does not provide facet measures), and the NEO-4, which was developed expressly for career counseling applications and excludes the Neuroticism factor. Widely used public domain measures of the Big Five and numerous specific personality constructs (including constructs assessed in the NEO PI-R, CPI, 16PF) are available from Goldberg's (1999) International Personality Item Pool (IPIP) collaboratory. A significant amount of the career-related research using the Big Five has focused on connections with Holland interest types, yielding points of convergence between Extraversion and Social and Enterprising interests, Openness to Experience and Investigative and Artistic interests, and Agreeableness and Social interests (Larson et al., 2002). Additional research on the Big Five supports their wide application to career counseling and industrial-organizational settings, especially regarding job performance and satisfaction (see Brown & Hirschi, Chapter 11; Lent & Brown, Chapter 22, this volume; Walsh & Eggerth, 2005). A series of meta-analytic investigations have concluded that Conscientiousness significantly relates to job performance across all occupations (cf. Barrick & Mount, 1991), whereas Emotional Stability and Extraversion also show significant, yet smaller effects (Tett, Jackson, & Rothstein, 1991). A similar meta-analysis by Judge, Heller, and Mount (2002) reported significant mean correlations between job satisfaction and the following Big Five traits: Emotional Stability (.29), Conscientiousness (.26), and Extraversion (.25). It is important to note that relationships involving Conscientiousness may differ, depending on the type of occupation (scientific versus artistic), and specific facets of Conscientiousness (e.g., dependability, achievement) may be more useful than other facets (e.g., organization) (Mount, Barrick, & Stewart, 1998; Tett et al., 1991). Thus, assessing the Big Five via one of the versions of the NEO personality inventories may yield valuable information about clients who are currently experiencing dissatisfaction or poor performance at work, as well as those who are having difficulty in the job search process. High Neuroticism (and perhaps low Conscientiousness) may contribute to clients' feelings of dissatisfaction at work; low Conscientiousness (and some of its facets) may contribute to performance and job-finding problems. Personality information can also be incorporated with RIASEC information to help clients make more fully informed career choices.

Myers-Briggs Type Indicator–3rd edition (MBTI; Myers et al., 1998). Unlike the atheoretical empirical approach used in developing measures based on the Big Five, the MBTI was derived from Carl Jung's personality types by Isabel Briggs Myers and Katherine Cook Briggs. The MBTI is commonly used in organizational and career counseling settings to facilitate clients' understanding of their natural tendencies across the following four areas: (1) Extraversion versus Introversion (the focus of one's energy), (2) Sensing versus Intuition (how one gathers information), (3) Thinking versus Feeling (how one makes decisions), and (4) Judging versus Perceiving (how one plans and deals with the outer world). Based on the highest scores within each dichotomy, combinations across these four dichotomies yield a four-letter MBTI type (e.g., ENFP, ISTJ) that can aid team building within organizations and inform clients about how their tendencies may relate to academic and career decisions. Although numerous guidebooks (e.g., Kirby & Barger, 2011) are available to support interpretations of results based on one of 16 resulting types, a relatively small literature has examined the utility of the MBTI in counseling settings and yielded inconclusive results regarding its effectiveness for the stated purposes. However, the MBTI Career Report (Hammer, 2009) does link MBTI types with occupational groups based on the preferred tasks and work environments of satisfied incumbents.

Personal Style Scales.   The five Personal Style Scales (PSS) of the Strong Interest Inventory (SII; Donnay et al., 2005; Hansen, Chapter 14, this volume) include Work Style, Learning Environment, Leadership Style, Risk Taking, and Team Orientation. As the newest set of scales in the SII, PSSs reflect distinctive personality features addressing how individuals approach learning, work, and leisure.

The Work Style scale distinguishes individuals who prefer to work with people versus ideas, data, or things. The Learning Environment scale identifies those who prefer hands-on, practical, or applied learning settings versus academic settings that emphasize conceptual ideas, including cultural and scientific content. The Leadership Style scale measures the degree to which people prefer leading by directing others versus leading by example. The Risk Taking scale distinguishes people who are comfortable taking chances in physical, financial, or general settings versus those who would rather play it safe. Introduced in 2005, the Team Orientation scale distinguishes those who prefer engaging in team-based versus individual activities.

These relatively new scales have generated a growing body of research demonstrating their utility in career-related applications. For example, the PSSs collectively predict college major and occupational choices above and beyond Holland themes (Donnay & Borgen, 1999; Lindley & Borgen, 2000). The Learning Environment scale predicts educational aspiration level among undergraduate students (Rottinghaus, Lindley, Green, & Borgen, 2002). Hees (2010) found that different PSS scales added significant unique variance in the prediction of work satisfaction beyond Holland RIASEC scales for different occupations. For example, higher Teamwork Orientation scores significantly distinguished satisfied from dissatisfied workers in five of the eight occupational samples, including engineering manager, computer support specialist, lawyer, elementary school teacher, and administrative assistant, suggesting that satisfied employees in these occupations value working in teams. Similarly, satisfied engineering managers and lawyers seemed to value taking on direct leadership responsibilities more than those who were less satisfied in these fields. Overall, the PSSs appear to complement the interest results on the SII. For example, the Learning Environment scale might provide additional useful information for clients trying to decide among occupations requiring different amounts of education. Persons scoring low on this scale (suggesting a preference for hands-on versus academic settings) may opt for interesting occupations requiring less formal education than others. At the very least, scores on this scale may provide clients with information about their likely comfort if they decide to pursue occupations requiring substantial academic education.

This section presented a brief overview of prominent personality measures used in career counseling settings. Career counselors traditionally embrace a normal view of personality and strengths instead of pathological features. Although personality assessment has not been emphasized in career settings as much as other individual differences (e.g., interests, abilities), their potential value is suggested by research examining the Big Five dimensions related to vocational interests, work performance, career satisfaction, and the job search process among other career outcomes (See Brown & Hirschi, Chapter 11, this volume). In addition to the Big Five, it may be useful to assess specific facets of the Big Five, as well as the Personal Style Scales on the SII and tendencies reflected in the MBTI.

CAREER DECISION-MAKING DIFFICULTIES

The processes involved in constructing a clear vocational identity are crucial precursors to implementing appropriate career plans. Throughout their careers, individuals must thoughtfully engage in career exploration tasks and overcome numerous barriers that can be external (e.g., disability, racism, poor economy) or internal (e.g., lack of confidence, negative outlook). The literature on career decision-making difficulties can inform practitioners in helping their clients navigate the challenges of making career decisions. Next, we summarize crucial information about career decision-making difficulties.

Career decision-making is a complex process, by which clients are required to process information about themselves and the world of work. Difficulties in making decisions could occur if clients do not possess relevant information, have conflicting information, or do not know how to process the information (Gati, 1986). Difficulties could also arise when the psychological characteristics of the individual interfere with decision-making tasks (Crites, 1969). There are several approaches to measuring career indecision, including My Vocational Situation (Holland, Daiger, & Power, 1980), the Career Decision Difficulties Questionnaire (CDDQ; Gati, Krausz, & Osipow, 1996), and the Emotional and Personality Related Career Decision-Making Difficulties questionnaire (EPCD; Saka, Gati, & Kelly, 2008).

Sources of indecision. Gati and his colleagues developed two systems to identify underlying sources of indecision. The first system is based on a decision theory approach (Gati et al., 1996) and distinguishes between difficulties that may arise prior to decision making (i.e., lack of readiness due to low motivation, general indecisiveness, dysfunctional beliefs) and those that occur as a person is deciding (i.e., lack of information about the process, self, and occupations; inconsistent information due to unreliable information). The second system suggests that personality and emotional factors interfere with career decision-making in three different ways: (1) pessimistic views about the process of decision making, the world of work, and personal control;

(2) anxiety about the process, uncertainty, choice making, and outcomes; and (3) self and identity factors related to generalized anxiety, self-esteem, and interpersonal conflicts. Both systems have yielded a measure that can be used in research and career counseling (Amir, Gati, & Kleiman, 2008; Gati et al., 1996).

More recently, Brown and colleagues (2012) showed empirically that a variety of internal (self-esteem, neuroticism, trait anxiety) and contextual (e.g., external barriers and external conflicts) variables that had been found in prior research to be related to career indecision intercorrelated in such a way to suggest four major sources of career indecision difficulties. Brown and colleagues (2012) labeled these factors (1) neuroticism/negative affectivity (i.e., persons scoring high on this factor may have chronic problems with decision making because they tend to focus on the negative aspects of different options and to be relatively dissatisfied with available options), (2) choice/commitment anxiety (i.e., persons scoring high on this factor may perceive a number of acceptable options but feel unable to commit), (3) lack of readiness (i.e., persons scoring high on this factor may lack planfulness and goal directedness and demonstrate low career decision-making self-efficacy beliefs), and (4) interpersonal conflicts. Hacker, Carr, Abrams, and Brown (in press) developed and evaluated the 65-item Career Indecision Profile (CIP) to measure each of these sources of career indecision. Although the research on the CIP is not as extensive as research on the two measures derived from the Gati and colleagues model, these measures have the goal of helping counselors more specifically target their counseling efforts to the sources of their clients' difficulties. For example, a high score on one of these measure's interpersonal conflicts scales suggests that identifying and managing this source of conflict should be a primary focus of counseling. Similarly, clients scoring high on the chronic indecisiveness, neuroticism/negative affectivity, or choice/commitment anxiety scales may need more intensive counseling than those scoring lower on these scales. As counselors work with their clients toward developing their vocational self-concepts and overcoming career decision-making difficulties, it is also important to consider cultural and contextual factors that may be influencing these processes.

Barriers. Counselors need to understand factors that may interfere with their clients' career development process to help them overcome various obstacles. One such factor is the perception of barriers that hinder an individual's ability to make and implement career choices. Swanson and Woitke (1997) defined *career barriers* as "events or conditions, either within the person or in his or her environment, that make career progress difficult" (p. 434). Accordingly, barriers may originate from intrapersonal (e.g., lack of confidence) or environmental (e.g., weak job market) sources and are modifiable to varying degrees. Lent, Brown, and Hackett's (1994, 2000) SCCT is a useful model for examining contextual features, such as barriers and supports, that affect career development. Counselors may facilitate clients' exploration of these barriers by reflecting on their own skills (e.g., "Do I have the capability to succeed as an engineer?"), their perceptions of various academic or work environments (e.g., "If I pursue this nontraditional career, will I experience discrimination?"), or their perceptions of the resources that they have available to them (e.g., "Can I financially afford to pursue this option?"). Barriers can also be explored by using one of the following barriers measures.

Swanson and Tokar (1991) developed the Career Barriers Inventory (CBI), a self-report measure designed to assess a wide range of barriers that individuals may face throughout the career development process (e.g., career choice, job performance, work–family interface). The Career Barriers Inventory–Revised (CBI-R; Swanson, Daniels, & Tokar, 1996) is a 70-item instrument scored on 13 scales that broadly cover several dimensions of barriers, including sex discrimination, lack of confidence, multiple-role conflict, conflict between children and career demands, racial discrimination, inadequate preparation, disapproval by significant others, decision-making difficulties, dissatisfaction with career, discouragement from choosing nontraditional careers, disability/health concerns, job market constraints, and difficulties with networking/socialization. The CBI-R can be used to gather information about the client's awareness of current barriers or those that may arise in the future. Once barriers have been identified, the counselor and client can then work collaboratively to garner resources and support to overcome or cope with these concerns. For example, a client facing a mid-career transition can explore ways to plan for the demands of changing job requirements (and affiliated skills) and potential health concerns and role conflicts that may limit future employability.

Another commonly used measure of barriers is the Perceptions of Barriers Scale (POB; McWhirter, 1997). The POB is a 24-item scale that measures barriers related to ethnic and gender discrimination, obstacles in the pursuit of postsecondary education, overall perception of barriers, and confidence level in overcoming them (McWhirter, Hackett, & Bandalos, 1998). One advantage of this measure is the inclusion of a confidence scale that can be used to assess clients' feelings of self-efficacy about overcoming identified barriers. For clients with low barrier-coping self-efficacy beliefs, counselors and clients can work toward enhancing clients' coping efficacy beliefs to overcome these structural and personal barriers by using skill-building interventions (Hackett & Byars, 1996). In addition to interventions aimed at modifying Bandura's (1977) four sources of self-efficacy (i.e., performance accomplishments, modeling, emotional arousal, verbal persuasion), this process can include identifying past situations in which clients have successfully overcome obstacles. Other strategies that have been proposed to help the client prepare for potential barriers include Brown and Lent's (1996) suggestion of having clients list the potential gains and losses associated with specified goals and develop methods to cope with or overcome identified losses (i.e., barriers; see Lent, Chapter 5, this volume).

CONCLUSIONS AND PRACTICE IMPLICATIONS

Throughout the history of the career counseling profession, assessment efforts have emphasized the traditional constructs of interests, needs/values, and abilities. However, various additional constructs that we have discussed in this chapter are also relevant to a comprehensive approach to career counseling. We have focused on specific measures and assessment strategies that have received empirical support and that offer insights for their use in career counseling practice. Next, we provide take-home messages to practitioners that give an overview of how and when these assessment procedures are commonly used. In this final section, we seek to guide practitioners in their pursuit of effective assessment decisions.

In relation to Super's theory of career development, career maturity has been considered to be a particularly important variable to assess during career exploration with adolescents. Adolescents frequently encounter important decisions that can affect their developmental and career trajectories. When faced with these decisions, many adolescents fail to consider and integrate their interests, skills, and abilities and thus find it difficult to progress toward a specific career goal. Assessing the barriers that have hindered adolescents' development and helping them establish strategies to overcome barriers may be an important initial goal in career counseling with adolescents. Career salience is often assessed with clients who are finding it difficult to commit to tentative career choices or who are struggling to balance the dual roles of both family and work.

Holland's theory encourages us to consider clients' vocational identities. Assessing vocational identity informs practitioners of the degree to which their clients' perceptions of their goals, interests, and abilities are clear and realistic. Essentially, assessing vocational identity serves as a needs assessment to help identify interventions that may optimize the counseling process. For example, career counseling and providing career information to clients has been shown to increase the level of vocational identity (Schmidt & Callan, 1992). In turn, higher levels of vocational identity have been associated with more congruent college major choices, planning about preferred occupations, and forming success-creating work attitudes (Wallace-Broscious, Serafica, & Osipow, 1994).

In relation to social cognitive career theory, self-efficacy, outcome expectations, goals, supports, and barriers can all be helpful constructs to assess in career counseling. SCCT specifically suggests that many people may eliminate potentially satisfying career options prematurely because of unrealistically low self-efficacy beliefs or inaccurate outcome expectations. Thus, an exploration of clients' self-efficacy beliefs and outcome expectations may allow them to reconsider occupations they previously eliminated. SCCT also outlines how contextual factors may impede (e.g., barriers) or facilitate (e.g., supports) clients' abilities to translate interests into satisfying occupational decisions. Thus, assessing the barriers and supports that clients may perceive for different career options may be crucial aspects of counseling by broadening options for clients and minimizing impediments to choice.

Personality assessment, although not as commonly used in career counseling, undoubtedly serves a purpose by providing information helpful for conceptualization, treatment planning, and building the therapeutic alliance. In conjunction with other types of assessments, such as an interest assessment, information about a client's personality can help enhance the information yielded by traditional career assessments. Similar to other assessments, the process of interpreting the results of a personality assessment facilitates discussion with the client and stimulates self-reflection that informs career choice and adjustment decisions. Personality is also related to work satisfaction and performance (see Lent and Brown, Chapter 22, this volume) and to job search success (see Jome & Phillips, Chapter 21, this volume). Thus, personality assessment can provide valuable information for working with persons seeking counseling for help in increasing work satisfaction, work performance, or job search success.

Assessing how clients approach the process of career decision-making is necessary because not all clients are similarly skilled at, or confident about, making a career choice, even after exploring their interests, skills/abilities, and values. Although making a career or educational choice is not always the ideal outcome of career counseling, counselors need to attend to personal concerns and other factors that may limit effective decision-making in clients. Counseling interventions may then be employed to assist clients to develop the confidence, skills, coping strategies, and information necessary to make career choices both now and in the future. Assessment of clients' problems in choice-making via the inventories we discussed in this chapter can also be used to tailor their counseling efforts. For example, clients with long-standing problems in decision-making (i.e., chronically indecisive clients) will probably require a different, more intensive type of counseling than clients who simply need additional information to clarify a potential career choice. Similarly, clients experiencing interpersonal conflicts with significant others about their choices may need help only in managing this conflict.

Vocational psychologists have examined cultural and contextual aspects related to career behavior (Bingham & Ward, 1994; Fouad & Kantamneni, 2008; Lent et al., 2000). We believe that the career adaptations discussed previously in this chapter are clearly contoured by the culture and the social ecology of everyday life (i.e., one's situations, role demands, developmental tasks, and challenges). Culturally sensitive counselors avoid inappropriate assessment strategies (Fouad & Bingham, 1995) by considering detailed connections between culture, relationships, and work when assessing career constructs.

It is critical for counselors to be guided by a framework that enhances understanding of the reciprocal influences of context on individuals' career decisions. Fouad and Kantamneni (2008) defined *context* as the "interrelated, reciprocal, and dynamic environment in which career decisions are made" (p. 408). Their model incorporates two levels of contextual influences: group level factors (e.g., gender, race and ethnicity, social class, family, religion, sexual orientation, and relationships) and societal factors (e.g., acculturation, influences from majority culture). These different factors intersect and include a third dimension that considers individual differences (e.g., interests, abilities) to help shape career decisions. Thus, counselors must consider aspects of clients' culture (e.g., values, barriers, and supports), as well as influences from mainstream culture (e.g., schooling, media influences).

It is important to emphasize that several of the constructs and associated measures cited in this chapter have been normed and developed with European Americans and therefore may not always align with minority group individuals' worldviews, career decision-making processes, and other influential factors in career counseling. In conducting career counseling assessments with culturally different clients, counselors should consider the value that each client places on these traditionally assessed constructs and take into account the relevance of each variable in the context of his or her cultural background. Moreover, by assessing for cultural aspects that are relevant to each client, this process should facilitate building a therapeutic alliance and ideally allow clients to develop positive attitudes toward career counseling.

Navigating the process of career choice and development is complex and multifaceted. Today's clients must routinely take stock of who they are and be ready to deploy adaptability skills and knowledge in response to changing circumstances. The assessment process should be done collaboratively with clients by combining multiple sources of information. In addition to the traditional focus on the big three assessment constructs—interests, abilities, and needs/values—specifically examined in earlier chapters, we elaborated on process variables. Indeed, knowledge of self and the world of work are necessary but not sufficient for achieving successful outcomes. Career adaptability begins to fill in the gaps by emphasizing the *process* of coping with career development tasks (Savickas, 1997, 2005). Attending to this critical aspect of career development brings necessary focus on more fluid constructs that can extend the career development literature to meet contemporary challenges. We agree with van Vianen, De Pater, and Preenan (2009), who noted that "career adaptability rather than decision making should become the focal concept of career theory and practice" (p. 307).

Ongoing theoretical and empirical work addressing career adaptability will aid work with clients attempting to overcome the demands of managing careers. Career-related agency, self-efficacy, and other theory-driven constructs addressed herein are important components of adaptive career decision-making. Ultimately, reflection of integrative career assessment within a cultural context can aid clients in making adaptive decisions that will increase their employability and support the development of a clear and integrated vocational identity that informs the construction of their career story.

REFERENCES

Ackerman, P. L., & Heggestad, E. D. (1997). Intelligence, personality, and interests: Evidence for overlapping traits. *Psychological Bulletin, 121,* 219–245.

Ajzen, I. (1988). *Attitudes, personality, and behavior.* Stony Stratford, UK: Open University Press.

Amir, T., Gati, I., & Kleiman, T. (2008). Understanding career decision-making difficulties. *Journal of Career Assessment, 16,* 281–309.

Bandura, A. (1977). Self-efficacy: Toward a unifying theory of behavioral change. *Psychological Review, 84,* 191–215. doi:10.1037/0033-295X.84.2.191

Bandura, A. (1986). *Social foundations of thought and action.* Englewood Cliffs, NJ: Prentice Hall.

Bandura, A. (2001). Social cognitive theory: An agentic perspective. *Annual Review of Psychology, 52,* 1–26.

Bandura, A. (2006a). Guide for constructing self-efficacy scales. In F. Pajares & T. C. Urdan (Eds.), *Self-efficacy beliefs of adolescents* (pp. 307–337). Charlotte, NC: Information Age.

Bandura, A. (2006b). Toward a psychology of human agency. *Perspectives on Psychological Science, 1,* 164–180. doi:10.1111/j.1745-6916.2006.00011.x

Barrick, M. R., & Mount, M. K. (1991). The big five personality dimensions and job performance: A meta-analysis. *Personnel Psychology, 44,* 1–26.

Betz, N. E. (1989). Implications of the null environment hypothesis for women's career development and for counseling psychology. *Counseling Psychologist, 17,* 136–144. doi:10.1177/0011000089171008

Betz, N. E., & Borgen, F. H. (2010). The CAPA integrative online system for college major exploration. *Journal of Career Assessment, 18,* 317–327. doi:10.1177 /1069072710374492

Betz, N. E., Borgen, F. H., & Harmon, L. W. (1996). *Skills Confidence Inventory applications and technical guide.* Palo Alto, CA: Consulting Psychologists Press.

Betz, N. E., Borgen, F. H., Rottinghaus, P. J., Paulsen, A., Halper, C., & Harmon, L. W. (2003). The Expanded Skills Confidence Inventory: Measuring basic dimensions of vocational activity. *Journal of Vocational Behavior, 62,* 76–100.

Betz, N. E., & Hackett, G. (1981). The relationship of career-related self-efficacy expectations to perceived career options in college women and men. *Journal of Counseling Psychology, 28,* 399–410.

Betz, N. E., & Rottinghaus, P. J. (2006). Current research on parallel measures of interests and confidence for basic dimensions of vocational activity. *Journal of Career Assessment, 14,* 56–76.

Betz, N. E., & Schifano, R. (2000). Evaluation of an intervention to increase Realistic self-efficacy and interests in college students. *Journal of Vocational Behavior, 56,* 35–52. doi:10.1006/jvbe.1999.1690

Betz, N. E., & Taylor, K. M. (2001). *Manual for the Career Decision Self-Efficacy Scale and CDMSE–Short Form.* Columbus: Ohio State University.

Bieschke, K. J. (2000). Factor structure of the Research Outcome Expectations Scale. *Journal of Career Assessment, 8,* 303–313.

Bingham, R. P., & Ward, C. M. (1994). Career counseling with ethnic minority women. In W. B. Walsh & S. Osipow (Eds.), *Career counseling with women* (pp. 165–195). Hillsdale, NJ: Erlbaum.

Blustein, D. L. (2001). The interface of work and relationships: A critical knowledge base for 21st century psychology. *Counseling Psychologist, 29,* 179–192.

Blustein, D. L. (2011). A relational theory of working. *Journal of Vocational Behavior, 79,* 1–17. doi:10.1016/j.jvb.2010.10.004

Brooks, L., & Betz, N. E. (1990). Utility of expectancy theory in predicting occupational choices in college students. *Journal of Counseling Psychology, 37,* 57–64.

Brown, S. D., Hacker, J., Abrams, M., Carr, A., Rector, C., Lamp, K., Siena, A. (2012). Validation of a four-factor model of career indecision. *Journal of Career Assessment, 20,* 3–21. doi:10.1177/1069072711417154

Brown, S. D., & Lent, R. W. (1996). A social cognitive framework for career choice counseling. *Career Development Quarterly, 44,* 354–366.

Brown, S. D., Lent, R. W., & Gore, P. A. (2000). Self-rated abilities and self-efficacy beliefs: Are the empirically distinct? *Journal of Career Assessment, 8,* 223–235.

Campbell, D. P., Hyne, S. A., & Nilsen, D. L. (1992). *Manual for the Campbell Interest and Skills Survey: CISS.* Minneapolis, MN: National Computer Systems.

Cattell, R. B., Cattell, K., & Cattell, H. (1993). *16PF Fifth Edition questionnaire.* Champaign, IL: Institute for Personality and Ability Testing.

Costa, P. T., Jr., & McCrae, R. R. (1992). *NEO PI-R professional manual.* Odessa, FL: Psychological Assessment Resources.

Creed, P. A., Fallon, T., & Hood, M. (2009). The relationship between career adaptability, person and situation variables, and career concerns in young adults. *Journal of Vocational Behavior, 74*, 219–229.

Crites, J. O. (1961). A model for the measurement of vocational maturity. *Journal of Counseling Psychology, 8*, 255–259.

Crites, J. O. (1969). *Vocational psychology.* New York, NY: McGraw-Hill.

Crites, J. O. (1973). *Theory and research handbook for the Career Maturity Inventory.* Monterey, CA: CTB/McGraw-Hill.

Crites, J. O., & Savickas, M. L. (1996). Revision of the Career Maturity Inventory. *Journal of Career Assessment, 4*, 131–138.

Crites, J. O., & Savickas, M. L. (2011). *Career Maturity Inventory-Form C.* Rootstown, OH: Vocopher.

Dawis, R. V. (2005). The Minnesota Theory of Work Adjustment. In S. D. Brown & R. W. Lent (Eds.), *Career development and counseling: Putting theory and research to work* (pp. 3–23). Hoboken, NJ: John Wiley and Sons, Inc.

Digman, J. M. (1990). Personality structure: Emergence of the five-factor model. *Annual Review of Psychology, 41*, 417–440.

Donnay, D. A., & Borgen, F. H. (1999). The incremental validity of vocational self-efficacy: An examination of interest, self-efficacy, and occupation. *Journal of Counseling Psychology, 46*, 432–447.

Donnay, D. A. C., Morris, M. A., Schaubhut, N. A., & Thompson, R. C. (2005). *Strong Interest Inventory manual: Research, development, and strategies for interpretation.* Palo Alto, CA: Consulting Psychologists.

Edwards, J. R., & Rothbard, N. P. (2000). Mechanisms linking work and family: Clarifying the relationship between work and family constructs. *Academy of Management Review, 25*, 178–199.

Fouad, N. A., & Bingham, R. P. (1995). Career counseling with racial and ethnic minorities. In W. B. Walsh & S. H. Osipow (Eds.), *Handbook of vocational psychology* (2nd ed., pp. 331–365). Hillsdale, NJ: Erlbaum.

Fouad, N. A., & Guillen, A. (2006). Outcome expectations: Looking to the past and potential future. *Journal of Career Assessment, 14*, 130–142. doi:10.1177 /1069072705281370

Fouad, N. A., & Kantamneni, N. (2008). Contextual factors in vocational psychology: Intersections of individual, group, and societal dimensions. In S. D. Brown & R. W. Lent (Eds.), *Handbook of counseling psychology* (4th ed., pp. 408–425). Hoboken, NJ: Wiley.

Fouad, N. A., Smith, P. L., & Enochs, L. (1997). Reliability and validity evidence for the Middle School Self-Efficacy Scale. *Measurement and Evaluation in Counseling and Development, 30*, 17–31.

Gati, I. (1986). Making career decisions: A conceptual frame of reference for counseling. *Journal of Counseling Psychology, 9*, 240–245.

Gati, I., Krausz, M., & Osipow, S. H. (1996). A taxonomy of difficulties in career decision-making. *Journal of Counseling Psychology, 43*, 510–526. doi:10.1037/0022 -0167.43.4.510

Goldberg, L. R. (1999). A broad-bandwidth, public domain, personality inventory measuring the lower-level facets of several five-factor models. In I. Mervielde, I. Deary, F. De Fruyt, & F. Ostendorf (Eds.), *Personality psychology in Europe* (vol. 7, pp. 7–28). Tilburg, The Netherlands: Tilburg University Press.

Gore, P. A., & Leuwerke, W. C. (2000). Predicting occupational considerations: A comparison of self-efficacy beliefs, outcome expectations, and person-environment congruence. *Journal of Career Assessment, 8*, 237–250.

Gough, H. G., & Bradley, P. (1996). *CPI Manual* (3rd ed.). Palo Alto, CA: Consulting Psychologists Press.

Hacker, J., Carr, A., Abrams, M., & Brown, S. D. (in press). Development of the Career Indecision Profile: Factor structure, reliability, and validity. *Journal of Career Assessment.*

Hackett, G., & Betz, N. E. (1981). A self-efficacy approach to the career development of women. *Journal of Vocational Behavior, 18*, 326–336.

Hackett, G., & Byars, A. M. (1996). Social cognitive theory and development of African American women. *Career Development Quarterly, 44*, 322–340.

Hammer, A. L. (2009). *MBTI career report user's guide*. Palo Alto, CA: CPP.

Harmon, L. W., Hansen, J. C., Borgen, F. H., & Hammer, A. L. (1994). *Strong Interest Inventory applications and technical guide*. Palo Alto, CA: Consulting Psychologists Press.

Hees, C. K. (2010). *Personally satisfying: Using personal style scales to enhance the prediction of career satisfaction*. Unpublished doctoral dissertation. Southern Illinois University, Carbondale, IL.

Holland, J. L. (1997). *Making vocational choices: A theory of vocational personalities and work environments* (3rd ed.). Odessa, FL: Psychological Assessment Resources, Inc.

Holland, J. L., Daiger, D., & Power, P. (1980). *My vocational situation*. Palo Alto, CA: Consulting Psychologists Press, Inc.

Holland, J. L., & Holland, J. E. (1977). Vocational indecision: More evidence and speculation. *Journal of Counseling Psychology, 24*, 404–414.

Judge, T. A., Heller, D., & Mount, M. K. (2002). Five-factor model of personality and job satisfaction: A meta-analysis. *Journal of Applied Psychology, 87*, 530–541.

Kirby, L. K., & Barger, N. J. (2011). *MBTI practitioner's field guide: Activities and strategies for type learning and engagement*. Palo Alto, CA: CPP.

Larson, L. M., Rottinghaus, P. J., & Borgen, F. H. (2002). Meta-analyses of Big Six interests and Big Five personality factors. *Journal of Vocational Behavior, 61*, 217–239.

Lent, R. W. (2012). Work and relationship: Is vocational psychology on the eve of construction? *Counseling Psychologist, 40*, 268–278. doi:10.1177/0011000011422824

Lent, R. W., & Brown, S. D. (2006). On conceptualizing and assessing social cognitive constructs in career research: A measurement guide. *Journal of Career Assessment, 14*, 12–35.

Lent, R. W., Brown, S. D., & Hackett, G. (1994). Toward a unifying social cognitive theory of career and academic interest, choice, and performance. *Journal of Vocational Behavior, 45*, 79–122.

Lent, R. W., Brown, S. D., & Hackett, G. (2000). Contextual supports and barriers to career choice: A social cognitive analysis. *Journal of Counseling Psychology, 47,* 36–49.

Lent, R. W., Brown, S. D., Schmidt, J., Brenner, B., Lyons, H., & Treistman, D. (2003). Relation of contextual supports and barriers to choice behavior in engineering majors: Test of alternative social cognitive models. *Journal of Counseling Psychology, 50,* 458–465.

Lindley, L. D., & Borgen, F. H. (2000). Personal style scales of the Strong Interest Inventory: Linking personality and interests. *Journal of Vocational Behavior, 57,* 22–41.

Locke, E. A., & Latham, G. P. (1990). *A theory of goal setting and task performance.* Englewood Cliffs, NJ: Prentice Hall.

McWhirter, E. H. (1997). Perceived barriers to education and career: Ethnic and gender differences. *Journal of Vocational Behavior, 50,* 124–140.

McWhirter, E. H., Hackett, G., & Bandalos, D. I. (1998). A causal model of the educational plans and career expectations of Mexican American high school girls. *Journal of Counseling Psychology, 45,* 166–181.

Mount, M. K., Barrick, M. R., & Stewart, G. L. (1998). Five-Factor model of personality and performance in jobs involving interpersonal interactions. *Human Performance, 11,* 145–165. doi:10.1080/08959285.1998.9668029

Myers, I. B., McCaulley, M. H., Quenk, N. L., & Hammer, A. L. (1998). *Manual for the Myers-Briggs Type Indicator* (3rd ed.). Mountain View, CA: CPP.

Nevill, D. D., & Calvert, P. D. (1996). Career assessment and the Salience Inventory. *Journal of Career Assessment, 4,* 399–412.

Neville, D., & Super, D. E. (1986). *The Salience Inventory: Theory, application and research.* Palo Alto, CA: Consulting Psychologists, Press, Inc.

Phillips, J. M., & Gully, S. M. (1997). Role of goal orientation, ability, need for achievement, and locus of control in the self-efficacy and goal-setting process. *Journal of Applied Psychology, 82,* 792–802.

Richardson, M. S. (2012). Counseling for work and relationship. *Counseling Psychologist, 40,* 190–242.

Rottinghaus, P. J. (2009). The *Kuder Skills Assessment–College and Adult* version: Development and initial validation in a college business sample. *Journal of Career Assessment, 17,* 56–68.

Rottinghaus, P. J., Buelow, K., Matyja, A., & Schneider, M. (2012). The Career Futures Inventory–Revised: Assessing multiple dimensions of career adaptability. *Journal of Career Assessment, 20,* 123–139. doi:10.1177/1069072711420849

Rottinghaus, P. J., Day, S. X., & Borgen, F. H. (2005). The Career Futures Inventory: A measure of career-related adaptability and optimism. *Journal of Career Assessment, 13,* 3–24.

Rottinghaus, P. J., Lindley, L., Green, M. A., & Borgen, F. H. (2002). Educational aspirations: The contribution of personality, self-efficacy, and interests. *Journal of Vocational Behavior, 61,* 1–19.

Rottinghaus, P. J., & Van Esbroeck, R. (2011). Improving person-environment fit and self-knowledge. In P. J. Hartung & L. M. Subich (Eds.), *Developing self in work and career: Concepts, cases, and contexts* (pp. 35–52). Washington, DC: American Psychological Association.

Saka, N., Gati, I., & Kelly, K. R. (2008). Emotional and personality-related aspects of career decision-making difficulties. *Journal of Career Assessment, 16*, 403–424.

Savickas, M. L. (1997). Career adaptability: An integrative construct for life-span, life-space theory. *Career Development Quarterly, 45*, 247–259.

Savickas, M. L. (2005). The theory and practice of career construction. In S. D. Brown & R. W. Lent (Eds.), *Career development and counseling: Putting theory and research to work* (pp. 42–70). Hoboken, NJ: Wiley.

Savickas, M. L. (2011). *Career counseling.* Washington, DC: American Psychological Association.

Savickas, M. L., & Hartung, P. J. (1996). The Career Development Inventory in review: Psychometric and research findings. *Journal of Career Assessment, 4*, 171–188. doi:10.1177/106907279600400204

Savickas, M. L., & Porfeli, E. J. (2011). Revision of the Career Maturity Inventory: The Adaptability Form. *Journal of Career Assessment, 19*, 355–374. doi:10.1177/1069072711409342

Savickas, M. L., & Porfeli, E. J. (2012). The Career-Adapt-Abilities Scale: Construction, reliability, and measurement equivalence across 13 countries. *Journal of Vocational Behavior, 80*, 661–673. doi:10.1016/j.jvb.2012.01.011

Schmidt, A. M., & Callan, V. J. (1992). Evaluating the effectiveness of a career intervention. *Australian Psychologist, 27*, 123–126.

Schultheiss, D. E. (2003). A relational approach to career counseling: Theoretical integration and practical application. *Journal of Counseling & Development, 81*, 301–310.

Smith, P., & Fouad, N. (1999). Subject-matter specificity of self-efficacy, outcome expectations, interests, and intentions and goals: Implications for the social cognitive model. *Journal of Counseling Psychology, 46*, 461–471.

Solberg, V. S. (1998). Assessing career search self-efficacy: Construct evidence and developmental antecedents. *Journal of Career Assessment, 6*, 181–193. doi:10.1177/106907279800600205

Super, D. E. (1955). The dimensions and measurement of vocational maturity. *Teachers College Record, 57*, 151–163.

Super, D. E., & Kidd, J. M. (1979). Vocational maturity in adulthood: Toward turning a model into a measure. *Journal of Vocational Behavior, 14*, 255–270.

Super, D. E., & Knasel, E. G. (1979). *Specifications for a measure of career adaptability in young adults.* Cambridge, UK: National Institute for Career Education and Counseling.

Super, D. E., & Knasel, E. G. (1981). Career development in adulthood: Some theoretical problems and a possible solution. *British Journal of Guidance and Counseling, 9*, 194–201.

Super, D. E., Savickas, M. L., & Super, C. M. (1996). The life-span, life-space approach to careers. In D. Brown & L. Brooks (Eds.), *Career choice and development: Applying contemporary theories to practice* (3rd ed., pp. 121–178). San Francisco: Jossey-Bass.

Super, D. E., Thompson, A. S., Lindeman, R. H., Jordaan, J. P., & Myers, R. A. (1981). *Career Development Inventory: College form.* Palo Alto, CA: Consulting Psychologists Press.

Swanson, J. L., & D'Achiardi, C. (2005). Beyond interests, needs/values, and abilities: Assessing other important career constructs over the life span. In S. D. Brown & R. W. Lent (Eds.), *Career development and counseling: Putting theory and research to work* (pp. 353–381). Hoboken, NJ: Wiley.

Swanson, J. L., Daniels, K. K., & Tokar, D. M. (1996). Measuring perceptions of career related barriers: The Career Barriers Inventory. *Journal of Career Assessment, 4,* 219–244. doi:10.1177/106907279600400207

Swanson, J. L., & Tokar, D. M. (1991). Development and initial validation of the Career Barriers Inventory. *Journal of Vocational Behavior, 39,* 344–361.

Swanson, J. L., & Woitke, M. B. (1997). Theory into practice in career assessment for women: Assessment and interventions regarding perceived career barriers. *Journal of Career Assessment, 5*(4), 443–462.

Tett, R. P., Jackson, D. N., & Rothstein, M. (1991). Personality measures as predictors of job performance: A meta-analytic review. *Personnel Psychology, 44,* 703–742. doi:10.1111/j.1744-6570.1991.tb00696.x

Thompson, A. S., & Lindeman, R. H. (1981). *Career Development Inventory: User's manual.* Palo Alto, CA: Consulting Psychologists Press.

van Vianen, A. E. M., De Pater, I. E., & Preenan, P. T. Y. (2009). Adaptable careers: Maximizing less and exploring more. *Career Development Quarterly, 57,* 298–309.

Vaux, A., Riedel, S., & Stewart, D. (1987). Modes of social support: The social support behaviors (SS-B) scale. *American Journal of Community Psychology, 15,* 209–237.

Vroom, V. H. (1964). *Work and motivation.* New York, NY: Wiley.

Wallace-Broscious, A., Serafica, F. C., & Osipow, S. H. (1994). Adolescent career development: Relationships to self-concept and identity status. *Journal of Research on Adolescence, 4,* 127–149.

Walsh, W. B., & Eggerth, D. E. (2005). Vocational psychology and personality: The relationship of the five-factor model to job performance and job satisfaction. In W. B. Walsh & M. L. Savickas (Eds.), *Handbook of vocational psychology* (3rd ed., pp. 267–296). Mahwah, NJ: Erlbaum.

Zytowski, D. G., Rottinghaus, P. J., & D'Achiardi, C. (2007). *The Kuder Skills Assessment user manual.* Adel, IA: National Career Assessment Services.

CHAPTER 18

The Structure, Sources, and Uses of Occupational Information

PAUL A. GORE JR., WADE C. LEUWERKE, AND ALEXANDRA R. KELLY

O CCUPATIONAL INFORMATION HAS BEEN a pillar of vocational and career guidance since the beginning of the 20th century. Parsons (1909) first identified the importance of understanding and evaluating the suitability of occupational alternatives. Unfortunately, his work and that of his colleagues was limited by the lack of available occupational information. An Advisory Committee on Education (1938) established under the Roosevelt administration wrote:

> At present, no one can advise young people with any assurance as to the relative opportunities in the various occupational fields to which their abilities may be suited. The available information is scattered, fragmentary, and frequently unreliable . . . An occupational outlook service is needed that will provide a clear description of each of the major occupations or groups of minor occupations, the kind of life each occupation offers, the character of the preparation essential to enter it, the numbers employed and the trend of employment, the numbers of new employees taken on each year, and the numbers of youth in each year of college or secondary school preparation who have the intention of entering the occupation, if possible.

Soon after the publication of this report, the Bureau of Labor Statistics was charged with this responsibility, and it continues to provide most of this information today.

A review of the professional literature around this same time is replete with examples of suggestions for developing and distributing occupational information (Brayfield & Reed, 1950; Brewer, 1942; Clark & Murtland, 1946; Hoppock & Spiegler, 1941; Markham, 1943; Rohr & Speer, 1948; Shartle, 1946).

Authors described methods for distributing information (Rohr & Speer, 1948) and its effective use in career counseling (Strang, 1945). Markham (1943) included the use of occupational information as one of his six facets of vocational guidance, the remaining five of which were assessment, counseling, exploration of training opportunities, placement, and follow-up. Williamson (1937) described the early development and evaluation of a course for college freshman that emphasized gathering occupational information in support of career decision making.

Early authors were also concerned with the quality of occupational information. For example, Shartle (1946) recommended that individuals responsible for developing occupational information have a background in information development techniques and that they be acquainted with the particular specialties being described. Shartle includes recommendations for occupational classification, industrial classification, the development of information for both military and civilian occupations, development of occupational information for the disabled, and methods for assessing occupational outlook—all elements that can be found in contemporary sources of occupational information. Other authors focused on the readability of occupational information and the extent to which individuals would find the information "interesting." Brayfield and Reed (1950) assessed the readability and interest level of 24 published sources of occupational information. They judged over two-thirds of the published occupational information sources to be "dull" or only "mildly interesting" and "very difficult" to read.

Today, career counselors have access to many sources of occupational information, including resources published by the U.S. Department of Labor, private publishers, and companies that aggregate and resell occupational information. Occupational information is available through print and electronic sources and can be linked to assessment results, opportunities for training and educational advancement, and local job openings. Unlike our professional predecessors, we now face issues related to having too many sources of occupational information. Similar to those predecessors, however, we are concerned with the quality of the available information, its appropriateness for different client populations, and how to best use occupational information to the advantage of our students and clients.

This chapter provides an overview of important issues in the use of occupational information in career education and counseling. To balance breadth and depth of coverage of this topic, we chose to focus on issues relevant to professionals working with school-age children and clients in the early stages of career choice and implementation. Although the sources of occupational information used for workforce development, employment transition, and retirement planning may be similar to those described in this chapter, their uses may differ. Additionally, we chose to limit our review of print and electronic sources of occupational information to those that are mostly widely available to career practitioners today. As such, this chapter will not include a comprehensive list of available sources of information. The National Career Development Association and American School Counseling Association Web sites are recommended for readers interested in more comprehensive lists of available resources. Finally, we restricted our discussion to *occupational information*. We recognize that gathering career-related information might involve acquiring information about occupations, jobs, organizations, and job-search processes, among other topics, but we believe that a focus on occupational information is consistent with our developmental focus on school-age children and clients in the early stages of career choice and implementation. Readers interested in these other topics are referred to Kanfer, Wanberg, and Kantrowitz (2001); Posthuma, Morgeson, and Campion (2002); Saks (2005); and Zikic and Saks (2009); also see Jome and Phillips, Chapter 21, this volume.

This chapter begins with an empirical justification for the importance of occupational information. We follow this with a brief discussion of the occupational classification systems used in the major information sources available today. The sheer number of different occupations and their manifestation across industries necessitates classification, and familiarity with these classification systems is necessary for career educators and counselors to use these systems effectively in their work. Next, we present an overview of some of the most widely available print and electronic sources of occupational information. We then discuss ethical issues in the use of career information resources and end by offering practical suggestions for integrating occupational information systems into career interventions.

RESEARCH ON THE IMPORTANCE AND USE OF OCCUPATIONAL INFORMATION

The acquisition, evaluation, and use of occupational information play a pivotal role in most career theories (Crites, 1976; Hartung, 1999). Thus, it is not surprising that occupational information has been the focus of a number of empirical studies. Career information gathering behavior has been treated as both a precursor to other career outcomes and as a desirable outcome itself, and lack of career information has been identified as a major contributor to career decision-making difficulties (Gati & Amir, 2010; Gati, Krausz, & Osipow, 1996). Career information has also been examined using a developmental lens. In this section, we provide a brief overview of recent research exploring the role of occupational information in career development.

Research focusing on developmental aspects of early childhood and adolescence illuminate the importance of early and accurate occupational information (Porfeli, Hartung, & Vondracek, 2008). Research suggests that very young children learn a great deal about the world of work, although the accuracy of their information varies (Walls, 2000). For example, children appear to have a better understanding of incomes associated with occupations than they do the availability of those occupations in the workforce. Moreover, students' preferences for an occupation are associated (not always accurately) with perceived prestige and length of preparatory time (Walls, 2000). Investigators reviewing the primary sources of occupational information for children and adolescents suggest that media (most notably television) and the family are dominant sources of occupational knowledge for many young children (Hoffner et al., 2006; McMahon, Carroll, & Gillies, 2001).

Formal occupational information resources were identified as salient by one group of investigators (Patton & McCrindle, 2001), though other findings suggest that the information available in primary sources of occupational information may not be what young children want. For example, using large samples of Australian and South African 11- to 14-year-olds, McMahon and Watson's (2005) results suggest that students are most interested in learning about the life and career implications of various career choices. A very small minority of students (less than 8%) expressed a desire to understand elements such as the nature of work or the relationship between interests or personal characteristics and occupations—information that is highlighted in many occupational information systems designed for students.

Porfeli and his colleagues (2008) suggest that occupational aspirations in children are often influenced by occupational stereotypes—stereotypes that could be checked and invalidated using sources of occupational information. Occupational stereotypes, along with persistent gender-role expectations and socialization, are often cited as explanations for continued gender imbalances in careers involving science, technology, engineering, and math (see Heppner, Chapter 7, this volume).

A recent study by Hirschi (2011) further illustrates the importance of occupational information in early career development. Hirschi studied the development of career-choice readiness in a sample of Swiss students over a 2-year period and found that, other than age, occupational information was the strongest predictor of career choice readiness. Predicting and promoting occupational information-seeking behavior may be a complex process. Although many career education and counseling interventions promote information-seeking behavior, recent research suggests that this behavior is partially a function of deterministic factors, such as family socioeconomic status and early childhood cognitive development (Jordan & Pope, 2001). More optimistic findings are offered by Millar and Shevlin (2003), who report that the primary determinants of occupational information-gathering behavior include the extent of past information gathering and attitudes related to those past experiences. Their findings have clear implications for school counselors and other career educators and counselors and are echoed by recent research by Brown and his colleagues (Brown & Ryan Krane, 2000; Brown et al., 2003), described later.

Systems designed to foster occupational information-gathering behavior may not be as effective as we would like them to be. Using a sample of over 80,000 users from an online computer-assisted career guidance program, Gore, Bobek, Robbins, and Shayne (2006) identified three types of users: focused users, general browsers, and in-depth users. Among high school users, general browsers made up almost 70% of the sample. General browsers visited the system an average of 1.3 times, spent approximately 20 total minutes in the session, and recorded only approximately four page hits in the occupational information session. In contrast, focused users (making up approximately 28% of the users) visited the system approximately three times, spent over an hour total in the system, and recorded 19 page hits in the occupational information session. The in-depth user is what most school counselors would like to see more frequently. Unfortunately, this group made up less than 4% of the high school sample, though it was characterized by heavy use: over eight sessions on average for a total system use of over 1.5 hours. In-depth users were far more likely to discuss their educational and career plans with school counselors and parents than were other user types. Based on results from this study and those of Millar and Shevlin (2003), it is clear that efforts need to focus on getting students more engaged in using sources of occupational information.

Perhaps some of the strongest evidence arguing for the use of accurate and reliable sources of occupational information comes from the work of Brown and his colleagues (Brown & Ryan Krane, 2000; Brown et al., 2003). In reporting on the results of a meta-analysis of published intervention studies targeting career-choice clients, Brown and Ryan Krane (2000) identified five intervention techniques that were most highly and positively associated with beneficial outcomes. These "critical ingredients" included individualized one-on-one interpretation and feedback of assessment results, modeling, attention to building support networks, the use of writing assignments, and the use of career information. Further, their findings suggest that by combining these ingredients, practitioners can obtain almost linear increases in desirable outcomes. In a follow-up study, Brown and colleagues (2003) found that simply introducing students and clients to sources of occupational information is suboptimal. Instead, career educators and counselors should (a) introduce students or clients to reliable and valid sources of occupational information, (b) work with students and clients "in session" to make sure they develop confidence in their ability to navigate and use the system or resource effectively, and (c) prescribe specific information-gathering behavior rather than allowing students and clients to determine which system or resource elements to explore.

OCCUPATIONAL CLASSIFICATION SYSTEMS

Occupational information is consumed by a variety of individuals, from children and adolescents to college students, working adults, job analysts, state and federal government agencies, and companies responsible for packaging and distributing this information to consumers. Organizational classification systems impose structure on an expansive body of occupational information and make this information accessible to a range of audiences. In this section, we discuss four occupational classification systems (Standard Occupational Classification System, Holland's hexagon, the World of Work Map, and the Minnesota Occupational Classification System) frequently used by career counselors and popular occupational information products.

THE STANDARD OCCUPATIONAL CLASSIFICATION SYSTEM

First introduced in 1977, the Standard Occupational Classification System (SOC) was developed to unify the language used by U.S. federal and state employment agencies to communicate about occupations and jobs. The SOC system classifies occupations based on the nature of the work activities and on the skills, education, and training requirements for the job. The system groups occupations at four levels of specificity; it currently includes 840 detailed occupations within 23 major groups, 97 minor groups, and 461 broad occupations. By including multiple levels of specificity, the SOC system can be used by agencies or organizations with differing needs or capabilities with respect to data collection and analysis. A more detailed description of elements and uses of the SOC can be found in Gore and Hitch (2005).

The SOC system is also dynamic in that it can accommodate occupational consolidation as easily as it can respond to the growth and development of new occupations. In a 2010 revision, a Standard Occupational Classification Policy Committee (SOCPC) reviewed existing occupations and potential additions based on public input and a review of changes in the economic landscape since the last revision. Ultimately, the SOCPC introduced 24 new detailed occupations, many of them related to health care, information technology, and renewable energy; refined the definitions of existing SOC occupations based on changes in the nature of the work performed; and combined occupations that had become more similar since the last revision.

Access to the SOC system has increased significantly with the development of the Occupational Information Network (O*NET), a network of products, databases, and services designed to enhance the availability and usability of occupation and workforce information (described in more detail later). The O*NET includes the characteristics of both occupations and the people who inhabit those occupations, and it employs the SOC system as its organizing schema. Because the system clusters occupations that are similar with respect to the work performed and training required, a user who enters the SOC system to gather information about the occupation of Health Educator (21-1091), for example, will have easy access to information about related occupations such as Community Health Worker (21-1094) and Rehabilitation Counselor (21-1015). The SOC system is also used to organize occupations in the Occupational Outlook Handbook (OOH; U.S. Department of Labor, 2010).

Overseas, the International Standard Classification of Occupations (ISCO) system serves a similar purpose, providing a structure for aggregating survey and census data about occupations across a range of nations and economies. Developed by the International Labor Organization, a United Nations agency comprising 183 member countries, the ISCO system groups occupations based on similarity of the skill level required and nature of the activities performed. The most recent version, adopted in 2008, clusters occupations within 10 major groups, 43 submajor groups, 131 minor groups, and 425 unit groups.

The SOC and ISCO systems represent atheoretical models of occupational classification, with occupations organized based solely on the similarity of the tasks performed in each. The three models that follow, in contrast, organize occupations based on specific theories about the preferences and motivational factors that drive individuals' career choice and satisfaction.

HOLLAND'S HEXAGON

Nauta (Chapter 3, this volume) provides a comprehensive overview of John Holland's theory of career choice (Holland, 1997). Holland believed that most individuals' work personalities closely resemble a subset of one or more of six distinct types. Holland also suggested that these six dimensions could be used to characterize work environments based on aspects of job function and organizational structure. A basic premise of Holland's theory is that individuals will find satisfaction to the extent that their work personalities are congruent with the characteristics of their work environment.

Today, a number of career inventories and resources use Holland's typology as their primary organizing schema. The Self-Directed Search (SDS; Holland, 1987) can assist career counselors in assessing the work personalities of their clients by providing users with scores on each of Holland's six personality dimensions. Several additional career assessment instruments, such as the Strong Interest Inventory (Donnay, Morris, Schaubhut, & Thompson, 2005), the O*NET Interest Profiler (Lewis & Rivkin, 1999), and the Skills Confidence Inventory (Betz, Borgen, & Harmon, 2005), provide users with information using Holland's organizational structure.

A comprehensive list of occupational titles and college majors organized by Holland types is available in the *Dictionary of Holland Occupational Codes* (Gottfredson & Holland, 1996). Meanwhile, the O*NET online database allows users to browse occupations by each of Holland's six dimensions or to search occupations based on a two- or three-letter Holland code.

WORLD-OF-WORK MAP

Developed by ACT, the World-of-Work Map (WWM) elaborates on Holland's hexagon by adding two bipolar and bisecting work task dimensions (Data/Ideas and Things/People) that seem to underlie Holland's six work personality dimensions (Prediger, 1982; Rounds, 1995). As shown in Figure 18.1, occupations are positioned on the WWM based on the degree to which they involve working with data versus ideas on one dimension and with people versus things on the other. The precise placement of occupations on this matrix is informed by expert evaluations of the occupations in question, as well as interest inventory scores for persons working in these roles.

The WWM comprises 26 career areas that contain occupations that are relatively homogeneous with respect to the work tasks that are required. For example, career area V, Applied Arts (Written, Spoken) includes the professions of reporter, ad copywriter, and editor. These areas are nested within 12 career regions used to provide directional interest information to students or clients. For example, a client interested broadly in the helping professions might be encouraged to explore all occupations in Region 12 (i.e., Career Areas W, X, and Y).

The WWM is found in a range of academic and career-related products. In conjunction with products that contain the Unisex Edition of the ACT Interest Inventory (UNIACT; ACT, 2009), such as the Career Planning Survey, EXPLORE, PLAN, and the ACT Assessment, counselors can use the WWM to suggest career areas that a client might want to explore more thoroughly based on his or her UNIACT scores. Prediger (2002) described how the WWM could also be used to integrate results obtained from other vocational interest inventories, ability self-estimate measures, and measures of work-relevant values. DISCOVER, a computer-based career guidance

Your Career Possibilities

STEP 1: You and the World of Work

The World-of-Work Map is your key to hundreds of jobs in the work world. The map shows 26 Career Areas (groups of similar jobs) according to their basic work tasks involving people, things, data, and ideas.

The map is divided into 12 regions. Each region has a different mix of work tasks. For example, Career Area P (Natural Science & Technologies) mostly involves working with ideas and things. Which Career Areas mostly involve working with people and data?

STEP 2: Your Interests

When you completed EXPLORE, you were asked to:
- choose a Career Area you would like.
- complete an interest inventory.

Your results are shown on the World-of-Work Map below.
- You chose Career Area P: Natural Science & Technologies
- Your interest inventory results suggest that you may enjoy jobs in map regions 9, 10, and 11. See the Career Areas in those regions.

There are many jobs in these Career Areas. For example, Nurse Practitioners are registered nurses with advanced education. They diagnose and treat health problems.

STEP 3: Exploring Career Options

The Career Area List below shows examples of jobs in each of the 26 Career Areas. Review all of the Career Areas, especially any that are shaded.

Circle at least two Career Areas that have jobs you might like best.

Find out more about jobs that are right for you. Use the tips in your booklet, or go to **www.explorestudent.org**

Career Area List

A. Employment-Related Services
Human Resources Manager; Recruiter; Interviewer

B. Marketing & Sales
Agents (Insurance, Real Estate, etc.); Retail Salesworker

C. Management
Executive; Office Manager; Hotel/Motel Manager

D. Regulation & Protection
Food Inspector; Police Officer; Detective

E. Communications & Records
Secretary; Court Reporter; Office Clerk

F. Financial Transactions
Accountant; Bank Teller; Budget Analyst

G. Distribution & Dispatching
Warehouse Supervisor; Air Traffic Controller

H. Transport Operation & Related
Truck/Bus/Cab Drivers; Ship Captain; Pilot

I. Agriculture, Forestry & Related
Farmer; Nursery Manager; Forester

J. Computer & Information Specialties
Programmer; Systems Analyst; Desktop Publisher; Actuary

K. Construction & Maintenance
Carpenter; Electrician; Bricklayer

L. Crafts & Related
Cabinetmaker; Tailor; Chef/Cook; Jeweler

M. Manufacturing & Processing
Tool & Die Maker; Machinist; Welder; Dry Cleaner

N. Mechanical & Electrical Specialties
Auto Mechanic; Aircraft Mechanic; Office Machine Repairer

O. Engineering & Technologies
Engineers (Civil, etc.); Technicians (Laser, etc.); Architect

P. Natural Science & Technologies
Physicist; Biologist; Chemist; Statistician

Q. Medical Technologies (also see Area W)
Pharmacist; Optician; Dietitian; Technologists (Surgical, etc.)

R. Medical Diagnosis & Treatment (also see Area W)
Physician; Pathologist; Dentist; Veterinarian; Nurse Anesthetist

S. Social Science
Sociologist; Political Scientist; Economist; Urban Planner

T. Applied Arts (Visual)
Artist; Illustrator; Photographer; Interior Designer

U. Creative & Performing Arts
Writer; Musician; Singer; Dancer; TV/Movie Director

V. Applied Arts (Written & Spoken)
Reporter; Columnist; Editor; Librarian

W. Health Care (also see Areas Q and R)
Recreational Therapist; Dental Assistant; Licensed Practical Nurse

X. Education
Administrator; Athletic Coach; Teacher

Y. Community Services
Social Worker; Lawyer; Paralegal; Counselor; Clergy

Z. Personal Services
Waiter/Waitress; Barber; Cosmetologist; Travel Guide

World-of-Work Map

Working with **DATA**

Working with **THINGS**

— DATA & THINGS —

IDEAS & THINGS

PEOPLE & DATA

PEOPLE & IDEAS

Working with **IDEAS**

Working with **PEOPLE**

Region 99

6. H. Transport Operation & Related
J. Computer/Info Specialties
N. Mechanical & Electrical Specialties
7. M. Manufacturing & Processing
K. Construction & Maintenance
L. Crafts & Related
I. Ag/Forestry & Related
G. Distribution and Dispatching
E. Communications & Records
F. Financial Transactions
D. Regulation & Protection
C. Management
B. Marketing & Sales
A. Employment-Related Services
Z. Personal Services
Y. Community Services
X. Education
W. Health Care
U. Creative & Performing Arts
V. Applied Arts (Written & Spoken)
T. Applied Arts (Visual)
S. Social Science
R. Medical Diagnosis & Treatment
Q. Medical Technologies
O. Engineering & Technologies
P. Natural Science & Technologies

Information for Counselors

Scores: R6 I8 A6 S6 E5 C5
%Like, Indifferent, Dislike: 43—22—35

Figure 18.1 ACT's World-of-Work Map With Student's Results Shaded in Gray as Presented on the EXPLORE Score Report. UNIACT Interest Inventory results displayed using ACT's World-of-Work Map. Students are encouraged to further explore shaded map regions and career areas. Copyright 2011 by ACT, Inc. Reproduced with permission.

program, is an excellent example of how assessment results from these three sources can be combined to encourage focused occupational exploration.

THE MINNESOTA OCCUPATIONAL CLASSIFICATION SYSTEM

The Minnesota Occupational Classification System (MOCS III) (Dawis, Dohm, Lofquist, Chartrand, & Due, 1987) was developed to support applications of the Minnesota theory of work adjustment (TWA). According to TWA, individuals will experience longevity on the job to the extent to which (a) their needs are being met by reinforcers (such as sense of achievement, variety of tasks, or recognition from others) in the work environment and (b) their abilities correspond to the work requirements of the job.

Consistent with its theoretical underpinnings, the MOCS III classifies occupations according to the abilities that are required for successful performance, as well as the reinforcer patterns that are commonly experienced in the work environment. The MOCS III classifies the 1,769 occupational titles found in the 1977 edition of the *Dictionary of Occupational Titles* (U.S. Department of Labor, 1977). One of the benefits of the MOCS III is that it provides clients with a tool that can assist them in matching their values to occupations that are likely to reinforce those values while simultaneously suggesting the degree to which their skills will match the ability requirements of the job.

Although much of the data used to develop the MOCS III is now dated, the work of Dawis and colleagues (Dawis, England, & Lofquist, 1964) has been updated to serve the career development and counseling needs of O*NET users. Through the Work Importance Profiler (WIP; McCloy et al., 1999a) and Work Importance Locator (WIL; McCloy et al., 1999b) questionnaires built into the O*NET system, users can identify reinforcers that are important to them and learn about settings and occupations where their needs are most likely to be met. The O*NET online database also allows users to browse occupations by six salient work values: achievement, independence, recognition, relationships, support, and working conditions.

SOURCES OF OCCUPATIONAL INFORMATION

Sources of occupational information have evolved from simple pamphlets describing a single occupation to comprehensive printed volumes and computer databases describing thousands of occupational titles. Similar to the use of occupational classification systems, these sources of occupational information are used by a range of individuals for a variety of purposes. In this section, we describe several printed and Internet-based sources of occupational information that are of particular use to career educators and counselors. In doing so, we focus on sources that are either (a) in the public domain or (b) available for purchase from vendors and widely distributed throughout the United States.

DICTIONARY OF OCCUPATIONAL TITLES

The Dictionary of Occupational Titles (DOT; U.S. Department of Labor, 1991) was one of the first printed products developed in response to the call for more accurate and comprehensive occupational information in the 1930s. It was maintained by the U.S. Employment Service from 1939 until the late 1990s and has now been abandoned and replaced by the O*NET. The DOT is still available online on several sites (see, for example, http://www.occupationalinfo.org/) and in most public libraries. The DOT provides brief information about thousands of occupational titles, including job duties, occupational classification, and the level of skill needed for working with data, people, and things.

OCCUPATIONAL OUTLOOK HANDBOOK

The Occupational Outlook Handbook (OOH; U.S. Department of Labor, 2010) resulted from calls for workforce projections by the Advisory Committee on Education (1938), the Serviceman's Readjustment Act of 1944, the Veterans Administration (which requested data to support returning veterans' employment searches), and consultation with the National Vocational Guidance Association (now the National Career Development Association, NCDA). First released in 1949, the OOH continues to be published in print and electronic form by the Bureau of Labor Statistics.

The OOH includes detailed information for hundreds of occupations (over 100 occupations in Spanish), including descriptions of the nature of work, working conditions, the number and distribution of workers, training and educational requirements, and the average earnings of job incumbents. The OOH is unique compared to other sources of occupational information in that it provides specific workforce projections by occupation or occupational group. Future job openings are influenced by a complex set of factors, including population demographics, labor force trends, technological developments, demand for goods and services, and overall economic conditions. When these factors are systematically analyzed by the BLS, they result in projected changes in the size of the workforce for a 10-year period.

For example, logging occupations are expected to grow more slowly than the average for all U.S. occupations, due primarily to increased mechanization in this industry. In contrast, jobs in occupational therapy are expected to grow by over 25% in the next decade—much faster than the national average—as a result of the increasing size of the elderly population. Alpert and Auyer (2003) found that the employment projections published in the OOH have tended to be reasonably accurate. Specifically, in reviewing the projections offered between 1988 and 2000, they found that projections were in the correct direction more than 70% of the time.

The OOH includes additional sections that may be of assistance to career educators and counselors. One supplemental section includes descriptions of informational interviews, the role of guidance and school counselors, the importance of professional organizations and societies, and resources for populations such as blind and disabled individuals, veterans, women, and elderly workers. Another section includes detailed recommendations for finding job openings, job search methods, applying and interviewing for openings, and evaluating job offers. Finally, the OOH includes information to assist students and clients in understanding their educational options for advanced training and how to finance those options.

THE OCCUPATIONAL INFORMATION NETWORK

The Occupational Information Network (O*NET) was developed in 1998 primarily as a replacement for the DOT. Far from being a static electronic resource, however, the O*NET is best characterized as a network of products, databases, services, and projects designed to enhance the availability and usability of occupational information by a wide range of individuals and organizations. Data from the O*NET may be used directly by career educators and counselors when working with individuals or small groups, uploaded and supplemented by companies developing comprehensive computer-assisted career guidance systems (described in more detail later), and used by organizations to inform performance evaluation rubrics, job announcements, or advanced training for job incumbents.

A complete description of the elements of the O*NET is beyond the scope of this chapter. We focus exclusively on the O*NET database itself and recently released products that can be used by counselors and career educators working with students, young adults, and veterans. Readers interested in more detailed descriptions of the projects, services, and products available through the O*NET are encouraged to visit http://www.onetcenter.org/. Additional information describing the career assessments available in the O*NET are described by Hansen (Chapter 14, this volume), Rounds and Jin (Chapter 15, this volume), and Metz and Jones (Chapter 16, this volume).

At the heart of the O*NET is an occupational database that serves as the primary source of occupational information in the United States. The organization and elements of this database are best described by the O*NET Content Model shown in Figure 18.2. These data include information about occupational requirements (e.g., work activities, work context, and tools used in

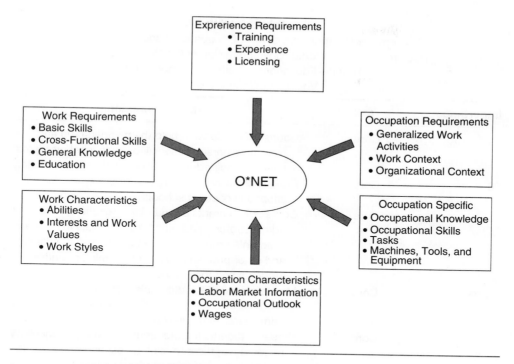

Figure 18.2 O*NET Content Model
Adapted from http://www.onetcenter.org/content.html.

the occupation), worker requirements (e.g., skills requirements, knowledge, and education), and worker characteristics (e.g., interests, abilities, values, and work styles). Additionally, the database includes information describing the specific training and experience needed for a given occupation, as well as any specific certification or licensing required for job entry. Finally, the database hosts national information about the labor market, including wage information, current employment numbers, and employment projections. Users can also search similar state-specific information (including job postings) through a link to Career Onestop, an online service sponsored by the U.S. Department of Labor Employment and Training Administration. An example of output from the O*NET online database is included in Table 18.1 for the occupation 21-1012.00—Educational, Guidance, School, and Vocational Counselors.

Until recently, data in the O*NET were accessible only through the O*NET Online (http://www.onetonline.org). The O*NET Online provides a functional interface for searching and accessing occupational information but is not very client friendly. Now, career educators and counselors can use the My Next Move website (http://www.mynextmove.org) at no cost to help students search for occupations by title, browse occupations by industry,

Table 18.1

Abbreviated Output from O*NET. Occupational and Worker Requirements and Worker Characteristics for the Occupation of 21-1012.00—Educational, Guidance, School, and Vocational Counselors

Importance	Task	Task Description
90	Core	Counsel individuals to help them understand and overcome personal, social, or behavioral problems affecting their educational or vocational situations.
86	Core	Provide crisis intervention to students when difficult situations occur at schools.
85	Core	Confer with parents or guardians, teachers, administrators, and other professionals to discuss children's progress, resolve behavioral, academic, and other problems, and to determine priorities for students and their resource needs.
83	Core	Maintain accurate and complete student records as required by laws, district policies, and administrative regulations.
82	Core	Prepare students for later educational experiences by encouraging them to explore learning opportunities and to persevere with challenging tasks.
81	Core	Evaluate students' or individuals' abilities, interests, and personality characteristics using tests, records, interviews, or professional sources.
81	Core	Identify cases of domestic abuse or other family problems and encourage students or parents to seek additional assistance from mental health professionals.
80	Core	Counsel students regarding educational issues, such as course and program selection, class scheduling and registration, school adjustment, truancy, study habits, and career planning.

Importance	Knowledge	Knowledge Description
95	Psychology	Knowledge of human behavior and performance; individual differences in ability, personality, and interests; learning and motivation; psychological research methods; and the assessment and treatment of behavioral and affective disorders.
91	Therapy and Counseling	Knowledge of principles, methods, and procedures for diagnosis, treatment, and rehabilitation of physical and mental dysfunctions, and for career counseling and guidance.

Table 18.1 *(Continued)*

Importance	Skill	Skill Description
85	Active Listening	Giving full attention to what other people are saying, taking time to understand the points being made, asking questions as appropriate, and not interrupting at inappropriate times.
85	Speaking	Talking to others to convey information effectively.
81	Reading Comprehension	Understanding written sentences and paragraphs in work related documents.
81	Social Perceptiveness	Being aware of others' reactions and understanding why they react as they do.

Importance	Ability	Ability Description
85	Oral Expression	The ability to communicate information and ideas in speaking so others will understand.
81	Oral Comprehension	The ability to listen to and understand information and ideas presented through spoken words and sentences.
81	Written Comprehension	The ability to read and understand information and ideas presented in writing.

Importance	Work Activity	Work Activity Description
91	Establishing and Maintaining Interpersonal Relationships	Developing constructive and cooperative working relationships with others, and maintaining them over time.
91	Assisting and Caring for Others	Providing personal assistance, medical attention, emotional support, or other personal care to others such as coworkers, customers, or patients.
90	Communicating with Supervisors, Peers, or Subordinates	Providing information to supervisors, coworkers, and subordinates by telephone, in written form, e-mail, or in person.

Note: Importance and other ratings are measured on different scales. To provide users with more intuitive scores, ratings are standardized and presented on a scale ranging from 0 to 100. Higher scores reflect higher levels of importance.

or match occupations to assessed interests and degree of desired training. Results are delivered in a colorful and easily digested presentation and filtered to provide only the most salient elements (e.g., knowledge, skills, abilities, educational requirements, and job outlook). An additional site (http://www.mynextmove.org/vets/) has been established to permit veterans to search for civilian occupations that are similar to their military occupational specialty. These two sites represent the O*NET's ongoing effort to provide resources for career educators and counselors working with school-age children and young adults. More counselor resources, including free access to interest, values, and ability assessments, can be found at http://www.onetcenter.org/tools.html

COMPREHENSIVE INTERNET-BASED SOURCES OF CAREER INFORMATION

It is probably safe to assume that a large percentage of career exploration today occurs on the Internet. Computer-assisted career guidance (CACG) systems (also referred to as career information delivery systems or CIDS) have been available since the 1960s, though recently made more accessible as systems became available on personal computers and through the Internet. These systems have many advantages over print-based resources in that CACG systems can deliver and score career assessment tools in real time and provide results to clients and counselors immediately. Moreover, those results can be logically linked to congruent occupational and educational information to facilitate the transition from self-understanding to occupational and educational exploration (Gore et al., 2006).

There currently exist dozens of CACG systems. These systems are available to individuals, schools, districts, colleges and universities, and workforce development services. A growing number of U.S. states are choosing to adopt a CACG system for use by all state citizens and organizations. Next we review a subset of CACG systems that are widely available in the United States today.

intoCareers (CIS). The University of Oregon has a not-for-profit outreach center, intoCareers (http://www.intocareers.org), that has been producing career information system (CIS) products for over 30 years. Products developed by intoCareers are currently in use by over 20 states and include (a) the basic CIS system for career and educational exploration (designed for high school students and beyond), (b) CIS Junior, which includes a suite of academic planning and career exploration tools for middle school students, and (c) Career Trek, a career awareness program for younger children in the elementary grades. CIS includes a suite of formal interest assessments (O*NET Interest Profiler, IDEAS, Career Cluster Inventory), as well as a skills self-rating instrument and the O*NET Work Importance Locator (values), among other features. CIS Junior and Career Trek include fewer, and more informal (Career Trek), assessment materials.

The model of intoCareer is to deliver state-specific data combined with national data in an Internet-based platform that can be customized to meet the specific needs of each state. The backbone of the CIS database consists of occupational information based on data obtained from the O*NET and supplemented with additional information from the OOH and publications produced by professional organizations and state-specific sources. Users can access the occupational database using an occupational sort by linking from assessment results or by selecting one of the U.S. Department of Education's 16 career clusters. The occupational model includes interviews with job incumbents, occupational videos, the identification of environment-friendly or green jobs, and links to related military careers. Additional data sets describe postsecondary programs of study and colleges and universities.

State-level customization provides opportunities to extend the role of the CIS beyond what is typically encountered in stand-alone products such as those described here later. For example, the State of Utah decided to include a measure of noncognitive strengths and deficits, the Student Strengths Inventory (http://www.campuslabs.com/products/beacon/), in UtahFutures, the Utah state CIS (http://www.utahfutures.org). Using this information, Utah school counselors are able to assess college and work readiness in their upper-level high school students with more than grades and standardized achievement test scores. Other states have created data shares between the CIS and their state workforce development services and jobs sites (e.g., Idaho, Illinois, and New Jersey). Finally, customization at the state level also permits users to preload a database describing high school course numbers and names by school so that the CIS system can be used by school counselors to create academic course sequences and plans when meeting with their students.

SIGI³. SIGI³ (http://www.sigi3.org) is the most recent version of a system that was originally developed by Martin Katz (1963) as the system for interactive guidance information (SIGI). Originally designed to help students identify occupational alternatives based on assessment of work values and skills, SIGI³ continues this tradition today by including a values card-sort activity, a skills self-assessment, and two interest assessments.

The Values card-sort exercise uses a forced-preference technique (24 value statements) similar to that found in the Work Importance Locator (McCloy et al., 1999a). Values assessment results are organized in eight categories (Contribution to Society, High Income, Independence, Leadership, Leisure, Prestige, Security, and Variety); users can select value categories to see a list of occupations likely to reinforce that value. The more formal interest assessment includes 30 forced-choice items and results in a profile with scores on eight dimensions (Arts and Humanities; Business; Education; Engineering; Health; Science, Math and Agriculture; Social and Behavioral Sciences; and Trades and Technology). Similar to results from the values assessment, users can view a list of occupations that are congruent with high interest scores. The skills self-assessment includes 35 items organized into six Holland-like domains (six or seven items in each domain). Users are first asked to rate themselves as "good" or "not good" on each item and then to select the strongest skill from their "good" list. Users are then linked to occupational titles that require skills reflected in their assessment results.

Like other systems described in this chapter, users can search for occupations using assessment results and combinations of assessment results or by title or postsecondary academic major title. Occupational information in SIGI[3] appears to be directly exported from the O*NET database and is presented in a functional, albeit not very user-friendly form. Unlike some other systems, SIGI[3] does not contain its own postsecondary educational database. The system includes a module for users to maintain their portfolio (e.g., assessment results, favorite occupations, and educational aspirations), a basic resume-building module, and links to standardized achievement test prep sites.

Career Cruising. Established in 1997, Career Cruising (http://public.career cruising.com/us/en) is one of the more recent additions to the family of online career guidance systems and is currently used by over 19,000 institutions across North America. Career Cruising is part of a broader network of services that also includes a high school Course Planner, a college Application Planner, a Test Prep platform, and a Network platform that allows users to connect to local businesses for the purposes of coordinating internships, arranging field trips, or viewing available employment opportunities.

Career Cruising includes six primary modules: Main, Assessments, Careers, Schools, Employment, and the Portfolio. The Main module serves as a landing portal and a place where occupations can be featured. The Assessments module hosts four primary assessment instruments: interests, skills, abilities, and learning styles. The foundation of the Career Cruising assessment is the Career Matchmaker. Users complete the 39 items that make up the core Matchmaker inventory using a 5-point response system ("dislike very much" to "like very much"). Users have the option of completing an additional 77 items. Unlike many interest inventories in use today, linkages between Matchmaker assessment results and occupational recommendations are based on a detailed job analysis of primary occupational activities rather than Holland codes. A recent analysis of the core items of the Matchmaker system, however, revealed that the items more than adequately reproduce a Holland-like factor structure (Gore & Leuwerke, 2011).

Rather than relying solely on self-assessments of skills or abilities, Career Cruising includes the O*NET Ability Profiler (McCloy, Campbell, Oswald, Lewis, & Rivkin, 1999), a timed and proctored paper-and-pencil assessment of six ability domains (for more information, see Metz & Jones, Chapter 16, this volume). For career educators and counselors looking for a less formal instrument, Career Cruising also includes a 45-item skills self-assessment, the results of which are linked to appropriate occupational titles. Finally, Career Cruising includes a 20-item measure of visual, tactile, and auditory learning preferences that can be used to provide students with recommendations that may optimize their approach to academic coursework or enhance decisions regarding future educational and training opportunities.

The Careers and Schools modules are portals to internal databases of occupations and postsecondary educational opportunities and sites. The Careers module includes detailed information about each occupation, including a job description, working conditions, earnings, educational requirements, career paths, and related careers. The data appear to supplement those provided by O*NET databases. Also in this module are interviews with male and female job incumbents and a photo file of pictures related to the occupation. The Schools database includes profiles of 2- and 4-year colleges, as well as vocational schools. Users can search for schools or academic programs using a number of search criteria and identify schools that offer training programs or academic majors that lead to specific careers through a "related college programs" option that links the school and career databases.

The Employment module contains helpful information about preparing a resume, conducting a job search, interviewing, and evaluating job offers. Additionally, Career Cruising has partnered with Indeed (http://www .indeed.com), an online job listing site, allowing users to search for current openings. The Portfolio module provides the option to save favorites, review assessment results, or authorize portfolio access by others, and it also features an online journal that the client can use to reflect on his or her career exploration. Features like the Portfolio Completion Standards, messaging tools, and Assignments and Activities support structured portfolio development. Career counselors have access to a suite of administrative tools for tracking users' progress, configuring the system to meet their specific needs, and generating aggregate reports on system usage and stored portfolio data.

ETHICAL ISSUES IN THE USE OF CAREER INFORMATION

Career practitioners must understand the ethical challenges of using occupational information systems and take appropriate precautions to ensure that students and clients are well served by career interventions. In this section, we highlight several ethical issues that can arise when working with occupational information systems and offer guidelines related to integrating Internet-based applications into existing career counseling and education interventions. These ethical issues are drawn, in part, from the publications noted here, and career practitioners who regularly use occupational information systems are encouraged to download and integrate the following resources into their practice. The National Career Development Association (NCDA) and the Association of Computer-Based Systems for Career Information (ACSCI) provide ethical standards, practice guidelines, and implementation standards to promote appropriate utilization and presentation of career information. In addition to its *Code of Ethics* (NCDA, 2007), NCDA has published *Career Counseling Competencies* (NCDA, 2009) and *NCDA Guidelines for the Use of the Internet for the Provision of Career Information and Planning Services* (NCDA, 1997). ACSCI (2009) has also published *Standards Implementation Handbook*, which outlines minimum qualifications in the areas of core standards, components, integration, and information delivery aspects of career information systems.

Career counselors working with students and clients in any setting should be aware of the following general ethical practices. First, career professionals should utilize systems with which they are competent to work. This requires proper education, training, and/or supervision in the use of each system. Second, because many occupational information systems contain assessment tools (e.g., interests, values, skills), counselors must consider the psychometric properties of all instruments and evaluate their appropriateness for particular client groups. Third, counselors who encourage clients to explore occupational information systems on their own need to establish processes to monitor their progress. Current occupational information systems are vast stores of occupational content that can easily overwhelm users. Practitioners who are working with clients at a distance or with students with whom they do not meet regularly should create procedures to evaluate progress and ensure that information exploration goals are being met. For example, the second author recommends that his clients set time and occupation limits, such as 45 minutes and three occupations for each search, to help them effectively manage exploration sessions.

Fourth, as supported by research mentioned earlier, practitioners should use occupational information systems as one component of a comprehensive career intervention rather than simply referring clients to a source of information and leaving them to explore it on their own (Brown et al., 2003). Finally, counselors should evaluate the appropriateness of a given occupational information system for their clients. Young students or individuals with intellectual or reading disabilities might not benefit from computer-based information systems or may need additional supports to achieve positive outcomes (Hutchinson, Freeman, Downey, & Kilbreath, 1992).

Many occupational information systems, such as the *Occupational Outlook Handbook* (U.S. Department of Labor, 2010), have migrated from print to computer-based applications and then onto the Internet (http://www.bls.gov/oco/). Although this evolution has been tremendously beneficial in expanding access to this information, it also raises ethical challenges that practitioners must address. Career professionals should caution students about transmitting personal information online and alert them that confidentiality cannot be guaranteed. To maximize safety, counselors should also determine whether Web sites requiring clients to provide personal information hold an SSL (Secure Sockets Layer) certificate documenting the use of encryption methods to protect information transmitted over the Internet. This information can normally be found at the bottom of the browser window or in a Web site's security information section. Practitioners should also develop procedures to ensure that client information stored on their computers is secure and that records are purged according to applicable laws and guidelines. Awareness of these ethical issues positions career professionals to appropriately and responsibly use occupational information systems to help students and clients achieve their career development goals.

PRACTICAL APPLICATIONS

Occupational information sources and CACG systems provide tremendous opportunities for career counselors and educators to connect individuals to career information, encourage exploration, and facilitate the process of making academic and career choices. Moreover, the integration of career assessments and easy online access create opportunities for career professionals to integrate career information into their classes and practices, both inside and outside of session. This section describes practices that integrate occupational information systems into career interventions organized around tasks of exploration, choice, and implementation when working with school-age students and early career clients.

EXPLORATION

Students frequently begin active career exploration in secondary school. The American School Counseling Association (ASCA, 2005) identifies individual student planning as one of the core activities that professional school counselors conduct in their practice. Many students' first exposure to a career information system might occur as part of a classroom guidance lesson or in a small group in the school counselor's office. Other counselors meet individually with students to go through occupational information systems or to plan high school coursework based on interests and academic goals.

Many states, meanwhile, either encourage or require career and academic exploration starting in middle school. This exploration is often facilitated by statewide adoption of CACG systems that allow students, counselors, teachers, and parents to access career information. The longitudinal utilization of these systems represents an additional benefit of this approach. Students who create an account in middle school can continue to utilize a CACG system through high school and into postsecondary education or training, providing continuity in their career exploration, as well as comfort and familiarity with the system (Kucker, 2000).

Career development goals at the middle school and high school levels include exposing students to career information and information systems; providing students with information search skills; fostering self-understanding of interests, skills, and values; and engaging in academic and career planning (Dahir, Burnham, & Stone, 2009). These activities can be accomplished through the effective use of career information systems (Turner & Lapan, 2005). For example, intoCareers offers CIS Junior, a set of tools for middle school students to engage in self-assessment, begin academic planning, and start exploring careers. Systems such as CIS Junior often include lesson plans that counselors can use to deliver classroom-based guidance or consult with teachers who wish to integrate guidance elements into their existing lesson plans. For example, a history teacher might develop an assignment called "Careers Now, Careers Then" and require students to compare a contemporary career of their choice to a comparable occupation in the historical period being studied. This might include a description of typical daily activities, core competencies, educational requirements, and a forecast of future employment opportunities. Such exercises provide students with an opportunity to learn how to access and evaluate career information and simultaneously support the existing academic curriculum.

Individuals at secondary and postsecondary levels benefit from systematic individual student planning, as well as regular academic and career exploration activities (Paisley & McMahon, 2001). CACG systems that integrate portfolios, resume builders, and saved assessment results facilitate these activities and provide students with long-term access to career information. At this level, counselors and career educators can also support career exploration through reflection on completed coursework and experience outside the classroom (e.g., job shadowing, service learning experiences, internships, and volunteer or paid work), which students can then connect to information exploration using a computer-based system. Programs such as My Next Move (http://www.mynextmove.org) provides easily navigable search tools by keyword, industry, or completion of the O*NET Interest Profiler and can be used at no cost to the school or student. Older students and individuals preparing to enter the workforce can utilize the OOH (U.S. Department of Labor, 2010) to identify professional associations that provide information about training, internship, or shadowing opportunities, as well as potential mentors who might facilitate career exploration and entry.

CHOICE

Career choice at the secondary level typically includes selection of high school coursework, articulation of career/technical training goals, development of plans for college coursework, and possibly college major decisions (Peterson, Long, & Billups, 1999). CACG systems support these choices by storing students' plans in portfolios and by integrating academic and vocational information to facilitate the choice process. Some states go so far as to mandate the creation of an academic/career plan at the secondary level. School counselors can input high school course schedules to support students' articulation of their academic plans, and parents, teachers, and mentors can access this information and provide input as students prepare for work and education beyond high school.

Career and educational choices following high school involve pursuing postsecondary education or training, identifying college majors, and choosing a career path. The role of career professionals at this point is to highlight and process the actions involved in making a choice based on the information clients have acquired in school and through their own exploration. CACG systems that maintain portfolios allow individuals to engage in goal setting, creating new career plans, and continued exploring as they continue to make career choices. The critical task of the career professional is to aid individuals in understanding how career development is a lifelong skill. A CACG system that maintains client information over time is an ideal framework for counselors to engage with clients to attain current career goals while also preparing individuals to tackle future career challenges, such as acquiring new skills or responding to an unexpected career change (Bobek et al., 2005). Career information websites also include tools to directly connect clients to careers. The Network platform of the Career Cruising system allows counselors to collaborate with local employers to create resources for students to learn about and select internships, training opportunities, or job openings. For instance, a counselor might create pages for all construction companies within 100 miles of campus. The employers have the opportunity to connect with current students and new graduates and communicate the skills they are seeking in new employees. At the same time, clients can learn about companies and make choices based on information tailored to their specific field.

IMPLEMENTATION

Individuals implement academic and career choices through enrolling in courses, engaging in job shadowing, and pursuing early work experiences. Career counselors serve as a tremendous resource to students and early career entrants by providing interventions that promote college and career readiness. For instance, career professionals can use the ability assessments incorporated into most CACGs to assist individuals in evaluating their skills and develop plans to enhance their college and career readiness. ACT's Explore platform combines assessment results with specific activities students can use to improve skills in the assessed areas (e.g., mathematics, reading). Counselors and clients can use this information to write and implement plans to improve skill deficit areas. Also, intoCareers includes a skill assessment that connects users' skills to occupations. As individuals acquire knowledge about critical skills in their future occupation, they can take active steps to build the habits critical to success in their field of interest. For example, understanding the importance of communication, accountability, and attention to detail will motivate some students to improve their present performance to achieve longer-term goals. Teachers and counselors, meanwhile, can highlight the importance of teamwork and oral communication through class projects, reinforce accountability through class deadlines, or build conscientiousness by encouraging students to arrive on time prepared to actively participate. Early career clients can work with their career counselor to identify ways to build these skills (e.g., oral communication, teamwork) on the job, such as taking lead responsibility for the presentation of a new product. These noncognitive or "soft skills" were recently identified as some of the most sought-after skills in a large national sample of U.S. employees and employers (U.S. Chamber of Commerce & University of Phoenix, 2011).

CACG systems also include resources that clients can utilize throughout their lifetimes. Resume-building templates allow individuals to craft a resume from information they have already entered regarding work, volunteer, and extracurricular activities and may also have the capacity to build objective statements from individuals' academic and career goals or develop a summary profile based on skills and values assessment results. Many systems also include online modules or classroom activities to support career educators and counselors in educating clients about cover letters, personal statements, and preparing for interviews. As an example, the CACG system available to all Iowa residents includes an interview practice tool that provides job seekers common interview questions, tips for responding, and an opportunity to write out answers. Counselors can bolster their clients' interview performance through activities such as assigning these modules as homework and then practicing interviewing in session (Maurer, Solamon, Andrews, & Troxtel, 2001). This is just one example of the tremendous career information tools available to counselors to support clients throughout the career development process.

CONCLUSIONS

Occupational information is a critical element of career development and counseling at all ages and is now more widely available to career educators and counselors and to their students and clients than ever before in history. Clearly, additional work remains as we develop our understanding of how to best promote the exploration of occupational information. In a recent review of the career exploration literature, Taveira and Moreno (2003) offer a rubric to guide future research and practice in this area. Their rubric poses a number of questions that remain to be answered: Why do people explore, how much value do they attribute to exploratory behavior, how confident are they exploring, where and how do they explore, what kind of conditions promote or inhibit exploration, and what occurs after information is acquired? Answers to these questions would greatly assist career educators and counselors in their efforts to provide more effective and efficient services to their students and clients.

The following are some useful recommendations related to the use of career information in career education and counseling:

- Educators and counselors should be familiar with current systems of classifying occupational information and how those systems might be used most appropriately based on student and client needs.
- Educators and counselors should be familiar with comprehensive computer-assisted career guidance systems and recognize their appropriateness for use with students and clients of varying ages and needs.
- Educators and counselors need to use sources of occupational information in an ethical manner, which means being familiar with the psychometric properties and appropriate uses of assessment instruments, as well as the currency and appropriateness of occupational information for students and clients at varying developmental levels.
- Advances in our understanding of the developmental precursors to career exploration and occupational information gathering offer opportunities for educators and counselors working with younger children to better tailor their interventions and be more helpful to their students.
- Educators and counselors should familiarize themselves with recent research on the effectiveness of occupational exploration and how the effectiveness of exploration can be enhanced by combining occupational information gathering and exploration with other key intervention strategies.

REFERENCES

ACT. (2009). *ACT Interest Inventory technical manual (UNIACT)*. Iowa City, IA: American College Testing.

Advisory Committee on Education. (1938). *Report of the committee* (p. 104). Washington, DC: Government Printing Office.

Alpert, A., & Auyer, J. (2003, Spring). The 1988–2000 employment projections: How accurate were they? *Occupational Outlook Quarterly*, 2–21.

American School Counseling Association. (2005). *The ASCA national model: A framework for school counseling programs* (2nd ed.). Alexandria, VA: Author.

Association of Computer-Based Systems of Career Information. (2009). *Standards implementation handbook*. Stillwater, OK: Author.

Betz, N. E., Borgen, F. H., & Harmon, L. W. (2005). *Manual for the Skills Confidence Inventory* (rev. ed.). Mountain View, CA: Consulting Psychologists Press.

Bobek, B. L., Robbins, S. B., Gore, P. A., Jr., Harris-Bowlsbey, J., Lapan, R. T., Dahir, C. A., & Jepsen, D. A. (2005). Training counselors to use computer-assisted career guidance systems more effectively: A model curriculum. *Career Development Quarterly, 53*, 363–371.

Brayfield, A. H., & Reed, P. A. (1950). How readable are occupational information booklets? *Journal of Applied Psychology, 34*, 325–328.

Brewer, J. M. (1942). Using existing facilities and developing new. In J. M. Brewer, E. J. Cleary, C. C. Dunsmoor, J. S. Lake, C. J. Nichols, C. M. Smith, & H. P. Smith (Eds.), *History of vocational guidance: Origins and early development* (pp. 121–136). New York, NY: Harper & Brothers.

Brown, S. D., & Ryan Krane, N. E. (2000). Four (or five) sessions and a cloud of dust: Old assumptions and new observations about career counseling. In S. D. Brown & R. W. Lent (Eds.), *Handbook of counseling psychology* (3rd ed., pp. 740–766). New York, NY: Wiley.

Brown, S. D., Ryan Krane, N. E., Brecheisen, J., Castelino, P., Budisin, I., Miller, M., & Edens, L. (2003). Critical ingredients of career choice interventions: More analyses and new hypotheses. *Journal of Vocational Behavior, 62*, 411–428.

Clark, F. E., & Murtland, C. (1946). Occupational information in counseling: Present practices and historical development, *Occupations, 24*, 451–475.

Crites, J. O. (1976). Career counseling: A comprehensive approach. *Counseling Psychologist, 3*, 2–12.

Dahir, C. A., Burnham, J. J., & Stone, C. (2009). Listen to the voices: School counselors and comprehensive school counseling programs. *Professional School Counseling, 12*, 182–192.

Dawis, R. V., Dohm, T. E., Lofquist, L. H., Chartrand, J. M., & Due, A. M. (1987). *Minnesota occupational classification system III*. Minneapolis: Vocational Psychology Research, University of Minnesota.

Dawis, R. V., England, G. W., & Lofquist, L. H. (1964). A theory of work adjustment: Minnesota studies in vocational rehabilitation, no. 15. Minneapolis: University of Minnesota Industrial Relations Center.

Donnay, D. A. C., Morris, M. L., Schaubhut, N. A., & Thompson, R. C. (2005). *Strong Interest Inventory manual*. Mountain View, CA: Consulting Psychologists Press.

Gati, I., & Amir, T. (2010). Applying a systemic procedure to locate career decision-making difficulties. *Career Development Quarterly, 58,* 301–320.

Gati, I., Krausz, M., & Osipow, S. H. (1996). A taxonomy of difficulties in career decision making. *Journal of Counseling Psychology, 43,* 510–526.

Gore, P. A., Jr., Bobek, B. L., Robbins, S. B., & Shayne, L. (2006). Computer-based career exploration: Usage patterns and a typology of users. *Journal of Career Assessment, 14,* 421–436.

Gore, P. A., Jr., & Hitch, J. L. (2005). Occupational classification and sources of occupational information. In S. D. Brown & R. W. Lent (Eds.), *Career development and counseling: Putting theory and research to work* (pp. 382–413). Hoboken, NJ: Wiley.

Gore, P. A., Jr., & Leuwerke, W. (2011). Career cruising: *Matchmaker scale evaluation report.* Unpublished manuscript.

Gottfredson, G. D., & Holland, J. L. (1996). *Dictionary of Holland occupational codes* (3rd ed.). Odessa, FL: Psychological Assessment Resources.

Hartung, P. J. (1999). Work illustrated: Attending to visual images in career information materials. *Career Development Quarterly, 44,* 234–241.

Hirschi, A. (2011). Career-choice readiness in adolescence: Developmental trajectories and individual differences. *Journal of Vocational Behavior, 79,* 340–348.

Hoffner, C. A., Levine, K. J., Sullivan, Q. E., Crowell, D., Pedrick, L., & Berndt, P. (2006). TV characters at work: Television's role in the occupational aspirations of economically disadvantaged youth. *Journal of Career Development, 33,* 3–18.

Holland, J. L. (1987). *The Self-Directed Search professional manual.* Odessa, FL: Psychological Assessment Resources.

Holland, J. L. (1997). *Making vocational choices: A theory of vocational personalities and work environments* (3rd ed.). Odessa, FL: Psychological Assessment Resources.

Hoppock, R., & Spiegler, S. (1941). 66 best books on occupational information and guidance. Arranged in suggested order of purchase for an average public school library. Oxford, UK: Occupational Index.

Hutchinson, N. L., Freeman, J. G., Downey, K. H., & Kilbreath, L. (1992). Development and evaluation of an instructional module to promote career maturity for youth with learning difficulties. *Canadian Journal of Counselling, 26,* 290–299.

Jordan, T. E., & Pope, M. L. (2001). Developmental antecedents to adolescents' occupational knowledge: A 17-year prospective study. *Journal of Vocational Behavior, 58,* 279–292.

Kanfer, R., Wanberg, C. R., & Kantrowitz, T. M. (2001). Job search and employment: A personality-motivational analysis and meta-analytic review. *Journal of Applied Psychology, 86,* 837–855.

Katz, M. R. (1963). *Decisions and values.* New York, NY: College Entrance Examination Board.

Kucker, M. (2000). South Dakota's model for career and life planning. *Journal of Career Development, 27,* 133–148.

Lewis, P., & Rivkin, D. (1999). *Development of the O*NET Interest Profiler.* Raleigh, NC: National Center for O*NET Development.

Markham, W. T. (1943). Occupational guidance has six facets. *School Executive, 62,* 20–23.

Maurer, T. J., Solamon, J. M., Andrews, K. D., & Troxtel, D. D. (2001). Interviewee coaching, preparation strategies, and response strategies in relation to performance in situational employment interviews: An extension of Maurer, Solamon, and Troxtel (1998). *Journal of Applied Psychology, 86,* 709–717.

McCloy, R., Campbell, J., Oswald, F. L., Lewis, P., & Rivkin, D. (1999). *Linking client assessment profiles to O*NET occupational profiles.* Raleigh, NC: National Center for O*NET Development.

McCloy, R., Waugh, G., Medsker, G., Wall, J., Rivkin, D., & Lewis, P. (1999a). *Development of the O*NET computerized Work Importance Profiler.* Raleigh, NC: National Center for O*NET Development.

McCloy, R., Waugh, G., Medsker, G., Wall, J., Rivkin, D., & Lewis, P. (1999b). *Development of the O*NET paper-and-pencil Work Importance Locator.* Raleigh, NC: National Center for O*NET Development.

McMahon, M., Carroll, J., & Gillies, R. M. (2001). Occupational aspirations of sixth-grade children. *Journal of Career Development, 10,* 25–31.

McMahon, M., & Watson, M. (2005). Occupational information: What children want to know. *Journal of Career Development, 31,* 239–249.

Millar, R., & Shevlin, M. (2003). Predicting career information-seeking behavior of school pupils using the theory of planned behavior. *Journal of Vocational Behavior, 62,* 26–42.

National Career Development Association. (1997). *NCDA guidelines for the use of the Internet for provision of career information and planning services.* Columbus, OH: Author.

National Career Development Association. (2007). *Code of ethics.* Columbus, OH: Author.

National Career Development Association (2009). *Career counseling competencies.* Columbus, OH: Author.

Paisley, P. O., & McMahon, H. G. (2001). School counseling for the 21st century: Challenges and opportunities. *Professional School Counseling, 5,* 106–115.

Parsons, F. (1909). *Choosing your vocation.* Boston, MA: Houghton Mifflin.

Patton, W. A., & McCrindle, A. R. (2001). Senior students' views on career information: What was the most useful and what would they like. *Australian Journal of Career Development, 10,* 32–36.

Peterson, G. W., Long, K. L., & Billups, A. (1999). The effect of three career interventions on educational choices of eighth graders. *Professional School Counseling, 9,* 136–143.

Porfeli, E. J., Hartung, P. J., & Vondracek, F. W. (2008). Children's vocational development: A research rationale. *Career Development Quarterly, 57,* 25–37.

Posthuma, R. A., Morgeson, F. P., & Campion, M. A. (2002). Beyond employment interview validity: A comprehensive narrative review of recent research and trends over time. *Personnel Psychology, 55,* 1–81.

Prediger, D. J. (1982). Dimensions underlying Holland's hexagon. *Missing link between interest and occupations. Journal of Vocational Behavior, 21,* 259–287.

Prediger, D. J. (2002). Abilities, interest, and values: Their assessment and their integration via the World-of-Work Map. *Journal of Career Assessment, 10*(2), 209–232.

Rohr, E., & Speer, D. (1948). The guidance service uses the school newspaper. *Occupations, 26,* 363.

Rounds, J. B. (1995). Vocational interests: Evaluating structural hypotheses. In D. J. Lubinski & R. V. Dawis (Eds.), *Assessing individual differences in human behavior: New concepts, methods, and findings* (pp. 177–232). Palo Alto, CA: Consulting Psychologists Press.

Saks, A. M. (2005). Job search success: A review and integration of the predictors, behaviors, and outcomes. In S. D. Brown & R. W. Lent (Eds.), *Career development and counseling: Putting theory and research to work* (pp. 155–179). Hoboken, NJ: Wiley.

Shartle, C. L. (1946). *Occupational information: Its development and application.* New York, NY: Prentice Hall.

Strang, R. (1945). Use in counseling of information about vocations. *School Review, 53,* 526–529.

Taveira, M. D. C., & Moreno, M. L. R. (2003). Guidance theory and practice: The status of career exploration. *British Journal of Guidance and Counselling, 31,* 189–207.

Turner, S. L., & Lapan, R. T. (2005). Evaluation of an intervention to increase non-traditional career interests and career-related self-efficacy among middle school students. *Journal of Vocational Behavior, 66,* 516–531.

U.S. Chamber of Commerce, & University of Phoenix. (2011, September 27). Life in the 21st century workforce, A national perspective. Retrieved from http://icw.uschamber.com/sites/default/files/Life%20in%20the%2021st%20Century%20Workforce.pdf

U.S. Department of Labor. (1991). *Dictionary of occupational titles* (4th ed.). Washington, DC: U.S. Government Printing Office.

U.S. Department of Labor. (2010). *Occupational outlook handbook* (2010–2011 ed.). Washington, DC: U.S. Government Printing Office.

Walls, R. T. (2000). Vocational cognition: Accuracy of 3rd-, 6th-, 9th-, and 12th-grade students. *Journal of Vocational Behavior, 56,* 137–144.

Williamson, E. G. (1937). A college class in occupational information. *School Review, 45,* 123–129.

Zikic, J., & Saks, A. M. (2009). Job search and social cognitive theory: The role of career relevant activities. *Journal of Vocational Behavior, 74,* 117–127.

COUNSELING, DEVELOPMENTAL, AND PREVENTIVE INTERVENTIONS

Promotion of Career Awareness, Development, and School Success in Children and Adolescents

SHERRI L. TURNER AND RICHARD T. LAPAN

THE PRIMARY GOAL OF this chapter is to discuss how professional school counselors, career counselors, career educators, and psychologists can create career awareness, support career development, and promote school success in children and adolescents. The discussion of creating career awareness focuses on the types and nature of career information that young people need, and how this information can be shared most effectively with them. The discussion of supporting career development is organized around the Integrative Contextual Model of Career Development (Lapan, 2004; Turner & Lapan, 2005b). The discussion of promoting school success focuses on the importance of offering both academic and career development counseling interventions for young people. Assisting K–12 young people in these areas can help them create more satisfying, productive, and fulfilling adult lives. Other chapters in this book, most notably those on major theories (see, for example, Chapters 3, 4, and 5), diversity, and individual differences, also attend to issues of career awareness, career development, and school success. We cite these chapters as appropriate. The reader is also referred to these chapters to supplement what we cover in the present chapter.

CREATING CAREER AWARENESS

Career awareness, or what people know about the occupational world and the types of work they might want to do, is foundational to career exploration, which in turn can lead to career preparation, career choice, and career attainment. In the Developmental Theory of Occupational Choice, Ginzberg, Ginsburg, Axelrad, and Herma (1950) proposed that children's initial career awareness is founded more on fantasy than on reality. In this fantasy stage, young children's career awareness is based on a "rather loose integration of fantasies or assumptions as well as actual observations of adults working" (Hill, 1969). Children enter the tentative stage at about age 11, when they begin to become aware of themselves in relation to the world of work, and then at about age 18 they enter the realistic stage, where interests and choices become more crystallized.

Super, in building on the Ginzberg et al. theory, proposed that career awareness is born out of curiosity, fantasies, capacities, and interests (see Hartung, Chapter 4, this volume). Through a process of orientation to vocational choice, gathering information and planning, and developing one's self-concept, career choices are eventually made. Assisting children in this process, by providing appropriate and timely information, can be fundamental to helping them become aware of a broad range of career possibilities.

Gottfredson (1981), in building on Super and Ginzberg, highlighted the process that socialization plays in children's developing career awareness. In her Theory of Circumscription and Compromise (1981), she proposes that young people are highly motivated by their understanding of socially prescribed gender and prestige roles. Thus, social class and background become integrated into their view of self and their place in the world as they consider their own interests, values, competencies, and intelligence. In this theory, children (ages 3 to 5) become oriented to size and power, or what it means to be an adult in their world. From ages 6 to 8, they become aware of socially prescribed sex roles. Between 9 and 13, they become oriented to social valuation (i.e., the roles that social class and abilities play in their occupational aspirations and choices). As discussed later in this chapter, at age 14, they begin to more actively circumscribe their aspirations based on these views until they finally compromise in their educational and vocational choices so that their own interests and abilities are sacrificed, at least partially, to their views of societal expectations. Research that has tested this theory has shown that young people indeed identify occupations as gender-appropriate or gender-inappropriate, and that there is high agreement among them regarding this gender-based identification (e.g., Turner & Lapan, 2005a).

In examining ways to create career awareness among young people, researchers have found that "the top sources of information are family (parents and relatives), school personnel (teachers and counselors), and friends" (Lane Workforce Partnership, 2011). According to this study, to search out information about careers, 56% of young people go to websites first, followed by television. Less than half find information at job fairs or in the newspaper (Lane Workforce Partnership, 2011). Researchers have also explored the types of information that young people desire to have. In a study conducted in South Africa and Australia among English-speaking, middle- and upper-strata socio-economic 11- to 14-year-olds (McMahon & Watson, 2006), participants expressed a need for information related to life/career implications and life/career management tasks, and to a lesser extent, for information related to interests, personal characteristics, and the nature of work. Life/career implications included information related to stress, earnings, lifestyle, and conditions of employment. Life/career management tasks included information such as how to find jobs or apprenticeships. Information regarding the nature of work included information such as job requirements and skills needed.

Several authors have suggested other ways that career awareness can be promoted among children and adolescents. For example, among elementary children, career awareness can be enhanced by taking them to visit various places of work and discussing with them the types of jobs that people do there (e.g., Beale, 2000). When doing so, counselors can help these children explore what it would be like for a person of the opposite gender to work in the jobs they are exploring (Turner & Lapan, 2005a).

For older children and adolescents, mentoring can help broaden their awareness of various types of occupations, including the job tasks, attitudes, and supports needed to work successfully in that occupation. Research has suggested that mentoring is especially important for young people in rural areas who have less access to role models with expertise in particular types of work. They may also have fewer opportunities to explore through their school curricula how the skills they are learning in school apply to work. In particular, e-mentoring through using advanced technologies, such as video-conferencing, has been shown to be a promising intervention. For example, Li, Moorman, and Dyjur (2010) conducted a mixed-methods study of a semester-long intervention that combined e-mentoring with inquiry-based learning in order to facilitate math performance and the awareness of math careers. Results showed gains in math scores for the treatment group who did receive the intervention, but not the control group who did not receive the intervention. Further, treatment group participants reported a broader understanding of the relevance of math and science, an increased awareness of math and science careers, and a greater engagement and motivation to learn math and science.

Finally, research has suggested that in order for young people to pursue certain specialized careers, they need to gain early awareness of these careers so that they can prepare adequately in pre-high school and high school for entry into training facilities. An example of this is the pursuit of higher-level health careers (e.g., medical doctors, physician assistants), where solid progress in math and science in high school is necessary for subsequent entry into corresponding training programs. In a study that demonstrates how young people can be helped to explore these specialized careers, African American middle-school students participated in a 3-year health career awareness program that emphasized lectures, video presentations, interactive discussions, and college campus visits. Results showed that 55% of the students indicated an interest in pursuing health professions at post-test (Balogun, Sloan, & Hardney, 2005).

Taken together, the literature indicates that young people benefit from interventions designed to enhance their career awareness. These interventions can include (a) providing information in ways that are accessible to young people, (b) helping young people confront gender biases concerning the appropriateness of various careers for men and women at an early age, (c) providing technology-enhanced mentoring, and (d) concentrating on strategies that can help them become aware of specialized careers that require early planning, sometimes prior to entering college, and that are dependent on both high school and college academic performance.

SUPPORTING CAREER DEVELOPMENT

Despite limited research concerning the career development of young children, relationships among such variables as personality traits, vocational interests, perceived competencies, vocational aspirations, and career orientations have been found in children as young as 8 years old (e.g., Prime et al., 2010; Whiston & Brecheisen, 2002). Several studies have yielded evidence supporting hypothesized relationships among personality and career variables (e.g., congruence between interests, intentions, and choices) among early and later adolescents as well (see Brown & Hirschi, Chapter 11, this volume). The results of these and other investigations have led researchers and practitioners toward the goal of more thoroughly understanding the career development needs of young people, and toward establishing empirically supported career interventions.

THE INTEGRATIVE CONTEXTUAL MODEL (ICM) OF CAREER DEVELOPMENT: INTRODUCTION

Career development, as the word suggests, is a "developmental" learning process that evolves throughout our lives (McDaniels & Gysbers, 1992). The term also pertains to the interventions used by practitioners to facilitate age- and situation-appropriate career behaviors across one's lifetime (Herr, 2001; Jones, Dominguez, & Durodoye, 2011). In the Integrative Contextual Model of Career Development, Lapan contends that both aspects of career development need to be considered when preparing school-age youth to creatively and proactively manage the significant challenges they face. School-age youth need to learn sets of skills and develop the types of motivational styles and approaches that will assist them in their efforts to establish satisfying life structures across their lifespans (Super, Savickas, & Super, 1996).

THE INTEGRATIVE CONTEXTUAL MODEL (ICM) OF CAREER DEVELOPMENT: TASKS

At the heart of providing career development services to children and adolescents is the recognition of their need to develop more adaptive, resilient, and proactive approaches to their present situations and possible future career selves (Markus & Nurius, 1986). Lapan (2004) argued that youth are more likely to develop such an approach to the present and future if they can accomplish the following separate, but interrelated tasks: (a) develop positive career-related self-efficacy expectations and attributional styles; (b) form a vocational identity by engaging in more self-directed career exploration and planning activities, setting effective educational and career goals, and making a commitment to reach these goals; (c) learn effective social, prosocial, and work readiness skills and behaviors; (d) construct a better understanding of self, the world of work, and how to best fit in the work world; (e) crystallize personally valued vocational interests; and (f) become empowered to achieve academically and become self-regulated learners. Although these tasks are drawn from different theoretical perspectives, young people who accomplish them are hypothesized to gain adaptive advantages as they enter a world of work characterized by rapid and unpredictable changes (Savickas, 1995), a high demand for personal responsibility and self-determination (Watts, 1996), and an expectation that people should be both agentic and able to adapt flexibly to new challenges without losing their core identities (Flum & Blustein, 2000). These career development tasks are detailed below.

Developing positive career-related self-efficacy expectations and attributional styles. Self-efficacy expectations refer to "beliefs concerning one's ability to successfully perform a given behavior" (Betz, 1994, p. 35). Self-efficacy is task-specific; in the context of this chapter, self-efficacy refers to a person's belief that he or she can successfully engage in academic or career-related tasks (see Lent, Chapter 5, this volume). Self-efficacy expectations have been shown to be predictive of both academic and career outcomes among children and adolescents. For example, self-efficacy has been associated with subject matter interests and persistence in such subjects as math, science, and English (Larose, Ratelle, Guay, Senecal, & Harvey, 2006; Lopez, Lent, Brown, & Gore, 1997; Smith & Fouad, 1999). Self-efficacy expectations have been positively linked to intermediate career developmental tasks, such as career planning and exploration, and to overcoming personal challenges in academic and occupational settings (O'Brien, Dukstein, Jackson, Tomlinson, & Kamatuka, 1999; Turner & Conkel, 2010). Finally, self-efficacy expectations have been found to be correlated with the interests, aspirations, outcome expectations, goals, career pursuits, and career trajectories of both majority and minority youth (e.g., Alliman-Brissett & Turner, 2010; Bandura, Barbaranelli, Vittorio-Caprara, & Pastorelli, 2001).

Research offers some clues about how to develop academic and career-related self-efficacy beliefs in K–12 youth. Bandura (1997) suggested that self-efficacy beliefs develop from four primary sources of information. The first and usually most potent source is personal performance accomplishments (e.g., receiving an A in a math course will increase math self-efficacy if the young person understands that receiving the A is the result of his or her own efforts). The other three sources of information are modeling or vicarious learning (e.g., seeing someone of the same race and gender receive an A in math will strengthen math efficacy), social persuasion (e.g., being complimented for math performance versus being ignored or belittled by teachers, friends, or parents will strengthen math efficacy), and physiological arousal (e.g., heightened perceptions of one's own anxiety while taking a math test will make a student question his or her math abilities). These four sources of self-efficacy information have been found to relate to the development of social (Anderson & Betz, 2001), academic (Usher & Pajares, 2006), math (Joet, Usher, & Bressoux, 2011), science (Britner, 2008), language (Joet et al.), self-regulatory (Usher & Pajare), and career-related (Turner, Alliman-Brissett, Lapan, Udipi, & Ergun, 2003) self-efficacy. For example, in the Turner et al. (2003) study, parents' provision of efficacy information about each of the four source dimensions was positively related to four important adolescent career development outcomes: (a) efficacy to engage in academic and career planning, (b) knowledge of self and others in career and academic contexts, (c) understanding of the relationships between academic achievement and occupational opportunities, and (d) early career decision-making. The results of this study led Turner et al. (2003) to recommend further investigations into how extended families, teachers, and school and career counselors can provide opportunities for adolescents to develop career-related self-efficacy beliefs using Bandura's schema to focus their efforts.

Research on attributional styles also offers potential implications for the development of self-efficacy and related psychological variables (Luzzo, Funk, & Strang, 1996). Positive self-attributional styles refer to young people's confidence that their own skills, abilities, and efforts will determine the bulk of their life experiences, including their educational and career success. More specifically, people with positive attributional styles attribute their successes to themselves, while people with negative attributional styles attribute their failures to themselves. Positive attributional styles have been shown to be related to decreases in perceptions of career barriers among children and adolescents (Albert & Luzzo, 1999). Among high school adolescents, significant positive relationships were found between optimistic attributional styles and career maturity (i.e., vocationally mature attitudes, behavior, and knowledge that characterize adaptive career development during late adolescence and early adulthood) (Powell & Luzzo, 1998). In another study of high school adolescents, relationships were found among internal attributions for success, career planning and exploration, general self-esteem, and school/academic self-esteem (Janeiro, 2010). Among African American adolescents, positive self-attributions predicted work salience (i.e., the perceived importance of work), which in turn predicted career maturity (Naidoo, Bowman, & Gerstein, 1998). Among British final-year school leavers, self-attributions for employment success were found to relate to the use of positive job search strategies (Furnham & Rawles, 1996).

One study examined the effects of attributional retraining on the self-attributions of college students (Luzzo, James, & Luna, 1996). After viewing an eight-minute video presentation designed to foster internal, controllable attributes for career decision making and to challenge faulty attributional beliefs, experimental group participants displayed more positive career beliefs and attributional styles, and exhibited significantly more career exploratory behaviors than did control group participants. Although this type of training has not yet been evaluated among K–12 students, we suggest that developmentally appropriate attributional style training may positively affect the career development of this population as well.

Forming a vocational identity. Vocational identity refers to the integration and crystallization of one's energy, aptitudes, and opportunities into a consistent sense of the uniqueness of one's self and one's fit in the vocational world (see Nauta, Chapter 3, this volume). An adolescent's vocational identity will give clarity and stability to her or his current and future career goals, and will set the stage for her or his future career development. Vocational identity is related to the concept of ego identity (Erikson, 1968) and is achieved through the same cognitive processes as ego identity (i.e., exploration, observation, reflection, and commitment). Vocational identity has been shown to be clearly achieved before ideological, political, or religious identity (Skorikov & Vondracek, 1998). This finding is indicative of the leading role that vocational development plays in adolescent identity formation.

Significant associations between vocational identity and many desirable career outcomes in adolescents have been demonstrated. For example, greater vocational identity clarity was related to the ability to identify and surmount sociopolitical barriers among urban adolescents (Diemer & Blustein, 2006). Higher levels of vocational identity have been associated with more congruent college major choices among gifted high school students (Leung, 1998), and with greater career certainty and career choice commitment among high school adolescents (Ladany, Melincoff, Constantine, & Love, 1997; Schulenberg, Vondracek, & Kim, 1993). The achievement of vocational identity in adolescents has further been associated with (a) strengthening and solidifying reality-based vocational aspirations (Sarriera, Silva, Kabbas, & Lopes, 2001); (b) vocational choice orientation, planning about preferred occupations, and formation of success-creating work attitudes (Wallace-Broscious, Serafica, & Osipow, 1994); and (c) positive mental health indicators, including self-esteem and psychological adjustment (Munson, 1992; Skorikov & Moore, 2001).

Learning effective social, prosocial, and work readiness skills. Work readiness skills are composed of general employability skills (e.g., the ability to accept responsibility and make sound decisions), social competency skills (e.g., the ability to appropriately initiate conversations and appropriately regulate emotions), and prosocial skills (i.e., voluntary behavior intended to benefit another) (Lapan, 2004). Intuitively, one might think that learning these skills is a natural function of the socialization process. Yet in today's complex world, with understaffed schools, fluctuating economies, increasing family and educational transitions, increased residential mobility, and increasing demographic and cultural diversity, counselors concerned with the career development of children and adolescents may need to take a deliberate and proactive stance in the development of these career-related competencies.

Both career researchers and governmental policy makers have recommended a number of other work readiness skills (Bloch, 1996). For example, the Job Training Partnership Act of 1982 identified work readiness skills believed to be necessary to the retraining of displaced workers. These skills include maintaining regular attendance, being punctual, displaying positive work attitudes and behaviors, completing tasks effectively, presenting an appropriate appearance, and demonstrating good interpersonal relationship skills. Lapan (2004) outlined a comprehensive set of skills to help children and adolescents maximize their career potential. These are: (a) social competence (i.e., the ability to build effective relationships), (b) diversity (i.e., the ability and flexibility to successfully interact with coworkers, clients, customers, or students from different cultures), (c) positive work habits (including sound judgment, responsibility, dependability, punctuality, attendance, life planning and management skills, and recognition of and adherence to the legal and ethical standards that govern one's profession), (d) personal management skills (including positive self-attitudes, cleanliness, appropriate dress, both verbal and nonverbal communication skills), and (e) entrepreneurship (including leadership, creativity, desire, motivation, and openness to opportunity). In sum, work readiness skills encompass a diverse range of attitudes and skills, and include positive work habits and attitudes (including punctuality and attendance, taking responsibility and completing tasks effectively, demonstrating sound judgment and dressing appropriately), social and prosocial competencies (including initiating conversations, interacting successfully with diverse persons, regulating emotions, and building relationships), and entrepreneurship skills (including taking on leadership roles and added responsibilities at work).

Research has shown that adult workers who possess adequate work readiness skills experience greater work satisfaction (Meir, Melamed, & Abu-Freha, 1990). Other investigators have found that greater work readiness skills lead to more integration into the work environment (Ashford & Black, 1996), a stronger commitment to the organization in which one is employed (Fisher, 1985), more successful job performance (Ashford & Black), fewer job turnovers, and greater workplace rewards (Wanberg & Kammeyer-Mueller, 2000).

A small body of literature suggests that work readiness skills can be developed within family and classroom environments. For example, Naimark and Pearce (1985) hypothesized that children learn skills within the family that can be transferred to the workplace, such as goal setting, decision making, scheduling, budgeting, leading, nurturing, and communicating. Harkins (2001) suggested that work readiness skills can be learned through direct instruction and should be infused into the classroom curriculum. Munson and Rubenstein (1992) suggested that school personnel, such as school counselors and career educators, are in an ideal position to contribute to a student's sense of work, work values, work habits, and work behaviors.

A more extensive body of literature suggests that work readiness skills can also be developed through children's friendships and peer group interactions. For example, researchers have shown that, within peer groups, children have opportunities to learn (a) social skills, such as successfully exchanging information, being clear in one's communication with others, and engaging in appropriate self-disclosure (Gottman, 1983), and (b) prosocial skills such as empathy and treating others with justice and kindness (Youniss, 1980). Gaining these social and prosocial skills can facilitate greater workplace stamina and adjustment (Ladd & Kochenderfer, 1996) by promoting such worker characteristics as stability, resilience, self-esteem, self-efficacy, and adaptability (Rigby & Slee, 1993). We maintain that psychologists, counselors, and career educators can help shape children's family, school, and community contexts (e.g., facilitating peer groups in the community) in ways that promote the growth of those critical work readiness skills that are the foundation for a wide range of work readiness behaviors in adulthood (Lapan, 2004).

Constructing a better understanding of oneself, the world of work, and one's fit in the work world. Constructing a better understanding of oneself, the world of work, and how one best fits in the world of work has been the foundation of vocational psychology since Frank Parsons (1909) first introduced these concepts. Both career development researchers and counselors have focused on helping career clients understand their abilities, interests, values, and personality styles; the specifics of current labor market information; and how to make better and more satisfying career decisions. However, in the past several years, researchers have noted that children and adolescents experience special challenges in constructing their career pathways. Three of these challenges, discussed in this section, are gender-based circumscription of vocational aspirations, career decision-making readiness, and school-to-school/school-to-work transitioning.

Gottfredson's Theory of Circumscription and Compromise (1981, 2002, 2005) has generated much research and has helped us better understand the process of *gender-based circumscription of vocational aspirations*. These studies generally have shown that adolescents do indeed circumscribe their vocational interests, self-efficacy expectations, outcome expectations, and prestige expectations according to their social valuation of occupations as either gender appropriate or gender inappropriate (e.g., Lapan, Hinkelman, Adams, & Turner, 1999). This process of circumscription (i.e., continual narrowing of occupations that one will consider) and compromise (i.e., eliminating the most preferred options for less compatible ones) can result in young people sacrificing the fulfillment of their "internal unique selves" by choosing occupations that they perceive to be more socially acceptable (Gottfredson, 2002). Circumscription of vocational aspirations has been shown to begin in early childhood (Henderson, Hesketh, & Tuffin, 1988), with children identifying segments of the occupational world as unattainable. The process continues throughout middle and later adolescence during which time adolescents make vocational preparation decisions that can affect their ability to enter into more prestigious, lucrative, or congruent occupations (Leung & Harmon, 1990; Mendez & Crawford, 2002). One of the most disturbing outcomes of the circumscription process is young women's frequent avoidance of the more highly paid and higher prestige math, science, and technology-based careers (Lapan & Jingeleski, 1992).

However, research has shown that the process of circumscription can be countered. In a study conducted with middle school students (Turner & Lapan, 2005a), young people participated in constructing a map that reflected their career interests, efficacy concerning working in specific careers, and gender-typing of careers in which they were both interested and not interested. Overall, constructing these maps demonstrated to participants that they had greater interests and efficacy for careers that they also believed were more gender-appropriate for them. They then participated in group discussions with their peers and a group leader that were intended to increase their understanding of ways that women and men can enter into and become successfully employed in gender-nontraditional careers. Results indicated that young adolescents' career-related self-efficacy and interests in non-traditional careers can be increased through participation in this type of career intervention. Thus, helping young people understand how socialization has impacted their own views of acceptable careers, and helping them to make informed choices that can counter those views, can be important targets for career development interventions, especially during the years before their occupational possibilities become substantially circumscribed (see Gottfredson, 2005; Lent, Chapter 5, this volume).

Career decision-making readiness represents the second challenge that many adolescents face in constructing their career pathways. Piaget (1977) theorized that sometime during early adolescence (approximately at age 12), young people undergo a fundamental shift in the way they view the world by moving away from concrete thinking toward more abstract, logical thinking. During this stage of cognitive development, adolescents begin to think more scientifically, design and test multiple hypotheses, and manipulate objects, operations, and future outcomes in their minds. Physical maturation, experience, and socialization allow young adolescents to envision not only what they will be like in the future, but also how they will implement what they conceive themselves to be.

Building on Piaget (1977) and Gottfredson (1981, 2005), information processing theorists have argued that cognitive development can be strongly influenced and circumscription lessened through cognitive interventions (e.g., information sharing, knowledge construction, learning critical thinking skills; Case, 1991; Siegler, 1991). Career theorists who adhere to an information processing approach advocate sequential training in problem-solving as a prerequisite to adolescent career decision-making (see Gottfredson, 2005 for a more complete discussion). For example, Sampson, Peterson, Lenz, and Reardon (1992) proposed that adolescents be trained in the cycle of information processing skills used in career decision-making, which are: (a) problem identification, (b) analyzing the causes of the problem and the relationships among the problem components, (c) synthesizing possible courses of action through elaboration and crystallization, (d) evaluating each course of action, and (e) implementing and executing a plan of action. Despite disagreement in the research literature concerning when adolescents have the cognitive maturity to make career decisions, there is general agreement about the value of improving students' problem-solving and career decision-making competencies (Patton & Creed, 2001).

Helping children and adolescents know how best to fit into the world of work can also be accomplished through *facilitating school-to-school and school-to-work transitioning*. Transitioning has been described as a prolonged and increasingly complex process for young persons (Bynner, Chisholm, & Furlong, 1997; Jones & Wallace, 1992). Transitioning is characterized for many children by few institutional supports, the prolongation of education, and a multitude of options that combine school, work, and family in unique ways (Mortimer, Zimmer-Gembeck, Holmes, & Shanahan, 2002). Although the literature is sparse in this area, research has shown that transitioning can be accompanied by negative thoughts and emotions that may diminish children's and adolescents' ability to achieve, explore, and plan at the level of their abilities, especially for students who are already vulnerable.

For example, transitioning from grade school to junior high school has been associated with decreases in self-esteem in ethnically diverse adolescents living in poverty (Seidman, Lambert, Allen, & Aber, 2003). Transitioning from primary to secondary school has been found to be accompanied by fears of bullying, getting lost, increased workload, and more challenging peer relationships (Zeedyk et al., 2003). Among young adults, the deployment of maladaptive strategies, such as passive avoidance and external control attributions (i.e., a sense that one's personal destiny is controlled more by others than by oneself), has been associated with increased difficulties in dealing with school-to-work transitions (Maeaettae, Nurmi, & Majava, 2002). This avoidance behavior could arguably be said to begin in childhood, which suggests that earlier interventions might provide young people with the cognitive behavioral strategies to be more successful in their school-to-school and school-to-work transitioning.

Research and theory have suggested ways to help children and adolescents engage in school-to-school and school-to-work transitioning (Juntunen & Wettersten, 2005). For example, Phillips, Blustein, Jobin-Davis, and Finkelberg White (2002) argued that the use of resources in an adolescent's environment (e.g., supportive available adults, siblings, peers) can be associated with clearer transitional plans. Lapan, Tucker, Kim, and Kosciulek (2003) found that the career development activities recommended by the School-To-Work Opportunities Act—in particular, school-based learning, work-based learning, connecting activities (e.g., job shadowing), and stakeholder support (e.g., from teachers, counselors, parents)—predicted grades, interests, expectations, goals/actions, and person–environment fit among high school students. Shanahan, Mortimer, and Krueger (2002) proposed that helping adolescents recognize connections between school and work might assist them in preparing for school-to-work transitions. Worth (2002) suggested that assisting adolescents to enhance their flexibility in decision making might help them to better adapt to more precarious employment situations and increase their opportunities in a quickly changing labor market. Together, these studies suggest a number of activities that might promote more successful school-to-school and school-to-work transitions among children and adolescents, including helping them to (a) marshal appropriate support from their family, friends, and school environments; (b) engage in school- and work-based learning opportunities that would help them appreciate the important connection between school achievement and later work attainment, and (c) develop flexible, but effective, decision-making skills.

Crystallizing personally valued vocational interests. Many theorists have highlighted the importance of interests in young people's career development (see earlier chapters in this volume). The foundation of career interests is hypothesized to be based on genetic factors, accounting for about a third of the variance in interests (Betsworth & Fouad, 1997), as well as such factors as young people's self-exploration activities, self-efficacy expectations, and outcome expectations (e.g., values) (see Nauta, Chapter 3, Hartung, Chapter 4, and Lent, Chapter 5, this volume).

The crystallization of interests implies the formation of young people's career interests into a defined and somewhat permanent structure. Career interests begin to develop and become clarified during the early high school years and often crystallize at the point of educational and vocational transitions (Mortimer et al., 2002). The crystallization of interests occurs when adolescents recognize that they must make choices about how to fit into a complex world (Sharf, 2002). Crystallization requires adolescents to weigh their values (for instance, choosing occupations that are altruistic, or ones that are expressive of their personal moral views), clarify their vocational goals, and begin to commit to occupational preparation. During subsequent developmental stages, this initial commitment is reanalyzed, with continuing reflection on the value of previous occupational choices (Cochran, 1997).

Research has suggested that not all children and adolescents have the opportunity to crystallize personally valued vocational interests. Social forces, such as uneven educational opportunities, uneven environmental supports, discrimination, and cultural and gender-based valuing of various careers (Gottfredson, 2005) may seriously hinder the crystallization of personally valued interests. Indeed, recent research has shown that the value systems underlying young people's vocational interests are systematically tied to social origin and early experiences, are highly influenced by the social manifestations of race and gender, and change the most when adolescents come to terms with the limits of their opportunities (Johnson, 2002). We suggest that career counselors are in key positions to help all young people crystallize personally valued interests by (a) designing strategies to help them explore the underlying dimensions of their interests and expand their awareness of vocational possibilities, and (b) working for community awareness, social justice, and advocacy for children and adolescents who may be disadvantaged in the marketplace due to their race, socio-economic status, or gender.

Empowering all students to achieve academically and become self-regulated learners. *Self-regulated learning* is defined as an active, constructive process whereby learners set goals for their learning and then attempt to monitor, regulate, and control their cognitions, motivations, and behaviors (Pintrich, 2000). Zimmerman (2000) construed self-regulated learning as the monitoring of one's own planning, performance, and the expected and real outcomes of any learning activity, whether interesting or uninteresting. Self-regulated learning promotes both academic achievement and lifelong learning (Lapan, Kardash, & Turner, 2002).

Research has shown that self-regulation promotes goal motivation and direction (McWhaw & Abrami, 2001), effort intensity and task performance (Boekaerts, 1997), academic performance and achievement (Pintrich & de Groot, 1990; Wolters, 1999), and positive self- and other-expectations (Zimmerman, 2000). Further, schools, families, and communities can work together to promote and enhance self-regulated learning among K–12 youth through identifying programs that effectively promote academic achievement, instituting mutual accountability structures and practices, and supporting the learning of children from different social contexts (Lapan & Kosciulek, 2001).

THE INTEGRATIVE CONTEXTUAL MODEL (ICM) OF CAREER DEVELOPMENT: MOTIVATIONS AND MOTIVATIONAL APPROACHES

Motivations, such as hope or the desire for enjoyment, provide persons with a reason to act in a certain way. Motivations are related to initiation, persistence (Lapan, 2004), and production. Motivational approaches (i.e., those behaviors that are engaged in to satisfy one's motivations) are both the antecedents to and the consequences of the interrelationships between the ICM skills and career outcomes, meaning that young people who have certain motivations (e.g., hope) are more likely to engage in skill development and that skill development and positive outcomes from this development serve to further reinforce or increase their motivations. An example of this is seen in a study (Sung, Turner, & Kaewchinda, in press) in which researchers examined the relationships among hope, ICM skills, and outcomes. Results showed that hope predicted both skills and outcomes, and that developing skills and experiencing positive outcomes in turn predicted hope.

In addition to hope, other studies have found relationships among ICM skills, motivational approaches, and career development outcomes, such as proactivity, assertiveness, problem-solving orientation, awareness of opportunity, seeking opportunities, creating opportunities, capitalizing on skills and abilities, active preparation, adaptability, and flexibility (Turner, Conkel, Starkey, & Landgraf, 2010). The next section summarizes the results of studies investigating the usefulness of the ICM model to describe the career development of young people and a study on the effectiveness of an intervention based on ICM.

Research on the Integrative Contextual Model of Career Development

When examining the usefulness of the ICM model to describe the career development of young people, researchers have deconstructed the ICM career development tasks into a set of six interrelated career development skills (career exploration, person–environment fit, goal setting, social/prosocial/work readiness, self-regulated learning, and the utilization of emotional and instrumental support) and six vocational outcomes (academic achievement, educational and career-related self-efficacy expectations, positive self-attributions, vocational interests, vocational identity, and proactivity). Tests of the model among Native American adolescents (Turner et al., 2006) that was replicated in undergraduate college students (Sung et al., in press) showed that ICM skills together predicted from 65% to 75% of the variance in five of the six vocational outcomes (the exception was academic achievement).

The ICM model has also been used to develop a career intervention. In a pre-post study among multiethnic seventh- and eighth-grade students, Turner and Conkel (2010) compared the ICM intervention, and a traditional career counseling intervention to a no-treatment condition. The traditional intervention consisted of students completing the Self-Directed Search (Holland, 1997), participating in a discussion of individual results, and completing a structured protocol of occupational exploration activities based on these results. They were then assisted by the researchers in considering the pros and cons of working in their top choice career, and how aspects of their vocational personalities matched with the occupational requirements of this choice. Finally, they discussed how they could work toward the goal of entering their top occupational choice, and how they could obtain the required education for that occupation.

The ICM intervention was a combination of the traditional career counseling intervention, in which participants completed all of the activities completed by students in the traditional intervention group, plus a set of activities based on the ICM model. These additional activities were focused on assisting students to develop skills related to (a) social/prosocial/work readiness, (b) career exploration, (c) person–environment fit, (d) goal setting, (e) self-regulated learning, and (f) garnering emotional and instrumental support for overcoming educational and career barriers.

Results showed that only adolescents who participated in the combined traditional and ICM intervention reported improved career development outcomes in comparison to the control-group participants. Specifically, students in the combined intervention condition reported greater (a) person–environment fit; (b) social, prosocial, and work readiness skills; (c) efficacy for reaching their career goals; and (d) emotional and instrumental support than did control group participants who completed no career development activities. There were no differences in reported skills or outcomes between students who completed only the traditional career counseling intervention and control group students.

Collectively, the results of these studies suggest that the ICM is useful when describing the career development of young people and that interventions based on the ICM seem to be effective when used to increase career development skills and outcomes among adolescents. Because research based on the ICM model is still limited, more investigation of this model and how it can be used to enhance young people's career development is necessary.

PROMOTING SCHOOL SUCCESS

In today's global economy, school success is foundational to career development success. For example, research has shown that students who take and pass a rigorous set of core courses in high school, in which they achieve subject matter mastery, are more likely to achieve success in college than students who take a less rigorous high school curriculum (for a review, see American College Testing, 2010). Achieving academic success in the middle school years seems to be related to achieving high school academic success and to the types of educational and career aspirations that students report when they graduate from high school. In fact, one large-scale study showed that the educational and occupational aspirations that students reported in eighth grade were the strongest predictors of these students' twelfth-grade educational and occupational aspirations (Rojewski & Yang, 1997). Even more troubling was the finding that the best predictor of students' eighth-grade aspirations was their academic performance in their elementary and middle school years. This research, therefore, suggests that efforts to help elementary and middle school students achieve academic success may have long-term positive consequences on their later levels of academic success and on their educational and career aspirations. Indeed, Lapan, Turner, and Pierce (in press) suggested that the academic deficits that students bring with them into high school are not likely to be overcome unless they receive substantial remediation while they are in the seventh and eighth grades.

Other research has shown that academic discipline (i.e., student effort and conscientiousness), academic challenge, and having opportunities for active and collaborative learning are all also related to high school academic achievement (Fuller, Wilson, & Tobin, 2011; Robbins, Allen, Casillas, Peterson, & Le, 2006). Academic challenge and support seem to be especially critical to school success. For example, in a 10-year longitudinal intervention study designed to increase graduation rates, researchers found that achievement in both reading and math was related to teachers' expectations and the degree to which classes were challenging (i.e., more successful students reported that their teachers had high expectations for them and challenged them in class) (Mason-Chagil et al., 2011).

Parent support has also been shown to be important to school and career success. Marjoribanks (2002) demonstrated that parents' perceived aspirations for their adolescent children had medium to large associations with their adolescents' educational aspirations and small but significant associations with their occupational aspirations. Smith and Hausafus (1998) found that middle school minority students had higher test scores in math when their parents helped them to see the importance of taking advanced math courses, emphasized the importance of math for today's careers, and supported their children's participation in extracurricular math/science activities. Hoyt (2001) argued that young people do not necessarily understand the link between higher education and more lucrative employment opportunities. Therefore, parents should be enlisted to help adolescents explore a wide variety of educational options in order to choose those that are best suited to their needs.

Research has also shown that academic achievement and school success can be promoted by career development interventions, especially if career interventions are intensive and integrated into the school curriculum, and students receive more than one year of career services (Evans & Burck, 1992). Other research has found positive relations between diverse students' level of involvement in career planning activities and school engagement (Kenny, Blustein, Hasse, Jackson, & Perry, 2006), and one study found that the relation between career planning activities and academic performance among a diverse sample of urban high school students could be fully explained by school engagement (Perry, Liu, & Pabian, 2010). Thus, career development activities may promote academic success because students who participate in these activities show more school involvement and engagement than students who do not participate or who are not afforded such opportunities.

One example of an intensive and integrated intervention was provided by Lapan, Gysbers, Hughey, and Arni (1993). This joint program between school counselors and language arts teachers was offered to 166 high school juniors. School counselors presented extensive in-class career exploration exercises. These included opportunities for adolescents to understand their own goals, interests, personalities, and talents, to gather information about the world of work through computer-assisted and other reference materials, and to reflect upon how to create more career support from other students within their immediate peer group. At the same time, the language arts teachers worked with students on composing a research paper that addressed their post–high school transition plans. After statistically controlling for prior academic achievement, gains in the students' career development competencies (e.g., career planning and exploration, understanding how being male or female relates to jobs and careers, understanding how education and careers are related) were significantly associated with grades.

Other studies have shown that work-based learning and community/career partnerships can support greater school success. Results of studies of workplace learning activities suggest that those who participate in workplace learning programs, versus those who do not, gain employment at higher rates, obtain larger initial salaries, and show longer retention rates (U.S. Department of Labor, 1996).

Community/career partnerships allow students as young as 15 years old to hold part-time jobs during part of their school day while they are under the supervision of both their career education instructor and their employer. In the career education classes, students learn job and life skills such as interviewing and job acquisition techniques (e.g., using labor market information to find jobs), how to manage personal resources (e.g., balancing a checking account), and skills needed for self-sufficient living (e.g., preparing a budget). While at work, they practice the interpersonal skills, basic literacy skills (e.g., writing, math, and English language skills), and job skills required to become successful full-time employees. The results of the studies discussed in this section of the chapter suggest that counselors providing career services to K–12 clients in order to promote school success should carefully plan interventions so that they incorporate and integrate both academic and career development activities (e.g., Kenny et al., 2006), involve parents whenever possible, connect to real-world work-related experiences, and achieve support from community/career partnerships.

CONCLUSIONS AND PRACTICE IMPLICATIONS

In this chapter, we have examined how career development professionals can assist K–12 youth to develop career awareness, acquire career development strategies and skills, and experience school success. We have maintained that career awareness is developmental and have suggested that to enhance career awareness, young people should be (a) given developmentally appropriate career information, (b) assisted in confronting gender biases at an early age, (c) provided opportunities to participate in technology-enhanced mentoring, and (d) introduced to specialized careers that require earlier planning and educational attainment that begins in high school.

In the area of career development strategies and skills, we have reviewed the Integrative Contextual Model (ICM) of Career Development (Lapan, 2004), and discussed emerging research that indicates that learning ICM skills and developing specific, positive motivations and motivational approaches can support young people's career development success. Critical ICM skills appear to be (a) developing positive career-related self-efficacy beliefs and attributional styles, (b) forming a vocational identity, (c) learning effective social, prosocial, and work readiness skills and behaviors, (d) constructing an understanding of the self, the world of work, and the fit between the two, (e) crystallizing personally valued vocational interests, and (f) becoming empowered to achieve academically and engage in self-regulated learning.

In the area of promoting school success, we have demonstrated that both academic and career development interventions are important in supporting school achievement and that school achievement as early as junior high school can have long-range ramifications on later academic and occupational achievement. We suggest that career interventions should be consistently and intentionally provided for all children and adolescents, according to their individual needs and circumstances, and that incorporating support from parents, encouraging teachers to challenge students, and engaging in community/career partnerships are also important to fostering school achievement via career development.

Finally, we hope that this chapter has acquainted the reader with some of the positive results that career interventions can offer to children and adolescents. Creating career awareness, supporting career development, and promoting school success can be accomplished through providing skillful and informed career services to school-age youth and can meaningfully assist them in establishing more satisfying, productive, and fulfilling adult lives.

REFERENCES

Albert, K. A., & Luzzo, D. A. (1999). The role of perceived barriers in career development: A social cognitive perspective. *Journal of Counseling and Development, 77*, 431–436.

Alliman-Brissett, A. E., & Turner, S. L. (2010). Racism, parent support, and math-based career interests, efficacy, and outcome expectations among African American adolescents. *Journal of Black Psychology, 36*, 197–225.

American College Testing. (2010). *Issues in college readiness: What are ACT's college readiness benchmarks?* Retrieved from http://www.act.org/research/policymakers/pdf/benchmarks.pdf

Anderson, S. L., & Betz, N. E. (2001). Sources of social self-efficacy expectations: Their measurement and relation to career development. *Journal of Vocational Behavior, 58*, 98–117.

Ashford, S. J., & Black, J. S. (1996). Proactivity during organizational entry: The role of desire for control. *Journal of Applied Psychology, 81*, 199–214.

Balogun, J. A., Sloan, P. E., & Hardney, K. (2005). Health professions career awareness program for seventh- and eighth-grade African-American students: A pilot study. *Journal of Allied Health, 34*, 236–243.

Bandura, A. (1997). *Self-efficacy: The exercise of control.* New York, NY: W. H. Freeman/Times Books/Henry Holt.

Bandura, A. Barbaranelli, C., Vittorio-Caprara, G., & Pastorelli, C. (2001). Self-efficacy beliefs as shapers of children's aspirations and career trajectories. *Child Development, 72*, 187–206.

Beale, A. V. (2000). Elementary school career awareness: A visit to a hospital. *Journal of Career Development, 27*, 65–72.

Betsworth, D. G., & Fouad, N. A. (1997). Vocational interests: A look at the past 70 years and a glance at the future. *Career Development Quarterly, 46*, 23–47.

Betz, N. E. (1994). Basic issues and concepts in career counseling for women. In B. W. Walsh & S. H. Osipow (Eds.), *Career counseling for women: Contemporary topics in vocational psychology* (pp. 1–41). Hillsdale, NJ: Erlbaum.

Bloch, D. T. (1996). Career development and workforce preparation: Educational policy versus school practice. *Career Development Quarterly, 45*, 20–40.

Boekaerts, M. (1997). Self-regulated learning: A new concept embraced by researchers, policy makers, educators, teachers, and students. *Learning & Instruction, 7*, 161–186.

Britner, S. L. (2008). Motivation in high school science students: A comparison of gender differences in life, physical, and earth science classes. *Journal of Research in Science Teaching, 45*, 955–970.

Bynner, J., Chisholm, L., & Furlong, A. (1997). *Youth, citizenship, and social change in a European context.* Brookfield, VT: Ashgate.

Case, R. (1991). *The mind's staircase: Exploring the conceptual underpinnings of children's thought and knowledge.* Hillsdale, NJ: Erlbaum.

Cochran, L. (1997). *Career counseling: A narrative approach.* Thousand Oaks, CA: Sage.

Diemer, M. A., & Blustein, D. L. (2006). Critical consciousness and career development among urban youth. *Journal of Vocational Behavior, 68*, 220–232.

Erikson, E. (1968). *Identity: Youth and crisis.* New York, NY: W. W. Norton.

Evans, J. H., & Burck, H. D. (1992). The effects of career education interventions on academic achievement: A meta-analysis. *Journal of Counseling & Development, 71,* 63–68.

Fisher, C. D. (1985). Social support and adjustment to work: A longitudinal study. *Journal of Management, 11,* 39–53.

Flum, H., & Blustein, D. L. (2000). Reinvigorating the study of vocational exploration: A framework for research. *Journal of Vocational Behavior, 56,* 380–404.

Fuller, M. B., Wilson, M. A., & Tobin, R. M. (2011). The National Survey of Student Engagement as a predictor of undergraduate GPA: A cross-sectional and longitudinal examination. *Assessment & Evaluation in Higher Education, 36,* 735–748.

Furnham, A., & Rawles, R. (1996). Job search strategies, attitudes to school and attributions about unemployment. *Journal of Adolescence, 19,* 355–369.

Ginzberg, E., Ginsburg, S. W., Axelrad, S., & Herma, J. L. (1950). The problem of occupational choice. *American Journal of Orthopsychiatry, 20,* 166–201.

Gottfredson, L. S. (1981). Circumscription and compromise: A developmental theory of occupational aspirations. *Journal of Counseling Psychology, 28,* 545–579.

Gottfredson, L. S. (2002). Gottfredson's theory of circumscription, compromise, and self-creation. In D. Brown (Ed.), *Career choice and development* (4th ed., pp. 85–148). San Francisco, CA: Jossey-Bass.

Gottfredson, L. S. (2005). Applying Gottfredson's theory of circumscription and compromise in career guidance and counseling. In S. D. Brown & R. W. Lent (Eds.), *Career development and counseling: Putting theory and research to work* (pp. 71–100). Hoboken, NJ: Wiley.

Gottman, J. M. (1983). How children become friends. *Monographs of the Society for Research in Child Development [No. 201], 48,* 86.

Harkins, M. A. (2001). Developmentally appropriate career guidance: Building concepts to last a lifetime. *Early Childhood Education Journal, 28,* 169–174.

Henderson, S., Hesketh, B., & Tuffin, K. (1988). A test of Gottfredson's theory of circumscription. *Journal of Vocational Behavior, 32,* 37–48.

Herr, E. L. (2001). The impact of national policies, economics and school reform on comprehensive guidance programs. *Professional School Counseling, 4,* 236–245.

Hill, J. M. M. (1969). *The transition from school to work: A study of the child's changing perception of work from the age of seven.* London, UK: Tavistock Institute of Human Relations.

Holland, J. L. (1997). *Making vocational choices: A theory of vocational personalities and work environments* (3rd ed.). Odessa, FL: Psychological Assessment Resources.

Hoyt, K. B. (2001). Helping high school students broaden their knowledge of postsecondary education options. *Professional School Counseling, 5,* 6–12.

Janeiro, I. N. (2010). Motivational dynamics in the development of career attitudes among adolescents. *Journal of Vocational Behavior, 76,* 170–177.

Joet, G., Usher, E. L., & Bressoux, P. (2011). Sources of self-efficacy: An investigation of elementary school students in France. *Journal of Educational Psychology, 103,* 649–663.

Johnson, M. K. (2002). Social origins, adolescent experiences, and work value trajectories during the transition to adulthood. *Social Forces, 80,* 1307–1341.

Jones, B., Dominguez, C. S., & Durodoye, B. (2011). Career maturity and ethnically diverse high school students. *Career Convergence Web Magazine.* Retrieved from http://associationdatabase.com/aws/NCDA/pt/sd/news_article/5522/_PARENT/layout_details_cc/false

Jonesa, G., & Wallace, C. (1992). *Youth, family and citizenship.* Buckingham, UK: Open University Press.

Juntunen, C. L., & Wettersten, K. B. (2005). Broadening our understanding of work-bound youth: A challenge for career counseling. In S. D. Brown, & R. W. Lent (Eds.), *Career development and counseling: Putting theory and research to work* (pp. 573–599). Hoboken, NJ: Wiley.

Kenny, M. E., Blustein, D. L., Haase, R. F., Jackson, J., & Perry, J. C. (2006). Setting the stage: Career development and the student engagement process. *Journal of Counseling Psychology, 53,* 272–279.

Ladany, N., Melincoff, D. S., Constantine, M. G., & Love, R. (1997). At-risk urban high school students' commitment to career choices. *Journal of Counseling & Development, 76,* 45–52.

Ladd, G. W., & Kochenderfer, B. J. (1996). Linkages between friendship and adjustment during early school transitions. In W. M. Bukowski, A. F. Newcomb, & W. W. Hartup (Eds.), *The company they keep: Friendship in childhood and adolescence. Cambridge studies in social and emotional development* (pp. 322–345). New York, NY: Cambridge University Press.

Lane Workforce Partnership. (2011). *Youth awareness of middle skill jobs.* Retrieved from http://laneworkforce.org/youth-services/youth-career-awareness-task-force/youth-career-awareness-task-force-survey-results/

Lapan, R. T. (2004). *Career development across the K–16 years: Bridging the present to satisfying and successful futures.* Alexandria, VA: American Counseling Association.

Lapan, R. T., Gysbers, N., Hughey, K., & Arni, T. J. (1993). Evaluating a guidance and language arts unit for high school juniors. *Journal of Counseling & Development, 71,* 444–451.

Lapan, R. T., Hinkelman, J. M., Adams, A., & Turner, S. (1999). Understanding rural adolescents' interests, values, and efficacy expectations. *Journal of Career Development, 26,* 107–124.

Lapan, R. T., & Jingeleski, J. (1992). Circumscribing vocational aspirations in junior high school. *Journal of Counseling Psychology, 39,* 81–90.

Lapan, R. T., Kardash, C. A. M., & Turner, S. (2002). Empowering students to become self-regulated learners. *Professional School Counseling, 5,* 257–265.

Lapan, R. T., & Kosciulek, J. F. (2001). Toward a community career system program evaluation framework. *Journal of Counseling & Development, 79,* 3–15.

Lapan, R. T., Tucker, B., Kim, S., & Kosciulek, J. F. (2003). Preparing rural adolescents for post high-school transitions. *Journal of Counseling and Development, 81,* 329–342.

Lapan, R. T., Turner, S. L., & Pierce, M. E. (in press). College and career readiness: Policy and research to support effective counseling in schools. In N. A. Fouad, J. A. Carter, & L. M. Subich (Eds.), *APA handbook of counseling psychology.* Washington, DC: American Psychological Association.

Larose, S., Ratelle, C. F., Guay, F., Senecal, C., & Harvey, M. (2006). Trajectories of science self-efficacy beliefs during the college transition and academic and vocational adjustment in science and technology programs. *Educational Research and Evaluation, 12,* 373–393.

Leung, S. A. (1998). Vocational identity and career choice congruence of gifted and talented high school students. *Counselling Psychology Quarterly, 11,* 325–335.

Leung, S. A., & Harmon, L. W. (1990). Individual and sex differences in the zone of acceptable alternatives. *Journal of Counseling Psychology, 37,* 153–159.

Li, Q., Moorman, L., & Dyjur, P. (2010). Inquiry-based learning and e-mentoring via videoconference: A study of mathematics and science learning of Canadian rural students. *Education Technology, Research, and Development, 58,* 729–753.

Lopez, F. G., Lent, R. W., Brown, S. D., & Gore, P. A. (1997). Role of social-cognitive expectations in high school students' mathematics-related interest and performance. *Journal of Counseling Psychology, 44,* 44–52.

Luzzo, D. A., Funk, D. P., & Strang, J. (1996). Attributional retraining increases career decision-making self-efficacy. *Career Development Quarterly, 44,* 378–386.

Luzzo, D. A., James, T., & Luna, M. (1996). Effects of attributional retraining on the career beliefs and career exploration behavior of college students. *Journal of Counseling Psychology, 43,* 415–422.

Maeaettae, S., Nurmi, J. E., & Majava, E. M. (2002). Young adults' achievement and attributional strategies in the transition from school to work: Antecedents and consequences. *European Journal of Personality, 16,* 295–312.

Marjoribanks, K. (2002). Family contexts, individual characteristics, proximal settings, and adolescents' aspirations. *Psychological Reports, 91*(3, Pt1), 769–779.

Markus, H., & Nurius, P. (1986). Possible selves. *American Psychologist, 41,* 954–969.

Mason-Chagil, G., Turner, S. L., Pabon, M., Conkel, J. L., Joeng, J., Landgraf, R., ... Dade, S. N. (2011). *Bush high school completion program.* Unpublished report, Bush Foundation, Minneapolis, MN.

McDaniels, C., & Gysbers, N. C. (1992). *Counseling for career development: Theories, resources, and practice.* San Francisco, CA: Jossey-Bass.

McMahon, M., & Watson, M. (2006). Occupational information: What children want to know. *GIPO Giornale Italiano Di Psicologia Dell'Orientamento, 7*(3), 41–46.

McWhaw, K., & Abrami, P. C. (2001). Student goal orientation and interest: Effects on students' use of self-regulated learning strategies. *Contemporary Educational Psychology, 26,* 311–329.

Meir, E. I., Melamed, S., & Abu-Freha, A. (1990). Vocational, avocational, and skill utilization congruences and their relationship with well-being in two cultures. *Journal of Vocational Behavior, 36,* 153–165.

Mendez, L. M. R., & Crawford, K. M. (2002). Gender-role stereotyping and career aspirations: A comparison of gifted early adolescent boys and girls. *Journal of Secondary Gifted Education, 13,* 96–107.

Mortimer, J. T., Zimmer-Gembeck, M. J., Holmes, M., & Shanahan, M. J. (2002). The process of occupational decision making: Patterns during the transition to adulthood. *Journal of Vocational Behavior, 61,* 439–465.

Munson, H. L., & Rubenstein, B. J. (1992). School IS work: Work task learning in the classroom. *Journal of Career Development, 18,* 289–297.

Munson, W. W. (1992). Self-esteem, vocational identity, and career salience in high school students. *Career Development Quarterly, 40*, 361–368.

Naidoo, A. V., Bowman, S. L., & Gerstein, L. H. (1998). Demographics, causality, work salience, and the career maturity of African-American students: A causal model. *Journal of Vocational Behavior, 53*, 15–27.

Naimark, H., & Pearce, S. (1985). Transferable skills: One link between work and family. *Journal of Career Development, 12*, 48–54.

O'Brien, K. M., Dukstein, R. D., Jackson, S. L., Tomlinson, M. J., & Kamatuka, N. A. (1999). Broadening career horizons for students in at-risk environments. *Career Development Quarterly, 47*, 215–229.

Parsons, F. (1909). *Choosing a vocation*. Boston, MA: Houghton Mifflin.

Patton, W., & Creed, P. A. (2001). Developmental issues in career maturity and career decision status. *Career Development Quarterly, 49*, 336–351.

Perry, J. C., Liu, X., & Pabian, Y. (2010). School engagement as a mediator of academic performance among urban youth: The role of career preparation, parental career support, and teacher support. *Counseling Psychologist, 38*, 269–295.

Phillips, S. D., Blustein, D. L., Jobin-Davis, K., & Finkelberg White, S. (2002). Preparations for the school-to-work transition: The views of high school students. *Journal of Vocational Behavior, 61*, 202–216.

Piaget, J. (1977). *The development of thought: Equilibration of cognitive structures*. New York, NY: Viking.

Pintrich, P. R. (2000). The role of goal orientation in self-regulated learning. In M. Boekaerts, P. R. Pintrich, & M. Zeidner (Eds.), *Handbook of self-regulation* (pp. 452–502). New York, NY: Academic Press.

Pintrich, P. R., & de Groot, E. V. (1990). Motivational and self-regulated learning components of classroom academic performance. *Journal of Educational Psychology, 82*, 33–40.

Powell, D. F., & Luzzo, D. A. (1998). Evaluating factors associated with the career maturity of high school students. *Career Development Quarterly, 47*, 145–158.

Prime, D. R., Nota, L., Ferrari, L., Schultheiss, D. E. P., Soresi, S., & Tracey, T. J. G. (2010). Correspondence of children's anticipated vocations, perceived competencies, and interests: Results from an Italian sample. *Journal of Vocational Behavior, 77*, 58–62.

Rigby, K., & Slee, P. T. (1993). Dimensions of interpersonal relations among Australian school children and their implications for psychological well-being. *Journal of Social Psychology, 133*, 33–42.

Robbins, S. B., Allen, J., Casillas, A., Peterson, C. H., & Le, H. (2006). Unraveling the differential effects of motivational and skills, social, and self-management measures from traditional predictors of college outcomes. *Journal of Educational Psychology, 98*, 598–616.

Rojewski, J. W., & Yang, B. (1997). Longitudinal analysis of select influences on adolescent occupational aspirations. *Journal of Vocational Behavior, 51*, 375–410.

Sampson, J. P., Peterson, G. W., Lenz, J., & Reardon, R. C. (1992). A cognitive approach to career services: Translating concepts into practice. *Career Development Quarterly, 41*, 67–74.

Sarriera, J. C., Silva, M. A., Kabbas, C. P., & Lopes, V. B. (2001). Occupational identity formation in adolescents. *Estudos de Psicologia, 6,* 27–32.

Savickas, M. L. (1995). Current theoretical issues in vocational psychology: Convergence, divergence, and schism. In W. B. Walsh & S. H. Osipow (Eds.), *Handbook of vocational psychology* (2nd ed., pp. 1–34). Mahwah, NJ: Erlbaum.

Schulenberg, J., Vondracek, F. W., & Kim, J. (1993). Career certainty and short-term changes in work values during adolescence. *Career Development Quarterly, 41,* 268–284.

Seidman, E., Lambert, L. E., Allen, L., & Aber, J. L. (2003). Urban adolescents' transition to junior high school and protective family transactions. *Journal of Early Adolescence, 23,* 166–193.

Shanahan, M. J., Mortimer, J. T., & Krueger, H. (2002). Adolescence and adult work in the twenty-first century. *Journal of Research on Adolescence, 12,* 99–120.

Sharf, R. S. (2002). *Applying career development theory to counseling* (3rd ed.). Belmont, CA: Brooks/Cole.

Siegler, R. S. (1991). *Children's thinking.* Englewood Cliffs, NJ: Prentice-Hall.

Skorikov, V. B., & Moore, S. (2001, August). *Relationships between career development and mental health: Implications of research.* Paper presented at the 109th annual convention of the American Psychological Association, San Francisco, CA.

Skorikov, V., & Vondracek, F. W. (1998). Vocational identity development: Its relationship to other identity domains and to overall identity development. *Journal of Career Assessment, 6,* 13–35.

Smith, F. M., & Hausafus, C. O. (1998). Relationship of family support and ethnic minority students' achievement in science and mathematics. *Science Education, 82,* 111–125.

Smith, P. L., & Fouad, N. A. (1999). Subject-matter specificity of self-efficacy, outcome expectancies, interests, and goals: Implications for the social-cognitive model. *Journal of Counseling Psychology, 46,* 461–471.

Sung, Y., Turner, S. L., & Kaewchinda, M. (in press). *Career development skills, outcomes, and hope among college students.*

Super, D. E., Savickas, M. L., & Super, C. M. (1996). The life-span life-space approach to careers. In D. Brown, L. Brooks, & Associates (Eds.), *Career choice and development* (3rd ed., pp. 121–178). San Francisco, CA: Jossey-Bass.

Turner, S. L., Alliman-Brissett, A. E., Lapan, R. T., Udipi, S., & Ergun, D. (2003). The Career-Related Parent Support Scale. *Measurement and Evaluation in Counseling and Development, 36,* 83–94.

Turner, S. L., & Conkel, J. L. (2010). Evaluation of a career development skills intervention with adolescents living in an inner city. *Journal of Counseling & Development, 88,* 457–465.

Turner, S. L., Conkel, J., Starkey, M., & Landgraf, R. (2010). Relationships among middle school adolescents' vocational skills, motivational approaches, and interests. *Career Development Quarterly, 59,* 154–168.

Turner, S. L., & Lapan, R. T. (2005a). Evaluation of an intervention to increase adolescents' efficacy and interests in non-traditional careers. *Journal of Vocational Behavior, 66,* 516–531.

Turner, S. L., & Lapan, R. T. (2005b). Promoting career development and aspirations in school-age youth. In S. D. Brown & R. W. Lent (Eds.), *Career development and counseling: Putting theory and research to work* (pp. 417–440). Hoboken, NJ: Wiley.

Turner, S. L., Trotter, M. J., Lapan, R. T., Czajka, K. A., Yang, P., & Brissett, A. E. (2006). Vocational skills and outcomes among Native American adolescents: A test of the Integrative Contextual Model of Career Development. *Career Development Quarterly, 54,* 216–226.

U.S. Department of Labor, Employment and Training Administration. (1996). *Involving employers in training: Best practices.* Retrieved from http://wdr.doleta .gov/opr/fulltext/97-practices.pdf

Usher, E. L., & Pajares, F. (2006). Sources of academic and self-regulatory efficacy beliefs of entering middle school students. *Contemporary Educational Psychology, 31,* 125–141.

Wallace-Broscious, A., Serafica, F. C., & Osipow, S. H. (1994). Adolescent career development: Relationships to self-concept and identity status. *Journal of Research on Adolescence, 4,* 127–149.

Wanberg, C. R., & Kammeyer-Mueller, J. D. (2000). Predictors and outcomes of proactivity in the socialization process. *Journal of Applied Psychology, 85,* 373–385.

Watts, A. G. (1996). Toward a policy for lifelong career development: A transatlantic perspective. *Career Development Quarterly, 45,* 41–53.

Whiston, S. C., & Brecheisen, B. K. (2002). Practice and research in career counseling and development–2001. *Career Development Quarterly, 51,* 98–154.

Wolters, C. A. (1999). The relation between high school students' motivational regulation and their use of learning strategies, effort, and classroom performance. *Learning & Individual Differences, 11,* 281–299.

Worth, S. (2002). Education and employability: School leavers' attitudes to the prospect of non-standard work. *Journal of Education & Work, 15,* 163–180.

Youniss, J. (1980). *Parents and peers in social development.* Chicago, IL: University of Chicago Press.

Zeedyk, M. S., Gallacher, J., Henderson, M., Hope, G., Husband, B., & Lindsay, K. (2003). Negotiating the transition from primary to secondary school: Perceptions of pupils, parents and teachers. *School Psychology International, 24,* 67–79.

Zimmerman, B. J. (2000). Attaining self-regulation: A social cognitive perspective. In M. Boekaerts, P. R. Pintrich, & M. Zeidner (Eds.), *Handbook of self-regulation* (pp. 13–39). New York, NY: Academic Press.

CHAPTER 20

Promotion of Career Choices

SUSAN C. WHISTON AND BARBARA NOBLIN JAMES

A S MILLER AND BROWN (2005) wrote, most individuals in developed countries at some time during their lives either make or remake decisions about work. Career choice or decision making is often the focus of career counseling: The counselor helps an individual or group of individuals decide on a career path and make academic decisions related to that choice, to select types of occupations to pursue, to decide whether to leave one occupational field and pursue another, or to make other work-related decisions. Various environmental and contextual factors can impede career development and the career choice process; therefore, it is important that counselors know about strategies to promote the career choices. This chapter is based on more than 50 years of research related to career counseling in which the goal is to help individuals choose or decide on a career path. Our aim with this chapter is to summarize this research with the intent of providing practical suggestions for practitioners who are working with clients who are struggling with career choices and decisions.

In a chapter on the promotion of career choice interventions, it is first important to define what is meant by both promotion and career choice. We define *career choice* very broadly to include decisions that are made throughout the life span, and our discussion includes both proximal and distal factors related to career choice. Following the lead of Ryan (1999), we suggest that career choice consists of intentions, plans, or aspirations related to engaging in a career direction and that proximal measures are indices of career certainty, decidedness, or commitment. We further view career choice as a process and suggest that there are also distal factors that contribute to career choice. Ryan labeled these as intermediate outcome variables and contended that a number of theoretically derived factors ultimately influence career choice, such as vocational identity and congruence (from person–environment fit approaches), career maturity (from developmental approaches), and career decision-making self-efficacy, perceived environmental supports, and perceived career choice barriers (from social cognitive career approaches) (see, respectively, Chapters 3, 4, and 5, this volume). Therefore, in our summary of activities that promote career choice, we have included both proximal and distal measures of outcome.

Concerning the term *promotion*, we have primarily focused on interventions or activities counselors or clinicians can implement that promote or facilitate career choice or career choice-related outcomes. In this focus on interventions, we do not intend to dismiss the aspects of society (e.g., educational systems) that either promote or stifle career choice; however, the audience for this book is practitioners. Therefore, we address what clinicians can do to facilitate career choice. This clinical focus is based on a growing body of research that provides insight into specific types of interventions found to facilitate career choice, which ultimately results in people selecting occupations that optimize their chances of being successful in and satisfied with their work.

EFFECTIVENESS OF CAREER CHOICE INTERVENTIONS

Meta-analytic studies are often used to determine the effectiveness of psychological and educational interventions because meta-analyses combine the results from many individual studies quantitatively and yield an overall index of the magnitude of the effects of the intervention (often called an effect size). The most common effect size used in counseling outcome research is the standardized mean difference effect size. This effect size index can be interpreted as how far one group's mean (e.g., the counseled group) fell from the other group's mean (e.g., a control group who received no counseling). Thus, for example, an effect size of 1.00 suggests that the counseled clients improved a standard deviation more than control clients, whereas an effect size of 0.00 means that there was no difference between the two groups. Obviously, the larger the effect size, the stronger the treatment effect. Cohen (1988) provided some guidelines with which to interpret effect sizes, suggesting that effect sizes of .20, .50, and .80 represent small, medium, and large effects, respectively. In career counseling, a number of meta-analyses (e.g., Brown & Ryan Krane, 2000; Oliver & Spokane, 1988; Spokane & Oliver, 1983; Whiston, Sexton, & Lasoff, 1998) have examined whether those who received a career intervention fare better on outcome measures than those who did not receive any type of career intervention. Of these meta-analyses, Brown and Ryan Krane's (2000) study is the only one that examined the effectiveness of career counseling interventions specifically on measures of career choice. Brown and Ryan Krane's study was an extension of Ryan's (1999) series of meta-analyses, which provide unique insight into the overall effectiveness of career choice-related interventions. Using a sophisticated weighting system to calculate effect size, Brown and Ryan Krane (2000) found that career choice interventions had an average effect size of .34. This means that those who received the career choice intervention improved on the outcome measures about one-third of a standard deviation more than those who did not receive the intervention. Whiston and colleagues (1998) did not limit their meta-analysis to career choice-related outcomes; however, they did calculate separate average effect sizes based on categories of outcome measure. They found a sufficient number of studies to calculate effect sizes for two outcomes related to career choice (i.e., level of decidedness and career maturity). Whiston and colleagues found an average effect size of .19 for decidedness and .55 for career maturity. Using Cohen's (1988) commonly used method, the effect sizes for career choice interventions found by Brown and Ryan Krane and Whiston and colleagues would range from small to moderate. Brown and Ryan Krane, however, found that the magnitude of the effect sizes varied depending on the types of interventions that were used to facilitate career choice.

Although the findings regarding overall effect sizes for career counseling interventions that promote career choice are somewhat mixed, there is a growing body of literature indicating that certain interventions can have long-terms effects. For example, Hirschi and Läge (2008) found that Swiss middle school students who received a 2-day, nine-module career intervention had higher scores in terms of both career exploration and vocational identity than the control group 3 months after completing the interventions. Also with Swiss clients, Perdrix, Stauffer, Masdonati, Massoudi, and Rossier (2012) examined the effectiveness of four to five sessions of career counseling based on work adjustment theory (see Swanson & Schneider, Chapter 2, this volume) and social cognitive career theory (see Lent, Chapter 5, this volume) at a 3-month and 1-year follow-up. They found that the majority of clients followed an *implementation* path (64%), meaning that most clients had implemented the career project developed during counseling within a year after completing career counseling. Further, Perdrix and colleagues found that increases in life satisfaction evident immediately after counseling remained stable for a year after treatment and that career decision-making difficulties showed a continual decline during the year. Finally, Lapan, Aoyagi, and Kayson (2007) found that enhanced career development in high school was significantly connected to more successful career transitions and to greater satisfaction with life 3 years after graduation from high school.

FACTORS THAT CONTRIBUTE TO EFFECTIVENESS

For practitioners, it is not enough to know that career choice interventions are, on average, moderately effective and that their effects appear to be sustained over time. Practitioners need also to understand factors that contribute to effectiveness so that they can consider these when choosing strategies to help clients with career choice difficulties. For this reason, we dedicate the largest portion of this chapter to summarizing factors that have emerged as salient to the creation of effective career choice interventions with the caveat that this list is ever growing and that future research is needed to flesh out and add to this list. We cover here the following factors: client preferences, dose effects, critical ingredients, process factors, modalities, and client factors. Before beginning these sections, however, note that much of this research has been conducted with college students. As an example, Whiston (2002) found that of the studies published between 1950 and 1996 that compared a career counseling intervention to a control group, 49% of the studies were conducted with a college-age sample.

CLIENT PREFERENCES

In terms of their preferences before seeking career counseling, Galassi, Crace, Martin, James, and Wallace (1992) found that college students prefer to talk about specific careers or decision making, explore careers in general, explore self, and gain new information about careers and majors. These clients, however, anticipated that the career counseling would primarily involve exploring self and taking tests. Shivy and Koehly (2002) found that college students prefer career services involving direct interaction with employed individuals, such as participation in an internship experience, the opportunity to interview people at their worksite, or attending a career fair.

In developing a measure to assess clients' attitudes toward career counseling, Rochlen, Mohr, and Hargrove (1999) found that male college students were more likely to report a higher stigma attached to career counseling than female college students. In contrast, Shivy and Koehly (2002) found college students' perceptions of, and preference for, career services did not vary based on gender. In examining why male college students would or would not seek career counseling, Rochlen and O'Brien (2002a) found that males would seek career counseling to receive direct advice, general career assistance, and help with job placement, as well as to increase career options; their reasons for not seeking career counseling were inconvenience, preferences for solving problems without assistance from others, a lack of need (i.e., already decided), and doubts about the potential utility of the service. Therefore, these studies tended to indicate that men prefer career counseling that involves a more directive, advice-giving style and a reluctance to become involved in a process that involves self-exploration. This is consistent with Rochlen and O'Brien's (2002b) findings that after viewing two videotaped career counseling sessions, men tended to prefer a more directive approach to career counseling over a more contextual, emotionally oriented approach. What is noteworthy is that more recent research has tended to focus on the preferences of men and that clinicians have less information related to women's career counseling preferences.

In addition, two recent studies have explored whether individuals' expectations and attitudes toward career counseling can be changed based on some type of role induction. Fouad and colleagues (2007) compared two role induction protocols—one focusing on the holistic nature of career counseling and the other offering a very narrow definition of career counseling—versus a no role induction control group. They found very few differences among the three conditions. Conversely, Whitaker, Phillips, and Tokar (2004) hypothesized that people often believe the role of the career counselor is to inform them of what they "should be." These researchers tested whether viewing a video of an initial session in which the counselor focused on the client's involvement in the process and the counselor's role as a guide through the process would affect expectations of career counseling. Whitaker and colleagues found that those who viewed the preparatory video as compared to a nonpreparatory video reported higher levels of personal commitment to career counseling and viewed the counselor as less of an expert who would inform them of their career direction than as a guide who would help them through the process of deciding. Particularly with career counseling that focuses on career choice, it may be important for practitioners to consider some form of role induction, which encourages client participation and clearly articulates the role of the counselor as a guide through the process and not as an authority on the client's future career direction.

Dose Effect

Analogous to medical or pharmaceutical research, where the interest is on how much of the prescribed treatment is necessary, the area in intervention research that examines the number of sessions or the length of the treatment is often called the dose effect. In Oliver and Spokane's (1988) meta-analysis, the only significant predictor of effect size was treatment intensity (number of hours and number of sessions entered as a block). In plotting the number of sessions by outcome, Brown and Ryan Krane (2000) found an interesting relationship between effect size and number of sessions. They found an effect size (ES) of .24 with one session, an ES = .47 for two to three sessions, and an ES = 1.26 for four to five sessions; however, the effect sizes precipitously decreased after four to five sessions. These results led Brown and Ryan Krane to conclude that career choice counseling can probably best be implemented in four to five sessions. However, Brown and Ryan Krane found that it was not simply the number of sessions that influenced outcome; what mattered most was whether certain ingredients were contained in the career choice counseling.

CRITICAL INGREDIENTS

Ryan (1999) proposed that although past meta-analyses (Oliver & Spokane, 1988; Whiston et al., 1998) were helpful in determining the overall effectiveness of career counseling interventions and in beginning to identify variables that underlie effectiveness, further investigation was warranted to tease out the processes that are involved in effective career choice counseling interventions. Stated more specifically, she sought to determine what was actually *happening in* effective career choice counseling sessions. Her series of meta-analyses yielded the identification of five broad categories of interventions that were present in and associated with higher effect sizes on measures of career choice outcomes (most often in career maturity). These interventions yielded larger effect sizes beyond what could be accounted for by client, modality, treatment intensity, therapist, or method variables.

These five broad categories were later labeled the "critical ingredients" of career choice counseling by Brown and Ryan Krane (2000). Brown and Ryan Krane found not only that they seemed to be individually important to at least one career choice outcome but also that combinations of them yielded larger effect sizes than did any one individually. They found that interventions that included none of the critical ingredients resulted in an effect size of only .22, whereas adding one, two, and three of the critical ingredients resulted in effect sizes of .45, .61, and .99, respectively. Because none of the studies involved in the meta-analyses employed more than three of the critical ingredients, it was not possible for them to determine the aggregate effect size of the use of all five together. However, Brown and colleagues (2003) were able to verify that the linear pattern created by the addition of each component was not due to the alternative explanation that "more of anything" is better. They found, in fact, random combinations of the five noncritical ingredients produced either flat or no relationship at all to effect size, which is in stark contrast to the linear model produced by the addition of each of the critical ingredients.

The following is a brief description of the five critical ingredients: workbook/written exercises, counselor–client dialogue (later called "interpretations and feedback"), information about the world of work, modeling, and increasing environmental supports. These five critical ingredients provide the foundation for evidence-based career choice interventions and speak directly to what practitioners can do to help clients in choosing or rechoosing careers.

Workbook/written exercises. The workbook activities that were effective ranged from sentence completion to journaling and included prescribed activities completed by clients in booklets, as well as personal logs and diaries. Brown and Ryan Krane (2000) reported that this group of interventions has the goal of getting clients to reflect on their own thoughts, concerns, questions, or curiosities related to their personal career development while helping clients to establish and plan activities toward meeting career goals. Brown and colleagues (2003) found that larger effect sizes were associated with written exercises that included two notable activities: (1) opportunities for written occupational analysis and comparison and (2) an opportunity to engage in goal setting and future planning at the end of the intervention. This critical ingredient involved in getting clients to physically write down information related to their career search is consistent with instructional effectiveness research, which indicates that *written* note taking, homework, and summarization are among the most effective teaching and learning strategies because they increase understanding and retention of information (Marzano & Brown, 2009; Marzano, Pickering, & Pollock, 2001).

Individualized interpretations and feedback. This ingredient is made up of face-to-face interactions (or other direct forms of communication such as telephone) between client and counselor, regardless of whether the intervention is performed in a classroom, a group, or individually. Group interventions in which individualized attention was provided yielded better career choice outcomes than ones that did not include this critical ingredient (Brown et al., 2003). Individualized interpretation and feedback could involve the counselor providing written or verbal feedback to the client on specific assignments (e.g., on goal setting) or throughout the process of counseling. Additionally, helping clients understand and use personal assessment data is part of this ingredient, especially if the assessment results are anomalous or otherwise hard to understand (e.g., inconsistent RIASEC profiles; see Nauta, Chapter 3, this volume).

Although Brown and Ryan Krane (2000) identified individual interpretations as one of the critical ingredients, there is little outcome research related to precisely how practitioners should interpret the results of career assessments. In analyzing studies published between 1983 and 1995, Whiston and colleagues (1998) found no treatment/control comparison studies that addressed individual test interpretation. Based on only two studies, Oliver and Spokane (1988) found an unweighted effect size of .62 for individual test interpretation. Fortunately, Chapters 14 through 17 of this book address assessment in career counseling and provide practitioners with detailed suggestions on using assessments in the areas of interests; needs and values; abilities, aptitudes, and skills; and other career constructs.

Information about the world of work. Brown and colleagues (2003) defined this ingredient as the provision of opportunities in session to gather information on the world of work and on specific career options. This ingredient can seem even more critical today when one considers the enormous changes that have occurred in the world of work due to the changing global economy, changing gender roles, and the technology boom of the last two decades. Now, more than ever, clients who are making or remaking career choices need to be armed with information about the environment, expectations, and options within the world of work (DeBell, 2006). Clients can easily become overwhelmed in the face of such enormity and benefit from gathering some of this information and processing it in session. Although occupational information has typically been a part of career counseling, Brown and Ryan Krane's (2000) findings clearly indicate that it is important to process that information in session.

Modeling. Providing clients with examples of others who have been successful in making or remaking a career choice decision is the basis of modeling (Ryan, 1999). This process can actually take many forms. For instance, practitioners can model this personally through sharing career experiences, personal illustrations of using the Holland codes to select careers for exploration, or other career decision-making experiences. Other forms of modeling include exposing clients to mentors or guest speakers (e.g., in workshops or class interventions). Video presentations may also be implemented as part of this ingredient as a substitute or supplement to other forms of modeling. Group career counseling or class modalities could include opportunities for participants to learn from each other's successful career choice-making experiences. However, it is important to note that although all of the studies in the Ryan (1999) meta-analysis that implemented modeling strategies yielded significant effect sizes, Brown and colleagues (2003) found that those studies that employed "expert" modeling yielded much larger effect sizes than those that used "peer" modeling. Therefore, although peer-to-peer modeling may benefit clients, clinicians should consider avoiding its use as the sole modeling intervention in a career-choice program.

Increasing environmental supports. Ryan (1999) defined this critical ingredient as "providing clients with practical suggestions, information, or assistance concerning how to obtain more financial or emotional support from their environment" (p. 88). Because career choice making or remaking is a process accomplished in a context and not in isolation within a client's life, many factors could serve to spur on or inhibit a client's career choices. For instance, perceived barriers (e.g., family role definition or family responsibilities) might impede implementation of a career goal, whereas a myriad of protective factors (e.g., supportive family or school environment) may facilitate confidence in the career choice, ultimately leading to successful transition into that occupation.

Brown and colleagues (2003) found surprisingly few studies that examined attention to building support, but those that did yielded an average effect size of .83. Of those studies included in Brown and colleagues' analysis, most concerned building parental support for career choice. These findings are consistent with Whiston and Keller's (2004) finding that parental support, particularly for individuals of color, plays a key role in the career development of adolescents and young adults. These findings are also consistent with some of the central tenets of social cognitive career theory (see Lent, Chapter 5, this volume), in which support plays a critical role in overcoming career barriers and influences both self-efficacy and outcome expectations. Nevertheless, this critical ingredient, out of the five critical ingredients, has the least research supporting it. Therefore, Brown and colleagues encouraged practitioners to combine this intervention with written exercises by having clients write down potential obstacles to successful choice making and possible sources from which to draw support for overcoming these obstacles.

Although none of the studies in Brown and Ryan Krane's (2000) meta-analysis included more than three of the five critical ingredients, some recent studies have included more or all of the ingredients with primarily positive results. Hirschi and Läge (2008) conducted workshops based on all of the critical ingredients with Swiss adolescents. They found that, compared to a control condition, the intervention group had higher scores on career decidedness, career planning, career exploration, and vocational identity measures at both postintervention and at a 12-week follow-up. Also with clients from Switzerland, Masdonati, Massoudi, and Rossier (2009) evaluated the effectiveness of individual career counseling that included four of the five critical ingredients (i.e., workbooks and written exercises, individualized interpretation and feedback, world of work information, and attention to building support). The pretest–posttest comparisons reflected quite large effect sizes, with the effect size for life satisfaction of .68 and the effect size for career decision-making difficulties of .98. Perdrix and colleagues (2012), following up with these same clients a year later, found a continued decrease in career indecision and maintenance of gains in clients' satisfaction with life. In refining a career counseling course for American college students based on the critical ingredients, Reese and Miller (2010) found that the course consistently improved career decision-making self-efficacy but had a less consistent influence on career decision-making difficulties.

For practitioners involved in career choice counseling, there is strong empirical support for the five critical ingredients. Juntunen (2006) hypothesized that sometimes practitioners shy away from addressing clients' vocational issues because they have little knowledge about best practices, and the five critical ingredients provide sound guidance for these clinicians. The five critical ingredients can be applicable either for clients who present with career choice dilemmas or for clients in which vocational choice issues unfold during the counseling process. What is important is the degree of empirical support for the five critical ingredients and, therefore, the confidence practitioners can have in using these interventions in session with clients.

OTHER PROCESS FACTORS

Heppner and Heppner (2003) referred to career counseling process variables as the overt and covert thoughts, feelings, and behaviors of both clients and counselors while engaged in counseling. The five critical ingredients found by Brown and colleagues (Brown & Ryan Krane, 2000; Brown et al., 2003) are process factors that a counselor would engage in while conducting career choice counseling; however, there are other process factors in career choice counseling that have been empirically explored. These process factors may influence career choice outcomes, but the research results are not so compelling as to merit the label of critical ingredients.

Although Meara and Patton (1994) contended that the client–counselor working alliance is an essential process component within career counseling, there has been limited research on the influence of the working alliance in career counseling compared to psychotherapy (Heppner & Heppner, 2003). Lewis (2001) did not find a difference between the working alliance scores of clients in either career or personal counseling. Perdrix, de Roten, Kolly, and Rossier (2010) compared the working alliance scores of Swiss clients in career counseling and those in personal counseling. They found no difference in terms of bond or agreement on tasks, but they did find that career counseling clients tended to report higher scores related to agreement on goals than the clients in personal counseling. In another study with Swiss clients, Masdonati, Massoudi, and Rossier (2009) found that the working alliance at the end of four to five sessions of individual career counseling was significantly related to outcome measured as increased life satisfaction and decreased career decision-making difficulty.

In an interesting study of process variables, Littman-Ovadia (2008) examined the interaction among clients' attachment styles and counselors' functioning as a secure base. Not all of the clients in this study were in counseling to address career choice issues, although career choice was the focus of counseling for the majority (65%). In a general indication of the effectiveness of career counseling, Littman-Ovadia found that all clients, irrespective of attachment style, were more likely to engage in career exploration at the end of the career counseling as compared to the beginning. She also found that clients either high or low in anxiety or avoidance tendencies were equally likely to engage in career exploration after working with counselors who were adept at providing a secure base. Hence, counselors who were high in caregiving behaviors appeared to have a crucial influence on the career exploration activities of clients across attachment styles.

MODALITIES

Although Brown and Ryan Krane (2000) found that the five critical ingredients influenced career choice outcome measures across different treatment modalities, there is a body of research related to the effectiveness of different treatment modalities. Whiston and colleagues (1998) found individual career counseling to have the largest effect size (ES = .75) as compared to other modalities (e.g., group, classes), and the gains associated with individual counseling were accomplished on average in less than a single hour. In calculating effect sizes related to career choice, Brown and Ryan Krane (2000) found that group counseling had the largest effect sizes (ES = .55), followed by class (ES = .43) and individual counseling (ES = .41). In considering career interventions for the promotion of career choice, Folsom and Reardon (2003) examined the effectiveness of career courses at colleges and universities. They found that in 34 of the 38 studies identified, career counseling courses resulted in positive outcomes related to career maturity, career decision making, vocational identity and thoughts, and locus of control. Further, when the outcomes were course satisfaction and retention (both to the next semester and until graduation), 13 of the 15 studies had positive findings.

Whiston, Brechiesen, and Stephens (2003) compared the effectiveness of different career modalities and did not find that one approach was significantly more effective than another. Conversely, they did find that one modality, counselor-free interventions (e.g., computers program used in isolation), was significantly *less* effective than any other type of treatment that involved counseling. This finding was consistent with Whiston and colleagues' (1998) earlier report of a nonsignificant effect size (ES = .11) for counselor-free interventions.

Practitioners should consider Whiston and colleagues' (2003) finding that counselor-free interventions are less effective than modalities that involve counselors in the development of career interventions, and, whenever possible, counseling activities should be integrated into career development programming. Some schools and counseling organizations are investing in computer-assisted career guidance systems (e.g., DISCOVER, SIGI³) to provide career assistance. These programs are also available through the Internet, and individuals can easily use them in isolation. Although some of these programs are quite comprehensive, Gore, Bobek, Robbins, and Shayne (2006) found that only 3% of students could be classified as "in-depth" users who utilized a comprehensive program for more than 1 hour; the majority used one of these programs only once and for less than 30 minutes. It may be difficult for a 30-minute intervention to have much impact, which reinforces the need for career counseling to accompany the use of computer-assisted career guidance systems. This is consistent with Whiston and colleagues' (2003) findings that computer-assisted career guidance systems supplemented by counseling were found to have significantly better outcomes than interventions that relied solely on the computerized system. Hence, practitioners can be assured that their role in career counseling is particularly vital and adds value beyond simple exposure to computerized programs.

CLIENT FACTORS

In a seminal article, Fretz (1981) made a plea for more research related to the question of which clients benefit from what type of career counseling. Fretz's call for research on client aptitude-by-treatment interactions is still relevant today as we are beginning to examine client attributes or aptitudes and how they interact with certain types of career counseling. Although there are many client factors that may be of interest to practitioners, we have limited our discussion to client factors that have been empirically investigated and where there is sufficient research to draw some conclusions related to practice.

Age. In considering client factors that may contribute to the promotion of career choice, practitioners may be interested in whether different types of treatments work better with clients of different ages. Related to college students, Mau and Fernandes (2001) found that younger college students (i.e., less than 26 years old) were more likely to use career counseling services than older students, but there were no differences between the two age groups related to their satisfaction with career counseling.

Sometimes there are questions about whether interventions designed to promote career choice are most effective for adolescents and college students and less effective with other age groups. In an interesting study of Swiss clients, Perdrix and colleagues (2012) compared career choice counseling received by younger clients (14 to 21 years old) versus older clients (22 to 56 years old). The clients received four or five sessions of career counseling that contained four of five of Brown and Ryan Krane's (2000) critical ingredients. At the 1-year follow-up, both groups had the same sustained satisfaction, but some interesting differences occurred in changes in career decision-making difficulties between the two groups: Younger clients' career decision difficulties continued to decrease between the time they finished counseling and the time of the 1-year follow-up. However, older clients' career decision-making difficulty decreased only during the time of the counseling and then stabilized. In general, however, Perdrix and colleagues' results indicate that career choice counseling is effective with adolescents, young adults, and older adults.

Gender. In their meta-analysis, Brown and Ryan Krane (2000) found 18 studies that compared whether males or females benefited more from career counseling. Only 3 of the 18 studies reported significant outcome differences between men and women. Interestingly, in each of those three studies, women had higher levels of career maturity at posttreatment than men. Mau and Fernandes (2001) found no significant gender difference in terms of usage of career counseling services at a university; however, they found that women reported slightly higher levels of satisfaction with career counseling than men. Conversely, Healy (2001) did not find gender differences in terms of satisfaction with either a brief career program or a more in-depth individual career counseling approach.

Race and ethnicity. In terms of race and ethnicity, neither Ryan (1999) nor Whiston and colleagues (1998) were able to analyze effect sizes with diverse groups because race and ethnicity information was so infrequently reported. Carter, Scales, Juby, Collins, and Wan (2003), however, found that race was related to the number of sessions students attended at a university-based career development center. They found that, on average, Black students were most likely to attend only one session, whereas Asian and Hispanic students were most likely to attend two to nine sessions. White students were most likely to attend 10 or more sessions. This trend is disturbing, as Fouad and Byars-Winston's (2005) meta-analysis found that racial and ethnic minorities perceived fewer career opportunities and greater career barriers than their White counterparts. Interestingly, in a meta-analysis,

Nichols (2009) hypothesized that there would be an inverse relation between the percentage of racial and ethnic minorities in a study and effect size (i.e., effect size would go down as the percentage of people of color increased). Although they did not find support for this hypothesis, they did find a relationship between career maturity effect sizes and the degree to which the career interventions were intentionally tailored to clients' developmental levels and to cultural factors.

An excellent example of a research program related to career interventions with one group of clients is Kim and colleagues' research related to the career counseling process with Asian American clients. Kim and Atkinson (2002) examined the impact on the career counseling process of Asian American clients' adherence to Asian values and counselors' ethnicity and expression of cultural values. Counselors were trained to conduct a career counseling session based on a trait-factor theory and to express either Asian or U.S. cultural values during the session. Although the researchers postulated that the Asian American clients would evaluate the sessions conducted by Asian American counselors more positively than those conducted by European American counselors, they found that the Asian American clients rated the sessions as more positive and arousing if they were conducted by European American counselors. However, clients' adherence to cultural values played an important role in their evaluation of the session: Clients with high (versus low) adherence to Asian values rated the Asian counselors as being more empathetic and credible.

Kim, Li, and Liang (2002) also evaluated Asian American clients' experiences in career counseling based on their level of adherence to Asian values, and their results were also somewhat contradictory. In general, Asian American clients rated the session as being better if the counselors focused on immediate problem resolution as compared to insight attainment. However, contrary to expectations, clients with high adherence to Asian cultural values tended to evaluate the counselors as being more empathic and the working alliance as stronger than clients with low adherence to Asian cultural values. In addition, clients with high adherence to Asian values tended to perceive the counselor as being more cross-culturally competent if the counselor focused on the expression of feelings as compared to counselors who focused on the expression of cognition.

Li and Kim (2004) had less equivocal results when they examined Asian American clients' cultural values and a directive versus a nondirective form of career counseling. They found that regardless of cultural values, Asian American clients preferred a directive style of career counseling. These findings are noteworthy, as they indicate that in practice, clinicians should not just consider race or ethnicity but also consider adherence to cultural values. Moreover, the results indicate that adherence to cultural values and evaluation of the career counseling process is complex; therefore, counselors should not make assumptions about the counseling process based on simplistic stereotypes.

In a rare study that compared treatment designed specifically for diverse adolescents (i.e., integrative contextual model) versus treatment as usual, Turner and Conkel (2010) found that those in the integrative contextual model group (see Turner & Lapan, Chapter 19, this volume) reported more emotional support than those in the treatment as usual group. This finding may be related to the integrative contextual model's focus on the utilization of social support in regard to overcoming societal and career barriers, which is similar to Brown and Ryan Krane's (2000) critical ingredient of building support. Therefore, the critical ingredient of building social support for a career decision may be particularly germane in working with diverse clients.

Problem-solving appraisal. Making a career choice is similar to solving a problem, and, thus, better problem solvers may have better outcomes in career counseling. Heppner and colleagues (2004) examined the role of clients' problem-solving appraisal on process and outcome factors in career counseling. Not only did these researchers examine clients' problem-solving abilities at the start of counseling and how they affected outcome but also they examined whether changes in problem-solving appraisal during the course of career counseling affected outcome (i.e., did those whose abilities to solve problems increased during career counseling have better outcomes?). Their adult clients participated in at least three sessions of career counseling. Heppner and colleagues (2004) found that problem-solving appraisal scores and other measures of outcome increased between the beginning and the end of career counseling. They also found that clients who entered counseling with high versus low problem-solving appraisal skills were more likely to become more decisive about their careers as a result of the career counseling.

Lee, Park, and Heppner (2009) reanalyzed Heppner and colleagues' (2004) data using a cross-lagged panel design and verified Heppner and colleagues' contention that counselors should consider clients' precounseling problem-solving abilities in designing career interventions. Heppner and colleagues (2004) also found that if clients experience a positive change in terms of problem-solving appraisal during career counseling, they were more likely to have better psychological resources in career transitions and greater goal directedness at the end of the career counseling than clients whose problem-solving abilities did not increase. These results indicate that practitioners should consider clients' abilities to solve problems at the beginning of career counseling and attempt to increase their abilities to solve problems through the career counseling process.

In conclusion, as this discussion reflects, researchers have not been very successful in identifying which types of career choice interventions are more effective with different types of clients. This may be related to the client characteristics that researchers have been studying, which have primarily been demographic variables (e.g., age, gender). What may be more pertinent is to use diagnostic criteria as the basis for treatment decisions. Using psychotherapy as an analogy, researchers may not be considering that some clients are depressed whereas others are anxious and are providing the same treatment to both sets of clients. Rounds and Tinsley (1984) called for the development of a vocational problem diagnostic scheme that both researchers and practitioners could use to identify clients who need more in-depth services versus those who may need help in a single area. Therefore, the development of a vocational diagnostic system may provide a good starting point for tailoring treatment to the needs of the client.

DECISION-MAKING DIFFICULTIES

In terms of diagnostic schemes relevant to career choice counseling, researchers have made significant progress in targeting clients' difficulties with career decision making. One of the first to make a diagnostic distinction was Salomone (1982), when he differentiated between undecided and indecisive clients. According to Salomone, an undecided client is someone who has yet to make a decision but for whom the process is normal and common; by contrast, an indecisive client is someone who has chronic problems with decision making, and the chronicity of the decision-making problems is rooted in psychological issues. Salomone's distinction between undecided and indecisive clients drew from Holland and Holland's (1977) description of an indecisive disposition in which individuals are difficult to treat because they suffer from a complex cluster of maladaptive attitudes and coping behaviors.

According to Salomone, indecisive clients suffer from identity diffusion and substantial anxiety and, therefore, are diagnostically different from undecided individuals who may experience some mild anxiety related to having not yet reached a decision. This diagnostic distinction is important because more traditional career counseling techniques may be extremely helpful to the undecided individual but significantly less helpful in address-ing the chronically maladaptive personality characteristics of the indecisive client. Hence, Salomone (1982) urged practitioners to distinguish between these two forms of indecision and provide appropriate career counseling based on the diagnostic decision.

A prominent researcher in vocational psychology, Itamar Gati, has been instrumental in developing two taxonomies related to career decision-making difficulties. According to Gati and Amir (2010), locating clients' career decision-making difficulties is one of the first steps in career counseling. Gati, Krausz, and Osipow (1996) proposed a taxonomy of career decision-making difficulties by starting with the "ideal career decision maker" and then identifying deviations from this theoretical ideal. They proposed that career decision-making difficulties are comprised of three major clusters: lack of readiness, lack of information, and inconsistent information. Gati and colleagues' taxonomy is hierarchical, with 10 subcategories that further identify and specify the career decision-making difficulty. For example, under the lack of readiness cluster, three subcategories further delineate the lack of readiness as being related to (a) lack of motivation, (b) general indecisiveness, or (c) dysfunctional beliefs. In the category of lack of information, the subcategories concern lack of information on (a) the career decision-making process, (b) self, (c) occupations (i.e., alternatives), and (d) obtaining information. The last category concerns inconsistent information due to (a) unreliable information, (b) internal conflicts, and (c) external conflicts. On the basis of the taxonomy, Gati and colleagues (1996) developed the Career Decision-Making Difficulties Questionnaire (CDDQ). A number of studies have been conducted related to the psychometric qualities of the CDDQ, which have supported its use with clients from various countries (e.g., Amir & Gati, 2006; Creed & Yin, 2006; Gati, Osipow, Krausz, & Saka, 2000; Mau, 2001).

Saka, Gati, and Kelly (2008) hypothesized that there is a distinction between developmental indecision and more chronic, pervasive indecisiveness mainly stemming from personality and emotional factors, and they focused on developing a theoretical framework for understanding the emotional and personality-related aspects of career decision-making difficulties. Based on a review of the literature, they first identified variables that were consistently correlated with career indecision and indecisiveness, which were pessimistic views, anxiety, and self-concept and identity. Similar to Gati and colleagues' (1996) model of cognitive decision making, the emotional and personality-related model is hierarchical, and there are 11 subcategories that correspond to the categories of pessimistic views, anxiety, and self-concept and identity. Under the category of pessimistic views are the subcategories of pessimistic views about (a) the process, (b) the world of work, and (c) one's control. In terms of anxiety, the subcategories are anxiety about (a) the process, (b) uncertainty, (c) the choice, and (d) the outcomes. The subcategories within the category of self and identity are (a) general anxiety, (b) self-esteem, (c) uncrystallized identity, and (d) conflictual attachment and separation. Based on this model, Saka and colleagues (2008) developed the Emotional and Personality Career Difficulties Scale (EPCD), which measures the 11 subcategories and 3 categories. Using eight Israeli samples and eight iterations of the EPCD, Saka and colleagues arrived at a 53-item instrument with strong psychometric indicators. They also examined an English version of the EPCD with an American sample and found the instrument held up well, with the exception that the uncrystallized identity scale was included in the anxiety cluster instead of that of self-concept and identity.

Another significant researcher conducting studies of types of career indecision is Steven Brown, whose research has taken a different approach from Gati and colleagues. Rather than taking the rational or top-down approach of Gati and colleagues, Brown and Rector (2008) took a bottom-up approach by extracting latent variables from the correlations matrices from already published studies of career indecision. To identify the latent factors of career indecision, Brown and Rector used an iterative technique of factor analyzing these correlation matrices and a meta-analytic factor analysis to arrive at a four-factor solution.

The first factor identified by Brown and Rector (2008) was labeled indecisiveness/trait negative affect as the loadings were consistent with previous literature on indecisiveness (e.g., Salomone, 1982) and the core trait of negative affect (e.g., Watson & Clark, 1984). The construct of trait negative affect concerns negativity to work and life satisfaction with difficulties in making decisions in various aspects of life (see Lent & Brown, Chapter 22, this volume). In a follow-up factor analysis, Brown and colleagues (2011) developed a 167-item instrument and found that indecision-related items loaded on both of the first two factors of Brown and Rector; hence, they renamed the first factor *neuroticism/negative affectivity*. The second factor identified by Brown and Rector concerned the latent dimension of lack of information and includes deficiencies in terms of information regarding both self and occupations. A set of variables that loaded on this factor concerned an approach–approach conflict, in which an individual needs information to choose between or among some appealing options. In the factor analysis conducted by Brown and colleagues (2011), additional items reflecting an inability to commit to, and anxiety about, making a decision also loaded highly on the second factor, and this factor was renamed *choice/commitment anxiety factor*.

The third factor related to vocational decision-making problems found by Brown and Rector (2008) involved *interpersonal conflicts and barriers*. Similar to Gati and colleagues' (1996) external conflict subscale, this latent factor related to conflicts or disagreements with significant others and differing opinions on preferred career directions. The fourth factor in Brown and Rector's taxonomy was labeled *lack of readiness*. This factor is defined by identity diffusion (see Brown & Ryan Krane, 2000), lack of self-clarity, and low career decision-making self-efficacy beliefs. Hence, high scores in this area reflect a pattern of developmental deficits in terms of self-knowledge, decision-making attitudes and skills, and goal-setting abilities. Brown and colleagues' (2011) factor analysis supported the structure of the third and fourth factors. In our view, clinicians should consider all four factors (i.e., neuroticism/negative affectivity, choice/commitment anxiety factor, interpersonal conflicts and barriers, and lack of readiness) in career decision-making case conceptualization because considering only the most apparent problematic factor may impede the clinician's abilities to adequately conceptualize the complexities associated with career indecision.

Certainly, there are similarities between Brown and colleagues' (2011) four-factor model and Gati and colleagues' (1996) and Saka and colleagues' (2008) models of career decision-making difficulties. Brown and colleagues explored these similarities by factor-analyzing the interfacet correlation matrices published by Gati and colleagues and Saka and colleagues and found that, in part, Gati and colleagues' cognitive and personality/emotional models could be recast in terms of Brown and colleagues' four-factor model. Whereas Brown and colleagues' model has some clinical parsimony and utility for practitioners over using Gati and colleagues' two models and instruments (i.e., the CDDQ and the EPCD), there are also some limitations. First, more research has been conducted related to Gati and colleagues' models, as this research began in the early 1990s, whereas Brown and Rector's (2008) model is a more recent contribution, and there has been less time for researchers to validate and corroborate their findings. Second, although Brown and colleagues have recently developed an instrument, Gati and colleagues have developed and refined two existing instruments. Conversely, using two instruments to identify career decision-making difficulties may be unrealistic in many field-based settings. Currently, Hacker, Carr, Abrams, and Brown (in press) have developed a 65-item instrument (Career Indecision Profile-65) to measure their four factors. Although this instrument needs additional psychometric investigation, it may ultimately be a useful tool to identify major sources of clients' decision-making difficulties.

In conclusion, we anticipate that this resurgence in research related to career decision-making difficulties or factors underlying career indecision will result in practitioners having a better understanding of the process of making career decisions and better tools for diagnosing types of career indecision with clients. What is particularly encouraging about research on decision-making difficulties or types of indecision is the quality of the research currently being conducted by these well-respected scholars in the field of career counseling. Based on the research in this area, when clinicians are working with clients, they should consider both the level and type of indecision. Although the field has yet to reach consensus about the precise types of career indecision or decision-making difficulties, researchers have clearly found that both cognitive and emotional-affect components contribute to difficulties in making career choices.

FUTURE RESEARCH

We now focus briefly on needs for future research on career choice and its promotion. There have been numerous calls for more process and outcome research in career counseling (Brown et al., 2003; Whiston & Rahardja, 2008), particularly with international populations (Bernes, Bardick, & Orr, 2007; Hartung, 2005). Recent research related to the process of career counseling has provide some information, but Heppner and Heppner's (2003) contention that "remarkably little is known about what underlying processes and mechanisms lead to effective change in career counseling" (p. 429) is still relevant to career choice counseling.

Although Brown and Ryan Krane's (2000) five critical ingredients provide an empirically based foundation for career choice interventions, further research is needed to verify these ingredients. In psychotherapy research, there is a history of using dismantling and constructive design strategies in which interventions or components are added, subtracted, or varied, and outcome is then assessed (Høglend, 1999). Conducting dismantling and constructive strategies with the five critical ingredients and other process variables with different populations could provide more detailed information to practitioners about which factors are truly critical with which types of clients. With advances in diagnostic systems, we may learn that some of the critical ingredients may be needed for certain clients, whereas other clients may need treatments that include more than these particular ingredients. Therefore, the development of a vocationally oriented diagnostic system is critical for answering the question of what works with which type of client and under what conditions. This recommendation is consistent with Brown and McPartland's (2005) assertion that little can be gained from additional studies that employ vague, one-size-fits-all treatments.

In our view, there is a need to examine career choice interventions with individuals from different socioeconomic classes, as we found very few studies that directly considered socioeconomic status. This is somewhat surprising, given Blustein and colleagues' (2002) finding that social class plays a significant role in vocational development and that individuals from a lower (versus higher) socioeconomic status were less likely to see work as a means for satisfaction and had fewer academic and vocational resources (see also Juntunen, Ali, & Pietrantonio, Chapter 9, this volume). In our opinion, the lack of research targeted at helping individuals from lower socioeconomic strata is one of the largest gaps in career choice counseling research. Therefore, practitioners who are committed to social justice issues should work in concert with researchers to conduct studies about which career interventions will lead to better career outcomes for those who may face both perceived and real environmental barriers as a result of their social class.

Although there has been some research related to career choice interventions with individuals from different racial and ethnic groups, much of the research has involved Asian American clients. As indicated earlier, Fouad and Byars-Winston's (2005) meta-analysis found that racial and ethnic minorities perceived fewer career opportunities and greater career barriers than their White counterparts. Hence, there is also a need to conduct intervention research with diverse racial and ethnic groups, particularly with African American and Latino clients, who represent a significant proportion of the population in the United States. Working with diverse clients should not be restricted to the United States; many international scholars are investigating the effectiveness of career choice interventions, and they also should be encouraged to use samples reflecting the diversity of clients within their countries.

There have been a number of calls for methodological diversity in regard to research designs used in evaluating the effectiveness of career interventions. Perry, Dauwalder, and Bonnett (2009) asserted that both qualitative and quantitative methods are needed to answer questions regarding the efficacy of career interventions and that the choice of methodology should be dependent on the research question. Moreover, Perry (2009) argued that tests of the efficacy of vocational guidance, particularly with underserved populations, can best be accomplished with mixed-methods approaches. We reiterate the call for methodological diversity and believe the research methodology should match the research questions; however, we suggest that there is a significant need for large-scale, clinical trials research.

Clinical trials research has evolved from medical research in which individuals are randomly assigned to either the treatment group or the placebo or treatment as usual group. Clinical trials research is also common in psychotherapy and, to some extent, educational research. Analogous to medical research, where the researcher must ensure that the medical or pharmaceutical intervention is properly administered, vocational researchers must ensure that a specific career intervention is administered. In psychotherapy research, this is labeled treatment integrity, and issues of treatment integrity are typically met by using treatment manuals and supervising psychotherapists to certify that clients are actually receiving the intended treatment. One of the limitations in career choice counseling is the lack of treatment manuals (Bernes et al., 2007; Whiston, 2002). To conduct large-scale clinical trials research, vocational researchers will probably need to work with multiple sites; thus, issues of treatment integrity and the development of treatment manuals are essential. Once treatment manuals are tested in the field with a large number of participants and found to be effective, then practitioners can use these treatment approaches and be confident in their effectiveness.

Furthermore, unless there is a clear understanding of the status and quality of the outcome measures used, conclusions about the gains clients are experiencing have little practical utility. Savickas (1989) called for the development of a standard battery of sound, career-related instruments that could be used in career counseling outcome research. We would like to reiterate this call and suggest that this goal is attainable for career choice counseling. A battery of assessments is needed because outcome assessment is best accomplished when researchers use multiple assessments from multiple perspectives (Hill & Lambert, 2004). Based on that premise, Whiston (2001) provided a scheme for selecting multiple career outcome assessments.

Regarding a battery of outcome assessments, it has been observed that researchers are moving away from using measures of career maturity and more frequently using measures of decidedness (Folsom & Reardon, 2003; Whiston, 2002). As noted earlier, advances are being made at developing and validating instruments to assess career decision-making difficulties. We also noted the increased usage of measures of career decision-making self-efficacy in career intervention outcome research. These advances related to career decision making are laudable; however, we suggest that researchers focus on developing other domain-specific measures of career choice counseling, such as measures of the degree to which choices are being implemented.

Perry and colleagues (2009) suggested that researchers conduct more studies of the cost-effectiveness of career counseling. Whiston (2011) indicated that, for some policy makers and stakeholders, the major question is not whether vocational or career interventions can help people; for them, the question is rather whether these interventions are cost-effective. Whiston suggested further examination of the degree to which career interventions influence gains in employment and decreases in school dropout rates and then the evaluation of the economic benefits associated with those outcomes. To conduct some cost-benefit analyses, such as whether career choice interventions affect unemployment rates and save on governmental expenditures, researchers will need to conduct more longitudinal studies of career choice interventions (Bernes et al., 2007).

Although we are calling for research in a number of areas, we would like to conclude this section by applauding the research that has been and is being conducted on the promotion of career choice. The extant research can inform practitioners globally on methods for intervening to assist people in making sound career decisions. As is evident from this chapter, researchers are working internationally to provide insight into what types of intervention facilitate career choice or decision making. The following provides a brief summary of these research findings, with a focus on informing practitioners about relevant trends that can enhance their work with clients.

CONCLUSIONS AND PRACTICE IMPLICATIONS

In reflecting on the literature related to the promotion of career choice, we offer the following conclusions and suggestions. These comments are not inclusive of all the research discussed in this chapter but are intended to highlight major themes and findings.

- On average, career choice counseling is moderately effective, and the results appear to be long-term. The effectiveness of career choice interventions, however, seems to vary, depending on what is included in the career counseling.
- Career choice counseling can probably best be implemented in four or five sessions, yet it appears that it is not solely the length of the counseling that influences effectiveness but, once again, what is included in the counseling.
- Practitioners should incorporate five critical ingredients that have been shown to increase the effectiveness of career choice counseling. These ingredients are (a) workbooks and written exercises (especially written goal setting and occupational comparisons), (b) individualized interpretations and feedback on written goals and hard-to-interpret assessment results, (c) in-session occupational information exploration; (d) modeling, and (e) increasing environmental support. Not only do the five critical ingredients seem to be individually important but also combinations of them yield larger effect sizes than any one individually. Hence, these five ingredients do, indeed, seem to be *critical* in influencing career choice outcomes.
- Many potential clients have expectations about the career choice counseling process (e.g., wanting simply to be given occupational information) that do not align well with the critical ingredients. If not addressed, such incompatible expectations may hamper the effectiveness of the counseling process. Some research supports the use of role induction activities, in which clients are provided with information regarding the importance of their active participation in career choice counseling.
- Counselor involvement seems to play an important role in the process, as counselor-free interventions have been found to be less effective than

any other type of career counseling modality (e.g., individual or group career counseling). Furthermore, there is empirical evidence that many users of computerized career guidance systems use these systems only briefly, so practitioners should not rely on them as the sole provider of career guidance.

• Although there has been research related to client factors that may influence career choice outcome, the findings are generally equivocal. One of the reasons for this lack of definitive results may be the slow pace of developing diagnostic taxonomies that could be used to match interventions to clients' diagnostic needs. The development of a vocational diagnostic system would be beneficial for practitioners, who could use it for screening, case conceptualization, treatment planning, and evaluative purposes.

• Two researchers (i.e., Itamar Gati and Steven Brown) are developing diagnostic systems and assessment instruments related to career decision making that have practical utility. According to Gati and colleagues (Gati et al., 1996), career decision-making difficulties are primarily related to lack of readiness, lack of information, and inconsistent information; Saka and colleagues (2008) also maintain that emotional or personality-related problems associated with career decision making are represented by the constructs of pessimistic views, anxiety, and self-concept and identity. Using a different approach, Brown and colleagues (2011) identified four primary career decision difficulties: neuroticism/negative affectivity, choice/commitment anxiety, interpersonal conflicts and barriers, and lack of readiness. Both approaches show promising empirical support, overlap somewhat, and should be considered by practitioners to diagnose career choice-making difficulties. Doing so can help to develop differential treatment plans specific to client need and, therefore, avoid a one-size-fits-all approach that may be less efficient or effective.

• There is a need for a standard outcome assessment battery related to career choice counseling that could be used by both clinicians and researchers.

• There are a number of research areas related to the promotion of career choice where practitioners and researchers could collaborate, thus enriching our knowledge of what counseling interventions facilitate career choice. In particular, we suggest that this research focus on clients living in poverty and other marginalized groups.

Although we have discussed research related to the promotion of career choice in this chapter, it would be negligent to conclude without addressing the point made by a number of noted vocational psychologists (e.g., Blustein,

2006, 2008; Fouad, 2007) who have asserted that career choice is a luxury not afforded to the working poor and other marginalized groups. As indicated by Fouad (2007), one "cannot assume that all individuals have work choices, that they will enter a career until they choose to leave it, or that opportunities are open to all" (p. 544). Blustein (2006, 2008) argued that career counseling theories and research have often overlooked millions of individuals globally for whom career choice is an elusive construct that does not fit their working lives, in which work serves more as a means of survival than an expression of talents or personality. Therefore, we would like to encourage practitioners to be agents of social justice and deliberately work toward changing social structures that impede the career opportunities of all. The second section of this book addresses many of the inequities that currently exist and provides practitioners with suggestions for remedying these inequities. In a perfect world, career choices would not be a luxury afforded to some, but an aspect of everyone's life. In concluding this chapter, we would like to encourage readers to consciously identify ways in which they can influence society so that opportunities for career choice become a reality for all individuals.

REFERENCES

Amir, T., & Gati, I. (2006). Facets of career decision-making difficulties. *British Journal of Guidance & Counselling, 34*(4), 483–503. doi:10.1080/03069880600942608

Bernes, K. B., Bardick, A. D., & Orr, D. T. (2007). Career guidance and counselling efficacy studies: An international research agenda. *International Journal for Educational and Vocational Guidance, 7*(2), 81–96. doi:10.1007/s10775-007-9114-8

Blustein, D. L. (2006). *The psychology of working: A new perspective for career development, counseling, and public policy.* Mahwah, NJ: Erlbaum.

Blustein, D. L. (2008). The role of work in psychological health and well-being: A conceptual, historical, and public policy perspective. *American Psychologist, 63,* 228–240. doi:10.1037/0003-066X.63.4.228

Blustein, D. L., Chaves, A. P., Diemer, M. A., Gallagher, L. A., Marshall, K. G., Sirin, S., & Bhati, K. S. (2002). Voices of the forgotten half: The role of social class in the school-to-work transition. *Journal of Counseling Psychology, 49*(3), 311–323. doi:10.1037/0022-0167.49.3.311

Brown, S. D., Hacker, J., Abrams, M., Carr, A., Rector, C., Lamp, K., Siena, A. (2011). Validation of a four-factor model of career indecision. *Journal of Career Assessment, 20,* 1–19. doi:10.1177/1069072711417154

Brown, S. D., & McPartland, E. B. (2005). Career interventions: Current status and future directions. In W. B. Walsh & M. L. Savickas (Eds.), *Handbook of vocational psychology: Theory, research, and practice* (3rd ed., pp. 195–226). Mahwah, NJ: Erlbaum.

Brown, S. D., & Rector, C. C. (2008). Conceptualizing and diagnosing problems in vocational decision making. In S. D. Brown & R. W. Lent (Eds.), *Handbook of counseling psychology* (4th ed., pp. 392–407). Hoboken, NJ: Wiley.

Brown, S. D., & Ryan Krane, N. E. (2000). Four (or five) sessions and a cloud of dust: Old assumptions and new observations about career counseling. In S. D. Brown & R. W. Lent (Eds.), *Handbook of counseling psychology* (3rd ed., pp. 740–766). New York, NY: Wiley.

Brown, S. D., Ryan Krane, N. E., Brecheisen, J., Castelino, P., Budisin, I., Miller, M., & Edens, L. (2003). Critical ingredients of career choice interventions: More analyses and new hypotheses. *Journal of Vocational Behavior, 62*(3), 411–428. doi:10.1016/S0001-8791(02)00052-0

Carter, R. T., Scales, J. E., Juby, H. L., Collins, N. M., & Wan, C. M. (2003). Seeking career services on campus: Racial differences in referral, process, and outcome. *Journal of Career Assessment, 11*(4), 393–404. doi:10.1177/1069072703255835

Cohen, J. (1988). *Statistical power analysis for the behavioral sciences* (2nd ed.). Hillsdale, NJ: Erlbaum.

Creed, P. A., & Yin, W. O. (2006). Reliability and validity of a Chinese version of the career decision-making difficulties questionnaire. *International Journal for Educational and Vocational Guidance, 6*(1), 47–63. doi:10.1007/s10775-006-0003

DeBell, C. (2006). What all applied psychologists should know about work. *Professional Psychology: Research and Practice, 37*(4), 325–333. doi:10.1037/0735-7028.37.4.325

Folsom, B., & Reardon, R. (2003). College career courses: Design and accountability. *Journal of Career Assessment, 11*(4), 421–450. doi:10.1177/1069072703255875

Fouad, N. A. (2007). Work and vocational psychology: Theory, research, and applications. *Annual Review of Psychology, 58*, 543–564. doi:10.1146/annurev.psych.58.110405.085713

Fouad, N. A., & Byars-Winston, A. M. (2005). Cultural context of career choice: Meta-analysis of race/ethnicity differences. *Career Development Quarterly, 53*, 223–233.

Fouad, N. A., Chen, Y., Guillen, A., Henry, C., Kantamneni, N., Novakovic, A., Terry, S. (2007). Role induction in career counseling. *Career Development Quarterly, 56*(1), 19–33.

Fretz, B. R. (1981). Evaluating the effectiveness of career interventions. *Journal of Counseling Psychology, 28*(1), 77–90. doi:10.1037/0022-0167.28.1.77

Galassi, J. P., Crace, R. K., Martin, G. A., James, R. M., & Wallace, R. L. (1992). Client preferences and anticipations in career counseling: A preliminary investigation. *Journal of Counseling Psychology, 39*(1), 46–55. doi:10.1037/0022-0167.39.1.46

Gati, I., & Amir, T. (2010). Applying a systemic procedure to locate career decision-making difficulties. *Career Development Quarterly, 58*(4), 301–320.

Gati, I., Krausz, M., & Osipow, S. H. (1996). A taxonomy of difficulties in career decision making. *Journal of Counseling Psychology, 43*(4), 510–526. doi:10.1037/0022-0167.43.4.510

Gati, I., Osipow, S. H., Krausz, M., & Saka, N. (2000). Validity of the career decision-making difficulties questionnaire: Counselee versus career counselor perceptions. *Journal of Vocational Behavior, 56*(1), 99–113. doi:10.1006/jvbe.1999.1710

Gore, P. A., Bobek, B. L., Robbins, S. B., & Shayne, L. (2006). Computer-based career exploration: Usage patterns and a typology of users. *Journal of Career Assessment, 14*(4), 421–436. doi:10.1177/1069072706288939

Hacker, J., Carr, A., Abrams, M., & Brown, S. D. (in press). Development of the Career Indecision Profile: Factor structure, reliability, and validity. *Journal of Career Assessment.*

Hartung, P. J. (2005). Internationalizing career counseling: Emptying our cups and learning from each other. *Career Development Quarterly, 54*, 12–16.

Healy, C. (2001). A follow-up of adult career counseling clients of a university extension center. *Career Development Quarterly, 49*, 363–373.

Heppner, M. J., & Heppner, P. P. (2003). Identifying process variables in career counseling: A research agenda. *Journal of Vocational Behavior, 62*(3), 429–452. doi:10.1016/S0001-8791(02)00053-2

Heppner, M. J., Lee, D., Heppner, P. P., McKinnon, L. C., Multon, K. D., & Gysbers, N. C. (2004). The role of problem-solving appraisal in the process and outcome of career counseling. *Journal of Vocational Behavior, 65*(2), 217–238. doi:10.1016/S0001-8791(03)00100-3

Hill, C. E., & Lambert, M. J. (2004). Methodological issues in studying psychotherapy processes and outcomes. In M. J. Lambert (Ed.), *Bergin and Garfield's handbook of psychotherapy and behavior* (5th ed., pp. 84–135). New York: Wiley.

Hirschi, A., & Läge, D. (2008). Increasing the career choice readiness of young adolescents: An evaluation study. *International Journal for Educational and Vocational Guidance, 8*(2), 95–110. doi:10.1007/s10775-008-9139-7

Høglend, P. (1999). Psychotherapy research: New findings and implications for training and practice. *Journal of Psychotherapy Practice & Research, 8*(4), 257–263.

Holland, J. L., & Holland, J. E. (1977). Vocational indecision: More evidence and speculation. *Journal of Counseling Psychology, 24*(5), 404–414. doi:10.1037/0022-0167.24.5.404

Juntunen, C. L. (2006). The psychology of working: The clinical context. *Professional Psychology: Research and Practice, 37*(4), 342–350. doi:10.1037/0735-7028.37.4.342

Kim, B. S. K., & Atkinson, D. R. (2002). Asian American client adherence to Asian cultural values, counselor expression of cultural values, counselor ethnicity, and career counseling process. *Journal of Counseling Psychology, 49*(1), 3–13. doi:10.1037/0022-0167.49.1.3

Kim, B. S. K., Li, L. C., & Liang, T. H. (2002). Effects of Asian American client adherence to Asian cultural values, session goal, and counselor emphasis of client expression on career counseling process. *Journal of Counseling Psychology, 49*(3), 342–354. doi:10.1037/0022-0167.49.3.342

Lapan, R. T., Aoyagi, M., & Kayson, M. (2007). Helping rural adolescents make successful postsecondary transitions: A longitudinal study. *Professional School Counseling, 10*(3), 266–272.

Lee, D., Park, H., & Heppner, M. J. (2009). Do clients' problem-solving appraisals predict career counseling outcomes or vice versa? A reanalysis of Heppner, et al. *Psychological Reports, 105*(3), 1159–1166.

Lewis, J. (2001). Career and personal counseling: Comparing process and outcome. *Journal of Employment Counseling, 38*, 82–90.

Li, L. C., & Kim, B. S. K. (2004). Effects of counseling style and client adherence to Asian cultural values on counseling process with Asian American college students. *Journal of Counseling Psychology, 51*(2), 158–167. doi:10.1037/0022-0167.51.2.158

Littman-Ovadia, H. (2008). The effect of client attachment style and counselor functioning on career exploration. *Journal of Vocational Behavior*, 73(3), 434–439. doi:10.1016/j.jvb.2008.08.004

Marzano, R. J., & Brown, J. L. (2009). *A handbook for the art and science of teaching*. Alexandria, VA: Association for Supervision and Curriculum Development.

Marzano, R. J., Pickering, D. J., & Pollock, J. E. (2001). *Classroom instruction that works: Research-based strategies for improving student achievement*. Alexandria, VA: Association for Supervision and Curriculum Development.

Masdonati, J., Massoudi, K., & Rossier, J. (2009). Effectiveness of career counseling and the impact of the working alliance. *Journal of Career Development*, 36(2), 183–203. doi:10.1177/0894845309340798

Mau, W. (2001). Assessing career decision-making difficulties: A cross-cultural study. *Journal of Career Assessment*, 9(4), 353–364. doi:10.1177/106907270100900403

Mau, W., & Fernandes, A. (2001). Characteristics and satisfaction of students who used career counseling services. *Journal of College Student Development*, 42(6), 581–588.

Meara, N. M., & Patton, M. J. (1994). Contributions of the working alliance in the practice of career counseling. *Career Development Quarterly*, 43(2), 161–177.

Miller, M. J., & Brown, S. D. (2005). Counseling for career choice: implications for improving interventions and working with diverse populations. In S. D. Brown & R. W. Lent (Eds.), *Career development and counseling: Putting theory and research to work* (pp. 441–465). Hoboken, NJ: Wiley.

Nichols, G. C. (2009). *Career interventions in context: A meta-analysis examining the influence of environmental factors on outcome* (Doctoral Dissertation, University of Wisconsin).

Oliver, L. W., & Spokane, A. R. (1988). Career-intervention outcome: What contributes to client gain? *Journal of Counseling Psychology*, 35(4), 447–462. doi:10.1037/0022-0167.35.4.447

Perdrix, S., de Roten, Y., Kolly, S., & Rossier, J. (2010). The psychometric properties of the WAI in a career counseling setting: Comparison with a personal counseling sample. *Journal of Career Assessment*, 18(4), 409–419. doi:10.1177/1069072710374583

Perdrix, S., Stauffer, S., Masdonati, J., Massoudi, K., & Rossier, J. (2012). Effectiveness of career counseling: A one-year follow-up. *Journal of Vocational Behavior*.

Perry, J. C. (2009). A combined social action, mixed methods approach to vocational guidance efficacy research. *International Journal for Educational and Vocational Guidance*, 9(2), 111–123. doi:10.1007/s10775-009-9158-z

Perry, J. C., Dauwalder, J. P., & Bonnett, H. R. (2009). Verifying the efficacy of vocational guidance programs: Procedures, problems, and potential directions. *Career Development Quarterly*, 57(4), 348–357.

Reese, R. J., & Miller, C. D. (2010). Using outcome to improve a career development course: Closing the scientist-practitioner gap. *Journal of Career Assessment*, 18(2), 207–219. doi:10.1177/1069072709354309

Rochlen, A. B., Mohr, J. J., & Hargrove, B. K. (1999). Development of the attitudes toward career counseling scale. *Journal of Counseling Psychology*, 46(2), 196–206. doi:10.1037/0022-0167.46.2.196

Rochlen, A. B., & O'Brien, K. M. (2002a). Men's reasons for and against seeking help for career-related concerns. *Journal of Men's Studies, 11*(1), 55–63. doi:10.3149/jms.1101.55

Rochlen, A. B., & O'Brien, K. M. (2002b). The relation of male gender role conflict and attitudes toward career counseling to interest in and preferences for different career counseling styles. *Psychology of Men & Masculinity, 3*(1), 9–21. doi:10.1037/1524-9220.3.1.9

Rounds, J. B., & Tinsley, T. J. (1984). Diagnosis and treatment of vocational problems. In S. D. Brown & R. W. Lent (Eds.), *Handbook of counseling psychology* (pp. 137–177). New York, NY: Wiley.

Ryan N. E. (1999). *Career counseling and career choice goal attainment: A meta-analytically derived model for career counseling practice.* Unpublished dissertation, Loyola University, Chicago.

Saka, N., Gati, I., & Kelly, K. R. (2008). Emotional and personality-related aspects of career-decision-making difficulties. *Journal of Career Assessment, 16*(4), 403–424. doi:10.1177/1069072708318900

Salomone, P. R. (1982). Difficult cases in career counseling: II. The indecisive client. *Personnel and Guidance Journal, 60*, 496–499.

Savickas, M. L. (1989). Annual review: Practice and research in career counseling and development, 1988. *Career Development Quarterly, 38*(2), 100–134.

Shivy, V. A., & Koehly, L. M. (2002). Client perceptions of and preferences for university-based career services. *Journal of Vocational Behavior, 60*(1), 40–60. doi:10.1006/jvbe.2001.1811

Spokane, A. R., & Oliver, L. W. (1983). Outcomes of vocational intervention. In S. H. Osipow & W. B. Walsh (Eds.), *Handbook of vocational psychology* (pp. 99–136). Hillsdale, NJ: Erlbaum.

Turner, S. L., & Conkel, J. L. (2010). Evaluation of a career development skills intervention with adolescents living in an inner city. *Journal of Counseling & Development, 88*(4), 457–465.

Watson, D., & Clark, L. A. (1984). Negative affectivity: The disposition to experience aversive emotional states. *Psychological Bulletin, 96*(3), 465–490. doi:10.1037/0033-2909.96.3.465

Whiston, S. C. (2001). Selecting career outcome assessments: An organizational scheme. *Journal of Career Assessment, 9*(3), 215–228. doi:10.1177/106907270100900301

Whiston, S. C. (2002). Application of the principles: Career counseling and interventions. *Counseling Psychologist, 30*, 218–237. doi:10.1177/0011000002302002

Whiston, S. C. (2011). Vocational counseling and interventions: An exploration of future "big" questions. *Journal of Career Assessment, 19*, 287–295.

Whiston, S. C., Brecheisen, B. K., & Stephens, J. (2003). Does treatment modality affect career counseling effectiveness? *Journal of Vocational Behavior, 62*(3), 390–410. doi:10.1016/S0001-8791(02)00050-7

Whiston, S. C., & Keller, B. K. (2004). The influences of the family of origin on career development: A review and analysis. *Counseling Psychologist, 32*(4), 493–568. doi:10.1177/0011000004265660

Whiston, S. C., & Rahardja, D. (2008). Vocational counseling process and outcome. In S. D. Brown & R. W. Lent (Eds.), *Handbook of counseling psychology* (4th ed., pp. 444–461). Hoboken, NJ: Wiley.

Whiston, S. C., Sexton, T. L., & Lasoff, D. L. (1998). Career-intervention outcome: A replication and extension of Oliver and Spokane (1988). *Journal of Counseling Psychology*, *45*(2), 150–165. doi:10.1037/0022-0167.45.2.150

Whitaker, L. A., Phillips, J. C., & Tokar, D. M. (2004). Influencing client expectations about career counseling using a videotaped intervention. *Career Development Quarterly*, *52*(4), 309–322.

CHAPTER 21

Interventions to Aid Job Finding and Choice Implementation

LARAE M. JOME AND SUSAN D. PHILLIPS

HAVING ARRIVED AT A promising vocational direction, the next task in the career development process is to implement one's choice. Toward that end, counselors may be called on to assist clients in identifying opportunities and helping them develop the skills to successfully present themselves to potential employers. It is clear that the work world has been undergoing vast changes since the first edition of this book. Factors such as technological advances, the global marketplace, and economic crises have affected almost all aspects of society (see Lent & Brown, Chapter 1, this volume) and, in turn, the job-finding and implementation processes have shifted as well. One of the most profound areas of change has been in the use of the Internet and other electronic technology (Selden & Orenstein, 2011; Tso, Yau, & Cheung, 2010). Today, for example, job seekers are likely to use the Internet and e-mail to explore career information, find resources for creating resumes and tips for interviewing, post their resumes, network, scroll through job listings, and submit job applications. Another major change in the current work world is the shift in the nature and availability of work in the United States and worldwide.

With this current context in mind, we approach the question of what the vocational literature can offer researchers and practitioners seeking to facilitate the choice implementation and job-finding process with clients. Choice implementation refers to the process by which individuals identify career goals and then seek opportunities for work in areas that reflect those goals. Job finding encompasses the search behaviors of job seekers in pursuing the goal of obtaining employment. Although these may be distinct processes at times, we focus on the totality of the implementing and searching process; thus, we use terms such as *job searching, job finding*, and *choice implementation* interchangeably throughout the chapter.

How can job seekers best prepare for and engage in the job-search process? What strategies and characteristics are most helpful in this process, and what characteristics make the process more difficult? What advice can be gleaned from the research literature for career counselors and students learning about career counseling? We consulted the literature from a broad range of fields (i.e., vocational psychology, industrial/organizational psychology, rehabilitation psychology, sociology) from the last decade and summarize here the kinds of job-seeking strategies and interventions suggested by this literature.

Scholars (Blau, 1994; Kanfer, Wanberg, & Kantrowitz, 2001; Van Hooft & Noordzij, 2009) have conceptualized the job search as a self-regulatory process with multiple phases. In the initial phase, an individual makes a decision—voluntary or otherwise—to search for a job and become a job seeker. Essentially, the individual develops the goal of searching for a job, and this goal then guides the individual's job-searching intentions and behavior. Following this preparatory stage, individuals engage in an active job search and put time and effort into job search behaviors, with the final goal of obtaining employment or reemployment. This chapter highlights the active search phase, focusing first on methods of job searching (i.e., the ways in which job seekers locate job openings and possibilities). The second section discusses how individuals convince others to employ them (e.g., preparing a compelling resume, developing interviewing skills). Following this, we focus on various moderating factors that affect how individuals engage in the job search process (i.e., what demographic, motivational, and cognitive factors play a role in how individuals navigate the search and persuasion processes). Finally, we highlight recent intervention studies designed to increase individuals' success in the job-finding process and discuss their implications for practice and research.

JOB SEARCH METHODS

One of the major questions faced by potential job seekers, whether they are currently employed or unemployed, is what job openings are available and accessible to them. In this section, we discuss the different job search methods that are documented in the literature and commonly used by job seekers and career practitioners; we also note additional, less mainstream methods that are used by individuals who are excluded for various reasons from more formal, traditional methods of job searching.

How do job seekers identify potential job openings? What methods do job seekers use to identify accessible jobs? Van Hoye and Saks (2008) compiled a list of six job-searching methods that capture the various methods used by job seekers: "looking at job ads [in newspapers or job postings on the Internet], visiting job sites, networking, contacting employment agencies, contacting employers, submitting applications" (p. 362). Technology has greatly expanded the avenues by which job seekers track down open positions. Although the basic methods of searching through job advertisements, networking, completing applications, and sending resumes persist, the Internet has made it possible for job seekers to do many of these activities from one location with the help of a computer, Internet connection, and e-mail account.

Van Hoye and Saks (2008) found some evidence that individuals might use different search methods, depending on their specific job objective. Among employed Belgian and Romanian individuals who had a master's degree and were enrolled in graduate business classes, those whose main job search objective was to find a new job tended to use all the job search methods; those whose objective was to stay abreast of alternative job possibilities tended to engage in more passive search methods, such as looking at job ads and visiting Web sites. Those who wanted to develop a network of professional relationships employed relational strategies, such as contacting employers and networking, and those who wanted leverage against a current or potential employer tended to contact other employers. Although this study did not make any connections between search methods and outcomes, the findings suggest the value of career counselors making sure that they understand the many possible objectives of the job seeker and not assuming that the individual is always focused on finding new employment.

We next discuss some of the most common methods of job searching: using job ads, networking, and internships and volunteer opportunities. In addition, we briefly discuss alternative methods of job searching that are more commonly used by immigrants, illegal residents, and others who are barred from typical routes to finding employment.

JOB ADVERTISEMENTS

As documented in the research literature, the most common method of identifying potential jobs is looking at job advertisements, whether they are printed in newspapers or posted on Internet sites (e.g., Cannata, 2010; Try, 2005; Wanberg, Glomb, Song, & Sorenson, 2005). For example, in Wanberg and colleagues' (2005) study on job search persistence, unemployed job seekers reported that the most popular and consistent job search strategies they used were newspaper advertisements and Internet job postings, followed by networking and sending out resumes. Modern job seekers, especially those who are under 40, are likely to go to the Internet as the first source for exploring job ads. Job-seeking materials and books in the popular literature (e.g., Bolles, 2011) are full of tips on using the Internet to search and typically provide listings of websites that post job advertisements.

In the days before the Internet, employers looking to hire would take out an advertisement in a local or national paper or place a sign out in front of the place of business. Today, in addition to, and sometimes instead of, these methods, employers may post the job advertisement on the company website. Given that job seekers would need to identify the specific company or institution to locate these job ads, a number of larger electronic recruitment websites have been developed, at which companies can pay a third party to post information about job openings, search resumes, and collect resumes from interested job seekers (Lin, 2010). These e-recruitment service providers list openings in a variety of fields and occupations (e.g., http://www.monster.com); other websites are focused on jobs in a particular subfield or geographical area or are websites for local, state, or federal government jobs (e.g., http://www.usajobs.gov). It is typically free for job seekers to use the Web site to search for jobs as well as to post their resumes, and the cost is passed on to employers.

We found two studies that highlighted the role of the Internet in identifying specific job advertisements. In a study on teachers' job-searching decisions, Cannata (2010) found that all of the newly graduated teachers in her study used the Internet as the primary source for identifying open positions. Interestingly, three-quarters of the applicants searched the websites of the school districts with which they were familiar, rather than doing a broader search of school district websites, despite the extremely tight job market for teachers. Lin (2010) studied the intentions of graduating Taiwanese high school and college seniors to use e-recruitment websites for job searching. Job seekers were more likely to have stronger intentions to use e-recruitment websites when they had more positive attitudes about them (largely based on how easy and useful they found them), perceived some social pressure from others in their social network to use the websites, and felt more efficacious in navigating the websites.

Despite the limited generalizability of these studies, the findings raise interesting issues. Clients might need information about where to search on the Internet and which specific websites to explore; they might also need encouragement (or social pressure) to go beyond their familiar spaces (both geographically and in cyberspace) to expand the number and types of websites they explore. The studies also highlight potential generational differences in familiarity with and confidence in using the Internet as a search method. Today's job searchers are at a distinct disadvantage if they do not have an e-mail account or consistent access to the Internet because many job applications and hiring procedures require individuals to submit job materials electronically. Older job seekers, in particular, may have lower self-efficacy for using the Internet as a job search tool and may need training on how to use the computer to search for information generally, as well as additional help navigating particular websites.

NETWORKING

Among the most common pieces of advice for the modern job seeker is to use networking as a job search strategy (e.g., Bolles, 2011)—that is, to use one's personal connections with friends, family, and acquaintances to garner information about potential job leads that are not available through formal means, such as job ads. Granovetter (1973) distinguished between formal (e.g., answering job ads) and informal (e.g., networking) methods of job searching and further conceptualized informal networks as consisting of strong (i.e., family and friends) and weak (i.e., acquaintances, friends-of-friends) ties. More recently Huang and Western (2011) differentiated between market and social network methods of job searching. Market methods describe ways that individuals seek out jobs using formal methods such as sending out resumes, applying for jobs through advertisements, and attending job fairs. Network methods, on the other hand, refer to informal search methods in which job seekers use their relationships with other people and their social connections to find job leads.

Evidence in support of using one's informal network suggests that it is an effective tool in obtaining employment. Previous research findings suggested that using weak ties, rather than strong ties, was a more effective strategy to finding a job (e.g., Granovetter, 1995). Indeed, there is evidence in the research literature that networking is a very important method for identifying potential job leads. About half of the teachers in Cannata's (2010) study relied heavily on their professional social contacts and personal contacts for identifying open positions, as well as for other aspects of the job search process, such as providing information, feedback, and interview preparation. A study of women working in the textile and apparel industry found that informal networks of other women in the industry played a key role in securing an initial position in the field (Hodges, Karpova, & Lentz, 2010).

Although networking is certainly an important job search method, recent research findings have also drawn attention to some of the factors that might hinder or limit the usefulness of this method. In a sample of Norwegian college graduates, Try (2005) found that graduates with restricted social capital (e.g., fewer highly educated friends and family) had less access to informal search networks. Studying Australian employed adults, Huang and Western (2011) found that using weak ties was more effective in finding higher-paying jobs, whereas obtaining a job through strong ties was associated with lower-paying jobs. Additionally, Van Hoye, van Hooft, and Lievens (2009) found that unemployed Flemish adults who spent more time networking were more likely to be reemployed; however, those who had connections with higher-status others in their social network were more likely to be reemployed than those with strong, low-status connections. Redline and Rosenbaum (2010) also noted that individuals without a college education and those from poorer families with lower levels of education may have limited personal networks or have a social network comprised mainly of strong, low-status ties that are not as likely to be facilitative in the job-seeking process. They described a community college placement program aimed at students whose personal social networks may not be helpful in securing high-quality employment (i.e., low-income, students from underrepresented groups) and found that participants benefited most from the use of institutional contacts in the job search process.

The research findings suggest that using social networking as a job search method continues to be good advice for some job seekers. Networking can provide information about job leads that are not found in other places. Those with college degrees and those who can make connections with high-status individuals (i.e., those individuals who are in positions of influence and could help the job seeker get in the door for an interview) may be especially able to benefit from using their social network. Like most human endeavors, however, the job-seeking situation is complex and influenced by multiple factors, such as cultural context (Huang & Western, 2011) and the type of social network one has (Redline & Rosenbaum, 2010; van Hoye et al., 2009). Networking may not be the most efficient method to use for job seekers who have few connections with higher-status individuals.

Job seekers and counselors need to realize that "networking is not a panacea" (van Hoye et al., 2009, p. 678). Rather than simply suggesting that clients use their social network, a counselor might discuss how job seekers can use their networks and encourage them to identify the weak ties in their networks and not to rely entirely on close friends and family (van Hoye et al., 2009). In addition, counselors need to recognize that networking may be much easier for more extraverted individuals. With shyer, less extraverted clients, they may need to go beyond providing basic advice about networking to discuss and implement (e.g., role-playing) strategies for overcoming anxieties about networking.

INTERNSHIPS, APPRENTICESHIPS, AND VOLUNTEER OPPORTUNITIES

Students and new graduates are often encouraged to explore internships as a way to learn more about a particular career and gain entrance to that occupation. Very little research exists about the role of internships in the job-finding and implementation process. Hodges and colleagues (2010) found that about half of a sample of women who had entered the textile and apparel industry obtained their positions by first securing an internship in their current company. Research on apprenticeships is even sparser, especially in the United States. Studies conducted in Europe found that adolescents who successfully obtained apprenticeship positions had stayed focused on the goal of obtaining an apprenticeship, engaged in more job searching behaviors, and downgraded the level of prestige of their aspirations as the search continued (Haase, Heckhausen, & Köller, 2008; Tomasik, Hardy, Haase, & Heckhausen, 2009).

Another potential job search method is to volunteer one's time and services at an agency or program in one's area of interest. There may be multiple benefits of volunteering, such as using the experience gained at the site to enhance one's resume, making important networking connections, and obtaining employment. Volunteering may not be feasible for many job seekers, such as those with great financial needs, and may be a more attractive job search method for students and retirees.

ALTERNATIVE JOB SEARCH METHODS

Other job search methods suggested in the popular literature (e.g., visiting job sites, using employment agencies, contacting employers directly) have, unfortunately, received little, if any, research attention. Although there is little reason to believe that these methods would be detrimental to the job search process, there is no evidence that they add to the effectiveness of the more established methods discussed. The job search methods outlined earlier—ads, networks, and internships—are viable tools for some job seekers, yet it is clear that their effectiveness may be limited in more challenged educational or socioeconomic circumstances. More research is needed on effective job search methods used by individuals with lower levels of education and restricted access to employment resources, such as recent immigrants, those with little or no English proficiency, those who lack familiarity with U.S. culture, or workers who are in the U.S. illegally or who have engaged in illegal behavior in the past (e.g., ex-prisoners and prostitutes). Clearly, much additional research is necessary to identify the potentially unique needs of, and services for, these and other less privileged job seekers.

PERSUASION METHODS

Once individuals have identified one or more potential job possibilities, they begin the process of trying to convince employers to hire them. Job seekers essentially engage in a process of self-presentation and persuasion, which comes more naturally to some clients than others. We describe here the two main components of this process: resumes and interviewing.

THE RESUME

For many positions, especially professional positions requiring higher education, the first step in the persuasion process is to submit a resume that lists one's credentials and experience. The resume often represents the first interaction with the potential employer. The content and appearance of the resume can be essential in getting called for an interview or being placed immediately in the reject pile. The resume may be printed out on high-quality paper and mailed to prospective employers or may be submitted electronically either via e-mail or through a particular website application. Job searching websites are rife with advice on how job seekers can put together a winning resume. Given that assistance with resume preparation is one of the most common tasks of career counselors, it is vital that they are knowledgeable about resumes and trained in how to help a diverse array of clients create and revise effective resumes that best showcase the strengths and skills of that individual, given their job goal.

Much of the extant research about job resumes is from the perspective of the recruiter and organization and examines the cognitive processes recruiters use in making judgments about resumes. For example, Tyler and McCullough (2009) found that resumes of women who presented with more agentic characteristics (e.g., competitive and boastful) that violated feminine stereotypes were rated as less socially skilled by male raters. As another example, Tsai, Chi, Huang, and Hsu (2011) found that based on the content of job applicants' resumes, campus recruiters in Taiwan made inferences about the fit of the applicant with the job and the organization, which influenced recruiters' hiring recommendations. The authors recommend that job applicants tailor their resumes so that they highlight the fit between the applicants' educational background and work experience and the particular position and organization to which they are applying.

A number of recent studies and articles provide some good information for counselors to consider in helping clients construct effective resumes. Johnson and Lahey (2011) found that resumes of middle-aged female applicants to entry-level positions that listed at least 1 year of post–high school vocational training or computer training had a higher chance of being selected for an interview than resumes with no additional vocational education or computer training. Additionally, their results found that age was significantly related to the chance of receiving an interview, confirming other findings suggesting that older applicants are likely to have a harder time securing interviews and employment. Adding information about hobbies, sports, and volunteering did not greatly increase the chance of an interview, although the authors caution that it may not hurt applicants to remain active and to consider adding these characteristics to their resumes. One of the major implications of the study is that job seekers, especially middle-aged women who may have gaps in their experience in the paid workforce, could benefit from additional training and education. Counselors should be knowledgeable about opportunities to help older job searchers overcome financial barriers to seeking additional training.

Toporek and Flamer (2009) discussed a narrative approach to resume development. They noted that although counselors often focus on the content of the resume and approach it from the perspective of the role of editor, critique, or coach, it may be beneficial to approach the resume task from the perspective of a counselor and advocate who helps the client construct the story of his or her working life. Counselors can glean ideas about the client's interests, personality, barriers, anxieties, and unfinished business and engage them in a process of rewriting their career story that includes making changes to the resume document. In addition to the traditional resume, some fields lend themselves well to the development of portfolios, where individuals can visually display their work. Willis and Wilkie (2009) described the process by which business majors developed digital portfolios that helped them see the connections between their academic work and the competencies they were developing that could be presented to potential employers.

Job seekers often need to submit a cover letter that accompanies their resume in which they briefly state their interest in and expertise for the position. The cover letter, like the resume, provides a verbal snapshot of the job seeker. Counselors can play a vital role in the process by critiquing these documents to ensure that they are neat, concise, free of typographical errors, and aesthetically pleasing and present the most accurate and appealing picture of the job seeker. In addition, counselors might be especially important in facilitating a self-exploration process. Job seekers who have a clear understanding of themselves and their search goals may find it easier to present a clear picture of themselves to employers via the resume and cover letter.

THE JOB INTERVIEW

The interview can be both one of the most important steps in the hiring process and a source of anxiety for many job seekers. For some jobs, there may be multiple stages of the hiring process, with interviews with different levels of management at each stage. The research in personnel psychology examines interviewing from the perspective of the interviewer and has called attention to issues of bias and fairness in the interview process (e.g., de Meijer, Born, van Zielst, & van der Molen, 2007; Leasher, Miller, & Gooden, 2009). Derous (2007) found that job applicants and recruiters differed in the characteristics they valued in the application process. Applicants valued transparency and feedback in the selection process and desired tailor-made interview processes and being interviewed by warm, engaging interviewers. Recruiters valued objectivity and preferred more standardized interviews. Their results suggested that job applicants' expectations for what they will encounter in the interview may not match those of the interviewer. Counselors can help clients adjust their expectations so they are not discouraged by a more formal, impersonal interview process.

Very few recent studies focus on methods for enhancing applicants' interviewing skills. Given that the interview can often make or break the hire and that this can be a major source of worry for job seekers, discussing the interviewing process and preparing clients for interviews is an important topic in career counseling. It is vital that counselors become knowledgeable about interviewing skills and competent at helping clients to develop these skills. For example, given the anxiety-provoking nature of interviews, counselors can teach clients behavioral techniques to help them manage their anxiety levels before and during an interview. Role-playing may be especially effective because it allows the client to practice interviewing in a safe environment and get immediate feedback from the counselor about their behavior.

Counselors should be familiar with commonly asked interview questions (e.g., "What are your strengths and weaknesses?" "Tell me about yourself," and "What interests you about this position?") and questions that are illegal to ask in the United States (e.g., "How old are you?" "Are you married?" "Have you had any recent health issues?"). In some job settings, employers and search committees may not be up-to-date on the current legal issues with regard to hiring and inadvertently ask the applicant illegal questions. Counselors and clients can role-play how they might respond to such questions in an interview. For example, if a client is asked, "How many children do you have?" the counselor can help the client brainstorm ways in which they might answer. Additionally, counselors can raise issues related to contextual factors that might influence the interview. For example, ample research suggests that gender and racial biases exist in the interviewing and hiring process. Counselors can help clients be prepared for these realities of the work world and develop coping skills in advance for dealing with these issues.

As noted in our discussion of job search methods, for immigrants and others new to the United States, it can be helpful for counselors to ensure that clients have some familiarity with U.S. cultural norms and the expectations that potential employers will have for workers during the interview and hiring process. Cultural differences can be a potential source of confusion and lost job opportunities, as immigrant interviewees and U.S.-born bosses may have very different expectations regarding interpersonal behaviors, such as shaking hands, degree of eye contact, types of questions that are appropriate to ask, and the degree to which one might openly disagree with a potential employer.

PREDICTORS OF JOB SEARCH AND PERSUASION BEHAVIORS AND OUTCOMES

In the previous sections, we discussed the basic methods job seekers might use to search for job openings and persuade employers to hire them. We now consider the person and contextual variables that predict how individuals approach and participate in the job search and persuasion process. Searching for a job is not a linear and consistent process, but rather a highly individualized process that waxes and wanes over time and is influenced by multiple internal and external factors (Kanfer et al., 2001; Wanberg et al., 2005). Given the unique personalities and contextual factors of job seekers, the great variation in how job seekers go about the job search process is not surprising. Some job seekers devote many hours to the job search; others struggle to put in a few hours each week. Some may possess a great sense of confidence in their abilities to search for a job and believe strongly that their searching will have positive results; others are pessimistic about their employment prospects and struggle with depressive feelings.

Kanfer and colleagues (2001) conceptualized the job search process as a self-regulatory, dynamic, volitional, and autonomous process. Job seekers must ultimately decide to engage in the search and take responsibility for navigating the process. They must cope with the emotions and cognitions that accompany the inevitable ups and downs of the job search process and find ways to stay motivated through the process. According to Kanfer and colleagues' model, multiple factors influence job seekers' search behaviors and employment outcomes, including their personality characteristics, general beliefs about themselves and the world, search motives and intentions, the larger social context, and aspects related to their life history. Kanfer and colleagues conducted a meta-analysis to examine the degree to which these antecedents predicted both job search behaviors and employment outcomes. In the following sections, we discuss the individual differences, variables, and contextual factors that influence the job search and persuasion processes and discuss how counselors can apply these research findings in the counseling process. First, however, we note how the research literature has defined the goals and objectives of the job search and summarize research findings related to job search behaviors and outcomes.

JOB SEARCH BEHAVIORS AND OUTCOMES

In the research literature, the job search process has typically been operationalized as job search behaviors and employment outcomes. These behaviors and outcomes are used to indicate whether a job seeker has engaged in a more (or less) successful search. Typically, job search behaviors have been defined as the intensity and effort with which individuals engage or persist in the search process, that is, the amount of time and degree of effort devoted to specific job search tasks (e.g., searched job ads, submitted resumes, went on interviews). Scholars have also examined the clarity of the job search goal (i.e., how clearly the job seeker defines the objective of the search).

Some studies focus on job search behaviors; others examine the outcomes of the search process. Employment-related outcomes include variables such as employment status (i.e., whether the individual obtained employment or reemployment), the number of interviews or job offers received, degree of satisfaction with the job, duration of the search, and the quality of the reemployment (i.e., satisfaction, turnover intentions, person–job fit). Although the bulk of the job-searching research has focused on employment-related outcomes, there is growing attention to the negative psychological and physical effects of unemployment (e.g., McKee-Ryan, Song, Wanberg, & Kinicki, 2005).

One consistent finding, regardless of whether the job seeker is a college student, unemployed adult, or employed worker, is that there are clear benefits to spending more time and putting in more effort in the job search if the main objective is to obtain employment (Creed, King, Hood, & McKenzie, 2009; Crossley & Stanton, 2005; Kanfer et al., 2001; Van Hooft, Born, Taris, and van der Flier, 2005; Wanberg, Hough, & Song, 2002). For example, Creed and colleagues (2009) found that Australian job seekers who engaged in a more intense job search and spent more time examining job ads, sending out resumes, networking, and using other resources increased their chances of obtaining employment. As another example, Saks (2006) found that U.S. college students with greater job search intensity and job search self-efficacy received more interviews, received more job offers, and were more likely to be hired.

These findings highlight the importance of preparing job seekers for an intensive job search because a more active, intense search is more likely to result in successfully finding a job.

In addition to encouraging job seekers to put as much time and effort into job searching as possible, counselors can also facilitate the self- and job-exploration process. Job seekers who jump into the active phase of the job search without having clear job-searching goals may not present a cohesive picture of themselves to potential employers in their resume and in the interview. Clients with less insight into their interests and personalities and with fuzzier ideas about the types of jobs they want to search for could, therefore, benefit from traditional career assessment of interests, values, skills, and personality.

FACTORS THAT INFLUENCE THE JOB SEARCH PROCESS

Knowing that a more intense, active job search increases the chances for a positive search outcome gives counselors some general ideas for increasing the amount of job-searching behaviors in clients; however, it can be helpful to have a more complete picture of the job seeker and understand the factors that might facilitate or hinder the process. Scholars have identified a number of variables related to the job-searching behaviors of job seekers, and counselors can benefit from understanding how these aspects might influence the unique search process of individual clients. In the next sections, we discuss the results of Kanfer and colleagues' (2001) meta-analysis and other studies within the past decade to shed light on the factors that influence how job seekers approach and participate in the job search and persuasion processes.

Personality characteristics. Personality traits have been found to relate to job seekers' behavior and to employment outcomes. Extraversion and conscientiousness show the strongest relationships with job search behaviors and outcomes. Regardless of whether job seekers are unemployed adults (Kanfer et al., 2001; Van Hoye et al., 2009), high-level managers (Boswell, Roehling, & Boudreau, 2006), or college students (Turban, Stevens, & Lee, 2009), those who are more extraverted and conscientious tend to engage in more job search behaviors and report more interview and job offers. Kanfer and colleagues also found that greater openness to experience and agreeableness were predictive of positive search behaviors and outcomes, although these relationships tended to be weak. The effects of neuroticism are more mixed and point to a complex picture of how neuroticism might influence the job search process. Boswell and colleagues (2006) found that more neurotic job seekers reported more job search behaviors. Kanfer and colleagues, however, noted that measurement issues were influential: Neuroticism was related negatively to job search intensity (typically measured as the amount of time devoted to specific job search tasks) but positively to job search effort (the degree of effort individuals put into their job search). Other studies have found that one's general disposition to experience positive and negative emotional states also relates to job search success. Positive affectivity relates positively to job search clarity (Côté, Saks, & Zikic, 2006) and job offers (Turban et al., 2009); experiencing greater negative affect can inhibit job search success (Crossley & Stanton, 2005).

Although counselors cannot necessarily change clients' personality traits, these findings nevertheless have relevance for serving individual clients' needs and addressing barriers in the search and persuasion processes. Clients who are naturally extraverted may have an easier time with the social interaction that accompanies many job search tasks, and greater conscientiousness is associated with more successful search outcomes. Therefore, clients who are less extraverted, less conscientious, and more neurotic may find job search activities more daunting and potentially more anxiety-producing, making them good candidates for individual career counseling or support via job clubs. Similarly, clients with less positive affect or more negative affect might benefit from cognitive restructuring techniques that help them reframe their negative feelings about the job search and induce more positive emotions. Having a more positive outlook may help them cope more effectively with the inevitable disappointments in the job search process, as well as present themselves more positively in interviews.

Expectancies and self-evaluations. It likely comes as no surprise to counselors that how individuals feel about themselves and their general expectations and perceptions of the world may influence the job search process. Kanfer et al.'s (2001) findings suggest that when job seekers perceive that they have some control in the job search process, they engage in a more active job search. Although optimism was not significantly related to job search behaviors, it was predictive of positive employment outcomes (Kanfer et al., 2001). In addition, self-esteem has been found to be associated with job search behaviors and employment outcomes (Kanfer et al., 2001; Slebarska, Moser, & Gunnesch-Luca, 2009), suggesting that fostering greater self-esteem in job seekers can be beneficial. Job search self-efficacy, or the belief that one can successfully master the job search tasks and process, has been positively related to greater search behavior, as well as more positive interview and employment outcomes (Côté et al., 2006; Kanfer et al., 2001; Saks, 2006; Wanberg et al., 2005), and has also been found to mediate the relationships between other antecedents (e.g., distress and negative affect) and job search behaviors or outcomes (e.g., Crossley & Stanton, 2005). These findings again highlight the importance of maintaining a positive outlook through the job search process and having a positive self-concept. Job seekers with less positive self-concepts and lower self-esteem might benefit from individual counseling or participating in job clubs to keep them motivated through the job search process (Wanberg et al., 2005).

Job search motives, social support, and intentions.   Kanfer et al. (2001) identified a number of situational, motivational, and cognitive variables that were influential in the job search process, including financial need, employment commitment, and social support. The degree of financial need or economic hardship of the job seeker has been found to be related positively to job search behaviors (Van Hooft & Crossley, 2008), although not necessarily to employment outcomes (Kanfer et al., 2001; Wanberg et al., 2002). Although counselors cannot directly control the degree of financial need or stress related to economic hardship that clients experience, it can be helpful to understand that these may not necessarily be counterproductive character-istics for job seekers because they may help motivate individuals to be more active in this process.

Other motivational and cognitive variables that have been found to be related to job search behaviors among unemployed adults include employ-ment commitment or placing a high value on having a job (Creed et al., 2009; Kanfer et al., 2001; Vansteenkiste, Lens, De Witte, & Feather, 2005), having a greater learning goal orientation (Vansteenkiste et al., 2005), and greater use of self-regulation strategies such as emotional and motivation control (Creed et al., 2009). Taken together, these results suggest job seekers' motivations for engaging in the job search—especially their commitment to being employed and their ability to approach the job search process with an attitude of learning and growing—may be important in facilitating a more intense search. Counselors can also teach clients strategies to manage their emotions related to the job search process to help them maintain a high level of job search activities.

Feeling supported by others can increase job search behaviors and increase the chance of a positive employment outcome (Kanfer et al., 2001). Slebarska et al. (2009) suggested that in addition to the overall level of social support, it may be important to assess whether individuals perceive that the support is adequate. Not all job seekers may need the same level of support; for example, some individuals may be receiving very little support, but it is just enough or from the right source to be perceived as beneficial.

There is a burgeoning body of research that applies Ajzen's (1991) theory of planned behavior framework to the job search process. We mention it here because this line of research has focused on predicting job search intentions, which can be conceptualized as a motivational antecedent of job search behaviors (especially job search intensity). In general, research findings have demonstrated empirical support for the theoretical model in which job attitudes, subjective norms, perceived behavioral control, and self-efficacy are predictive of intentions to search, and these intentions, in turn, are predictive of job search behaviors and employment outcomes (Jaidi, Van Hooft, & Arends, 2011; Van Hooft & De Jong, 2009; Van Hooft et al., 2005; Wanberg et al., 2005; Zikic & Saks, 2009). For example, Wanberg et al. (2005) found that unemployed job seekers with more confidence for engaging in job search behaviors, who believed that their family and friends wanted them to be searching for a job, reported greater intentions to work hard at finding a job; those with greater job search intentions reported engaging in more job search behaviors. The findings related to social norms highlight the importance of other people in the behavior of the job seeker. Wanberg et al. (2005) noted that family members might not appreciate how much time and energy are required for a successful job search and expect the unemployed individual to take on additional household chores and activities. Counselors can provide some psychoeducational materials to job seekers and their family members to give friends and family specific ideas of how they can be most helpful and to facilitate realistic expectations for the process (Wanberg et al., 2005).

Life history and demographic characteristics. Kanfer et al. (2001) identified a number of demographic and human capital variables that were related to different aspects of the job search process, such as age, race, gender, educational level, and job tenure. There is evidence that age is an influential factor in getting hired and that older individuals may have a more difficult time in obtaining employment. Nakai, Chang, Snell, and Fluckinger (2011) coined the phrase "mature job seeker" to refer to those individuals who are mid-career (typically age 40) and above but not necessarily chronologically "older" workers. They identified three clusters of mature job seekers: (1) *satisficers*, whose main goal was to find a job to meet financial obligations; (2) *maximizers*, who reported a diverse range of needs and desires largely centered on the parameters of the job (i.e., benefits, full-time versus part-time); and (3) *free agents*, who tended to be older with fewer family obligations and were focused on fulfilling individual needs in their job. Nakai and colleagues suggested that each type may profit from different forms of help (e.g., satisficers may need to be encouraged to search as broadly as possible). In general, because it may take longer for older workers to find a job, counselors can provide support during periods of discouragement. The social support provided in a job club may also be beneficial for keeping motivation up and coping with disappointments in the job search process.

Kanfer et al. (2001) found some interesting patterns related to race and gender. Racial and ethnic minority job seekers reported a longer job search than

Whites, although race was not related to employment outcomes. Similarly, gender was related to job search behaviors but not employment outcomes. Men tended to engage in more job-searching behaviors than women, and when the type of search measure was examined, women reported greater job search effort, and men reported a more intense search. These findings highlight how the job search process and hiring are not immune from the effects of racial and gender socialization, as well as societal prejudice and discrimination. Although race and gender reflect individual characteristics that are not malleable, counselors need to be aware of how stereotypes can influence the hiring process and be prepared to help those most affected—women and job seekers from racial and ethnic minority groups—to cope effectively with potential discrimination experiences.

Having more education is associated with greater job search behavior and likelihood of reemployment (Kanfer et al., 2001; Wanberg et al., 2002). It may be beneficial for clients to obtain additional job training or degrees (Johnson & Lahey, 2011). Although research findings suggest that individuals with higher educational levels are more successful in the job search, in difficult economic times when jobs are scarce, individuals may opt to work in jobs that are beneath their training, educational level, or skill level. There is a growing research literature on underemployment (i.e., "working in a job that is below the employee's full working capacity"; McKee-Ryan & Harvey, 2011, p. 963) and overqualified employees (i.e., having "surplus skills, knowledge, abilities, education, experience, and other qualifications that are not required by or utilized on the job"; Erdogan, Bauer, Peiró, & Truxillo, 2011, p. 217). Recruiters may be less likely to consider applications from overqualified individuals because they perceive that overqualified employees will be dissatisfied and disgruntled (Erdogan et al., 2011; Luksyte & Spitzmueller, 2011). Erdogan and colleagues (2011) suggest that job applicants acknowledge their overqualification very early on in the application process and make a compelling case for why they should be considered, such as highlighting the potential advantages and strengths they would bring to the job. Counselors can help clients decide how they will market themselves to alleviate managers' fears that they will not be good employees.

JOB SEARCH PROGRESS AND STRATEGIES

Counselors can benefit from having a clear idea of the factors related to search behaviors and employment outcomes, yet it might be even more important to understand *how* individuals engage in the search process (Koen, Klehe, Van Vianen, Zikic, & Nauta, 2010). Recent studies have focused on understanding the progression of the search or the day-to-day activities, as well as the strategies that individuals use to search. Wanberg, Zhu, and

Van Hooft (2010) noted that most of the job seekers in their sample spent between 2 and 6 hours a day in job-searching activities. They examined the daily progress of job seekers and found that on days that job seekers perceived they made more progress on their job search, they reported more positive affect and greater confidence in finding a job. Those with greater financial hardship were more likely to perceive they had not made good progress in the job search and reported more negative affect. When job seekers reported low positive affect on one day, on the following day those job seekers who had more difficulty disengaging from negative thoughts tended to report less job search progress. In contrast, job seekers who could more easily disengage from negative thoughts tended to report greater job search progress on the next day. The implication of these findings is that clients may cope very differently with the inherent ups and downs of the job search process. Counselors need to assess to what degree their clients might ruminate on their negative thoughts, which may impede their ability to take action on search tasks. These clients may need more encouragement to help them feel more positive and maintain their motivation to continue job search efforts, whereas clients who are more action oriented might not need as much cheerleading from the counselor.

Additionally, Wanberg and colleagues (2010) found that on days that job seekers perceived that they had made good progress, the following day they tended to not work as hard on job search tasks; conversely, not making progress on one day was associated with greater progress the next day. These findings suggest that job seekers might tend to take a break after working hard on one day, and, at times, this strategy may not be in the best interest of job seekers. Counselors may want to encourage job seekers to maintain a consistent pace of job-finding activity from day to day (e.g., by putting in at least a minimum number of hours).

The strategy that individuals use to search for jobs has been associated with employment outcomes. A focused job search strategy (i.e., gearing the search to specific jobs and organizations) might be the most effective approach for job seekers who want to find a high-quality (i.e., highly satisfying and good person–job fit) position. Job seekers using a focused search strategy received more job offers (Koen et al., 2010) and reported more satisfying reemployment (Crossley & Highhouse, 2005). An exploratory search strategy (i.e., pursuing a broad array of opportunities) was associated with more job offers yet, surprisingly, offers of lower quality (e.g., lower satisfaction, poorer job–person fit) (Crossley & Highhouse, 2005; Koen et al., 2010). These findings suggest that although an exploratory strategy may be effective in getting job offers, in the absence of clear goals for the job search, individuals may be tempted to take the first job offer that comes their way, even it if might not be the best fit. Finally, a haphazard strategy in which individuals do not have a clear approach and use random methods to search unsystematically may be the least effective strategy, as it was unrelated to employment outcomes (Koen et al., 2010), and haphazard searchers tended to be less satisfied with the jobs they found (Crossley & Highhouse, 2005).

JOB-FINDING INTERVENTIONS

In the preceding sections, we explored the methods job seekers use to search for jobs, the strategies they employ to persuade others to hire them, and the characteristics that influence how they engage in the job search process. We end by discussing job-finding interventions reported in the research literature and summarizing their effectiveness in helping participants obtain employment, decrease psychological distress, and increase self-efficacy for the job-searching process.

Interventions for facilitating the job search behavior of job seekers have largely employed a structured group model that relies on social learning principles in teaching and reinforcing job search skills, as well as providing emotional support through the job search process. The two most popular of these group interventions are the Job Club (Azrin & Besalel, 1980; Azrin, Flores, & Kaplan, 1975) and JOBS (Caplan, Vinokur, Price, & van Ryn, 1989). Evidence of the efficacy of these intervention programs has accumulated since the early 1980s (Brown & McPartland, 2005).

In our current literature search, we found a number of diverse studies examining the effectiveness of Job Club interventions for groups that ranged from downsized executives to food service workers (e.g., Della-Posta & Drummond, 2006; Franze & Ferrari, 2002; Van Hooft & Noordzij, 2009). Although not all of the studies adhered to the specific Job Club procedures, they all used a group format with unemployed or job-seeking adults that provided information about the job search process; practice with specific job searching, interviewing, or networking skills; and a focus on enhancing coping skills needed for a long-term job search. In general, the results suggested that participants perceived interventions as effective (e.g., Kondo, 2009). Providing additional treatment aimed at reducing anxiety and preparing job seekers for the inevitable ups and downs of the job search process may be especially helpful in maintaining high levels of motivation and self-efficacy for the job search.

There were a number of studies in the recent literature on the effectiveness of the JOBS program that strictly adhered to the guidelines of the program. This program is focused on five elements: (1) increasing job search knowledge and skills; (2) using active teaching methods (e.g., small and large group exercises, role-plays); (3) using trainers who are skilled at group facilitation and have adequate job search knowledge; (4) creating a positive, supportive learning environment; and (5) preparing job seekers for setbacks by increasing problem-solving skills, identifying potential barriers, and enhancing motivation. The program has been found to be effective in reducing job seekers' psychological distress and facilitating reemployment (Vuori, Price, Mutanen, & Malmberg-Heimonen, 2005; Vuori & Silvonen, 2005; Vuori & Vinokur, 2005). In particular, the components of increasing job seekers' confidence in job-seeking tasks and preparing them to antici- pate the ups and downs of the job search process contribute to the positive employment outcomes.

In general, there is strong support for the effectiveness of Job Club groups (Brown & McPartland, 2005). Although we uncovered a few studies that did not report significant effects on employment or psychological outcomes (e.g., Foley et al., 2010; Shirom, Vinokur, & Price, 2008), unique characteristics of those samples (American Indians in substance abuse treatment, long- term unemployed adults) might account for these findings. Given that the prevailing job-finding intervention uses a group format, these studies raise a number of issues for counselors to consider in developing and implementing job-finding groups. The group intervention has the potential to provide individual group members with built-in social support for coping with the multiple stressors associated with job seeking. Thus, facilitating cohesion among the group members will be a vital task in successful group interventions.

Research studies note attrition rates for participants, and although group members may drop out for a variety of reasons, it raises the concern that the group may have a negative influence on some individuals. Thus, it is impor- tant to have trained facilitators who are competent to observe and address group dynamics (Curan, Wishart, & Gingrich, 1999). The constellation of the group members may be important because it may be easier to bring about cohesion when members have a shared experience such as unemployment that brings them together. For example, Rutter and Jones (2007) ran a focus group for counselor education students and found some evidence that Job Club members might prefer a homogeneous group (i.e., individuals from similar programs looking for similar jobs). In reflecting on the success of a career intervention for battered women, Chronister (2006) noted that having very heterogeneous groups with respect to ethnicity and social class made it more difficult for some groups to develop cohesion, and some members eventually dropped out because they could not relate to the other members.

CONCLUSIONS AND TAKE-HOME MESSAGES

Additional research on effective job search and persuasion methods is needed, particularly for individuals whose lives and circumstances are encumbered by special challenges, such as recent immigrants with low English proficiency, workers who are not legal residents, and individuals transitioning from illegal work (e.g., selling drugs, prostitution) to legal employment. However, the existing choice implementation and job-finding literature does offer useful ideas for career counselors working with many job seekers, whether they are new job entrants, job changers, or unemployed workers.

- Technological innovations have permeated all aspects of modern life, and this is clearly evident in the methods job seekers use to locate open positions, communicate with potential employers, and apply for jobs. The Internet provides job seekers with information and resources at their fingertips, yet some job seekers may need assistance in navigating the available information. Older workers in particular might need additional training or encouragement to feel comfortable using technology in the job-finding process.
- Many job seekers can benefit from networking or using their personal connections to identify potential job openings; however, this strategy is especially effective for those with large social networks who can make connections with people in positions of authority.
- Some job seekers can probably benefit from using alternative job search methods such as internships, co-op experiences, and volunteer activities, yet we need to learn more about how these methods facilitate the process of obtaining formal employment.
- There is some evidence that elements of vocational maturity, particularly clarity of self-concept, continue to be implicated in successful implementation outcomes. Having greater clarity about one's self and one's employment goals might facilitate a more focused, successful search. Traditional career assessment activities that facilitate self- and world-of-work exploration might be especially helpful for clients with less clarity about themselves and their employment goals.
- Career counselors should be knowledgeable about resume preparation so they can help job seekers present themselves most accurately and persuasively in their resumes and cover letters.
- The results provide some clear evidence that job seekers who are more active in the job search process greatly increase their chances of finding a job. It may be helpful for counselors to provide clients with the gentle push they need to be more active and help them cope more effectively with the inevitable ups and downs of the process.
- The literature has identified a number of individual characteristics that facilitate the job-finding process. These characteristics include qualities such as being comfortable interacting with others, being conscientious,

having a positive outlook on life and a positive attitude toward the job search, feeling good about oneself, having high job search self-efficacy, experiencing support from others, and being focused or intentional about finding a job.

- Some characteristics of job seekers can hinder their ability to keep up an active search. Clients who feel less control over the process, who struggle with negative views about themselves, who experience high amounts of anxiety, or who have little confidence in their ability to search for a job might benefit from greater focus on these issues in individual counseling or Job Club groups, rather than the simple message to be more active.
- There is good evidence that structured interventions (e.g., JOBS, the Job Club) can aid the employment and mental health needs of many unemployed individuals. It would be helpful to learn more about the active elements of these interventions and to be able to include them in both group and individual counseling contexts.

REFERENCES

Ajzen, I. (1991). The theory of planned behavior. *Organizational Behavior and Human Decision Processes, 50*, 179–211.

Azrin, N. H., & Besalel, V. A. (1980). *Job club counselor's manual: A behavioral approach to vocational counseling*. Baltimore, MD: University Park Press.

Azrin, N. H., Flores, R., & Kaplan, S. J. (1975). Job-finding club: A group assisted program for obtaining employment. *Behavior Research and Therapy, 13*, 17–27.

Blau, G. (1994). Testing a two dimensional measure of job search behavior. *Organizational Behavior and Human Decision Processes, 59*, 288–312.

Bolles, R. N. (2011). *What color is your parachute? A practical manual for job-hunters and career-changers*. Berkeley, CA: Ten Speed Press.

Boswell, W. R., Roehling, M. V., & Boudreau, J. W. (2006). The role of personality, situation, and demographic variables in predicting job search among European managers. *Personality and Individual Differences, 40*, 783–794. doi:10.1016/j.paid.2005.09.008

Brown, S. D., & McPartland, E. B. (2005). Career interventions: Current status and future directions. In W. B. Walsh & M. L. Savickas (Eds.), *Handbook of vocational psychology* (3rd ed., pp. 195–242). Mahwah, NJ: Erlbaum.

Cannata, M. (2010). Understanding the teacher job search process: Espoused preferences and preferences in use. *Teachers College Record, 112*(12), 2889–2934.

Caplan, R. D., Vinokur, A. D., Price, R. H., & van Ryn, M. (1989). Job seeking, reemployment, and mental health: A randomized field experiment in coping with job loss. *Journal of Applied Psychology, 74*, 759–769.

Chronister, K. M. (2006). Social class, race, and ethnicity: Career interventions for women domestic violence survivors. *American Journal of Community Psychology, 37*(3–4), 175–182. doi:10.1007/s10464-006-9017-8

Côté, S., Saks, A. M., & Zikic, J. (2006). Trait affect and job search outcomes. *Journal of Vocational Behavior, 68*, 233–252. doi:10.1016/j.jvb.2005.08.001

Creed, P. A., King, V., Hood, M., & McKenzie, R. (2009). Goal orientation, self-regulation strategies, and job-seeking intensity in unemployed adults. *Journal of Applied Psychology, 94*(3), 806–813. doi:10.1037/a0015518

Crossley, C. D., & Highhouse, S. (2005). Relation of job search and choice process with subsequent satisfaction. *Journal of Economic Psychology, 26*, 255–268. doi:10.1016/j.joep.2004.04.001

Crossley, C. D., & Stanton, J. M. (2005). Negative affect and job search: Further examination of the reverse causation hypothesis. *Journal of Vocational Behavior, 66*, 549–560. doi:10.1016/j.jvb.2004.05.002

Curan, J., Wishart, P., & Gingrich, J. (1999). *JOBS: A manual for teaching people successful job serach strategies.* Ann Arbor: Michigan Prevention Research Center, Institute for Social Research, University of Michigan.

de Meijer, L. A. L., Born, M. P., van Zielst, J., & van der Molen, H. T. (2007). Analyzing judgments of ethnically diverse applicants during personnel selection: A study at the Dutch police. *International Journal of Selection and Assessment, 15*(2), 139–152.

Della-Posta, C., & Drummond, P. D. (2006). Cognitive behavioral therapy increases re-employment of job seeking workers' compensation clients. *Journal of Occupational Rehabilitation, 16*, 223–230. doi:10.1007/s10926-006-9024-5

Derous, E. (2007). Investigating personnel selection from a counseling perspective: Do applicants' and recruiters' perceptions respond? *Journal of Employment Counseling, 44*, 60–72.

Erdogan, B., Bauer, T. N., Peiró, J. M., & Truxillo, D. M. (2011). Overqualified employees: Making the best of a potentially bad situation for individuals and organization. *Industrial and Organizational Psychology, 4*, 215–232. doi:1754-9426/11

Foley, K., Pallas, D., Forcehimes, A. A., Houck, J. M., Bogenschutz, M. P., Keyser-Marcus, L., & Svikis, D. (2010). Effect of job skills training on employment and job seeking behaviors in an American Indian substance abuse treatment sample. *Journal of Vocational Rehabilitation, 33*, 181–192. doi:10.3233/JVR-2010-0526

Franze, I. J., & Ferrari, J. R. (2002). Career search self-efficacy among an at-risk sample. *Journal of Prevention and Intervention in the Community, 23*(1–2), 119–128. doi:10.1300/J005v23no01_07

Granovetter, M. S. (1973). The strength of weak ties. *American Journal of Sociology, 78*, 1360–1380.

Granovetter, M. S. (1995). *Getting a job: A study of contacts and careers* (2nd ed.). Chicago, IL: University of Chicago Press.

Haase, C. M., Heckhausen, J., & Köller, O. (2008). Goal engagement during the school-work transition: Beneficial for all, particularly for girls. *Journal of Research on Adolescence, 18*(4), 671–698.

Hodges, N., Karpova, E., & Lentz, H. (2010). An investigation of women's early career experiences in the textile and apparel industries. *Family and Consumer Sciences Research Journal, 39*(1), 75–89. doi:10.1111/j.552-3934.2010.02046.x

Huang, X., & Western, M. (2011). Social networks and occupational attainment in Australia. *Sociology, 45*(2), 269–286. doi:10.1177/0038038510394029

Jaidi, Y., Van Hooft, E. A. J., & Arends, L. R. (2011). Recruiting highly educated graduates: A study on the relationship between recruitment information sources, the theory of planned behavior, and actual job pursuit. *Human Performance*, *24*(2), 135–157. doi:10.1080/08959285.2011.554468

Johnson, E., & Lahey, J. (2011). The resume characteristics determining job interviews for middle-aged women seeking entry-level employment. *Journal of Career Development*, *38*(4), 310–330. doi:10.1177/0894845310372772

Kanfer, R., Wanberg, C. R., & Kantrowitz, T. M. (2001). Job search and employment: A personality-motivational analysis and meta-analytic review. *Journal of Applied Psychology*, *86*, 837–855. doi:10.1037//0021-9010.86.5.837

Koen, J., Klehe, U., Van Vianen, A. E. M., Zikic, J., & Nauta, A. (2010). Job search strategies and reemployment quality: The impact of career adaptability. *Journal of Vocational Behavior*, *77*, 126–139. doi:10.1016/j.jvb.2010.02.004

Kondo, C. T. (2009). Benefits of job clubs for executive job seekers: A tale of hares and tortoises. *Journal of Employment Counseling*, *46*, 27–37.

Leasher, M. K., Miller, C. E., & Gooden, M. P. (2009). Rater effects and attitudinal barriers affecting people with disabilities in personnel selection. *Journal of Applied Social Psychology*, *39*(9), 2236–2274.

Lin, H. (2010). Applicability of the extended theory of planned behavior in predicting job seeker intentions to use job-search websites. *International Journal of Selection and Assessment*, *18*(1), 64–74.

Luksyte, A., & Spitzmueller, C. (2011). Overqualified women: What can be done about this potentially bad situation? *Industrial and Organizational Psychology*, *4*, 256–259.

McKee-Ryan, F. M., & Harvey, J. (2011). "I have a job, but . . .": A review of underemployment. *Journal of Management*, *37*(4), 962–996. doi:10.1177/0149206311398134

McKee-Ryan, F. M., Song, Z., Wanberg, C. R., & Kinicki, A. J. (2005). Psychological and physical well-being during unemployment: A meta-analytic study. *Journal of Applied Psychology*, *90*(1), 53–76. doi:10.1037/0021-9010.90.1.53

Nakai, Y., Chang, B., Snell, A. F., & Fluckinger, C. D. (2011). Profiles of mature job seekers: Connecting needs and desires to work characteristics. *Journal of Organizational Behavior*, *32*, 155–172. doi:10.1002/job.697

Redline, J., & Rosenbaum, J. E. (2010). School job placement: Can it avoid reproducing social inequities? *Teachers College Record*, *112*(3), 843–875.

Rutter, M. E., & Jones, J. V. (2007). The job club redux: A step forward in addressing the career development needs of counselor education students. *Career Development Quarterly*, *55*, 280–288.

Saks, A. M. (2006). Multiple predictors and criteria of job search success. *Journal of Vocational Behavior*, *68*, 400–415. doi:10.1016/j.jvb.2005.10.001

Selden, S., & Orenstein, J. (2011). Government e-recruiting web sites: The influence of e-recruitment content and usability on recruiting and hiring outcomes in US state governments. *International Journal of Selection and Assessment*, *19*(1), 31–49.

Shirom, A., Vinokur, A., & Price, R. (2008). Self-efficacy as a moderator of the effects of job-search workshops on re-employment: A field experiment. *Journal of Applied Social Psychology*, *38*(7), 1778–1804.

Slebarska, K., Moser, K., & Gunnesch-Luca, G. (2009). Unemployment, social support, individual resources, and job search behavior. *Journal of Employment Counseling, 46*, 159–170.

Tomasik, M., Hardy, S., Haase, C. M., & Heckhausen, J. (2009). Adaptive adjustment of vocational aspirations of German youths during the transition to work. *Journal of Vocational Behavior, 74*, 38–46. doi:10.1016/j.jvb.2008.10.003

Toporek, R. L., & Flamer, C. (2009). The résumé's secret identity: A tool for narrative exploration in multicultural career counseling. *Journal of Employment Counseling, 46*, 4–17.

Try, S. (2005). The use of job search strategies among university graduates. *Journal of Socio-Economics, 34*, 223–243. doi:10.1016/j.socec.2004.09.009

Tsai, W. C., Chi, N. W., Huang, T. C., & Hsu, A. J. (2011). The effects of applicant resume contents on recruiters' hiring recommendations: The mediating roles of recruiter fit perceptions. *Applied Psychology: An International Review, 60*(2), 231–254. doi:10/1111/j.1464-0597.2010.00434.x

Tso, G. K. F., Yau, K. K. W., & Cheung, M. S. M. (2010). Latent constructs determining Internet job search behaviors: Motivation, opportunity and job change intention. *Computers in Human Behavior, 26*, 122–131. doi:10.1016/j.chb.2009.10.016

Turban, D. B., Stevens, C. K., & Lee, F. K. (2009). Effects of conscientiousness and extraversion on new labor market entrants' job search: The mediating role of metacognitive activities and positive emotions. *Personnel Psychology, 62*, 553–573.

Tyler, J. M., & McCullough, J. D. (2009). Violating prescriptive stereotypes on job resumes: A self-presentational perspective. *Management Communication Quarterly, 23*(2), 272–287. doi:10.1177/089331890341412

Van Hooft, E. A. J., Born, M. P., Taris, T. W., & van der Flier, H. (2005). Predictors and outcomes of job search behavior: The moderating effects of gender and family situation. *Journal of Vocational Behavior, 67*, 133–152. doi:10.1016/j.jvb.2004.11.005

Van Hooft, E. A. J., & Crossley, C. D. (2008). The joint role of locus of control and perceived financial need in job search. *International Journal of Selection and Assessment, 16*(3), 258–271.

Van Hooft, E. A. J., & De Jong, M. (2009). Predicting job seeking for temporary employment using the theory of planned behaviour: The moderating role of individualism and collectivism. *Journal of Occupational and Organizational Psychology, 82*, 295–316. doi:10.13-48/096317908X325322

Van Hooft, E. A. J., & Noordzij, G. (2009). The effects of goal orientation on job search and reemployment: A field experiment among unemployed job seekers. *Journal of Applied Psychology, 94*(6), 1581–1590. doi:10.1037/a0017592

Van Hoye, G., & Saks, A. M. (2008). Job search as goal-directed behavior: Objectives and methods. *Journal of Vocational Behavior, 73*, 358–367. doi:10.1016/j.jvb.2008.07.003

Van Hoye, G., van Hooft, E. A. J., & Lievens, F. (2009). Networking as a job search behavior: A social network perspective. *Journal of Occupational and Organizational Psychology, 82*, 661–682. doi:10.1348/096317908X36067S

Vansteenkiste, M., Lens, W., De Witte, H., & Feather, N. T. (2005). Understanding unemployed people's job search behavior, unemployment experience and well-being: A comparison of expectancy-value theory and self-determination theory. *British Journal of Social Psychology, 44,* 269–287. doi:10.1348/014466604X17641

Vuori, J., Price, R. H., Mutanen, P., & Malmberg-Heimonen, I. (2005). Effective group training techniques in job-search training. *Journal of Occupational Health Psychology, 10*(3), 261–275. doi:10.1037/1076-8998.10.3.261

Vuori, J., & Silvonen, J. (2005). The benefits of a preventative job search program on re-employment and mental health at 2-year follow-up. *Journal of Occupational and Organizational Psychology, 78,* 43–52. doi:10.1348/096317904X23790

Vuori, J., & Vinokur, A. D. (2005). Job-search preparedness as a mediator of the effects of the Työhön Job Search Intervention on re-employment and mental health. *Journal of Organizational Behavior, 26,* 275–291. doi:10.1002/job.308

Wanberg, C. R., Glomb, T. M., Song, Z., & Sorenson, S. (2005). Job-search persistence during unemployment: A 10-wave longitudinal study. *Journal of Applied Psychology, 90*(3), 411–430. doi:10.1037/0021-9010.90.3.411

Wanberg, C. R., Hough, L. M., & Song, Z. (2002). Predictive validity of a multidisciplinary model of reemployment success. *Journal of Applied Psychology, 87,* 1100–1120.

Wanberg, C. R., Zhu, J., & Van Hooft, E. A. J. (2010). The job search grind: Perceived progress, self-reactions, and self-regulation of search effort. *Academy Management Journal, 53*(4), 788–807.

Willis, L., & Wilkie, L. (2009). Digital career portfolios: Expanding institutional opportunities. *Journal of Employment Counseling, 46,* 73–81.

Zikic, J., & Saks, A. M. (2009). Job search and social cognitive theory: The role of career-relevant activities. *Journal of Vocational Behavior, 74,* 117–127. doi:10.1016/j.jvb.2008.11.001

CHAPTER 22

Promoting Work Satisfaction and Performance

ROBERT W. LENT AND STEVEN D. BROWN

P EOPLE WORK FOR MANY reasons and differ in the rewards they receive from their work (Blustein, 2006; Lent & Brown, Chapter 1, this volume), yet they generally wish to be satisfied with and effective at their jobs. Work organizations also have a strong desire to hire workers who will be both happy and productive on the job. These two outcomes—work satisfaction and satisfactory performance—have, understandably, been the focus of a great deal of theory and research, given their profound consequences (e.g., emotional, economic) for both worker and employer. Although they are often studied separately, they can be seen as representing complementary views on effective adjustment to work. When the focus is on how the worker feels about his or her work (including its conditions and rewards), the commonly used term is *job satisfaction;* when the perspective shifts to the question of how well the worker performs his or her job, we may speak about his or her *job satisfactoriness* (Lofquist & Dawis, 1984). These language conventions in the vocational literature imply that, as in any contract, it is important for both parties to be satisfied—in this case, the worker with the job (and what it offers) and the employer with the worker (and what he or she contributes to the work organization).

According to the theory of work adjustment (TWA), the worker's job satisfaction and satisfactoriness are, together, expected to lead to job tenure, the length of time that the worker will stay in a particular job or work environment (see Swanson & Schneider, Chapter 2, this volume). That is, satisfied workers are assumed to be motivated to remain in their jobs. Likewise, employers have a vested interest in retaining satisfactory (i.e., productive) workers. The reasonableness of these twin assumptions is immediately obvious. Imagine a work organization populated mostly by miserably unhappy and poorly performing workers. Over time, one would expect a great deal of turnover: those who can do so will tend to seek more satisfying work elsewhere, and the least productive will risk losing their jobs (or experiencing other negative consequences, such as frozen wages or demotions, which may exacerbate their dissatisfaction).

Research findings generally support the expectation that satisfaction and satisfactoriness should each predict job tenure (Swanson & Schneider, Chapter 2, this volume). However, these relationships are complicated by many factors. For example, some workers remain in unsatisfying jobs because they perceive few good alternatives (e.g., given their age, skill set, geographical location, family responsibilities), have limited support for making a job change, or fear jumping from the frying pan into the fire during difficult economic times. Likewise, employers may either retain workers or lay them off for reasons other than the strength of their work performance (e.g., seniority, outsourcing, corporate mergers, plant closings).

Although satisfaction and satisfactoriness offer no unconditional guarantee of job stability, and even though the world of work has been undergoing dramatic change in recent years (Lent & Brown, Chapter 1, this volume), these two outcomes are still considered important markers of work adjustment, albeit with some key qualifications. In particular, although everyone who works would most likely prefer to have a satisfying job, there are many situations in which job choices are dictated more by economic need or other considerations (e.g., family wishes, job availability, skill or educational limitations) than by work enjoyment. Also, as noted by Super's life space theory (see Hartung, Chapter 4, this volume), the work role varies in its centrality for different people. Work satisfaction is, therefore, more likely to be especially meaningful for those who view work as among their most significant life roles than for those who are more psychologically invested in other roles, such as family member or community volunteer. Different people also hold varying standards for their work performance, with some focused on doing the minimum required and others wishing to excel, either for intrinsic (e.g., self-satisfaction) or extrinsic (e.g., pay) reasons.

In this chapter, we draw on a variety of perspectives—especially person–environment (P-E) fit and social cognitive career theories—that may be used to help counselors conceptualize and assist clients experiencing problems with work dissatisfaction or substandard performance. Although our primary focus is on remedial counseling (i.e., where existing problems have motivated help seeking), the practical implications we derive from the literature are also relevant for developmental and preventive interventions, that is, for promoting work satisfaction and performance proactively or for nipping problems in the bud where they do occur. We divide the chapter into two main sections focusing, respectively, on factors that promote job satisfaction and performance. Within each section, we offer examples of how the theoretical and research literatures may be used to inform interventions. Although we believe these literatures also have valuable implications for providing counseling aimed at role satisfaction and success to students and to those engaged in nonpaid work activities, our primary focus here is on adult employees who have made the transition from school (or college) to work.

JOB SATISFACTION

This section (a) considers the typical ways in which job or work satisfaction has been defined and measured; (b) discusses major sources of, and theoretical views on, job satisfaction, particularly those that may have particular relevance for counseling; and (c) identifies suggestions for promoting work satisfaction that can be derived from research and theory. Although the literature on job satisfaction is voluminous, the limited scope of this chapter requires a highly selective review. A variety of sources are available for readers who wish a more comprehensive or different (e.g., organizational psychology) perspective on job satisfaction theories and research (e.g., Brief, 1998; Fritzsche & Parrish, 2005; Locke, 1976; Spector, 1997). The approach taken here is adapted from Lent's (2008) recent review of the literature, offered from the perspective of vocational psychology.

DEFINITION AND FRAME OF REFERENCE

Because most people spend a sizable portion of their lives working, how they feel about their work can be quite important to them, their significant others, and their work organizations. For example, meta-analytic evidence supports the popular belief that job satisfaction is related to job success; that is, happy workers are likely to be productive workers, both in doing the formal parts of their jobs (task performance) and in making informal contributions to their organizations (contextual performance) (Fritzsche & Parrish, 2005; Judge, Thoresen, Bono, & Patton, 2001). Affect at work may also spill over into people's nonwork lives (e.g., Judge & Ilies, 2004; Rain, Lane, & Steiner, 1991). In addition, job satisfaction may contribute to overall life satisfaction, mental health, physical health, and even longevity (Fritzsche & Parrish, 2005; Lofquist & Dawis, 1984; Spector, 1997).

Job satisfaction has been formally defined as "a pleasurable or positive emotional state resulting from the appraisal of one's job or job experiences" (Locke, 1976, p. 1300). In simpler terms, it refers to the *extent to which people like their jobs* (Spector, 1997). Common synonyms for *job satisfaction* include *work/job enjoyment, happiness,* and *well-being.* Although its basic definition may appear to be fairly straightforward, as we will see, job satisfaction becomes a more complex matter when theorists and researchers need to be more precise about such things as which aspects of the job to focus on, from whose perspective, and over what length of time.

Job satisfaction is typically assessed by asking for a worker's self-report, allowing the individual to consider and weigh whatever specific factors are deemed relevant to their overall level of work enjoyment. It is also possible to obtain satisfaction ratings through external means, for example, by asking Suzie's supervisor, romantic partner, or coworkers about her degree of job satisfaction. These alternative perspectives are useful for some research purposes, but in most inquiry on job satisfaction, Suzie would be seen as the key arbiter of how she feels about her own job or work situation; that is, satisfaction is usually viewed as a subjective matter.

OVERALL RATES OF JOB SATISFACTION

Perhaps surprisingly, when asked by opinion researchers, most people report fairly high levels of overall job satisfaction. For instance, in a 2008 Gallup poll, 48% of U.S. workers reported being completely satisfied with their jobs, and 42% said they were somewhat satisfied; 7% reported being somewhat dissatisfied, and 2% were completely dissatisfied; 1% reported no opinion (http://www.gallup.com/poll/109738/us-workers-job-satisfaction-relatively-high.aspx). Respondents gave more variable responses, however, when they were asked about their satisfaction with particular parts of their jobs. For instance, over two-thirds were completely satisfied with the safety conditions of their jobs and with their relations with their coworkers, whereas less than a third were completely satisfied with their amount of work stress or pay.

The 90% of respondents who were at least partly satisfied with their jobs overall had dipped only slightly by 2011 (http://www.gallup.com/poll/147833/job-satisfaction-struggles-recover-2008-levels.aspx), despite 3 years of economic recession. Of course, responses to the 2011 survey may have been affected by workers' relief over simply having a job during the recession. The percentages of those who were at least partly satisfied with their jobs did vary somewhat as a function of demographic group membership. For example, older, higher paid, better educated, and racial/ethnic majority workers reported the highest rates of satisfaction—generally 90% or higher. However, no demographic group that was examined reported less than an 82% overall rate of job satisfaction either in 2008 or 2011. Although it is certainly a positive sign that most people in the United States tend to be satisfied with their jobs, the 10% or so who are unhappy (including up to

18% from some demographic groups) constitute literally millions of people who may, theoretically, be aided by career practitioners.

Global Versus Facet Job Satisfaction

The Gallup poll used about the simplest possible method of assessing job satisfaction—essentially, asking people a single question about how satisfied they were with their jobs, with two response options reflecting satisfaction (completely or somewhat satisfied) and two others reflecting dissatisfaction (completely or somewhat dissatisfied). A similar method was used when asking about satisfaction with particular aspects of one's job (e.g., pay). The only simpler approach would be to ask for a single "are you satisfied or dissatisfied?" judgment. Indeed, for some reporting purposes, the Gallup poll aggregated the two satisfaction response options into a single "satisfied" rating and the two dissatisfaction options into a single "dissatisfied" rating, thereby dichotomizing workers into satisfied versus unsatisfied categories.

Whereas the Gallup approach may be sufficient for purposes of a general opinion survey, most vocational researchers prefer scales that are more sophisticated from a psychometric standpoint (e.g., use of multiple items and response options, asking about satisfaction in different ways) yet that are still fairly straightforward, brief, and easy to use. The measures they use tend to assess either *global* or *facet* satisfaction. Global measures reflect overall feelings about one's job. Two popular examples include the Index of Job Satisfaction (Brayfield & Rothe, 1951) and the Job in General Scale (JIG; Ironson, Smith, Brannick, Gibson, & Paul, 1989), from which very brief (five- to eight-item) forms have been devised. The JIG, for example, asks workers to rate their job using a variety of feeling-oriented and evaluative (e.g., "enjoyable," "good") terms. Facet measures assess satisfaction with specific aspects of one's job, such as the work activities one performs, the rewards offered by the job, the nature of the work conditions, and the people with whom one works. Examples of facet measures include the Job Descriptive Index (Smith, Kendall, & Hulin, 1969) and the Minnesota Satisfaction Questionnaire (MSQ; Weiss, Dawis, England, & Lofquist, 1967). They naturally tend to be a bit longer (e.g., 72 to 100 items) than general measures of job satisfaction because they cover more content areas, but briefer forms, such as a 20-item version of the MSQ, have also been developed. Researchers sometimes assess both forms of satisfaction or average together facet item responses to yield a composite measure of job satisfaction.

Apart from the general versus facet focus, researchers must also decide on the time frame of the assessment. Job satisfaction can be measured in terms of how people feel about their jobs either over nonspecific time periods (e.g., "most of the time"; Ironson et al., 1989) or over particular time periods (e.g., the past week, today). More immediate feeling judgments tend to be easier to make and may be more likely to capture responses to particular work events (e.g., conflict with a supervisor). Retrospective or indefinite time periods require people to remember or reconstruct how they might have felt in the past (e.g., "let's see, how did I feel about my work last year?"). Such summary judgments involve simplifying cognitive strategies that can distort self-reports of past feelings (Kahneman, 1999) and confound people's perceptions of their jobs with their more general affective or personality traits (e.g., general tendencies to be happy or unhappy or to see the positive or negative sides of most life situations).

THE MANY SOURCES OF JOB SATISFACTION—AND DISSATISFACTION

Job satisfaction can stem from many different factors. We consider here four major views on the origins of work satisfaction: person, environment, P-E interaction (or fit), and integrative positions. The distinction between these categories is not always crisp, particularly when the individual is the sole source of information about self, environment, or P-E fit. For instance, in rating one's work environment, the person is telling us how he or she experiences that environment, which may or may not be consistent with the views of coworkers. Despite potential overlap among them, it may nevertheless be useful to present these putative sources of satisfaction under different headings.

Person variables. This category includes personality and affective traits that have been linked to satisfaction outcomes. Personality researchers assume that job satisfaction reflects more global tendencies to feel or act in certain ways, regardless of the specific life context. In this view, job satisfaction may be less about the job than it is about the person—how he or she generally experiences the world in relation to the self. In a meta-analysis, Judge, Heller, and Mount (2002) found that three of the Big Five personality traits (extraversion, neuroticism, conscientiousness) yielded small to medium correlations with job satisfaction (see also Brown & Hirschi, Chapter 11, this volume). Other meta-analyses have found that the traits of positive affect and negative affect were moderately associated with job satisfaction (e.g., Bowling, Eschleman, & Wang, 2010). Ilies and Judge (2003) reported that 29% of the variance in job satisfaction may be due to genetic factors, lending support to the argument that "job satisfaction is, in part, dispositionally based" (Judge et al., 2002, p. 530).

Job satisfaction ratings have been found to be somewhat stable over time. For example, Staw and Ross (1985) reported moderate stability coefficients over 3- and 5-year intervals. It is noteworthy, however, that job satisfaction ratings tended to be more stable when workers remained in the same positions than when they changed employers or occupations. Other research suggests that job satisfaction can fluctuate over time and conditions (Judge & Ilies, 2004), particularly when job satisfaction is assessed over shorter time periods (e.g., on a daily basis). Moreover, situational and cognitive variables have been found to predict job satisfaction independently of traits (e.g., Watson & Slack, 1993). Thus, the trait and heritability findings do not rule out the operation of nongenetic sources of job satisfaction.

What might we conclude from a counseling perspective? Our main interpretation of the findings is that job satisfaction is responsive both to dispositional and situational factors. If job satisfaction were only an immutable quality of the person (e.g., people are born to be happy or unhappy), as some writers believe (e.g., Lykken & Tellegen, 1996), then one would expect very high stability of job satisfaction over time and despite changing contexts. The moderate stability coefficients—and the sensitivity of satisfaction ratings to work events, situational influences, and cognitions—suggest that job satisfaction is potentially modifiable (rather than merely a matter of genetic fate). However, efforts to enhance job satisfaction will no doubt profit from additional research on the specific pathways (intermediate variables and processes) through which traits are linked to job satisfaction (Brief, 1998; Heller, Watson, & Ilies, 2004).

Environment variables. This category includes a variety of work condition and climate factors (e.g., social support, role stressors). Job satisfaction has been linked to many features of the work environment, particularly as people experience this environment subjectively. One influential view is that job satisfaction depends on the degree to which people perceive that their work environment provides a general set of favorable conditions, characteristics, or opportunities to fulfill their values. Warr (1999) organized commonly studied work characteristics and values into a set of 10 job features (e.g., opportunity for personal control, supportive supervision, valued social position, availability of money) that have been associated with job-specific well-being indices. It is noteworthy that several of Warr's categories involve social features of work. Other writers have noted that work environments offer opportunities for companionship, emotional support, belongingness, and practical assistance (Turner, Barling, & Zacharatos, 2002). Indeed, findings show that the perceived social climate of work relates substantially to job satisfaction (Carr, Schmidt, Ford, & DeShon, 2003).

Many studies have examined particular positive and negative work conditions, such as supports and stressors. A number of distressing work conditions—such as role stressors (e.g., role ambiguity, conflict, and overload), incivility, and harassment—have been linked to job (dis)satisfaction, with some findings showing that such work conditions account for significant unique variance in job satisfaction apart from affective dispositions (cf. Lent, 2008). Organizational support theory (Rhoades & Eisenberger, 2002; Shore & Shore, 1995) offers a larger conceptual umbrella within which to view supportive or hostile work conditions. Perceived organizational support refers to the degree to which workers feel that their organization cares about their welfare, appreciates their contributions, and is committed to them. For instance, the experience of stressful work conditions or unfair pay may lead people to see their workplace as unsupportive, which, in turn, diminishes their satisfaction. Perceived organizational support may, therefore, be a central mediating variable that helps explain how diverse work conditions affect satisfaction.

Person–environment fit. Another perspective—one that has particularly influenced the thinking of career counselors—assumes that it is not the presence of generally favorable job characteristics or conditions per se that leads to job satisfaction, but rather the capacity of the work environment to provide specific conditions or rewards that individuals desire, based on aspects of their work personalities. This is the P-E fit perspective on job satisfaction. For instance, TWA posits that individuals will be satisfied to the extent that the work environment provides a set of reinforcers (e.g., variety, autonomy) that meet their personal work needs/values (e.g., Swanson & Schneider, Chapter 2, this volume). Holland's theory maintains that people will be more satisfied when their vocational interests/personalities match (are highly congruent with) those of others in their work environment (Nauta, Chapter 3, this volume)—for example, when an Investigative type person works in Investigative type environment. Research findings suggest that P-E fit, as defined by TWA and Holland's (1997) theory, tends to be modestly related to job satisfaction (e.g., Tranberg, Slane, & Ekeberg, 1993). It has also been found that value-reinforcer correspondence accounts for unique variance in job satisfaction beyond interest congruence (e.g., Rounds, 1990).

An integrative perspective. A recent trend has been to develop integrative models of work satisfaction that bring together person, environment, and P-E fit perspectives. Social cognitive career theory (SCCT), presented in Chapter 5, is one such approach. SCCT includes a variety of cognitive, behavioral, and environmental variables that are assumed, individually and jointly, to promote job satisfaction. In particular, the theory posits that people are likely to be happy at work to the extent that they are engaged in valued activities, are making progress toward personal goals, feel self-efficacious at meeting their goals and performing their jobs, believe that their work will produce valued outcomes, and perceive ample supports (and minimal barriers) for their work behavior and goal pursuit. Research findings generally provide support for the relations of these individual variables to work satisfaction, and several recent studies suggest that the model as a whole (or subsets of it) is tenable (Lent & Brown, 2006, 2008; Sheu & Lent, 2009), though not all hypothesized paths are uniquely predictive of job satisfaction in all studies. (See Lent, 2008, for coverage of additional integrative models of job satisfaction.)

From a counseling perspective, research on work conditions, P-E fit, and social cognitive variables offers an important counterpoint to the literature on dispositional predictors of job satisfaction. The dispositional research produces a view of job and other aspects of satisfaction as relatively fixed (e.g., Lykken & Tellegen, 1996), whereas situational and cognitive approaches encourage a focus on antecedents of job satisfaction that are potentially modifiable via counseling or other means (e.g., self-help, organizational interventions). For example, by setting and pursuing personal goals or by identifying organizations (or niches within organizations) where they are likely to find support and a sense of reciprocated loyalty, people may be partly able to promote their own work satisfaction—rather than merely feeling forced to either "grin and bear it" or defect to a different job. This is not to imply that everyone will be equally able to make changes in themselves or their work environments to enhance their job satisfaction, but even small exercises of personal control may be good for one's morale.

IMPLICATIONS FOR ASSESSMENT AND INTERVENTION

It should be clear from the preceding review that job satisfaction is a "multiply determined phenomenon" (Lent, 2008, p. 475) in the sense that a number of different variables contribute to its prediction when it is studied in groups of people. However, when individual clients seek counseling because they are dissatisfied with their job or career, our experience has been that they often perceive a particular factor (or small set of factors) to be at issue. They may be able to point to fairly specific conditions, events, or relationships that they do not like (or that they may feel anxious, angry, or depressed about) in their current work situation. By contrast, some clients may have a difficult time articulating what "just *feels* wrong"; they may experience job dissatisfaction as a vague sense of ennui or as a growing conviction that their work has come to lack meaning or purpose for them (Lent, in press-b).

In many cases, clients may enter counseling asking for assistance in changing their jobs or careers. This is often a sign of work dissatisfaction that has reached a point where the client feels that escape may be the best or even the only viable answer. How the counselor defines the problem will partly determine whether counseling is directed at environmental change, self-change, or both. For example, will the counselor take the client's desire to leave the current job at face value or dig deeper to identify the source(s) of dissatisfaction? Can something be done to manage the condition(s) that seem to be behind the client's dissatisfaction? If so, is the client likely to be happy remaining in the current job—or is the P-E gulf just too wide to be bridged?

As should be apparent, the first step in counseling for job satisfaction (and change) is to assess the problem carefully. How dissatisfied is the client and with *what* in particular? Fortunately, the literature can be used to provide a structure for assessing job satisfaction and its sources. For example, if formal assessment is preferred, a very brief measure, such as the JIG, can be used to gauge the client's overall level of job satisfaction. If the counselor is comfortable with a more informal approach, he or she can simply ask the client to rate his or her current or usual level of job satisfaction on a scale of 1 (totally miserable) to 10 (totally happy). Although some counselors would simply infer the client's degree of satisfaction from information provided in the first interview, an advantage of obtaining numeric ratings as a part of problem assessment is that they provide an explicit baseline against which efforts to enhance job satisfaction can later be compared.

Where it is clear, either from the client's presenting problem or targeted assessment, that dissatisfaction is likely to be the focus of counseling, it is useful to explore the source of the dissatisfaction and to ascertain whether it appears limited to the current job situation or extends beyond it (e.g., poor fit with one's larger occupation in terms of values or interests). Our review suggests that most specific sources of work dissatisfaction are likely to fall within several broad categories, such as environmental conditions (e.g., a nonsupportive supervisor), cognitive-person factors (e.g., self-efficacy, goal progress), traits (e.g., negative affect), and P-E fit (e.g., not getting what one wants from work). Table 22.1 lists common causes of job dissatisfaction, which can be used to structure the assessment process and to identify possible targets for counseling.

Despite their placement in different conceptual categories in the table, it is important to keep in mind that the attribution of the problem's source generally lies in the eye of the beholder. Although it is important to respect the client's point of view, it is also important to appreciate that this view is usually not the only one possible. For example, the client may feel certain that his or her supervisor is *the* cause of the client's dissatisfaction when, in fact, others generally find it pleasant to work with the supervisor. Such differences in perception may mean that what the client sees as a problem

Table 22.1
Common Sources of Work Dissatisfaction

- **Environmental sources**
  - Stress
  - Role conflict (e.g., work/family, dual career), ambiguity, or overload
  - Interpersonal conflict, adverse social climate
  - Harassment
  - Incivility
  - Discrimination
  - Amount of support from supervisor, co-workers, larger organization for P's goals, personal growth, or well-being
  - Barriers to career or goal progress
  - Amount of opportunity to engage in personally valued (meaningful) work activities
  - Job characteristics (e.g., low skill variety, task significance, autonomy)
- **Person sources**
  - Affective and personality dispositions
    - Negative affect and neuroticism
    - Positive affect and extraversion
    - Conscientiousness
  - Cognitive-person variables
    - Self-efficacy regarding job tasks and personal goals
    - Outcome expectations regarding work conditions and rewards
    - Goals (e.g., progress toward central goals)
- **Person–Environment fit**
  - Interests
    - Congruence between P and occupation in measured interests (Holland)
  - Values
    - Correspondence between P and occupation in measured values (TWA)
    - Perceived fit between what P wants and what the job supplies
  - Abilities
    - Perceived fit between P's abilities and the ability demands of the job
  - Other or multiple P-E fit dimensions
    - Perceived fit of P to the job, work organization, work group, or supervisor in terms of values, goals, personality, and/or interpersonal compatibility

with the work environment could also be viewed as a matter of P-E fit (e.g., the client's difficulty interacting with the supervisor around particular issues). We find it helpful, like most counselors, to start off by exploring the client's perspective. But it can also be invaluable to seek additional sources of information that can support, challenge, or broaden that perspective. For example, the client can be encouraged to discuss with coworkers how they experience or deal with a particular issue that the client experiences as problematic. The counselor could also form hypotheses based on aspects of the client's in-session presentation (e.g., low affect, lack of assertion, difficulty listening, lack of follow-through on homework assignments) that may be relevant to his or her work relationships or experience of work dissatisfaction.

At the broadest level, work dissatisfaction is likely to be caused either by the *absence* of something positive that the client wants (e.g., engrossing work activities, better pay, fun coworkers) or by the *presence* of something negative that he or she does not want (e.g., stress, role conflicts, harassment). The client's decision to seek counseling likely implies that he or she feels unable to access the positive things or to neutralize the negative ones. To clarify these perceptions, the counselor might ask the following sorts of questions: (a) What do you want from your work that you are currently not getting (or not getting enough of)? (b) What parts of your job or work situation do you dislike the most (or even dread)? (c) How do you like to spend your time when you are not working? How does your work life fit with these other parts of your life?

Although they may capture overlapping information, the first question is intended to help clarify needs or values that are not being adequately met at work (e.g., insufficient variety, growth opportunities); the second and third sets of questions seek to identify negative work conditions or role strain issues (e.g., overwork, interpersonal tensions, work–family conflict). Yet another way to get at these issues is through a version of the "magic question": "Imagine you were to wake up one day to find yourself truly happy at work. What would need to change for that to happen in real life?" The responses to any of these questions could lead to more in-depth exploration of the sources of dissatisfaction, conditions that exacerbate or lessen it, and the usefulness of current coping strategies. Although clients often provide a window on their primary perceived source of dissatisfaction without much prompting, more thorough exploration may reveal secondary sources of dissatisfaction and hypotheses about coping options.

Where a more structured or thorough approach is preferred, a facet measure of job satisfaction, like the Minnesota Satisfaction Questionnaire, could be used to survey a range of potential job-setting-based sources of dissatisfaction. To explore potential trait-based reasons for job dissatisfaction, a simple, brief measure like the Positive and Negative Affect Schedule (PANAS; Watson, Clark, & Tellegen, 1988) can be administered. The PANAS contains two 10-item scales that measure, respectively, characteristic levels of positive (e.g., enthusiastic) and negative (e.g., scared) affect. Clients can be instructed to indicate how they "generally feel" (i.e., without respect to life context) or how they feel specifically, most of the time, when at work.

Once the counselor has integrated various sources of assessment data to conceptualize the problem—and once the client and counselor have arrived at a shared construction of the likely source(s) of the dissatisfaction—a counseling plan can be designed to address it. The plan might include a variety of options for the client to consider, such as (a) making changes in the self (e.g., managing time differently to deal with work overload, developing ways to manage problematic affective tendencies; Brown, Ryan, & McPartland, 1996; Lent, 2004), (b) making changes in the work environment (e.g., negotiating for more challenging work assignments, finding advocates to redress unfair conditions), or (c) making a job or occupational change. When none of these options is feasible (and if the client feels that continuing to endure job dissatisfaction is a lesser evil than leaving his or her current job), compensatory strategies might be considered, such as increased involvement in nonwork activities that allow for personal growth, valued goal pursuit, or social participation.

The approach we have described is largely derived from the literature on work satisfaction and integrates ideas from P-E fit theories, SCCT, and more general cognitive-behavioral counseling theories. The methods of other career theories presented in the first section of this book could also be assembled to inform interventions designed to prevent or treat work dissatisfaction. For example, career construction theory (Savickas, Chapter 6, this volume) could suggest narrative methods to help clients "edit" unsatisfying work stories and envision new scripts for more fulfilling or meaningful work. The important thing, we think, is for counseling to proceed from a reasonably thorough and shared assessment of the problem. Where career change seems indicated, the typical methods of career choice counseling can be adopted (e.g., see Whiston & James, Chapter 20, this volume). Where job change (within the same career) is desired, the client can be assisted with job search methods described by Jome and Phillips (Chapter 21, this volume). However, in such cases, it may still be valuable to explore and deal with sources of dissatisfaction (e.g., affective traits, unreliable coping methods) that may follow the client to a new job or career path.

WORK SATISFACTORINESS OR PERFORMANCE

We turn now to a discussion of satisfaction from the perspective of the work organization, that is, to the employee's satisfactoriness in performing his or her work roles. Counselors working with adults frequently encounter clients seeking help with problems that involve job performance. Such problems may be a client's primary reason for entering counseling (perhaps to stave off an impending job loss or to deal with blocked advancement opportunities) or may be contributory to, or exacerbated by, other presenting concerns (e.g., depression). The primary purposes of this section are to summarize relevant research and theory and to draw implications for promoting work performance. As in the satisfaction section of this chapter, we begin by considering key ways that job satisfactoriness has been defined and measured and then turn to a discussion of major sources of satisfactoriness, drawing on theoretical perspectives that are relevant to career counseling. Finally, we summarize counseling implications that may be derived from research and theory.

Definition and Frame of Reference

Job satisfactoriness refers to the organization's satisfaction with the employee and is assessed in most organizations by supervisor performance appraisals. Although research on job satisfactoriness typically uses standardized measures like the Minnesota Satisfactoriness Scales (MSS; Carlson, Dawis, England, & Lofquist, 1963), most employers have their own performance appraisal systems that reflect their focus on particular work tasks and performance criteria. Poor appraisals from an employing organization may lead people to seek help from a counselor or, in some cases (especially with managers and executives), to assignments to work with a job coach.

Work or job performance is a related but broader term that refers to the adequacy with which a person fulfills his or her job-specific tasks or other behaviors that contribute to the organization. Research on work performance often uses supervisor appraisals to index employees' levels of work performance but may also include other types of measures (e.g., job simulations and work sample tests, records of customer satisfaction or complaints, measures of productivity, job knowledge tests, and measures of performance in training). Work performance has historically been a major focus of research in industrial/organizational psychology and has greatly informed understanding of employee satisfactoriness.

It is possible to differentiate performance and satisfactoriness at a conceptual level: performance may connote objective or data-driven indicators of role functioning, whereas satisfactoriness involves a summary judgment (usually made by a supervisor) of the individual's performance, taking into account various (objective and subjective) data sources. In other words, satisfactoriness reflects how happy the organization (or a representative of the organization) is with the employee, given assessments of his or her work behavior. These terms are, however, often used as synonyms in the literature and, in practice, satisfactoriness and performance appraisal ratings may be considered an efficient way to index performance, at least from the perspective of the work organization. Because the distinction between the two is often muddied in practice and because the larger literature on this topic in organizational psychology more often uses the term *performance* (though *satisfactoriness* remains popular with some in vocational psychology), we use these terms interchangeably here.

THE MULTIPLE DIMENSIONS OF WORK PERFORMANCE

Job performance is one of the central constructs in organizational psychology (Campbell, Gasser, & Oswald, 1996). Not surprisingly, a vast literature focuses on the antecedents and consequences of job performance. Research has recently produced an expanded view of work performance. Results of this body of research have revealed that job performance is not a unidimensional construct, but instead involves several aspects of employee behavior, all of which may influence the performance appraisals of individual employees. In other words, the question of how well a person does his or her job is often not so simple; the answer may well differ, depending on which dimension of performance one considers.

Task and contextual performance. Contemporary conceptions of work performance include two to four broad classifications of employee behavior that contribute to organizational effectiveness. The first, usually labeled as *task performance*, focuses on how well employees perform the specific work tasks prescribed by their jobs or job descriptions (e.g., selling, teaching, writing, plumbing). Task performance, which reflects the common image of what people do when they are at work, has been a major focus of research since the beginning of organizational psychology and has been shown to be an important factor underlying performance appraisals (e.g., Rotundo & Sackett, 2002).

Organizational psychology scholars have, in more recent years, recognized the importance of employee behaviors that are not strictly prescribed by job descriptions but that nevertheless contribute to organizational effectiveness by enhancing the psychological and social context in which work occurs (Katz & Kahn, 1978). These extra-role, beyond the call of duty behaviors—typically labeled *contextual performance* (CP) or *organizational citizenship behaviors* (OCB) (Borman & Motowidlo, 1993, 1997; Organ, 1988, 1997; Smith, Organ, & Near, 1983)—include helping and cooperating with others, volunteering to do more than the minimum required in the job, following procedures even when personally inconvenient, persisting to accomplish tasks, and defending and supporting the organization's objectives (Borman & Motowidlo, 1993).

Borman (2004) suggested that the various OCB behaviors can be subclassified within a three-category system. The first OCB category, *personal support*, describes behaviors that are intended to facilitate coworker performance and includes helping others by offering suggestions, teaching skills, assisting on tasks, and providing emotional support. This category also includes cooperative behaviors (e.g., accepting suggestions, putting team needs ahead of one's own needs) and courteous behaviors (e.g., showing consideration and confidence in others). The second OCB category, *organizational support*, involves behaviors aimed at the organization rather than individual employees. Such behaviors include representing the organization favorably and promoting its public image, showing loyalty despite temporary hardships, supporting the organization's mission and objectives, complying with organizational rules, and suggesting improvements. The third OCB category, *conscientious initiative*, includes behaviors that are less interpersonally or organizationally directed but that show effort and initiative on the part of the employee (e.g., persisting on difficult tasks, taking on extra work to get the job done, finding additional work to do when one's own tasks are completed, and taking the initiative to develop new knowledge and skills).

Similar taxonomies focus on the value of both interpersonally and organizationally directed citizenship behaviors. For example, Organ and colleagues (e.g., Organ & Paine, 1999; Smith et al., 1983) suggest that prosocial behaviors directed at other individual employees (OCB-I) and those directed at the organization as a whole (OCB-O) represent conceptually and empirically distinct types of organizational citizenship behavior. The former (OCB-I), like Borman's personal support dimension, generally involve cooperating with and helping others, being courteous to fellow employees, and displaying an altruistic attitude to others in the organization. The latter (OCB-O), similar to Borman's organizational support dimension, are defined as behaviors that demonstrate identification with and allegiance to the organization, defend the organization against threats, and endorse and support the organization's objectives (e.g., Borman & Motowidlo, 1993; Graham, 1991).

Both types of OCBs (in addition to behaviors involving conscientious initiative) have been hypothesized to contribute to the performance appraisals of employees, above and beyond their task performance. In the case of OCB-I, it has been suggested that a reciprocity norm may operate between supervisor and subordinate. For example, employees who perform these types of citizenship behaviors (e.g., helping a worker who has fallen behind on a task) often free up supervisors' time to work on other important tasks. As a result, supervisors may reciprocate this help by providing positive performance appraisals. OCB-O may form an important aspect of performance appraisals, especially today when perceptions of commitment to organizations seem to be declining (e.g., Johnson, 2005), by demonstrating to managers and supervisors loyalty and commitment to the organization.

OCB researchers have noted that the current economic environment requires organizations to be flexible and able to adapt quickly to changing local, national, and worldwide trends to improve their products and services and remain competitive in the global marketplace (e.g., Jelinek &

Schoonhoven, 1993). Accordingly, scholars have begun to recognize that another type of OCB may contribute significantly to the productivity or efficiency of work organizations. Called *voice* behaviors by Van Dyne and LePine (1998), this type of OCB includes "making innovative suggestions for change and recommending modifications to standard procedures even when others disagree" (p. 109), challenging the status quo, and promoting change in the organization. There are several reasons that voice may contribute to performance appraisals independent of both task performance and other types of organizational citizenship behavior. First, as suggested earlier, employee voice may be seen as integral to initiating the types of changes and adaptability required in today's business climate. Second, employees who provide valuable suggestions to managers on how to improve the organization are likely to help managers be more successful in their own jobs. Third, voice behaviors may be seen as a reflection of the employee's commitment to the organization, much like OCB-O type behaviors.

Counterproductive behaviors. A third set of employee behaviors has also been seen as contributing to performance appraisals separately from task and contextual performance but in the opposite direction—*counterproductive work behaviors* (CWB). CWB involves voluntary behaviors that harm the well-being of the organization (Rotundo & Sackett, 2002) and negatively affect an organization's productivity and culture. Examples of CWB behaviors that have been studied include (a) personally deviant behaviors (e.g., substance and alcohol abuse, other illegal behaviors), (b) destructive or hazardous behaviors (e.g., violating security and safety, destroying equipment), (c) aggression and unruliness (e.g., actions that harm other workers, such as gossiping and spreading rumors), and (d) behaviors that diminish organizational productivity (e.g., taking overly long breaks, being tardy, missing work, sabotaging the work of others, behaving in an unprofessional manner with customers).

Adaptive performance. The changing nature of the work world has also led some investigators to posit that a fourth class of performance behaviors may be critical in the current marketplace and that supervisors may also consider these behaviors when making performance appraisals. Called *adaptive performance* (e.g., Pulakos, Arad, Donovan, & Plamondon, 2000), these behaviors include employees' facility at handling emergency or crisis situations and work stress, solving problems creatively, dealing with uncertain and unpredictable work situations, and adapting to new cultures. Adaptive performance is conceptually related to career adaptability (Savickas, Chapter 6, this volume), career preparedness (Lent, in press-a), and similar constructs that are of current interest in career counseling and vocational psychology. Research on adaptive performance, however, seems to be less well developed at this time than research on task performance, organizational citizenship, and counterproductive work behaviors and, therefore, is not discussed further here.

Relations among the types of work performance. Researchers have examined the relations among the various types of work performance to determine whether they truly represent distinct psychological dimensions. LePine and Van Dyne (2001) explored the relations among task performance, voice, and other forms of organizational citizenship behavior and found that voice was sufficiently distinct from other forms of organizational citizenship to warrant its separate assessment in the study of work performance. However, studies of the relations between individually focused (OCB-I) and organizationally focused (OCB-O) citizenship behaviors suggest that they may not be empirically distinguishable when assessed from the perspective of supervisors. LePine, Erez, and Johnson (2002) found large meta-analytic correlations among measures of OCB-I and OCB-O. They also found that potential antecedents of OCB (e.g., job satisfaction) produced similar relations to OCB-I and OCB-O behaviors. Together, these results suggest that OCB-I and OCB-O behaviors may form a single underlying psychological construct. Whether they are considered as distinct manifestations of OCB or as a single category, an adequate understanding of clients' organizational citizenship behavior may require exploration of his or her interactions with fellow employees, contributions to the organization's culture and objectives, and voice (or demonstration of independent initiative) in the organization.

Research has also shown that counterproductive work behavior is empirically distinguishable from the other forms of work performance. Dalal (2005), for example, reported only moderately sized meta-analytic correlations between measures of organizational citizenship behaviors and counterproductive work behaviors. Understandably, prosocial behaviors are inversely related to CWBs (i.e., those who demonstrate good organizational citizenship are less likely to engage in organization-harming behaviors). However, the negative correlations between these two constructs are not so large as to suggest that they are just opposite poles of a good-to-bad worker continuum. Others have found that task performance relates only weakly to organizational citizenship and counterproductive work behaviors (LePine & Van Dyne, 2001).

Types of performance and supervisor appraisals of work effectiveness. From a counseling perspective, it is important to note that task performance, organizational citizenship behavior, and counterproductive work behavior all contribute to performance appraisals (i.e., ratings of employee satisfactoriness). Researchers have found that task performance and OCBs both correlate substantially with overall performance ratings (e.g., .43 for task performance and .41 for contextual performance; Motowidlo & Van Scotter, 1994). Counterproductive work behaviors seem to also contribute importantly to overall performance appraisals, apart from the contributions of task performance and OCBs. In a study of performance appraisals in five occupational groups, Rotundo and Sackett (2002) found that task performance and counterproductive work behaviors each correlated more highly with overall performance appraisals (average *r*s of .50 and −.52 for task performance and counterproductive behaviors, respectively) than did OCBs (average *r* = .29).

Finally, research has explored the unique contribution of employee voice, as an aspect of OCB, to overall performance appraisals. Whiting, Podsakoff, and Pierce (2008) reported that task performance, OCB-I, OCB-O, and voice behaviors all explained significant unique variance in performance appraisal ratings. It is interesting that they also found significant interactions among these sources of performance appraisal, suggesting that voice influences performance appraisals positively only if task performance, citizenship behavior, or both are high. In other words, supervisors in this study gave more weight to voice when employees were also contributing to the organization via acceptable task or contextual performance. Because voice behaviors have the potential to threaten the status quo and engender organizational defensiveness, it may be that employees who exercise their voice have credibility only if they are seen as effective performers in other ways. Otherwise, supervisors and coworkers may take the position, "Why should we listen to *you?*"

In summary, the research in this area suggests that work performance encompasses more than just task performance. In addition to how well people perform the tasks that are formally required of them, performance appraisals can be influenced by the prosocial behaviors that employees display at work, including the degree to which they cooperate with and help others (OCB-I), support and defend the organization as a whole (OCB-O), demonstrate conscientious initiative, and offer challenging and innovative suggestions to improve the organization's effectiveness (voice). Performance appraisals also take into account counterproductive behaviors that detract from or harm the organization. In terms of organizational citizenship, supervisors may attend to behaviors that challenge the status quo (voice), as well as to more cooperative types of behaviors aimed at helping fellow employees or promoting the organization as a whole. The impact that voice behaviors have on employee satisfactoriness may depend on the other types of contributions that employees make to the organization. Voice may not be well accepted by supervisors unless employees are performing their job tasks well or contributing in other ways to the performance and climate of their organization. It is also possible that voice behaviors are more likely to be heeded and rewarded if offered in constructive ways rather than seen as rabble-rousing—a style issue that may be explored in counseling.

THE MANY SOURCES OF JOB SATISFACTORINESS—AND UNSATISFACTORINESS

Many variables discussed earlier in this chapter as sources of job satisfaction have also been found to be important sources of job satisfactoriness. These include person variables, the work environment, person–environment fit, and various social cognitive variables.

Person variables. Certain personality variables, especially the Big Five trait of conscientiousness (see Brown & Hirschi, Chapter 11, this volume), have been shown to reliably predict work performance. Several large-scale meta-analyses (e.g., Barrick & Mount, 1991; Salgado, 1997) have found that employee conscientiousness may, in fact, represent one of the strongest predictors of work performance for most jobs. Finer-grained analyses have suggested that conscientiousness is an important predictor of task performance, as well as organizational citizenship behavior and counterproductive work behavior (Chiaburu, Oh, Berry, Li, & Gardner, 2011). Some researchers have also reported that other Big Five traits rival conscientiousness in predicting organizational citizenship behaviors. For example, Chiaburu and colleagues (2011) found that openness, agreeableness, and conscientiousness were all good predictors of both OCB-I and OCB-O, while extraversion and openness were good predictors of voice.

These findings suggest that work performance is partly linked to the personality dispositions that people bring with them to their work settings. For example, employees who tend to be cooperative (agreeable) and open to new experiences and ideas (open) may be more likely to engage in the types of citizenship behaviors that are seen as valuable in performance appraisals. Similarly, persons who are relatively outgoing (extraversion) and comfortable with change (open) may be more likely to effectively challenge the status quo when such behavior is desirable. Conscientious employees (those who are goal directed, organized, planful, and achievement oriented) seem to have an advantage over less conscientious employees in most, if not all, performance domains that are included in performance appraisals.

Another type of person variable, general cognitive ability, has been studied extensively in relation to work performance. General cognitive ability (or intelligence), which reflects the ability to learn new tasks (Schmidt, 2002), is indexed by a variety of commercially available intelligence and ability tests. It has been found to be a strong predictor of work performance (see Metz & Jones, Chapter 16, this volume). Meta-analytic correlations between intelligence and work performance are some of the largest that have been reported in the literature and suggest that as much as 25% of the variance in work performance is accounted for by employee general cognitive ability, irrespective of type of job, though more complex jobs seem to require more general learning ability than less complex jobs (e.g., Gottfredson, 1997; Schmidt, 2002). Intelligence also seems to be more strongly related to task performance than to organizational citizenship behavior (although it is involved in both), whereas personality traits relate more strongly to organizational citizenship behavior (although they, too, especially conscientiousness, relate to both; e.g., Borman & Motowidlo, 1993). General cognitive ability appears to relate to task performance in at least two ways, both directly (i.e., higher levels of cognitive ability enable stronger performance) and indirectly, through the acquisition of job knowledge (see Schmidt, 2002). That is, those with higher levels of general cognitive ability learn what is required on their jobs (acquire job knowledge) more quickly and easily than do those with lesser ability.

For a variety of reasons, the contributions of general cognitive ability and personality to work performance remain sensitive topics in the counseling field. For example, counselors may lack clear guidelines about how to approach variables that have a heritable component or feel that adherence to social justice values is incompatible with acknowledgment of person qualities that may be used to label people in negative, static ways or contribute to their oppression. At the same time, it is difficult to ignore findings that general cognitive ability and conscientiousness each account for substantial amounts of the variance in work performance (Schmidt & Hunter, 1998). Hence, there remains a tension between, on the one hand, viewing ability and personality as undeniable aspects of individual difference and, on the other hand, seeking avenues to change features of persons and environments that can enable people to lead more fulfilling work lives.

Environment variables. Several features of the work environment have also been found to relate to employee satisfactoriness, most notably role stressors and strains (role ambiguity, conflict, and overload), perceived organizational support, job autonomy, and organizational climate (Carr et al., 2003; Langford, & Moye, 2004; Morgeson, Delaney-Klinger, & Hemmingway, 2005). There is also evidence that these environmental factors may be linked to performance indirectly through the intervening variable of employee satisfaction. This indirect pathway may be more pronounced in the case of organizational citizenship and counterproductive work behaviors than task performance (Eatough, Chang, Miloslavic, & Johnson, 2011). In other words, employees who view their work environments as nonsupportive (e.g., because they routinely receive ambiguous assignments or have low levels of autonomy) are likely to become dissatisfied at work. Dissatisfied workers are, in turn, less likely to engage in organizational citizenship behaviors and more likely to exhibit counterproductive work behaviors than satisfied workers, whose more supportive environments encourage goodwill and loyalty toward the organization.

Person–environment fit. P-E fit has also been found to predict job performance as well as job satisfaction (see the satisfaction section of this chapter). For example, Holland's theory (see Nauta, Chapter 3, this volume) hypothesizes that work performance, like satisfaction, results from working in an occupational environment that is congruent with one's personality. Thus, an IA person working in an IA environment will tend to like the job more and perform better in it than a person with an SE personality working in the same type (IA) environment. The theory of work adjustment (TWA; see Swanson & Schneider, Chapter 2, this volume) also maintains that harmonious P-E matches produce both worker satisfaction and satisfactoriness. In the case of satisfactoriness, better fit between the employee's abilities and the ability requirements of the work environment are assumed to lead to better work performance. Findings indicate that both forms of P-E fit (RIASEC congruence and TWA correspondence) are modestly related to various indices of work performance and that TWA correspondence accounts for unique variance in the prediction of job satisfactoriness beyond RIASEC congruence (e.g., Dawis & Lofquist, 1984).

An integrative perspective. Social cognitive career theory's performance model (SCCT; see Lent, Chapter 5, this volume) attempts to integrate several sets of variables that, together, are seen as promoting work performance. While acknowledging various person, learning, and environmental variables that contribute to performance, this model highlights the joint roles of cognitive ability and work-related skills, self-efficacy beliefs, outcome expectations, and performance goals relative to work performance. More specifically, SCCT hypothesizes that general cognitive ability and the specific work skills that people develop (through prior mastery experiences and by observing others) influence task performance both directly and indirectly via self-efficacy beliefs. Self-efficacy is seen as enabling performance in several ways, in particular, by helping people organize and deploy their cognitive abilities more effectively and form more optimistic outcome expectations (see Lent, Chapter 5).

SCCT also posits that self-efficacy and outcome expectations affect work performance, at least in part, via their influence on the types of work goals that people set for themselves. Persons with more robust self-efficacy beliefs and positive outcome expectations are likely to set more challenging performance goals than workers with weaker self-efficacy beliefs and less positive (or more negative) outcome expectations. More challenging goals, in turn, are expected to motivate people to work harder at goal attainment, leading to higher levels of performance. In a meta-analysis of research on a portion of the performance model, cognitive ability and self-efficacy were found to jointly predict both work goals and performance (Brown, Lent, Telander, & Tramayne, 2011). When conscientiousness was added to the model test, findings suggested that this variable related to task performance directly as well as indirectly through self-efficacy (presumably, more conscientious persons may hold stronger beliefs in their work capabilities, which, in turn, motivate greater effort).

Although SCCT's performance model was specifically developed to account for task performance, it may also have implications for under-standing how much and how well people engage in contextual performance. In particular, the performance model might be extended to posit that work-ers are more likely to perform extra-role citizenship behaviors when they possess both strong self-efficacy beliefs and favorable outcome expectations related to these behaviors (i.e., when they believe they can perform the OCBs successfully and that doing so will produce positive rather than negative out-comes). A growing body of research suggests that engaging in OCB, though positively valued by employers, is not without its costs for employees; it can, for example, be associated with work overload, job stress, and work–family conflict (e.g., Bolino & Turnley, 2005). Some employees may, understand-ably, be reluctant to engage in OCBs because of such anticipated costs (i.e., negative outcome expectations may outweigh positive ones). Although there is need to test the SCCT performance model in the context of organizational citizenship, these speculations suggest the potential value of helping clients to consider both the pros and cons of engaging in increased OCB.

Implications for Assessment and Intervention

Like satisfaction, job satisfactoriness is multiply determined. Thus, it is useful for counseling aimed at performance problems to begin by determining the major sources of a client's lack of satisfactoriness at work. We typically start by exploring the degree to which inadequate task performance, organiza-tional citizenship behaviors (including voice), and counterproductive work behaviors might be contributing to clients' performance appraisals. We try to determine whether clients are aware of the importance of citizenship behaviors and other extra-role behaviors (e.g., counterproductive work behavior) to performance appraisals. We have found that some clients think that doing their official job tasks well is all that is required of them. Although this might be an accurate assumption in some work settings, an exploration of the degree to which extra-role behaviors are positively valued in their organizations can be enlightening to clients.

One possible strategy for gathering data on task performance, organizational citizenship, and counterproductive work behaviors is to ask clients to describe their past work day or week. Counselors can, for example, listen for instances of citizenship and counterproductive behaviors and probe for examples of each (e.g., What did you do last week to help a fellow employee? How do you feel about your organization's goals and values? What do you do when you disagree with the direction your organization or work unit is going?). Counselors can also develop checklists of potential organizational citizenship and counterproductive behaviors. Clients can be asked to complete the checklist between the first and second session, or the counselor may present items orally to the client for in-session discussion. Table 22.2 provides a summary of behaviors that can be used to create such a checklist.

It may be also be helpful for clients to seek the perspectives of a supervisor or trusted coworkers on their task and extra-role behaviors at work, because external feedback may help clients to peer around their own blind spots. In fact, in some cases, consultation with several other feedback sources may be useful in creating a composite picture of one's performance. To the extent that perceptions of satisfactoriness lie in the eye of the beholder, and in situations where work performance appraisals are heavily based on subjective data, such interpersonal feedback may prove very informative.

This suggestion is similar to the practice of "360-degree feedback" in organizational consultation, where, for example, performance feedback is sought from a sample of a target individual's supervisors, coworkers, and subordinates or customers. If such options are pursued, it may be important to discuss or role-play with clients how to gather and respond nondefensively to constructive feedback. It may also be valuable to employ performance instruments that closely reflect the actual tasks and organizational citizenship behaviors of the employee's work environment. A possibly less threatening approach to assessment may be to rely on prior performance appraisals that the client has received, possibly augmented by follow-up discussions between the client and his or her supervisors to get a clearer sense of areas for improvement and how they will be assessed.

We have often found it beneficial to explore specifically the extent to which feelings of job satisfaction might be affecting clients' performance. For example, unhappiness at work may serve as a negative motivational force, contributing to diminished task performance, withholding of citizenship

Table 22.2

Examples of Organizational Citizenship and Counterproductive
Work Behaviors

- **OCB-I***
  - ○ Helping others by offering suggestions
  - ○ Teaching others useful knowledge and skills
  - ○ Helping others to perform their tasks
  - ○ Accepting others' suggestions
  - ○ Providing emotional support
  - ○ Showing courtesy to others
  - ○ Showing confidence in others
  - ○ Being tactful

- **OCB-O***
  - ○ Representing the organization favorably
  - ○ Defending the organization
  - ○ Promoting the organization
  - ○ Supporting the organization's mission and objectives
  - ○ Complying with reasonable organization rules and procedures

- **Conscientious Initiative***
  - ○ Persisting with extra effort when the task requires it
  - ○ Taking initiative to do all that is required even if not part of one's job duties
  - ○ Finding additional productive work when one's own duties are completed

- **Voice**
  - ○ Making innovative suggestions for change
  - ○ Challenging the status quo
  - ○ Recommending changes in standard procedures even when others disagree

- **Counterproductive Work Behaviors**
  - ○ Frequent absences
  - ○ Arriving late to work
  - ○ Gossiping or spreading rumors about others
  - ○ Behaving disrespectfully to customers or co-workers
  - ○ Engaging in dangerous or unsafe behaviors
  - ○ Destroying equipment
  - ○ Sabotaging the work of others

*Adapted from Borman (2004), Table 1.

behavior, or involvement in counterproductive work behaviors (e.g., frequent absences, tardiness, brusqueness with customers or coworkers). (Of course, there may be bidirectional relations as well, with performance problems serving to diminish work satisfaction, resulting in a negative satisfaction–performance cycle.) Should lack of satisfaction seem to be contributing to satisfactoriness problems, we typically shift our focus to identifying the underlying sources of clients' dissatisfaction and proceed with counseling strategies outlined in the first section of this chapter.

Where assessment results suggest that clients' unsatisfactoriness is due primarily to task performance problems, we try to ascertain the work tasks that seem to be problematic for them, their abilities to meet task demands, and their self-efficacy beliefs. Should assessment results reveal that citizenship behaviors are contributing to unsatisfactory performance appraisals, we attempt to identify the basis for these appraisals (e.g., lack of knowledge of their importance, negative outcome expectations, lack of skill or low self-efficacy beliefs at citizenship behaviors) and then proceed to explore options for improving contextual performance in ways that parallel the promotion of task performance. Strategies derived from SCCT or P-E fit theories can be used to target features of the client, work setting, or their possible mismatch that, if addressed, could enhance performance (e.g., identifying and accessing desired organizational supports or reinforcers). Where ability or skill limitations, in particular, are implicated, these can be approached in several ways. For example, intervention could focus on motivational variables (e.g., self-efficacy, goals) that may optimize use of one's abilities (see Lent, Chapter 5, this volume). Training or continuing education might also be used to strengthen or update work-specific skills that can enhance performance. Especially when other options may not be viable, efforts can be made to identify new job roles or tasks (either within the current environment or elsewhere) that may better match the client's current abilities and desired level of effort.

Finally, it can be helpful to assess performance-related aspects of personality (see Brown & Hirschi, Chapter 11; Rottinghaus & Hauser, Chapter 17, this volume) early in counseling. In particular, where clients score low on measures of conscientiousness, the counselor can explore the degree to which specific aspects of conscientiousness (e.g., lack of goal directedness or organization, poor time management or follow-through) may be contributing to unsatisfactory performance appraisals. Although conscientiousness is usually conceptualized as a cluster of traits in the personality literature, we find it useful to view it as a set of behaviors that, like most other behaviors, can be broken into smaller segments and learned through observation and practice. This focus on conscientious *behaviors* may be extremely valuable for certain clients in that it frames the problem in motivational or self-regulation terms that can be tackled via social learning strategies, rather than construing it as necessarily a matter of static disposition.

SUMMARY AND TAKE-HOME MESSAGES

Problems of work satisfaction and satisfactoriness represent primary reasons for some adult clients to seek counseling. For others, these may be secondary to their main presenting concerns (e.g., depression, lack of life satisfaction). In either case, the promotion of greater satisfaction or satisfactoriness represents an important goal for counseling. The approaches that we have described in this chapter integrate ideas from organizational and personality psychology research, as well as from P-E fit and social cognitive career theories. All of these sources of evidence converge to suggest that work satisfaction and satisfactoriness are multiply determined (and related to each other). For this reason, it is useful to begin by trying to understand the reasons underlying clients' dissatisfaction or unsatisfactoriness and then working collaboratively with clients to set goals and develop specific interventions. Although tailored to a given client's needs, useful general strategies include (a) self-change (e.g., developing better time management skills, displaying more frequent organizational citizenship behaviors), (b) modifying the current work environment or P-E fit conditions (e.g., arranging more challenging work assignments or ones that require more or less interpersonal interaction), or (c) pursuing counseling for job or career change.

REFERENCES

Barrick, M. R., & Mount, M. K. (1991). The Big Five personality dimensions and job performance: A meta-analysis. *Personnel Psychology, 44,* 1–26.

Blustein, D. L. (2006). *The psychology of working: A new perspective for career development, counseling, and public policy.* Mahwah, NJ: Erlbaum.

Bolino, M. C., & Turnley, W. H. (2005). The personal costs of organizational citizenship behavior: The relationship between individual initiative and role overload, job stress, and work–family conflict. *Journal of Applied Psychology, 90,* 740–748.

Borman, W. C. (2004). The concept of organizational citizenship. *Current Directions in Psychological Science, 13,* 238–241.

Borman, W. C., & Motowidlo, S. J. (1993). Expanding the criterion domain to include elements of contextual performance. In N. Schmitt & W. C. Borman (Eds.), *Personnel selection in organizations* (pp. 71–98). San Francisco, CA: Jossey-Bass.

Borman, W. C., & Motowidlo, S. J. (1997). Task performance and contextual performance: The meaning for personnel selection research. *Human Performance, 10,* 99–109.

Bowling, N. A., Eschleman, K. J., & Wang, Q. (2010). A meta-analytic examination of the relationship between job satisfaction and subjective well-being. *Journal of Occupational and Organizational Psychology, 83,* 915–934.

Brayfield, A. H., & Rothe, H. F. (1951). An index of job satisfaction. *Journal of Applied Psychology, 35,* 307–311.

Brief, A. P. (1998). *Attitudes in and around organizations.* Thousand Oaks, CA: Sage.

Brown, S. D., Lent, R. W., Telander, K., & Tramayne, S. (2011). Social cognitive career theory, conscientiousness, and work performance: A meta-analytic path analysis. *Journal of Vocational Behavior, 79,* 81–90.

Brown, S. D., Ryan, N. E., & McPartland, E. B. (1996). Why are so many people happy and what do we do for those who aren't? A reaction to Lightsey (1996). *Counseling Psychologist, 24,* 751–757.

Campbell, J. P., Gasser, M. B., & Oswald, F. L. (1996). The substantive nature of job performance variability. In K. R. Murphy (Ed.), *Individual differences and behavior in organizations* (pp. 258–299). San Francisco, CA: Jossey-Bass.

Carlson, R. E., Dawis, R. V., England, G. W., & Lofquist, L. H. (1963). The measurement of employee satisfactoriness. *In Minnesota studies in vocational rehabilitation, XIV*, Bulletin 37. Minneapolis: University of Minnesota Press.

Carr, J. Z., Schmidt, A. M., Ford, J. K., & DeShon, R. P. (2003). Climate perceptions matter: A meta-analytic path analysis relating molar climate, cognitive and affective states, and individual level work outcomes. *Journal of Applied Psychology, 88,* 605–619.

Chiaburu, D. S., Oh, I. S., Berry, C. M., Li, N., & Gardner, R. G. (2011). The five-factor model of personality traits and organizational citizenship behavior: A meta-analysis. *Journal of Applied Psychology, 96,* 1140–1166.

Dalal, R. (2005). A meta-analysis of the relationship between organizational citizenship behavior and counterproductive work behavior. *Journal of Applied Psychology, 90,* 1241–1255.

Dawis, R. V., & Lofquist, L. H. (1984). *A psychological theory of work adjustment.* Minneapolis, MN: University of Minnesota Press.

Eatough, E. M., Chang, C. H., Miloslavic, S. A., & Johnson, R. E. (2011). Relationship of role stressors with organizational citizenship behavior: A meta-analysis. *Journal of Applied Psychology, 96,* 619–632.

Edwards, J. R., Cable, D. M., Williamson, I. O., Lambert, L. S., & Shipp, A. J. (2006). The phenomenology of fit: Linking the person and environment to the subjective experience of person–environment fit. *Journal of Applied Psychology, 91,* 802–827.

Fritzsche, B. A., & Parrish, T. J. (2005). Theories and research on job satisfaction. In S. D. Brown & R. W. Lent (Eds.), *Career development and counseling: Putting theory and research to work* (pp. 180–202). Hoboken, NJ: Wiley.

Gottfredson, L. S. (1997). Why *g* matters: The complexity of everyday life. *Intelligence, 24,* 79–132.

Graham, J. W. (1991). An essay on organizational citizenship behavior. *Employee Responsibilities and Rights Journal, 4,* 249–270.

Heller, D., Watson, D., & Ilies, R. (2004). The role of person versus situation in life satisfaction: A critical examination. *Psychological Bulletin, 130,* 574–600.

Holland, J. L. (1997). *Making vocational choices: A theory of vocational personalities and work environments* (3rd ed.). Odessa, FL: Psychological Assessment Resources.

Ilies, R., & Judge, T. A. (2003). On the heritability of job satisfaction: The mediating role of personality. *Journal of Applied Psychology, 88,* 750–759.

Ironson, G. H., Smith, P. C., Brannick, M. T., Gibson, W. M., & Paul, K. B. (1989). Construction of a job in general scale: A comparison of global, composite, and specific measures. *Journal of Applied Psychology, 74,* 193–200.

Jelinek, M., & Schoonhoven, C. B. (1993). *The innovation marathon: Lessons from high-technology companies.* San Francisco, CA: Jossey-Bass.

Johnson, L. K. (2005). The new loyalty: Make it work for your company. *Harvard Management Update, 10*(3), 3–5.

Judge, T. A., Heller, D., & Mount, M. K. (2002). Five-factor model of personality and job satisfaction: A meta-analysis. *Journal of Applied Psychology, 87,* 530–541.

Judge, T. A., & Ilies, R. (2004). Affect and job satisfaction: A study of their relationship at work and at home. *Journal of Applied Psychology, 89,* 661–673.

Judge, T. A., Thoresen, C. J., Bono, J. E., & Patton, G. K. (2001). The job satisfaction–job performance relationship: A qualitative and quantitative review. *Psychological Bulletin, 127,* 376–407.

Kahneman, D. (1999). Objective happiness. In D. Kahneman, E. Diener, & N. Schwarz (Eds.), *Well-being: The foundations of hedonic psychology* (pp. 3–25). New York, NY: Russell Sage Foundation.

Katz, D., & Kahn, R. L. (1978). *The social psychology of organizations* (2nd ed.). New York, NY: Wiley.

Kristof-Brown, A. L., Zimmerman, R. D., & Johnson, E. C. (2005). Consequences of individuals' fit at work: A meta-analysis of person–job, person–organization, person–group, and person–supervisor fit. *Personnel Psychology, 58,* 281–342.

Langford, C. W., & Moye, N. A. (2004). Effects of task autonomy on performance: An extended model considering motivational, informational, and structural mechanisms. *Journal of Applied Psychology, 89,* 934–945.

Lent, R. W. (2004). Toward a unifying theoretical and practical perspective on well-being and psychosocial adjustment. *Journal of Counseling Psychology, 51,* 482–509.

Lent, R. W. (2008). Understanding and promoting work satisfaction: An integrative view. In S. D. Brown & R. W. Lent (Eds.), *Handbook of counseling psychology* (4th ed., pp. 462–480). New York: Wiley.

Lent, R. W. (in press-a). Career-life preparedness: Revisiting career planning and adjustment in the new workplace. *Career Development Quarterly.*

Lent, R. W. (in press-b). Promoting meaning and purpose at work: A social cognitive perspective. In B. J. Dik, Z. S. Byrne, & M. F. Steger (Eds.), *Purpose and meaning in the workplace.* Washington, DC: American Psychological Association.

Lent, R. W., & Brown, S. D. (2006). Integrating person and situation perspectives on work satisfaction: A social-cognitive view. *Journal of Vocational Behavior, 69,* 236–247.

Lent, R. W., & Brown, S. D. (2008). Social cognitive career theory and subjective well-being in the context of work. *Journal of Career Assessment, 16,* 6–21.

LePine, J. A., Erez, A., & Johnson, D. E. (2002). The nature and dimensionality of organizational citizenship behavior: A critical review and meta-analysis. *Journal of Applied Psychology, 87,* 52–65.

LePine, J. A., & Van Dyne, L. (2001). Voice and cooperative behavior as contrasting forms of contextual performance: Evidence of differential relationships with Big Five personality characteristics and cognitive ability. *Journal of Applied Psychology, 86,* 326–336.

Locke, E. A. (1976). The nature and causes of job satisfaction. In M. D. Dunnette (Ed.), *Handbook of industrial and organizational psychology* (pp. 1297–1349). Chicago, IL: Rand McNally.

Lofquist, L. H., & Dawis, R. V. (1984). Research on work adjustment and satisfaction: Implications for career counseling. In S. D. Brown & R. W. Lent (Eds.), *Handbook of counseling psychology* (pp. 216–237). New York, NY: Wiley.

Lykken, D., & Tellegen, A. (1996). Happiness is a stochastic phenomenon. *Psychological Science, 7*, 186–189.

McCrae, R. R., & Costa, P. T. (1991). Adding *liebe und arbeit*: The full five-factor model and well-being. *Personality and Social Psychology Bulletin, 17*, 227–232.

Morgeson, F. P., Delaney-Klinger, K., & Hemmingway, M. A. (2005). The importance of job autonomy, cognitive ability, and job-related skill for predicting role breadth and job performance. *Journal of Applied Psychology, 90*, 399–406.

Motowidlo, S. J., & Van Scotter, J. R. (1994). Evidence that task performance should be distinguished from contextual performance. *Journal of Applied Psychology, 79*, 475–480.

Organ, D. W. (1988). *Organizational citizenship behavior: The good soldier syndrome.* Lexington, MA: Lexington.

Organ, D. W. (1997). Organizational citizenship behavior: It's construct clean-up time. *Human Performance, 10*, 85–97.

Organ, D. W., & Paine, J. B. (1999). A new kind of performance for industrial and organizational psychology: Recent contributions to the study of organizational citizenship behavior. *International Review of Industrial and Organizational Psychology, 14*, 337–368.

Pulakos, E. D., Donovan, M. A., & Plamondon, K. E. (2000). Adaptability in the workplace: Development of a taxonomy of adaptive performance. *Journal of Applied Psychology, 85*, 612–624.

Rain, J. S., Lane, I. M., & Steiner, D. D. (1991). A current look at the job satisfaction/life satisfaction relationship: Review and future considerations. *Human Resources, 44*, 287–307.

Rhoades, L., & Eisenberger, R. (2002). Perceived organizational support: A review of the literature. *Journal of Applied Psychology, 87*, 698–714.

Rotundo, M., & Sackett, P. R. (2002). The relative importance of task, citizenship, and counterproductive performance to global ratings of job performance: A policy-capturing analysis. *Journal of Applied Psychology, 87*, 66–80.

Rounds, J. B. (1990). The comparative and combined utility of work value and interest data in career counseling with adults. *Journal of Vocational Behavior, 37*, 32–45.

Salgado, J. F. (1997). The five factor model personality and job performance in the European community. *Journal of Applied Psychology, 82*, 30–43.

Schmidt, F. L. (2002). The role of general cognitive ability and job performance: Why there cannot be debate. *Human Performance, 15*, 187–210.

Schmidt, F. L., & Hunter, J. (1998). The validity and utility of selection methods in personnel psychology: Practical and theoretical implications of 85 years of research findings. *Psychological Bulletin, 124*, 262–274.

Sheu, H., & Lent, R. W. (2009). A social cognitive perspective on well-being in educational and work settings: Cross-cultural considerations. *International Journal for Educational and Vocational Guidance, 9*, 45–60.

Shore, L. M., & Shore, T. H. (1995). Perceived organizational support and organizational justice. In R. S. Cropanzano & K. M. Kacmar (Eds.), *Organization politics, justice, and support: Managing the social climate of the workplace* (pp. 149–164). Westport, CT: Quorum.

Smith, C. A., Organ, D. W., & Near, J. P. (1983). Organizational citizenship behavior: Its nature and antecedents. *Journal of Applied Psychology, 68*, 653–663.

Smith, P. C., Kendall, L. M., & Hulin, C. L. (1969). *The measurement of satisfaction in work and retirement: A strategy for the study of attitudes.* Chicago, IL: Rand McNally.

Spector, P. E. (1997). *Job satisfaction: Application, assessment, causes, and consequences.* Thousand Oaks, CA: Sage.

Staw, B. M., & Ross, J. (1985). Stability in the midst of change: A dispositional approach to job attitudes. *Journal of Applied Psychology, 70*, 469–480.

Tranberg, M., Slane, S., & Ekeberg, E. (1993). The relation between interest congruence and satisfaction: A metaanalysis. *Journal of Vocational Behavior, 42*, 253–264.

Turner, N., Barling, J., & Zacharatos, A. (2002). Positive psychology at work. In C. R. Snyder & S. J. Lopez (Eds.), *Handbook of positive psychology* (pp. 715–728). New York, NY: Oxford University Press.

Van Dyne, L., & LePine, J. A. (1998). Helping and voice extra-role behaviors: Evidence of construct and predictive validity. *Academy of Management Journal, 41*, 108–119.

Warr, P. (1999). Well-being and the workplace. In D. Kahneman, E. Diener, & N. Schwarz (Eds.), *Well-being: The foundations of hedonic psychology* (pp. 392–412). New York, NY: Russell Sage Foundation.

Watson, D., Clark, L. A., & Tellegen, A. (1988). Development and validation of brief measures of positive and negative affect: The PANAS scales. *Journal of Personality and Social Psychology, 54*, 1063–1070.

Watson, D., & Slack, A. K. (1993). General factors of affective temperament and their relation to job satisfaction over time. *Organizational Behavior and Human Decision Processes, 54*, 181–202.

Weiss, D. J., Dawis, R. V., England, G. W., & Lofquist, L. H. (1967). *Manual for the Minnesota Satisfaction Questionnaire.* Minneapolis: University of Minnesota Press.

Whiting, S. W., Podsakoff, P. M., & Pierce, J. R. (2008). Effects of task performance, helping, voice, and organizational loyalty on performance appraisal ratings. *Journal of Applied Psychology, 93*, 125–139.

CHAPTER 23

Counseling Adults for Career Transitions

BECKY L. BOBEK, MARY ANN HANSON, AND STEVEN B. ROBBINS

O N GOING SHIFTS IN THE condition of the U.S. economy and the job market have compelled more adults to make job and career transitions. Career transitions are becoming the norm, and counselors can play a critical role in helping adults adapt and navigate successfully through these transitions. To provide effective interventions, counselors must take into account both individual and environmental influences. They can draw from a variety of theoretical orientations to organize this information and use available research results and recommendations from researchers and practitioners to guide counseling of transitioning adults. In this chapter, we review the following topics relevant to counseling for adult career transitions: (a) the increasing prevalence of adult career transitions, (b) challenges unique to different types of adult transitions, (c) some common challenges faced regardless of specific transition, (d) the implications of current theories for counseling adults in transition, and (e) research relevant to career transition interventions. We conclude by considering implications for counseling practice with career-transitioning adults.

CAREER TRANSITIONS: A COMMON EXPERIENCE FOR ADULTS

Most adults can no longer expect lifetime employment within a single organization or steady movement up a predetermined career ladder. Rather, individuals will typically negotiate a lifetime of job changes, work task restructuring, and employer demands for new or higher-level skills. Up to 80% of employees expect to leave their job for a new employer within 1, 2, or 3 years (Glassdoor, 2011). Based on results from the 2011 National

Survey of Working America (National Career Development Association, 2011), nearly half (45%) of working adults indicated that they will need more training or education to increase their skills either to maintain or enhance their financial status during the coming years. Thirty-six percent of these adults also believed it would be difficult to find a new job with their current skills, given the current job market. Regardless of whether adult career transition decisions are driven by personal choice, a rapidly changing and unpredictable world of work, or some combination of the two, "the need to change jobs or occupations multiple times must be considered the rule and not the exception" (Ebberwein, Krieshok, Ulven, & Prosser, 2004, p. 292). Individuals must be able to adapt effectively to the changing nature of work to make successful career transitions.

Current market forces, opportunity structures, and technology also have increased the need for transition counseling. A continuing rise in service-producing jobs and corresponding fall in manufacturing or goods-producing jobs has concentrated employment opportunities in the service sector, which relies on many part-time and temporary workers and has a large proportion of lower-wage jobs that are routine and require lower-level skills. According to labor market projections by the U.S. Department of Labor, Bureau of Labor Statistics (2011), food preparers and servers, cashiers, retail salespersons, office clerks, and customer service representatives will be among the fastest-growing occupations over the next few years. However, these occupations typically provide limited opportunities for adults to experience occupational advancement.

Although a high school diploma granted access to a wide range of jobs in the past, postsecondary education or training is now needed for more and more jobs across the job market. Nearly two-thirds (63%) of projected jobs will require education above a high school diploma over the next decade (Carnevale, Smith, & Strohl, 2010). These jobs are in areas such as education, health care, community services, STEM (science, technology, engineering, and mathematics) fields, managerial and office professionals, and higher-level positions in sales and food service. Further, jobs that require higher levels of education will, on average, pay higher wages and provide a wider range of benefits than jobs requiring less education. For example, in 2008, men with an associate's degree or bachelor's degree earned a median annual income that was $11,696 or $39,032 higher, respectively, than those with a high school diploma (Infoplease, n.d.). Women with an associate's degree or bachelor's degree earned a median annual income that was $8,415 or $22,671 higher, respectively, than those with a high school diploma (Infoplease, n.d.).

Shifts in the concentration of jobs across sectors and education requirements also contribute to restrictions in advancement opportunities. With the expansions of lower-skilled jobs in the service sector, declines in traditional low-skilled manufacturing jobs, and the more professional, managerial, and higher-level technical jobs reserved for the better educated, there are few opportunities for workers to advance if they are in manufacturing or service jobs and have only a high school diploma. Given that these workers generally earn relatively low wages, presenting a financial impediment to accessing additional education, they can feel trapped. The prospect of making a career transition, let alone an upwardly mobile one, can be severely constrained by economics and the structure of the job market.

Advancing technologies continue to change the landscape of work as well. Technology allows for continuous forms of production across the globe and enables more routine tasks to be performed by computers rather than people. Today's work environments are often fast paced, and workers are expected to be increasingly productive. In some instances, technological advances also require workers to upgrade their skills in their current jobs or move into different jobs for continued employment. Technology has also led to increases in the use of e-mail communication, text messaging, teleconferencing, and telecommuting. These tools are used to different degrees by different workers, but given their increased availability, workers must be competent in using these tools to interact effectively with coworkers.

In sum, organizational downsizing, rightsizing, outsourcing, fluctuating markets, advances in technology, changes in opportunity structures, and increased job skill demands have contributed to an uncertain work life for adults, both those just entering the labor market and those with workforce experience. This uncertainty, coupled with the career needs and expectations of adults, has resulted in more frequent and more varied adult career transitions.

TYPES OF ADULT CAREER TRANSITIONS

Career-related transitions involve "change and adaptation" throughout the "unfolding sequence of any [adult] person's work experiences over time" (Arthur & Rousseau, 1996, pp. 30, 34). For an individual, a particular transition may be anticipated or unanticipated and can be perceived as positive or negative. Transitions occur in a social, cultural, and political context and have the potential to impact individuals' relationships, assumptions, routines, and roles (Anderson, Goodman, & Schlossberg, 2011). Multiple transitions can produce a cumulative decrease in well-being if an individual is unable to recover before another transition occurs (Williams, 1999). The duration of time it takes to make and adjust effectively to a career transition varies, depending on factors both internal and external to the individual and on the type of transition. The transition process itself is more complex than can be thoroughly described in this chapter. Bridges (2004),

Bright and Pryor (2008), Hudson (1999), Nicholson (1990), and Schlossberg, Waters, and Goodman (1995) provide in-depth discussions of models of the transition process.

The adult career-related transitions considered in this chapter include (a) adults who have graduated from high school and are unprepared for the transition to work, (b) adults who are currently employed and want to shift their career direction (e.g., by moving up, down, or across) or to enrich their current employment, and (c) adults who are not employed and want to reenter the labor market, shift from welfare to work, or respond to job loss. These three types of career transitions are the most prevalent and have a wide range of potential consequences. These career transitions also require varied degrees of coping and adaptability, and counselors who better understand the contexts in which these transitions occur can be more effective in assisting those affected.

ADULTS WHO HAVE GRADUATED AND ARE UNPREPARED FOR WORK

For emerging adults who have recently graduated from high school and are looking for jobs, full-time entry into the workforce and adjustment has become increasingly difficult. Adults with only a high school diploma experience one of the highest rates of unemployment, second only to adults with less than a high school diploma. Further, a high school diploma qualifies these adults for only about a third of U.S. jobs, and these jobs have lower wages and fewer opportunities for advancement. In a competitive job market, employers are able to hire workers with more education and skills rather than workers with less education and fewer skills at the same, or similar, cost. Given these circumstances, high school graduates often struggle with attaining economic stability and self-sufficiency (Danziger & Ratner, 2010). These young adults also have less labor market experience, and experience is preferred, if not required, by many employers. Work experience exposes young adults to the realities of work, which can help them reassess their own career expectations. High school graduates transitioning to work with little or no work experience do not have the benefit of that experience to aid their work adjustment.

High school graduates transitioning to work may also have unrealistic expectations. Some graduates think they have unlimited work options and earning power, which can quickly lead to unfulfilled expectations. Others graduate without ever having considered their future career direction and become paralyzed without the tools needed to engage in their own career planning. Many do not recognize the need for additional training and better developed skills until they start looking for jobs. Further, once these young adults find employment, they must understand the expectations of their coworkers and supervisors and learn about the norms of the organizations in which they work. These early work transition experiences can foster feelings of marginality and impede adjustment (Anderson et al., 2011). A lack of realistic, well-informed personal expectations and understanding about actions that support employability is a significant barrier for high school graduates to transition effectively into the workforce.

Employed Adults Who Are Shifting Career Direction

For adults who are currently employed in the workforce, there are a variety of career direction alternatives (moving up, down, across, or enriching their current employment) available for workers to transition into positions that better suit their current needs and circumstances. Working adults wanting to advance into higher-level positions or move up the career ladder are looking to make a vertical move. Adults who want to shift to a different but comparable position are sometimes looking to engage in a lateral move. Adults who are generally satisfied with their current positions may still want to enrich their work experiences or may recognize the need to develop additional skills to keep pace with workplace demands. Adults in high-stress, high-demand positions; older workers with shifting priorities; or adults in the midst of organizational restructuring may want or need to explore options for moving down the career ladder.

With increased job instability, working adults often confront both antici-pated and unanticipated shifts in career direction (Danziger & Ratner, 2010). Although moving up the career ladder or laterally to a different position may be perceived as exciting opportunities, there may be concerns about having the necessary skills to effectively perform the new job and meet competing demands, as well as a fear of failure. Adults who are satisfied with their current positions may have concerns about the skills they need to keep their jobs. For workers wanting to move down, there may be a desire for more work options, such as flexible work arrangements, job sharing, or phased retirement (U.S. Department of Labor, 2008) but concerns about whether these are viable options in their organizations. There may also be concerns about the financial repercussions of shifting jobs. Mature adults are more likely to consider quality of life or work–life balance and may want to spend more time with family and on hobbies and less time on work. For older workers wanting to shift career direction, there can be concerns about age discrimination and skill obsolescence. Finances and health benefits can also contribute to delays in retirement or a desire for partial retirement (U.S. Department of Labor, 2008).

UNEMPLOYED ADULTS WHO ASPIRE TO WORK

Adults who are not employed and want to reenter the labor force, move from welfare to work, or respond effectively to job loss generally face the most challenges.

Labor force reentry. Labor market reentry applies to individuals who have focused their time (usually a number of years) and energy on roles other than that of paid worker in the civilian labor force. Both women and men may desire reentry, but it is primarily women who consider reentry when they are single heads of households, displaced homemakers, empty-nesters, or married with children but seeking opportunities for additional fulfillment or income (Padula, 1994). Men primarily reenter the workforce as veterans after completing their military service.

For women, reentry may be motivated by vocational, family, or financial factors (Padula, 1994). Many women may delay establishing their vocational role until after their children start school or grow up and leave home. These women are often looking for a career and an opportunity to become more financially independent. Another reason for reentry among homemakers who have primarily worked without remuneration to care for home and family is that they become financially responsible for themselves due to disability, divorce, death, or other circumstances related to their spouses or partners (Moss & Baugh, 1983). These women may never have anticipated working outside the home, may think they lack marketable skills, and may be unsure of how and where to seek help (Moss & Baugh, 1983).

Reentry women often have multiple responsibilities, including caring for children, maintaining a home, and volunteering in the community. They may experience role conflict and emotional distress as they attempt to balance family demands and work obligations (see Vetter, Hull, Putzstuck, & Dean, 1986, for a more complete discussion). Other common difficulties include low self-concept, lack of confidence regarding abilities, and relatively lower autonomy and assertiveness than women who are already engaged in careers.

For veterans, their top reentry priority is usually to secure employment. The military provides reentry programs to service members, including preseparation counseling and transition assistance workshops, but these programs are underutilized (Clemens & Milsom, 2008). As a result, counseling professionals are likely to encounter veterans as they transition into the civilian labor force. Available research highlights a number of career transition concerns for veterans including culture shock, identifying transferable skills, lack of job preparation and job search skills, and financial concerns (Simpson & Armstrong, 2009). One of the most challenging concerns is transitioning from a highly regimented military culture to more unstructured and individual-focused work environments. The loss or change of identity from a ranked position to a work role may also affect a veteran's transition adjustment. In addition, it can be difficult and overwhelming for veterans to articulate how their military skills translate into skills that are relevant to civilian jobs. Veterans may be unfamiliar with typical job search rituals (e.g., resumes, cover letters, and interviewing) and job search strategies. They may experience unrealistic expectations related to civilian salaries, given their education and experience, as well as the time it may take to obtain a job. Financial concerns are another salient issue, as veterans wonder about their ability to find stable positions in a competitive job market.

Combat veterans and veterans with disabilities face additional challenges. Combat veterans may experience challenges resulting from the consequences of combat stress and trauma (e.g., posttraumatic stress disorder). Some of these stress reactions include depression, irritability, difficulty relating to others, anxiety, and flashbacks, which can make reentry difficult, if not impossible (Clemens & Milsom, 2008). Veterans who have disabilities may confront barriers related to perceived inability to perform job tasks, perceived emotional instability from having a disability, lack of accommodations, and a lack of technology that would allow for higher level functioning (Ruh, Spicer, & Vaughan, 2009). Although veterans have career transition needs, they may also need to address psychological issues that, if left unchecked, could impede their career transition effectiveness.

Welfare to work.   For adults transitioning from welfare to work, the objective is to move from having fiscal dependency on state government to becoming economically self-sufficient through work. Welfare recipients transitioning into the labor force face a number of challenges. A study involving 750 employers in four major metropolitan areas highlighted that newly hired welfare recipients tended to experience problems with child care and transportation, contributing to problems with absenteeism, and problems with turnover and job performance (Holzer, 2000). A welfare reform study in Wisconsin identified additional barriers to economic self-sufficiency for welfare recipients. These barriers include "housing instability or unstable housing accommodation, providing care for a child or adult with disabilities, and being victimized by crimes" (Alfred & Martin, 2007, p. 8). Other barriers may include limited work and literacy skills, negative work attitudes, limited work experiences, negative interpersonal interactions and behaviors, and a lack of work motivation (Alfred & Martin, 2007). Welfare recipients who are transitioning to work often experience high levels of financial anxiety and, upon entry into the workforce, tend to be concentrated in low-skilled and low-wage jobs (Holzer, 2000).

Job loss. Adults can experience a host of adverse effects in response to job loss. Job loss is associated with an increased likelihood of prolonged unemployment, fewer opportunities, and decreased wages (Farber, 2005) compared to working adults. Adults coping with job displacement due to organizational downsizing, restructuring, or relocation may have substantial periods of unemployment, sometimes lasting years (Brand, 2004). These adults often also participate less in social activities, which can reduce networks of people available to provide information about potential employment possibilities (Brand & Burgard, 2008). Depending on the type of job that has been lost, similar job opportunities may be limited, and those opportunities that are available may be incompatible with these individuals' education or experience. For example, midlife adults who have advanced within a corporate structure are "faced with the prospect of being unable to find a position of comparable status" (Aiken, 1998, p. 274). Given the competitive job market, these adults often face the prospect of temporary jobs and downward mobility. In one study, unemployed managers and executives perceived themselves as having constraints that included employer preferences for younger, lower-paid workers and pressures to devalue or hide their skills and experience to counter potential age discrimination (Mendenhall, Kalil, Spindel, & Hart, 2008).

Job loss can also lead to compromised physical and psychological health. Job loss is associated with increased anxiety, depression, feelings of isolation, feelings of failure and rejection, lowered confidence and self-esteem, and stress-related somatic complaints (DeFrank & Ivancevich, 1986; Eby & Buch, 1994; Kelvin & Jarrett, 1985). In addition, job displacement is related to lower levels of self-acceptance, lower morale, and greater dissatisfaction with life (Brand & Burgard, 2008). The increased likelihood of marital or relationship difficulties and financial problems resulting from job loss may also exacerbate these health-related issues.

As described here, adults may experience an array of presenting issues as they navigate career transitions. Some issues are unique to the particular type of transition; other issues are more common across career transitions. In the next section, we highlight common issues that are especially critical to making effective transitions.

COMMON ISSUES ACROSS CAREER TRANSITIONS

Adults in career transition range from young adults (ages 18–25) just entering the workforce to mature adults (ages 45 and older) with a history of work and life experiences. A focus on adults across the age spectrum is important because they contend with many similar life and work context issues and are often in need of similar types of assistance with career transitions.

Despite some issues (e.g., unrealistic expectations) facing younger adults that are different from those of thirty-somethings (e.g., career stagnation), and from those of mature adults (e.g., age discrimination, health concerns), there are three major career transition issues that seem to be common for all transitioning adults regardless of age: (a) conducting a realistic self-appraisal of existing skills, (b) recognizing the need for career adaptability, and (c) dealing with the psychological effects related to financial difficulties and job uncertainty.

An important issue that adults confront across all career transitions considered in this chapter is the need to identify current skills and, in many cases, develop new skills. Many emerging adults who have just graduated from high school are inadequately prepared for work, lacking basic cognitive skills and the skills that enable them to behave effectively in work settings. They may also have a limited understanding of the skills needed to be successful in specific jobs. It may be difficult for these young adults to realistically identify their current skills because of lack of previous work experiences.

Adults reentering the workforce (homemakers, veterans) and adults responding to job loss often have rich life, military, and work experiences to draw from, but they may not consider how their skills can be deployed in new work contexts. Homemakers, for example, may not see how their numerous responsibilities and skills generalize to job requirements in the workplace. Veterans may have difficulty articulating how skills used in the military relate to the skills needed for civilian job options (Simpson & Armstrong, 2009). Similarly, mature adults with a wealth of work experience may not think about their skills until they have to search for a new job after job loss. The accurate appraisal of skills, and subsequent skill building, is critical to the development of a transportable, broad, flexible skill base that bolsters employability and eventual career success (Eby, Butts, & Lockwood, 2003; O'Connell, 2008).

Given the unpredictability of work and the personal life challenges faced by adults in career transition, another issue of increasing relevance is the need for career adaptability. Career adaptability is the ability to recognize and respond positively to or "cope with changing work and work conditions" that emphasize the interaction between individual and environmental contexts (Super & Knasel, 1981, p. 195). It is characterized by a high level of reality orientation and planfulness. Career adaptability allows one to engage in recurrent decision making throughout the adult work life and, especially, to make new choices that fit current circumstances (Anderson et al., 2011). It also allows adults to approach career changes proactively as they anticipate ongoing shifts in work and learn to assess their personal contexts realistically.

A few examples highlight the importance of career adaptability for making effective career transitions. Mature adults who experience job loss may have received training specific to their jobs, but those jobs may no longer be viable because of outsourcing. Their initial response to job loss may be to try to find the same job elsewhere in the United States, but this would be a maladaptive response if such jobs are no longer available for adult job seekers. Adults who engage in a more adaptive course of action by considering how their prior training might be relevant to different types of jobs may have greater transition success. Similarly, veterans reentering the civilian workforce may be inclined to look for jobs similar to those held during their military service, but this approach may severely limit the work options available to them. Veterans who focus on how the competencies they developed during their service could be used in novel work settings may better adapt to the change in their work circumstances.

Financial uncertainty can be a critical issue for adults who are just entering the workforce, those contemplating career shifts, and those who have lost jobs or are reentering the workforce. In an effort to become economically self-sufficient, emerging young adults must attempt to manage expenses against costs and learn that fiscal responsibility is a constant challenge. With the exception of those anticipating upward moves, adults considering a career shift are often concerned about whether they will earn sufficient wages to meet their financial needs when they enter a new job. Adults experiencing job loss may also have a loss of income, and reentry adults may already live with limited income. Decreases in income can have significant financial and personal consequences.

Many adults do not have sufficient savings to sustain them during periods of unemployment. Without financial security, these individuals experience considerable stress about paying monthly expenses, affording health insurance, retaining their homes, and providing for the needs of family members. Financial problems can be a major cause of family conflict and marital discord. People may feel powerless when they struggle with finances because they have little control over their options. In addition, some adults are not comfortable discussing their financial situation and may be embarrassed to divulge their limited resources.

The effects of job uncertainty can also be significant for adults in career transition. Adults who have difficulty finding jobs (as emerging or reentry workers or after unexpected job loss) and those unable to change jobs because of an unstable market may experience a lack of confidence and self-esteem and a fear of failure. Without sufficient job qualifications, people can lose confidence in their ability to meet expectations and to succeed in the job search process. With the loss of a job, people can experience diminished self-worth and feel devalued as less productive members of society. The loss of a job also translates into a loss of career identity and colleagues, which alters an individual's regular activities and social relationships. The loss of social supports and daily routines may compromise an individual's ability to mobilize psychological resources. For people who have worked comfortably in a job for years or who are reentering the workforce, the prospect of entering a completely new position can lead to fear of failure because they are unsure of their ability to adjust and perform different tasks.

When faced with unclear or inadequate skills, limited career adaptability, and uncertain circumstances related to one's finances and one's job, the ability to cope may be compromised during all types of career transitions. To help adults address these common issues and other transition-specific concerns effectively, counselors need to be prepared to incorporate pertinent theoretical and research perspectives into their practice. These perspectives are considered next.

THEORETICAL PERSPECTIVES ON CAREER TRANSITIONS

Counselors have a variety of theoretical perspectives available to them to enhance their understanding of adult career transition issues and guide the process by which they assist adults in making successful transitions. During the counseling process, the counselor's first major task is to organize the complex, multifaceted information they collect from the client. Once this information is organized, it must be put into a conceptual framework that helps to identify the salient issues, desired outcomes, and plan of action. At this point, the counselor and client must enter into a shared agreement and commitment to pursue these agreed-upon actions.

Theory serves as the overarching framework by which counselors implicitly or explicitly organize information, create an explanation for the client's expressed and implied difficulties or desires, and determine action steps (Robbins, 1989). Given the potential complexity of adult issues, counselors need a coherent conceptualization of the salient or defining constructs of interest in clients' lives, including both the individual and environmental issues that have implications for expected outcomes. Career and adult development theories help to (a) identify the critical connection between a counselor's worldview and the actions taken to assist clients, (b) reinforce the need for conceptual and practical consistency in action, and (c) integrate career and personal issues in addressing the needs of adults in transition.

Here we provide a brief overview of four career development theories that provide well-established and supported approaches to understanding career development. The first two represent person–environment (P-E) fit models, with an emphasis on the assessment and exploration of personal and work environment attributes and the corresponding congruence or fit between the person and environment. The third is a developmental approach, and the fourth has its roots in social learning theory. We also provide an overview of two adult development theories. All six theories lend themselves to identifying both personal and career issues and to establishing clear, measurable client outcomes.

PERSON–ENVIRONMENT (P-E) FIT PERSPECTIVE

Both the Minnesota theory of work adjustment (see Swanson & Schneider, Chapter 2, this volume; Hesketh, 2000) and Holland's theory of vocational types (Nauta, Chapter 3, this volume) focus on the interrelationships between personal and work environment characteristics that affect career satisfaction and work productivity. Counselors have historically used assessments to identify and match key constructs with the intent of ensuring appropriate placement and training. The ultimate goal is to find employment that enhances both satisfaction and productivity outcomes.

The P-E fit perspective emphasizes the importance of identifying and matching key abilities, values, and interests with the attributes of potential work settings and occupations. A critical issue in this process is the notion of transfer of skills or of articulating skills developed through past work and life experiences in the context of novel or alternative work-related settings. This is critical to the success of adult workers who face the pressure of entering the work world with limited skills, obtaining a new job after experiencing job loss, a dramatic revision of their career path, or reentry into the workforce. Thus, P-E fit theories can be used to help clients select potentially satisfying and satisfactory work options by helping them identify their major interests, skills, and values and then consider occupational possibilities that match these characteristics. Each of the P-E fit theories also suggests some additional factors that may influence this matching process, such as client and work environment flexibility and the consistency and differentiation of clients' interest profiles. The reader is referred to Swanson and Schneider (Chapter 2) and Nauta (Chapter 3) of this volume for more detailed discussion of these factors.

Note that personal responses to a career transition may impede the systematic analysis and execution of a career search plan using a P-E fit approach. For example, feelings of failure, reduced self-esteem, unrealistic expectations, and anxiety associated with financial and job uncertainty may need to be acknowledged and managed. Thus, counselors following a P-E fit perspective must remain sensitive to these additional issues in working with clients experiencing a career transition.

Super's Career Development Theory

Super's life-span/life-space career development theory offers another approach to understanding issues facing adult workers (Hartung, Chapter 4, this volume; Savickas, Chapter 6, this volume; Super, Savickas, & Super, 1996). With Super's emphasis on the importance of the development of self-concept, which changes over time and develops as a result of experience, this theory complements the notion of lifelong career transitions. As adults' occupational preferences, skills, and life situations change, understanding individuals' life stages and roles is critical to helping them frame their needs and expectations. Within this theoretical framework, adults seek career satisfaction through work roles in which they can implement and further develop their self-concepts. Counselors can support clients throughout this process by helping them elaborate their work self-concepts, exposing them to information and opportunities for growth, and assisting them in developing attitudes and behaviors associated with career adaptability. Adult clients will be better enabled to address career concerns, including the establishment of clear work goals and the skills necessary to compete with others and identify and obtain desired work.

Social Cognitive Career Theory

More contemporary models of career development have drawn heavily on Bandura's (1986) social cognitive theory. Social cognitive career theory (SCCT; Lent, Chapter 5, this volume) emphasizes motivational factors such as self-efficacy beliefs, outcome expectations, and goals to explain how vocational interests develop, choices are made, and various levels of work satisfaction and success are attained. SCCT offers at least two suggestions for working with adults in career transition. The first is that career possibilities may be substantially truncated by inaccurate self-efficacy beliefs and outcome expectations. That is, clients who underestimate their capabilities (self-efficacy beliefs) or have inaccurate or underdeveloped knowledge of occupations (outcome expectations) may fail to consider occupations that might give them satisfaction and success.

The second implication of SCCT centers around the role that environmental barriers and supports play in the interest development, choice, and job attainment process. Clients will be more able to implement their desired career plans if they experience few barriers and seek substantial supports for their career plans. As Lent (in press) argues, "matching" theories, such as those represented in the P-E fit perspective, must take into account the client's capacity to manage change and loss, respond realistically and proactively to a shifting and uncertain work environment, and internalize a sense of resiliency and purpose necessary to navigate painful and stressful transitions.

Taken together, these two implications suggest that in working with adults in transition, counselors should help clients (a) gain a realistic appraisal of their skills and abilities, (b) develop accurate occupational information, (c) learn how to overcome or manage barriers to their preferred occupational choices, and (d) build supports for these choices. Brown and Lent (1996) discuss strategies that can be used in implementing these suggestions (see also Lent, Chapter 5, this volume).

ADULT DEVELOPMENT THEORIES

Our discussion of the conceptual underpinnings for career counseling with adult clients can also be embedded in the broader adult development theoretical literature. Two theories that address potential personal and career issues are Baltes's (1997) selective optimization with compensation theory and Atchley's (1989) continuity theory.

Baltes's (1997) theory holds that people engage in lifelong processes of selection, optimization, and compensation (SOC) to maximize gains and minimize losses, which are most likely to result in successful development. In the SOC model, *selection* refers to developing and choosing goals, *optimization* involves applying and refining means to achieve goals, and *compensation* entails substituting other means when prior means are no longer available. With a focus on proactive strategies, this model would consider it adaptive to set clear career goals, obtain and invest in the means to pursue these goals, and persist in the face of challenges through compensatory efforts. Individuals are able to develop successful careers and maintain high levels of work performance over time by using SOC-related strategies that address shifts in means, which may result from personal characteristics (e.g., decreased physical strength or stamina), macroeconomic conditions, or other contextual circumstances. The SOC model adds to career theories by suggesting that career development can be conceptualized as a gain-loss dynamic with a focus on employing strategies to maximize work-related gains and minimize losses. This theory offers a guide for counselors with regard to the allocation of resources, given competing goals, and highlights how interrelationships between personal and career domains and their respective goals are critical in examining the allocation of these resources (Vondracek & Porfeli, 2002).

Although not as germane to younger adults, Atchley's (1989) continuity theory of aging observes that older adults strive to maintain their same activities, behaviors, and relationships over time by adapting strategies that are connected to past experiences. This theory describes how people adapt to their situations and set goals via internal and external structures in an effort to preserve continuity. For example, making adaptive or realistic career-related choices is a matter of connecting past work with future work within the context of personal ideas and beliefs and supportive social roles and relationships. This theory reflects the emphasis on maintaining a sense of meaning and stability across important transition points during middle age (cf. Robbins, Lee, & Wan, 1994). As Robbins et al. (1994) found, goal continuity—the ability to maintain a sense of equilibrium or balance as evidenced by an inner sense of goal direction, life meaning, and purpose—was a critical mediator of adjustment as middle-age adults moved into alternative work settings from what was considered their primary careers or jobs. Goal directedness also contributed to a person's ability to access and use necessary financial, health, and social resources. Conversely, a sense of discontinuity, or an inability to create and sustain goal-directed behavior, is viewed as contributing to poor adaptation. The implications for career counseling are clear: Clients demonstrating inability to sustain purpose and direction during times of transition may not be able to access available resources or use them in achieving a career plan. They may also demonstrate decreased personal and interpersonal satisfaction.

RESEARCH PERSPECTIVES ON CAREER TRANSITIONS

Interventions are at the center of counseling adults in career transition, but there is limited empirical research on the efficacy of various interventions for adults experiencing the types of transitions described in this chapter. Although the literature provides suggestions for practice related to adult transition issues, most interventions lack an evaluation component (Kerka, 1995; Whiston & Brecheisen, 2002).

RESEARCH SUPPORT FOR INTERVENTIONS

The broader career counseling literature provides some information about which interventions are more generally effective. There is research support for the effectiveness of interventions designed to assist individuals with issues such as making or remaking a career choice (e.g., results include increased career decidedness and career decision-making self-efficacy) and conducting a job search (e.g., Job Club participants have job placement success) (Brown & McPartland, 2005), but these interventions do not fully address the multifaceted nature of transitions such as job loss or reentry. According to Brown and McPartland (2005), the career intervention research "seems to treat all participants not only as if they are seeking additional career options but also as if they are all seeking help to make an initial choice" (p. 210). Efforts to empirically examine the effectiveness of various interventions with adult clients who are experiencing different types of transitions and facing a wide range of issues and challenges would certainly help determine how to better meet the needs of these clients.

Likewise, the effectiveness of career interventions delivered via different formats has received attention but not specifically for adults who are experiencing particular types of career transitions. For example, Whiston, Brecheisen, and Stephens (2003) conducted a meta-analysis of studies comparing one career intervention format to another. The most robust findings were that structured group experiences were more effective than less structured groups, that self-directed computer-guided interventions were much improved with counselor contact during computer use, and that totally self-directed interventions were less effective than most other delivery formats.

Robbins, Chartrand, McFadden, and Lee (1994a) compared leader-led and self-directed career workshops for mature adults undergoing a career transition. In this research, an AARP program was originally developed as a leader-led, group-oriented, 7-week program using a combination of minilectures, in-class group exercises, and homework assignments. Robbins, Chartrand, and colleagues (1994a) evaluated this program, then modified it into a self-directed and self-paced program, and compared the differential effects of leader-led and self-directed programs. They found that the career workshops were highly regarded and resulted in knowledge and behavior change regardless of format. More research is needed on a variety of topics related to adults in career transition. The Robbins, Chartrand, and colleagues (1994a) findings provide an excellent start, but more research is needed on the effectiveness of interventions with differing formats for this group. More research is also needed on the effectiveness of various interventions for transitioning clients with specific needs and circumstances.

Identifying Effective Interventions

Given recent changes in the frequency of adult career transitions and in the world of work, Krumboltz and Chan (2005) have advocated a shift from the traditional conception of career counseling to "transition counseling." This more comprehensive vision of career counseling includes (a) helping clients create satisfying and successful lives; (b) considering career, personal, family, and other life concerns as central to counseling; (c) ensuring counselors receive more comprehensive training that includes learning about the interaction among personal, family, and career concerns; (d) dealing with all types of transitions; and (e) fostering an ongoing counselor–client relationship as needed by the client (Krumboltz & Chan, 2005).

Multon, Wood, Heppner, and Gysbers (2007) identified subtypes of adult career counseling clients with their own distinct constellations of career and psychological issues (e.g., goal instability, lack of career transition readiness, high psychological distress, career decision-making discomfort). These findings lend support to more holistic approaches to counseling adults, especially approaches that consider both career and personal-emotional issues and that focus on establishing goals, developing transition coping skills, managing psychological stress, and developing career decision-making skills and confidence. Within such a comprehensive approach, potentially effective interventions could incorporate a range of theories into the intervention designs and implementation to help counselors synthesize information related to, and plan action around, the general and transition-specific issues faced by adult career clients, such as the increased need for career adaptability and the pressure for new or upgraded skills.

Research with career transitioning adults also provides information concerning which interventions are likely to be effective. For example, case studies with emerging adults transitioning to work suggest that social supports are vital during and after transition and that having advance awareness of the challenges they may encounter in the work world might help young adults anticipate and better respond to these difficulties (Murphy, Blustein, Bohlig, & Platt, 2010). Based on these results, activities that encourage social networks, training on what organizations expect from new workers, and programs or workshops that raise awareness of common transition issues (e.g., unmet expectations) are likely to be effective for recent high school graduates preparing to move into the workforce.

A program called Year to Career, developed by Jobs for the Future (http://www.jff.org), focuses on young adults seeking entry into high-demand, high-wage employment after high school and has shown some early improvements in postsecondary employment outcomes. This program includes short-term, intensive postsecondary experiences designed to provide young adults with career-based training (including instruction in basic literacy skills), ongoing social supports (including counseling), connections with employers, and work opportunities through internships. This type of program addresses a number of issues confronting the emerging adult, including the need to develop skills, obtain work experience, and generate more informed and realistic expectations.

Based on a review of studies and models pertaining to adults transitioning across and within organizations, Banks and Nafukho (2008) identified some behaviors important for successfully shifting career direction. They conclude that the career transition issues of these adults require their active participation in managing their own careers by being innovative and creative about career development, willing to learn informally and formally, and communicating the desire for career growth or change within and outside the organization. They also concluded that adults should be proactive and take advantage of organizational opportunities for career development, such as career coaching. According to Schlossberg (1990), counselors can also develop general and specific transition workshops to help adults cope more effectively with their career transitions. These workshops can help adults learn about coping, transitions, and steps to master change. The aim is to help adults build skills that allow them to help themselves and enhance ongoing career adaptability.

Research pertaining to adults dealing with job loss and other stressful unemployment-related transitions can also inform interventions. For example, midlife managers experiencing job loss perceived that strategies related to acquiring new skills, pursuing entrepreneurial options, and adopting an attitude of career flexibility would help them better cope with the challenges of reentering the workforce (Mendenhall et al., 2008). One intervention for these adults might focus on enhancing work-related skills (e.g., teamwork skills, technology skills) or building new job-specific skills. Another intervention might emphasize helping these adults adopt a "free agent" mentality to adjust to the notion that they must reconstruct themselves as consultants or contractors independent of the employer, which requires these adults to accept that they may have limited value as a long-term employee.

Case studies with career-transitioning combat veterans indicated that those who transitioned well relied on emotion-focused coping strategies initially but abandoned them for problem-focused approaches as the transition process progressed (Haynie & Shepherd, 2011). Veterans in this study also reported seeking support from other veterans and from professional counselors. Other literature (Simpson & Armstrong, 2009) suggests that veterans may benefit from assistance with articulating their transferable skills and pursuing options for self-employment. Based on available research, effective interventions for transitioning veterans are likely to need to respond to psychological needs, enable the identification of skills developed in the military that are relevant to the civilian work, and include social supports.

Social, family, and peer supports are powerful tools for all of the groups of adults discussed here seeking entry or reentry into employment. This support is exemplified by the tradition of job clubs, vocational support groups, and the increasing emphasis on building networks of people in education and the workplace to function as support systems (Banks & Nafukho, 2008; Brown & McPartland, 2005; Murphy et al., 2010). Support-related interventions appear to be an important strategy for encouraging and mobilizing adults in transition.

Given the diverse issues confronting adults transitioning from welfare to work, it has been suggested that targeting programs to match individual circumstances may be most effective for this group (Miller, Deitch, & Hill,

2010). Some programs aim to enhance employment retention once recipients leave welfare (Hendra et al., 2010). For example, one approach is to provide financial incentives to supplement earnings, in combination with other support services, which seems to promote employment retention among low-wage workers. For adults moving from welfare to work, employer-sponsored education or training programs and counseling services are also generally thought to be effective interventions (Alfred & Martin, 2007).

Finally, career interventions can be understood within a "phase-of-treatment model" that is often part of career counseling models (e.g., Swanson, 1995; Swanson & Fouad, 1999). Spokane's (1991) career intervention model, for example, organizes individual and group career interventions into beginning, activation, and completion stages. Hackney and Cormier (2005) incorporate relationship building, problem assessment, goal setting, initiating interventions, and termination/follow-up in their counseling model, with assessment, goal setting, and intervention as the major action phases of the model. Krumboltz and Chan (2005) articulate the goals of career counseling with clear implications for intervention, which include taking action, increasing overall client life satisfaction, and dealing with a broad array of complex issues. These models and intervention research inform counseling practices used with career-transitioning adults.

IMPLICATIONS FOR PRACTICE

What elements are essential to counseling adults in career transition? How might targeted approaches help counselors address the issues presented by transitioning adults, particularly those that are common across the various types of transitions?

Four key elements should be incorporated into the counseling process:

1. Recognizing the importance of individual client background and base-line data
2. Understanding the environmental context surrounding the adult in career transition
3. Determining the internal and external resources available to transition-ing adults using appropriate assessment and interviewing
4. Selecting appropriate activities and modes of delivery to help meet client needs

CLIENT BACKGROUND AND BASELINE DATA

A detailed account of a client's work, social, and educational history is critical to understanding the range of issues they may face during the process of making a career transition. This information can provide baseline data on the individual's attitudes and behaviors that may facilitate or impede transition progress and adjustment. The strain associated with changes in work makes it especially important for counselors to ascertain potentially negative physiological and psychological responses to transitions. For example, the client's response to the request "Tell me how you responded at other times in your life when stressed" may reveal considerable information about how the individual approaches task demands and the adaptation process.

Complete background data concerning adults' educational and work-related experiences can identify skills and experiences that can be generalized or transferred to new situations. This type of information is especially helpful when counseling clients who are reentering the labor force or dealing with job loss. Although it may feel unfamiliar or overwhelming for some clients to identify how their skills relate to possible work options, counselors can use this information to help clients learn more about potential jobs, recognize assets they bring to their transition experiences, and determine where gaps may exist between available skills and job demands. Throughout this process, clients should be positively recognized for their activities and accomplishments while helped to consider whether they need to upgrade their skills. Measures of abilities and skills can also help clients develop a better understanding of their talents. An advantage of such measures is that they can generate occupational options for clients that they might not have considered previously (see Metz & Jones, Chapter 16, this volume).

Building a detailed history that charts the range of skills, experiences, and supports for adult clients also presents an excellent opportunity to help them enhance their career adaptability. Counselors can use their clients' information to jump-start self-development efforts that can keep working adults more marketable and enhance coping strategies. Lent (in press) suggests activities such as updating one's skills, expanding one's interests, and redesigning one's job as ways to renew one's career that build on one's current skills and characteristics. Further, through actions such as maintaining social support and job contact networks, periodically exploring job opportunities, and envisioning future possibilities, clients can engage in proactive coping strategies and assert "agency" despite uncertain and shifting home and work environments (Lent, in press). Counselors can be critical to helping adults become active participants in this process by encouraging attitudes and behaviors that promote adaptation. Hartung (Chapter 4) and Savickas (Chapter 6) also discuss strategies to promote greater adaptability and active engagement in the career exploration, search, and interviewing process.

Environmental Context

As discussed earlier, career transitions occur in an environmental context, and contexts differ for different individuals. The economic, social, cultural, and political environment can affect adult perceptions of transition events and their responses to them, particularly in transitions where feelings of lack of control, anxiety, and uncertainty can magnify perceived threats. SCCT underscores the importance of environmental influences on self-efficacy beliefs throughout the transition process. For counselors working with adults in an era of job uncertainty, support, encouragement, and active preparation are crucial to their clients' adjustment and success. It is incumbent on the counselor to be familiar with and comfortable responding to differences in perceptions of environmental influences such as social class, cultural values, and opportunity structures in the job market. It is not just a matter of promoting the factors associated with adaptive transitions (e.g., agency, optimism, clear and realistic planning) but rather embedding these factors within the cultural and social framework of the client.

Côté's (2000, 2002) seminal work on identity capital development highlights the importance of viewing perceptions of and reactions to the world within an environmental framework. He proposed that navigation of life transitions is dependent on a combination of tangible resources (e.g., parents' social class, gender, other structural factors) and intangible resources (e.g., agentic personality, psychosocial and intellectual development, past experience). The acquisition of identity capital reflects the ability to capitalize on agentic and structural or environmental factors to achieve positive personal and occupational outcomes. This theory reinforces the importance of contextual factors in understanding adult development. For example, perceptions of being a productive older worker in the labor force can depend as much on environmental influences, such as mass marketing and peer pressure, as they do on internal forces of psychological development. It is critical for counselors to determine how variations in environmental context influence the perceptions and behaviors of their clients.

Internal and External Resources

A realistic assessment of available internal and external resources is critical to negotiating and adjusting to career transitions. There are several key internal resources associated with adult worker adjustment, especially regarding life transition or life stress events, including having a sense of agency, optimism, and positive coping (Lightsey, 1996); the ability to engage in clear and realistic planning and to identify opportunities (Peterson, Lumsden, Sampson,

Reardon, & Lenz, 2002); and having a sense of continuity, purpose, and direction (Robbins, Lee, et al., 1994). Other resources include the cognitive skills and personality characteristics needed for success in a job or the ability to develop new skills and behaviors associated with success. These can aid individuals in their efforts to obtain jobs and to be successful once in the workplace. Externally, relying on family supports and social supports facilitates transition (Murphy et al., 2010), as does the ability to network with others and engage in new experiences that can produce valuable contacts (Eby et al., 2003). It is imperative for counselors to help clients identify and access the internal and external resources that contribute to positive transition adjustment. For example, a client responding to job loss may not have adequately dealt with related psychological issues or responses. They may not have the supports in place (e.g., sufficient savings) to delay a new job search and work on psychological adjustment first. The counselor can determine which resources are available that may help the client mount an effective job search despite the psychological distress.

A transition model proposed by Anderson and colleagues (2011) provides a structure for identifying and organizing available supports. It is designed to "help clients enhance their resources for coping by assessing their (1) Situation, (2) Self, (3) Support, and (4) Strategies" (p. 195). Based on this model, clients are expected to cope better with change if they perceive the transition to be a challenge rather than a threat. Encourage clients to marshal their internal and external resources, including external supports for personal encouragement and for professional networking, to cope with transitions that may evoke feelings of uncertainty, loss of control, and lowered self-esteem.

Counselors can use clarifying interview techniques and relevant assessments to identify the resources available to their clients. For example, interviews can help a counselor gauge propensity for coping, whether expectations are realistic, and the degree to which a client is likely to use social supports. From another perspective, realistic appraisal of the match between client abilities and job possibilities or the need for further education may require not only transfer of skill activities but formal assessment of cognitive ability (e.g., ACT's WorkKeys tests, job-specific skill and certification exams). The counselor can also employ personality and behavior-based assessments to determine the extent to which a client exhibits behaviors and attitudes that are important for success in the workplace. In essence, the counselor needs a range of assessment alternatives at his or her disposal to address the variety of client needs likely to be encountered.

APPROPRIATE DEVELOPMENT ACTIVITIES AND MODES OF DELIVERY

Counselors working with adults in career transition also need to understand, and appropriately select from, the varied development activities and delivery platforms that are available to help clients meet their transition goals. For example, traditional education programs may serve adults who have sufficient time and whose career goals require a specific type of educational program, and other options, such as short-term training, mentoring, and internship opportunities, may serve adults who seek more immediate results or desire development within the workplace (as is the case with mentoring and internship). Identifying the mode of delivery (e.g., structured one-on-one, group workshop or class, self-paced computer, or some combination of delivery modes) that best suits the adult client is also critical. For instance, short-term traditional counseling may be an appropriate delivery format for those adults who approach career development and search experiences with trepidation (e.g., those who prefer the familiar and see changes as threats to their self-esteem, as opposed to those who seek out new experiences and view changes as challenges to be overcome). Adults who have a positive history of coping with stress and strain from job loss or job reentry may be prime candidates for action-oriented career counseling (Maslach, Schaufeli, & Leiter, 2001), which can employ a variety of different development activities and delivery formats.

In sum, by analyzing a client's background information, environmental context, and the availability of internal and external resources, the counselor can help the client clarify goals, understand the obstacles that may hinder the realization of those goals, and identify the tools they have available to work toward goal achievement. The counselor and client may consider the fit between client skills and the requirements of jobs or the needs of employers or the fit between the client's education or training needs and the different venues available to provide relevant training as they work to identify appropriate development activities and modes of delivery.

SUMMARY AND TAKE-HOME MESSAGES

Based on the theory, research, and best practices reviewed here, successful intervention with career-transitioning adults requires combining many different elements, including (a) the use of one or more sound theoretical approaches to guide the collection and organization of information, (b) the use of information on individual background and environmental contexts, (c) the use of assessments to fill in additional client information, (d) the development and execution of targeted and concrete plans of action, (e) evaluation of the actions and outcomes for effectiveness, and (f) preparation of clients to use new skills in future situations. Within the context of their expanding role, counselors can facilitate the interconnection between an evolving world of work and individuals who are increasingly expected to "own" or manage their own job transitions and career paths. Figure 23.1

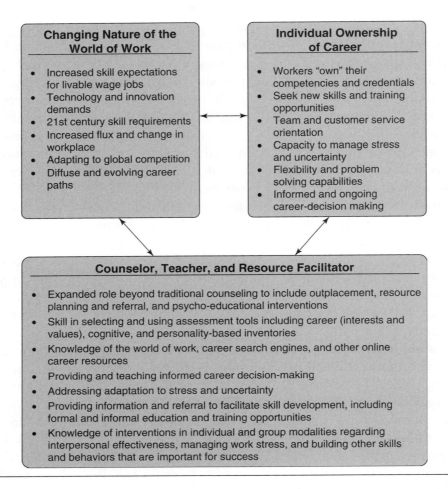

Figure 23.1   Expanded Role of Counselors in Working With Adults Making Career Transitions

illustrates this interconnection and summarizes what counselors can do to help adult clients undergoing career transitions.

This figure illustrates a range of knowledge, skills, and resources that counselors can employ to enable individuals to be competitive and productive members of the workforce. Because clients may grapple with a number of different issues, counselors need to be knowledgeable about career information and work-related resources; sufficiently flexible to move between assessment, counseling, coaching, and teaching roles; and able to help the client assemble a broader referral and support network or system. For example, counselors need to understand the changing technology and innovation demands of the world of work and be proficient in selecting and using a wide variety of assessments to ascertain client skills, place them in context, and facilitate opportunities for skill training to help clients meet their needs.

There are five areas of focus that are especially important for counselors who are working with adults experiencing career transitions:

- *Action orientation.* Counselors should reinforce the connections between concrete activities and behaviors and clients' transition issues and goals throughout the process. By making these connections more transparent to clients, counselors are able to help them document their progress and motivate them to continue pursuing a successful career transition plan.
- *Wide-ranging interventions and supports.* To respond to the diverse support needs of adults in transition, counselors must remain up-to-date on the range of services available to assist with specific types of career transition issues. By understanding the types (e.g., support groups for veterans entering the civilian labor force) and locations (e.g., local community colleges, state agencies) of services, counselors can better determine which interventions may be appropriate and useful for their adult clients.
- *Work context.* To help career-transitioning adults respond more effectively to the work context in which they find themselves, counselors need to understand the characteristics of the current economy and the world of work at all levels (e.g., local, state, and national). Employment rates, industries that are growing, organizations hiring locally, the changing skill requirements for occupations, and the skills desired by employers all are important characteristics of the work context. This information can help counselors to (a) better understand the environmental contexts in which clients experience their career transitions and (b) work with clients to generate realistic solutions that are likely to enhance transition success.
- *Cue up for adaptability.* Counselors need to promote career adaptability in their clients and provide them with tools, skills, and knowledge for dealing with career change. In addition to assisting clients with finding solutions that address more immediate issues, counselors should think about ways in which they might help clients proactively approach future career change.
- *The whole person.* To respond to the range of issues encountered by career-transitioning adults, counselors have to attend to the whole person. The multifaceted issues that often surface during counseling often demand varied interventions that go beyond career tasks and involve other parts of life (e.g., psychological symptoms, relationship demands).

In summary, more adults are experiencing a wider range of career transitions in the United States than ever before. We have highlighted the context in which these transitions occur, including continuing economic upheavals, occupational shifts, and changes in the workplace itself. We have reviewed the most prevalent types of career transitions, including high school graduates who are unprepared for work, employed adults wanting to shift their career direction, and unemployed adults seeking entry into employment, including those responding to job loss. These adults are challenged by myriad issues, such as the need to identify current skills and develop new skills, the need for career adaptability, and the need to cope with job and financial uncertainty. We considered several career and adult development theories that can inform career counseling with transitioning adults. Unfortunately, there is limited research available on the effectiveness of various career interventions for adults going through career transitions. However, the available literature does offer a number of suggestions for helping adults cope with current challenges, as well as preparing them to proactively manage their future career and life development. Helping adults learn to realistically appraise their life circumstances, respond adaptively and flexibly to these life demands, and effectively engage available supports is critical to successful counseling with career-transitioning adults.

REFERENCES

Aiken, L. R. (1998). *Human development in adulthood*. New York, NY: Plenum Press.

Alfred, M. V., & Martin, L. G. (2007). The development of economic self-sufficiency among former welfare recipients: Lessons learned from Wisconsin's welfare to work program. *International Journal of Training and Development, 11*(1), 2–20.

Anderson, M. L., Goodman, J., & Schlossberg, N. K. (2011). *Counseling adults in transition: Linking Schlossberg's theory with practice in a diverse world*. New York, NY: Springer.

Arthur, M. B., & Rousseau, D. M. (1996). A career lexicon for the 21st century. *Academy of Management Executives, 10*(4), 28–39.

Atchley, R. (1989). A continuity theory of normal aging. *The Gerontologist, 29*, 183–190.

Baltes, P. (1997). On the incomplete architecture of human ontogeny. *American Psychologist, 52*, 366–380.

Bandura, A. (1986). *Social foundations of thought and action: A social cognitive theory*. Englewood Cliffs, NJ: Prentice-Hall.

Banks, C. H., & Nafukho, F. M. (2008, February). Career transitions across and within organizations: Implications for human resource development. Paper presented at the Academy of Human Resource Development International Research Conference in the Americas, Panama City, FL. Retrieved from http://www.eric.ed.gov/PDFS/ED501678.pdf

Brand, J. E. (2004). *Enduring effects of job displacement on career outcomes* (Unpublished doctoral dissertation). University of Wisconsin, Madison.

Brand, J. E., & Burgard, S. A. (2008). Job displacement and social participation over the lifecourse: Findings for a cohort of joiners. *Social Forces, 87*(1), 211–242.

Bridges, W. (2004). *Transitions: Making sense of life's changes.* Cambridge, MA: Da Capo Press.

Bright, J. E. H., & Pryor, G. L. (2008). Shiftwork: A chaos theory of careers agenda for change in career counseling. *Australian Journal of Career Development, 17,* 63–72.

Brown, S. D., & Lent, R. W. (1996). A social cognitive framework for career choice counseling. *Career Development Quarterly, 44,* 354–366.

Brown, S. D., & McPartland, E. B. (2005). Career interventions: Current status and future directions. In W. Walsh & M. Savickas (Eds.), *Handbook of vocational psychology* (pp. 195–226). Mahwah, NJ: Erlbaum.

Carnevale, A. P., Smith, N., & Strohl, J. (2010). *Help wanted: Projections of jobs and education requirements through 2018.* Retrieved from University of Georgetown, Center on Education and the Workforce: http://www9.georgetown.edu/grad/gppi/hpi/cew/pdfs/FullReport.pdf

Clemens, E. V., & Milsom, A. S. (2008). Enlisting service members' transition into the civilian world of work: A cognitive information processing approach. *Career Development Quarterly, 56,* 246–256.

Côté, J. E. (2000). *Arrested adulthood: The changing nature of maturity and identity.* New York, NY: New York University Press.

Côté, J. E. (2002). The role of identity capital in the transition to adulthood: The individualization thesis examined. *Journal of Youth Studies, 5*(2), 117–134.

Danziger, S., & Ratner, D. (2010). Labor market outcomes and the transition to adulthood. *The Future of Children, 20*(1), 133–158.

DeFrank, R., & Ivancevich, J. M. (1986). Job loss: An individual level review and model. *Journal of Vocational Behavior, 19,* 1–20.

Ebberwein, C. A., Krieshok, T. S., Ulven, J. C., & Prosser, E. C. (2004). Voices in transition: Lessons on career adaptability. *Career Development Quarterly, 52,* 292–308.

Eby, L. T., & Buch, K. (1994). The effect of job search method, sex, activity level, and emotional acceptance on new job characteristics: Implications for counseling unemployed professionals. *Journal of Employment Counseling, 31,* 69–82.

Eby, L. T., Butts, M., & Lockwood, A. (2003). Predictors of success in the era of the boundaryless career. *Journal of Organizational Behavior, 24,* 689–708.

Farber, H. S. (2005). What do we know about job loss in the United States? Evidence from the displaced workers survey, 1984–2004. *Economic Perspectives, 29*(2), 13–28.

Glassdoor. (2011). *Employee confidence survey: Overview, methodology & highlights.* Retrieved from http://www.glassdoor.com/press/wp-content/files_mf/13014 04295Glassdoor_Q1_2011SummaryFINAL.pdf

Hackney, H., & Cormier, S. (2005). *The professional counselor: A process guide to helping* (5th ed.). Boston, MA: Pearson.

Haynie, J. M., & Shepherd, D. (2011). Toward a theory of discontinuous career transition: Investigating career transitions necessitated by traumatic life events. *Journal of Applied Psychology, 96*(3), 501–524.

Hendra, R., Dillman, K. N., Hamilton, G., Lundquist, E., Martinson, K., Wavelet, M., & Williams, S. (2010). *How effective are different approaches aiming to increase employment retention and advancement? Final impact for twelve models.* Retrieved from MDRC: http://www.mdrc.org/publications/558/full.pdf

Hesketh, B. (2000). Prevention and development in the workplace. In S. D. Brown & R. W. Lent (Eds.), *Handbook of counseling psychology* (pp. 471–498). New York, NY: Wiley.

Holzer, H. (2000). *Employers and welfare recipients in Milwaukee and other metropolitan states: Summary of findings from employer survey.* San Francisco, CA: UCLA School of Public Policy and Research.

Hudson, F. M. (1999). *The adult years: Mastering the art of self renewal* (rev. ed.). San Francisco, CA: Jossey-Bass.

Infoplease. (n.d.). *Median annual income, by level of education, 1990–2008.* Retrieved from http://www.infoplease.com/ipa/A0883617.html

Kelvin, P., & Jarrett, J. A. (1985). *Unemployment: Its social and psychological effects.* Cambridge, England: Cambridge University Press.

Kerka, S. (1995). *Adult career counseling in a new age* (ERIC Digest No. 167). Retrieved from http://www.eric.ed.gov/ERICWebPortal/detail?accno=ED389881

Krumboltz, J. D., & Chan, A. (2005). Career interventions: Current status and future directions. In W. Walsh & M. Savickas (Eds.), *Handbook of vocational psychology* (pp. 347–370). Mahwah, NJ: Erlbaum.

Lent, R. W. (in press). Career-life preparedness: Revisiting career planning and adjustment in the new workplace. *Career Development Quarterly.*

Lightsey, O. R., Jr. (1996). What leads to wellness? The role of psychological resources in well-being. *Counseling Psychologist, 24,* 589–759.

Maslach, C., Schaufeli, W., & Leiter, M. (2001). Job burnout. *Annual Review of Psychology, 52,* 397–422.

Mendenhall, R., Kalil, A., Spindel, L. J., & Hart, C. M. D. (2008). Job loss at midlife: Managers and executives face the "new risk economy." *Social Forces, 87*(1), 185–209.

Miller, C., Deitch, V., & Hill, A. (2010). *Paths to advancement for single parents.* [Executive summary]. Retrieved from MDRC: http://www.mdrc.org/publications/582/execsum.pdf

Moss, W., & Baugh, J. (1983). Displaced homemakers: An overlooked extension audience. *Journal of Extension 21*(4). Retrieved from http://www.joe.org/joe/1983july/a3.html

Multon, K. D., Wood, R., Heppner, M. J., & Gysbers, N. C. (2007). A cluster-analytic investigation of subtypes of adult career counseling clients: Toward a taxonomy of career problems. *Journal of Career Assessment, 15,* 66–86. doi:10.1177/1069072706294508

Murphy, K. A., Blustein, D. L., Bohlig, A. J., & Platt, M. G. (2010). The college-to-career transition: An exploration of emerging adulthood. *Journal of Counseling and Development, 88,* 174–181.

National Career Development Association. (2011). *National survey of working America 2011.* Retrieved from http://associationdatabase.com/aws/NCDA/asset_manager/get_file/37267

Nicholson, N. (1990). The transition cycle: Causes, outcomes, processes, and forms. In S. Fisher & C. Cooper (Eds.), *On the move: The psychology of change and transition* (pp. 83–108). West Sussex, England: Wiley.

O'Connell, D. J. (2008). *Unpacking personal adaptability at work*. Retrieved from http://www.courts.michigan.gov/mji/curricula_guide/Unpacking_Personal _Adaptability_at_work.pdf

Padula, M. (1994). Reentry women: A literature review with recommendations for counseling and research. *Journal of Counseling & Development, 73*, 10–16.

Peterson, G. W., Lumsden, J. A., Sampson, J. P., Reardon, R. C., & Lenz, J. G. (2002). Using a cognitive information processing approach in career counseling with adults. In S. G. Niles (Ed.), *Adult career development: Concepts, issues and practices* (pp. 98–117). Tulsa, OK: National Career Development Association.

Robbins, S. (1989). The role of contemporary psychoanalysis in counseling psychology. *Journal of Counseling Psychology, 36*, 267–278.

Robbins, S., Chartrand, J., McFadden, K., & Lee, R. (1994). Efficacy of leader-led and self-directed career workshops for middle-aged and older adults. *Journal of Counseling Psychology, 41*, 83–90.

Robbins, S., Lee, R., & Wan, T. (1994). Goal continuity as a mediator of early retirement adjustment: Testing a multidimensional model. *Journal of Counseling Psychology, 41*, 18–26.

Ruh, D., Spicer, P., & Vaughan, K. (2009). Helping veterans with disabilities transition to employment. *Journal of Postsecondary Education and Disability, 22*(1), 67–74.

Schlossberg, N. K. (1990). Training counselors to work with older adults. *Generations, 14*(1), 7–10.

Schlossberg, N. K., Waters, E. B., & Goodman, J. (1995). *Counseling adults in transition: Linking practice with theory* (2nd ed.). New York, NY: Springer.

Simpson, A., & Armstrong, S. (2009). From the military to the civilian work force: Addressing veteran career development concerns. *Career Planning and Adult Development Journal, 25*(1), 177–187.

Spokane, A. (1991). *Career intervention*. Englewood Cliffs, NJ: Prentice-Hall.

Super, D. E., & Knasel, E. G. (1981). Career development in adulthood: Some theoretical problems and a possible solution. *British Journal of Guidance & Counselling, 9*, 194–201.

Super, D. E., Savickas, M. L., & Super, C. M. (1996). The life-span, life-space approach to careers. In D. Brown & L. Brooks (Eds.), *Career choice and development* (3rd ed.) (pp. 121–178). San Francisco, CA: Jossey-Bass.

Swanson, J. (1995). The process and outcome of career counseling. In W. B. Walsh & S. H. Osipow (Eds.), *Handbook of vocational psychology* (pp. 217–259). Mahwah, NJ: Erlbaum.

Swanson, J., & Fouad, N. (1999). *Career theory and practice: Learning through case studies*. Thousand Oaks, CA: Sage.

U.S. Department of Labor, Bureau of Labor Statistics. (2011). *2008–2018 Employment projections*. Retrieved from http://www.bls.gov/emp/#tables

U.S. Department of Labor, Employment & Training Administration. (2008). *Current strategies to employ and retain older workers* (ETA Occasional Paper 2008–1). Washington, DC: Author.

Vetter, L., Hull, W., Putzstuck, C., & Dean, G. (1986). *Adult career counseling: Resources for program planning and development.* Bloomington, IL: Meridian Education.

Vondracek, F., & Porfeli, E. (2002). Life-span developmental perspectives on adult career development: Recent advances. In S. Niles (Ed.), *Adult career development: Concepts, issues and practices* (pp. 20–38). Tulsa, OK: National Career Development Association.

Whiston, S., & Brecheisen, B. (2002). Evaluating the effectiveness of adult career development programs. In S. Niles (Ed.), *Adult career development: Concepts, issues and practices* (pp. 370–388). Tulsa, OK: National Career Development Association.

Whiston, S., Brecheisen, B., & Stephens, J. (2003). Does treatment modality affect career counseling effectiveness? *Journal of Vocational Behavior, 62,* 390–410.

Williams, D. (1999, January). *Life events and career change: Transition psychology in practice.* Paper presented at the British Psychology Society's Occupational Psychology Conference, Blackpool, UK.

Author Index

Subject Index